이성현

textbook*plus⁺*

Equipping Instructors and Students with
FREE RESOURCES *for Core Zondervan Textbooks*

Available Resources *for* Pilgrim Theology

Teaching Resources

- Instructor's manual
- Presentation slides
- Chapter quizzes
- Midterm and final exam
- Sample syllabus

Study Resources

- Quizzes
- Flashcards
- Exam study guides

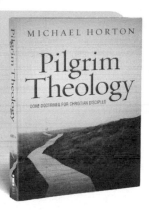

MICHAEL HORTON

Pilgrim Theology

CORE DOCTRINES FOR CHRISTIAN DISCIPLES

*How To Access Resources

- Go to www.ZondervanAcademic.com
- Click "Sign Up" button and complete registration process
- Find books using search field or browse using discipline categories
- Click "Teaching Resources" or "Study Resources" tab once you get to book page to access resources

▶ www.ZondervanAcademic.com

Pilgrim Theology

CORE DOCTRINES FOR CHRISTIAN DISCIPLES

MICHAEL HORTON

ZONDERVAN®

ZONDERVAN

Pilgrim Theology
Copyright © 2011, 2012 by Michael Horton
Abridged from *The Christian Faith*

This title is also available as a Zondervan ebook. Visit www.zondervan.com/ebooks.

This title is also available in a Zondervan audio edition. Visit www.zondervan.fm.

Requests for information should be addressed to:

Zondervan, 3900 *Sparks Dr. SE, Grand Rapids, Michigan 49546*

Library of Congress Cataloging-in-Publication Data

Horton, Michael Scott.
   Pilgrim theology : core doctrines for christian disciples / Michael Horton.
      p. cm.
   Includes bibliographical references and indexes.
   ISBN 978-0-310-33064-6 (hardcover : alk. paper)
   1. Theology, Doctrinal. 2. Reformed Church–Doctrines. I. Title.
BT75.3.H675 2012
230'.42—dc23
                                                      2012023993

Cover design: Ron Huizinga
Cover photography: istockphoto
Interior design: Matthew Van Zomeren

Printed in the United States of America

---

15 16 17 18 19 20 21 /DCI/ 23 22 21 20 19 18 17 16 15 14 13 12 11 10 9 8 7 6 5

To James, Olivia, Adam, and Matthew
For challenging and encouraging me to keep on
growing up into Christ even as you are, by his grace

Contents

Acknowledgments

O nce again I have had the pleasure of working with the excellent team at Zondervan and am indebted especially to the expert labors of Ryan Pazdur and Verlyn Verbrugge. Their editorial input improved this work greatly and their keen eyes caught glaring mistakes, though I do not mean to implicate them in any remaining errors. I am grateful to my colleagues and students at Westminster Seminary California, who have taught me a great deal over the years by their lives as much as by their instruction. The same can be said of my colleagues at the White Horse Inn and *Modern Reformation* magazine, who not only indulge but encourage me in the writing projects that distract me frequently from that gratifying work. Most of all, I am thankful to Lisa for loving patience, wise counsel, and the sense of mission that we share in this calling.

Abbreviations

ANF	*Ante-Nicene Fathers* (ed. Alexander Roberts and James Donaldson; Grand Rapids: Eerdmans, repr. 1976)
Church Dogmatics	Karl Barth, *Church Dogmatics* (ed. G. W. Bromiley and T. F. Torrance; trans. G. W. Bromiley; Edinburgh: T&T Clark, 1956–1975)
ESV	English Standard Version
HCSB	Holman Christian Standard Bible
Institutes	John Calvin, *Institutes of the Christian Religion* (ed. J. T. McNeill; trans. Ford Lewis Battles; Philadelphia: Westminster, 1960)
KJV	King James Version
NIV	New International Version, 2011
NPNF2	*Nicene and Post-Nicene Fathers* (ed. Philip Schaff et al.; 2nd series; Grand Rapids: Eerdmans, repr. 1982)
NRSV	New Revised Standard Version
PG	Patrologia graeca (ed. J.-P Migne; 162 vols.; Paris, 1857–1886)

Why Study Theology?

Whether you realize it or not, you are a theologian. You come to a book like this with a working theology, an existing understanding of God. Whether you are an agnostic or a fundamentalist—or something in between—you have a working theology that shapes and informs the way you think and live. However, I suspect that you are reading this book because you're interested in *examining* your theology more closely. You are open to having it challenged and strengthened. You know that theology—the study of God—is more than an intellectual hobby. It's a matter of life and death, something that affects the way you think, the decisions you make each day, the way you relate to God and other people, and the way you see yourself and the world around you.

I. Pilgrims on the Way

I have written this book on the heels of another theology book entitled *The Christian Faith: A Systematic Theology for Pilgrims on the Way*.[1] As I explained in the introduction to that book, the old Reformed theologians would sometimes refer to their summaries of the faith as "*our* theology." They referred to it this way for two reasons. First, to indicate that what they were writing was distinct from God's own self-understanding. This is why they would sometimes use the term *ectypal* when talking about their theology. Though it sounds somewhat technical, an ectype is simply a copy, with the archetype as the original. Talking about theology as "ectypal," then, is a humble admission that only God's own self-knowledge is original (archetypal). All that we say about God is a copy, subject to error. We will never know anything exactly as God knows it. Instead, we know things as he has revealed them to us, accommodating his knowledge to our feeble capacity to understand.

Second, the older theologians referred to their summary of faith as "*our* theology" to make it clear that it was not just "*my* theology"—their own

---

1. Michael Horton, *The Christian Faith: A Systematic Theology for Pilgrims on the Way* (Grand Rapids: Zondervan, 2011).

individualistic understanding of God. To study theology involves entering into a long, ongoing conversation, one that we did not begin. Others have been talking about God long before you or I entered this discussion. We do not read the Bible somewhere off by ourselves in a corner; we read it as a community of faith, together with the whole church in all times and places.

Because our theological understanding is necessarily limited and finite, subject to our sinful biases, affections, and errors, I follow a venerable Christian tradition by referring to this volume as a "pilgrim theology" for those on the way—Christians who humbly seek to understand God but who are aware of their own biases and sinful tendencies to distort the truth. Older theologians used this term to distinguish our theological understanding from that of the glorified saints. A day will yet come when we are glorified and the effects of sin fully conquered, and our understanding of God will be fuller, more complete. Even in this condition, however, we will still be finite and our theology will remain ectypal—creaturely. Yet it will no longer be a theology for pilgrims. It will no longer be subject to sinful error. Then, we shall know, even as we are fully known.

So consider this book a map for pilgrims—people "on the way," those on a journey seeking theological understanding for life in this world and the world to come. This book is more than simply an abridgment of *The Christian Faith*. Instead, I have sought to write for an entirely new and wider audience. I've intentionally tried to make it useful for both group and individual study, and have included key terms, distinctions, and questions at the end of each chapter that are linked to words in bold font within the text. Though this book is less detailed than my longer systematic theology, it is written to serve as something of a travel guide to help you on your own journey of theological understanding, showing you the proper coordinates and important landmarks you'll need to recognize along the way.

II. Drama to Discipleship

Although it is "the study of God," theology has a reputation for being dry, abstract, and irrelevant for daily living. Many Christians assume that we can just experience God in a personal relationship apart from doctrine, but that's impossible. You cannot experience God without knowing who he is, what he has done, and who you are in relation to him. Even our most basic Christian experiences and commitments are theological. "I just love Jesus," some say. But who is Jesus? And why do you love him? "I just try to live for the Lord." Is this Lord *Yahweh*, the Creator and Redeemer who reveals himself in Scripture, or an idol? What is this Lord like, what does he approve? What are his attributes? And is there any good news to report concerning this God's actions in our history, or are you just trying to be a "good person"? What happens when you die? What's the future of this world? These are not abstract questions, but questions that haunt our hearts and minds from childhood to old age. We can suppress these questions, but we cannot make them go away. Reality forces us to bump into them. The burden of this book is to elaborate the claim that God has revealed answers, though we will not like all of them.

In this regard, Christianity is a unique religion. The starting point and endgame of the Christian faith are distinct from every other way people tend to approach religion and spirituality. Today, especially in the West, most people tend to associate religion with the inner realm of the individual soul (mysticism) or with principles for individual or social behavior (morality), or perhaps—though less often these days—with intellectual curiosity and speculation (philosophy). Mix elements of these three—mysticism, morality, and philosophy—together and stir in a generous dose of Yankee pragmatism, and the result is an eclectic soup that is easy to swallow. The goal of life is often viewed as some form of personal or collective happiness. If a person can mix in a bit of wisdom from various other perspectives to spice things up, all the better!

The faith that springs from the Bible's story of God is entirely different. We could even say that it has a different horizon. The triune God is the sun on this horizon, and we orient ourselves to this sun, not the other way around. Instead of starting with ourselves—our plans, purposes, dreams, and accomplishments—and seeking to learn how God can serve our goals and desires, we begin with God, who *is* life, and who freely created, sustains, and directs history to his ends. In this strange new world of the Bible, religion is not something that I can use for my own fulfillment. I do not come to Christianity to find truths that confirm me and strengthen my resolve to live better, try harder, or make more of myself. Rather, when I encounter the God of the Bible I come to see that my very questions are skewed, badly ranked, and disordered—even before I try to give my answers. In other words, the Bible is not primarily concerned with me and my quest for personal meaning and fulfillment. It's a story about God, who is good enough to tell us about himself, about ourselves, and about this world, and to give us the true meaning of history. Yes, in the process of being swept away into this story, we do indeed find personal meaning and fulfillment for ourselves in ways that we could never have imagined, much less arranged. But we don't get those things by starting with them. Instead, we need a compass to guide us.

A compass orients us. It helps us on our journey by helping us to grasp that the Bible is not chiefly about me and my personal experience or morality. Rather, it is the revelation of God and God's history with us. Its relevance lies not in helping the pious individual to attain spiritual well-being, but in the way it actually introduces us to reality. It is not a flight *away* from the world into the inner recesses of the soul, but a completely new existence *within* the world that God has made, sustains, has redeemed, and will one day transform fully and forever into his everlasting home. As we shall see, the theology of the Bible leads us away from the high places of the religious, the moral, and the spiritual specialists. It keeps our boots firmly on the ground. Instead of ascending to spiritual heights, we meet God in his gracious descent to us.

Like the directions on a compass, there are four coordinates that guide us in our journey to know God:

Drama
Doctrine
Doxology
Discipleship

All of our faith and practice arise out of the *drama* of Scripture, the "big story" that traces the plot of history from creation to consummation, with Christ as its Alpha and Omega, beginning and end. And out of the throbbing verbs of this unfolding drama God reveals stable nouns—*doctrines*. From what God does in history we are taught certain things about who he is and what it means to be created in his image, fallen, and redeemed, renewed, and glorified in union with Christ. As the Father creates his church, in his Son and by his Spirit, we come to realize what this covenant community is and what it means to belong to it; what kind of future is promised to us in Christ, and how we are to live here and now in the light of it all. The drama and the doctrine provoke us to praise and worship—*doxology*—and together these three coordinates give us a new way of living in the world as *disciples*.

Unlike the directions on a common compass, all of these coordinates are engaged simultaneously. We do not begin our journey in the direction of the drama, then move on to the doctrine and doxology and finally arrive at discipleship. Often, as we will see later, doctrinal gold is discovered in Scripture's rich veins of prayer and praise. Doctrines like the Trinity did not emerge out of ivory-tower theorizing, but out of the worship of Jewish

Christians who acknowledge one God yet were baptized into the name of the Father, the Son, and the Holy Spirit, and gave praise to each of them as a distinct person of the one God. At no point was doctrine conceived merely as an intellectual enterprise. In Scripture and in the best of church history, doctrinal reflection has maintained a deeply integrated connection with the biblical narrative, the desire of the heart, and the engagement of the will and the body in worship and life.

The Bible knows nothing of any contrast between truth and experience, head and heart, theology and practical living. On the contrary, Israel lived out of its unfolding story. Every year when Passover was celebrated, each participant was to think of himself or herself as one who had escaped God's judgment and slavery in Egypt, along with the ancient fathers and mothers whom God led through the sea. The children asked, "What does this mean?" and the parents explained the meaning of the story, not only as the narrative of a mighty act of God in the past, but as a living reality that continued to shape their identity. Attentive to the doctrines that arose from this drama, and with an entire hymnal that expressed and structured the people's appropriate response, each generation rediscovered itself in this covenantal drama, somewhere between promise and fulfillment. The story of God and his history with Israel became their story as well. How did the people know that God was all-powerful and full of mercy (i.e., the doctrine)? Without hesitation, they would have spoken of how God had redeemed his people from the heavy hand of Pharaoh and promised an even greater exodus in the future (i.e., the drama). An outsider might have learned this story by overhearing believers in prayer and in praise:

> Give thanks to the LORD, for he is good, for his steadfast love endures forever.... Give thanks ... to him who alone does great wonders, for his steadfast love endures forever ... to him who spread out the earth above the waters, for his steadfast love endures forever; to him who made the great lights [sun, moon, and stars], for his steadfast love endures forever ... to him who struck down the firstborn of Egypt ... and brought Israel out from among them ... with a strong hand and an outstretched arm, for his steadfast love endures forever. (Ps 136:1 – 12)

God's mighty acts, which happened apart from them (in the drama), were done for them (identified as doctrine) and were now enveloping them (in doxology) and shaping their way of living in the world (discipleship).

The New Testament also begins with a dramatic story of God's mighty deeds, recounted in the Gospels and Acts. In the Epistles, doctrinal explanations explore the significance of these deeds for us here and now, as do early liturgical elements (hymns, confessions of sin and faith, and prayers) and commands that specify the sort of life in the world that this paradigm shift entails. Paul's famous Letter to the Romans is densely packed with depth charges that explode in our minds and hearts. Even in the first verse, Paul announces that his central focus is "the gospel of God," and this good news is first of all a dramatic story: "the gospel of God, which he promised beforehand through his prophets in the holy Scriptures, concerning his Son, who was descended from David according to the flesh and was declared to be the Son of God in power according to the Spirit of holiness by his resurrection from the dead" (vv. 1–4).

Paul unpacks the glories of this gospel—its doctrines. We find our place in the story of God's gracious covenant. From the drama we learn that Christ died and was raised on the third day. And then from the doctrine we discover that he "was delivered up for our trespasses and raised for our justification" (Ro 4:25). Like a hiker reaching alpine vistas, Paul is provoked by each of these doctrinal arguments to rest a spell and take in the view, yielding to exclamations of wonder and praise (8:31–39; 11:33–36). Along the way, the apostle relates doctrine and practice: "What shall we say then? Are we to continue in sin that grace may abound? By no means!" To explain his answer, Paul returns to the drama and doctrine: "How can we who died to sin still live in it? Do you not know that all of us who have been baptized into Christ Jesus were baptized into his death? We were buried therefore with him by baptism into death, in order that, just as Christ was raised from the dead by the glory of the Father, we too might walk in newness of life" (Ro 6:1–4). Discipleship—through "the renewing of [the] mind" by the word and Spirit—now becomes, in the language of the old King James Version, the "reasonable service" offered not to attain God's favor, but in view of the mercies of God (12:1–2).

Drama, doctrine, doxology, and discipleship—the four coordinates of our compass—integrate our faith and practice. We will keep our eyes on these four coordinates throughout this volume, as we endeavor not to separate what God has united in his infinite wisdom.

III. The Gospel of God's Son

Especially in the modern era, summaries of Christian doctrine often begin with the least controversial premises: things that all reasonable people can agree upon. First, you prove God's existence, then you unpack the essence of who God is, and this gives you the building blocks for a doctrine of Scripture. Only after all of this preparatory work can you begin "doing theology."

This is a problem for several reasons.

First, nobody comes to any serious discussion without already believing something—lots of things, in fact. There is no "view from nowhere," an unbiased perspective of neutrality. Our starting point already presupposes many things that we already believe, explicitly or implicitly. People change their minds, especially when God graciously opens them, but all of us come to the big questions of life with a host of assumptions that we already hold.

In addition, becoming a Christian is more than simply signing on to a belief that God exists or that the case for Christ's resurrection is better than alternative explanations of the data. I have never met anyone who became a Christian simply because of good arguments. Those arguments are important and necessary; in fact, I will lay out a case for the central Christian claims in short order. They can play a critical role in exploding our assumptions about the sort of claims that Christianity makes. However, as in any science, a paradigm shift in our theology requires more than a single piece of data; it is the result of feeling the total inadequacy of one paradigm to account for the broadest available evidence. As the new paradigm proves its greater explanatory power, conversion occurs. We repent of the old scheme and embrace another.

Consider the case of Copernicus. At first, Copernicus was mocked by his peers for insisting that the earth orbits the sun instead of the other way around. It ran against common sense. Everyone knew that the sun rises in the east and sets in the west; clearly, the sun was the body that moved, not the earth! Eventually, experiments confirmed that Copernicus was correct, and the older scientific models were seen as inadequate. They simply *could not* account for the data that the Copernican theory explained. Revolutions in any field are difficult to come by—as they should be, or we would never have stable sciences. Paradigms remain resilient against particular challenges, but they can be overthrown.

Of course, the paradigm shift of conversion to Christ is complicated by our spiritual condition. It requires something more than being convinced, rationally, that Christianity is true. The Bible reveals that we intentionally and systematically suppress and distort the evidence that would lead us to the God to whom we must give an account. Yet the truth still has revelatory power. Even many who do not yet believe the Christian story are haunted by its explanatory power over against rival paradigms. Because the world is more radically grand and more tragically disfigured than our reigning set of working assumptions, we will sense our need of a different paradigm.

To have a "pilgrim" theology, you must begin with reality. Christian faith requires commitment to a relentless pursuit of reality, come what may. What finally turns the switch of conversion is not an argument here or there, but the emergence of a new interpretation of reality, disclosed by God's revelation. More than just a few religious beliefs, Christianity is a whole web of beliefs and assumptions.

This is why I want to begin our journey of understanding—the pilgrim way—with the central claim to which all of Scripture leads and from which it all flows. In other words, we begin by turning to the climax of the novel and then going back to read the pages leading up to it. We begin with the most scandalous of all claims made by the Christian faith: the gospel—the good news concerning Jesus Christ. The gospel is not something you can just tack on to another worldview. On the contrary, it makes you rethink everything from the ground up, from the center out. Only when we start with the gospel—the *most* controversial point of Christian faith—are we ready to talk about who God is and how we know him.

I do not believe the gospel because I believe in God; rather, I believe in God because of the gospel. There are great arguments for the existence of a supreme being, but unless the gospel is true, the claim that a god exists is either personally meaningless or a horrible threat. God's existence and moral attributes are revealed in nature, but it's only after we embrace the gospel that we see the truth about God and ourselves in full color. There is more for us to know in the Bible than the gospel, but apart from it there is nothing worth knowing. Some Christians think it's better to move people to theism (belief in a deity) and then introduce them to the gospel, but I would argue that it is the gospel that makes it even *possible* for me to believe in God—not only to believe that someone or something exists beyond us all, but to trust in this particular God who is known in Jesus Christ.

In the end, it all comes down to a simple question: what kind of "God" are we talking about? If we're just talking about a higher power, a vague God defined by beliefs that we all share in common, then theology seems like a pretty trivial affair. Nor am I suggesting that we should begin with great arguments for the reliability and authority of the Bible. I'll be offering some of those in the next chapter. Yet my confidence in Scripture, too, is first established by the gospel. As Herman Bavinck observed, faith in Scripture rises and falls with faith in Christ.[2]

In a sense, this entire volume is an exploration of the message richly summarized in Romans 1:1–6 as

---

2. Quoted in G. C. Berkouwer, *Holy Scripture* (Grand Rapids: Eerdmans, 1975), 44.

the gospel of God, which he promised beforehand through his prophets in the holy Scriptures, concerning his Son, who was descended from David according to the flesh and was declared to be the Son of God in power according to the Spirit of holiness by his resurrection from the dead, Jesus Christ our Lord, through whom we have received grace and apostleship to bring about the obedience of faith for the sake of his name among all the nations, including you who are called to belong to Jesus Christ.

First, the gospel I am talking about is "the gospel of *God.*" Every field of study requires an *object.* Astronomy is the study of stars (and other celestial bodies), botany is the study of plants, sociology studies society, and so forth. The object is evident in the name of the discipline. Similarly, theology (*theologia*) is the study of God. The object of theology is not the church's teaching or the experience of pious souls. It is not a subset of ethics, religious studies, cultural anthropology, or psychology. *God* is the object of this discipline.

And the gospel is the good news *of* God, *from* God: the announcement of God's purposes, promises, and achievements — not ours. God can be the object of our knowledge only because he has freely and actively revealed himself. Whenever God is revealed, he is also the revealer. If God doesn't reveal himself, we're just talking to ourselves in a godlike voice, spiritual ventriloquists who make our wooden partner speak the lines we have written for it. Saying that God is the object of theology entails a pretty strong claim: namely, that God can be *known.* Yet that is precisely Paul's claim here: "the gospel of God, *which he promised beforehand through his prophets in the holy Scriptures.*" God can be known because he has revealed himself. We will be exploring this point — as well as the God who is known — in the first two chapters.

Second, the main message of Scripture is "the gospel of God ..., *concerning his Son.*" There is, of course, more in the Bible than just the gospel. In Scripture God reveals himself as creator, sustainer, and judge as well as savior and shepherd of his people. God's moral as well as saving will is clearly taught in the Bible. However, as Paul argues elsewhere, all people know *by nature* that God exists — they even know his invisible attributes of power and justice — and they know that they are obligated to this God. "So they are without excuse" (Ro 1:20). Even if the Bible had never been written, there would be a certain degree of law and order, morality and religion, in the world. However, we twist and distort even this truth, so that our morality becomes a path to self-justification and pride rather than thanksgiving and our religion becomes superstition and idolatry. What we need — what all of us need — is another word, something other than the general revelation of

God's existence, power, glory, justice, and law. We need a saving revelation if we are to be reconciled to this Creator. For those who stand in a broken covenantal relationship, the only safe encounter with God is as he has revealed himself in Christ through the gospel. In addition, this gospel—the heart and soul of special revelation—is not just about something that happens in our hearts. It is not an inner experience or subjective moral impulse, but rather a revelation of particular historical events. This gospel of God concerns his Son, "who was *descended from David* according to the flesh and was declared to be the Son of God in power according to the Spirit of holiness by *his resurrection from the dead.*"

Finally, although the gospel itself is an announcement about God's mighty deeds in Christ, apart from us, in history, the Spirit applies the benefits to us here and now through preaching and sacrament. Even those who were formerly not part of Israel, strangers to the covenants and promises, are now included as coheirs with Christ. Effectually calling us through this gospel, the Spirit unites us to Christ for justification, sanctification, and future glorification. Paul's sentence concludes by identifying "Jesus Christ our Lord" as the one "through whom we have received grace and apostleship to bring about the obedience of faith for the sake of his name among all the nations, *including you who are called to belong to Jesus Christ*" (emphasis added). The latter half of this volume (chs. 8–18) unpacks this rich treasure, from the Spirit's application of redemption to the nature of the church and the return of Christ to judge and reign as the Alpha and Omega of a restored creation.

"Faith comes from hearing, and hearing through *the word of Christ*" (Ro 10:17). We "have been born again, not of perishable seed but of imperishable, through the living and abiding word of God ... And this word is *the good news* that was preached to you" (1Pe 1:23, 25). Every word that comes from the mouth of God is essential. God's moral will has not changed, and his law remains its perfect expression. However, Peter marvels at the fact that by his preaching "the Gentiles should hear the *word of the gospel* and believe" (Ac 15:7, emphasis added in all quotes).[3]

Sound theology, then, does not start with something else, something more basic and universal, and then add the gospel later on. Even when evaluating a wider horizon, the Christian is wearing "gospel" glasses. C. S. Lewis put the matter well: "I believe in Christianity as I believe that the Sun has risen not only because I see it but because by it I see everything else."[4] In his preface to the first Bible translated into French from the Hebrew and

---

3. In this and the other quotations in this paragraph, the emphasis is added.
4. "Is Theology Poetry," 1944, in *They Asked for a Paper* (London: Geoffrey Bles, 1962), [154–65.]

Greek, John Calvin expresses the conviction that will guide our course in this volume:

> Without the gospel everything is useless and vain; without the gospel we are not Christians; without the gospel all riches is poverty, all wisdom, folly before God; strength is weakness, and all the justice of man is under the condemnation of God.
>
> But by the knowledge of the gospel we are made children of God, brothers and sisters of Jesus Christ, fellow townsmen with the saints, citizens of the Kingdom of Heaven, heirs of God with Jesus Christ, by whom the poor are made rich, the weak strong, the fools wise, the sinners justified, the desolate comforted, the doubting sure, and slaves free. It is the power of salvation of all those who believe....
>
> It follows that every good thing we could think or desire is to be found in this same Jesus Christ alone. For, he was sold, to buy us back; captive, to deliver us; condemned, to absolve us; he was made a curse for our blessing, sin offering for our righteousness; marred that we may be made fair; he died for our life; so that by him fury is made gentle, wrath appeased, darkness turned into light, fear reassured, despisal despised, debt cancelled, labor lightened, sadness made merry, misfortune made fortunate, difficulty easy, disorder ordered, division united, ignominy ennobled, rebellion subject, intimidation intimidated, ambush uncovered, assaults assailed, force forced back, combat combated, war warred against, vengeance avenged, torment tormented, damnation damned, the abyss sunk into the abyss, hell transfixed, death dead, mortality made immortal.
>
> In short, mercy has swallowed up all misery, and goodness all misfortune. For all these things which were to be the weapons of the devil in his battle against us, and the sting of death to pierce us, are turned for us into exercises which we can turn to our profit.... And we are comforted in tribulation, joyful in sorrow, glorying under vituperation [verbal abuse], abounding in poverty, warmed in our nakedness, patient amongst evils, living in death.
>
> This is what we should in short seek in the whole of Scripture: truly to know Jesus Christ, and the infinite riches that are comprised in him and are offered to us by him from God the Father.[5]

---

5. John Calvin, "Preface to Pierre Olivetan's 1534 Translation of the New Testament," in *Calvin: Commentaries* (ed. and trans. Joseph Haroutunian; Library of Christian Classics 23; Philadelphia: Westminster, 1958), 66, 69–70.

Chapter One

Knowing God

Can we know God, and if so, how? No one comes to that question from a neutral, unbiased perspective. Right out of the gate, we all have some assumptions that predispose us to accept some beliefs and discount others. Our beliefs are part of a web or paradigm. Some of these convictions are explicit. We're conscious of them, particularly when someone asks us to weigh in on them. Many others are implicit or tacit. Habitually using the same route to get to work each day, we are not always vividly aware of the road we travel upon or the various subway stops along the way. But If we're first-time visitors, the various roads, signs, turnoffs, or stations become objects of our focal awareness. The same is true with respect to our religious convictions.

According to "New Atheists" like Richard Dawkins, "Faith is the great cop-out, the great excuse to evade the need to think and evaluate evidence. Faith is belief in spite of, even perhaps because of, the lack of evidence."[1] Unfortunately, many Christians reinforce the impression that faith and reason are like an old-fashioned pair of scales: as one goes up, the other goes down. However, this misunderstands both faith and reason. Reason is no less biased than faith, and faith — genuine faith — is no less intelligent than reason. In both cases, everything turns on the object and the justification: in other words, what we believe and why we believe it. Faith in God as he has

---

1. Richard Dawkins, untitled lecture, Edinburgh International Science Festival, April 15, 1992.

revealed himself in his Word, consummately in Jesus Christ, is not a subjective leap. Nor is it merely an act of will. It involves a personal commitment, to be sure, but a commitment to a truth claim about something that has happened in history, which is available for public inspection. Some people trust in Christ with minimal arguments and evidence, just as most of us believe that the earth orbits the sun without investigating the science behind it. Yet in both cases, the arguments and evidences are there for anyone who is interested in pursuing the claim further. Whatever one concludes concerning the claims of Christianity, they cannot be dismissed as belonging to an irrational sphere called "faith" that is sealed off from reason.

"After being dead for three days, Jesus rose from the dead, bodily." This is the heart of the gospel, the central truth claim of Christian proclamation. It is not an eternal truth of reason, since there was a time when Jesus was not incarnate, much less raised. Nor is it a logical truth, like "All unmarried men are bachelors" or "a triangle has three sides." Yet it cannot be reduced to a subjective personal commitment, as if to say, "We should all live as if Jesus rose from the dead."

Acts 17 records the apostle Paul's famous speech in Athens. The seedbed of Western thought, Athens had been home to Socrates, Plato, and Aristotle—and to any school vying for the minds and hearts of civilization. After discussing and debating the resurrection in the synagogues and the marketplace, Paul received the invitation to address the Areopagus, where the leading philosophers "would spend their time in nothing except telling or hearing something new" (Ac 17:21). Luke tells us that the two major schools represented were the Epicureans and the Stoics (v. 18). In the view of Epicureans old and new, god or the gods—if they exist—are conveniently tucked away in their heaven, quite unconcerned with and largely oblivious to worldly happenings. Nature and fate rule the world. At the other end of the spectrum, the Stoics believed that nature itself was divine and every living thing had a spark of divinity in it. Imagine a daytime talk show with New Atheists and New Agers on the panel and you have a serviceable idea of Paul's audience.

Paul began his speech, "Men of Athens, I perceive that in every way you are very religious. For as I passed along and observed the objects of your worship, I found also an altar with this inscription, 'To the unknown god'" (vv. 22–23a). "Religious" here is a double entendre in Greek; it could as easily be translated "superstitious." In any case, the compliment turns out to be offered tongue in cheek. Trying to cover all of their bases, the Athenians were so religious—or superstitious—that they had the equivalent of a manger scene, Hanukkah lights, a winter solstice flag, and a statue of the Buddha or storm god Thor on the lawn at city hall. Paul does not say, "Whoever bet his money on Apollo is closest to the winning number." He does not pick out one of the idols to tweak in the direction of the biblical God. Rather, he says, "What therefore you worship as unknown, this I proclaim to you" (v. 23b).

Paul tells them that this unknown God is the Creator and Lord of everything — visible and invisible — who gives everything and doesn't need anything, least of all from us. Thus, God is completely independent from the world (vv. 24 – 27). Paul is declaring that God is clearly distinct from the created order. So much for the Stoics. On the other hand, the Epicureans don't have it right either. This God, though distinct, freely relates the world to himself and enters it as he pleases, so near to us in his self-revelation that we have no excuse for ignoring him (vv. 27 – 28). If God is our Creator, then we have no business worshiping golden images fashioned by human art (v. 29).

What Paul says about God's relationship to the world would have sparked a lively debate by itself, but the apostle hurries on to his central point: "The times of ignorance God overlooked, but now he commands all people everywhere to repent, because he has fixed a day on which he will judge the world in righteousness by a man whom he has appointed; and of this he has given assurance to all by raising him from the dead" (vv. 30 – 31). While those in his illustrious audience thought of themselves as the trustees of the world's wisdom, Paul included the golden age of Greek philosophy in "the times of ignorance." But Paul isn't talking philosophy anymore. He moves on to focus his audience's attention on a historical event that has happened just a little more than seven hundred miles away, a little more than two decades ago. Suddenly, the subject has shifted from philosophy to history — and not just any history, but the very particular (and peculiarly Jewish) expectation of a final resurrection of the dead. Why would this shift have been so jarring?

Epicureans believed that dead people stay dead. Reality consists of atoms and is therefore material. Thinking is simply the random swerving of atoms. Given the fact of evil and suffering in the world, the gods are (or god is) either evil or impotent — or, more likely, they just do not care about the world. From these doctrines, the Epicureans developed a particular way of living and discipleship: the chief end of human beings is to maximize happiness, and this can be best attained by avoiding extremes. You had best make this life count, because it is the only one you have. From Ludwig Feuerbach, Friedrich Nietzsche, Karl Marx, and Sigmund Freud to Richard Dawkins, modern atheism is largely neo-Epicureanism.

The Stoics, on the other hand, believed that nature is divine. God is the world and the world is God, consisting of passive matter and active energy (Logos or reason, also identified with fate). If you believe that you are suffering, you will suffer; if you dedicate yourself through meditation to inner calm, then you will avoid suffering. Stoicism was revived in the Enlightenment, especially by Baruch Spinoza, and its chief patterns of thought and life may be seen in German idealism (especially Friedrich Schelling and G. W. F. Hegel) as well as in Romanticism, American Transcendentalism and a host of theosophical movements (such as Christian Science and New Thought) that feed into what is often identified popularly as the New Age movement. Many similarities have been drawn also to Eastern religions and philosophies.

The following table explains some common terms that are helpful for our theological journey:

Worldview Paradigms	
Polytheism	Belief in many gods.
Pantheism	All is divine.
Panentheism	All is within divinity; the divine and worldly principles are mutually dependent.
Deism	God created the world but does not intervene miraculously within it.
Atheism	God does not exist.

The deities of ancient polytheism were consigned by most Greek philosophers to the myths and cults of popular piety. Based on the definitions in this table, Epicureanism fits most closely with deism and atheism, while Stoicism is basically pantheistic or at least panentheistic.

A revived Platonism was also important in the first century. At first, Platonism might seem to be closer to the biblical view of reality, since Plato held that there was one god (though not personal) who transcended the world. However, Plato's worldview divided reality into the "upper world" (perfect, spiritual, unchanging, divine, and eternal forms) and a "lower world" (imperfect, material, ever-changing, temporal). Out of a cosmological drama, doctrines emerged, provoking distinct ways of experiencing and living in the world. Platonists believed that the transcendent One could not have created the material world since it represents a "falling away" from divine perfection, so the world was instead created by a semidivine workman (or "demiurge"). They believed that the soul is immortal (eternally existing in the upper world), but that it has been imprisoned in a material body. Our lives should therefore be dedicated to contemplation of the eternal forms, by transcending our bodies and fastening our souls' gaze on their divine origin in the upper world. The good life is that of the philosopher, who can give his or her life to the soul's ascent. "Salvation," therefore, is death—the liberation of the divine soul from its bodily prison.

None of these ancient schools—indeed, none of the religions of the East or West—had a map for understanding God and the world that even came close to resembling the gospel that Paul proclaimed in Athens that day. By pursuing either happiness or virtue, Epicureans and Stoics (then as now) were trying to find the best path for personal and social improvement by their own effort. The drama of creation, the fall, and redemption within history and of the consummation at the end of this age was incomprehensible to those who presupposed an entirely different story. The notion of God's coming cataclysmic judgment of the world, already rendered certain by the resurrection of the incarnate Son, was a *stumbling block* to Jews. Understanding what Jesus and his apostles were claiming, many of their fellow Jews charged Christianity not with being incomprehensible or irrational but with being blasphemous and false. However, for Greeks and those unfamiliar with the Jewish story (the Gentiles), the gospel was simply *folly* (1Co 1:23).

So what happened in the theater of the philosophers that day? "Now when they heard of the resurrection of the dead, some mocked. But others said, 'We will hear you again about this.' So Paul went out from their midst. But some men joined him and believed, among whom also were Dionysius the Areopagite and a woman named Damaris and others with them" (vv. 32–34).

I. Knowledge of God

How you know something depends on what it is that you are studying. Knowing your spouse is different from knowing atomic energy or the history of Renaissance art. We cannot come up with a universal method and criteria for knowing God before identifying the sort of God we have in mind.

In his speech before the Greek philosophers, Paul affirms the biblical teaching that God is neither separated from the world (pagan transcendence) nor one with it (pagan immanence). Though independent of the world, God is free to act in it as he pleases. God is qualitatively distinct from the world—that is, transcendent. And yet this same God created the world, pronouncing it good. In this, we see that God is immanent, present in the world, entering into a covenantal relationship with human beings and sustaining all of his creatures. God judges and saves human beings, even to the point of actually assuming their humanity, bearing their curse in his body on the cross, and raising their humanity to the Father's right hand in his resurrection and ascension. The prophets and the apostles believe more deeply in God's **transcendence** of and independence from the world than the most ardent deists and more deeply in God's **immanence** than the most ardent pantheists. No religion faces, welcomes, and proclaims this paradox as does the Christian faith. No religion is more convinced simultaneously of God's radical difference from creatures and God's radical identification with them.

God's radical difference from creatures is sometimes referred to by theologians as God's **incomprehensibility**. The difference between God and creation is not merely *quantitative* ("more than"), but *qualitative* ("different from"). This marks the chasm separating biblical faith from **polytheism**, **pantheism**, and **panentheism** (see page 28). In its attempt to conquer heaven, the fallen heart climbs ladders of rational speculation, mystical experience, and moral effort. However, the vision of God in his majestic glory is deadly, according to Scripture. No one can see God's face and live (Ex 33:20); the immortal, invisible and eternal God "dwells in inapproachable light" (1Ti 6:15–16). No mortal "has known the mind of the Lord" (Ro 11:34). "For my thoughts are not your thoughts, neither are your ways my

---

Key Distinction:
transcendence/immanence (God's relationship to the world)

God not only is higher or greater than all creatures (a quantitative distinction), but transcends the world infinitely (qualitatively). Incomprehensible in his majesty, God eludes our direct knowledge or experience. At the same time, in his condescending goodness and love, God has chosen freely to relate us to himself and engage us as covenant partners. He freely speaks and acts in our history, dwells in the midst of his people, and even became human in the incarnation of the Son.

Like all great truths of revelation, God's transcendence and immanence are a paradox, intended to be adored rather than resolved. The God of love who does not need the world nevertheless chooses freely to bind creaturely reality (including us) to himself. In order to keep these from becoming abstract categories, we need to allow the biblical story to identify what is meant by the transcendent-immanent God.

ways, declares the LORD. For as the heavens are higher than the earth, so are my ways higher than your ways and my thoughts than your thoughts" (Isa 55:8–9). At the end of our zealous ascent we discover God as blinding glory, terrifying justice, and a love that destroys unlovely and unwelcome intruders. Any union we achieve with divinity in this enterprise will be like that of a dry branch within "a consuming fire" (Heb 12:29). If this were all we were told, then we might throw up our hands, concluding with radical mystics and skeptics throughout the ages that we cannot know God—at least in a rational way that can be put into words. However, Scripture tells us more.

Together with the absolute incomprehensibility of God (transcendence), Scripture affirms just as clearly the free decision of God to condescend beneath his majesty and reveal himself to us as he sees fit. Although we cannot ascend to God's incomprehensible majesty, God stoops to our capacity, descending and **accommodating** his speech to our understanding. We know God *not according to his essence, but according to his works.*[2] This formula, found frequently in the ancient fathers (especially in the East), was repeated often by Martin Luther, John Calvin, and their theological successors. We know that God is merciful, for example, because he has acted mercifully in history and revealed these actions as well as their interpretation through prophets and apostles.

A. How We Know God

So we can know God truly precisely because he makes himself known to us. We do not rise up to God; he descends to us. As God assured Moses, we cannot behold God in a beatific vision, because we are mere creatures—and sinners to boot (Ex 33:20). And yet God condescends to reveal himself by hiding himself in a gracious display of accommodated speech—even as he hid Moses and allowed his "back" (33:23) to pass by as he proclaimed himself as the one who freely shows mercy on whom he will.

Staring into the sun will blind us, yet we can find contentment simply being warmed by its rays. In the same way, trying to ascend to heaven to capture God's essence with our speculative, moral, or mystical gaze would not just blind us; it would destroy us. "They are mad who seek to discover what God is," Calvin says.[3] "What is God? Men who pose this question are merely toying with idle speculations. What help is it, in short, to know a

---

2. Gregory of Nyssa, *On 'Not Three Gods,' to Ablabius* (*NPNF²*, 5:333); Basil, "Epistle 234" (*NPNF²*, 8:274); John of Damascus, *An Exact Exposition of the Orthodox Faith* (*NPNF²*, 9:1).

3. John Calvin, *Commentaries on the Epistle of Paul the Apostle to the Romans* (ed. and trans. John Owen; Grand Rapids: Baker, 1996), 69.

God with whom we have nothing to do?... The essence of God is rather to be adored than inquired into."[4] God shows himself "not as he is in himself," Calvin cautioned (invoking the ancient fathers), "but as he is toward us"— in his energies (works), not in his essence.[5] God clothes himself in frail human language—and, ultimately, with the incarnation, in our human nature.

Furthermore, we dare not approach this God apart from the Mediator, his own Son who became flesh. A God who eludes our comprehending gaze—who masters but is never mastered—is a terrifying prospect for the sinful heart until Christ steps forward as our mediator. Calvin reminds us,

> In this ruin of mankind no one now experiences God either as Father or as Author of salvation, or favorable in any way, until Christ the Mediator comes forward to reconcile him to us.... It is one thing to feel that God as our Maker supports us by his power, governs us by his providence, nourishes us by his goodness, and attends us with all sorts of blessings—and another thing to embrace the grace of reconciliation offered to us in Christ.[6]

Apart from the gospel we flee from God's self-revelation, dressing folly in the robe of wisdom and ungodliness in the garments of virtue. It is ultimately an ethical revolt against the God who made us. There is no other "God" who exists, much less who is worth talking about, than the Father who is known in his Son and by his Spirit according to his Word, Calvin adds. In other words, we cannot just talk about a divine being, with certain ideal attributes, and then somehow add the Trinity and Jesus Christ to this understanding of the divine being. No, we must come to the Father in the Son by the Spirit through his Word.

Through revelation, the incomprehensible and utterly transcendent God places himself within our reach. The sovereign God, who eludes our attempts at mastery, by speculation, good works, or mystical experience, places himself in our hands as a free gift. Instead of being consumed, we are reconciled, redeemed, and made adopted heirs of his kingdom in the Son and by his Spirit, through his Word. Just as we are created in God's image and likeness, yet intersecting with divinity at no point, our knowledge is a creaturely version of truth, which God accommodates to our capacity and

---

4. John Calvin, *Institutes* 1.2.2. Early Reformed writers such as Musculus repeated this approach, launching their discussion of God with the question of *who* God is rather than *what* God is. See Richard Muller, *Post-Reformation Reformed Dogmatics: Divine Essence and Attributes* (2nd ed.; Grand Rapids: Baker Academic, 2003), 228.

5. Calvin, *Institutes* 1.10.2.

6. Ibid., 1.2.1.

reveals through ordinary speech and speakers. As the infinite Creator, God alone possesses absolute knowledge. Every fact is interpreted, and we need God's interpretation if we are to know reality properly.

There are obvious differences between human beings: height, age, skin color, gender, ethnicity, and so forth. Some people are stronger, while others are wiser; some are more attractive, while others are more skillful, and so on. Yet all of these are *finite-quantitative* differences—that is, differences in degree rather than kind. Even when comparing different classes we see some points of complete overlap. As different as they are, humans and whales have enough in common to belong to the same class (mammal). There are even shared characteristics across classes—for example, between mammals and reptiles. As vast as differences may be between humans, sparrows, and oak trees, they share at least one thing in common: creaturely existence.

However, there is an *infinite-qualitative* distinction between God and creatures. This applies at the level of reality (ontology). At no point do God's essence and existence overlap or intersect with ours. Even when we use a predicate like "good" to describe God and our neighbor, God is not only greater or better, but is in a class of his own. It also applies at the level of how we know things (epistemology). As in our being, so in our knowing, we are always creatures and God is the creator. We are incapable of knowing anything as God knows it. Another way of putting this is to say that God is infinitely transcendent.

Does this mean that we cannot know God at all? Are comparisons meaningless? Not at all, because God has revealed himself through everyday language. Like "baby talk," God speaks in ways that we can understand. His communication is effective, though he infinitely transcends his own revelation. When he tells us that he is good, speaks of himself as a loving parent or king, and responds to our prayers, we can be confident that he is telling us the truth as far as we can know it—even though it is not the Truth as he knows it. God's knowledge is **archetypal** (original), while ours is **ectypal** (a finite copy). God is not only infinitely transcendent, but freely immanent as well—that is, coming to us, getting involved in our lives. Because our God does not remain aloof in blissful detachment but enters into our history by speaking his Word and then sending his incarnate Word to us for our redemption, we can know God truthfully as finite creatures.

This traditional Christian view avoids the extremes of rationalism and irrationalism that continue to dominate modern and postmodern thinking. On the one hand, *rationalism* assumes that whatever we know truthfully, we know exactly as God knows it. In fact, as the ancient philosophers

> ## Key Distinction:
> ### *archetypal/ectypal*
>
> Coined by an early Reformed theologian (Franciscus Junius), this distinction affirms that God is just as different from us in his knowledge as in his being. Since he is the Creator and we are his creatures, God's being and knowledge are not just greater quantitatively, but also differ qualitatively from ours.

understood it, our reason itself is a spark of infinite and eternal divinity. So "good" means exactly the same thing when we are talking about God as it does when we are referring to our neighbor. The predicate "good" here is used **univocally** (the same meaning). On the other hand, *irrationalism* assumes that just because we cannot know anything perfectly, we cannot know anything truly; "truth" is just a subjective opinion that we imagine to be anchored somehow in a world outside of our own thoughts and feelings. In this view, we have no idea what "good" means applied to God, since God is nothing like my neighbor ("good" is used here **equivocally**).

However, Christian theology maintains that even though we do not have absolute truth, God does, and he has communicated all of the truth he deems sufficient in ways that we can understand and respond to accordingly. We are not divine at any point, but we are created in God's image—as his analogy. Similarly, while our finite and creaturely knowledge is never exactly the same as God's (univocal), it is also not irrational (equivocal). Rather, we know God **analogically**. Our knowledge (like our being) is analogical of God's, since we receive both as his gift.

By exclaiming, "Your mother roared," one is suggesting neither that Mom is a lion (using "roared" univocally) nor that there is no similarity between the mother's manner of speaking and a lion's native tongue (understanding "roared" equivocally—bearing no relation). Rather, one is drawing an analogy, a similarity without exact correspondence. A time-honored axiom in theology is that in every analogy between God and human beings, there is always more dissimilarity than similarity. Nevertheless, because God is the creator who made us in his image and left traces of his own character through the whole fabric of the whole world, there is sufficient basis for analogies that make their point.

Even to predicate "existence" of God and creatures, one cannot assume a univocal correspondence without falling into pantheism (divine and human beings differing in degree but not in kind). Strictly speaking, God does not "exist"; rather, he has life in himself. Existence is inherently dependent, while God is the source of our being. Nevertheless, the Living God does certainly exist in the way that an average person intends by asking whether God exists.

The point is that we do not have to possess absolute life or absolute knowledge in order to receive from God our creaturely existence and truth. Because this God is the Father, the Son, and the Spirit, and because this God has related the world to himself from creation to consummation — even entering history by becoming flesh — his immanent nearness is just as great as his infinite transcendence. We can know God because he has revealed himself.

B. Meeting a Stranger

Coming to "know" God is like meeting a stranger. God is a stranger to us in three senses. First, God is a stranger in the *ontological* sense. That is, in his very being, God is not like any person you've ever met. A popular poster said it best: "Two Basic Truths: There is a God and You Are Not He." Far from being seen as something negative, this truth is something to be celebrated. It explains why it is right to worship God rather than ourselves or other creatures. If you are not God, there is no crime in being finite, dependent, embodied creatures who belong to the register of space and time. Contrary to Plato, Hegel, and a host of contemporary philosophers, being a stranger

Key Distinction:
univocal/equivocal/analogical

God infinitely transcends us in knowledge as well as being. Therefore, for example, the word "good" cannot be univocal (= means exactly the same thing) in relation to God and creatures alike. At the same time, it's not as if there is no basis for using "good" to describe God and creatures, as an equivocal (= no relation) view assumes. Created in God's image, we are his analogies, and God reveals himself in familiar terms so that we can understand what he is like, though not exactly what he is in himself. Our knowledge is therefore *analogical* of God's. A univocal view tends toward rationalism, while an equivocal view tends toward irrationalism or skepticism. An analogical view affirms that we can know reality truly as creatures who attend to God's Word, even though we do not know reality absolutely, as does God.

to God, ontologically, is not negative—a falling away from pure being. It is the gift of a distinct creaturely existence.

Second, God is a stranger in the *ethical* sense. Unlike our ontological difference from God, this "strangeness" in our relationship to God is negative. Because we are strangers to God in the ethical sense, we are estranged from him, marked by the tragic condition of human beings "in Adam," under the reign of sin and death. It is in this sense that the Bible speaks about us as enemies of God, hostile, separated, and condemned. Our ethical rebellion corrupts not only our will and action, but also our reasoning. We still will, act, and reason, but we do all of this as covenant breakers. We still encounter reality, but our interpretations are out of whack. We are not neutral, autonomous, independent, and unbiased investigators, but those "who by their unrighteousness suppress the truth" (Ro 1:18).

Finally, God is a stranger in a third sense, *redemptively*, as he issues the surprisingly wonderful announcement that in spite of human rebellion he will redeem us by grace alone in Christ alone. For reasons we will explore later, this gospel is counterintuitive—strange to us in our fallen state of death and estrangement from God. It does not resonate with us in our natural condition because we are hostile to the God who commands and saves us. Because it entails the surrender of our autonomy—our "right" to determine good and evil for ourselves—it sounds foreign and unusual to us. When we meet God in the gospel, we first encounter him as a stranger, come to rescue us from a danger we did not even realize we were in.

II. God Reveals Himself

Contrary to what many assume, revelation is not something that wells up within pious souls who seek it. As we have just discussed, God is a stranger and we meet him when and where he chooses to introduce himself. Strictly speaking, we do not come to know God; God *reveals* himself. In our fallen condition, "None is righteous, no, not one; no one understands; no one seeks for God" (Ro 3:10–11). Yet God does not wait for the impossible move on our part. "I revealed myself to those who did not ask for me; I was found by those who did not seek me" (Isa 65:1 NIV). Like a parent playing hide-and-seek with a child, the ungraspable God allows himself to be "caught," as it were. In creation as well as redemption, God is always the initiator. He is never revealed passively, like someone who is caught changing clothes without the blinds being drawn. Rather, God makes himself known on his own terms, when, where, and how he chooses. God can be an object of our knowledge only if he has revealed himself to us. Consequently, *theology can exist as a legitimate enterprise only when it begins with God's self-revelation.*

A. General and Special Revelation

I know my wife because she communicates with me. Likewise, I know that there is a purpose for my life and for the world and history because God has communicated his acts, intentions, and promises. We know God as the sovereign maker and judge from his works in creation and providence. This is what is commonly referred to as **general revelation**. The Psalmist exclaims, "The heavens declare the glory of God, and the sky above proclaims his handiwork" (Ps 19:1). Even the testimony yielded by the inanimate creation is described poetically in terms of living speech (vv. 2–4). Besides the Psalms (especially Pss. 8:1–9; 19:1–6; 102:25), the wisdom literature appeals to God's design in nature as revealing the love, justice, righteousness, sovereignty, and wisdom of God in everyday life. Jesus also teaches us to trust in God's providential care by appealing to the obvious order in nature (Lk 12:24, 27).

Here we encounter the important distinction between **law** and **gospel**. Taken in the broadest senses, law refers to the revelation of God as our loving yet just Creator, Lawgiver, and Judge. As Paul argues, it is the righteousness *of* God that is revealed in the law, and this condemns us all (Ro 1:18–3:20), while the gospel reveals the righteousness *from* God, namely, that we "are justified by his grace as a gift, through the redemption that is in Christ Jesus" (Ro 3:24). The great Roman writer Seneca gave eloquent testimony to many truths that, according to Romans 1 and 2, God has inscribed on the human conscience in creation. Paul sometimes calls this natural law the "elementary principles of the world" (*stoicheia tou kosmou*), as in Galatians 4:3, 8–9 and Colossians 2:8, 20.

No one, Jew or Gentile, can claim ignorance on the day of judgment, since they have suppressed the knowledge that they do in fact have of their Creator and Judge. Paul can even call pagan poets to witness in his speech in Athens (Ac 17:28). Predating the Mosaic law by at least five centuries, the Babylonian Code of Hammurabi issues remarkably similar commands, even appealing to divine sanction.[7] In our own day, Muslims, Jews, Christians, Buddhists, Hindus, and others have every reason to reflect together on the universal moral imperatives that they affirm together. Jordan's Prince

---

7. C. H. W. Johns, trans., *Babylonian and Assyrian Laws, Contracts and Letters* (Whitefish, Mont.: Kessinger, 2004), 390.

Key Distinction:
law/gospel

God's Word has two parts—the law and the gospel—and there is a danger in either confusing or separating them. The law commands and the gospel gives. The law says, "Do," and the gospel says, "Done!" Equally God's Word, both are good, but God does different things through them.

In the widest sense, the law is everything in Scripture that commands, and the gospel is everything in Scripture that makes promises based solely on God's grace to us in Christ. But in a narrower sense, the gospel is 1 Corinthians 15:3–4: "For I delivered to you as of first importance what I also received: that Christ died for our sins in accordance with the Scriptures, that he was buried, that he was raised on the third day in accordance with the Scriptures." The content of the gospel is the announcement that Christ was crucified and raised for our salvation in fulfillment of the Scriptures. At the same time, the gospel includes God's gracious fulfillment in Christ of *all* of the promises related to the new creation. That's why Paul can answer his question, "Shall we then sin that grace may abound?" with *more* gospel: union with Christ in his death, burial, and resurrection, so that we're no longer under sin's dominion. The gospel isn't just enough to justify the ungodly; it's enough to regenerate and sanctify the ungodly. However, only because (in the narrower sense) the good news announces our justification are we for the first time free to embrace God as our Father rather than our Judge. We have been saved from the condemnation *and* tyranny of sin. Both are essential to the "glad tidings" that we proclaim.

We can also speak of the law and the gospel in the redemptive-historical sense, as the covenantal principle of inheritance. The history of salvation moves from promise to fulfillment, from shadows to reality. In this sense, the law is not opposed to the gospel.

Yet when it comes to how we receive this gift—how redemption is applied to us by the Spirit—we are saved apart from the law. Law and gospel are completely opposed in this sense, since they are two different bases or principles of inheritance. We are saved by Christ or by our own obedience, but we cannot be saved by both. Interestingly, Paul includes both senses in Romans 3:21: "But now the righteousness of God has been manifested apart from the law [justification in the order of salvation], although the Law and the Prophets [i.e., the Old Testament writings] bear witness to it."

Finally, Lutheran and Reformed traditions distinguish (without separating) *three uses of the law*: the first (pedagogical), to expose our guilt and corruption, driving us to Christ; the second, a civil use to restrain public vice; and the third, to guide Christian obedience. Believers are not "under the law" in the first sense. They are justified. However, they are still obligated to the law, both as it is stipulated and enforced by the state (second use) and as it frames Christian discipleship (third use). We never ground our status before God in our obedience to imperatives, but in Christ's righteousness; yet we are also bound to Christ, who continues to lead and direct us by his holy will.

Hassan bin Talal, a Muslim, has remarked, "I keep saying that if we all observed the Ten Commandments, we would not have succumbed to so much grief in the first place. Whether it is the Golden Law, the Straight Path, or the Ten Commandments, we recognize that we do not need to reinvent the code of conduct."[8]

There is a lot of consensus on the law. The Golden Rule ("Do unto others as you would have them do unto you" [see Mt 7:12; Lk 6:31]) is not a precept unique to Christianity, and it is arrogant for Christians to assume that they have a corner on personal and civic virtue. Even well-known atheist Sam Harris once wrote that "there is clearly a sacred dimension to our existence, and coming to terms with it could well be the highest purpose of human life."[9] Harris added that he is "interested in spiritual experience." "There is such a thing as profoundly transformative, meaningful experience that can be very hard won. You might have to go into a cave for a month or a year to have certain experiences. The whole contemplative literature is something I read and I take very seriously. The problem is it is also riddled with religious superstition and dogma, [so] that you have to be a selective consumer of this literature."[10] Harris repeats a familiar refrain of the Enlightenment philosophers: universal moral intuitions that can be known without special revelation are fine; where religions go off the rails is in their miraculous claims. The law is familiar, innate, and written on everyone's conscience; the gospel is strange, astonishing—even offensive—and can be

---

8. Prince Hassan, interview by Cornelis Hulsman, "The Peacebuilding Prince," *Christianity Today*, February 2008, 64.

9. Quoted in Steve Padilla, "Rabbi, Atheist Debate with Passion, Humor," *Los Angeles Times*, December 29, 2007, B2.

10. Ibid.

announced only by a herald. The law is in our conscience by creation, part of what it means to be created in God's image. Philosophers like Kant can speak of the sufficiency of this "moral law within," however, only because they have denied that they are in a precarious situation that requires special revelation and redemption.

Creation reveals God's law—"his eternal power and divine nature," as well as his commands that render us "without excuse" (Ro 1:19–20). However, the "gift of righteousness" by which God justifies the guilty in Christ is known only in the gospel (Ro 3:21–26). In its grandeur, the Grand Canyon displays the majesty of its Artist, but it speaks not a word of forgiveness for sinners. For this, we need another word that comes after the fall, after the "No!" that our race has issued to its kind Creator. Because the law is natural to us, the average person is inclined to think that religion is primarily about inner experience and moral improvement. However, the gospel is alien to us, even counterintuitive. As a surprising announcement of God's free mercy, it requires a lot of words—many sermons—for God to preach Christ into our hearts. When people call for "deeds, not creeds," asking, "What Would Jesus Do?" without much interest in the query, "What has Jesus done?" identifying themselves as "spiritual but not religious," they are asking for the law without the gospel.

Special revelation, the particular knowledge of God that we attain through the illumination of the Spirit in the written Word of God, corrects our systematic distortion of **general revelation**. Not only do we need special revelation to correct our interpretation of creation and "the good, the true, and the beautiful," but we would have absolutely no knowledge of God's saving work for us in Christ apart from it. In our sinful condition, we need not only a clearer revelation of God's moral will, but an entirely different message, a word of rescue, an announcement of what God has done to forgive, justify, and liberate us from our treason against that moral will and the law's just sentence. It is just that new word that God speaks to Adam and Eve after the fall, in the promise of a redeemer. The rest of the Bible, after Genesis 3:15, traces the unfolding promise of redemption in Christ. All of the laws, wisdom, narratives, poetry, and prophecies coalesce around this thickening plot. The gospel is the heartbeat of the triune God and his revelation in Scripture. It is an announcement that we never could know—or can know—apart from someone bringing the good news to us. The law keeps stopping history in its tracks—not because it is defective, but because we are depraved. Whenever history moves forward, human rebellion provokes God's judgment. It is the gospel that keeps covenantal history rushing forward, in spite of the dams erected by the unfaithfulness

> ## Key Distinction:
> ### general/special revelation
>
> God has revealed himself to us in general revelation by what he has created, although we actively suppress and distort this truth as sinners. Creation (general revelation) displays the existence, wisdom, power, goodness, and righteousness of God "so that everyone is without excuse" (Ro 1:20). However, in special revelation God more clearly discloses these attributes, correcting our sinful distortions, and also reveals the gospel of his Son, which is not known apart from this source. The normative canon of special revelation is Holy Scripture.

of the covenant partner. This promise begins in Genesis 3:15 and concludes with the vision of that day when the elect are given the right to eat freely from the Tree of Life in the true garden of which Eden was merely a type (Rev 2:7; 22:1 – 5).

B. The Death of Reason

Whether by collapsing the creation into the Creator (as in Stoicism) or by sweeping from our horizon any transcendent and self-revealing God (as in Epicureanism), the modern age has been characterized by radical swings between rationalism and irrationalism. In this regard, though, modern thought is hardly unique; there are not many options once one jettisons God's own self-revelation. "Claiming to be wise, they became fools, and exchanged the glory of the immortal God for images.... They exchanged the truth about God for a lie and worshiped and served the creature rather than the Creator, who is blessed forever!" (Ro 1:22, 25). The story of modern thought begins with the enthronement of autonomous reason.

Since the Enlightenment (1650 – 1800), the modern individual was called to a thorough house-cleaning, rejecting all outside authorities and sweeping beneath his feet all inherited beliefs, institutions, and practices. Everything, we were told, would rest now on the sure foundation of reason. The assumption here was that reason, unlike authority, was unbiased. Aware that the fire they had started might burn down the house of morality upon which civilization depended, many of these thinkers tried to rescue some indispensable remnants for the palace they would erect on the ashes of Christendom. We cannot know anything objectively about God, Immanuel Kant argued; God is not an object of our reason or our sense experience. Universal reason is implanted in all of us, and there is much in the Bible as well as other sacred texts to support "the moral law within," but we do not base our convictions on any external authority.

Furthermore, the enthronement of reason meant that there was now no special revelation—that is, no miraculous word from God revealed to a particular people, in particular times and places. Because natural reason is sufficient, we do not need such a revelation. In addition, any true knowledge must be *universal* and absolutely *certain*, grounded in the rational ideas of our mind. Even if its reports are accurate, historical knowledge is not capable of yielding rational certainty, and a particular revelation to a particular people cannot command universal assent. At most, Jesus can be a model for us, but even that is unnecessary, Kant said, because we already have "the idea of a life well-pleasing to God" in our own minds and are capable of doing our duty ourselves. Still, we cannot eliminate all theistic belief. We must continue to presuppose God's existence as a necessary prerequisite for the moral principles that we know according to our practical reason. Without "God," the immortality of the soul, and rewards and punishments in the hereafter, we will descend into anarchy. But "God" was no longer regarded as knowable in terms of public reason or historical evidence delivered through special envoys. If he were, then Kant's entire system would be threatened. Basically, this reflects a *deistic* worldview.

At the other extreme, G. W. F. Hegel argued that God actually comes to realize his own existence in and through the world, especially through human spiritual consciousness. Hegel represents a panentheistic paradigm. We can know God as he is in himself, even as God comes to know himself through the unfolding of history. Hegel believed that it was possible for us to have absolute (archetypal) knowledge by *immediate intuition*, not through a finite (ectypal) revelation like the Bible. As Enlightenment rationalism turned to Romantic sentiment, Friedrich Schleiermacher—the father of modern theology—argued that although we cannot know God, we can experience him in the universal *feeling* of absolute dependence. The scriptures of various religions are expressions of that universal experience, but they issue from the work of God in the soul, not as an external word from heaven. It was out of these presuppositions that liberal scholars went to work, critiquing and redacting the biblical text with an assumed, naturalistic bias they identified as "unprejudiced" reason.

The net effect of this modern criticism has been the denial that God speaks and acts within history. Either we know God in the same way as he knows himself, or we cannot know God at all—even as finite creatures, through his self-revelation. Many modern theologians not only accepted the critical terms of surrender, but help to write them. No longer the study of God, theology became a subjective discourse about human feelings, cultures, values, and religious practices.

In recent decades this Tower of Babel has come crashing down all around us, collapsing under its own weight. However, we should bear in mind that the assault on rationalism is nothing new. Rationalism and irrationalism have always formed a secret alliance against God's authoritative Word.[11] The question of whether modernity is really over and we have now truly entered a "postmodern" era is beside the point. The swinging pendulum remains—and will remain—a constant in all forms of pagan thinking.

As the pretensions of modernity are unmasked today, it is a good time for us to recover our nerve, "always being prepared to make a defense to anyone who asks [us] for a reason for the hope that is in [us]" (1Pe 3:15). By breaking into our history, sharing our history, and transforming that history from the inside out, God has indeed made himself the object of our knowledge. "That which was from the beginning, which we have heard, which we have seen with our eyes, which we looked upon and have touched with our hands, concerning the word of life—the life was made manifest, and we have seen it, and testify to it and proclaim to you the eternal life, which was with the Father and was made manifest to us" (1Jn 1:1–2).

There is much that the Stoics had right, as Paul himself acknowledged. There is a general revelation of God's existence, power, wisdom, and justice that permeates the whole creation. There is indeed "the moral law within," as Kant insisted. This revelation is universal, whereas the Bible and other sacred texts are particular revelations, made to particular peoples, in particular times and places. However, these philosophers rejected not only the possibility, but also the need of special revelation/redemption by assuming that human beings are good people who could become better rather than sinners who need to be saved. Modernity had an allergic reaction to "the scandal of the particular," and today, when many people identify themselves as "spiritual, not religious," they show themselves to be heirs of this modern, Enlightenment way of thinking. In the modern and postmodern understanding, spirituality is something general, with no particular object of worship, no specific story (external to "my story"), and no specific doctrines, worship, or discipleship that flow out of it. It leaves us free to worship ourselves. We have everything we need within ourselves. Universal reason and morality—the nucleus of general revelation—will create a better world, whereas the claims

---

11. So Cornelius Van Til, *The Defense of the Faith* (Philadelphia: Presbyterian and Reformed, 1955), 143.

concerning particular revelations create creeds, rituals, and dead institutions. It is the specificity and the particularity of Christian truth claims that are a scandal to today's Stoics and Epicureans alike.

However, this general revelation—universal reason and morality—is sufficient to convict us of our crimes against our Creator and just Judge. What we need now is more than this general revelation. We need an external revelation, a particular revelation, of God's saving mercy toward us in his Son. In other words, our attention must turn from ascending to eternal truths above and within, from the script we are writing for ourselves, to the grand drama that God is unfolding before us—and with us—in history. And even though the resurrection of Jesus, by itself, is meaningless apart from the unfolding biblical drama that begins with creation and leads to the consummation, nevertheless, by beginning with this unique event in history, we are led to a particular claim that can unsettle our settled assumptions. So that is where we must begin: with the particular and unique claim that Jesus Christ has been raised from the dead.

III. Revelation within the Realm of History Alone: The Resurrection

The heart of special revelation is "good news," what we commonly call *the gospel.* The New Testament word translated "gospel" (*euangelion*) refers to a report brought by an official herald from the frontlines of the battlefield, announcing that victory has been achieved and the war is over. As we discussed earlier, the gospel is "folly to Gentiles" (1Co 1:23) not only because of its message (namely, a crucified Messiah crowned King of kings in his bodily resurrection as the beginning of the new creation) but because of its very form. Jesus does not found a new school of philosophy with its own version of "the good life." Though the gospel does generate a new worldview, a new way of ethical living, these are the fruit of the gospel, not its source. The gospel is not something you come to understand from reflection, a truth based on a new metaphysical worldview taught by Jesus. It is a message, declared to us from God.

Uniquely, Christianity is a message much closer to the grammar of politics than to that of religion, though the military conquest of its King is nothing that the rulers of this age could even imagine. It is a conquest of grace, not oppression; of the will to forgiveness rather than to brute power. In the first song of the New Testament, Mary testifies to this gospel in the Magnificat: Israel's God has acted in history, fulfilling his promise of salvation, bringing the powerful to nothing and raising up the poor and lowly.

So everything turns on whether the reported events actually happened. *No other religion bases its entire edifice on datable facts.* The events it reports either happened or they didn't, but the result is that the gospel creates heralds, not speculative pundits, mystics, and moralists. Jesus Christ does not create a school or a pious community for the spiritually and morally gifted. Rather, he brings a kingdom — the kingdom of God — which casts down the proud and lifts up the downcast.

We must not miss this striking truth — that the Christian creed turns on *historical* events rather than eternal truths or principles. Just as we were trying to ascend away from historical particulars to universal and eternal truths — the Word became flesh. The universal God became a zygote in the womb of a Jewish virgin. Confirmed by extrabiblical sources, Luke places Jesus' birth in the days when Caesar Augustus issued a decree for a census, "when Quirinius was governor of Syria" (Lk 2:1 – 2). An otherwise obscure Roman bureaucrat became one of history's most recognizable names because Jesus was "crucified under Pontius Pilate." The eternal God dates himself, so to speak.

"And the Word became flesh and dwelt among us, and we have seen his glory, glory as of the only Son from the Father, full of grace and truth" (Jn 1:14). Notice the physical senses included in John's reference elsewhere:

> That which was from the beginning, which we have *heard*, which we have seen with our eyes, which we looked upon and have touched with our hands, concerning the word of life — the life was made manifest, and we have *seen* it, and testify to it and proclaim to you the eternal life, which was with the Father and was made manifest to us — that which we have seen and heard we proclaim also to you, so that you too may have fellowship with us; and indeed our fellowship is with the Father and with his Son Jesus Christ. (1Jn 1:1 – 3, emphasis added)

Here, speculation is useless. It does not matter what we thought reality was like, whether we believed in thirty gods or none. Something has happened in history, and we cannot wish it away. Now that the apostles have entered Jesus' existence and message in the rolls alongside other public, historical claims, that existence and message can no longer be treated as purely subjective beliefs.

Those who argue that God cannot be the object of our empirical knowledge ignore the heart of the Christian message: namely, that God became flesh and lived, died, rose again, ascended to his throne, and will return again in datable history. These claims are now open to countertestimony in the public square. This either happened or it didn't happen, but the claim itself is hardly meaningless or beyond investigation. The apostolic testimony was not about what happened to the apostles; it was about what happened to Jesus—and through him, to the whole world. And in the summary that follows, we examine the central elements of the testimony they gave. Even though this summary includes extrabiblical references, the New Testament itself represents the most reliable basis for the resurrection of Jesus Christ. Compared with other ancient texts, the New Testament texts enjoy an unrivaled transmission history.[12]

The earliest Christians testified to the following elements of the resurrection claim, even to the point of martyrdom:

A. Jesus Christ Lived, Died, and was Buried

Only those in the popular media still ask the question whether Jesus was a historical person. As the liberal Jewish scholar Rabbi Samuel Sandmel observes, "The 'Christ-myth' theories are not accepted or even discussed by scholars today."[13] Even Marcus Borg, cofounder of the radical "Jesus Seminar," concedes that Christ's death by Roman crucifixion is "the most certain fact about the historical Jesus."[14] There are numerous attestations to these facts from ancient Jewish and Roman sources. According to the Babylonian Talmud, "Yeshua" was a false prophet hanged on Passover eve for sorcery and blasphemy. Joseph Klausner, an eminent Jewish scholar, identifies the following references to Jesus in the Talmud: Jesus was a rabbi whose mother, Mary (Miriam), was married to a carpenter who was nevertheless not the natural father of Jesus. Jesus went with his family to Egypt, returned to Judea and made disciples, performed miraculous signs by sorcery, led Israel astray, and was deserted at his trial without any defenders. On Passover eve he was crucified.[15] Late in the first century, the great Roman historian Tacitus (*Annals*

---

12. Historians today rely on classics like Thucydides' *History of the Peloponnesian War*, Caesar's *Gallic War*, and Tacitus's *Histories*. The earliest copies we have for these date from 1,300, 900, and 700 years after the original writing, respectively, and there are eight extant copies of the first, ten of the second, and two of the third. In contrast, the earliest copy of Mark's gospel is dated at AD 130 (a century after the original writing), and there are 5,000 ancient Greek copies, along with nearly 20,000 Latin and other ancient manuscripts. The sheer volume of ancient manuscripts provides sufficient comparison between copies to provide an accurate reproduction of the original text. Ironically, a number of fashionable scholars attracted to the so-called gnostic gospels as an "alternative Christianity" have far fewer manuscripts, and the original writings cannot be dated any earlier than a century after the canonical Gospels.

13. Rabbi Samuel Sandmel, *A Jewish Understanding of the New Testament* (3rd ed.; Woodstock, Vt.: Jewish Lights Publications, 2010), 197.

14. Marcus Borg, *Jesus: A New Vision* (San Francisco: HarperCollins, 1987), 179.

15. Joseph Klausner, *Yeshu ha-Notzri* (Hebrew; Jerusalem: Shtible, 1922; trans. and repr. as *Jesus of Nazareth*; New York: Bloch, 1989), 18–46. Collected over the several centuries following Christ, the Talmud is of course further removed from the events than the New Testament. However, it contains a number of older fragments. Even the liberal Sandmel observes, "Certain bare facts are historically not to be doubted. Jesus, who emerged into public notice in Galilee when Herod Antipas was its Tetrarch, was a real person, the leader of a movement. He had followers, called disciples. The claim was made,

15.44) referred to the crucifixion of Jesus under Pontius Pilate. In AD 52, the Samaritan historian Thallos recounts the earthquake and strange darkness during Christ's crucifixion (reported in Luke 23:44–45), although he attributes the darkness to a solar eclipse.[16]

Of course, alternative explanations to Christ's death have been offered. The so-called swoon theory speculates that Jesus did not really die, but was nursed back to health to live out his days and to die a natural death. In Surah 4:157, Islam's Qur'an teaches that the Romans "never killed him," but "were made to think that they did." However, we know also from ancient sources how successful the Romans were at crucifixions. The description in the Gospels of the spear thrust into Christ's side and the ensuing flow of blood and water fit with routine accounts of crucifixion from Roman military historians as well as with modern medical examinations of the report.[17] As for the Islamic conjecture, no supporting argument is offered, and the obvious question arises: are we really to believe that the Roman government and military officers as well as the Jewish leaders and the people of Jerusalem "were made to think that" they had crucified Jesus when in fact they did not do so? Furthermore, why should a document written six centuries after the events in question be given any credence when we have first-century Christian, Jewish, and Roman documents that attest to Christ's death and burial? Roman officers in charge of crucifixions knew when their victims were dead. Another liberal New Testament scholar, John A. T. Robinson, concluded that the burial of Jesus in the tomb is "one of the earliest and best-attested facts about Jesus."[18]

The burial of Jesus in the tomb of Joseph of Arimathea is mentioned in all four Gospels (Mt 27:57–60; Mk 15:43–46; Lk 23:50–53; Jn 19:38–42). This is a specific detail that lends credibility to the account. Furthermore, it's an embarrassing detail that the disciples would not likely have forged. After

---

either by him or for him, that he was the long-awaited Jewish Messiah. He journeyed from Galilee to Jerusalem, possibly in 29 or 30, and there he was executed, crucified by the Romans as a political rebel. After his death, his disciples believed that he was resurrected, and had gone to heaven, but would return to earth at the appointed time for the final divine judgment of mankind" (Sandmel, *Jewish Understanding*, 33). The basic historical claims of the Apostles' Creed are present in this description of the earliest belief of the Jewish Christians.

16. Robert E. Van Voorst, *Jesus outside the New Testament* (Grand Rapids: Eerdmans, 2000), 19–20.

17. See, e.g., William D. Edwards, Wesley J. Gabel, and Floyd E. Hosmer, "On the Physical Death of Jesus Christ," *Journal of the American Medical Association* 255 (1986): 1455–63. See also the extensive bibliography on this point in Gary R. Habermas, "The Core Resurrection Data," in *Tough-Minded Christianity* (ed. William Dembski and Thomas Schirrmacher; Nashville: B&H Academic, 2008), 401 nn10–11.

18. John A. T. Robinson, *The Human Face of God* (Philadelphia: Westminster, 1973), 131. I refer to these sources merely to underscore the implausibility of popular dismissals of the evidence among nonspecialists, especially in the media.

all, according to the Gospels, the disciples fled and Peter even denied knowing Jesus. Yet here is a wealthy and powerful member of the ruling Jewish Council (Sanhedrin), coming to Pilate to ask for permission to bury Jesus in his own tomb. Adding to the embarrassment, according to John 19:38–42, Joseph was assisted in the burial by another leader of the Pharisees, Nicodemus (who met with Jesus secretly in John 3). Joseph was of such a stature that Pilate agreed to deliver the body over to him, but only after confirming with the centurion that Jesus was in fact dead (Mk 15:44–45).

B. Jesus Christ's Tomb was Empty after Three Days

Not even this claim should be controversial today, since it was acknowledged by Romans and Jews as well as by the first Christians. Of course, there were widely divergent explanations, but there was a remarkable consensus on this point—three days after his burial, the tomb of Jesus was empty. According to Matthew 28:11–15, the Jewish leaders maintained that the body was stolen by the disciples, and this is confirmed by the polemic that endured all the way to *Toledoth Yeshu*, a fourth- or fifth-century anti-Christian polemic.[19]

Romans, too, were concerned about the disruption caused by Jesus' empty tomb. A marble plaque was discovered with an "Edict of Caesar" commanding capital punishment for anyone who dares to "break a tomb." Called the *Nazareth Inscription*, the decree was provoked by disturbances in Jerusalem, and the plaque has been dated to somewhere near AD 41. Giving specific references to distinctively Jewish burials (tombs and other cemeteries), the edict targets the Jewish community.[20] Suetonius (AD 75–130), a Roman official and historian, recorded the expulsion of Jews from Rome in 48 because of controversy erupting over "a certain Chrestus" (*Claudius* 25.4). In a letter to the Emperor Trajan around the year 110, Pliny the Younger, imperial governor of what is now Turkey, reported that Christians gathered on Sunday to pray to Jesus "as to a god," to hear the letters of his appointed officers read and expounded, and to receive a meal at which they believed Christ himself presided (*Epistle* 10.96). The very fact that Jewish and Roman leaders, though unable to locate Jesus, dead or alive, sought alternative expla-

---

19. This widespread belief among early Jewish critics of Christianity is evident also in Justin Martyr's *Dialogue with Trypho*. See Sara Parvis and Paul Foster, eds., *Justin Martyr and His Worlds* (Minneapolis: Fortress, 2007), 83, 163.

20. Bruce M. Metzger, "The Nazareth Inscription Once Again," in *New Testament Studies: Philological, Versional, and Patristic* (New Testament Tools and Studies 10; Leiden: Brill, 1980), 76–90; cf. Clyde E. Billington, "The Nazareth Inscription: Proof of the Resurrection of Christ? Parts I and II," accessed at www.biblearchaeology.org (July 9, 2012).

nations for the resurrection demonstrates that the empty tomb is a historical fact. For the gospel story to have come to an easy and abrupt end, the authorities would only have had to produce a body.

In 1982, noted Jewish scholar Pinchas Lapide surprised many (especially liberal Protestants) with his book, *The Resurrection of Jesus: A Jewish Perspective*. Although Lapide does not believe that Jesus is the Jewish Messiah, after careful evaluation he concludes that Jesus was indeed raised by God from the dead after three days. Unsatisfied by alternative explanations (mass hallucination, a mere vision of a spiritually risen Christ, the disciples' theft of the body from the tomb, etc.), Lapide concludes that "some modern Christian theologians are ashamed of the material facticity of the resurrection." Their "varying attempts at dehistoricizing" the event reveal their own anti-supernatural prejudices more than they offer serious historical evaluation. "However, for the first Christians who thought, believed, and hoped in a Jewish manner, the immediate historicity was not only a part of that happening but the indispensable precondition for the recognition of its significance for salvation."[21]

Today, like every day since the first Easter, some mock, others express openness to further discussion, while still others embrace the risen Christ, exclaiming with Thomas, "My Lord and my God!" (Jn 20:28). If faith involves knowledge that Christ is the risen Lord, faith is also more than mere knowledge—it is trust. Faith is not merely believing *that* Jesus of Nazareth is the risen Christ; it is embracing him as *our* Lord and Savior. "*My* Lord and *my* God!"

True faith calls on the name of Jesus for salvation from death, hell, sin, and Satan. Therefore, sound theology has its source in a founding *drama* with its revealed *doctrines*. Through the drama and the doctrine together the Spirit produces *doxology*—repentance and trust—and brings us into the unfolding story of God, no longer as spectators, but as *disciples* on pilgrimage to the everlasting city.

Key Terms

- polytheism, pantheism, panentheism, deism, atheism
- incomprehensibility
- accommodation
- doctrine of analogy (or analogical)

---

21. Pinchas Lapide, *The Resurrection of Jesus: A Jewish Perspective* (trans. Wilhelm C. Linss; Minneapolis: Augsburg Fortress, 1982), 130.

Key Distinctions

- transcendence/immanence
- archetypal/ectypal
- univocal/equivocal/analogical
- law/gospel
- general/special revelation

Key Questions

1. What is the doctrine of analogy, and how does it differ from other views?
2. In what senses can we call God a "stranger"—in other words, qualitatively different from us?
3. Why do we need special revelation?
4. What are some of the principal alternatives to the resurrection of Jesus as the explanation for the empty tomb? Are they plausible? Why, or why not?
5. How much rests on the claim that God reveals himself?

Chapter Two

God's Written Word

Long ago, at many times and in many ways, God spoke to our fathers by the prophets, but in these last days he has spoken to us by his Son, whom he appointed the heir of all things, through whom he also created the world" (Heb 1:1–2). We know God as our redeemer through his saving work in Jesus Christ. Yet this revelation is strange to our fallen hearts, counterintuitive and even offensive. Contrary to our distorted intuitions, the gospel does not encourage our conquest of heaven through intellectual, mystical, or moral striving. It announces that even while we were enemies of God, he reconciled us (Ro 5:10). While we were dead in sins, he made us alive in Christ (Eph 2:5). We are saved by God's good works, not our own (Eph 2:8–9). Because we are sinners, God's speech is disruptive and disorienting. We are not the ones who overcome our estrangement from God; he heals the breach by communicating the gospel of his Son.

Jesus claimed to be the eternal Son of the Father who came down from heaven in order to reveal and fulfill his Father's will by saving sinners. He does not merely speak the words of God; he *is* the Word of God incarnate (Jn 1:1–4, 14). Whereas Moses, speaking from Mount Sinai, mediated the words of God, Jesus, in his Sermon on the Mount, issues his own commands as God himself (Mt 5:21–22, 27–28, 31–32, 33–34, 38–39, 43–44). Jesus prophesied his own death and resurrection, as well as the destruction of the temple (which occurred a little over three decades later). The religious leaders were able to conclude from Jesus' words and deeds that he "[made] himself equal with God" (Jn 5:18), and Jesus did not dispute this charge. Jesus assumed the role of judge on the last day, a role the prophets had reserved exclusively for Yahweh.

Since he has certified his claims by his resurrection, Jesus' view of Scripture must also be our view. Jesus submitted himself to Scripture, and we see that the phrase "It is written" was for Jesus the highest court of appeal. For Jesus, the words of the prophets are simply the word of God (Mt 4:4, 7, 10; 5:17–20; 19:4–6; 26:31, 52–54; Lk 4:16–21; 16:17; 18:31–33; 22:37; 24:25–27, 45–47; Jn 10:35–38). Jesus assumes as historical truth the creation of the human race "from the beginning" as male and female, "one flesh" in the covenant of marriage (Mt 19:4–5). He treats Abel and Zechariah as historical figures who encompass the whole of Old Testament history (Mt 23:35). The stories of Noah and the flood and of the destruction of Sodom he regards as historical events (Lk 17:26–30), as well as the stories of God's miraculous provision of manna and quail in the wilderness (Jn 6) and of Jonah being swallowed by the large fish (Mt 12:39).

Also well attested is the calling and authorization of the Twelve as his apostles (although Judas was later replaced with Matthias). Jesus said that to hear the apostles is to hear Jesus himself, and to receive them is to receive the Father and the Son (Mt 16:16–20; 18; 28:16–20; Ac 1:8). The apostles themselves understood that they were speaking authoritatively in Christ's name, and in spite of some friction early on, Peter acknowledges Paul's writings as "Scriptures" (2Pe 3:16).

From the claim of the resurrection, we can launch out into the vast reaches of our Lord's own testimony concerning himself, the Father and the Spirit, and the writings of the Old Testament as well as his authorization of the apostolic writings. Taken together these writings are called a **canon** (from the Greek *kanōn*, "rule"): the norm for faith and practice.

I. The Inspiration and Authority of Scripture

In our early childhood, we are trained simply to accept our parents' authority. Only later do we begin to trust their wisdom, and much depends on what they do with that trust. In a similar manner, there is sufficient basis for the authority of Scripture in the testimony of the triune God. Only God himself is an adequate source of his word's authority. That is to say, Scripture's status is inherent. The authority of the Scriptures does not depend on the decision of the church or the individual to validate it. To paraphrase the

Westminster Confession, we receive it as the word of God because of what it is, not because of what we make of it.[1]

Still, it would be reductionistic for us to argue that there is one argument for the Christian claim. It is important, first of all, to distinguish the basis for biblical authority from the reasons that we have come to trust it and, in fact, grow in that confidence more and more. With this in mind, we can see that the Bible's inherent authority does not prohibit secondary arguments and evidences that may convince us and others of its uniqueness. *The reason for its authority is distinct from the various means by which we come to embrace it.* The Westminster Confession adds, following its affirmation of the inherent authority of Scripture, that "we may be moved and induced by the testimony of the church to an high and reverent esteem of the Holy Scripture. And the heavenliness of the matter, the efficacy of the doctrine, the majesty of the style, the consent of all the parts, the scope of the whole (which is to give all glory to God), the full discovery it makes of the only way of salvation, the many other incomparable excellencies, and the entire perfection thereof, are arguments whereby it doth abundantly evidence itself to be the Word of God."

In addition to the Bible's inherent authority and additional secondary evidences, "the inward work of the Holy Spirit" produces "our full persuasion and assurance of the infallible truth and divine authority" of Scripture.[2] The medieval church had usurped this role, claiming that the church's sanctioning of this canon was sufficient witness to its authority. The Protestant Reformers, especially John Calvin, emphasized the point that only God himself is a sufficient witness to his own word and that the same Spirit who inspired the sacred text also illumines us to receive and respond to it. They were arguing that the inward testimony of the Spirit is not a subjective experience that happens apart from Scripture, but is, rather, the Spirit's witness within us to the truth of Scripture itself. The Spirit's inward witness is neither the *basis* of nor a secondary *reason for* our confidence in Scripture's authority, but is the *source* of that faith.[3] Just as our confidence in a parent

---

1. Westminster Confession of Faith (1647), 1.4, in *Trinity Hymnal* (Atlanta: Great Commission Publications, 1990), 848: "The authority of the Holy Scripture, for which it ought to be believed and obeyed, dependeth not upon the testimony of any man or church; but wholly upon God (who is the truth itself) the author thereof: and therefore it is to be received, because it is the Word of God."

2. Ibid., 1.5.

3. These same emphases are found in the Belgic Confession (1561), including the point that we are moved by the Holy Spirit to receive the Scriptures as coming from God "and also because they carry the evidence thereof in themselves. For the very blind are able to perceive that the things foretold in them are being fulfilled" (Belgic Confession, art. 5, in *Doctrinal Standards of the Christian Reformed Church*, in *Psalter Hymnal* [Grand Rapids: Board of Publications of the Christian Reformed Church, 1976], 71).

> ## Key Distinction:
> ### inspiration/illumination (Scripture)
>
> Scripture is inspired—that is, God-breathed (2Ti 3:16), whereas our interpretation is illumined by the Spirit. Thus, Scripture is infallible and inerrant, whereas our interpretations as churches and as individuals are always fallible and subject to revision in the light of Scripture.

or spouse rises and falls with experience, God's faithfulness to his word—in spite of our unfaithfulness—strengthens our faith in the Scriptures through which he reveals himself.

Historically, Christians have held that God is the ultimate author of Scripture. This is summarized by the term **verbal-plenary inspiration**: *verbal*, meaning in its words, and *plenary* meaning in its entirety. We are used to loose talk of people being "inspired," as if the muse were at work in the artist or pious sage to express universal spiritual sentiments in terms that illuminate existence. This view dominates Romantic theories of art, and liberal theologians like Friedrich Schleiermacher assumed it when they spoke about biblical inspiration. There is a universal feeling for the infinite, which spiritually sensitive souls express in their own way. However, Scripture never refers to the inspiration of *persons* (or communities). Rather, it is the *speech* of the prophets and the apostles that is inspired.

Jesus equated the word of the prophets with the word of God, and therefore he submitted himself to the Scriptures (Mt 4:4, 7, 10; 5:17–20; 19:4–6; 26:31, 52–54; Lk 4:16–21; 16:17; 18:31–33; 22:37; 24:25–27, 45–47; Jn 10:35–38). He also drew a qualitative distinction between "the tradition of the elders" and "the word of God" (Mt 15:2, 6). Because it is "breathed out by God," Scripture is "profitable for teaching, for reproof, for correction," to complete God's people as the church's canon or normative constitution (2Ti 3:16). The Greek adjective in 2 Timothy 3:16 (*theopneustos*) is not really "inspired" but "God-breathed." In other words, it is not that God breathes into the prophets and apostles, the way we speak loosely of great poets or other geniuses being "inspired." Nor is it that the Spirit breathes into the Scriptures, making them holy and useful when he sees fit. Rather, *the words of the prophets and the apostles are exhaled—as God's own speech to us.* Peter tells us that the prophets did not speak from themselves, from their own experiences, theoretical speculations, or moral intuitions, but as they "were carried along by the Holy Spirit" (2Pe 1:21).

This does not mean that the Bible fell from heaven. False prophets from Muhammad to Joseph Smith have claimed that they received God's word as mere secretaries taking down dictation. However, Scripture itself teaches an **organic** rather than **mechanical** view of revelation. That is to say, God revealed himself in the natural circumstances, environment, culture, language, and gifts of the human writers. The revelation did not come all at once, but "in many times and in many ways" (Heb 1:1). Sometimes it was a direct word, something close to dictation (e.g., "Thus says the Lord," or "Write this"). More frequently, though, it was an edited summary of what God had said and done, drawn from previous oral or written sources. Far from suppressing human involvement, God wrapped his gospel in the swaddling cloths of human speech. Though the inspiration of Scripture is qualitatively different from the incarnation of the Living Word, the latter proves that God enters into our world fully without losing any of his transcendence or truthfulness. If the eternal Son could become fully human without sin (Heb 4:15), then surely God can communicate his truth through thoroughly human ambassadors while preserving their writings from error.

A properly Christian doctrine of inspiration must take its coordinates from the doctrines that Scripture itself teaches. First among these is the doctrine of the Trinity. Each person — the Father, the Son, and the Holy Spirit — shares equally the one essence. Yet each has his own personal attributes as well. Throughout God's acts revealed in history, from creation to the exodus to the exile to redemption and on into the consummation, we discern a clear pattern: every good gift comes *from* the Father, *in* the Son, *by* the Spirit. The Father is the origin of the Son and the Spirit and therefore of all the works that they accomplish. The Father created and upholds the world in his Son (Jn 1:1–3; Col 1:15–17; Heb 1:1–4; Rev 19:13). The Spirit is at work within creation to bring about its appropriate response.

Key Distinction:
organic/mechanical (view of inspiration)

A mechanical view of inspiration assumes that God suspended ordinary human agency, perhaps even dictating his revelation word for word. An organic view recognizes the fully human character of Scripture, evident in the diversity of style, interest, and cultural-linguistic context of each author. In this view, Scripture is from God, yet written through human beings, compiled over many centuries as the history of redemption progressed.

In the creation account, God issues two kinds of commands: a fiat declaration ("'Let there be.... ' And there was...."), and a summons for the creature's fruitfulness ("'Let the earth bring forth....' And the earth brought forth...."). We have a tendency to think that when God commands, his command is always of the fiat variety: an ex nihilo creation of something out of nothing. However, God not only acts *upon* the world; he acts *in* the world (through the Son) and *within* creatures (by his Spirit). Both in the ordinary fruitfulness of creaturely response and in the extraordinary creation of life itself is the Spirit to be praised as the perfecting agent of God's works. The Spirit is the person especially associated with sanctification: the process of making creatures fruitful. However, he always does this through the medium of the word spoken by the Father in the Son.

Sometimes the revelation of Scripture comes in the form of the direct word spoken by God: "'Let there be....' And there was...." We find instances of this in the prophets: "And the word of the LORD came to me, saying...." or "Thus says the LORD...." But in many other places in the Bible we find biblical writers drawing on their own eyewitness testimony, cultural contexts, and peculiarities in personality, emphasis, and manners of speaking. Luke says nothing about the Spirit directly telling him what to write in his gospel or in Acts. Rather, he tells us that he set about to write an authoritative record of what happened by interviewing living eyewitnesses (Lk 1:1–5; Ac 1:1–3). Peter even tells us that the prophets "searched diligently" to figure out the Spirit's ultimate meaning in what they wrote and how their prophecies would be fulfilled (1Pe 1:10–12).

If we limit inspiration to the Father's role in speaking, we can easily fall into a **mechanical** theory. In this view, God operated on the human writers as if they were uninvolved in the process—nothing more than secretaries taking dictation. If we reduce inspiration to the content—namely, the Son's person and work, the temptation becomes to adopt a *canon-within-a-canon* approach, regarding as authoritative only that which we think preaches Christ explicitly (i.e., only in matters of salvation). If we reduce inspiration to only the Spirit's work, we may lose the proper origin of biblical authority in the external voice of the Father and the Son as his message, locating God's word in our own *inner experience*. However, the Spirit never speaks apart from the Father who addresses and the Son as the content. As Jesus taught his disciples in John 14–16, the Spirit focuses all of his energies on spotlighting the Son and illumining our hearts and minds to embrace him.

So our doctrine of inspiration rests on this three-legged stool, as it were, and this stool collapses if any leg is removed. We receive Scripture as God's authoritative word because it comes from the Father, with the Son as its content, and the Spirit testifies within us to its inherent truthfulness. And yet, analogous to the Son's humanity, Scripture everywhere exhibits the finitude, weakness, and limitations of its human authors. There was not one moment of revelation, downloading eternal truths; rather, Scripture has grown organically out of the history of God's redemptive acts, leading to the arrival of the Messiah "when the fullness of time had come" (Gal 4:4).

We can also affirm that Scripture is God's speaking. We must resist the false choice of either identifying it with God's essence (reserved for Jesus Christ, the hypostatic Word, alone) or identifying it as a merely creaturely witness or effect of God's action. Scripture is not just a *witness* to God's action, but is the *means* through which God acts in every time and place, liberating and ruling, judging and justifying, threatening and comforting, uprooting and planting.[4] God accomplishes his purposes in history through speech.

As "God-breathed," Scripture has historically been held by Christians to be inerrant—that is, free of error. Even with their humanity fully engaged, the prophets and apostles were preserved from error by the Holy Spirit. Again, this claim can be made only on the basis of the Trinitarian cooperation in the process of inspiration. The Father cannot be mistaken, much less mislead; the Son is the Truth in person; the Spirit works within whomever he will, to fulfill his purposes, yet without in any way subverting their ordinary characteristics, much less violating their will. How can the Spirit do this? How can a human act be freely willed while the Spirit is credited with bringing it about? Like Mary upon receiving the angel's announcement, we may ask, "How will this be?" but we must be content with the answer she heard: "For nothing will be impossible with God" (Lk 1:34, 37).

There are a few important points to mention on this topic.[5] First, **inerrancy** pertains to the original autographs. We do not say that our translations of the original texts (or even that the original-language copies available to us) are inspired and inerrant. In fact, they do contain errors of various kinds. However, the immense number of ancient copies allows textual scholars to determine the original reading with near certainty. Second, inerrancy

---

4. The view I am critiquing here is identified especially, though hardly exclusively, with Karl Barth. He so stressed divine transcendence, even to the point of contrasting divine and human action, that he had difficulty accepting that God works through creaturely means. The latter could only be witnesses to, not media of, God's direct word and work.

5. For a fuller delineation of inerrancy, see the Chicago Statement on Biblical Inerrancy. The statement, and an official commentary, are found in R. C. Sproul, *Explaining Inerrancy: A Commentary* (Oakland, Calif.: ICBI, 1980).

does not cancel human agency in the least; in other words, it does not entail a mechanical theory of dictation. Third, inerrancy does not mean that the human authors were omniscient or perfect in their understanding. Indeed, they openly exhibit their finitude and fallibility. The biblical writers assumed a cosmology that is quite different from our own, but it is not their cultural assumptions but their affirmations that we receive as God's word. In fact, there are many examples of prophets and apostles acknowledging their own errors of judgment and practice. Even Paul distinguished between his pastoral advice and the deliverances of his apostolic office (1Co 7:25).

Proponents of inerrancy have often pointed out that Scripture is inerrant *in all that it affirms*. Scripture never says that the prophets and apostles were inspired, but that Scripture (i.e., the canonical text) is God-breathed. The reason for this qualification is to counter the caricature (often validated among some conservatives) that inerrancy requires belief that everything in the Bible is true. Of course, this has never been held by the church. In Genesis 3 Satan speaks patent falsehoods; the speeches of Job's friends are littered with distortions. However, God steps in to clear things up in both cases. The point that inerrancy makes is that Scripture faithfully and truthfully reports these events and dialogues. Remember, God's truth is revealed not only in doctrinal propositions, but also in narrative (drama), praise (doxology), and commands (discipleship).

Fourth, inerrancy does not mean that the human authors were exhaustive or exact. God spoke to his people at different times, in their own context, and according to their ordinary capacities. We should not impose modern standards of exactitude on ancient texts. There are discrepancies in reports, which one would expect of any series of witnesses in a courtroom, but these are due to different perspectives (as in witnessing a traffic accident) rather than to error.

II. Scope and Clarity: Revealing Everything We Need for Faith and Practice

Many disagreements, even on the question of inerrancy, have turned on the *scope* of Scripture. It is beside the point to argue that the mustard seed is not the smallest seed known to botanists today. Jesus' example was fit for its intended purpose and the scope of his parable (Mt 13:31–32). We have to attend to the point being made—noting what Jesus is doing with his words, not what we want to do with them, namely, to turn them into statements of botanical science that should be refuted or defended. Scripture is clear only to the extent that we recognize its scope, both in its parts and in its whole teaching.

As the evangelical doctrine of Scripture was refined in the aftermath of the Reformation, Protestant orthodoxy emphasized the point that the law and the gospel, with Christ at the center, are the scope of Scripture. This is not an a priori decision to accept only that which preaches Christ, but the recognition that when the pieces of the puzzle are put together, the whole Bible focuses on the unfolding drama of redemption. If we go to the Bible looking for answers to questions that are beyond its purpose and scope, we will turn it into an entirely different book, like the Pharisees to whom Jesus said: "You search the Scriptures because you think that in them you have eternal life; and it is they that bear witness about me, yet you refuse to come to me that you may have life" (Jn 5:39–40).

The unfolding drama of redemption has its roots in eternity, but it is executed in history through various *covenants*. Reformed theology is hardly alone in recognizing the significance of covenants in the Bible. Combating the mystical flight away from history exhibited by the Gnostics, the second-century church father Irenaeus emphasized the unity of God's plan of salvation from Genesis to Revelation. This *history of salvation* is disclosed through various covenants, he argued. The first covenant, "under Adam," was a promise of immortality on condition of obedience; the second covenant was with Noah; the third, "under Moses," was a "law of works" that intervened between Abraham and Christ, while the fourth is the new covenant "which renovates man and sums up all things in itself by means of the Gospel, raising and bearing men upon its wings into the heavenly kingdom."[6] Irenaeus distinguishes frequently between a "covenant of works" (also "economy of law") and "a Gospel covenant."[7] Each covenant has its own role to play, "but the treasure hid in the Scripture is Christ, since he was pointed out by means of types and parables."[8]

Even before creation, the persons of the Trinity entered into a covenant of peace, known in Reformed theology as the **covenant of redemption** (*pactum salutis*). This plan was then executed in history through the **covenant of creation** (also called the covenant of works) and then, after the fall, through the covenant of grace. The covenant of creation, between God and Adam as the federal representative of the human race, was conditioned on Adam's perfect obedience in the trial that God placed before him. The **covenant of grace** began with God's promise to Adam and Eve after the fall that a redeemer would come. These three overarching covenants form the

---

6. Irenaeus, *Against Heresies* 1.10.3 (*ANF*, vol. 1, pp. 429).
7. Ibid., book 4, ch. 25 in *ANF*: 5.16.3 (1:554), 4.13.1 (1:24); 4.15.1 and 4.16.3 (1:25–26).
8. Ibid., 1:496.

architecture of Reformed theology, with other biblical covenants as subsets under these broader categories.[9] Like the framework of most buildings, these covenants are not always explicitly visible, much less the focus of a given passage. That is why we have to ask ourselves where a certain passage is located in the history of redemption, and how different covenantal economies are functioning in that period. This helps tremendously in identifying the scope of the passage. We will encounter these distinct covenants as we go along.

The scope of Scripture, then, is God's commands and promises — law and gospel — centering on the unfolding plan of redemption in Jesus Christ. It is crucial to recognize this point, because we can easily turn the Bible into a "handbook for life," an answer book or manual of supernatural information on anything that interests us. When we go to the Bible with our questions, demanding that it speak to whatever we find important or relevant, we force it to speak about things that it does not actually address. As Calvin observed, Moses was not an astronomer and the Pentateuch is not a science textbook.[10] Whatever Scripture does teach explicitly about such matters is authoritative, but its *purpose* is not to provide data for determining the age of the earth, the orbit of planets, or precise details concerning the earth's condition prior to the creation of human beings.

Others come to Scripture as one might explore the writings of Nostradamus, trying to correlate the Bible's prophecies with the daily headlines. However, the Old Testament prophets were not just predicting the future; they were pointing to Christ (1Pe 1:10–12). Jesus' own prophetic teaching turned on his crucifixion, resurrection, ascension, and return in glory (Mt 24–25). The book of Revelation was written to comfort persecuted saints in *all* times and places with the triumph of the Lamb in a consummated kingdom without sin and death.

Still others turn to Scripture expecting to find a catalog of moral advice for practical living, and they turn parables of the kingdom into quarries for defending capitalism or socialism, managing personal finances and family

---

9. I explore these covenants more fully in *Introducing Covenant Theology* (Grand Rapids: Baker, 2009).

10. For example, "Moses refers to two great luminaries [sun and moon], but astronomers prove, by conclusive reason, that the star of Saturn, which on account of its great distance, appears the least of all, but is greater than the moon. Here lies the difference: Moses wrote in a popular style things which without instruction all ordinary persons, endured with common sense, are able to understand, but astronomers investigate with great labor.... Nevertheless, this study [astronomy] is not to be reprobated, nor this science to be condemned, because some frantic persons are wont boldly to reject whatever is unknown to them." Moses "was ordained a teacher as well of the unlearned and rude as of the learned," and his teaching is adapted to ordinary experience rather than to scientific exactness (John Calvin, *Commentary on the Book of Genesis* [trans. John King; Grand Rapids: Baker, repr. 1996], 1:84–87.

life, and so forth. When we rifle through the Old Testament narratives for moral examples ("Dare to be a Daniel"), as if they were Aesop's Fables, we miss the point. In most cases, the lives of "Bible heroes" are quite mixed, morally speaking. Above all else, in these narratives, God is the real hero. David slays Goliath because the Spirit comes upon him, in contrast to Saul, whom the Spirit has abandoned. In each instance, the purpose is not to provide life lessons that we may apply directly to ourselves, but to see how God is fulfilling his purposes, which lead history to Jesus Christ. It is certainly true that the Bible includes wisdom for daily living (especially in Ecclesiastes, Proverbs, and Song of Solomon), but even these books direct us ultimately to Jesus Christ, "who became to us wisdom from God, righteousness and sanctification and redemption" (1Co 1:30).

So we must allow Scripture itself to identify its scope and purpose. We come to Scripture with humility, allowing it to give us its own questions as well as answers. This means that we need to interpret Scripture in its natural sense, recognizing the differences in genre between historical narrative and apocalyptic, poetry and prose, parable and doctrinal exposition. There is much in Scripture besides literal proposition, and a literalistic interpretation of nonliteral language is as misleading as is an allegorical reading of historical narrative. We also need to recognize the difference between covenants based on law and covenants based on promise, and covenants that are no longer in effect and covenants that are everlasting. In short, we come to Scripture expecting it to testify centrally to the interests that it has already displayed. Each passage has to be interpreted in the light of the whole while doing justice to each part.

When we approach Scripture in this way, its *clarity* becomes obvious. To justify its claim to be the infallible interpreter of Scripture and therefore the ultimate authority, the medieval church claimed that Scripture was a dark and mysterious book. However, this was at least in part due to the dominance of an interpretive method that included allegorical and other senses alongside the natural way of reading a passage. So, for example, the historical narrative of Moses climbing Mount Sinai to meet with God and receive his law became a spiritual allegory of our contemplative and moral ascent toward the beatific vision. A natural reading of the Song of Solomon might suggest that it is about the God-glorifying love between husband and wife, but the medieval church (and some Protestants) turned it into an elaborate allegory of Christ and the church. Most tragically, the clarity of the Bible's testimony to the gospel promised and fulfilled was obscured in medieval interpretation.

The Reformers called for a return to the Scriptures in their original languages, looking for Christ, following the natural sense of each passage. This did not imply a naïve or simplistic view of the interpretive task. As the Westminster Confession observes, different interpretations can arise, both because of the difficulty of certain passages and because of a diversity of understanding among interpreters: "All things in Scripture are not alike plain in themselves, nor alike clear unto all." "Yet," the Confession immediately adds, "those things which are necessary to be known, believed, and observed for salvation, are so clearly propounded, and opened in some place of Scripture or other, that not only the learned, but the unlearned, in a due use of the ordinary means, may attain unto a sufficient understanding of them" (1.7). This conviction of the Bible's clarity—specifically with respect to its scope or purpose—gave the Bible back to the people of God, translated into their own languages.

The Confession's counsel avoids the error that we easily fall into on either side. Scripture is clear enough in its principal commands and promises, sufficient for salvation and godliness. However, the Bible is not equally clear about everything, and while all of its teachings are to be received, it gives greater importance to some of its own teachings than to others. The enduring consensus reflected in the Nicene and Apostles' Creeds is a testimony to the fact that the Bible's central message, its basic plot, can be easily discerned and summarized by believers around the world throughout history, in a diversity of cultures and languages.

III. Form and Function: Covenant Canon

We move from the question of what Scripture is to how it functions, although these questions are integrally related. The key distinction here is between the Spirit-inspired canon and the Spirit-illumined community.

In Israel, the dominant analogies for understanding God come not from the field of religion, but politics. Yahweh is the Great King, who creates, liberates, judges, and fulfills his promises in history. Human beings are subjects (vassals) of the Great King who are formed into a special community by his Word and Spirit. The Bible, in this political analogy, is more like a nation's constitution than a collection of timeless truths and principles for living. In modern nations, constitutions are foundational in a sense in which no other document or decision is so. Drawing on the analogy of the United States, we see that there is first a founding event—such as a declaration of independence—but it is the constitution that literally "constitutes" the states into a single nation. In the Bible, we see a similar pattern. God's act of creation liberates the creature made in his image from the threat of being engulfed by the waters by making a safe place for communion. Then he issues his constitution or covenant, specifying the mandate for his creature and the conditions for blessing for the creature himself and for all whom he represents. In the calling of Israel, too, the exodus is the liberation of God's people from Egyptian bondage through the waters, but only at Sinai are they constituted the nation of Israel by receiving the law and pledging to obey its stipulations. In the upper room, just before his death, Jesus institutes the new covenant, ratified in his own blood. Then, after liberating his people from death and hell, he delivers a written constitution through his ambassadors the apostles. God liberates us in order to rule us, and he rules us in order to liberate us.

Unlike in modern democracies, however, none of God's covenants are "by the people." At Sinai, God gave his law. The covenant of grace does not arise because of the people's revolution, but in spite of their rebellion against his reign. The people of God do not liberate themselves, but are liberated by God. They do not even cooperate in this liberation, but in fact are redeemed and reconciled "while ... enemies" of God (Ro 5:10). God *gives* his covenant to his people; the people do not create the constitution. We cannot say that "the church created the Bible" or that "the Bible is the church's book." Rather, it is God's book. Although the church existed long before the canon was completed, the church has continued to exist by feeding off the Word that God spoke to it up to that point in history.

In other words, the canon is *inspired*; the community is *illumined* to understand, embrace, interpret, and obey it. Jesus taught that there is a qualitative distinction between the prophets and the tradition of the elders who were Israel's teachers after the Old Testament canon was closed (Mt 15:2, 6). Similarly, Paul distinguishes between the foundation-laying era of the apostles and the building-erecting era of the ordinary ministers who follow after them (1Co 3:11–12). Although Paul could appeal to no human authority higher than his own office, he encouraged Timothy to recall the gift he received at his ordination, "when the council of elders [*presbyteriou*] laid their hands on you" (1Ti 4:14). None of us, today, is a Moses. None is a Paul or a Peter. We are all "Timothys," no longer adding to the apostolic deposit, but guarding and proclaiming it (1Ti 6:20). The apostolic era has now come to an end; the office was a unique one, for a unique stage of redemptive history, a period of time used by God for the drafting of the new covenant constitution. Even in the days of the apostles, this transition was emerging. At the synod of Jerusalem, reported in Acts 15, the apostles and the elders met in solemn assembly to determine together what should be required of Gentile converts. The churches sent representatives, and the synod's decisions were reached, not by a single pastor (even Peter), but by mutual agreement between apostles and elders together. The Spirit did not give any new revelations, but illumined the minds and hearts of those gathered to understand what God was doing in breaking down the wall dividing Jew and Gentile. By his grace, the whole church came to one mind on this matter.

Today, the Spirit illumines the hearts and minds of his people to understand, interpret, and obey his Word. Apart from this gracious work of the Spirit, the church would eventually become a Tower of Babel, rather than an organized society of the new creation as we see in embryo at Pentecost. In spite of the tragic divisions in Christ's visible body today, there remains a remarkable consensus on the basic teachings of Scripture across many churches and denominations. In fact, it is precisely because Scripture is "God-breathed," and is therefore not only infallible but clear in its basic teachings, that we can be confident that the Spirit-illumined church will be able to interpret it faithfully from generation to generation. Again the Westminster Confession is instructive:

> The whole counsel of God concerning all things necessary for his glory, man's salvation, faith and life, is either expressly set down in Scripture, or by good and necessary consequence may be deduced from Scripture: unto which nothing at any time is added, whether by new revelations of the Spirit, or traditions of men. Nevertheless, we acknowledge the inward illumination of the Spirit of God to be necessary for the saving understanding of such things as are revealed in the Word: and that there are some circumstances concerning the worship of God, and government of the church, common to human actions and societies, which are to be ordered by the light of nature, and Christian prudence, according to the general rules of the Word, which are always to be observed.[11]

The Confession mentions an important distinction: between *elements*, based on whatever is "expressly set down in Scripture, or by good and necessary consequence may be deduced from Scripture," and *circumstances*, which are not determined by Scripture and may be left to godly wisdom. The danger comes when we confuse these categories. Antinomianism collapses elements into circumstances, as if the clear commands of Scripture could be relaxed. Everything becomes indifferent, determined by personal or collective whim. Legalism collapses circumstances into elements, demanding uni-

---

11. Westminster Confession of Faith 1.6.

formity in doctrine and practice even where Scripture has not clearly spoken directly or "by good and necessary consequence." The church's authority goes *only as far as* the canon allows, but must submit to *everything* that the canon contains. This is referred to as the **regulative principle**. The word *trinity* is nowhere found in Scripture, but the dogma of the Trinity is a "good and necessary consequence" that can be deduced from many passages. One may argue that a particular view of the age of the earth, a particular political policy, or a stance concerning the use of alcohol may seem like a *good* inference from Scripture, but is it a *necessary* one? If it falls below that bar, then Christians may differ freely on the matter; the church has no authority to teach or require it as Christ's will for his people and leaves this to godly wisdom and liberty.

The very notion of a canon is not imposed on these texts by the church, but arises from the Scriptures themselves. With parallels in the ancient Near Eastern treaties, the Old and New Testaments identify the great king (suzerain), provide a historical prologue justifying his right to determine the constitution, and stipulate commands and sanctions.[12] And like these treaties, both Testaments include a curse formula for anyone who amends the treaty (OT: Dt 4:2; 12:32; cf. Dt 28:15–68; NT: Rev 22:18–19). The Savior, not the saved, is the author of the covenant canon. The church is the offspring of the Word, not the mother.

This covenantal view of the biblical canon diverges sharply from the Roman Catholic view. There was no debate during the Reformation over the nature, authority, and inerrancy of Scripture. This was accepted on both sides. Differences turned on the sufficiency of Scripture—particularly the relationship between Scripture and tradition. Since Rome had argued that the church is the mother of Scripture, it was only natural for her to conclude that she alone could interpret it faithfully in the office of the magisterium, particularly the pope. The qualitative distinction between the founding constitution and its ongoing interpretation and application by the church was barely legible. A number of prominent medieval theologians (like Duns Scotus and Pierre D'Ailly—even Thomas Aquinas) maintained that Scripture alone was the church's ultimate authority. However, there also developed the view that Scripture and tradition represented two sources of revelation, of equal stature and authority, since the church was mother of both. However, at the Council of Trent (1545–63), the magisterium brought medieval and Reformation disputes to a halt, rejecting *sola scriptura* and affirming

---

12. See M. G. Kline, *The Structure of Biblical Authority* (Grand Rapids: Eerdmans, 1975); idem, *Treaty of the Great King* (Grand Rapids: Eerdmans, 1961).

the primacy of papal authority over councils. Though offered with greater nuance in the Second Vatican Council, this is the view that is still held by the Roman Catholic Church.[13]

This was not, however, the view of the ancient fathers. As we have seen, apostles themselves referred to each other's writings as "Scripture." Already in the second century, church fathers like Irenaeus and Tertullian were quoting from twenty-three of the twenty-seven New Testament books. In other words, these books were already being used in churches from Asia to Gaul (France) as the ultimate court of appeals for deciding controversies. An official list was necessitated, not by any widespread uncertainty among the churches, but because heresies (especially Gnosticism) were circulating their own texts in addition to Scripture. It is interesting that even these heterodox writers recognized the "working canon" when they added their spurious collection.

In 367, Athanasius drew up a list of all twenty-seven books, even identifying it as a canon, and maintained that "holy Scripture is of all things most sufficient for us."[14] Basil of Caesarea (330–79) instructed, "Believe those things which are written; the things which are not written, seek not." In fact, he added, "It is a manifest defection from the faith, a proof of arrogance, either to reject anything of what is written, or to introduce anything that is not."[15] By their own procedure of evaluation we can see that the early fathers were simply *discerning* or *recognizing* that which is canonical, not *creating a canon* by their own authority.[16] While some parts of the New Testament (James, Jude, 2 Peter, 2 and 3 John) were disputed early on, these finally won recognition. The Roman Catholic canon of the Old Testament adds certain books (the Apocrypha) that do not belong to the official canon recognized by Judaism.

Similar to Roman Catholicism, Eastern Orthodoxy also tends to blur the distinction between the extraordinary office of apostles (extant during the

---

13. Austin Flannery, OP, ed., *Vatican Council II: The Conciliar and Postconciliar Documents* (Northport, N.Y.: Costello, 1975), 754–55.

14. Athanasius, "Against the Heathen" (*NPNF²*, 4:23).

15. Basil, "On the Holy Spirit" (*NPNF²*, 8:41).

16. On this process, see Eusebius, "The Church History of Eusebius" (*NPNF²*, 1:155–57). It has become fashionable in recent years (especially in popular media) to advance the idea that the "heretics" were mainstream in the early church and the "orthodox" party was simply better at political maneuvering. Actually, this thesis goes back to F. C. Baur (1792–1860). Although discredited on historical grounds, it continues to carry a certain charm for contemporary crusaders against conservative theologies. An outstanding evaluation of this view is found in *The Heresy of Orthodoxy*, by Andreas J. Köstenberger and Michael J. Kruger (Westchester, Ill.: Crossway, 2010). Michael J. Kruger's *Canon Revisited: Establishing the Origins and Authority of the New Testament Books* (Wheaton: Crossway, 2012) is the best contemporary statement of various theologies of the biblical canon as well as perspectives on its historical development.

foundation-laying era of drafting the constitution) and the ordinary office of bishops (interpreting the canon). However, in the Christian East there has never been any notion of one pastor having supremacy over the church, much less being infallible. The truth of the faith—revealed in the Scriptures and the ecumenical creeds—always stands over a bishop, who may be deposed even by the laity if he strays from the orthodox faith. Among Orthodox theologians today, some affirm the unique authority of Scripture "above all the sources of faith, especially of all tradition in all its forms," while others treat Scripture and early tradition as belonging to a single source of revelation.[17] In my view, the best conclusion concerning the ancient writers of the East is that they held to the uniquely normative authority of Scripture, as interpreted by the churches whose bishops formulated the "rule of faith" in ecumenical councils.

To regard Scripture as the church's constitution is to directly counter the Roman Catholic claim that the church is the mother of Scripture. The canon, as the constitution of the church, is what constitutes a people as *this* people, under *this* government, in *this* body. Of course, the Reformers and their heirs never doubted that the church came before the completed canon of Scripture in history. However, they insisted that it is the word that always creates the church. Based on God's promise of the gospel in Genesis 3:15, a church was born. Already in Genesis 4 we hear of God replacing slain Abel with Seth. "At that time people began to call upon the name of the LORD" (v. 26). Covenant law guided and judged the church under the old covenant, and it was the covenant promise that kept the church alive, even during its exile. The law and the promise were God's sacramental word (faith-creating means of grace) even before they were committed to the canon. As that word became inscripturated, the church itself found its proper constitution. Christ was seen as the climax of revelation, the Mediator of the new covenant. Until he returns, therefore, we should not expect new incarnations, redemptions, or sendings of the Spirit. Likewise, we are not expecting new apostles or revelations, but rather seek the Spirit's illumination of the Word.

The churches of the Reformation do not deny the ongoing authority of the church in its representative assemblies, but the key difference is this: whereas the Roman Catholic Church combines Scripture and tradition as one source of **magisterial** (i.e., ruling) authority, we confess that this belongs

---

17. An example of the first view would be Sergius Bulgakov (1871–1944), in *The Orthodox Church* (London: Centenary, 1935), 28. An example of the latter view would be Vladimir Lossky (1903–58), in *The Mystical Theology of the Orthodox Church* (Crestwood, N.Y.: St. Vladimir's Seminary Press, 1976), 25.

Key Distinction:
magisterial/ministerial (authority)

Reformation theology applies the *magisterial-ministerial* distinction when it speaks about the authority of the Word over the subordinate authority of the church, reason, tradition, and experience. The church has received a legitimate authority from Christ to reach consensual interpretations of God's Word through its representative assemblies (as in the councils that led to the formation of the ecumenical creeds as well as the confessions, catechisms, and church orders of particular bodies). Nevertheless, this authority is always relative to and dependent upon the sovereign (magisterial) authority of God's revealed word. Like the church, reason and experience and culture are servants through which we apprehend God's Word, but we are never masters of it.

---

to Scripture alone, with tradition as **ministerial** (i.e., serving). Just as courts interpret the constitution, church courts interpret Scripture. This is why churches from the Reformation affirm the ecumenical creeds and subscribe to confessions and catechisms as communally valid interpretations of God's Word. Yet again, it must be emphasized that this authority does not arise from the church. It arises from the canon that the church seeks faithfully to interpret in dependence on the Spirit.

Roman Catholic arguments have often depended on the distinction between written traditions (Scripture) and unwritten traditions, the latter extending the apostolic office and authority to the pope. The Reformers and their heirs recognized that there were many traditions in the apostolic church that were unwritten. In that era, believers were to follow the teaching and example of the apostles in both written and unwritten forms: "So then, brothers, stand firm and hold to the traditions that you were taught by us, either by our spoken word or by our letter" (2Th 2:15; cf. 1Co 11:2; 2Th 3:6). These traditions are different from the "tradition of the elders" that Jesus challenged (Mt 15:2), because the apostles were on a par with the prophets. Similarly, the traditions received and handed down by the apostles were inspired, but their proper interpretation depends on the Spirit's illumination. Whatever unwritten traditions they may have promulgated, we are bound only to the ones that became part of the written canon. Like the rabbis and elders of Jesus' day, the ministers and elders of the postapostolic church may err even in solemn councils.

Even while the apostles were still living, Paul could warn the Corinthians "not to go beyond what is written" (1Co 4:6). The apostles laid the foundation, with Christ as the cornerstone, and the ordinary ministers who follow in their wake are building on that foundation rather than adding to it (1Co 3:10). Just as the Ethiopian court secretary acknowledged his need for a teacher to understand the Scriptures (Ac 8:30 – 39), churches today require this office, which Christ gave generously in his ascension (Eph 4:7 – 15). In addition to teachers, they need elders to exercise spiritual leadership in the churches. These pastors and elders have real authority, particularly when assembled in an official body together, but it is always ministerial rather than magisterial. Individual believers as well as churches seek the Spirit's illumination of the sacred text, but neither can claim infallibility or inspiration for their pronouncements.

Therefore, the churches of the Reformation have received the Scriptures as the sole magisterial authority without disregarding the ministerial authority of church councils. Special respect is accorded to those early assemblies that established orthodoxy in the face of heretical challenges and whose statements of faith enjoy ecumenical status. These statements include the Nicene Creed, Athanasian Creed, Chalcedonian Creed, and the later summary known as the Apostles' Creed. As in Acts 15, churches coming together in representative assemblies with pastors and elders can bind each other in mutual admonition and instruction. The arrangement determined by our King is neither hierarchical nor democratic, but covenantal (i.e., representative). Christ the King exercises his saving reign by his word and Spirit, through the ministers and elders whom he has appointed as heralds and guardians of this sacred treasure.

If the Roman Catholic position erases the line between the canonical (magisterial) authority of Scripture and the interpretive (ministerial) authority of church tradition, modern Protestantism has multiplied the threats to the normative authority of Scripture. John Wesley's appeal to Scripture, reason, tradition, and experience at least gave priority to the first. However, many of his more liberal heirs have transformed these checks and balances into the "Wesleyan Quadrilateral," treating reason, tradition, and experience as sources of revelation alongside Scripture. In recent years, some evangelical theologians have added culture as a source of revelation. Like the radical Anabaptists of the Reformation era, Pentecostalism has also extended the extraordinary office of apostle into the postapostolic era.

Even where this move is not made and formal adherence to the Protestant position is expressed, there is always a danger of allowing servants to become masters. Are our fundamental beliefs about God, creation and providence, the human person, Christ's person and work, the church and its mission, and the end times shaped decisively by Scripture? Or do we allow psychological, philosophical, cultural, marketing, and political assumptions a normative role, bringing in various biblical passages to support conclusions that we have already reached apart from them?

Conclusion: From Drama to Discipleship

I have drawn a line from the most particular fact of revelation — Christ's resurrection — to the authority of Scripture. It is true that Christ did not rise on the third day merely to prove the authority of Scripture. We would be saved by Christ's life, death, and resurrection regardless of whether God decided to give us an inspired and inerrant witness. Nevertheless, by going about the argument in this way, we ground the authority of Scripture in Christ and not the other way around.

In this chapter, I have also emphasized the covenantal context in which Scripture emerged and in which it now exercises its magisterial authority. With this covenantal horizon, we can see the dissolving of some of the tensions between faith and practice, doctrine and life, head and heart that modern thought has imposed upon us. The canon for this covenant gives us not only the doctrines we must intellectually grasp, but the inspired narrative and an inspired hymnal for worship. It gives us commands for living in a way that is consistent with the God who has revealed himself consummately in his Son. And it creates a discipleship that is shared in community, over against the authoritarianism and individualism that mark the societies of this passing age. To know God, in Scripture, is to understand who he is, what he has done, and the future he has promised, but it is also to follow him as our Great King and Savior in his body, the church.

Theology is the lived, social, and embodied integration of drama, doctrine, doxology, and discipleship. The organ of biblical faith is not the eye, which masters all that it surveys, but the ear, which hears someone else — the God of the universe — in command and promise. We hear the testimony of God to himself through the witness of the prophets and apostles. Here there is no sovereign self or community, but a triune God who gathers us to be made into a new self and a new community by his living speech. Here the yawning chasm between theory and practice that our culture has created for us vanishes in the mist of our imagination. To hear God's word is to be informed and transformed simultaneously in a relationship of fear and hope, distance and nearness, repentance and faith. None of this is something that we attain; it is something that God does to us—and gives to us—when he speaks.

Key Terms

- canon
- verbal-plenary inspiration
- inerrancy
- covenants of redemption, creation, and grace
- the regulative principle

Key Distinctions

- inspiration/illumination
- organic/mechanical (views of inspiration)
- magisterial/ministerial (authority)

Key Questions

1. What is the basis for saying that the Bible is God's word? How would you defend this claim?
2. Explain some of the differences between a Christian view of revelation and rival accounts. What do people you meet usually mean by "revelation"?
3. What is meant by "verbal-plenary inspiration"?
4. Discuss the relationship of the doctrine of the Trinity to biblical inspiration. How does this challenge inadequate views of inspiration?
5. What is the difference between inspiration and illumination, and how are they sometimes confused?
6. What is the scope of Scripture, and how does that relate to its clarity and sufficiency?
7. What is the relationship between Scripture and tradition—and, for that matter, between Scripture and reason, experience, and culture?

Chapter Three

The Living God

Every covenant has a lord, on whose name the lesser ruler calls in the case of extreme danger. And in the battle royal of the Old Testament between the great kings (suzerains), Pharaoh and Yahweh, the revelation of God's name is seen to be politically significant. Yahweh claims his lordship over his people—and over Pharaoh—by sending plagues upon Egypt. With each plague he sends, Yahweh mocks a particular deity in the Egyptian pantheon, and each plague further hardens Pharaoh's heart so that he will not let God's people go. All of this sets the stage for God's sovereign liberation, so that it is clear to all how the people are saved. The liberation of God's people will not be in any way credited to the leniency or acquiescence of the rival lord.

In fact, the specific purpose Moses is told to give to Pharaoh, the reason why Pharaoh should let the people go, is "that they may hold a feast to me in the wilderness" to celebrate Yahweh's victory (Ex 5:1). From this we begin to recognize a fact that becomes increasingly obvious in the unfolding drama of redemption—namely, that God reveals his attributes in the context of historical works. With the calling of Moses and the liberation of his people from Egypt, God gives his name as the guarantee for his people throughout all ages (Ex 3). God reveals his name, not for us to use like a magical charm for whatever purposes we desire, nor as a code that cracks open the secret chamber of God's majestic essence. God reveals his name to us as to be used as a political invocation in our distress and in our worship and celebration.

pantheon : 모든 신을 모신 신전, 만신전
acquiescence : 묵인, 아무말없는 동의
invocation : 신의 도움을 빎 · 기원

Yahweh : 여호와 (Jehovah) · 구약시대 '야훼' 의
독의 YHWH의 음역 · 고유명사이며
하나님 그분을 뜻한다.

As Yahweh speaks and acts, and interprets his actions, the drama gives rise to doctrines which evoke doxology and discipleship.

I. Incommunicable Attributes

Although God's "eternal power and divine nature.... have been clearly perceived, ever since the creation of the world, in the things that have been made" (Ro 1:20), it is in Scripture that we learn that God is "immortal, invisible, the only God" (1Ti 1:17), that he is spirit (Jn 4:24), "the only Sovereign, the King of kings and Lord of lords, who alone has immortality, who dwells in unapproachable light, whom no one has ever seen or can see. To him be honor and eternal dominion. Amen" (1Ti 6:15–16). Scripture reveals to us that God is independent of the world, even though the world is dependent on his word for its creation, preservation, redemption, and consummation. Scripture reveals that God has even determined where each person would live, and for how long (Ac 17:24–26). The attributes of God that are unique to him are considered **incommunicable**—they cannot be understood to be true, even analogically, of creatures. Most, but not all, of the terms for these incommunicable attributes have a negative prefix meaning "not": a- (alpha) in Greek and in Latin, in-/im- (e.g., *infinite, immortal, invisible*, etc.).

Worldview Paradigms	
ATTRIBUTE	DESCRIPTION
Simplicity	As infinite spirit, God is not made up of different parts; his attributes are identical with his being.
Aseity	Self-existence
Immutability	Unchangeableness
Impassibility	Incapacity for being overwhelmed by suffering
Eternity	God's transcendence of time

A. Simplicity (Unity)

"Simple" means undivided and indivisible; not complex or made up of different things. For example, a jacket made entirely out of wool is simple in its fabric, while one composed of different fibers is complex. To say that God is simple is to say, first of all, that he is pure spirit. We are made up of different parts. Not only are we composed of spiritual and physical aspects; even our soul and body are complex. The soul has capacities for thinking,

> ## Key Distinction:
> ### incommunicable/communicable (attributes of God)
>
> God's attributes of infinity (e.g., eternity, aseity, and immutability) are not shared with creatures, even analogically. Hence, they are incommunicable. God's communicable attributes (e.g., goodness, love, knowledge, wisdom, and righteousness) are shared analogically with human beings as his image-bearers.

desiring, and willing, and the body is composed of a host of different parts. However, God is not composed of different faculties or parts.

One of the important implications of divine **simplicity** is that God's attributes are not literally different aspects of God's essence but various descriptions of God's unified being. This does not mean that all of God's attributes are really the same. Love is not the same as justice; holiness is not merely a synonym for omniscience. These are distinct attributes. Nevertheless, they are differences with respect to what God is like, not divisions in his being. Especially in the Christian East, a helpful distinction was drawn between God's *essence* and God's *energies*. Like the sun and its rays, the essence of God is simple and transcendent while God's energies are his works—and the attributes that his working displays. As Basil expressed it, "The energies are various, and the essence simple, but we say that we know our God from his energies, but do not undertake to approach near to his essence. His energies come down to us, but his essence remains beyond our reach."[1]

This means that we cannot rank God's attributes. Gregory of Nyssa reminds us, "For all the divine attributes, whether named or conceived, are of like rank one with another."[2] There is a caution here against the tendency of hyper-Calvinism to rank God's sovereignty and justice over his love and of Arminianism to reverse the order. This comes perilously close to idolatry by worshiping an attribute of God rather than God himself. While we often experience inner turmoil or tension between various faculties, desires, and attributes of our character, God does not. God never wrestles with whether to be loving or just, righteous or good, omnipotent or kind. God's sovereignty and justice are never greater than his love, nor his love greater than his sovereignty and justice.

---

1. Basil, "Epistle 234" (*NPNF²*, 8:274).
2. Gregory of Nyssa, *On the Holy Trinity and of the Godhead of the Holy Spirit, to Eustathius* (*NPNF²*, 5:327 [PG 32, col. 689]).

If ever there could be a division in God's being, with different priorities to negotiate, surely it would have appeared in Christ's death: God's justice, holiness, and righteousness on one side and his love, mercy, and compassion on the other. Nevertheless, it is precisely here—in the specific way in which God saved us—that God did not sacrifice love to justice or justice to love. Rather, because Christ—no less than God himself—fulfilled the law and bore our curse, justice and love embrace. God is "just *and* the justifier of the one who has faith in Jesus" (Ro 3:26). All of God's actions are determined by the unity of his simple being.

B. Aseity (Independence)

Latin for "from-himself-ness," **aseity** refers to God's self-existence or independence from creation. There is God and there are creatures. There is no emanation of God's being, radiating from "the One" to ever-diminishing grades of being. The angels may be a lot older than we are, but they were created and continue to exist as created beings. Creation exists as a result of God's word freely spoken, not as a necessary and eternal extension of God's being.

Often the term *absolute* is used to illumine aseity. Literally, the word means "without relation." I am using the term *absolute* here in the traditional Christian, rather than ancient Stoic or modern panentheistic, sense. Particularly in recent years, many Christian thinkers have questioned whether the God of biblical revelation can be considered absolute in this strict sense. After all, the God of Israel is engaged deeply in history. How can he be considered "without relation" to creation? In its technical use, *absolute* simply refers to God's not being dependent on the world, his not having any *necessary* relation to the world. God would be who he is without the world. On the other hand, the world is related to God in a dependent sense. Without God, the world would not exist. What we mean by saying that God alone is absolute, then, is that God doesn't need the world, but the world needs God.

The world adds nothing to God, Paul argued in his speech to the philosophers in Athens, "since he himself gives to all mankind life and breath and everything" (Ac 17:25). So of course it is true that God can enter freely into the creation he has made, even as an actor within history, since nature and history are always dependent on his will and word. However, he does not have to. The world is not necessary for God's being or happiness. He could live without us—does live without us in that ultimate sense, but chooses not to live without us. It is not because God is related to (dependent on) the world that the world is related to him, but because he has related the world to himself, especially in a covenantal relationship, by the act of his own free speech. This means that <u>love is the ground of God's creation</u> of a world that is different from himself yet valuable as the work of his hands. As Karl Barth observed, precisely because God is free *from* creation, he is free *for* creation.[3]

This is precisely the relationship that we see in Scripture. As creatures, we are dependent on other people—indeed, on other creatures and natural conditions—for our well-being. What would be a deficiency in God (dependence) is in us a measure of our uniqueness—our difference—from God. For us, it is good to be finite, interdependent creatures who need each other. Nevertheless, "Our God is in the heavens; he does all that he pleases" (Ps 115:3). God is so independent of creation that, at the end of the day, even the comparisons that God himself reveals fall short of the majesty of his being (Isa 40:8, 15, 17–18, 25). No creature can determine God's happiness or the fulfillment of his purposes (Da 4:34–37). "The God who made the world and everything in it, being Lord of heaven and earth, does not live in temples made by man, nor is he served by human hands, as though he needed anything, since he himself gives to all mankind life and breath and everything" (Ac 17:24–25). "'Or who has given a gift to him that he might be repaid?' For from him and through him and to him are all things. To him be glory forever" (Ro 11:35–36).

We *live*, but only God *is* life and possesses life "in himself." In fact, this is the point that Jesus made in John 5:26, claiming this divine attribute for himself as well as the Father. God gives life to creatures, because he does not receive it; it is his alone to give. Even as God's image-bearers, we do not possess this kind of self-existence. So even existence is qualitatively different for God than it is for us.

Whatever relationship God chooses to have to that which is other than God is free rather than necessary. Scripture emphasizes that God has condescended freely to enter into an intimate relationship with human beings by means of a covenant. Inherent in the very idea of a covenantal relationship is a mutual exchange of oaths and bonds. This covenantal relationship, in which the transcendent God condescends to bind himself freely to creatures, <u>exhibits the utter freedom of God's love</u> and the significance of those he created in his own image for that relationship.

C. Immutability and Impassibility (Unchangeability)

If God is independent of creation, does that mean that he cannot be affected by creation? Before we answer too quickly one way or the other, it's

---

3. Karl Barth, *Church Dogmatics* (trans. G. W. Bromiley; Edinburgh: T&T Clark, 1957–1975), vol. 2, pt. 1, 310.

condescend : 겸손하게 굽다 · 이르르다 · 동참하다

important to acknowledge that this is a more complicated question than we might think at first. After all, to say that God is affected by creation implies change. If the world can somehow change God, then we can hardly say that he is independent and self-existent. Even more, we cannot say that God is eternally perfect, since change involves either improvement or loss.

However, this important question cannot be settled by logical speculation. When we turn to Scripture, questions still arise. On one hand, God reveals his character in an unfolding historical drama in which it would seem that he is affected by what human beings do. For example, in Exodus 32:10–14, God is about to carry out his threatened destruction of Israel for worshiping the golden calf, when Moses intercedes and God relents. Similarly, God relents from bringing the threatened judgment upon Nineveh when the people repent (Jnh 3:10). In 1 Samuel 15:11, God regrets having made Saul king. On the other hand, verse 29 adds, "And also the Glory of Israel will not lie or have regret, for he is not a man, that he should have regret."

Some conclude that while God does not change in his moral attributes, he changes his will and purposes in response to human actions. However, this distinction seems arbitrary. According to Scripture, it is not only God's character but also his eternal purposes that do not change. If they did, then the covenant partner would never have any future. In fact, this is Israel's only assurance in the face of God's judgment: "For I the LORD do not change; therefore you, O children of Jacob, are not consumed" (Mal 3:6). Even "if we are faithless, he remains faithful — for he cannot deny himself" (2Ti 2:13). It is God's immutable being and eternal oath that guarantee the salvation of the faithless covenant partner (Heb 6:17–18). Indeed, God works all things together for the good of his people (Ro 8:28), who were "predestined according to the purpose of him who works all things according to the counsel of his will" (Eph 1:11). There are more passages in Scripture affirming God's unchanging will than even his unchanging nature.

Nevertheless, we have to distinguish between God's *revealed will* and his *hidden or secret will*. Deuteronomy 29:29 distinguishes explicitly between "secret things" and "things that are revealed." The passages that speak of God relenting do not refer to God's secret plan, decreed from all eternity; indeed, these decisions are hidden from us. Rather, they refer to the revealed will of God in his word. God promised blessing for obedience and judgment for disobedience. Yet even in covenantal breach, the faithless partner is at the mercy of a God who is free to be compassionate toward whomever he will. He may relent from the judgment threatened in his revealed word, but this says nothing about what he has predestined.

Here is an amazing mystery that our minds cannot comprehend: even while relating the world to himself in an intimate bond, freely acting in history, upholding every atom, God nevertheless remains qualitatively distinct from creation. Totally involved (immanent), while remaining totally distinct (transcendent), God can be a character in his own story with us even while remaining qualitatively different from every other actor. In that story, God condescends to meet us at our own level. He represents himself as a player among other players: as a king, a shepherd, a judge, a warrior, a friend, a husband, a father and mother. God hides his majesty behind such masks in order to interact with us as covenant partners. While the analogies succeed for the purposes intended, they all finally break down if we try to measure God's hidden being. We have to let the analogies do their work as analogies, never turning them into exact and literal descriptions of God's eternal majesty, which will always elude our gaze. God reminds us that he transcends infinitely all creaturely comparisons (Nu 23:19; 1Sa15:29; Isa 44:8–9; 46:4; Hos 11:9). It should be noted that in his covenants, God binds himself freely to act in certain ways (judgment and grace). By acceding to the pleas of Moses (e.g., Nu 14:13–25), he strengthens the role and office of the covenant's mediator in the eyes of the people. All of this serves ultimately to point forward to Christ, the mediator of a better covenant (Heb 8:6–13).

With these categories in mind, we return to the question: if God does not change, either in his character or in his secret purposes, does that mean that he is unaffected by what we do? *Immutability* (changelessness) seems to imply *impassibility* (immunity to suffering). Yet this seems to fly in the face of explicit passages that represent God as being provoked by creaturely circumstances and actions. Of course, God did not change from being unloving to being loving by observing the oppression of his people in Egypt. Nevertheless, wasn't he moved to compassion when he heard the cry of his people?

It is important to define what we mean by "impassibility." Undoubtedly, for some philosophers and theologians it has meant that God is untouched and unprovoked by us and our circumstances. There is the danger of a Stoic ideal of a deity who is blissfully detached from others. However, this is hardly

Key Distinction:
hidden/revealed (the will of God)

God's word reveals his promises and commands, as well as his actual execution of judgments and deliverance. However, his eternal plan includes everything that happens, although not revealed to us.

immanent: ωਪਾਤ: inherent

a god worth praying to and is far from the biblical view of God. That the Greek word *apatheia* (translated into English, via Latin, as "impassibility") had such a connotation in Stoicism is true enough. However, as with many inherited terms, Christian theology transformed the concept in the light of biblical revelation. Most often, *impassibility* simply meant that God is not like the pagan deities, which were little more than exalted human beings. Determined by their passing whims and passions, the gods could without notice range from beneficent aid to benign neglect to a drunken rage. Slaves of their lust, greed, and power, they could also exhibit virtue on occasion. They were generally capricious and unpredictable.

However, everything that has been said so far in this chapter already eliminates such conceptions from the biblical doctrine of God. An implication of God's independence from the world is that he is who he is eternally and will always be. All of God's acts are consistent with his nature. God determines the world's course; the world does not determine God's course. As Gerald Bray observes concerning the patristic doctrine of impassibility, "The emphasis was not on tranquility in a state of indifference, but on the sovereignty of God."[4] So when the Westminster Confession says that God is "without parts or passions," it is not denying God's responsiveness to creaturely actions; rather, it is denying (a) that God is "made up" of various faculties or emotions and (b) that God is taken captive by anything other than his own nature. Like Greek *apatheia*, Latin *impassio* means "nonsuffering," in the sense of God's not being overwhelmed or overtaken by something external to himself.

The consistent biblical testimony is that while God may be opposed and provoked, God cannot be *overcome* by surprise, distress, anger, compassion, or opposition. Again, this is good news for us, because we do indeed provoke God's wrath. Yet God can execute or withhold his wrath, depending on the wisdom of his judgment and ultimate purposes: "I will not execute my burning anger; I will not again destroy Ephraim; for I am God and not a man, the Holy One in your midst, and I will not come in wrath" (Hos 11:9). God is always in charge; whatever occurs in creaturely affairs does not catch him off guard. As we have seen, this is good news for us. Those who attribute anthropopathisms (humanlike emotions) to God's essence ordinarily focus on passionate love and compassion. However, we know from Scripture that God is just as capable of wrath. If he were determined in his very being by what we do, then we would have no confidence that he, like Zeus, might not as easily destroy us in a fit of rage as weep helplessly over our condition.

---

4. Gerald Bray, *The Doctrine of God* (Downers Grove, Ill.: InterVarsity Press, 1993), 98.

If God's response were determined by what we do, rather than by his own eternal counsel, we would have long since perished from the earth (Mal 3:6). Only because God cannot be overwhelmed by his creatures can we be confident that he will indeed wipe away every tear of suffering in the age to come (Rev 21:4). Thank God that he is different from us!

D. Eternity (Immortality) and Omnipresence

"Of old you laid the foundation of the earth, and the heavens are the work of your hands," the psalmist praises. "They will perish, but you will remain; they will all wear out like a garment. You will change them like a robe, and they will pass away, but you are the same, and your years have no end" (Ps 102:25–27). In this doxology all that we have just affirmed is expressed, with the addition of God's eternity. God transcends the world in every respect, including time. Although God relates temporal creation to himself, he is not circumscribed by or contained within it. The world is changed by God, but God is not changed by the world.

While God freely bestows everlasting life and immortality on us in the resurrection (2Ti 1:10), God alone *is* eternal life in his very being (1Ti 1:17). Not even angels, or the human soul, are immortal by nature. They come into being by God's word and exist only by that same word. Yet God not only lives; he *is* life. The psalmist exults, "Lord, you have been our dwelling place in all generations. Before the mountains were brought forth, or ever you had formed the earth and the world, from everlasting to everlasting you are God. You return man to dust and say, 'Return, O children of man!' For a thousand years in your sight are but as yesterday when it is past, or as a watch in the night" (Ps 90:1–4). As with the other attributes we have considered, God's *eternity* marks the infinite-qualitative distinction between God and creation.

Again, affirming God's eternity depends to some extent on definitions. Traditionally, Christian theology maintains that God transcends time. Some, like Augustine, revised Plato's concept of **eternity**, reasoning that it is the fullness of time rather than a pure negation of time. Many today, however, prefer Aristotle's view of eternity as endurance in time without beginning or end. This view is usually called *sempiternity*. In my view, **sempiternity** means that at least at one point (time), God is not qualitatively but merely quantitatively distinction from creation. Does God just have infinitely more time than we do?

It might help if we think about God's relation to time together with his relationship to space. Scripture extols God for his transcendence of both. It is ludicrous to imagine that God could be contained within a particular space, even a temple (1Ki 8:27; Ac 17:24). "Am I a God at hand, declares the

sempiternity: eternal

Lord, and not a God far away? Can a man hide himself in secret places so that I cannot see him? declares the Lord. Do I not fill heaven and earth? declares the Lord" (Jer 23:23–24). God can dwell "in the midst of [his people]" (Ps 46:4), but even in doing so he remains omnipresent. Even in the incarnation, God assumes our nature fully while transcending it in infinite majesty. Again, this is a mystery beyond our comprehension—that a God who transcends spatial categories altogether can nevertheless be present, for us, in promised blessing and grace. Just as it is true that God not only has been everywhere but transcends the category of space, God not only endures through all ages but transcends time altogether. Precisely for this reason, he can be present for us simultaneously in all times and places.

With Augustine, I believe that time comes into being with creation itself.[5] Again, this underscores God's freedom *from* creation as the very presupposition of his total freedom *for* it. To draw an analogy, there is no more intimate connection than the mother-child relationship in the womb. And yet, from fertilization to delivery, the child is wrapped in an environment all its own. Of course, this analogy too breaks down—especially since it involves two *creatures*. Nevertheless, the point is that time, like the fetal sac, is intrinsic to creation—whether of angels or stars or earthly creatures. The God-world relation is different from that of the soul to the body; it is more like the relation of mother and child. Though always dependent on God's eternal Word, we are given our own creaturely space-time. We are not autonomous, but we are also not automatons. Not only in our dependence upon but also in our difference from God we find our own significance. Whenever we try to make God more like us, our distinct existence as well as God's sovereignty is threatened. Just as the God who *is* life gives us our own creaturely lives, the eternal God gives us time, our own way of being in the world.

II. Communicable Attributes

Only God is independent, immutable, immortal, and eternal. This cannot be said of any creature. That is why most of these attributes carry the negative prefix and we call them incommunicable attributes—attributes that are not shared with us, even analogically. However, because human beings are created in God's image, they do share other attributes with God, analogically. Where we have attributes similar (analogous) to God's, he is always qualitatively different and greater. Therefore, these **communicable** attributes will often have the "omni" (all) prefix attached to them.

---

5. Augustine, *Confessions* (trans. Henry Chadwick; Oxford: Oxford Univ. Press, 1991), bk. 11.

Communicable Attributes	
ATTRIBUTE	DESCRIPTION
Wisdom	The power to discern truth from error and righteousness from unrighteousness, and to make deliberate choices that eventuate in good rather than evil
Knowledge	Possession of truth, including contingencies; in God's case, knowledge of all things from eternity—includes the free acts of creatures
Power	Ability to act as a free agent; in God's case, comprehensive freedom as Lord of all
Holiness	As glory is a weightiness (significance), holiness is a separateness from all unrighteousness and injustice; for God, it is both an ontological uniqueness and an ethical purity.
Righteousness	Similar to justice, righteousness is integrity; in God's case, an inability to sin.
Justice	Conforming desires, actions, and judgments to the standard of truth rather than expediency, favoritism, or personal advantage; in God's case, absolute commitment to what is right and to judging transgressors
Jealousy	In God's case, a love for his people that zealously binds them to himself, over against both the involuntary servitude and voluntary embrace of other lords
Wrath	In God's case, the righteous and holy response to transgression
Goodness	Faithful to his own character, God also seeks the welfare of his people.
Love	Favor toward and regard for the other; mutually interdependent in the case of human beings, but utterly free of reciprocity in God's case
Mercy	God's favor toward those who deserve his wrath

A. Wisdom, Knowledge, and Power

Wisdom, knowledge, and power are predicated of human beings, yet God is all-wise, omniscient, and sovereign. Our knowledge is always piecemeal and partial. We learn this, now that; we never comprehend every piece perfectly, much less the whole puzzle. God's **knowledge** is different. First, he does not learn anything because his knowledge is eternally perfect and comprehensive (1Sa 23:10–13; 2Ki 13:19; Ps 139:1–6; Isa 40:12–14; 42:9; Jer 1:4–5; 38:17–20; Eze 3:6; Mt 11:21). God does not depend on the world for his knowledge any more than for his existence. No more than his omnipresence can his omniscience be limited or circumscribed within boundaries. God knows all things, including all future free actions of creatures (Pss 44:21; 94:11; Isa 44:7–8) because in his wisdom he has decreed the end from the beginning and "works all things according to the counsel of his will" (Eph 1:11). At the same time, we must recall that none of God's attributes is independent of the others. God's knowledge is inseparable from his **wisdom** (Ro 8:28; 11:33; 14:7–8; 1Co 2:7; Eph 1:11–12; 3:10; Col 1:16).

God has the kind of wisdom, knowledge, and power that are unique to the only sovereign of heaven and earth. "The earth is the LORD's and the fullness thereof" (Ps 24:1). We do not have even 1 percent of that kind of **power**. Rather, we have 100 percent of the natural freedom that God deemed appropriate to the creatures he made in his own image. Instead of pieces rationed between God (a larger portion) and creatures (a smaller portion), God has his "pie" (sovereign, Creator-style freedom) and we have our own as well from him (dependent, creature-style freedom). Our freedom is like his, but always with greater difference. "In him we live and move and have our being" (Ac 17:28), so even our ability to think, will, and act is dependent on God's sovereign gift. We reflect God's glory, but God does not give his own glory to a creature (Isa 48:11). "For my thoughts are not your thoughts, neither are your ways my ways, declares the LORD. For as the heavens are higher than the earth, so are my ways higher than your ways and my thoughts than your thoughts" (Isa 55:8–9).

So God is not just one player among others — one thinker, planner, and actor in the mix of agents. God's wisdom, knowledge, and activity are incomprehensible to us. No one has been his counselor or given him anything that obligates a gift in return (Ro 11:33–36). Nor is God a tyrant, smothering creaturely freedom in his own sovereignty. Rather, it is precisely because of his sovereignty that he freely chooses to give human beings their own creaturely freedom. The relationship between divine and human freedom is a deep mystery — indeed, a paradox. It is never resolved in Scripture, but simply affirmed. In retrospect, Joseph (raised by God to Pharaoh's prime minister) could tell his brothers who long before had thrown him into a pit, "You meant evil against me, but God meant it for good" (Ge 50:20). In the same breath, Peter could attribute Christ's death both to the wicked action of human beings and to God's gracious plan (Ac 2:23).

Sometimes it seems in Scripture that God's plans are frustrated by human beings. Even Jesus could lament, "O Jerusalem, Jerusalem, the city that kills the prophets and stones those who are sent to it! How often would I have gathered your children together as a hen gathers her brood under her wings, and you were not willing!" (Mt 23:37). Yet, at the same time, he says that no one can come to him apart from his gracious determination and activity (Jn 6:44; 14:6). This is not a contradiction, however, because God's secret decree is distinct from his revealed will (Dt 29:29). We do not know what God has planned from all eternity before it occurs, but we do know what God has said he will do under certain circumstances.

It is not God who is circumscribed by this relationship, but the covenant partner. In the historical drama of Scripture there is a genuine covenantal relationship, with give-and-take. This mutuality is entirely appropriate if God is to enter into genuine relationships with human beings, but this in no way entails that such mutuality is intrinsic to God's being. Though unbound in his eternal nature and purposes, God freely binds himself to relate to his people in certain ways. God promises blessing and warns of danger, depending on the response of the covenant partner. This does not mean that God's eternal purposes are determined or thwarted by human beings, but only that God's revealed plans may change. God says he will destroy Israel if the nation sins; the nation sins, but Moses intercedes, and God relents. However, there is no reason to infer from this that God has changed his eternal plan. Rather, he has in fact fulfilled his eternal plan — displaying his glorious grace — precisely in and through the give-and-take of the covenantal drama. As we have seen above, God could reveal his regret with having made Saul king (1Sa 15:10–11), and yet "the Glory of Israel will not lie or have regret, for he is not a man, that he should have regret" (v. 29). God changes his revealed plans, but not his secret plans, and this is a great assurance for us, whose fickleness and unfaithfulness would otherwise defeat God's saving work.

B. Holiness, Righteousness, and Justice

The noun **holiness** comes from the Hebrew verb meaning "to cut or separate" and is translated in Greek as *hagios* (verb: *hagiazō*). Set apart from creatures, Yahweh is transcendent in glory. It is especially God's *holiness* that underscores the strangeness of God that I discussed earlier (pp. 35-36). Thus, holiness refers to an *ontological* difference between God and creation. Beyond this, it refers also (and especially in the Scriptures) to God's *ethical* difference from sinners. God cannot tempt or be tempted to evil (Jas 1:13). God's holiness and glory are closely related, especially in passages like Isaiah

6. In that vision, the mere glimpse of God's holy majesty provokes in sinners an overwhelming xenophobia. Only this is a *healthy* fear of a stranger: "Woe is me! For I am lost; for I am a man of unclean lips, and I dwell in the midst of a people of unclean lips; for my eyes have seen the King, the LORD of hosts!" Only when the seraph touches his lips, announcing, "Behold ... your guilt is taken away, and your sin atoned for," can the forgiven prophet rise to his feet in joyful service to his commission: "Here I am! Send me" (Isa 6:5 – 8). The appropriate response to God's holiness is reverence and awe, as well as confession and repentance.[6]

Righteousness is a legal and ethical term that refers to a right relationship; the Hebrew and Greek terms translated "righteousness" are closely related to those languages' terms for "*justice*." Revealed especially in his law, God's holiness, righteousness, and justice are never abstract ideas but are exercised in concrete relationships with covenant creatures. God's moral commands are never arbitrary, but reflect the proper relationships that his eternal character demands of human beings—in relation both to him and to each other.

God can no more relax his holy justice than he can suspend his love, omniscience, or any other attribute. In the cosmic courtroom, God must be true to himself by punishing sin. Here, as in the other attributes, Christ—especially at the cross—most fully displays the coinherence of holy love and holy justice.

C. Jealousy and Wrath

God's jealousy and wrath are exercised only in the context of a violation of his holiness, righteousness, and justice. Once more we see that the difference between God and creatures is qualitative, not just quantitative. After all, jealousy is condemned in us, but praised in God. How can this be? It is because "the earth is the LORD's and everything in it" (Ps 24:1), while we pretend in our sin to possess that which does not truly belong to us. God's **jealousy** is revealed in the context of his covenant, analogous to the jealousy of ancient Near Eastern rulers for their name, people, and dominions. Any threat against the good of the empire is a threat against the emperor. Similarly, God declares, "I will be your God, and you shall be my people" (Jer 7:23; cf. Ex 5:1; Lev 26:12; Dt 7:6; 2Ch 7:14; Ps 53:6; Isa 52:6; Jer 11:4; 18:15; 24:7; Lk 1:17; Heb 11:25; Rev 21:3). The church is Christ's bride (Jer

---

6. R. C. Sproul explores this attribute (and this episode) richly in *The Holiness of God* (2nd ed.; Carol Stream, Ill.: Tyndale, 2000).

2:32; Hos 1–4; Jn 3:29; Eph 5:25–32; Rev 19:7; 21:9; 22:17). Although the bride is often unfaithful, he remains faithful—though jealous in judging her lovers and separating her from their fatal embrace.

Yahweh alone has a rightful claim on his people and this claim is exercised directly by Jesus Christ, who is the only mediator. There is no other name to call upon for deliverance, since Jesus has been raised and exalted to the seat of all authority (Jn 14:6; Ac 4:12; Php 2:9–11). So he is jealous for his people and also for his name. Challenges to these rightful claims provoke his wrath, which is "quickly kindled" toward rivals (Ps 2:12). Precisely because of the other attributes we have considered, his *wrath* is not the capricious willfulness or temper tantrum of sinful human beings—or of the gods of Mount Olympus. Rather, it is the holy and wise wrath of a just judge. Thus, even God's jealousy and wrath reveal his electing love for his people as well as for the honor of his own name.

D. Goodness, Love, and Mercy

God's knowledge, wisdom, and power are inseparable from his goodness. In fact, in the strict sense, Jesus said, "No one is good except God alone" (Mk 10:18). Whatever **goodness** we discern in creation—including each other—is but a reflection of its source. As with God's other attributes, goodness, love, and mercy are exhibited in his works—particularly in his relationship with human beings.

We have seen that God not only has life, as we do, but is life; similarly, God not only loves, he is **love** (1Jn 3:1; 4:8, 16). It is natural for us as interdependent creatures to love those who return love, but God loves without any compulsion or necessity. In fact, God "hates the wicked and the one who loves violence" (Ps 11:5). "The boastful shall not stand before your eyes; you hate all evildoers. You destroy those who speak lies; the LORD abhors the bloodthirsty and deceitful man" (Ps 5:5–6). Yet God's uniqueness means that he is free even to love his enemies, whom he is perfectly free (and just) to hate (Mt 5:44–45; Jn 3:16; 16:27; Ro 5:8). We do not determine the meaning of love from our own experience and then apply it to God, but define love according to God's works: "In this is love, not that we have loved God but that he loved us and sent his Son to be the propitiation for our sins" (1Jn 4:10).

God's **mercy** is the form that God's love takes when the objects of his love are sinners. Strictly speaking, God's mercy is something that could be revealed only after the fall. The Father, Son, and Holy Spirit never had any occasion to show mercy to each other, since there could never be any fault. There was no need for God to show mercy, even to human beings before the fall. God loved his faithful covenant partner and is good to all that he has made, but mercy is shown to sinners. With love as his essential being, God cannot choose to be unloving. God "is merciful and gracious ... abounding in steadfast love" (Ex 34:6; cf. Pss 86:15; 103:8; 116:5). Nevertheless, God is free to be merciful to whomever he will: "I will have mercy on whom I have mercy, and I will have compassion on whom I have compassion" (Ro 9:15, appealing to Ex 33:19). By definition, mercy is not required. God's freedom is nowhere more evident than in his merciful love and grace. And in Jesus Christ, God's grace "has been *manifested*" (2Ti 1:9 – 10; cf. Jn 1:17). Grace is not just a divine attribute, but the merciful action of God in history.

Key Terms

- simplicity (unity)
- aseity (independence)
- immutability and impassibility
- eternity and sempiternity
- knowledge, wisdom, and power
- holiness, righteousness, and justice
- jealousy and wrath
- goodness, love, and mercy

Key Distinctions

- incommunicable/communicable (attributes of God)
- hidden/revealed (the will of God)

Key Questions

1. How does the revelation of God's personal name arise from the covenantal drama of history?
2. Does God ever have to choose between his love and his justice?
3. How do we explain the apparent contradiction in Scripture between God's unchanging purpose and his being affected by what we do?
4. What's the difference between sempiternity and eternity?
5. Is it proper to speak of God as jealous and wrathful? How would you explain the difference between God's jealousy and anger and ours?
6. What is the relationship between God's love and mercy?

Chapter Four

The Holy Trinity

I n the doctrine of the Trinity," wrote Herman Bavinck, "beats the heart of the whole revelation of God for the redemption of humanity." As the Father, the Son, and the Spirit, "our God is above us, before us, and within us."[1] The doctrine of the **Trinity** — God as one in essence and three in person — shapes and structures Christian faith and practice in every way, distinguishing it from all world religions.

From the Enlightenment to the present day, it has been widely assumed that we all worship the same God with different names; every religion brings its piece of the puzzle to the game. Despite its cheery optimism, this is actually a disrespectful position to take, not only toward Christianity but toward other religions.

As a deliverance of special revelation, the doctrine of the Trinity most obviously distinguishes the Christian faith from all the world's religions. It is one thing to call the same animal a *horse* in English, *caballo* in Spanish, *cheval* in French, and *mǎc* in Mandarin, and quite another thing to imagine that a horse is also a dog, a fish, a vacation, and a dinner plate. We do not disagree merely over words or the finer points of theology, but over the identity of the object of our worship and the only name on whom we are to

---

1. Herman Bavinck, *Reformed Dogmatics: God and Creation* (ed. John Bolt; trans. John Vriend; Grand Rapids: Baker Academic, 2004), 2:260. Note that I am discussing the Trinity after the attributes not because God's unity is more important than his plurality, but because it makes sense to discuss first the characteristics that each person shares as God.

call for salvation. As I said in the introduction, the gospel defines who God is in Christian theology.

Central to the unfolding drama of Scripture, the Trinity is also a dogma that gives decisive shape to our worship and discipleship. As this chapter argues, these coordinates (drama, doctrine, doxology, and discipleship) are integrally related in the development of this central teaching.

I. Revelation of the Trinity in Scripture

Over against the polytheistic religions of Israel's neighbors, the first presupposition of the Bible is that there is one God. This is revealed in the *Shema* ("Hear, O Israel: The LORD our God, the LORD is one. You shall love the LORD your God with all your heart and with all your soul and with all your might" [Dt 6:4–5]), to which Jesus alluded when Satan tempted him to idolatry (Mt 4:10). Jesus honors his Father in all that he says and does (Jn 5:36), and his miracles testify to this God: "And they glorified the God of Israel" (Mt 15:31).

The apostles follow this emphasis. For example, Paul says that while the Gentiles worship many so-called gods, "yet for us there is one God, the Father, from whom are all things and for whom we exist, and one Lord, Jesus Christ, through whom are all things and through whom we exist" (1Co 8:6). There is "one God" (Eph 4:6). Paul's mission was to turn Gentiles "from idols to serve the living and true God" (1Th 1:9), as was Peter's mission as well (1Pe 4:3). Before the Roman governor Felix, Paul entreated, "This I confess to you, that according to the Way, which they call a sect, I worship the God of our fathers, believing everything laid down by the Law and written in the Prophets, having a hope in God" (Ac 24:14–15).

So how did it come to be that these apostles—and the first Christian communities—began to worship not only the Father but Jesus of Nazareth, as well as the Holy Spirit, as God? That they did so is an established fact, which we know not only from the biblical sources but also according to the description of early Christian worship by Jewish and Roman sources. Doesn't this practice contradict their repeated insistence that they worship only one God? To answer this question, we should remind ourselves of that inextricable link between drama, doctrine, doxology, and discipleship.

First, then, the drama. Like the person and work of Christ, or the union of Jews and Gentiles in one body—which Paul calls a "mystery" that has now been revealed—the Trinity is more clearly revealed as the history of redemption proceeds. However, when we reread the Old Testament in the light of the New, we pick up on many references that we (and old covenant believers) might easily have overlooked. Not only does Yahweh act through his angelic servants; in some passages, a particular servant is singled out for special mention. Distinguished from the other angels, this servant is even on occasion identified as Yahweh himself. This is especially true of the "Angel of the LORD" theophanies, in which the heavenly messenger is distinguished from other angels as well as from Yahweh but then identified with Yahweh as well (Ge 18; 22:11 – 18; 32:24 – 30; Ex 3:2 – 6). He is the Angel of God's Presence (Isa 63:9), and in Zechariah 3 there is an intriguing courtroom scene in which Yahweh himself (the personal name, not just the title) is identified with the Angel of the LORD (vv. 1 – 4). In the Psalms and prophets, there are references to the coming Messiah, who is laureled with attributes that can be predicated only of Yahweh. In Isaiah 42, the Servant is identified with Yahweh himself, and yet Yahweh says, "I have put my Spirit upon him" (v. 1). Reading such passages in the light of the fuller teaching of the New Testament, it made sense to say that the Father put his Spirit upon the incarnate Son.

The early Christians did not arrive at the doctrine of the Trinity by theological speculation. Rather, they simply found themselves at a significant moment in redemptive history, when God had acted climactically in Jesus Christ. It was held that this Jesus was the Son who existed with the Father before the ages and was made human "when the fullness of time had come" (Gal 4:4; cf. Ro 1:1 – 6). With intentional echoes of Genesis 1, John 1 begins, "In the beginning was the Word, and the Word was with God, and the Word was God. He was in the beginning with God. All things were made through him, and without him was not any thing made that was made" (vv. 1 – 3). Here, the Son is distinct from the Father, but is identified as God. He is "the only Son from the Father" (*monogenous para patros*, v. 14) and "the only God [*monogenēs theos*], who is at the Father's side" (v. 18).

Paul follows the same formula. Jesus Christ is "the image of the invisible God." "For by him all things were created, in heaven and on earth, visible and invisible, whether thrones or dominions or rulers or authorities—all things were created through him and for him. And he is before all things, and in him all things hold together" (Col 1:15 – 17). The author of creation is also the author of redemption. All things come from the Father, in the Son, by the Spirit. The doctrine arises out of the drama also in the event of Jesus' baptism. There are not only three names, but three actors on the scene (Mt 3:13 – 17; Mk 1:9 – 11; Lk 3:21 – 22; Jn 1:32 – 34). There is the Father who speaks ("This is my beloved Son"), the beloved Son who is baptized, and the dove who hovers above Jesus, as he did over the waters in creation. Jesus also identified himself as the Lord of the Sabbath (Lk 6:5) and as the Son of David who is nevertheless David's Lord (Lk 20:41–44, in fulfillment of Ps 110:1).

Jesus appropriates the attributes and actions reserved for Yahweh alone, including the personal name, Yahweh (I AM) (Jn 6:35, 48, 51; 8:12, 58; 9:5; 10:11, 14; 11:25; 14:6; 15:1, 5). In the upper room discourse (Jn 14–16), Jesus reveals the intimate relationship between himself and the Father and the Spirit—a relationship with precreation origins—and in his prayer in John 17 Jesus speaks of "the glory that I had with you before the world existed" (v. 5). He provokes the outrage of the religious leaders by forgiving sins directly in his person, bypassing the temple: "Why does this man speak like that? He is blaspheming! Who can forgive sins but God alone?" (Mk 2:7). Jesus was condemned on the charge of blasphemy, "making himself equal with God" (Jn 5:18). Jesus welcomes Thomas's confession, "My Lord and my God!" (Jn 20:28–29). It is prophesied in Isaiah 45:23 that "every knee shall bow… and every tongue shall swear allegiance" to Yahweh's sovereign lordship. Yet Paul says that Jesus is given "the name that is above every name, so that at the name of Jesus every knee should bow, in heaven and on earth and under the earth, and every tongue confess that Jesus Christ is Lord, to the glory of God the Father" (Php 2:9–11). Surely Paul knew that Yahweh was "put to the test" in the wilderness, but now he identifies the offended party with Christ (1Co 10:9). "For in him all the fullness of God was pleased to dwell" (Col 1:19). The "day of the Lord" is identified with Christ's return (1Th 5:2).

In the Apocalypse, Jesus is "the Alpha and the Omega … who is and who was and who is to come, the Almighty" (Rev 1:8); he is "the first and the last" and "the living one," who holds "the keys of death and Hades" (vv. 17–18). In fact, as Gerald Bray notes, this opening passage of John's revelation refers to the voice of the Father (v. 8) and the voice of the Son (vv. 17–18) and John received his vision "in the Spirit" (v. 10). "In the famous letters to the seven churches (chs. 2–3), it is Christ who speaks, yet each letter concludes with the solemn command: 'He who has an ear, let him hear what the Spirit says to the churches."[2] In the heavenly worship, the saints and angels worship the Lamb (Rev 5:13), although when John falls down before the angel who tells him what to write, the apostle is warned, "You must not do that! I am a fellow servant with you and your brothers who hold to the testimony of Jesus. Worship God." John adds, "For the testimony of Jesus is the spirit of prophecy" (Rev 19:9–10).

---

2. Gerald Bray, *The Doctrine of God* (Downers Grove, Ill: InterVarsity Press, 1993), 150.

The Spirit, distinct from the Father and the Son, is nevertheless worshiped with them as God and as the one who, with the Father, "raised Christ Jesus from the dead" and "will also give life to your mortal bodies… " (Ro 7:11). In both testaments, the Spirit possesses the name of Yahweh (Ex 31:3; Ac 5:3–4; 1Co 3:16; 2Pe 1:21) and his essential attributes (Ps 139:7–10; Isa 40:13–14; 1Co 2:10–11). To the Spirit are attributed works that are ascribed only to God (creation, Ge 1:2; cf. Job 26:13; Ps 33:6; providence, Ps 104:30; regeneration, Jn 3:4–6; Tit 3:5; resurrection of the dead, Ro 8:11). The Spirit also receives divine worship (Mt 28:19; Ro 9:1; 2Co 13:14). In fact, when Peter confronts Ananias and Sapphira in Acts 5, he warns that they have lied "to the Holy Spirit" (v. 3); therefore, they have "not lied to man but to God" (v. 4). Paul explains that "the Lord is the Spirit" (2Co 3:17). In short, with the progress of the drama there is a progressive revelation of the triune God.

Second, *doxology*. Besides arising from the unfolding drama, many New Testament trinitarian references occur in worship. The formal confession "one God in three persons" arises naturally from the triadic formulas in the New Testament, especially in the context of baptism (Mt 28:19) and liturgical blessings and benedictions (Mt 28:19; Jn 1:18; 5:23; Ro 5:5–8; 1Co 6:11; 8:6; 12:4–6; 2Co 13:13–14; Eph 4:4–6; 2Th 2:13; 1Ti 2:5; 1Pe 1:2).

Third, the Trinitarian confession also arises from the *discipleship* prescribed and practiced in the apostolic community. The father of liberal Protestantism, Friedrich Schleiermacher, dismissed the Trinity as nonessential because, he said, it makes no difference to religious experience. Since we experience only "God" and not "three persons," why should it matter? However, not only is Schleiermacher's method deeply flawed (based on our pious experience rather than an external revelation); he missed one of the most intriguing features that gave rise to belief in the Trinity in the first place: namely, that people did in fact experience the Father, the Son, and the Spirit as distinct yet divine persons. They encountered the incarnate Son at first hand (1Jn 1:1–4), and they experienced the Spirit as he descended at Pentecost and indwelled believers. Not even in terms of personal experience and response, then, can one regard the Trinity as nonessential to the apostolic community.[3] This practical experience of the apostolic community not only was a useful application or implication of the doctrine, but, along with the drama, demanded it.

Far from renouncing the God of Israel, the earliest Christians believed that they were worshiping the God of their fathers and mothers. Yet there they were, faced with Jesus as God the Son in human flesh and God the Spirit

---

3. This point is ably argued in relation to the Spirit by Gordon Fee, *God's Empowering Presence: The Holy Spirit in the Letters of Paul* (Peabody, Mass.: Hendrickson, 1994).

descending and indwelling. There they were, being baptized—at Christ's behest—in the name of the Father, the Son, and the Holy Spirit, and being blessed with benedictions from the Trinity. "One God, three persons": the formula was implicit already, but became explicit through hard-fought battles.

II. Postapostolic Development of the Doctrine

In its earliest years, the Christian church was a Jewish sect, preoccupied with the challenge of bringing the gospel to Jerusalem and Judea. Soon, however, it entered the Gentile world—first through the Diaspora (that is, Jews scattered throughout the Roman Empire). In the process, the gospel encountered different objections and challenges. On the popular level, Greeks and Romans were not offended by the addition of another foreign deity to the pantheon. Early Christians repeated traditional Jewish objections to polytheism. Yet as Christianity gained converts and critics among cultural elites, it had more philosophical challenges to face.

How do you explain and defend the Christian faith to those with a fundamentally different worldview—without accommodating that faith to the presuppositions of unbelief? That perennial question of Christian mission pressed itself on the consciousness of the ancient church. The dogma of the Trinity would never have emerged out of a synthesis of Christian and pagan thought. On the contrary, the early pioneers of Trinitarian theology were remarkably adept at exploiting their inherited vocabulary and philosophical concepts in service to revelation.

A. Early Trinitarian Debates

For centuries, the Greek mind had been preoccupied with the "one-and-many problem." **Essence** refers simply to reality: what is there to know. Something with certain definable characteristics is called an "essence" or "substance." Is reality ultimately one or many? Is plurality a falling away from the pure unity of being, into a mere appearance or shadow of its former self? That was the assumption of most Greek philosophers, including Parmenides, the Stoics, and Plato. Even Aristotle maintained the priority of the one over the many.

The great Jewish philosopher of Jesus' day, Philo, established a school in Alexandria, where he not only translated but transformed biblical teaching into the categories of Platonism. A little over a century later, Origen (185–254) founded a Christian school in Alexandria modeled on Philo's academy. Like Philo, Origen tried to merge the Bible with Plato. "The One"—Platonism's favored term for the divine principle—cannot be divided, Origen argued;

Key Distinction:
economic/immanent (Trinity)

Scripture reveals the three persons (Father, Son, and Spirit) as distinct actors in the economy (historical outworking) of creation, redemption, the application of salvation, and the consummation. Christianity teaches that this is a truth not only in revelation, but in reality. In other words, God reveals himself economically as one God in three persons because he *is* in fact such (ontologically).

plurality itself is a falling away from being. However, the Son is indeed held by the apostles to be divine. Furthermore, the radical New Testament identification of the Creator as God—and the Logos by whom he made the world as God (Jn 1:1–5)—had a weaker grip on Origen's thinking than the Platonist view of the logos as a semidivine being or principle responsible for creating the "lower" (material) world. Origen concluded that the Son is subordinate to the Father not only **economically** (i.e., with respect to God's works in the world), but *ontologically* (that is, in his essential nature). To many Christians, this suggested that the Son is less divine than the Father.

A third-century presbyter named Arius, who also served in Alexandria, went a step further, arguing that the Son is the first created being. "There exists a trinity [*trias*]," he said, "in unequal glories." The Father alone is God, properly speaking, while there was a time when the Son did not exist.[4] Seeking a middle way, Semi-Arians argued that the Son is of an essence *similar* to, though not exactly the same as, that of the Father. Orthodoxy hung on a vowel: **homoousios** ("of the same essence") versus *homoiousios* ("of a similar essence").

A somewhat different way of preserving the unity of God was struck by Sabellius. He argued that the Father, the Son, and the Spirit are "masks" or personae worn by the one divine person. Like an actor on the stage, God could appear sometimes as the Father, other times as the Son, and other times as the Spirit. However, these are not actually three different actors. Though the third-century Roman presbyter was excommunicated by the bishop of Rome in AD 220, Sabellianism—more commonly known as modalism—has remained a recurring challenge throughout church history.

All of these early challenges were the result of the inability of the Greek mind to comprehend a plurality that is not in some sense a division or falling away

---

4. Quoted from Arius's poem "Thalia," in Rowan Williams, *Arius: Heresy and Tradition* (Grand Rapids: Eerdmans, 2002), 102.

from the pure unity of being. To put it clumsily, there could only be *one* One at the top of the ladder, not three. An essence cannot be divided—certainly, not the essence of the divine One. To the Greek mind, the orthodox Christians were saying that God is one in essence and three in essence: an obvious contradiction. Part of the problem was that there just weren't enough conceptual tools in the toolbox to make the point that the threeness (plurality) did not pertain to the essence. Aristotle had coined the same term, **ousia**, to refer both to the essence and to individual bearers of it. For example, Susan is a bearer of the essence we call "humanity," but Susan and humanity were both called *essence*.

The real breakthrough at this point came with the Cappadocian theologians in the fourth century: Gregory of Nyssa, Gregory of Nazianzus, and Basil of Caesarea. Instead of calling the essence and the individual both "essence" (*ousia*), they coined the term **hypostasis** for individual persons who bear it. No longer did persons get swallowed up in generic essences. At the same time, the Greek word for *person* (*prosōpon*) had its own set of problems, because it was ordinarily used to refer to an actor's role (exactly what we mean by an actor's "persona"). Applied to the Trinity, that would mean modalism, the heresy of Sabellius.

Up to this point, Christians objected to the charge of logical contradiction but did not yet have the precise vocabulary for articulating it. Even though the philosophy here is complex, *hypostasis* (an individual subsistence with its own characteristics) was the right word for distinguishing the three persons from the one essence. Although a bearer of a shared essence, a hypostasis is a distinct entity with its own attributes as well. For the first time, "persons" attained their own ontological status. No longer was the Greek objection to a division in the divine essence even relevant: it is not God's essence that is plural, but the persons. There are not grades of being in God's essence, from the Father (pure being) to the Son and the Spirit (less being); rather, there is one essence that each person shares equally. In the process of defining the Trinitarian formula, the Cappadocians also introduced new conceptual space for a richer affirmation of human personhood that transformed Western culture.

These theologians of the East argued that while each person of the Trinity shares equally in the one divine essence (avoiding Origen's ontological subordinationism), the Son and the Spirit receive their personal existence from the Father. Thus, unity and plurality receive equal appreciation: "No sooner do I conceive of the One," said Gregory of Nazianzus, "than I am illumined by the Splendor of the Three; no sooner do I distinguish Them than I am carried back to the One."[5]

---

5. Gregory of Nazianzus, Oration 40: *The Oration on Holy Baptism*, ch. 41 (*NPNF²*, 7:375).

> ## Key Distinction:
> ### *essence/persons (Trinity)*
>
> God is one in essence and three in persons (or hypostases). An essence is simply something with characteristics — that is, an entity about which something can be said. A person (or hypostasis) is a distinct bearer of an essence. Applied to the Trinity, it means that the Father, the Son, and the Spirit are distinct persons, each with his own personal attributes, while each also shares equally the attributes of deity (i.e., the divine essence).

This interrelationship between persons is further underscored by the term **perichoresis**, which refers to the mutual indwelling of the persons in each other. This relationship is underscored in John's Gospel, where Jesus speaks of himself as being in the bosom or at the side of his Father from all eternity (Jn 1:18; 14:10; 17:5) and engaging, with the Father and the Spirit, in a mutual exchange of gifts and activities (Jn 16:14–15; 17:6, 21–23). No one comes to the Father except through the Son; in fact, to know the Son is to know the Father also (Jn 14:6–7). This notion of perichoresis — a unity of will and action — is not an alternative to a unity of essence, as is taught by Latter-Day Saints (Mormonism) as well as social Trinitarianism (especially Jürgen Moltmann). Rather, the essential unity of the persons is the presupposition for their shared life. There is therefore an intimate unity of these three persons that cannot be duplicated in any creaturely community. No human society, even the church, is more than an analogy of the Trinitarian life. That said, the analogy is one that is pregnant with implications for our life together in Christ.

B. The Ecumenical Consensus and East-West Tensions

It has become fashionable in recent theology to overemphasize the differences between the Eastern and Western formulations of the Trinity. To summarize briefly, it is frequently said that Western (Latin) reflection, especially from Augustine onward, is implicitly *modalistic*. Whereas the East locates the unity of the Godhead in a person — namely, the Father, who eternally begets and spirates the other persons — the West lodges it in the one essence. The result is that the "real God" is the essence, as if it were a person in its own right, and the persons are nothing more than relations (fatherhood, sonship, and bond of love). Like most rumors, this thesis has an element of truth that has been exaggerated into a caricature.

It is true that the unity of essence is more fully developed in Jerome, Augustine, and other Western theologians than the distinctness of persons. This is due in part to the fact that they were wrestling especially with Arian and Semi-Arian opponents, and were therefore eager to underscore the fact that the Son (and the Spirit, too) shares exactly and equally the same essence as the Father. It is also due in part to the fact that Latin fathers like Jerome and Augustine did not understand the point that the Cappadocian (Eastern) fathers were making when they seized upon the word *hypostasis*. Unable to read Greek fluently, Augustine himself expressed his confusion over the term and, like Jerome, preferred the Latin term *persona*. He compounded the suspicion of modalistic tendencies when he offered his infamous psychological analogy of the Trinity, as memory (the Father), understanding (the Son), and will (the Spirit). Augustine even says that "these three constitute" not only one divine essence but "one mind."[6] Although it is only an analogy, it is not a good one; it suggests one person, not three. (In fact, most Western analogies for the Trinity veer toward modalism, not doing justice to the distinct identity of the persons.) While the East seemed more worried about modalism, the West exhibited a greater suspicion of ontological subordination. Some on both sides increasingly traded charges that the other had in fact embraced these heresies.

Nevertheless, it is crucial to recognize and celebrate the fact that the whole church agreed upon the formula "one in essence and three in persons." In fact, this phrase was already coined by the Latin father Tertullian in the third century.[7] The remarkable ecumenical consensus reached at the Council of Nicaea in 325 (subsequently codified as the Nicene-Constantinopolitan Creed) remains the church's confession to this day. This illustrates an important distinction between dogmas (the church's statement of biblical doctrine) and formulations of theologians concerning the shared ecumenical consensus. Difference over nuances in formulations may affect the ecumenical dogma, but this need not be — and often has not been — the case.

In spite of this consensus, mutual suspicions (political as well as theological) deepened over the centuries after Nicaea. Confronting a revival of Arianism in Spain, the church received the repentant back only by amending the Nicene Creed to say that the Spirit proceeds from the Father *and the Son* (**filioque**). Again, the threat of Arianism made the Western church

---

6. Augustine, *The Trinity* 10.18–20.
7. This formula first appears in ch. 2 of Tertullian's *Against Praxeas* (*NPNF²*, 3:598).

especially sensitive to any challenge to the Son's equality with the Father. Soon, the additional clause was used in formal services, even in Rome. Named for the addition (*filioque*), the *filioque* controversy contributed significantly to a formal schism in 1054. Among the charges made by the East were the following: (1) Out of an exaggerated fear of ontological subordination, the West had abandoned the consensus that the Father is the principium (origin) of the Godhead. (2) What does this mean for the status of the Spirit? Had the West staved off the ontological subordination of the Son only to embrace the ontological subordination of the Spirit to the Father and the Son? The suspicions of modalism and a reduction of the Spirit to the "bond of love" between the Father and the Son seemed now to have been justified. (3) By definition, a unilateral amendment of an ecumenical creed by one branch of the church is an act of schism. In spite of a promising beginning, the Fourth Lateran Council (1215) failed to heal the East-West schism.

The Protestant Reformers championed the ecumenical consensus. Although they accepted the Latin version of the Nicene Creed, they did not spend much energy in defending the filioque clause and were obviously sympathetic to the East's grievance against Rome's pretensions even to the point of amending an ecumenical creed. Faced by challenges from radical Protestants—especially neo-Arians who became known as Socinians (forerunners of Unitarianism), Calvin was especially eager to draw from the best of Eastern and Western Trinitarian reflection.

I discuss Calvin's contributions more fully in *The Christian Faith*.[8] Here I offer only a brief summary. First, Calvin believed that the Trinity lies at the heart of the faith. Without it, "only the bare and empty name of God flits about in our brains, to the exclusion of the true God."[9] Second, Calvin also tried to understand the tensions between the Christian East and West that we have considered, even scolding Augustine and Jerome for being "confused .... by the word 'hypostasis'" instead of listening carefully to the Cappadocian insight.[10] While affirming the unity of the persons in one essence against his neo-Arian opponents, Calvin saw the wisdom in the East's emphasis on the persons as real "subsistences"—that is, as distinct entities, each with his own personal characteristics. "For in each hypostasis the whole divine nature is understood," he says, "with this qualification—

---

8. Michael Horton, *The Christian Faith: A Systematic Theology for Pilgrims on the Way* (Grand Rapids: Zondervan, 2011).

9. Calvin, *Institutes* 1.13.2.

10. Ibid., 1.13.5.

that to each belongs his own peculiar quality."[11] He adds, "It is not fitting to suppress the distinction that we observe to be expressed in Scripture. It is this: to the Father is attributed the beginning of activity, and the fountain and wellspring of all things; to the Son, wisdom, counsel, and the ordered disposition of all things; but to the Spirit is assigned the power and efficacy of all that activity."[12] Calvin is simply following the formulation of the Cappadocian fathers; for example, in Gregory of Nyssa's statement that all of God's external activity "has its origin from the Father, and proceeds through the Son, and is perfected in the Holy Spirit."[13] Third, Calvin argues that the Son and the Spirit do not receive their *divine nature* from the Father, but they do receive their *personal existence* from the Father. "In this sense the opinions of the ancients are to be harmonized, which otherwise would seem somewhat to clash."[14]

While affirming the Western position on the filioque (i.e., the procession of the Spirit from the Father *and the Son*), Calvin shared the East's concerns about the West's modalistic tendencies—even singling out Augustine's psychological analogy for criticism.[15] He was persuaded by the East's emphasis on the distinctness of the persons and on their distinct agency in every external operation. "And that passage in Gregory of Nazianzus vastly delights me: 'I cannot think on the one without quickly being encircled by the splendor of the three; nor can I discern the three without being straightway carried back to the one.'"[16] Ontological subordinationism (and Arianism) is contradicted by the fact that the persons share exactly and equally the same *essential* attributes. Modalism is rebuffed by affirming the reality of personal attributes that distinguish each person.

This path was taken by other Reformed theologians as well. They even went so far as to call the attributes of each person "incommunicable."[17] The Father is the source, the Son is the mediator, and the Spirit is the one who brings about the intended effect of God's speech within the world. As will become clearer as we move along, this point shapes the way we think about God's relation to the world and his creative and redemptive work in it.

---

11. Ibid., 1.13.19.

12. Ibid., 1.13.18.

13. Gregory of Nyssa, *On 'Not Three Gods'* (*NPNF²*, 5:334).

14. Augustine is correct to insist that the Son has his essential divinity from himself. "But when we mark the relation that he has with the Father," Calvin adds, "we rightly make the Father the beginning [origin] of the Son" (*Institutes* 1.13.19). See Brannon Ellis, *Calvin, Classical Trinitarianism, and the Aseity of the Son* (New York: Oxford Univ. Press, 2012).

15. Calvin, *Institutes* 1.13.18.

16. Ibid., 1.13.17.

17. Richard Muller, *Post-Reformation Reformed Dogmatics* (2nd ed.; Grand Rapids: Baker, 2003), 4:179.

Key Defenders of the Trinity in the Ancient Church	
Irenaeus **(second century)**	Bishop of Lyons and student of Polycarp (who was a disciple of John the apostle). Known especially for his defense of Christianity against gnosticism (*Against Heresies*).
Tertullian **(160–220)**	Carthage theologian who pioneered Trinitarian theology in the West; developed the formula "three persons, one essence."
Athanasius **(293–373)**	Bishop of Alexandria who helped to shape and defend Nicene orthodoxy.
The Cappadocian **Fathers** **(fourth century)**	Brothers Basil of Caesarea and Gregory of Nyssa, together with their friend Gregory of Nazianzus, were leaders in Cappadocia (modern Turkey) who played a formative role in developing the Trinitarian theology of the East.
Augustine **(354–430)**	Bishop of Hippo (in Northern Africa) who contributed important advances to Latin (Western) Trinitarian theology.

C. Modern Developments

The Enlightenment represents the triumph of a basically Socinian (neo-Arian) theology. Even many who did not identify formally with the Unitarian religion and remained within established churches either rejected the Trinity (along with other core Christian beliefs) or treated it as an irrelevant concept. After all, it was not a deliverance of unaided, autonomous, universal reason. Nor was it required by the necessities of universal, practical morality (as Kant argued), or religious experience (as Schleiermacher argued). So, with few exceptions, it was simply avoided until G. W. F. Hegel appropriated a Trinitarian scheme for his speculative philosophy.

Protestant liberalism added new chapters to the Socinian legacy, and while orthodox Christians continued to affirm the Trinity as an essential doctrine, its import was not always evident in faith and practice. It was Karl Barth who, in the twentieth century, revived widespread interest in the Trinity, in part through his reading of the older Reformed systems. Not only affirmed as one doctrine among many, Trinitarian thinking is evident across Barth's entire *Church Dogmatics*.

Nevertheless, some recent theologians have wondered if Barth's formulations emphasize the one God over the three persons. There is some basis for this concern, in my view.[18] However, Barth is often treated as the foil for sweeping indictments of Western Trinitarian reflection. More radical critiques, especially by Jürgen Moltmann and other advocates of *social Trinitarianism*, challenge the whole ecumenical consensus as a failure to give the plurality of persons its due. The Trinity is "one community of persons," not "one essence in three persons."[19] Although advocates of this view reject the label, in substance it represents *tritheism*: that is, belief in three Gods.

It has become increasingly popular in evangelical circles to reject the orthodox belief in the eternal generation of the Son. The concern is that it renders the Son ontologically subordinate (inferior) to the Father. However, this rests on a misunderstanding of the classic formulation and is easily resolved by a proper distinction between essence and persons.[20]

As the pendulum continues to swing between the "one" and the "many" in our own day as it did in the past, we should be impressed with that vast consensus that has bound Christians in all times and places to the formula "one God in three persons." This formula is sufficient for our faith and practice, Calvin reminds us. "Here, indeed, if anywhere in the secret mysteries of Scripture, we ought to play the philosopher soberly and with great moderation."[21]

Views of the Trinity	
Modalism and Subordinationism	• God is one person (the Father), manifested to us sometimes also as "Son" and "Spirit." Subordinationists (and Arians) taught that the Son and the Spirit are inferior ontologically to the Father. • Founder of Modalism: Sabellius (third-century Roman presbyter). Later proponents: Socinians, Unitarians. Origen and Eusebius were subordinationists, as were the Arians in a more radical way.
Orthodox Trinitarianism	• God is one in essence, three in persons. • Hippolytus, Tertullian, Athanasius, Augustine, the Cappadocian Fathers, Council of Nicaea (AD 325).
Tritheism	• God is three persons, with no unity of essence. • Founders: John Philoponus, Eugenius of Seleucia. Later proponents: Latter-Day Saints (Mormons).

---

18. For a fuller treatment, see *The Christian Faith*, 295–96. The principal places where Barth may be interpreted in a "modalistic" direction are in his *Church Dogmatics*, vol. 2, pt. 1, 350–53, 361.

19. Jürgen Moltmann, *Trinity and the Kingdom: The Doctrine of God* (trans. Margaret Kohl; Minneapolis: Augsburg Fortress, 1991), 92–98, 150. See also Elisabeth Moltmann-Wendel and Jürgen Moltmann, *Humanity in God* (Cleveland: Pilgrim Press, 1983), 96.

20. For a sound argument in favor of the orthodox understanding over against recent challenges, see Kevin N. Giles, *The Eternal Generation of the Son* (Downers Grove, Ill.: IVP Academic, 2012).

21. Calvin, *Institutes* 1.13.21.

III. Practical Benefits of the Doctrine of the Trinity

The Trinity is not one doctrine among others, but gives distinctive shape to Christian faith and practice—across all of the topics that we will cover in this volume. The Father, the Son, and the Spirit stride across the chapters of redemptive history toward the goal whose origin lies in an eternal pact between them. We worship, pray, confess, and sing our laments and praises to the Father, in the Son, by the Spirit. We are baptized and blessed in the name of the Father, and the Son, and the Holy Spirit. From the word of the Father concerning his Son in the power of the Spirit, a desert wasteland blooms into a lush garden in ever-widening patches throughout the world.

We are adopted as children, not of a unipersonal God, but of the Father, as coheirs with his Son as Mediator, united to the Son and his ecclesial body by the Spirit. Paul's doxology in Romans 11:36—"From him and through him and to him are all things"—now means more than a unipersonal God being the source, effectual agent, and end of all things; it means that all good gifts come from the Father, through the Spirit, and to the Son. As we noted earlier, "to the Father is attributed the beginning of activity, and the fountain and wellspring of all things; to the Son, wisdom, counsel, and the ordered disposition of all things; but to the Spirit is assigned the power and efficacy of that activity."[22] No less than the Father are the Son and the Spirit our Creator and preserver. No less than the Son are the Father and the Spirit our Savior and Lord. No less than the Father and the Son is the Spirit "worshiped and glorified."

One of the reasons that many Christians have found little practical relevance of this doctrine for their lives is that our public worship—and therefore private piety—has become increasingly emptied of Trinitarian references. As we've seen, one of the reasons for the controversies and greater refinements in formulating this doctrine is that monotheistic Jews were now offering worship to Christ and the Holy Spirit as well as to the Father. In addition to the New Testament formulas for baptism and benedictions, ancient prayers and hymns planted the Trinitarian faith deep in the hearts of Christian people across many times and places. Christians throughout the ages didn't just talk *about* the Trinity (which still, more often than not, happens today), but *to* the Father, in the Son, by the Spirit.

Many forms of worship today, however, have dispensed with these rich resources without replacing them with equally Trinitarian elements. So

---

22. Ibid., 1.13.18.

now when we raise the subject in catechism or youth group (which itself is increasingly rare), many find it unfamiliar to their Christian experience thus far. To the extent that our *experience* is not Trinitarian, it is not properly Christian. One of my goals in this book is to explore the relevance of the Trinity not only across the whole system of Christian doctrine, but in our lives as worshipers and disciples of Jesus Christ.

Many of the differences in faith and practice between Christian denominations and traditions can be attributed at least in part to a tendency to overlook this mutuality of the three persons in every work. It is not surprising that liberalism reduced the Trinity to the Father (as in Adolf von Harnack's oft-repeated formula, "the universal fatherhood of God and universal brotherhood of man") and therefore has had little interest in redemption by a divine Savior or its supernatural application by the Spirit. Deism needed only an Architect, not a Contractor and Builder. The tendency to focus on Christ apart from the Father and the Spirit has also led to a reductionistic view of redemption that is disconnected from creation and consummation. Placing the Spirit at the center—often in reaction against these other tendencies—one can easily treat the Spirit as a freelance operator rather than the one whose mission is to shine the spotlight on the Father's word concerning his Son's work. Throughout this volume we will be fleshing out what it means to say that in every external work of the Trinity all things are done by the Father, in the Son, through the Spirit.

Key Terms

- Trinity
- *homoousios*
- *hypostasis*
- *perichoresis*
- *filioque*

Key Distinctions

- economic/immanent (Trinity)
- essence/persons (Trinity)

Key Questions

1. As the drama unfolds in the New Testament, how did monotheistic Jews come to worship the Trinity?

2. What is the simplest and most widely embraced statement of the doctrine?
3. How significant was the distinction that emerged between essence (*ousia*) and person (*hypostasis*)?
4. The Christian East and West embraced a common Trinitarian faith. However, there are some important differences that contributed finally to schism. What are some of those differences?
5. Why is it important to talk about the personal attributes that distinguish the Father, Son, and Spirit, as well as the essential attributes that each person shares?

Chapter Five

Creation and Human Personhood

ᄀ하나님의 형.

J ust as we come to know God by attending to the covenantal drama rather than by speculating about his essence, the same is true for us. Again, the doctrine arises out of the drama—in this case, the doctrine of humanity. However, we need a wider view of creation and providence before focusing specifically on humanity in relation to God.

I. Creation by God's Word

With the doctrine of creation we discover one of the clearest points at which biblical faith contrasts sharply with rival worldviews. Whereas in pantheism and panentheism the world exists necessarily from God's own being, like the rays emanating from the sun, in the Bible there is the triune God with a retinue of angelic hosts perpetually worshiping him, and God freely speaks a declarative word to create a world that he does not need but simply desires in his loving joy and wise counsel. Trinity.

First, the author of creation is the triune God. The Creator is not a principle, force, or even a single person. This is not Plato's "One," Aristotle's "Unmoved Mover," or Islam's Allah. The God who exists in the unity of three persons created a community of persons as well as the radical diversity displayed on

pantheism : 범신론 · 자연론
panentheism : 만유 내재신론.

every hand. We often think of the Father in relation to creation, the Son in relation to redemption, and the Spirit in relation to the application of salvation. However, Scripture attributes all of these works to the Father, in the Son, by the Spirit. In every work of the Trinity, the Father is the source, the Son is the mediator, and the Spirit is the person who brings about within creation the appropriate effect of that living and active word. The Father speaks creation into being (Ge 1:3, 9, 11; Ps 33:9) in the Son (Jn 1:3; 1Co 8:6; Col 1:15–17) and by the Spirit (Ge 1:2; Job 26:13; Pss 33:6; Ps 104:30; Isa 40:12–13). The Logos by whom the worlds were made is not a silent principle or semidivine demiurge, but the second person, who is eternally begotten of the Father in the Spirit. The Spirit (*ruach*) of God who hovered over the watery depths to create dry land for the creature whom he, with the Father and the Son, would animate as "a living soul" (*nephesh*) is none other than the Holy Spirit who regenerates those who are "dead in ... trespasses and sins" (Eph 2:1).

Second, the source of God's creative act is loving freedom, not necessity. We say that something exists necessarily when it cannot be otherwise—in other words, when it is not contingent. God alone is necessary and eternal; everything else is contingent and temporal. "Before the mountains were brought forth, or ever you had formed the earth and the world, from everlasting to everlasting you are God" (Ps 90:2). This difference of creatures from their Creator is not a violent wound in a once-unified Being, but the kind of healthy difference you would expect in something that is not God. Not only the earth but "the heavens are the work of [his] hands" (Ps 102:25). "By faith we understand that the universe was created by the word of God, so that what is seen *was not made out of things that are visible*" (Heb 11:3, [emphasis added]). It is this powerful word that is spoken by God into nonexistence in the opening chapter of Genesis, and it is this pattern of *ex nihilo* ("out-of-nothing") creation that serves as a constant parallel for the "new creation" language that follows in redemptive history.

God created the world for his own glory. God does not say, as Jerry Maguire said to Dorothy in the 1996 film *Jerry Maguire*, "I love you ... You ... You ... complete me." Complete already in their shared essence and in their own loving communion, the Father, the Son, and the Spirit created the world out of pure freedom—an infinite love that gives without needing anything in return.

Neither divine nor demonic, all of creation is good in its intrinsic worldly difference from God. This also gives rise to a different conception of history. While the pagan myths treated earthly time as a projection of eternal cycles, the very notion of history as linear movement from origin to goal in time arose in Israel. This history and its revelation lead from *promise* to *fulfillment* rather than ~~from *lower* stages of being to *higher*~~.

At every point the world reflects its marvelous contingency—even to the point of apparent randomness. Far from the Enlightenment picture, post-Einsteinian science has become more aware of the dynamic natural processes that exhibit paradox and apparent chaos. Discerning something more like a complex organism involved in constant change than a cosmic machine running smoothly according to its own laws, the contemporary view of the world accents contingency. At no time in Western history has the dominant philosophical assumption of an eternal and necessary world become more unbelievable. Creation is intrinsically temporal, finite, contingent, and in constant flux. In this context, the deistic notion of God as a mere architect or watchmaker who designs the world and pushes the mighty "On!" button makes little sense. The amazing thing about the world is not that there are a few random anomalies, but that the apparently random accidents that are so pervasive nevertheless come together after all.

Third, the medium of God's creative work is his free speech. In our philosophical heritage of Platonism and Neoplatonism, the idea is (necessary) emanation rather than (free) creation. The usual analogies of the God-world relationship are those of a fountain with cascading waters or pure light emanating its rays in diminishing grades down the great chain of being. In contrast, the biblical analogy of speech highlights the absolute freedom and independence of God in this creative act. The world is the creation of God's word, not the extension of God's being. All three of these emphases become increasingly evident also in the new creation, as we will see in later chapters. If creation does not take place within God's being, as panentheists insist, it also does not generate itself, as naturalistic materialism holds. Nor is the world a self-sustaining mechanism in the way that deism supposed.

It is remarkable how frequently Scripture attributes creation to God's speech. "By the word of the LORD the heavens were made, and by the breath of his mouth all their host. . . . For he spoke, and it came to be; he commanded, and it stood firm" (Ps 33:6, 9). Walter Brueggemann notes, "Israel's testimony about Yahweh as Creator is fully embedded in Israel's larger covenant testimony. As Israel believes that its own life is covenantally ordered, so Israel believes that creation is covenantally ordered; that is, formed by continuing interactions of gift and gratitude, of governance and obedience."[1]

---

1. Walter Brueggemann, *Theology of the Old Testament: Testimony, Dispute, Advocacy* (Minneapolis: Fortress, 1997), 158–59.

This expresses the "relentless ethical dimension."[2] That the story of God's covenant with Israel emerges out of the story of God's covenant with creation (and vice versa) underscores the integral relationship between the universal and the particular. As the primary medium of world making, speech is also the primary medium of covenant making. The Son is eternally and necessarily the Word of the Father in his very essence, while the word spoken by the Father in creation is the contingent speech of his energies. And the Father sustains creation in his energetic speech by that same Word and Spirit: "The Mighty One, God the LORD, speaks and summons the earth from the rising of the sun to its setting" (Ps 50:1).

Notice the covenantal language for these communicative actions: "commanded" and "summons." Creation is in its very existence and from the very beginning covenantally ordered. Thus, as Brueggemann observes, "Creation has within it the sovereign seriousness of God, who will not tolerate the violation of the terms of creation, which are terms of gift, dependence, and extravagance. For those who refuse the doxology-evoking sovereignty of Yahweh, creation ends on an ominous warning."[3] It is to this covenant that the natural world gives its testimony (as in Psalm 19), and Yahweh even calls upon the natural world to testify both for (Ge 15:5–6; 8:22; 9:8–17; Mt 2:10) and against (Mt 24:28; 27:45; Ac 2:20) his covenant people in history. God's rule in nature and in history, in creation and redemption, is jointly celebrated repeatedly in the Psalms.

II. Providence

Although the whole cosmos came into being at a definite point in time (original or *ex nihilo creation*), the Father is still sustaining creation in his Son and by his Spirit, what we commonly refer to as God's *providence*. In Genesis 1 there are two distinct types of speech acts: the fiats of *ex nihilo* creation ("Let there be ..." with the report, "And it was so") and God's command to creation to put forth its own powers with which he has endowed it and within which the Spirit is operative ("Let the waters under the heavens be gathered together into one place, and let the dry land appear" [v. 9]; "Let the earth sprout vegetation, plants yielding seed ..." [v. 11]). In fact, it is reported, "The earth brought forth vegetation ..." (v. 12). God adds, "Let the waters swarm with swarms of living creatures, and let birds fly above the earth across the expanse of the heavens" (v. 20), and "Let the earth bring

---

2. Ibid., 158.
3. Ibid., 156.

> ## Key Distinction:
> ### *creation ex nihilo / providence*
>
> While God's fiat word brought the world into being out of no pre-existing matter (*ex nihilo*), God's providence governs history, so that his purposes are realized gradually in the world—yet without subverting the free agency of creatures.

forth living creatures according to their kinds ..." (v. 24). Furthermore, God commands the fish and fowl, as well as humans, "Be fruitful and multiply" (vv. 22, 28). We may put these two types of speech acts in the form of "Let there be ..." and "Let it become what I have 'worded' it to be." Anticipating my argument in later chapters, I would add that this is the same pattern that we find in the new creation, in justification and sanctification, respectively.

God not only speaks the world into being out of nothing; his speech also shapes creaturely response. In other words, God doesn't just act upon creation, but within it, as we see in the rich imagery of the Spirit sweeping across the earth with his fructifying energies. If my wife tells me, "I love you," she not only does something by her words (namely, speaking); she brings something about in me (namely, grateful affection). Of course, this is a pale analogy, but it makes the point that God's speech is not only of the fiat variety, creating something out of nothing, but includes those many instances in which creatures actually respond, grow, and bear the fruit that is in accord with that word.

This is a crucial point, especially at a time when some Christians over-react against the naturalistic assumptions of our modern world in the direction of a hypersupernaturalism. Every rustling of a leaf has to be seen as a direct act of God in this approach. In order to attribute everything to God, one must eliminate natural causes. If one is mysteriously cured of a disease, it must be an example of God's direct intervention. However, this inevitably reduces our sense of God's involvement to the miraculous, fiat, "Let there be *x*!" types of speech acts. Furthermore, we fall prey to the "God-of-the-Gaps" apologetic: treating God as the answer to mysteries in the natural sciences, only to be disappointed when science does in fact discover natural explanations that fill in those gaps. Scripture itself encourages us to think of God's lively speech as more than direct, creative, and fiat-type declarations. When the earth itself brings forth fruit, it is no less due ultimately to God's generous and sovereign involvement than when he created trees in the first place. God not only created the world with its own inherent potential for fruitfulness, but continues to work in the Son and by the Spirit to enable creation to bring forth fruit—that is, to enable each thing to do what it has been "worded" to do.

With this distinction I am making a transition from creation to providence. The danger in hypersupernaturalism is that of collapsing the latter into the former. Genesis 1 itself tells us that natural causes can be easily discerned: *the earth* brought forth fruit. Yet these natural explanations are not exhaustive. We can say that God healed someone of cancer *and* that the doctors healed him or her. God is no less to be praised when he works through ordinary means that he has created and sustains than when he acts unilaterally and miraculously. Childbirth is not a miracle, but one of the most marvelous examples of God's mighty providence. When we overreact against naturalism, we push God's agency out of our horizon unless we can somehow eliminate the natural means that he uses to accomplish his purposes. In other words, hypersupernaturalism is an unwitting ally of naturalism in downplaying the significance of God's ordinary providence.

Scripture has no difficulty attributing the same action or event both to God and creatures. Once again, we see the importance of the doctrine of analogy. Human agency no more intersects with God's in willing and choosing than in being or knowing. Everything that God does is *qualitatively* unique. It is misleading to assume that when God acts more, we act less. Rather, God is involved in every detail of our lives as Creator, and yet we are also active in our own creaturely way. Even John Calvin had no trouble speaking of "fortunate" or chance happenings, since that is exactly how they appear to us—and yet, even in those instances, God is sovereign over the contingencies.[4]

Christian theologians speak of **concursus** ("going together") between divine and human agency. God is always at work, but in his own way as the sovereign God. Sometimes God acts directly and immediately (as in the fiat word of ex nihilo creation or in the incarnation); at other times, indirectly and mediately (as in the "Let the earth bring forth" speech act). Because divine and creaturely agency are not on the same map, the latter is most directly evident to our empirical investigation while often the former remains largely hidden. God does not move birds miraculously in their annual migrations, and yet "not one of them will fall to the ground apart from your Father" (Mt 10:29).

---

4. Calvin, *Institutes* 1.16.9; 1.17.1.

Classic Reformed teaching on providence carries forward the Augustinian-Thomistic consensus. As Hodge nicely summarizes, "It is best, therefore, to rest satisfied with the simple statement that preservation is that omnipotent energy of God by which all created things, animate and inanimate, are upheld in existence, with all the properties and powers with which He has endowed them."[5] In this perspective, creaturely agency is real, even if (or rather, because) it is dependent ultimately on God's powerful word. In other words, we attribute the stability of planetary orbits ultimately to God, even though the means he employs have perfectly good natural explanations.

In treating providence, it is important to bear in mind some crucial distinctions. I will mention two here, although I have treated others elsewhere.[6]

First, there is the distinction between God's **common** and **saving grace**. "The LORD is good to all, and his mercy is over all that he has made.... The eyes of all look to you, and you give them their food in due season. You open your hand; you satisfy the desire of every living thing" (Ps 145:9, 15–16). Jesus reiterates this general kindness in his Sermon on the Mount: "For [God] makes his sun rise on the evil and on the good, and sends rain on the just and on the unjust" (Mt 5:45). We are no longer living in the old covenant theocracy, when the church was identified with a nation and God reigned directly, dispensing temporal blessings for obedience and curses for national disobedience. Believers and unbelievers alike share in the common curse of a fallen creation and the common grace of a generous King.

God has appointed the times and dwelling places of all people to the end that they will look to him as the source of all good (Ac 17:25–27). The most seemingly insignificant details are governed by God's providence. With the psalmist, we may wonder, "When I look at your heavens, the work of your fingers, the moon and the stars, which you have set in place, what is man that you are mindful of him, and the son of man that you care for him?" (Ps 8:3–4). Nevertheless, every hair of each person is numbered by God (Lk 12:7), and not a single bird falls to the ground without the Father's will (Mt 10:29). Even the results of every roll of dice in a game of chance are determined by God (Pr 16:33). God's majesty is revealed not only in his sovereignty over rising empires but in his tender concern for falling sparrows. The Father richly dresses the grass of the field and feeds the birds of the air (Mt 6:25–34).

---

5. Charles Hodge, *Systematic Theology* (Grand Rapids: Eerdmans, 1946), 1:581.
6. Michael Horton, *The Christian Faith* (Grand Rapids: Zondervan, 2011), 355–70.

Similarly, Paul calls for contentment, "for we brought nothing into the world, and we cannot take anything out of the world. But if we have food and clothing, with these we will be content" (1Ti 6:7–8). God "gives life to all things" (v. 13) and "richly provides us with everything to enjoy" (v. 17). Paul interpreted God's exhaustive providence over every detail of our lives, including where we would live and how long, not as an oppressive intrusion but as proof of God's generosity and nearness (Ac 17:26–28). Out of the lavishness displayed in the marvelous variety and richness of creation itself, God continues to pour out his common blessings on all people. Precisely because God does not depend on the world or share his own unique existence and freedom with creatures, he is an inexhaustible fountain of loving generosity. Therefore, we neither hoard possessions as if God's gifts were scarce nor deny ourselves good pleasures as if God were stingy.

It is always dangerous to interpret one's temporal circumstances as a sign of either God's favor or displeasure. Our natural reason tells us that good people finish first and cheaters never prosper. Of course, under the old covenant, God did promise temporal blessings (such as a long and fruitful life, many children, and peace) for obedience and temporal curses (such as disease, famine, and exile) for disobedience. However, with its thorough violation by the human partner, this national covenant came to an end. Today there is no holy nation or holy land, with promises of temporal and national blessings or judgments. Although the remnant of Israel and the nations, united to Christ, is the end-time sanctuary, all nations are common. Believers have no more right to God's common grace than to his saving grace; God remains free to show compassion to whomever he will, even to give breath, health, prosperity, and friends to those who breathe threats against him. For believers, every common blessing is a foretaste of heavenly joys, and "the sufferings of this present time are not worth comparing with the glory that is to be revealed to us" (Ro 8:18). From this assurance the Heidelberg Catechism confidently teaches in its first question and answer that "I am not my own, but belong—body and soul, in life and in death—to my faithful Savior Jesus Christ.... Not a hair can fall from my head without the will of my Father in heaven: in fact, all things must work together for my salvation."[7] These passages do not say that God *does* all things or that all things are *good*, but that *he works all things together for our good*—which means, ultimately, for our salvation.

Second, there is a distinction between God's hidden decree and his

---

7. Heidelberg Catechism, q. 1, in Doctrinal Standards of the Christian Reformed Church, in *Psalter Hymnal* (Grand Rapids: Board of Publications of the Christian Reformed Church, 1976), 8.

> ## Key Distinction:
> *common grace / saving grace*
>
> The civil kingdom (i.e., the particular government of nations) is no less under Christ's ultimate lordship than is his church. However, he rules the one through his providence and *common grace* in the world and the other through his miraculous *saving grace* in the church. Even non-Christian rulers are God's servants (Ro 13:1–5), but they are not given the spiritual ministry of word, sacrament, and discipline, just as pastors are not granted civil authority.

revealed will. We know from Scripture what God was doing in and through Israel, but we have no revelation about God's purposes for our own countries or even our own lives apart from his moral and saving will in Scripture. We cannot read God's purposes in the daily news or interpret prosperity or disasters as a sign of God's favor or disfavor toward us as individuals or nations. Often, the wicked prosper and the righteous suffer; the reasons lie hidden in God's purposes.

This distinction between things hidden and things revealed is maintained throughout Scripture (Dt 29:29; 1Co 2:7–10). Although God has decreed everything that comes to pass, he has not revealed everything that he has decreed. We must not try to figure out God's secret providence, but respect his majesty (Ro 11:34) and attend to the means that he has provided for our salvation (through word and sacrament) and earthly welfare (vocations, friendship, and other common gifts that we share with unbelievers). So we are directed to seek out God's will only in that which he has revealed: "in the law and the gospel," Calvin reminds us. Hidden in past ages, God's secret purpose in Christ has been revealed in these last days. "Yet his wonderful method of governing the universe is rightly called an abyss, because while it is hidden from us, we ought reverently to adore it."[8]

Romans 12:2 promises that "by testing you may discern what is the will of God, what is good and acceptable and perfect." On this basis, some have taught that God has a sovereign plan for our lives, but that we can step in and out of it. Often referred to as God's "perfect will," from this passage, the idea is that God's sovereign plan is merely a Plan A—God's best for our lives—rather than God's secret but certain decree. Many believers struggle

---

8. Calvin, *Institutes*, 1.17.2.

to discern God's secret will in daily decisions because they confuse it with his "perfect will" in this passage. However, Romans 12:2 is not speaking of God's eternal counsels, sure to be fulfilled yet hidden to us. Rather, the context (renewing the mind through the word) indicates that the perfect will that Paul calls us here to discern is God's moral and saving will (i.e., the law and the gospel) *insofar as he has revealed it in Scripture*. For example, we must marry fellow believers (2Co 6:14), but other considerations are left to our wisdom, the counsel of friends, and the desires of our heart. Although God has "determined allotted periods and the boundaries of [our] dwelling place" (Ac 17:26), we have no way of discovering the details that God wished to remain hidden to us.

Accordingly, there is great comfort for the believer. First, it's comforting to know that God's "Plan A" is sure to be realized because God is working everything—even our sins and mistakes in judgment, as well as external threats and calamities—together for good. We never have to fear falling into a "Plan B." Second, it's comforting to be liberated from the anxiety of having to figure out God's secret will for our lives and to focus on knowing his revealed word. Third, we are comforted by the fact that God has revealed his purposes in what seemed to human beings to be nothing more than the tragic end to a good man in the death of Jesus. I may not know how God will work together my mistakes, sins, and foolishness for my good and his glory. However, I do know that he has triumphed over evil ultimately in Christ. "None of the rulers of this age understood this, for if they had, they would not have crucified the Lord of glory" (1Co 2:8). The revelation now of this mystery is all we need for our confidence that our lives are not tragic and meaningless, as they might seem to us at times. With Christ's resurrection, we're already able to catch a glimpse of the ending (which is really the beginning) even in the middle of the story.

III. To Be Human

We have seen that the biblical identification of God arises out of a historical narrative. As the plot unfolds, throbbing verbs give rise to stable nouns. So we do not need to speculate about God's essence; we can attend to his own revelation concerning his works. The context of the relationship between God and human beings is *covenantal*. Having discussed the character of the Covenant Lord, we turn now to the identity of the covenant servant. The question, "What is it to be human?" can be answered, not by speculating on our human essence—particularly what distinguishes us from other creatures—but by listening to a story and the stable definitions that arise from this revelation. In this story, God not only reveals himself; he reveals us to ourselves.

A. Mapping Philosophical Options

"What is man that you are mindful of him, and the son of man that you care for him?" (Ps 8:4). The questions of the psalmist are not your typical philosophical speculations. Rather than regarding himself as a disinterested subject analyzing an objective "essence" of humanity, he places the question within the covenantal context. In other words, the question "what is man?" cannot even be asked apart from a reference to God: why does God care about this slight creature? The answer comes in the form of a story, about how God created human beings "a little lower than the heavenly beings," yet gave them royal dignity. Before we unpack this covenantal understanding of human beings, we should be aware of the dominant approaches to this topic in our culture.

At one extreme is Platonist/Neoplatonist **dualism**. Dualism is the long-influential idea that the mind or soul is the divine part of us struggling toward liberation from its bodily imprisonment. In Greek mythology, Prometheus was sentenced to death by Zeus for stealing fire from the sun—the divine spark within human beings that distinguishes them from the animals. As with other ideas in our Western bloodstream, stories like this one were "demythologized" in the form of a dogma: in this case, the immortality of the soul. Dualism holds that the soul is the real self, by nature eternal and pure.

Plotinus, the great third-century Neoplatonist, saw the human being as a microcosm: that is, a small-scale version of the cosmos. Just as the cosmos consists of three ranking orders from the unknowable One to Mind to matter, we are also divided into three parts: mind (or spirit), soul, and body, in descending ranks. As a result, there are three classes of people in the world: the *pneumatikoi* ("spirituals"), the *psychikoi* ("soulish") and the *sarkikoi* ("fleshly").[9] Although a minority view today in Christian circles,

---

9. Hans Jonas, *The Gnostic Religion* (Boston: Beacon, 1958); Kurt Rudolph, *Gnosis: The Nature and History of Gnosticism* (San Francisco: Harper and Row, 1983); Dan Merkur, *Gnosis: An Esoteric Tradition of Mystical Visions and Unions* (Albany: State Univ. of New York Press, 1993); Edwin M. Yamauchi, "The Descent of Ishtar, the Fall of Sophia, and the Jewish Roots of Gnosticism," *Tyndale Bulletin* 29 (1978): 143–75; Ugo Bianchi, ed., *Selected Essays on Gnosticism, Dualism, and Mysteriosophy* (Leiden: Brill, 1978). See also Rudolf Bultmann, *Theology of the New Testament* (trans. Kendrick Grobel; New York: Scribner's Sons, 1951), 1:166.

this anthropology, known as **trichotomy**, has been a perennial temptation among various Christian groups.[10]

René Descartes (1596–1650) brought this sort of sharp mind-body dualism into the modern era, transposed in a distinctly modern key. In this answer to the question of human essence the real self is a disembodied "thinking thing" (*res cogitans*), separated not only from the body but from everything in the "lower" realm of matter, including other people and the wider creation. Though this notion of rationalistic dualism was once the norm, it came under increasing attack throughout the twentieth century. Descartes's position was frequently characterized as considering the human being to be "the ghost in the machine."[11] Especially in Descartes's construction, this view inevitably pits human thinking against feeling and doing within the self and then pits this "thinking thing" against the rest of creation, which becomes little more than a machine or the raw materials for reason's calculative manipulation. Descartes failed to provide any satisfying account of how the mind and the body interact. Not only do mind and body seem unrelated in Descartes's system; individual thinkers do not seem related to each other, much less to the nonrational creation. Giving prominent space to Descartes, Charles Taylor documents the passage of modernity from a sense of the self defined by a complex web of relations to ever-narrower, autonomous, and individualistic concepts: a sense of the self disengaged from the world.[12]

At the other end of the spectrum—and in reaction against such dualistic thinking—there has been a growing trend toward anthropological **monism**. In monism there is no longer a sharp division between body and soul; in fact, there is no distinction between them at all. Some proponents of monism are atheistic naturalists who deny spiritual reality. Believing that classical theology has been too indebted to Plato, others (including some Jewish and Christian theologians) argue that while there is more to us than matter, there is no such thing as a soul that exists distinct from the body. Of course, it was sharp disagreement over this question that divided the Pharisees and Sadducees in Jesus' day. Nevertheless, the heirs of the latter party in the modern era have claimed that the Pharisees invented the idea of the soul, probably

---

10. In recent times it has been defended by C. I. Scofield in the *Scofield Reference Bible* (New York: Oxford Univ. Press, 1909), n 1 on 1Th 5:23; Watchman Nee, *The Spiritual Man* (3 vols.; New York: Christian Fellowship Publishers, 1968); Lewis Sperry Chafer, *He That Is Spiritual* (Grand Rapids: Zondervan, 1967). I respond to the exegetical arguments for trichotomy in *The Christian Faith*, 374–75.

11. Gilbert Ryle, "Descartes' Myth," in *The Concept of Mind* (Chicago: Univ. of Chicago Press, 1984), 11–23.

12. Charles Taylor, *Sources of the Self: The Making of the Modern Identity* (Cambridge, Mass.: Harvard Univ. Press, 1992).

> ## Key Distinction:
> ### *radical dualism/monism/biblical dualism*
>
> Radical dualism contrasts a divine soul with its bodily prison house (as in Plato); in Descartes's version, there is no interaction between mind and matter. Monism is equally radical in denying any distinction between body and soul. Biblical duality-in-unity recognizes a distinction without denying the unity of the human person.

due to Greek influences. Recent scholarship has challenged this thesis, demonstrating the pre-Pharisee belief in the soul's survival of bodily death and the hope of resurrection.[13]

Some orthodox Christians, especially in reaction against Greek and modern (Cartesian) dualism, advocate a **modified monism**, which emphasizes the psychosomatic (soul-body) unity of human beings. Advocates of this view are usually agnostic about whether the soul exists separately from the body at death until the final resurrection.[14] Against classical (and Christian) dualism, Nancey Murphy argues that we do not possess something like a soul distinct from the body, while she also rejects the naturalistic reduction of the human person to material processes. Identifying her view as "nonreductive physicalism," she prefers to speak of "spirited bodies" rather than of "bodies and souls."[15]

Criticism of dualism in general and a radical soul-body dualism in particular is a recurring motif in Reformed theology up to the present day.[16]

---

13. See especially Jon Levenson, *Resurrection and the Restoration of Israel: The Ultimate Victory of the God of Life* (New Haven, Conn.: Yale Univ. Press, 2006).

14. As we will see below, this is the view of G. C. Berkouwer. The strong criticism of dualism within the Reformed tradition can sometimes lead to an overreaction in this direction. The same tendency may be seen in Herman Ridderbos, *Paul: An Outline of His Theology* (trans. John R. de Witt; Grand Rapids: Eerdmans, 1975), 497–508, 548–50. More recently, some Christians working at the intersection of science and theology have developed a variation of modified monism known as "non-reductive physicalism," so called because it still acknowledges certain attributes and actions that transcend material substances. See Nancey Murphy, "Non-reductive Physicalism: Philosophical Issues," in *Whatever Happened to the Soul?* (ed. Warren S. Brown, Nancey Murphy, and H. Newton Maloney; Minneapolis: Fortress, 1998), 127–48; see also her more recently revised version of this essay in *Human Identity in Theological Perspective* (ed. Richard Lints, Michael Horton, and Mark Talbot; Grand Rapids: Eerdmans, 2009), 95–117.

15. See Murphy, "Non-reductive Physicalism: Philosophical Issues," 127–48. See also idem, *Bodies and Souls, or Spirited Bodies?* (Cambridge: Cambridge Univ. Press 2006).

16. Following Kuyper and Bavinck, G. C. Berkouwer explicitly defends a relational view of humanity over against abstract consideration of the nature or being of humanity as identified with the soul, heart, mind, or other faculties. See his *Man: The Image of God* (Grand Rapids: Eerdmans, 1962), 194–233. See also Anthony A. Hoekema, *Created in God's Image* (Grand Rapids: Eerdmans, 1986), 203–26.

However, we should beware of overreacting against one unbiblical view in favor of an equally unscriptural interpretation. So how do we evaluate these rival views? In contrast to the dualistic and monistic views, Scripture provides us with an entirely different map for understanding the human person.

To begin with, we must remember that the great ontological distinction in the Bible is between God and everything else, not between spirit (or mind) and body (or matter). Materialists are wrong, not when they say that human beings are thoroughly natural beings, but when they reduce human nature to physical-chemical components and processes. Plato, not the Scriptures, has taught us to think of the soul as a supernatural — even divine — part of us that has existed eternally. The soul is not an emanation of divinity entombed in a physical body; it is a natural but nonphysical aspect of our creatureliness. The soul is not divine, nor is the body demonic or evil; full humanity is a psychosomatic (body-soul) unity. We do not *have* a body (as if the soul were our real selves); we are created as a psychosomatic (soul-body) whole, as persons. Our bodies (including our brain) and souls are not separate compartments, but interactive aspects of our personal existence and activity. This holistic view of the human person is supported by research, especially in the neurological sciences. For example, severe depression cannot be regarded simply as a spiritual or moral problem, and there are often times when medical treatments may be of enormous benefit. Nevertheless, it is just as reductionistic to exclude spiritual and moral agency from the equation.

Some theologians (like G. C. Berkouwer) have gone so far in affirming the unity of the human person that they place in question the existence of the soul apart from the body in the intermediate state.[17] Earlier Reformed theologians were more judicious in this matter. "As flesh and spirit (taken physically) are *disparates, not contraries*," explains Turretin, "so also are the appetites, inclinations and habits of both in themselves. The repugnancy now found in them arises accidentally from sin" (emphasis added).[18] Peter Martyr Vermigli observed the close identification in the Old Testament of the soul (*nephesh*, "life") with the blood, highlighting the soul-body integration.[19] In fact, as Bavinck points out,

17. Berkouwer, *Man*, 194–233.

18. Quoted in Heinrich Heppe, *Reformed Dogmatics* (rev. and ed. E. Bizer; trans. G. T. Thomson; London: G. Allen and Unwin, 1950; repr., London: Wakeman Trust, 2002), 468.

19. Based on Ge 9:4, he argues that "the blood is the soul." This represents a metonymy: "Since the blood is a sign of the soul's presence, it may be called the soul itself ... I do not offer this as if I accept it

Adam's body was formed from the dust of the earth and then the breath of life is breathed into him. He is called 'Adam' after the ground from which he was formed; he is 'from the earth, a man of dust' (1 Cor. 15:47). The body is not a prison, but a marvelous piece of art from the hand of God Almighty, and just as constitutive for the essence of humanity as the soul (Job 10:8–12; Pss. 8; 139:13–17; Eccles. 12:2–7; Isa. 64:8).... Now, this body, which is so intimately bound up with the soul, also belongs to the image of God.... The incarnation of God is proof that the human body is an essential component of that image.[20]

Although the soul survives bodily death, it is only with the reintegration of body and soul in the resurrection that the whole person is finally saved. Immortality is not an attribute of the soul any more than of the body; it is God's gift of resurrection-glorification in Jesus Christ. To put it more simply, Platonism sees *embodiment* as a curse, while Christianity understands *disembodiment* to be the curse. While the body and soul *can* be separated, they are not *meant* to be separated, and our salvation is not complete until we are bodily raised as whole persons (Ro 8:23). The intermediate state is not the final state. The "real self" is the *whole self.*

Nevertheless, we should recognize that Scripture does presuppose and even explicitly teaches a distinction between the body and the soul, usually called **dichotomy**, especially in its affirmation of the soul's living presence before God at bodily death.[21] Since *dichotomy* suggests to some people the idea of separate—even disparate—things, I prefer to speak of a distinction between body and soul.

---

as the reason why God gave that commandment [against eating the blood of animals], but to indicate the communion of man's soul with the body" (Peter Martyr Vermigli, *Philosophical Works* [vol. 4 of *The Peter Martyr Library*; ed. and trans. Joseph C. McLelland; Kirksville, Mo.: Sixteenth Century Essays and Studies, 1996], 42).

20. Herman Bavinck, *Reformed Dogmatics: Abridged in One Volume* (ed. John Bolt; Grand Rapids: Baker Academic, 2011), 327.

21. See, for example, Wayne Grudem, *Systematic Theology* (Grand Rapids: Zondervan, 1994), 472–83, particularly for his exegetical summary of the dichotomist position and interaction with trichotomy and monism. Affirming the existence of the soul, distinct from the body, traditional Christian theologies have speculated as to whether the soul is passed down from our first parents through the entire human race (traducianism) or is immediately created in each instance by God (creationism). Traducianism maintains that individual souls are transmitted from the parents to their offspring, similar to the inheritance of physical traits. Creationism holds that each soul is a new creation of God. Although creationism is the dominant view at least in the West, traducianism has had notable defenders, including Tertullian, Augustine, and Gregory of Nyssa. These are interesting questions with valuable theological implications, but are unlikely to be settled conclusively on exegetical grounds.

Contrasting Anthropologies	
Trichotomy	Human beings are composed of spirit/mind, soul, and body (in descending rank).
Dichotomy	Human beings are composed of soul (synonymous with spirit or mind) and body.
Monism	Human beings are physical organisms; the characteristics traditionally associated with the soul or mind are attributable to chemical and neurological processes and interactions.
Mediating Views	(1) *Modified monism* (nonreductive physicalism) affirms spiritual causes and effects without identifying them with a nonphysical faculty; (2) *duality-in-unity* (my own term) is the view (which I prefer) that distinguishes soul and body without ranking them as higher and lower or more and less constitutive of human identity. In this distinction without dualism, human beings do not *have* bodies and souls; they *are* bodily souls. In the resurrection, this unity is restored.

On the one hand, our final salvation is identified in Scripture with the reunion of glorified body-soul existence. On the other hand, in between death and the resurrection the soul is present with Christ in heaven (Lk 23:43; 2Co 5:1 – 10; Php 1:21 – 24; Rev 6:9 – 10). Again, we must remember that Christian theology affirms a rich and complex anthropology, one that is determined not by speculation about essences but by an unfolding drama that leads from creation to consummation.[22] We understand who we are by seeing ourselves in light of the story, the drama of redemption in Christ.

B. The Image of God: A Biblical-Theological Account

Having briefly summarized the various philosophical perspectives, we now turn our attention to the biblical motifs of covenant and eschatology. *Covenant* refers to the *context* of our creation: God created us as covenant servants, and we will see the close connection between covenant and the "image of God" below. By *eschatology* we have in mind the *goal* of our creation. Creation was just the beginning of a relationship that would lead

---

22. John W. Cooper, *Body, Soul, and Life Everlasting: Biblical Anthropology and the Monism-Dualism Debate* (Grand Rapids: Eerdmans, 1989). This is the best exploration I have seen of the issues involved and the best defense of the traditional Christian view.

either to covenantal blessing or curse, everlasting life or death. The Tree of Life stood up ahead as the reward for covenantal obedience. By fulfilling all righteousness, Adam would have won for himself and his posterity not merely a continuance of temporal blessing but entrance into God's everlasting Sabbath rest. Swept into Adam's train, the whole creation would enjoy forever the liberty of God's children. In other words, the glorification that believers anticipate in the final resurrection of the dead, through the merit of the Last Adam, was already signified at the beginning with the trial in which God placed our first covenant head. Because of this, it is only by the revelation of Christ and the gospel that we come to understand properly what it means to be created in God's image.

The image of God (**imago dei**) is not something *in* us that is semidivine but something *between* us and God that constitutes a covenantal relationship. "The whole being, the whole human person and not just 'something' in us is the image of God," notes Bavinck. "Thus, a human being does not *bear* or *have* the image of God but *is* the image of God."[23]

To recall a point I have already made, the closest parallels to Israel's faith were not religious but political. The surrounding civilizations had developed elaborate mythopoetic religious cults, but this was idolatry in Israel. Yahweh was not just another god, lending transcendent authority to the earthly ruler, but the ruler himself — the suzerain or great king. For the idea of a covenant of a people *with their God* there are no parallels in the ancient world. Yahweh delivered his people and made them his nation. Israel's relationship to God was founded on a covenant, similar to the vassal-suzerain treaties of secular kingdoms. At the center of Israel's holiest shrine was not an image of the chief deity, as in pagan temples, but the ark (archive) of the covenant: a box in which God's covenant-law was placed. The prophets were God's lawyers, not life coaches, monks, or sages, and history (not just the inner self) was the courtroom.

So the concept of human beings as the image of God is not drawn from the usual stock of pagan religion (i.e., the idol as the replica of the deity). Rather, it is a political image. Just as the crown prince is the image of his imperial father, human beings are God's viceroys, his representatives among the creatures that God has made.

It's not just in a few doctrines here or there where biblical faith differs from its rivals; rather, biblical faith springs from a radically different paradigm. In addition to providing a different understanding of God and the

---

23. Bavinck, *Reformed Dogmatics*, 324.

God-world relationship generally, a covenantal paradigm grounds a fundamentally different view of human personhood. We do not meet God in the inner realm of our spirit or at sacred rivers, trees, or mountains. Rather, God hallows common places as historical venues of his discourse. Places are special (holy) in biblical faith because God met with his people there and spoke his covenant word. As covenantal, then, this faith is always social: meeting with God and others he has gathered, in public spaces, where we are constituted the people of God.

What defines human personhood, on this account, is not so much what happens within the self (i.e., the relation and ranking of faculties), or in the cycles of nature, but what happens between persons (God and human beings) in history. With God's act of creation, the relation between the persons of the Trinity finds its analogy in the relations between God and his people and the relations between the people themselves in the covenant community. This covenantal relationship is not something added to human nature, but is essential to it. To exist as human beings is not to be a "thinking thing," a disembodied and unrelated ego, but is already to be enmeshed in a web of relationships: a society.

This inherent sociality (analogous to the perichoretic relationship between the Father, the Son, and the Spirit) is evident in lonely Adam's delight upon meeting Eve (Ge 2:21–25) and the ever-expanding networks from the nuclear family to societies and cultures that follow from the patriarchal narratives (Ge 4:1–24), especially in the growth of the covenant community (Ge 4:25–26). At her creation, Eve is greeted by Adam in a way analogous to God's greeting of Adam. Hence, the Pauline implication (1Co 11:7) that Eve is Adam's image because she is consubstantial with him in humanity: "In the image of God he created *them, male and female*" (Ge 1:27, emphasis added). While both male and female are created in God's image, Adam could say of Eve, "This at last is bone of my bones and flesh of my flesh" (Ge 2:23). As Stanley Grenz observes, "Adam's cry of elation resembles the traditional kinship formula, 'my bone and (my) flesh' (cf. Gen. 29:14; Judg 9:3; 2 Sam 5:1; 19:12–13), which Walter Brueggemann suggests is actually a covenant formula that speaks of a common, reciprocal loyalty."[24]

The Bible places human beings in a dramatic narrative that defines their existence as inherently covenantal—fully engaged with God, with each other, and with the nonhuman creation. Instead of drawing us within our-

---

24. Stanley Grenz, *The Social God and the Relational Self* (Louisville: Westminster John Knox, 2001), 276.

selves in order to draw our contemplation upward from our lived experience in the world, a covenantal anthropology draws us outward, where we find ourselves responsible to God and our neighbors. Furthermore, the emphasis on eschatology underscores the point that "image of God" is not just something that human beings are in their essence (a private possession), but is a public vocation—a summons to fulfill a particular calling as God's covenant servants.

1. Being persons who answer, "Here I am"

The covenant of creation provides the context now for drawing conclusions about what it means to be human, especially to be created in God's image. To be created in God's image is to be called persons in communion: with God and each other, as well as with the whole creation.[25] There was no moment when a human being was actually a solitary, autonomous, unrelated entity; self-consciousness always included consciousness of one's relation to God and to each other and of one's place in the wider created environment. Our earliest moments of self-consciousness (even *in utero*) are dependent on our relation to others.

This covenantal understanding strikes at the heart of attempts to ground the image of God in any dualistic opposition between mind/spirit and body. Cornelius Van Til observed,

> Man is not in Plato's cave.... Man had originally not merely a capacity for receiving the truth; he was in actual possession of the truth. The world of truth was not found in some realm far distant from him; it was right before him. That which spoke to his senses no less than that which spoke to his intellect was the voice of God.... Man's first sense of self-awareness implied the awareness of the presence of God as the one for whom he had a great task to accomplish.[26]

Truth is a covenantal concept, something communicated between persons, within a context of hearing and answering. If we extend this reflection, we could say that human beings are those who reflect God's image not merely in *what they are essentially* but in *how they reply ethically*. Let me explain what I mean.

---

25. See Colin Gunton, "Trinity, Ontology and Anthropology," in *Persons: Divine and Human* (ed. Christoph Schwöbel and C. E. Gunton; Edinburgh: T&T Clark, 1991), 47–61. At the same time, I find such arguments as those employed by Harriet A. Harris (against a purely relational ontology of person) compelling ("Should We Say That Personhood Is Relational?," *Scottish Journal of Theology* 51, no. 2 [1998]: 222–23).

26. Cornelius Van Til, *The Defense of the Faith* (Philadelphia: Presbyterian and Reformed Publishing Company, 1955), 90.

First, we have seen how Genesis 1 refers to two distinct but united kinds of speech: God said, "'Let there be light,' and there was light" (Ge 1:3); yet he also summoned, "'Let the earth sprout vegetation.'... And the earth brought forth vegetation" (vv. 11–12). Throughout the narrative, there is this pairing of "Let there be *x*" and "Let *x* bring forth *y*." God made man in his image, male and female, and then issued his performative command, "'Be fruitful and multiply and fill the earth and subdue it, and have dominion over the fish of the sea and over the birds of the heavens and over every living thing that moves on the earth.' And God said, 'Behold, I have given you ... every tree with seed in its fruit....'And it was so" (vv. 28–30). God's word always accomplishes what it says (Isa 55:11)—not simply by direct fiat, but by the Spirit's work within creation, bringing about its appropriate response. In other words, the fiat-word brings something into being, but its effects are fully realized only when that something (or someone) "brings forth" that fruit that is consistent with what God worded the creature to be. This second type of speech act, then, is basically a summons for the various creatures to *become* what they *are*. Created in God's image, human beings are called to become the faithful image (servant/son) by fulfilling their vocation.

Second, in both Testaments there is a recurring Hebrew idiom for this proper response of the servant to the Lord of the covenant: "Here I am." In fact, the flight of Adam and Eve from the divine call, "Adam, where are you" (Ge 3:9) is contrasted with the "Here I am" of Abraham, Moses, Samuel, Isaiah, Mary, and Jesus. The focus in Genesis 1–3 is not on *what* Adam is in his inner essence, but on *who* he is and *where* he is in relation (ethically) to his Maker. By replying, "Here I am," the covenant servant acknowledges the suzerain's authority. The servant nails himself down, so to speak, in relationship to the covenant Lord. That is why the silence of Adam and Eve when God calls for them is so sinister. By contrast, after the angel's auspicious announcement, Mary declares, "[Here] I am your servant; let it be with me according to your word" (Lk 1:38). As humanity was created as a word from God, it was intended to respond to God's speaking by repeating back God's Word as its own. This "replying" began with the creation itself, but that was only the beginning. The full effect of God's speech was to be realized with Adam's successful fulfillment of his calling, his responding to God's word in the power of the Spirit. This underscores the significance of Jesus Christ as the Last Adam. It is noteworthy that Jesus announces his triumphant arrival in heaven with the words, "Here am I, and the children God has given me" (Heb 2:13b NIV).

A watch is a watch, but it is not a good watch—one that fulfills its purpose—unless it can tell time properly. Although everyone is God's image-bearer, this status is bound up with a summons to fulfill the vocation that the status identifies. Human existence is *human* regardless of any particulars, but it is "very good" insofar as human beings answer God according to the purpose of their existence. In his first two chapters of Romans Paul does not claim that the wicked are no longer human persons. It is precisely *because* they are human persons that they stand under judgment for having abused their office. The response of "Here I am" is diametrically opposed to the autonomous self, the product of introspective reflection. In fact, we cannot begin to think that we really know ourselves until we know someone other than ourselves. We do not possess ourselves, but were spoken into existence by our Covenant Lord. Because we were spoken by the Father *in the Son*, our personhood has a definite content, analogous to (but, of course, not identical with) the Father's begetting of the Son. Human beings are the created effect of God's speech, but the Son is the eternally begotten Word. Furthermore, it is only the Spirit who can open us up to the Father's summons in the brilliance of the Son's glory, so that we answer according to his word (Ps 143:10; Isa 32:15; 63:14; Eze 3:12; Ac 1:8; 2:17; 4:8; Ro 8:16, 26–27; 1Co 12:3; Gal 4:6). The covenantal relationality that is integral to human nature opens us up to say, "Here I am," not only to our Creator but also to our creaturely neighbors.

This covenantal pattern is undermined whenever we identify the image of God with something in the individual, such as a mind or soul. As we have seen, Scripture represents the image of God not as something *in* us, but as something that we *are*. In other words, the image of God is an office for which we are equipped, not simply by virtue of a rational soul, but by ethical qualities that we exhibit covenantally in relation to God and each other, such as "true righteousness and holiness" (Eph 4:24; cf. Lk 1:75).[27] The image is a gift, but also a task. Confirmation in this status was held out as the future glorification of the victorious servant.

2. Image and office

Human beings are more advanced in problem solving, evaluating, communicating, and creating societies, but piles of scientific data suggest that our fellow creatures, from octopuses to orangutans, possess intelligence. We

---

27. See also the Westminster Confession, ch. 4: In Adam human beings were "endued with knowledge, righteousness, and true holiness, after [God's] own image; having the law of God written in their hearts, and power to fulfil it: and yet under a possibility of transgressing, being left to the liberty of their own will, which was subject unto change. Beside this law written in their hearts, they received a command, not to eat of the tree of the knowledge of good and evil; which while they kept, they were happy in their communion with God, and had dominion over the creatures."

are creatures in time, and not even the highest creature, since God made us "a little lower than the heavenly beings" (Ps 8:5a). Contemplating the vast universe evident to the naked eye, the psalmist felt small and insignificant (vv. 3–4). Yet in spite of his apparently slight place in nature, he had been consecrated by God for a great task. "You ... ... *crowned* him with glory and honor. You have *given him* dominion over the works of your hands; you have *put* all things under his feet" (vv. 5b–6). The uniqueness of humankind is a gift, not a given. Our true uniqueness can be discovered only in relation to God, as we understand ourselves to be covenantal servants and ambassadors, created to lead the vast choir of creation in its "Hallelujah Chorus."

The image of God is constituted by the following characteristics: sonship/royal dominion, representation, glory, and prophetic witness. These marks of the image of God can also be expressed in terms that are typically connected with the threefold office of prophet, priest, and king. Concerning this original calling, Bavinck explains: "As prophet, man explains God and proclaims his excellence; as priest, he consecrates all that is created to God as a holy offering; as king, he guides and governs all things in justice and rectitude. In all this he points to One who in a still higher and richer sense, is the revelation and image of God, to him who is the only begotten of the Father, and the firstborn of all creatures. Adam, the son of God, was a type of Christ."[28]

As we will see in the next chapter, none of these aspects of the image-office was left unscathed by the fall, and at the same time, none of them has been entirely lost. Like Israel's wicked kings, we remain officials of God's court and bearers of his royal image — even in our treason. None of us can escape the experience of guilt, because we cannot escape the simple fact that to be human is to be accountable to the God as his covenant servants, made in his image.

Key Terms

- concursus
- dualism
- trichotomy and dichotomy
- monism and modified monism
- imago dei

---

28. Bavinck, *Reformed Dogmatics*, 328.

Key Distinctions

- creation ex nihilo/providence
- common grace/saving grace
- radical dualism/monism/biblical dualism

Key Questions

1. Compare and contrast pagan conceptions of the God-world relation with the biblical doctrine of *ex nihilo* creation.
2. How does God's providence affect our discipleship? If God's creative and providential love entails his abundant and generous provision, how should we live in the church and in the world?
3. Define *concursus*. How does this term shape our view of providence?
4. Is God's activity in nature and history always miraculous? Why or why not?
5. Is the soul-body distinction biblical? What about the immortality of the soul? Is our soul (or spirit) more divine than our body?
6. How do the biblical motifs of *covenant* and *eschatology* shape our concept of what it means to be human?

Chapter Six

The Fall

Solidarity of the human race under Adamic headship is the source of both the grandeur and the tragedy of our existence. If the world is a theater or a stage, as Calvin and Shakespeare have told us, then the play is a courtroom drama. Like Hamlet's play-within-a-play, the story of Israel can be read as a condensed version of the original covenant with our race in Adam. We are set before a great trial in which we ourselves are actors and not just the audience. This sets the stage for the final reenactment of all of covenantal history In Jesus Christ, the Last Adam and the true and faithful Israel.

I. The Covenant of Creation

The previous chapter emphasized the covenantal character of human identity. We do not find the essence of our humanness—that which makes us special in the cosmos—by looking within, but by looking outward to the one whose image we bear and to the others whose image we share. We discover our own identity not in our inner isolation, but in our historical interaction with God and others. However, before considering the outcome of Adam's royal embassy, we need to define more specifically the sort of covenant in which humanity was created.

I have already introduced the twin motifs of covenant and eschatology. Covenant provides the context, and eschatology indicates the goal.

Eschatology means "the study of last things," and it usually conjures up images of events that are yet to unfold in the future. Understandably, we identify these "last things" with the return of Christ, but it is crucial to recognize that from the very beginning Adam was promised a future consummation. The long and winding history of redemption that leads from Genesis 3 to Revelation 22 is actually a rescue operation, ensured by God's grace even in the face of human rebellion. If Adam had been faithful in his covenant trial, he would have entered the Sabbath consummation then and there, leading us and the whole creation in his train. From Adam's perspective, the "last things" (i.e., the consummation) lay just ahead, within his reach.

This eschatological perspective, which is in continuity with Irenaeus and the Cappadocians, is also extended by Reformed (covenant) theology. As Geerhardus Vos reminds us, "The universe, as created, was only a beginning, the meaning of which was *not perpetuation, but attainment*" (emphasis added). Creation began with a greater destiny lying before it (i.e., eschatology is prior to soteriology).[1] In the words of the Westminster Confession, "The first covenant made with man was a covenant of works, wherein life was promised to Adam; and in him to his posterity, upon condition of perfect and personal obedience."[2] If Adam had obeyed, he would have been granted the right (for himself and his posterity) to eat freely, then and there, of the Tree of Life. (This is especially clear from the promise that appears again in Revelation 2:7: "To the one who conquers I will grant to eat of the tree of life, which is in the paradise of God.")

Created in true righteousness and holiness, Adam was perfectly capable of fulfilling this commission. The commission was a covenant of law, which is why Reformed theologians refer to it variously as a covenant of nature or covenant of works (or sometimes as a covenant of creation, which I am using here). It is this original covenant that explains why all human beings retain—even after the fall—some sense of God and their relation to him as Judge, along with a lively sense of obligation to their neighbors.

Intrinsic to humanness, particularly the image, is a covenantal office or commission into which every person is born; this commission, therefore, being a phenomenon just as universal as our humanness, is the basis for God's righteous judgment of humankind, even apart from special revelation. This is to say that "law"—in particular, the divine covenant-law—is

---

1. Geerhardus Vos, *The Eschatology of the Old Testament* (ed. James T. Dennison Jr.; Phillipsburg, N.J.: P&R, 2001), 73–74. Vos goes on to write: "Eschatology aims at consummation rather than restoration.... It does not aim at the original state, but at a transcendental state of man."

2. Westminster Confession, 7.2, in *Trinity Hymnal* (Atlanta: Great Commission Publications, 1990), 852.

natural, a *verbum internum* (internal word) that rings in, yet is not identical to, the conscience. The covenant of creation renders every person a dignified and therefore accountable image-bearer of God. "So they are without excuse" (Ro 1:20b). This is why human rights do not derive from the authority of the individual or the state but from God alone. Ultimately, it is God's claim on us and our neighbors, not individual autonomy, that is determinative here—which is why, in a covenantal scheme, responsibilities (to others) are more basic than rights (for ourselves).[3] It is not simply that my neighbor has a natural right to be left unmolested, but that I have a responsibility to do everything in my power to love and respect God's image-bearers. This positive obligation is the real intention of the law, as the Reformed and Lutheran catechisms underscore in treating the second table of the Decalogue.

Therefore, believers and unbelievers alike retain some sense of justice, civic virtues, and even an awareness of God. It is that awareness, in fact, that the depraved heart suppresses and distorts into idolatry. The law is an internal word (*verbum internum*) that is known innately and universally, while the gospel is an external word (*verbum externum*) that is announced as good news. "Now we know that whatever the law says," whether written on the conscience or on tablets, "it speaks to those who are under the law, so that every mouth may be stopped, and the whole world may be held accountable to God" (Ro 3:19). The law brings no hope of relief, but only the knowledge of breach (v. 20). The gospel, by contrast, is entirely foreign to the human person in this natural state. It comes as a free decision on God's part in view of the fall and can be known only by a *verbum externum* (external Word), an astounding announcement proclaimed that brings hope and confidence in our standing before God (vv. 21–26). Since the gospel is God's free and gracious response to human treason, it is not at all natural to us. The covenant of creation (or works) explains why we crave law and order, justice and peace, and it is also the source of the myriad ways in which various religions attempt to mollify their deities by sacrifices, rituals, and duties. It also explains why we are goal oriented, with an insatiable work ethic. However inchoate and suppressed, there is some sense that we are on trial and there is something great to accomplish. These characteristics are intrinsic to being God's covenantal image-bearers.

---

3. This covenantal view of personhood represents an important area of convergence between Jewish and Christian theologies, as can be seen especially in David Novak, *Covenantal Rights: A Study in Jewish Political Theory* (Princeton, N.J.: Princeton Univ. Press, 2000).

Ancient theologians, including Irenaeus and Augustine, referred to this original relationship as a covenant.[4] In fact, Augustine writes, "The *first covenant* was this, unto Adam: 'Whensoever thou eatest thereof, thou shalt die the death,'" and this is why all of Adam's children "are breakers of God's covenant made with Adam in paradise" (emphasis added).[5]

Although this covenantal approach was refined by later Reformed theologians, its seeds can be easily discerned in the likes of Philipp Melanchthon, Heinrich Bullinger, Martin Bucer, and John Calvin.[6] Calvin writes, "Now that inward law [*lex interior*], which we have above described as written, even engraved, upon the hearts of all, in a sense asserts the very same things that are to be learned from the two Tables."[7] In contrast to Stoicism (and much of medieval natural law thinking), then, a covenantal perspective sees the **law of nature** as the consequence of our being in every moment summoned as covenant creatures by God's word, rather than of the participation of the mind or soul in divine being. Of Romans 2:14–15, Calvin says, "There is nothing more commonly recognized than that man is sufficiently instructed in a right rule of life by natural law (concerning which the apostle speaks here)."[8] "If the Gentiles by nature have law righteousness engraved upon their minds, we surely cannot say they are utterly blind as to the conduct of life."[9] In fact, Calvin praises "the sagacity" of the great scientists, philosophers, and jurists "in things earthly," scolding sectarians for insulting the Holy Spirit who gives such common gifts to humanity.[10] The covenant of works is assumed in all of the Reformed confessions, either explicitly or implicitly.[11]

---

4. Irenaeus, *Against Heresies*, bk. 4, ch. 25, 5.16.3 (*ANF* 1:544); see also 4.13.1; 4.15.1; 4.16.3; cf. Ligon Duncan, "The Covenant Idea in Irenaeus of Lyons," paper presented at the North American Patristics Society annual meeting, May 29, 1997 (Greenville, S.C.: Reformed Academic, 1998); Everett Ferguson, "The Covenant Idea in the Second Century," in *Texts and Testaments: Critical Essays on the Bible and the Early Church Fathers* (ed. W. E. March; San Antonio: Trinity Univ. Press, 1980); Augustine, *City of God* 16.28 (ed. David Knowles; trans. Henry Bettenson; New York: Penguin, 1972), 688–89. In fact, Augustine elaborates this point in considerable detail in these two pages, contrasting the creation covenant with the covenant of grace as we find it in the promise to Abraham. See also John of Damascus, "An Exact Exposition of the Orthodox Faith," *NPNF*[2], 4.

5. Augustine, *City of God* 16.28 (pp. 688–89).

6. For a definitive survey, see J. T. McNeill, "Natural Law in the Teaching of the Reformers," *Journal of Religion* 26 (1946): 168–69. Cf. Philipp Melanchthon, *Loci communes* (1555), ch. 7. See also, more recently, David VanDrunen, *Natural Law and the Two Kingdoms: A Study in the Development of Reformed Social Thought* (Emory University Studies in Law and Religion; Grand Rapids: Eerdmans, 2009).

7. Calvin, *Institutes* 2.8.1.

8. Ibid., 2.2.22.

9. Ibid.

10. Ibid., 2.2.15.

11. Herman Bavinck, *Reformed Dogmatics: Abridged in One Volume* (ed. John Bolt; Grand Rapids: Baker Academic, 2011), 330. It is assumed, for example, in the Belgic Confession (arts. 14–15), the

"Although the doctrine of the covenant of works also found acceptance with some Roman Catholic and Lutheran theologians," notes Bavinck, "it was vigorously opposed by Remonstrants [Arminians] and Rationalists."[12]

This original covenant is evident in Genesis 1–3. The structure of Genesis 1–3 is covenantal, similar to the historical prologue of ancient Near Eastern treaties. So too is the content. To be the "image" of the suzerain is a political, covenantal office—much like a viceroy or prime minister in relation to the monarch. Besides having a preamble (Ge 1:1a) and historical narrative (vv. 1b–27), Genesis 1 reveals stipulations (commands): "Be fruitful and multiply and fill the earth and subdue it, and have dominion" (vv. 28–29). And then in chapter 2, God commands, "You may surely eat of every tree of the garden, but of the tree of the knowledge of good and evil you shall not eat," along with the sanction, "for in the day that you eat of it you shall surely die" (vv. 16–17). The aftermath of Adam's disobedience confirms the sanction, with the announcement of God's covenant curses (Ge 3:14–19). While the word "covenant" (berith) does not appear, the structure and content offer unmistakable evidence that this is precisely the arrangement in view.

The covenant of works is also evident in the comparison that the prophets draw between it and the covenant that Israel swore to keep before Yahweh at Mount Sinai.[13] In this case, the preamble identifies the same suzerain (Yahweh), but the historical prologue presupposes God's deliverance of his people from Egyptian bondage. The stipulations—this time more than six hundred commands!—form the law, attended by the sanctions: blessing (long and fruitful life in the land) and curses (death and exile). Just as Adam assumed full responsibility for fulfilling all righteousness in his trial, Israel too assumes the burden of this covenant, as the people swear, "All that the LORD has spoken we will do," and Moses confirms their oath by splashing blood on the people, identifying it as "the blood of the covenant" (Ex 24:7–8). The

---

Heidelberg Catechism (qs. 6–11), and the Canons of Dort (3/4), and is explicit in the Irish Articles, the Westminster Confession, the Helvetic Consensus Formula, and the Walcheren Articles.

12. Bavinck, *Reformed Dogmatics*, 330.

13. While this parallel is drawn by a number of writers, it is given a thorough description and analysis in Herman Witsius (1636–1708), *The Economy of the Covenants* (Escondido, Calif.: den Dulk Christian Foundation, 1990). For a more contemporary summary, see Charles Hodge: "Besides this evangelical character which unquestionably belongs to the Mosaic covenant ['belongs to,' not 'is equivalent to'], it is presented in two other aspects in the Word of God. First, it was a national covenant with the Hebrew people. In this view the parties were God and the people of Israel; the promise was national security and land prosperity; the condition was the obedience of the people as a nation to the Mosaic law; and the mediator was Moses. In this aspect it was a legal covenant. It said 'Do this and live.' Secondly, it contained, as does also the New Testament, a renewed proclamation of the covenant of works" (*Systematic Theology* [Grand Rapids: Eerdmans, 1946], 117–22).

covenant code (Deuteronomy) makes it clear that although God has liberated his people from Egypt and brought them into his new Eden, it is theirs to keep or to lose by their faithfulness or unfaithfulness to all that the Lord has commanded. When Israel breaks this covenant, the prophets are sent to prosecute the case of Yahweh, and this case draws explicitly and frequently on the imagery of Adam and the garden of Eden. Just as God's favorable presence in the midst of his people produced a lush paradise in the beginning, so it has in Canaan; just as God's judgment and evacuation of his Spirit from Eden turned the garden into a wasteland of thorns, similar descriptions are offered for the consequence of the Spirit's evacuation from the temple in Jerusalem. Like Adam, Israel was God's "firstborn son," the servant-image of its suzerain. "But like Adam they transgressed the covenant; there they dealt faithlessly with me" (Hos 6:7).

The Abrahamic covenant of grace continued as the basis for the everlasting life of all who trust in the coming Messiah, and the Sinai covenant served this covenant of grace by pointing Israelites to Christ, especially through the typological rites of the sacrificial system. Nevertheless, the terms of the Sinai covenant (not to mention New Testament interpretations of it) show that it was a temporary parenthesis. It pertained to a temporal inheritance in a geopolitical territory, restricted to the physical descendants of Abraham, Isaac, and Jacob. In all of these ways, the Sinai covenant is distinguished from both the original covenant of creation with Adam and its fulfillment in Christ. Nevertheless, in its basis, the Sinai treaty was a covenant of law. Like the covenant of creation, it was based on the oath taker's personal fulfillment of the stipulations.

In the New Testament, the covenant of creation is implied as Jesus is given the Adamic commission to fulfill all righteousness as well as to bear the covenant curse of those whom he represents as covenant head. One clear example of this is Romans 5, in the comparison between Adam and Christ, but it is evident all throughout Paul's letter to the Romans. Paul's argument in the first three chapters culminates in 3:19–20: "Now we know that whatever the law says it speaks to those who are under the law, so that every mouth may be stopped, and the whole world may be held accountable to God. For by works of the law no human being will be justified in his sight, since through the law comes knowledge of sin." Not just Jews, but Gentiles are "under the law," Paul argues in Romans 1:18–20. "Are we Jews any better off? No, not at all. For we have already charged that all, both Jews and Greeks, are under sin" (3:9). How can Gentiles be "under the law" and therefore "under sin" and its condemnation apart from some covenantal arrangement? How can they be "held accountable to God" (3:19)—indeed, "without excuse" (1:20) — unless they were in fact bound to God in a covenantal relationship? Where there is no law, there is no sin, since sin is a transgression of the law (Ro 7:7). We die because we have sinned, and we have sinned in violation of God's law. "The sting of death is sin, and the power of sin is the law" (1Co 15:56). "For the law brings wrath, but where there is no law there is no transgression" (Ro 4:15). And where there is no covenant there is no law. Only within the context of a covenant are there stipulations (promises and commands) and sanctions (blessing and curse). Paul's contrast between the principle (*nomos*) of faith and that of works in salvation is identical with the contrast between the covenant of grace and the covenant of works.

It is within the context of the covenant of creation, therefore, that Christ's role as the Last Adam is revealed in all of its richness. The Gospels recount Christ's perfect obedience to God's law, his fulfilling all righteousness, and his undoing Adam's disobedience. In fact, right where Adam and Israel demanded the food they craved instead of heeding God's word, Jesus endures his trial, and instead of demanding an autonomous right to interpret good and evil for himself, he submits to "every word that comes from the mouth of God" (Mt 4:4). In our infancy, we Gentiles were "enslaved to the elementary principles of the world," just as Israel was under the tutelage of the written law. "But when the fullness of time had come, God sent forth his Son, born of woman, born under the law, to redeem those who were under the law, so that we might receive adoption as sons" (Gal 4:3–5). Christ fulfilled the covenant of works as our human representative, winning access for himself and for his posterity to eat from the Tree of Life, access that he dispenses in a covenant of grace (Rev 2:7). Jesus Christ, therefore, does not return us to the original state of human nature in Adam before the fall, but brings us into that everlasting blessedness that our race has never experienced, beyond the reach of death, sin, suffering, injustice, and war.

To refuse *in principle* the possibility of Adam's fulfillment of the covenant of works (or creation) is to challenge, first, the state of rectitude (not mere innocence) in which the race was created and, second, the justification of sinners by Christ's fulfillment of the law.[14] Many recoil at the idea that we

---

14. John Murray denied the covenant of works because he presupposed that a divine covenant must always be gracious. However, he did refer to "the Adamic administration." See John Murray, "The Adamic Administration," in *The Collected Writings of John Murray* (Edinburgh: Banner of Truth, 1977). Nevertheless, Robert Reymond properly replies, "But Murray fails to make clear what the 'Adamic administration' is an administration *of*" (Robert Reymond, *A New Systematic Theology of the Christian Faith* [Nashville: Nelson, 1998], 405).

were created originally in a covenant of works or law. How could there be any relationship with God that was not based on grace? Here "grace" is usually seen as synonymous with love—with both opposed to the idea of law. However, this opposition of love and law is a modern notion, which would have been foreign not only to Israel but to its neighbors. To love the great king is to obey him, to follow him, and to love fellow subjects is to follow the law that the great king lays down. Repeating Moses, Jesus taught that the whole law is summarized by love of God and neighbor (Mt 22:37–40). However, love (stipulated by the law) is not the same as grace, since the latter is God's merciful clemency on those who justly deserve the opposite. It would in fact be unjust for God to relate mercifully to Adam before he had sinned, while he remained a loyal covenant servant created in true righteousness and holiness.

We can really begin to understand love only when we come to know God in this history of the covenant—when we come to understand love as *hesed*, or *covenant* love. And in this state Adam could expect—for himself and his covenant heirs—royal entrance into the consummation, the Sabbath rest of God himself, and everlasting confirmation in righteousness. In the words of the Formula Consensus Helvetica, "the promise annexed to the covenant of works was not just the continuation of earthly life and felicity," but a confirmation in righteousness and everlasting heavenly joy.[15]

This covenant can be demonstrated even from non-Christian sources. This should not be surprising, since this covenant is the basis for universal religion and morality, the essence of which is fundamentally law. Along with its creation story (*Enuma Elish*), ancient Babylonian civilization produced the Code of Hammurabi, which bears striking resemblance to the Ten Commandments delivered to Moses centuries later. In fact, it was under king Hammurabi (1792–1750 BC) that the Enuma Elish poem was probably commissioned. The historical prologue to the Code even grounds its justice in the gods.[16]

Similarly, Judaism grounds human moral solidarity in an original covenant of creation, renewed in the covenant with Noah. In that covenant, David Novak argues, basic precepts of the moral law are made binding on all people, although the specific laws governing Israel's life in the land are not. A covenantal approach to rights, Novak argues, differs from Greek philosophi-

---

15. Heinrich Heppe, *Reformed Dogmatics* (rev. and ed. E. Bizer; trans. G. T. Thomson; London: G. Allen and Unwin, 1950; repr., London: Wakeman Trust, 2002), 295.

16. Alexander Heidel, *The Babylonian Genesis* (2nd ed.; Chicago: Univ. of Chicago Press, 1963), 14n9, quoted in R. F. Harper, *The Code of Hammurabi, King of Babylon* (Chicago: Univ. of Chicago Press, 1904); Bruno Meissner, *Babylonien und Assyrien* (Heidelberg: C. Winter, 1925), 2:46; and O. E. Ravn, *Acta orientalia* 7 (1929): 81–90.

cal theories of natural law on one side and modern autonomy on the other. It is, after all, a personal God and not an abstract concept of the Good that ultimately grounds a biblical sense of justice (equity). God establishes by his command the rights and duties that correspond to one another in all human relationships.[17] And it is not a silent principle within, emanating from higher to lower rungs in the chain of being; rather, it is a word that God spoke and keeps on speaking, obligating everyone to each other.[18]

God is the original rights-holder, and yet he condescends to enter into an unequal yet real relationship in which he accepts claims as well as makes them. This, in turn, provides the basis for the corresponding relationship between human beings.[19] According to Judaism, Novak explains, natural law and rights are universal, based on the covenant in paradise, repeated in God's covenant with Noah—even though the Mosaic laws are specific to the nation of Israel.[20] Thus, human solidarity is always more basic than national, racial, or cultural solidarity. It is not based on a social contract, but on a divine covenant.[21] Even in Islam, according to Osman bin Bakar, *shari'ah* includes both particular laws governing Muslims and laws that are regarded as universally binding as a result of a common Adamic origin.[22] Similarly, Confucius is reported to have said, "There may be someone who has perfectly followed the way [i.e., the Tao]: but I never heard of one."[23]

Every religion and culture professes some commitment to that which the Bible identifies as the law written on the human conscience in creation. Whether it is called the Tao, Dharma, Karma, Torah, the Universal Declaration of Human Rights, or "the little voice within," the most ineradicable report of general revelation is our moral accountability before a holy God for

---

17. Novak, *Covenantal Rights*, 20.

18. Ibid., 25 (emphasis added).

19. Ibid., 85.

20. Ibid., 86.

21. David Novak, *Jewish-Christian Dialogue: A Jewish Justification* (New York: Oxford Univ. Press, 1989), 27. I concur with Novak's assessment that Judaism and Christianity share a theocentric orientation against secularism that grounds human rights not in a social contract but in an original covenant God made with humanity in creation (140). "Creation itself is in essence a commandment, a speech-act establishing a reality that is to be" (142). "Speech precedes sight in the divine order of creation," and the human is a hearer first, someone commanded, not an autonomous moral legislator (143). Vision follows hearing, and Eve got this in reverse (143–44). "Holiness (*qedushah*) is not part of the cosmic order." Those in covenant with God are made holy by his address to them (154).

22. Osman bin Bakar, "Pluralism and the 'People of the Book,'" in *Religion and Security: The Nexus in International Relations* (ed. Robert A. Seiple and Dennis R. Hoover; Lanham, Md.: Rowman and Littlefield, 2004), 105, 108. Nevertheless, unlike Novak, bin Bakar exploits this universal dimension as a unifying religious factor among the "religions of the book." I would argue that law, whether natural or revealed, is a unifying human factor, but that the gospel is the only unifying religious factor.

23. Quoted in C. S. Lewis, *Collected Letters of C. S. Lewis* (San Francisco: HarperSanFrancisco, 2004), 2:561.

how we treat each other. This is the law above all positive laws of nations and international bodies. No matter how we try to suppress, distort, and deny it, our sense of being personally responsible for our sin is universal and natural. Even if Scripture did not teach it, experience would require something like the covenant of creation to account for this moral sensibility.

The implications of the covenant of creation for our concept of human personhood are many. Here, though, I will refer only to one, since it bears directly on the discussion of original sin below: namely, that the covenant of creation provides an ethical and historical rather than metaphysical interpretation of sin. Let me explain that point.

We have seen in the previous chapter that many ancient and medieval theologians were still under the thrall of Platonism and Neoplatonism with respect to human nature. They saw the human being as a microcosm of the cosmic ladder of being, divided between upper and lower worlds. The mind or soul corresponded to the upper realm of eternal ideas, while the body tended to drag the soul down by its passions to the lower realm of matter.

Paul's contrast between Spirit and flesh, however, is eschatological—not metaphysical. In other words, the contrast is not between two realms, but two ages. Paul is referring to the reign of the Holy Spirit in righteousness and life as opposed to the reign of sin and death. However, this contrast is often interpreted metaphysically, on the Platonic map of spirit and matter. This was a major impetus for the division of the church into the upper ranks of monks and clergy and the lower ranks of average believers, who were engaged in marriage and daily vocations in the world. Even Augustine represented Adam in a tension not only between eschatological probation and confirmation in everlasting blessing (which the covenant of works affirms), but between his higher and lower faculties. Adam could either ascend to the heavens and become like the angels or descend to the depths and become like the beasts of the earth.

At this point, the problematic notion of **concupiscence** was introduced. Concupiscence is not an actual transgression, but a tendency within human nature as such for sin—specifically, lust. Hence, to Adam's natural gifts there needed to be added a gift of grace (Latin, **donum superadditum**) to preserve Adam in his integrity. When God withdrew this gift of grace, Augustine argued, Adam fell. By identifying sin metaphysically with a falling away from being, as if natural finitude were inherently flawed, this influential tradition of interpretation fails to affirm the goodness of human nature as created by God. Furthermore, it attributes sin to some weakness in creation itself—and thus in God, rather than exclusively to a willful transgression of God's covenant in history.

By contrast, Scripture directs our attention to the sphere of history rather than metaphysics. God created human beings with all of the gifts necessary for fulfilling his commission. Calvin correctly saw this notion of a "weak spot" in human nature (as both concupiscence and the *donum superadditum* entail) to be nothing but a species of the Manichaean (gnostic) heresy, which made God the author of evil. In this understanding, the biblical opposition between sin and grace becomes the Neoplatonic opposition between nature and grace. According to Christian Neoplatonism, grace is a substance infused into the soul in order to elevate finite nature toward the Infinite. The Bible, however, teaches us that grace is God's favor and gift, given to sinners who have violated his law. In other words, grace is God's answer to our guilt, corruption, and death, not to our natural finitude and bodily constitution. Grace does not liberate us from nature; grace liberates nature from the reign of sin and death.

II. The Fall of the Covenant Servant

Genesis 3 provides the evidence for the case of "Yahweh vs. Humanity." Even before the infamous act of eating the forbidden fruit, Adam and Eve failed to execute their office. First, they refused to exercise their royal dominion. Instead of driving God's enemy from God's garden, they allowed the serpent to enter into the covenantal conversation. Only God is original; only he can truly create. Satan can only distort, pervert, and corrupt. His lies are parasitical on the truth, so he begins with just enough of God's word to twist (as he did with Israel and again in Jesus' temptation). Adam is not absent from the scene (since he "was with her," v. 6), but passively and silently observes the conversation, exposing his irresponsible sloth. Eve begins well, correcting Satan's obvious misstatement of God's command, but then she adds her own clause, "neither shall you touch it" (Ge 3:3). Satan then directly contradicts God's word: "You will not surely die. For God knows that when you eat of it your eyes will be opened and you will be like God, knowing good and evil" (v. 4–5). This appeal to autonomous pride has been successful ever since. Notice the emphasis on Eve's action as guided by what she saw, felt, and approved: "So when the woman saw that the tree was good for food, and that it was a delight to the eyes, and that the tree was to be desired to make one wise, she took of its fruit and ate, and she also gave some to her husband who was with her, and he ate" (v. 6). They were not enlightened, as the gnostic myths of the second century teach, but darkened. Their eyes were opened, but now to the horrible truth. Naked and ashamed, they were now appalled by their sinfulness, which the fading glory of their bodies now revealed. Their solution was as superficial as their diagnosis, as they strung together fig leaves for coverings (v. 7).

A. Corrupt Officer

Corruption can pertain only to something that is essentially good. Even after the fall, all of us are still office holders in the covenant of creation, still created in God's image. In one sense, this is a blessing—the foundation for upholding the dignity of every person. In another sense, it is a curse, because it means that everyone is born into the world under obligation and yet already corrupt. As soon as we are born, we are already living toward death. We cannot resign our office, refusing to have a personal relationship with God. We cannot even remain in hiding, trying to escape the approaching footsteps of the Covenant Lord. As prophets, we are false witnesses; as priests, we serve idols; and as kings we yield our allegiance to evil counselors, and when vested with power, abuse it for our own good rather than use it for the good of others. We are all ambassadors guilty of treason.

Satan is not creative. He cannot inaugurate a new office, but can only pervert the office holders so that they do not carry out the revealed will of the Great King. After the fall, official endowments are now devoted to treason. The excellencies of the image are not eradicated; rather, each one of them is deformed. Our powerful dominion becomes violent tyranny; pure love becomes warped by greedy self-interest; and our enormous capacities for sociality—no longer shaped by hearing God's word—become laced with half-truths, resentment, and misleading communication. The garden of Eden became a Tower of Babel. Each of the aspects of the image-office mentioned above becomes corrupted with the fall.

B. False Witness

The prophetic witness became a false witness in God's courtroom. It was Satan who first corrupted God's word by addition and then by subtraction and then finally by direct contradiction. Legalism and antinomianism still conspire to persuade us that God is a cosmic tyrant who does not deserve our allegiance. Once the most beautiful angel in God's court, Satan aspired to the throne itself. He is the one who "accuses [the saints] day and night before our God" (Rev 12:10). He is "a liar and the father of lies" (Jn 8:44). Once the chief magistrate under God in heaven, he has become the archetype and ruler of false witnesses on earth. Although Lucifer seduces the royal couple with the false promise of autonomy, he knows that this is impossible; his real intent is to make them his image-bearers rather than God's.

"The decisive point," notes Dietrich Bonhoeffer, "is that this question suggests to man that he should go behind the Word of God and establish what it is by himself, out of his understanding of the being of God... ... Beyond this given Word of God the serpent pretends somehow to know something about the profundity of the true God who is so badly misrepresented in this human word." The serpent claims a path to the knowledge of the real God behind the Word.[24] It is not atheism that is introduced by the serpent but idolatrous religion, says Bonhoeffer.[25] "The wolf in sheep's clothing, Satan in an angel's form of light: this is the shape appropriate to evil." This will be the doubt that Satan will introduce through false religion through the ages:

> "Did God say?" That plainly is the godless question. "Did God say," that he is love, that he wishes to forgive our sins, that we need only believe him, that we need no works, that Christ has died and has been raised for us, that we shall have eternal life in his kingdom, that we are no longer alone but upheld by God's grace, that one day all sorrow and wailing shall have an end? "Did God say," thou shalt not steal, thou shalt not commit adultery, thou shalt not bear false witness ... did he really say it to me? Perhaps it does not apply in my particular case? "Did God say," that he is a God who is wrathful towards those who do not keep his commandments? Did he demand the sacrifice of Christ? I know better that he is the infinitely good, the all-loving father. This is the question that appears innocuous but through it evil wins power in us, through it we become disobedient to God. ... Man is expected to be judge of God's word instead of simply hearing and doing it.[26]

Imitating the father of lies, the creature brought into being as God's star witness begins to interpret reality with himself rather than God at the center. "When man proceeds against the concrete Word of God with the weapons of a principle, with an idea of God, he is in the right from the first, he becomes God's master, he has left the path of obedience, he has withdrawn from God's addressing him."[27]

Indeed, the "I" in the "Here I am" that puts the covenant servant at the disposal of the covenant Lord becomes turned in on itself. Instead of hearing

---

24. Dietrich Bonhoeffer, *Creation and Fall: A Theological Exposition of Genesis 1–3* (ed. John W. de Gruchy; trans. Douglas Stephen Bax; Minneapolis: Augsburg Fortress, 1997), 66.

25. Ibid., 67.

26. Ibid., 68.

27. Ibid.

God's Word, the first couple sought to see, control, master, and determine it for themselves (Ge 3:3–6). "Then the eyes of both were opened, and they knew that they were naked. And they sewed fig leaves together and made themselves loincloths" (v. 7). "I heard the sound [*qol*, voice] of you in the garden," Adam answered God, "and I was afraid, because I was naked, and I hid myself" (v. 10). This will now be the tragic response of the human conscience in the presence of God.

In every subplot of the Bible we discover echoes of this trial of the covenant servant in the cosmic courtroom. The Israelites gathered at the foot of Sinai, filled with terror by the divine words, entreated Moses, "You speak to us, and we will listen; but do not let God speak to us, lest we die" (Ex 20:19). Moses even replies by calling this a trial (Ex 20:20; ESV "test"). Even Isaiah, caught up in a vision of God in holy splendor, could only reply, "Woe is me! For I am lost" (Isa 6:5). It was this same terror that gripped Peter's conscience when, after Jesus created a miraculous catch of fish, he could bring forth only the words, "Depart from me, for I am a sinful man" (Lk 5:8).

The covenantal structure of creation and the probationary trial that ensues underscore the ethical character of this situation. Rather than serve as God's witness, adding verbal testimony to the witness of the whole creation, Adam took the witness stand against God. Against the witness of the Spirit, the testimony of the whole creation, and even the glory, beauty, and integrity of his own high office, Adam perjured himself. Evil is not a principle in creation itself, but the willful distortion of good gifts into an arsenal deployed against God's reign.[28] This perversity corrupts that which is noble, suppresses that which is righteous, smears that which is beautiful, and smothers the light of truth.

Adam's role as false witness bears relation not only to God but to the whole creation, since he represents all human beings and humankind collectively as the chief of the rulers over the other creaturely realms. Every sign of human oppression, violence, idolatry, and immorality in the world can be seen as the perversion of an original good. The commission to be fruitful and to multiply, to guard, protect, and subdue God's garden so that its peace and righteousness extend to the ends of the earth is twisted into empires of oppression in order to secure a consummation without God.

Although pain in childbirth is dreaded in any circumstance, part of God's judgment in the curse is directed to Eve: "I will surely multiply your pain in childbearing; in pain you shall bring forth children" (Ge 3:16a).

---

28. Augustine, *Confessions* 7.15.22.

This increased pain undoubtedly included the emotional stress of bringing children into a world that was now fallen and that would be increasingly filled with violence, deprivation, and depravity. Furthermore, God adds, "Your desire shall be for your husband, and he shall rule over you" (v. 16b). Enmity with God will draw into its wake enmity against fellow human beings, including husband and wife. As male and female humanity was the image of God (Ge 1:27), but now they are at enmity not only with God but with each other.

The whole covenantal fabric of human life will become brittle and, in fact, broken. Childbirth and marriage are also joyful, to be sure, because God has not abandoned humanity to its own devices. Creation remains upheld by God's hand. And yet these common gifts are a mixed blessing. They involve pain not only at the beginning, but in the middle and at the end. Similarly, the curse imposed on Adam and the ground is commensurate with the fruitlessness and "vanity" that life now wears for human experience. Created to have dominion over the earth in order to bring forth its fruitfulness, those who turned their back on their covenant Lord now find that creation itself turns its back on them.

Adam blamed Eve, Eve blamed the serpent, and the serpent blamed God. At the end of the day, everybody blamed God, and ever since, we follow this course of vanity. In ancient as in modern dualism, the problem of evil is identified with created nature in an effort to externalize sin by attributing it to the "other" — "the woman you gave me," our physical or social environment, our family, or other circumstances beyond our control, but ultimately God. We look for scapegoats. Shifting the focus from our own sin to God (ontology and metaphysics) is one of the sources of dualism, ancient and modern. We must shift the ground back to covenantal transgression rather than ontological fault. Paul explains in Romans 1–3 that in Adam we have all become false witnesses. As Merold Westphal observes, the "hermeneutics of suspicion" was not invented by Marx and Nietzsche but finds "its true home in the Pauline teaching about the noetic effects of sin, the idea that in wickedness we 'suppress the truth' (Romans 1:18)."[29]

C. False Representative

This courtroom trial presents the accused in the most radical relation to justice—not to abstract justice but to the personal righteousness in which humanity was created and by which it was to enjoy unbroken communion

---

29. Merold Westphal, *Overcoming Onto-theology* (New York: Fordham Univ. Press, 2001), 105.

with God in a consummated Sabbath. The accused are discovered fleeing the scene of the crime, covering up the evidence. After this, all human beings will be born into the world "dead in the trespasses and sins" and "by nature children of wrath" (Eph 2:1, 3). Instead of representing the interests of the Great King in the world, the ambassador has defected to the enemy.

Humanity is driven deeper into the brush, ever more determined to suppress the truth; "none is righteous, no, not one; no one understands; no one seeks for God" (Ro 3:10). In fact, Paul adds in his litany, especially from the Psalms,

> "All have turned aside; together they have become worthless; no one does good, not even one." "Their throat is an open grave; they use their tongues to deceive." "The venom of asps is under their lips." "Their mouth is full of curses and bitterness." "Their feet are swift to shed blood; in their paths are ruin and misery, and the way of peace they have not known." "There is no fear of God before their eyes." (Ro 3:12–18)

Through the law that was once given as the way to everlasting life there is now, because of sin, only the expectation of death and judgment. The law announces this to everyone who is under it, whether in its written form or as it has been inscribed on the conscience, "so that every mouth may be stopped, and the whole world may be held accountable to God" (Ro 3:19).

Because of this original covenantal relation and revelation, there is, as in Aldo Gargani's vivid expression, "the nostalgia for God of every living person."[30] And this nostalgia drives us to idolatry and suppression of the truth—to a theology of glory that judges by appearances, rather than to the arms of God through the revelation of his Son. Together with this natural nostalgia for God, converted into idolatry, is the nostalgia for leading creation triumphantly into God's everlasting rest, converted into tyranny.

The accusation pronounced by God's law, however it is rebuffed, rationalized, therapeutically suppressed, or ignored through distraction, rings in the conscience and, as psychologist Robert Jay Lifton observes, drives our sense of guilt for a fault whose source seems forever ambiguous.[31] Thinking that their problem was merely shame rather than guilt, Adam and Eve covered themselves with loincloths, and ever since then we have found ourselves incapable of accepting—or rather, unwilling to accept—the radical diagnosis of our own depravity. We can talk about evil outside of us—the

---

30. Aldo Gargani, "Religious Experience," in *Religion* (ed. Jacques Derrida and Gianni Vattimo; Palo Alto, Calif.: Stanford Univ. Press, 1996), 132. See also his great Chekhov quote on 132–33.

31. Robert Jay Lifton, "The Protean Style," in *The Truth about the Truth: De-Confusing and Re-Constructing the Postmodern World* (ed. Walter Truett Anderson; New York: Putnam, 1995), 130–40.

"others," whoever they may be; evil places, structures, forces, and principles. But, like the religious leaders whom Jesus challenged, we refuse to locate evil within ourselves (Mt 12:33–37; 15:10–20; 23:25–28).

The accused, after offering countersuits, blaming each other for the fault, now face their sentence (Ge 3:16–19). In all of these sanctions, the generous giving and receiving embedded in God's natural order will yield to strife, control, exploitation, and manipulation at every level. And finally, instead of being confirmed in righteousness and everlasting life, Adam and his posterity will return to the dust (v. 19). This is a description of the fall, not of creation itself.

Guilt, strife, and vanity seem to be the dominant terms in this sentence. Instead of being eschatologically oriented toward Sabbath life with God, each other, and the whole creation, we grow increasingly aware that we are, in Heidegger's phrase, "being toward death." But this is not *natural*. This play was not intended to be a tragedy. There is no tragedy in God—no "dark side"—since only good comes from God, "with whom there is no variation or shadow due to change" (Jas 1:17), but only unmixed blessing and fulfillment that God longed to share with creatures.

In short, humanity in Adam is now the false prophet, who misrepresents God's Word in a futile and treasonous demand for autonomy; the false priest, who corrupts God's sanctuary instead of guarding, keeping, and extending it; and the false king, who is no longer the medium of God's loving reign but now exercises a cruel tyranny over the earth and other human beings.

III. Solidarity in Adam

Trying to avoid our guilt, we focus on the symptoms of sin. We complain of the boredom of life—which the preacher calls "vanity" in Ecclesiastes. No gospel note is struck in his conclusion of the matter, but what is clear is that the "eternity" that God has set in the heart of humanity is his law, the covenant of creation. Transgression of that covenant is the root of all human woe. Every person is now born estranged from the good Father, living in the far country in poverty and degradation. Unwilling to be a faithful son, humanity became a slave of sin and death.

A. Original Sin

Reading Genesis 3 in the light of the whole biblical story brings into still sharper focus the corporate and representational character of Adam's covenantal role. Not only was he in covenant with God; all of humanity is represented as being in covenant with God by virtue of participating covenantally in Adam. Indeed, all of creation was in some sense judged in Adam (Ge 3:17–18; Ro 8:20). It is with this simultaneously legal and relational background in mind that Paul makes his well-known statements on the imputation of Adam's guilt and corruption as the corollary of the imputation and impartation of the Second Adam's righteousness (esp. Ro 5) in justification and sanctification.[32]

The theme of covenant solidarity, otherwise regarded as congenial to relational and communal views of the self, is nevertheless put to the test when it involves collective human *guilt*: the tragic aspect of human solidarity and relationality. "The intersubjective matrix which forms individual, related persons," notes Francis Watson, "also simultaneously *de*forms them."[33] Together we stand or fall. The legal and relational basis for this solidarity is the covenant of creation.

Our collective human estrangement takes the form of what at least the Western church has identified as **original sin**. Like all of the important doctrines of the faith, original sin is a dogma that received greater refinement in the crucible of debate. At the turn of the fifth century, a British monk, Pelagius, arrived in Rome, with zeal to improve Christian morals. His views were popularized throughout the Roman world, and soon **Pelagianism** became identified with a denial of original sin. Pelagians argued that human beings are born in the same condition as Adam, with the free will to determine whether they will obey or disobey God's commands. If they do obey, then they will be saved. Thus, Adam's legacy condemns us only insofar as it offers a bad example to avoid. Jesus is our Redeemer by providing instruction and a unique example of godly living. Long before Ben Franklin coined his famous aphorism, "God helps those who help themselves," Pelagius and his followers were championing a self-help gospel. Pelagius's nemesis was Augustine, who turned his pen against this growing movement, and the Pelagian errors were condemned by successive church councils and popes. A softer version, known as Semi-Pelagianism, was also condemned at the Second Council of Orange in 529. But Pelagianism is far from dead. It is the native heresy of

---

32. This approach also rejects the stance often taken in the last half-century to set the "relational" category against the "legal" category of the divine-human relationship. "Covenant" is an inherently legal relationship. See also John Murray, *The Imputation of Adam's Sin* (Phillipsburg, N.J.: P&R, 1992).

33. Francis Watson, *Text, Church and World: Biblical Interpretation in Theological Perspective* (Edinburgh; T&T Clark, 1994), 110. See also Paul Ricoeur, *Figuring the Sacred: Religion, Narrative, and Imagination* (ed. Mark I. Wallace; trans. David Pellauer; Minneapolis: Fortress, 1995), esp. ch. 20, and Paul Ricoeur, *Oneself as Another* (trans. Kathleen Blamey; Chicago: Univ. of Chicago Press, 1992).

our fallen heart, and it is rife today—even in churches that identify with the heritage of the Reformation.

No doctrine is more crucial to our anthropology and soteriology than a clear doctrine of original sin, and yet no doctrine has been more relentlessly criticized since its articulation. Protestant liberalism has always had an optimistic view of human morality. Adolf von Harnack, a prominent German theologian writing near the end of the nineteenth century, once called original sin "an impious and foolish dogma."[34] That, however, was before two world wars, to which Harnack's own contribution should not be forgotten.[35]

Not surprisingly, the postwar years led to a fresh reappraisal of the classical doctrine of original sin. Reinhold Niebuhr correctly surmised, "The Christian doctrine of sin in its classical form offends both rationalists and moralists by maintaining the seemingly absurd position that man sins inevitably and by a fateful necessity but that he is nevertheless to be held responsible for actions which are prompted by an ineluctable fate."[36] As the natural theology par excellence, Pelagianism was the anthropological assumption of Kant's thought.[37] In other words, no one has to be taught the Pelagian heresy; it is our native tongue. Repeated attempts to dismiss the doctrine of original sin as a peculiarity of Calvin or Luther, Augustine or Paul fail to take seriously the fact that the same assumptions are articulated in the Psalms (Pss 51:5, 10; 143:2), the prophets (Isa 64:6; Jer 17:9), the Gospels (Jn 1:13; 3:6; 5:42; 6:44; 8:34; 15:4–5), and the Catholic Epistles (Jas 3:2; 1Jn 1:8, 10; 5:12).

Citing examples from Second Temple Judaism, Brevard Childs concludes, "Judaism shared the view that human sin derived from Adam (*4 Ezra* 3.7; *Sifre Deuteronomy* 323)."[38] In fact, one of the clearest examples of early Jewish belief in original sin is 2 Esdras (also *4 Ezra*):

> The same fate came upon all: death upon Adam, and the flood upon that generation [of Noah].... For the first man, Adam, burdened as he was with an evil heart, sinned and was overcome, and not only he but all who were

---

34. Adolf von Harnack, *History of Dogma* (trans. from 3rd German ed. by Neil Buchanan; Boston: Little, Brown and Company, 1899), 5:217.

35. Harnack helped to create Kaiser Wilhelm's "Deutschland über alles" war policy: one of the reasons for Barth's revulsion toward his liberal mentors.

36. Reinhold Niebuhr, *The Nature and Destiny of Man* (New York: Charles Scribner's Sons, 1964), 241.

37. Immanuel Kant, "Religion within the Boundaries of Mere Reason," in *Religion and Rational Theology* (trans. and ed. Allen W. Wood and George di Giovanni; Cambridge: Cambridge Univ. Press, 1996), 148, 150; Ricoeur, *Figuring the Sacred*, 84–86.

38. Brevard Childs, *Biblical Theology of the Old and New Testaments: Theological Reflections on the Christian Bible* (Minneapolis: Fortress, 1993), 579.

descended from him. So the weakness became inveterate, and although your law was in your people's hearts, a rooted wickedness was there too; thus the good came to nothing, and what was evil persisted ... behaving just like Adam and all his line; for they had the same evil heart. (2 Esdras 3:10, 21–22, 26)

These statements are in the context of explaining God's ways with Israel in her exile: the point is that Israel herself is "in Adam," and the first disobedience is lodged deep within the history of God's own people. The similarities to Paul's treatment, especially in Romans 1–3 and 5, are striking.

The concept of solidarity—solidarity of humanity in Adam and of Israel in Abraham and Sinai—is basic to the biblical worldview, however alien to our own. Paul simply elaborates this covenantal outlook when he explains that "sin came into the world through one man," in whom all people became henceforth sinners, condemned by the law and inwardly corrupt (Ro 5:12–21). It follows, then, that if Adam failed to carry out his commission as the servant-king of Yahweh, all of those who are "in Adam" are implicated as well, just as the people represented by the vassal in the Hittite treaties would share in the threatened sanctions in the case of a breach.

Moltmann concedes, "The Fathers of the church consistently followed the rabbinic and Pauline doctrine: suffering and death are the divinely appointed *punishment for human sin.* 'The wages of sin is death' (Rom. 6:23)." However, he rejects this view, preferring the path taken by Origen, namely, "that death belonged together with the creation of man as finite being." "It is therefore not a consequence of sin, and not a divine punishment either.... Augustine and the Latin Fathers, on the other hand, traced all forms of suffering and death back to sin, reducing the doctrine of redemption to juridical form into the doctrine of grace."[39] Sin brings its own misery, Moltmann concludes; it hardly needs any further punishment.[40] Once again we discern the natural tendency to identify sin merely with its symptoms rather than with its deeper heinousness as a criminal state and stance in relation to a holy God.

The effects of sin are both legal and transformative: we are guilty and corrupt. Ironically, both fundamentalism and liberalism tend to identify sin with something external to us, and both tend to reduce sin to actions. The basic assumption is that we become bad people by doing bad things and we can correct this by doing good things instead. By contrast, Scripture locates

---

39. Jürgen Moltmann, *The Trinity and the Kingdom: The Doctrine of God* (trans. Margaret Kohl; Minneapolis: Augsburg Fortress, 1991), 50.
40. Ibid.

sin deep within the fallen heart and treats it first of all as an all-encompassing *condition* that yields specific actions. If we cut off one branch, another one — pregnant with the fruit of unrighteousness — sprouts in its place.

One point at which fundamentalism and liberalism differ significantly is over what constitutes sinful actions. Where the one emphasizes personal morality, the other emphasizes social justice. In liberalism, sin is reduced to social, economic, and political structures that oppress and keep humanity from flourishing. Both errors are deeply reductionistic and allow us to take ourselves off the hook by transferring our own guilt to others: bad people or bad policies. However, by going deeper in its analysis and broader in its scope, the doctrine of original sin encompasses sinful actions and structures. Solidarity with Adam means that we suffer not just for specific sins we have committed, but because we are part of a corrupt race. We are sinners and sinned against, victims and oppressors, simultaneously — not equally and to the same degree, but of the same kind.[41] A particular act of sin may be the fault of someone else, but the sinful condition and the web of sinful actions and relationships that flow from it implicate us as well. It is true that we do not simply choose our vices but are conditioned by the malignant structures, contexts, and even genes that we have inherited. Yet it is also true that we yield ourselves to these vices and are responsible for our own actions.

Simplistic theories of sin result in Manichaean divisions between us and them, the good and the evil, whether cast in terms of private morality or public systems. From our throne of presumed exemption from the curse, we hurl our epithets at those who corrupt our decency and noble way of life. Yet as the biblical drama unfolds we recognize with increasing clarity that "all, both Jews and Greeks, are under sin, as it is written: 'None is righteous, no, not one; no one understands; no one seeks for God. All have turned aside; together they have become worthless; no one does good, not even one'" (Ro 3:10–12). Original sin makes us all equally condemned and corrupt, regardless of the wide variety of sin's expressions. Even at prayer, not only before idols but before the Living God in self-righteousness, we are digging our own grave (Lk 18:9–14).

It is our definition of sin that generates such radically different construals of redemption. As Robert Jenson notes, "The only possible *definition* of sin is that it is what God does not want done. Thus if we do not reckon with God, we will not be able to handle the concept; without acknowledging God, we

---

41. I have found no richer exposition of this point than in Miroslav Volf's *Exclusion and Embrace* (Nashville: Abingdon, 1996).

can—though perhaps not for long—speak meaningfully of fault and even of crime but not of sin."[42] As our confessions and liturgies remind us, there are sins of omission as well as commission; we fail God "in what we have done and in what we have left undone." Sin is a crime committed against a person, not just a principle; yet the law that is transgressed is the will of the personal Lord who institutes the relationship. The weight of the law is measured by the character of the one who gives it.

Furthermore, sin is not defined merely as "whatever causes harm to others." This is perhaps the prevailing view at least of crime or wrongdoing in Western-democratic jurisprudence today. One should be able to do whatever he or she chooses, unless it infringes the rights of another autonomous individual. However, sin is a God-centered rather than human-centered concept. Only when we are confronted with God in his holiness do we really understand something of the weight of sin (Isa 6:1–7). When reduced to the horizontal dimension (interhuman relationships), sin becomes negative behaviors that can be easily managed or a failure to live up to one's potential and expectations. Apart from its vertical reference, sin can produce shame but never guilt. The only judgment that matters in such a scheme is that of society or our own, rather than God's.

While enlightened modernity exhibits a Pelagianism that alternates between the serious tempo of a confident march and the nihilistic beat of self-indulgent consumerism, biblical faith cannot be sung without the blue note: the minor key. It is not all blues, of course, but without that note there is no hope. Blues is not nihilism—it is not opposed to hope. On the contrary, it is the unceasingly happy and upbeat jingles we hear in the supermarket or, with increasing frequency, at church that correlate with a denial of the reality of sin, evil, and pain and therefore deny their consumers any longing for something profoundly redemptive. Upbeat popular culture, feeding on images of the beautiful, well-adjusted, pleasant, happy, young, and vigorous, ignores the brutal reality of life that is the very condition for hope and its trigger-mechanism. Blues music is notoriously difficult to transpose into notations on a page, because it stretches and bends notes. With its doctrine of original sin, biblical faith comes to grips with the reality of human tragedy only to enter into the joyful comedy of which pagan revelry is only a pale parody. Deep despair and deep joy belong to those who have encountered God in his law and gospel. By contrast, denial of this doctrine gives to pagan thought a superficial happiness that hides a deeper and final despair.

---

42. Robert Jenson, *Systematic Theology* (New York: Oxford Univ. Press, 1997), 2:133.

B. Natural and Moral Ability: How Total Is Total Depravity?

Human beings remain human beings regardless of sin, and they remain covenant creatures in relation to God regardless of transgression. It is precisely this that holds everyone accountable for broken trust. When we say that we are *by nature* sinful or, in Paul's phrase, that "we ... were *by nature* children of wrath, like the rest of mankind" (Eph 2:3), the point is that each of us belongs to a species that is corrupt. It does not mean that the essence of our humanity is evil or that its created nature has been lost.

To underscore this point, over against Neoplatonic tendencies described earlier, Reformed theology distinguishes between **natural** and **moral** ability, as a way of guarding against two extremes: on the one end, a *Manichaean* identification of sin with God's creation itself and, on the other end, the *Pelagian* denial of total depravity. One of the interesting paradoxes of Calvin's thought is that he simultaneously affirmed the total integrity of humanity as created and the total depravity of humanity as fallen.[43] "For the depravity and malice both of man and of the devil, or the sins that arise therefrom, do not spring from nature, but rather from the corruption of nature."[44] Sin is accidental (not a necessary attribute) rather than essential to human nature (a necessary attribute), he insists. Calvin distinguishes this accidental view of sin's relation to human nature from what he calls the "Manichean error." "For if any defect were proved to inhere in nature, this would bring reproach upon [God]."[45]

Bringing such reproach upon God, deflecting our guilt ("the woman *you* gave me"; "the devil made me do it"; etc.), is itself a symptom of our disease. Yet God's judgment draws us out, summoning us to account for the fact that "the heart is deceitful above all things, and desperately sick; who can understand it?" "I the LORD search the heart and test the mind," and the verdict is never encouraging (Jer 17:9–10). Even more pointedly, Jesus excoriated the religious leaders for imagining that there was some innocent citadel of righteousness in the mind or heart, countering that it is from this seat that sin exercises its dominion (Mt 12:34–35; 15:10–11; 23:25). The inner self

---

43. He concurs with Aristotle's reference to humankind as a "microcosm" because "he is a rare example of God's power, goodness, and wisdom, and contains within himself enough miracles to occupy our minds, if only we are not irked at paying attention to them" (*Institutes* 1.5.3). He praises "the human body" as "ingenious" (ibid., 1.5.2). Yet in all this, humanity is "struck blind in such a dazzling theater" (ibid., 1.5.8). When we catch a glimpse of the "burning lamps" shining for us in God's works, including ourselves, we smother their light (ibid., 1.5.14). The dialectic here moves between the exquisite character of nature and the equally unfathomable ruin of that nature to which humans are inclined.

44. Calvin, *Institutes* 1.14.3.

45. Ibid., 1.15.1.

is not the innocent spark of divinity or island of purity, but is the fountain from which every act of violence, deceit, immorality, and idolatry flows out through the body and into the world.

Total depravity does not mean that we are incapable of any justice or good before fellow humans (civil righteousness). Instead, it says that there is no Archimedean point within us that is left unfallen, from which we might begin to bargain or to restore our condition (righteousness before God). As Berkhof points out, total depravity does not mean

> (1) that every man is as thoroughly depraved as he can possibly become;
> (2) that the sinner has no innate knowledge of the will of God, nor a conscience that discriminates between good and evil;
> (3) that sinful man does not often admire virtuous character and actions in others, or is incapable of disinterested affections and actions in his relations with his fellow-men; nor
> (4) that every unregenerate man will, in virtue of his inherent sinfulness, indulge in every form of sin.
>
> What is meant by "total" is that the whole nature of humanity, not only the body and its desires but the soul, mind, heart, and will, is corrupt.[46]

Therefore, when Pelagius, Kant, and Charles Finney insist that it would be unjust for God to require something of which we are not capable, they confuse our natural and moral ability. It is not that we are unable to freely will that which our mind and heart desire, but that our mind has been darkened and our heart is selfish. Everyone has the *natural* ability to render God faithful obedience, but after the fall, we are "sold into slavery under sin" (Ro 7:14 NRSV), and our *moral* ability is held captive not to a foreign army but to our own selfishness, idolatry, greed, and deceit. "None is righteous, no, not one; no one understands; no one seeks for God" (Ro 3:10–11). This is not hyperbole: even when we pretend to be seeking God, we are in fact running from the God who is actually there. If the self-help sections of the average bookstore are any indication, we are, like Paul's Athenian audience, "in every way ... very religious" (Ac 17:22). But God is not worshiped; he is used. "Spirituality" no less than atheism suppresses the specificity of the God revealed in Scripture.

The fact that we are still God's image-bearers and consequently possess all of the requisite *natural* ability for relating to God and others in covenant faithfulness—and the fact that this is even realized in our sense of duty to the rule of law, renders us culpable (Ro 1:18–2:16). The fault lies not in that we *cannot* but that we *will not* turn from our sin to the living God (Jn 8:44).

---

46. Louis Berkhof, *Systematic Theology* (Grand Rapids: Eerdmans, 1949), 246–47.

> ## Key Distinction:
> ### *natural/moral (ability)*
>
> The fall has not eradicated any aspect of our humanity (natural ability). Still God's image-bearers, we have everything with which God created us for fulfilling our purpose. However, since the fall we are in bondage to unbelief and unrighteousness (moral inability).

Captive to sin, "in Adam," we are nevertheless willing accomplices to our own imprisonment (Ro 5:12). Only when God seizes us and liberates us from our captivity are we truly free to be the human beings that we are (Jn 8:36).

IV. Stay of Execution

Our story of the fall concludes with a stay of execution. On the heels of the announcement that the woman's seed will triumph over the serpent is the surprising event of God's grace. It is the beginning of the covenant of grace: "And the LORD God made for Adam and his wife garments of skins, and clothed them" (Ge 3:21). Reading the Bible canonically, we cannot help but see in this gracious dispensation glimpses of "the Lamb of God, who takes away the sin of the world" (Jn 1:29).

We must repeat our refrain that "eschatology antedates redemption."[47] In other words, creation was only the beginning for Adam and Eve. Called to imitate their Creator and Covenant Lord's pattern of working and resting, they were to enter in to God's everlasting rest according to the covenant of creation. "That door, however, was never opened," notes Kline.

> It was not the Fall in itself that delayed the consummation. According to the conditions of the covenant of creation the prospective consummation was either/or. It was either eternal glory by covenantal confirmation of original righteousness or eternal perdition by covenant-breaking repudiation of it. The Fall, therefore, might have been followed at once by a consummation of the curse of the covenant. The delay was due rather to the principle and purpose of divine compassion by which a new way of arriving at the consummation was introduced, the way of redemptive covenant with common grace as its historical corollary.[48]

---

47. Meredith Kline, *The Structure of Biblical Authority* (2nd ed.; Eugene, Ore.: Wipf and Stock, 1997), 155.
48. Ibid.

Common grace opens up space for a delay of the consummation, in order to reverse the destiny of those thus fallen. "Consummation" after the fall would have proved the ultimate tragedy. The divine delay allows history to continue moving toward the consummation in God's eternal Sabbath as the fruit of God's own redemptive activity. And because of this stay of execution, "the promise of entering his rest still stands" (Heb 4:1).

The scene does not end there, however. Nor does the great trial of the covenant. But for now, we pick up the story with humanity barred from paradise, tilling the soil "east of Eden." Already in the following chapter we are introduced to Cain's fratricide of Abel over the former's jealousy that his brother's animal sacrifice was accepted by God while "for Cain and his offering he had no regard" (Ge 4:5). As a prelude to this story, Eve announces with Cain's birth, "Behold, I have brought forth the man with the help of the Lord" (v. 1, author's trans.). Without a definite article in this ancient text, we are especially dependent on the context. In light of the unfolding narrative, it makes sense to conclude that Eve is exclaiming that she has brought forth the offspring ("*the* man") who has been promised to her—the one who will crush the serpent's head and lift the bondage of the curse.

Eve will eventually learn that far from being the messiah, her firstborn son will be recorded as the Bible's first murderer. Yet even after the crime, God protects Cain and allows him to build a city and to produce descendants who eventually distinguish themselves as leaders in various cultural endeavors. Just at the point where this genealogy of Cain and the erection of his proud city are recounted (vv. 17–24), we read, by contrast, that another child was born to Adam and Eve. Eve named him "Seth [*appoint*], for she said, 'God has appointed for me another offspring instead of Abel, for Cain killed him.' To Seth also a son was born, and he called his name him Enosh. At that time people began to call upon the name of the Lord" (vv. 25–26).

From this point on, two cities rise in history: the one identified by violence, oppression, injustice, sin, and pride—as well as, let it be noted, cultural and technological advance; the other identified by that last sentence announcing Enosh's birth: "At that time people began to invoke the name of the Lord." The stay of execution opened up space within the history now defined by transgression and curse for the arrival of the promised redeemer and the gathering of a people who call on his name.

Key Terms

- law of nature (or natural law)
- concupiscence
- donum superadditum
- original sin
- Pelagianism

Key Distinction

- natural/moral (ability)

Key Questions

1. Define *original sin*. Why is it so difficult for us, today, to grasp the concept of an inherited guilt and corruption? Why does the concept of solidarity with Adam seem foreign to us?
2. Does *total depravity* mean that we are as sinful as we could possibly be? Does this doctrine mean that it is impossible for us to do anything good?
3. What's the significance of the cherubim guarding the Tree of Life after the fall?
4. How does our understanding of the fall and its effects inform our view of ourselves and our relationships with others, including non-Christians?

Chapter Seven

Jesus Christ: the Lord Who Is Servant

We can be fairly certain that the Jesus we like, that we feel most comfortable around, who arouses our sympathy for human goodness and reminds us of our highest ideals, is not the historical Jesus. Rabbi Samuel Sandmel reminds us that Jesus has been shaped like putty into myriad images. A great prophet. A charismatic leader. A healer. A sage. A political revolutionary. "More recently, some popular authors have indirectly depicted Jesus as a liberal rabbi, a Quaker, a Unitarian, or in one atrocity, an advertising expert."[1]

According to the New Testament, Jesus was and is the fulfillment of God's promises to Israel. Gentiles always will have to step inside the story of Israel in order to find their own redemption. As we do, we discover that Israel's God is indeed the Creator and Lord of all and that Israel's Messiah is indeed God incarnate, the Savior of the world.

---

1. Samuel Sandmel, *A Jewish Understanding of the New Testament* (3rd ed.; Woodstock, Vt.: Jewish Lights Publications, 2010), 194.

I. "Israel, My Beloved": Between the Two Adams

So decisive is the call of Abraham in Genesis 12 that it initiates the history of Israel and renders all that has preceded it a mere prologue to that story. The prophets, psalmists, Jesus, and the apostles "all teach us unanimously and clearly that the content of the divine revelation does not consist primarily in the unity of God, in the moral law, in circumcision, in the Sabbath, in short, in the law, but appears primarily and principally in the promise, in the covenant of grace, and in the gospel." The law was never confused with the promise, nor did it replace it. God's covenant with Abraham was a gracious promise, so that even the moral law that attended it "was not a law of the covenant of works, but a law of the covenant of grace, a law of gratitude."[2] Even circumcision was a sign and seal of the justification that Abram had through faith in the promise rather than a condition (Ro 4:11). It is not the mere presence of law (commands) that identifies a law-covenant (or covenant of works). There are commands in every covenant, since God is always the Lord and human beings are always his servants. What distinguishes a **covenant of law** (or works) is that God promises life and inheritance "upon condition of perfect and personal obedience."[3] The covenant partner's own covenant faithfulness is the basis for receiving the blessing. In the **covenant of grace**, law functions differently, as the appropriate response of those who have been forgiven, justified, and renewed solely on the basis of Christ's person and work.

Especially with Paul's interpretation, we can recognize within the Old Testament itself a clear distinction between the Abrahamic promise and the Mosaic law. These represent two antithetical ways of inheriting promised blessing. The Mosaic law (i.e., the Sinai covenant) was never given to save sinners from God's everlasting judgment. The promises of the Mosaic law were limited to a single nation and to temporal blessing ("long life") in a geopolitical theocracy ("in the land that I am giving you to possess"). Therefore, the Mosaic law is much more specific and limited than the promise that God made to Adam and Eve after the fall and renewed with Abraham. Like the "play-within-a-play" in Hamlet, the crucial importance of the Mosaic covenant is that by it God established an elaborate system of pointers to Jesus

---

2. Herman Bavinck, *The Philosophy of Revelation* (New York: Longmans, Green, and Co., 1909; repr., Grand Rapids: Baker, 1979), 192–93.

3. Westminster Confession of Faith, 7.2, in *Trinity Hymnal* (Atlanta: Great Commission Publications, 1990), 852.

> ## Key Distinction:
> ### *covenant of law/covenant of grace*
>
> There is law in the covenant of grace, but a *covenant* of law (or works) makes the oath taker's personal fulfillment of its commands the condition or basis of blessing or curse. Christ fulfilled the law so that we can inherit everlasting blessing by a covenant of grace. Thus, the law still obliges us, but cannot condemn those who are in Christ.

Christ long before his incarnation. Like mighty rivers that empty into the ocean, all subplots rush toward Christ as he is clothed in his gospel.

In the covenant that God made with Abraham (Ge 12 and 15), there are two distinct kinds of promises: an everlasting promise, with universal blessings for all nations, in a single seed of Abraham (Christ), and a conditional promise of a temporal land for Abraham's physical seed (Israelites). In Genesis 15, God is the oath maker and confirms the oath by passing through the halves, which was a customary political ceremony for ratifying international treaties. The Great King would make the lesser king pass through the halves of animal carcasses, assuming upon his own head the same fate if he should break the treaty. In this case, however, Yahweh—the Great King—reverses the roles and assumes full responsibility for the realization of this promise. In effect, God places himself on trial in the history of covenant faithfulness. Strangely, the Covenant Lord (suzerain) assumes the role of the servant (vassal).

Paul's whole point in Galatians is to resolve the confusion in his hearers' minds between the Abrahamic and Mosaic covenants. The Mosaic covenant was not at cross-purposes with the covenant of grace but was in service to it. The covenant of works and the covenant of grace were not offering two different ways of being saved. Rather, the Mosaic covenant was given to a temporary and typological theocracy designed to lead Israel to trust in Christ and his perfect obedience and sacrifice. A dollhouse is not a real house, but that does not make it superfluous or insignificant, if the child knows the difference. To use Paul's own analogy, a babysitter is essential until the parent comes home. Similarly, the Mosaic covenant was a "guardian" (schoolmaster, tutor, or governess; Gal 3:24) for a definite stage in the church's infancy until its Messiah himself should arrive. Understood in this sense, the Mosaic covenant was a distinct administration of the covenant of grace. As long as it pointed people to Christ, its purpose was being fulfilled. Yet when it was misunderstood as the means of inheriting the *everlasting* promise of *world-wide* blessing, this law pronounced its curse. "For the promise to Abraham and his offspring that he would be heir of the world did not come through the law but through the righteousness of faith. For if it is the adherents of the law who are to be the heirs, faith is null and the promise is void.... That is why it depends on faith, in order that the promise may rest on grace and be guaranteed to all his offspring," both Jews and Gentiles who trust in Christ as did Abraham (Ro 4:13–18).

From Sinai on, Israel inherits the land by promise but remains in the land by obedience. The promise is not everlasting life, but long life—temporal blessedness, in a land flowing with milk and honey. Like the covenant made with Adam, the Sinai covenant is anything but an unconditional oath (e.g., Dt 7:12–14). The language unmistakably echoes the creation narratives. Just as Israel has been brought out of the "darkness and void" of Egyptian bondage, so now she is to occupy the land as a new Adam under probation in anticipation of consummation. Israel's history is a trial within the larger trial of humanity. The passage just cited from Deuteronomy, and many others like it, draw on creation language to make this identification with the creation story. On this side of the curse—and in Israel's case, exile—there is flourishing: "Be fruitful and multiply." On the other side there are closed wombs, fallow fields with thorns, and famine and death (e.g., Dt 28).

The eventual exile of Israel, however, also tragically echoes the fall of Adam. "And those who transgressed my covenant and did not keep the terms of the covenant that they made before me, I will make like the calf when they cut it in two and passed between its parts" (Jer 34:18). The contrast with the covenant that God swore to Abraham in Genesis 15 could not be greater. The form and content of the treaty and the ratification ceremony (blood splashed on the people swearing the oath vs. Yahweh passing through the pieces assuming the curse) are enough to establish the difference. Yet the actual execution of the sanctions exposes the contrasts vividly as well. Here in Jeremiah 34, Israel is the oath maker ("the covenant that they made before me"); Israel has "transgressed [the LORD's] covenant," and Israel must now be torn in pieces like the calf between whose pieces they passed in order to ratify their oath.

Before and after the exile, the prophets take their place as prosecutors of the covenant law-suit. Further testimony to Israel's own realization that she had become the faithless servant of the covenant may be found, for example, in the Second Temple literature (i.e., Wisd. Sol. 6:3–7).

Yet, according to the Hebrew prophets themselves, the hope of entering God's Sabbath rest remains only on the basis of the Abrahamic promise rather than the Sinai covenant. The only hope is that the one will finally come who was promised unilaterally by God, in spite of our unfaithfulness. He will not only fulfill the Mosaic law in every detail, but will be the Abrahamic heir in whom all the nations will be blessed with everlasting life. The prophets repeatedly prosecute God's case against Israel on the terms of the Sinai covenant and announce God's mercy in Christ on the terms of the Abrahamic covenant. Thus, the new covenant promised in Jeremiah 31 echoes God's unilateral oath in Genesis 15: The "new covenant" will be firm, "not like the covenant that I made with their fathers" at Sinai — "my covenant that they broke, though I was their husband, declares the LORD." Rather, in this covenant *God* will write his law on their hearts; God will be their God, and they will be his people. "For *I will forgive* their iniquity, and I will remember their sin no more" (vv. 31–34, emphasis added). Furthermore, it is not just restoration to a former condition that is promised, but a greater future and a wider hope, with Jerusalem rebuilt and enlarged (vv. 38–40). It will not be paradise regained, but the consummation that had been forfeited by Adam's and Israel's disobedience.

But how will God be faithful to both covenants, to the law and the gospel? How will he be "just and the justifier" (Ro 3:26)? It will be by causing his own Son, the Last Adam and True Israel, to fulfill all righteousness and yet to pass through the judgment — cut off from the land of the living — for our sins, so that his righteousness becomes definitive for the solidarity of his new creation in and with him. Our focus now turns, therefore, from the dark night of human rebellion to this sunrise of the Messiah: the one who comes as Lord and Servant of the everlasting covenant.

II. Messiah

Unlike the second-century gnostic gospels, whose Jesus is more like Harry Potter in his youth and Zeus in his adulthood, the authentic Gospels of the New Testament locate Jesus in a thoroughly Jewish milieu. To capture this Jewish background, we must read the Scriptures as a whole canon, from promise to fulfillment, interpreting the Old Testament in the light of the New. We'll begin by focusing on five key messianic titles and motifs present throughout the Scriptures.

A. Faithful Adam and True Israel

Although Israel, like Adam, failed to drive the serpent out of God's holy land and instead succumbed to the seduction of God's archenemy, God pledges that he will not utterly destroy Israel, but will preserve a remnant. From this remnant—"the stump of Jesse"—God will raise up his Messiah (Isa 11:1–16). The representative roles of Adam and Israel merge in the messianic figure. Not only guarding and keeping God's sanctuary, he will be "a light to the nations" (Isa 49:6, with Jn 1:5; 3:19; 8:12; 12:36; Rev 21:24; 22:5). Pilgrims will arrive from the nations of Israel's erstwhile enemies— Egypt and Assyria—and from distant peoples (Isa 11:12, 16; 19:18–25). At last there will be one flock under one shepherd-king; "And this is the name by which he will be called: 'The LORD is our righteousness'" (Jer 23:1–8).

In his temptation (Mt 4:1–11; Lk 4:1–13), Jesus reenacts (recapitulates) the drama of the story, both Adam's trial in Eden and Israel's trial in the wilderness. Though Israel's forty years of faithless wandering are compressed into forty days and nights, the directness and intensity of Satan's temptation are greater. Satan even twists God's word to suit his scheme, but this time the faithful Adam untwists it and surrenders his whole heart to it.

In passages like Isaiah 60, we have set before us a marvelous vision of nations streaming to Zion, which is personified in messianic terms. "Nations shall come to your light, and kings to the brightness of your rising" (v. 3). A royal procession of prophets, priests, and kings from all nations enter through "gates [that] ... shall not be shut" (v. 11). All of this echoes the Sabbath enthronement of God in early days of creation, with the parade of the creature-kings before the Lord in Genesis 1 and 2. Now, however, the Last Adam leads creation in his train to the throne of conquest, instead of leading it away from the heavenly Sabbath in mutiny. Psalm 2 evokes a courtroom scene, with the creature-kings arrayed before the splendor of the Great King and his anointed one (Messiah), gathered together in war rather than tribute, with the Great King laughing at the self-confident posturing of the earth's mighty rulers who refuse to give homage to "the Son." Nevertheless, "Blessed are all who take refuge in him" (Ps 2:12). The contest between the City of God with its King and the earthly city and its rulers unfolds in the vision that John received on the isle of Patmos. Israel's Messiah is the true prophet, priest, and king that Adam and Israel failed to be for the world.

B. Messianic Savior: Son of David

Like the Abrahamic covenant, the covenant that God made with David and his seed in 2 Samuel 7 is inviolable. It does not depend on the personal performance of the beneficiaries, for God makes this covenant in full knowledge of their wickedness (and the history of the kings of Israel and Judah confirms this). God swears that he will always have a Davidic heir on the throne and that one from his own loins will establish an everlasting kingdom. This is not something that evolves from the powers of history itself or through the labors of human beings. "For *to us* a child *is born*, *to us* a son *is given*" (Isa 9:6, emphasis added). We are passive beneficiaries rather than agents of this messianic work. "Of the increase of his government and of peace there will be no end, on the throne of David and over his kingdom, to establish it and to uphold it with justice and with righteousness, from this time forth and forevermore. The zeal of the LORD of hosts will do this" (v. 7).

Just as the new covenant, unlike the Sinai covenant, will be founded on God's faithfulness and unilateral mercy, the kingdom that God builds is greater and more enduring than the Sinai theocracy. Not merely a provisional, conditional, geopolitical kingdom, the kingdom that God himself will build with his **Messiah** is everlasting, unconditional, and universal. In the last week leading to his crucifixion, Jesus assumes authority over the Temple Mount: inviting sinners to his wedding feast, pronouncing covenant curses on the religious leaders, cursing the fig tree (symbolic of the national theocracy), bypassing the temple by forgiving sins directly, foretelling the destruction of the earthly temple, telling parables of the kingdom, and prophesying his return in judgment at the end of the age (Mt 21–25). He is the true Son of David, the true Zion, the true Temple, and the true Vine in whom all branches draw their everlasting life. Jesus is Israel's seven-branched menorah that stood in the tabernacle and the temple, with its oil-fueled (Spirit-filled) lamps.

This is the major theme of the Epistle to the Hebrews, comparing the lesser glory of Moses' person and work with the greater glory of Christ's. With the coming of the Messiah, the old covenant is now "obsolete" (Heb 8:13). It has fulfilled its typological role, and now the reality has arrived. We have not come to Mount Sinai, but "to Mount Zion and to the city of the living God, the heavenly Jerusalem, and to innumerable angels in festal gathering, and to the assembly of the firstborn who are enrolled in heaven, and to God, the judge of all, and to the spirits of the righteous made perfect, and to Jesus, the mediator of a new covenant, and to the sprinkled blood that speaks a better word than the blood of Abel" (Heb 12:18–24). Because it is the kingdom founded on Christ's blood, which cries out for mercy, rather than the blood of Abel (and, we might add, the blood sprinkled on the people by Moses), which cries out for vengeance, we are not building a kingdom but "receiving a kingdom that cannot be shaken" (v. 28). Jesus is the High Priest of a better covenant, founded on better promises, sworn by God himself (chaps. 7 and 8).

Matthew's gospel especially focuses on Jesus as the fulfillment of Israel's messianic hope. From the prelude, listing the key figures in the genealogical record leading to Jesus, the first point made is not only the identity of Jesus with God (as in John's prologue), the Covenant Lord, but the identity of Jesus with the people of Israel, the Covenant Servant. The first line reads, "The book of the genealogy of Jesus Christ, the son of David, the son of Abraham," traced to "Jesse the father of David the king" and then, through David and his unfaithful heirs, to "Joseph the husband of Mary, of whom Jesus was born, who is called Christ" (Mt 1:1–16). Obviously, judging by the inclusion of nefarious figures in Israel's history, it is not the moral purity but the legal purity of the line that is highlighted. This once again emphasizes that the realization of this covenant depends wholly on God's faithfulness from beginning to end. Now we know why God tolerated so many centuries of wicked kings: it was faithfulness to his oath to David and his indefatigable purpose in sending his Son, the Messiah, to save sinners. This point is revealed further in the name that the angel announced: "you shall call his name Jesus [meaning, "Yahweh Saves!"], for he will save his people from their sins" (Mt 1:21).

Through the synoptic Gospels, Jesus receives — and welcomes — the title "Son of David." There were plenty of physical descendants of Israel's famous king, but this was a messianic title. Everyone knew that it designated the end-time king who would establish David's throne forever. Yet Jesus himself takes this a step further. In his conversation with the religious leaders he asks them how David could speak of his son as his Lord (Mk 12:35–37, from Ps 110). Rabbi Samuel Sandmel notes, "If it seems surprising that the passage implies that Christ was in existence in David's time, that is nevertheless exactly what the passage intends to say."[4] Jesus claimed authority over the temple as a greater king than David and a greater priest than Aaron (both anticipated in Ps 110).

C. Son of Man — Last Adam

We have seen that "Here I am" is the appropriate response of the covenant servant to the authoritative word of judgment and grace spoken by the Lord. Often spoken by the prophets and other servants in Israel's history (culminating in Mary's reply to the angel, "Behold, I am your servant; let it be to me according to your word" [Lk 1:38]), these words place one at God's disposal. It is a common idiom in ancient cultures, as a formal response to a

---

4. Sandmel, *A Jewish Understanding of the New Testament*, 132. It is significant that, unlike most liberal Protestants, a liberal Jewish scholar recognizes the clarity of the earliest Christian witness to Jesus' divinity.

royal summons. Yet the whole life of Jesus, not just his words, is this faithful reply of a covenant servant, "Here I am."

The phrase son of man (usually, *ben-'adam* but sometimes, *ben-'enosh*) is often used to refer simply to human beings (Ge 13:16; Nu 23:19; Job 16:18–21; 25:6; 35:8; Pss 8:4; 80:17; 144:3–4; 146:3–4; Isa 51:12; 56:2; Jer 49:18, 33; 50:40; 51:43). In Ezekiel, God addresses the prophet as "son of man," but the phrase also appears in reference to a future figure. In all, the phrase is used ninety-four times. The lodestar for the messianic import of the term is the book of Daniel, written during the exile in Babylon six centuries before Christ. In chapter 7 (vv. 9–27), the vision begins with the Ancient of Days taking his throne in majesty as he sits in court to judge the nations. Four beasts appear, one of which is destroyed by fire, while the other three are allowed to survive for a time. At this point, "there came one like a son of man, and he came to the Ancient of Days and was presented before him. And to him was given dominion and glory and a kingdom, that all peoples, nations, and languages should serve him; his dominion is an everlasting dominion, which shall not pass away, and his kingdom one that shall not be destroyed" (vv. 13–14). Alarmed by the vision, Daniel asks God to interpret it. The four beasts are earthly empires. "But the saints of the Most High shall receive the kingdom and possess the kingdom forever, forever and ever" (vv. 18). Prophesying the Roman Empire, Daniel is told that the fourth beast will be the most ferocious, devouring the whole earth, but ten kingdoms will arise from it, the last of which will speak blasphemies against Yahweh "and shall wear out the saints of the Most High" (v. 25). After God's court vanquishes this regime, the saints of the Most High will receive their everlasting dominion. This apocalyptic book concludes with the promise of the resurrection of the dead and the last judgment (ch. 12). Daniel 7 offers the most specific prophetic chronology of the Old Testament, and Jesus' Olivet Discourse (Mt 24–25) is its New Testament analogue.

Daniel played a major role in shaping postexilic eschatology, which most of Jesus' contemporaries (especially the Pharisees) would have embraced. There are similarities between the titles *Son of David* and *Son of Man*. Both emphasize the royal office of the Messiah. However, the latter is more universal. The Son of Man is not only King of the Jews, who will deliver the nation from oppressors, but the King of kings who will conquer the whole earth and judge all nations. Anyone who appropriated the title *Son of David* would earn the ire of Herod, but anyone who assumed to himself the title *Son of Man* claimed sovereignty over Caesar himself.

So it is significant that Jesus appropriates this title most frequently in connection with his conquest of Satan and death at the cross, his triumphant resurrection and enthronement, his return in glory to judge the living and the dead, and the everlasting kingdom (Mt 12:38–42; 13:37, 41–42; 16:27–28; 20:17–19; 24:30; 25:31–32; 26:64, with parallel passages in Mark and Luke). In Matthew 12:1–8 (with parallels), Jesus invokes the title to claim lordship over the Sabbath. In John's gospel also, "Son of Man" appears in connection with our Lord's claim to universal sovereignty. In John 1:49–51 he appropriates it as the personification of Jacob's Ladder (Ge 28). As Son of Man he has all authority to judge (Jn 5:25–27; 9:35–37), he is the light of the world (12:34–36), and will be "lifted up" on his crucifixion-throne to draw all people to himself (8:28; 12:32). At his martyrdom, Stephen sees a vision of Jesus Christ as the Son of Man standing in his defense at the Father's right hand (Ac 7:54–56). Upon hearing of his vision, Stephen's persecutors "cried out with a loud voice and stopped their ears and rushed together at him" (v. 57). Quoting Psalm 8, Hebrews 2:6–9 refers to Christ as the Son of Man to whom all things are subjected. In the book of Revelation, Jesus addresses the churches from his throne as the Son of Man (1:12–13; 14:14). Nothing could be a more obvious fulfillment of Daniel 7, with the paradox of a reigning King and a persecuted kingdom, than the persecution of the "saints of the Most High" (Da 7:18, 22, 25, 27) in Revelation.

It is worth noting that Second Temple Judaism held a similar expectation of the messianic Son of Man. In the first-century text *1 Enoch*, the Son of Man presides over the final judgment (*1 En.* 61:8–9; 62:11), is owed worship by the mighty of the earth (62:9), and in fact existed before the creation of the world (49:3). This is a remarkable development within early Judaism itself, given the charge of blasphemy against Jesus for making himself equal with God. Clearly, in this Jewish text, the messianic Son of Man is a divine figure. *First Enoch* celebrates the day when all people "shall fall down before him on their faces, and worship and raise their hopes in that Son of man," even to "beg and plead for mercy at his feet" (62:9). Therefore, the meaning of this title does not undergo significant change in the New Testament; the major difference between *1 Enoch* (as well as 2 Esdras 13) and the New Testament is that the latter identifies Jesus of Nazareth as this divine figure. The fact that the religious leaders react with such violence at this claim demonstrates the heavy and exalted freight that it carried.

D. Servant of the Lord

It is especially in the so-called Servant Songs of Isaiah that this title becomes inseparable from the messianic identity. In Isaiah 52:3–7, Israel is called to rejoice in the "good news" of the salvation that will appear when the Lord's people "shall be redeemed without money." "The LORD has bared his holy arm before the eyes of the nations, and all the ends of the earth shall see the salvation of our God" (v. 10). Once again, there is the dual aspect of divine glory and human humiliation in the messianic vocation of the **Servant** (vv. 13–15).

Much like *Son of Man*, this title is connected with eschatological judgment and salvation. Isaiah 53 focuses on the "Suffering Servant," who bears the judgment of his people, justifies them by his righteousness, and is enthroned as King (vv. 1–12). The unconditional basis of this covenant (compared with the unilateral oath God made to Noah) is the source of his people's comfort and security (Isa 54:9–10). This note is struck again in chapter 55, referring to "an everlasting covenant" that God swore to David. In that day, "a nation that did not know you shall run to you, because of the LORD your God, and of the Holy One of Israel, for he has glorified you" (vv. 3, 5).

Although "there was no justice" and "no one to intercede" (Isa 59:15, 16), the Great King himself was moved to compassion.

> "And a Redeemer will come to Zion,
> to those in Jacob who turn from transgression," declares the LORD.
>
> "And as for me, this is my covenant with them," says the LORD: "My Spirit that is upon you, and my words that I have put in your mouth, shall not depart out of your mouth, or out of the mouth of your offspring, or out of the mouth of your children's offspring," says the LORD, "from this time forth and forevermore." (Isa 59:20–21)

In chapter 60, the Servant is the locus of a great end-time ingathering that will be more extensive than the scattering of Israel and Judah had been. "Nations shall come to your light, and kings to the brightness of your rising" (v. 3). The sun will never set on this empire (vv. 19–20). "Your people shall all be righteous; they shall possess the land forever" (v. 21).

In chapter 61, the Servant of the LORD brings about an everlasting Year of Jubilee (typologically foreshadowed in Lev 25). "The Spirit of the Lord GOD is upon me, because the LORD has anointed me to bring good news to the poor; he has sent me to bind up the brokenhearted, to proclaim liberty to the captives, and the opening of the prison to those who are bound; to proclaim the year of the LORD's favor, and the day of vengeance of our God; to comfort all who mourn" (Isa 61:1–2). In the Servant will the servant people be righteous, "for he has clothed me with the garments of salvation; he has covered me with the robe of righteousness" (vv. 10–11; cf. 62:10–12). Launching his public ministry, Jesus read this passage in the synagogue and announced, "Today this Scripture has been fulfilled in your hearing" (Lk 4:21).

There is a close connection here between the Spirit and the Servant. The Spirit who hovered over the depths in creation, calling a world out of nothing, "will come upon you," the angel tells Mary, "and the power of the Most High will overshadow you; therefore the child to be born will be called holy—the Son of God" (Lk 1:35). It was the Spirit who led the Servant into the wilderness temptation, to endure the probation that Adam and Israel failed to fulfill (Mt 4:1), and who descended in the form of a dove above the waters in Jesus' baptism (Mt 3:16; Mk 1:9–11; Lk 3:21–22; Jn 1:32–34). As the Spirit led Israel through the waters and the wilderness to the promised land, he led Jesus through despair to victory. When we recall the Spirit's evacuation of the temple as the desacralizing of the land, leading to the exile (Eze 10:18–22; 11:23), the return of the Spirit to the earth—"upon" Jesus—identifies the Servant also as the end-time temple (Eze 43:1–12; Mt 12:6; Jn 2:19; 1Co 2:19; Eph 2:21; Rev 21:22).

E. Son of God

The humanity and deity of Christ cannot be identified directly by the titles *Son of Man* and *Son of God*. As we have seen, the relevant passages ascribe to the Son of Man divine attributes as well as divine actions (both words and deeds). Conversely, **Son of God** refers as much to human characteristics as divine identity. We have seen that "sonship" is an important aspect of humanity as God's image and likeness. The people of Israel are called collectively "son of God" (Ex 4:22–23; Ps 80:15; Hos 11:1–2, 8–11). And in the covenant that God makes with David he identifies David's heir as a "son" (2Sa 7:14). Psalm 2 speaks of the reign of Yahweh's Anointed (Messiah). David sings, "I will tell of the decree: The LORD said to me, 'You are my Son; today I have begotten you'" (v. 7). As the psalm unfolds, it is clear that David himself is not this royal figure who judges the kings of the earth and is accorded the honor due only to God: "Blessed are all who take refuge in him" (v. 12). Not surprisingly, then, Psalm 2 (along with Ps 110) served as a major source for Israel's longing for a Messiah, greater than David himself though from his royal line. The earth is God's footstool, and David and his heirs reign in Jerusalem, but this son possesses the everlasting kingdom and reigns at God's right hand in heaven.

Interestingly, it is Psalm 2 that is quoted in the opening argument of the Letter to the Hebrews. The writer introduces Jesus as God's "Son, whom he appointed the heir of all things, through whom also he created the world ... the radiance of the glory of God and the exact imprint of his nature," who "upholds the universe by the word of his power." "After making purification for sins, he sat down at the right hand of the Majesty on high, having become as much superior to angels as the name he has inherited is more excellent than theirs" (Heb 1:1–4).

Clearly, in the author's mind, Jesus is God's eternal Son, who shares the same nature as the Father. Jesus is Yahweh incarnate. The author's initial argument focuses on Jesus' superiority to angels. Many Jews of this period were fascinated with angels and their various ranks, and the primary audience of this letter were Jewish Christians who were in danger of returning to the shadows of the law, especially in the face of intense persecution. Jesus is not the mightiest of angels; rather, he is the divine Son, whom the angels are obliged to worship (Heb 1:5–14).

In the first two quotations (Ps 2:7 and 2Sa 7:14), the writer identifies Jesus as the "son of God" in the Davidic-messianic sense, fulfilling the covenant that God made with David to give his heir an everlasting kingdom. Yet the other citations identify Jesus, the bearer of the messianic title, as none other than God. It is he whom the angels themselves worship (Dt 32:43; Ps 97:7); he is addressed as God—and yet his God has anointed and elevated him above all others. He is the eternal and unchanging Lord who created all things—and yet the messianic ruler who sits at God's right hand.

The point to be drawn from this argument is that the Old Testament itself identifies the Messiah as God and yet distinguishes him from God as his Father. He is therefore related to God in a twofold manner. As the Covenant Lord, Jesus is not merely created in God's image and likeness—that is, he is not merely like him by analogy. Much more, Jesus is in fact the Creator himself, "the image and glory of God" (1Co 11:7); "the image of the invisible God ... in [whom] all the fullness of God was pleased to dwell" (Col 1:15a, 19a); "the radiance of the glory of God and the exact imprint of his nature" who "upholds the universe by the word of his power" (Heb 1:3a). Yet as the Covenant Servant, Jesus is the adopted and anointed son-messiah, the faithful Adam, Israel, and Davidic king. Jesus is both superior to angels, as God, and inferior to angels, as human (Heb 2:6–8, citing Ps 8). He is sovereign not only as God, but as the image-bearing son who finally fulfills the trial and commission he has been given as the covenantal head of his people. Hence, the complete humanity of Jesus is just as important in this argument (2:9–18; 4:14–16) as his deity as far as fulfilling this role of "son," which distinguishes him even above Moses (chap. 3). He had to "share in flesh and blood" with us so that "through death he might destroy the one who has the power of death, that is, the devil, and deliver all those who through fear of death were subject to lifelong slavery" (2:14–15). He was exalted to the Father's right hand not only because he is the eternal Son, but because he is the human image-son who accomplished our redemption. So Jesus had to be the Son of God in both senses, not only as the Covenant Lord but as the Covenant Servant.

The apostle Paul makes a similar point in his opening remarks in Romans "concerning [God's] Son, who was descended from David according to the flesh and was declared [*horisthentos*] to be the Son of God in power according to the Spirit of holiness by his resurrection from the dead, Jesus Christ our Lord" (Ro 1:3–4). The choice of the verb is important: *horisthentos* means declared, decided, or determined. Paul could have used *phaneroō*, "reveal/make known," as he does later in the chapter regarding general revelation (1:19). However, his point is that something happened in Christ's resurrection from the dead that changed his status, not ontologically, but judicially and eschatologically. His resurrection was not merely proof of his eternal sonship. Rather, through it he was declared to be "the Son of God in power." Although "our Lord" by eternal generation from the Father, he became the Lord—that is, the determinative actor—in history by what he achieved. He fulfilled the office of "Son of God" and thus not only became "a living being," like the first Adam and his posterity, but became, as the last Adam, "a life-giving spirit" (1Co 15:45).

A parallel argument is given in Philippians 2, where Jesus is identified as having been "in the form of God" and yet willing to empty himself of his rightful privileges, "taking the form of a servant, being born in the likeness of men," humbling himself even to the point of death on the cross. "*Therefore God has highly exalted him and bestowed on him the name that is above every name, so that at the name of Jesus every knee should bow, in heaven and on earth and under the earth, and every tongue confess that Jesus Christ is Lord, to the glory of God the Father*" (vv. 5–11, emphasis added). Once more, his exaltation is the result of his willing and successful humiliation for our salvation. The Son was exalted in eternal majesty with the Father, but became human and suffered for us, so that his exaltation now is not only that of the eternal Son returning to his pre-incarnate glory, but that of the one who returns this time as the victorious Son, glorified in our flesh at the Father's right hand. No Jewish person could have misunderstood the significance of the claim that Jesus now is given "the name that is above every name, so that at the name of Jesus every knee should bow." After all, this is taken from Isaiah 45:23, referring to Yahweh. As the name of the suzerain (great king) in the treaty, Yahweh is the only name that his people are to invoke for rescue, worship in reverence, and obey in fear. It is now transferred to Jesus, the son of Mary. So *Son of God* includes Christ's humanity as well as his deity, just as *Son of Man* also encompasses both natures.

In John's gospel, *Son of God* carries a heavy emphasis on Christ's essential unity with the Father. From the very beginning of this gospel, the point is underscored that Jesus is God's Son in a qualitatively different way than others—and, in fact, that believers can call God "Father" only because of their identification with the Son as their Mediator. Intentionally patterned on the Genesis prologue, John's prologue begins with the staggering announcement of the incarnation.

The Word is a person, and this person existed before creation. He was with God and in fact is God: "the only God, who is at the Father's side" (Jn 1:18; cf. 1:1). Therefore, he is distinguished from God (the Father) and yet is God in his essence. He is the Creator, who has life in himself (i.e., aseity). Finally, this Word became flesh, and it is only through him that we know the only living and true God.

Throughout John's gospel, Jesus is the **only begotten Son** who alone knows and reveals the Father; in fact, to know God is to know the Son whom he has sent. The economic submission of the incarnate Son to the Father's will and word is everywhere emphasized in this gospel, but Jesus speaks repeatedly of an intimate relation to the Father that is unique, eternal, and essential. He says that the Son was sent from the Father to save the world (3:17) and that "the light has come into the world" (v. 19). There is a recurring emphasis on the Son coming down from the Father into this world. John the Baptist testifies concerning Jesus, "He who comes from above is above all" (v. 31). "For he whom God has sent utters the words of God, for he gives the Spirit without measure. The Father loves the Son and has given all things into his hand. Whoever believes in the Son has eternal life; whoever does not obey the Son shall not see life, but the wrath of God remains on him" (vv. 34–36).

How can Jesus heal on the Sabbath? He is the "Lord of the Sabbath": "My Father is working until now, and I am working," he replied. "This was why the Jews were seeking all the more to kill him," John relates, "because not only was he breaking the Sabbath, but he was even calling God his own Father, making himself equal with God." Instead of qualifying this claim, Jesus went on to emphasize his unity with the Father: "For as the Father raises the dead and gives them life, so also the Son gives life to whom he will." In fact, "The Father judges no one, but has given all judgment to the Son, that all may honor the Son just as they honor the Father. Whoever does not honor the Son does not honor the Father who sent him." Jesus tells them that when he returns, "the dead will hear the voice of the Son of God, and those who hear will live. For as the Father has life in himself, so he has granted the Son also to have life in himself" (5:17–26). Jesus is the Son who has "come down from heaven" (6:33, 42, 62).

"Firstborn son," therefore, is a legal term transferred to the family of God. In the ancient world, the firstborn son was heir of the estate. What is truly remarkable is that in God's family, all children—males and females, regardless of birth order—are equal coheirs with Christ. In one sense, Jesus holds the office of adopted son. Fully human, he is, like us, God's image-bearer. As the last Adam and true Israel, he actually fulfilled this commission. In this sense, he is the faithful "firstborn son" and "the firstborn among many brothers and sisters" (Ro 8:29 NIV). Yet Christ himself is the "first-born son" in a qualitatively different sense, by eternal generation. He is God's Son ontologically (i.e., in his essence) and brings us by adoption into that same intimacy that he enjoys with the Father.

Interestingly, it was not only Jews for whom "Son of God" bore such weight. As Craig Evans points out, this was one of the titles that Caesar appropriated to himself as the incarnation of Zeus. "There is no reason to think that Jesus' Jewish contemporaries, who were themselves very much a part of the Greco-Roman world, would have thought of these expressions in terms significantly different from those held by Gentiles."[5] Against the background of Jewish and Roman culture, we can only imagine the astonishment of Mary at Gabriel's announcement, "The Holy Spirit will come upon you, and the power of the Most High will overshadow you; therefore the child to be born will be called holy—the Son of God" (Lk 1:35).

III. Two Natures in One Person: The Incarnation

Besides the select titles I have reviewed, our Lord's identity is revealed gradually through his words and deeds. At the heart of the Christian faith is the belief that Jesus of Nazareth is fully God and fully human: *two natures in one person*. This formula, "two natures in one person," is as significant for the church's Christology as the formula "one in essence and three in persons" is for its doctrine of the Trinity. This section explores the development of this doctrine of the incarnation in the early Christian community and its refinement in the controversies of the ancient church.

---

5. Craig Evans, "Jesus' Self-Designation 'The Son of Man' and the Recognition of His Divinity," in Gerald O'Collins, *The Trinity: An Interdisciplinary Symposium on the Trinity* (ed. Stephen T. Davis, Daniel Kendall, and Gerald O'Collins; New York: Oxford Univ. Press, 1999), 43.

A. Exegetical Sources

It is difficult to generalize about four gospels that have different authors, interests, perspectives, and organizing structures. Nevertheless, in the diversity of voices and aims, there is a common witness to the God who became incarnate "for us and for our salvation." The first half of the Nicene Creed's second article summarizes this message:

> We believe ... in one Lord Jesus Christ, the only-begotten Son of God,
> begotten of his Father before all worlds,
> God of God, Light of Light, very God of very God,
> begotten, not made, being of one substance with the Father;
> by whom all things were made;
> who for us and for our salvation
> came down from heaven, and was incarnate by the Holy Spirit of the Virgin
> Mary,
> and was made man.[6]

As we saw in relation to the Trinity, the early church's doctrine of Christ's person arose out of the one unfolding plot (drama) of both testaments, often presented in the form of doxology and exhibited in discipleship. The doctrinal refinement not only shaped but was often provoked by the practices commanded by Christ and his apostles: calling on the name of Jesus, baptizing in his name, praising him as God incarnate, and following him not merely as a rabbi but as God in flesh. The Nicene Creed and the earlier creeds it is based upon (going back to the first Christians) were (and are) used not merely as tests of orthodoxy but as confessions of faith and hymns of praise.

From the passages already considered, we learn that Jesus Christ is both God and human — not as a hybrid (a divinized man or a humanized god), nor as a two-headed hydra (two persons), but one person who is both God and human. The eternal Son assumed our human nature: this is the wonderful news that would form the baseline for early Christian confession in the face of challenges. Thus, the path from the earliest Christian community to the formal Christology of the ecumenical creeds is direct and straightforward. The Jesus of history, as prophesied in the Old Testament and witnessed to in the New Testament, is the Christ of faith, as confessed in the creeds.

As Brevard Childs notes, for Matthew, based on Isaiah 7:14, "The virgin birth is the sign which identifies [Jesus] as the Messiah." However,

---

6. The Nicene Creed, in *Trinity Hymnal* (rev. ed.; Philadelphia: Great Commission Publications, 1990), 846.

this already presupposes the existence of the Son prior to his incarnation.[7] Since the miracle was not Jesus' gestation and birth, it is more precisely correct to speak of the virginal *conception*. Rather than a human father, the Holy Spirit "overshadowed" Mary so that the person born of her would be the Son of God. At the same time, Mary was not a mere channel or surrogate mother: Jesus was born *of* the Virgin Mary, not just *from* her. Although he received his particular humanity from Mary, he did not have a human father and was therefore untainted by original sin (Heb 4:15; cf. Isa 7:14; Mt 1:18–20; Lk 1:34–35). Since sinfulness is accidental rather than essential to human nature (as we discussed in the previous chapter), Christ's exemption from it makes him no less human than Adam and Eve were before the fall. The maxim of Gregory of Nazianzus—"What he did not assume he did not redeem"—is already implied in Hebrews 2:10–18: he had to be made "like his brothers and sisters" in order to redeem them (v. 17 NIV).

Therefore, Jesus Christ is simultaneously Lord and Servant, God turned toward humanity and humanity turned toward God. He is "the faithful and true witness" (Rev 3:14). His temptations were real (Mt 4:1–11 and parallel passages; Jn 4:6; Heb 2:17–18). In fact, "The child *grew* and *became* strong, filled with wisdom. And the favor of God was upon him.... And Jesus *increased* in wisdom and in stature and in favor with God and man" (Lk 2:40, 52, emphasis added). His physical, psychological, social, and religious growth followed the normal course of his peers'. It is striking, in fact, that when he began his ministry his own childhood neighbors expressed astonishment at his words and deeds: "Is not this the carpenter's son? Is not his mother called Mary? And are not his brothers James and Joseph and Simon and Judas? And are not all his sisters with us? Where then did this man get all these things?" (Mt 13:54–56). Evidently, his childhood was quite ordinary, in contrast to the fables that one finds in the gnostic gospels. Jesus himself declared that the Father alone knew the day of his return (Mt 24:36). Agonizing over his impending crucifixion, he says, "My soul is very sorrowful, even to death" (Mt 26:38a), asking the Father to remove this cup, if it were possible, while nevertheless submitting to the Father's will (v. 39). On the cross he cries, "My God, my God, why have you forsaken me?" (Mt 27:46), and then commits his soul to the Father (Lk 23:46). The blood that he brings into the heavenly sanctuary is human (Heb 9:11–10:18), but it is also called the blood of God (Ac 20:28).

---

7. Brevard Childs, *Biblical Theology of the Old and New Testaments: Theological Reflections on the Christian Bible* (Minneapolis: Fortress, 1993), 470.

B. Historical Development

Reason quite properly rejects contradiction, but rationalism abhors mystery, which every heresy attempts in its own way to resolve. In this case, Christ's person is reduced either to his humanity or to his deity. The earliest challenges were directed at the deity of Christ. This is understandable, given the Jewish background, with its unqualified monotheism. The **Ebionite** heresy regarded Jesus as a superior prophet and moral teacher, who guides us to salvation through our own obedience to the law.[8] Similarly, **adoptionism** held that Jesus, though exclusively human, was adopted as God's son at his baptism or at some other point in his life. Both of these departures demonstrate the inextricable connection between Christ's person and his work. If salvation is achieved by our own obedience to the law, then Jesus need only be a great moral teacher.

Other heresies arose, mainly from the encounter with Hellenistic (Greek) culture. If the tendency of heresies in a Jewish milieu was to deny Christ's full deity, Greek-oriented heresies denied his full humanity. The Christ referred to in the canonical Gospels only appeared to have a human body, according to the early heresy of **Docetism** (from the verb *dokeō*, "to appear"). Already in 1 John 4:2–3, the apostles were battling this challenge to the full humanity of Christ, with John identifying this heresy as "the spirit of the antichrist." Perhaps the crucial test-question in contemporary terms would be, "Does the incarnation mean that God now has Mary's genes?" After being brought up to speed on what is meant by "genes," the orthodox would have answered yes without hesitation. The eternal Son assumed his humanity from Mary.

Gradually, the docetic tendency evolved into a formal movement. Known as **Gnosticism**, this movement spawned various sects, each with its own parallel canon (including the so-called gnostic gospels), sacraments (of course, without the use of material elements), church (the *gnōstikoi* — "enlightened ones," as they called themselves), and hierarchy of priests and bishops. From its founding drama and doctrines, to its doxology and discipleship (i.e., abandoning the official church and its ministry in favor of private ascetic practices), Gnosticism was a parody of Christianity, a completely different religion. It borrowed on Christian terms, themes, and figures, but reinterpreted them within a vastly different scheme.

Other early christological heresies emerged, reflecting these two extremes: denying either the full divinity or the full humanity of Christ. However, in

---

8. See the description of this group in Eusebius, *Ecclesiastical History* 3.27 (*NPNF²*, 1:159–60 [PG 20, col. 273]). See also Irenaeus, *Against Heresies* 1.26.2 (*ANF* 1:439, 507, 527).

this more Greco-Roman environment, challenges to Christ's full deity owed more to philosophical objections than to any defense of Jewish monotheism. "One" is the favorite number in Greek philosophy, so it was unimaginable that the ultimate reality might be three. Problems with Christ's deity were really problems with the Trinity, and vice versa. It has been argued that this tendency was already present in Origen of Alexandria (184–253), who emphasized the sole monarchy of the Father. Origen did teach that the Son was subordinate to the Father not only *economically* (that is, in his state of humiliation as the incarnate Lord), which the orthodox also affirmed, but *ontologically* (in his essence). This heresy is identified as **Subordinationism**.

However, Arius (AD 250/256–366), a presbyter in Alexandria, took a step beyond Origen, denying the essential unity of the Son with the Father. **Arianism** taught that there was a time when the Son did not exist. It was chiefly this heresy that the early creeds targeted when they affirmed that the Son is consubstantial—that is, of the same essence (Greek, *ousia*) or substance (Latin, *substantia*) with the Father (and the Spirit). Thus, according to Arians, the Son is God's first creation, through whom he then created the world. As the label suggests, **Semi-Arianism** (quite close to Subordinationism) proposed a middle way between Arianism and orthodoxy: although the Son is not of the same essence (*homoousios*), he is of a similar essence (*homoiousios*). It has been said that at this point in history the difference between Christianity and another religion depended solely on a vowel.

Toward the other end of the spectrum, downplaying Christ's true humanity, was **Apollinarianism**. Named after Apollinarius (d. 390), a bishop of Laodicea (in Syria), this heresy was not quite docetic or gnostic. Apollinarius held that Jesus possessed a truly human body. However, presupposing a Neoplatonic anthropology (body, soul, and spirit), he taught that the Logos (divine Son) had *replaced* the human soul (*nous*) of Jesus. Simply put, Jesus' humanity extended only as far as his body, which his true self—the Logos—wore like a garment. To use a modern illustration, Apollinarianism tends to think of Jesus like a car driven by the divine Spirit-Logos. Gregory of Nazianzus captured the problem with this view in his famous expression, "For that which He has not assumed He has not healed; but that which is united to His Godhead is also saved."[9] In other words, if

---

9. Gregory of Nazianzus, "Epistle 101, To Cledonius the Priest against Apollinarius," in *Select Letters of Saint Gregory of Nazianzen* (*NPNF*[2], 5:438 [PG 37, cols. 181, 184]). This principle is evident also in the Belgic Confession, art. 18: the Son "did not only assume human nature as to the body, but also a true human soul, that He might be a real man. For since the soul was lost as well as the body, it was

Jesus did not assume our full humanity, not only human flesh but a human soul and mind, then he did not redeem and glorify us in the totality of our human nature. Scripture speaks too clearly about Christ's genuine temptation, suffering, and even his anxiety in the face of the crucifixion; we have no grounds for downplaying the humanity either of his soul or of his body. Apollinarians could not deal adequately with these passages, because, on Apollinarius's account, there was no genuinely human nature to be disturbed by external circumstances. Therefore, the Council of Constantinople (381) condemned Apollinarianism as a denial of the true humanity of the God-Man.

But does this mean that Jesus had a truly human *will*? This question provoked the **Monothelite** (one-will) controversy. The church recognized from Scripture that Jesus, as God and human, possessed not only a divine but a human will, even to the point of his submission to the Father's will: "nevertheless, not as I will, but as you will" (Mt 26:39). In other words, there is *nothing* human that the eternal Son did not assume in his incarnation. If Jesus is God and human, he must have possessed both a divine and a human will. One more heresy in this class was **Monophysitism**, from a Greek phrase meaning "one nature." It is also known as Eutychianism, after Eutyches of Constantinople (380–456), who argued that Christ's deity had swallowed his humanity as an ocean absorbs a drop of vinegar. Whereas the orthodox spoke of Jesus Christ as one person *in* two natures (affirming the permanent distinction), Monophysites preferred "one person *of* two natures" (analogous to two substances poured into a container). After the incarnation, the two natures become one nature: a deified humanity.

In reaction against Monophysitism's confusion of natures, **Nestorianism** separated them. The test case was whether Nestorians could affirm that Mary is *Theotokos*, "God-bearer," or the "Mother of God." This title emerged not as a way of inflating Mary's person, but as a way of affirming that the one she bore was in fact God. Nestorians could not affirm that Mary was the mother of God, but merely that she was the mother of Jesus. But what does this say about the identity of Jesus? Are Jesus and God two different people?

Over against both heresies the Creed of Chalcedon (451) concluded that "the only-begotten Son of God must be confessed in two natures, unconfusedly, immutably, indivisibly, inseparably united.... without the

necessary that He should take both upon Him, to save both" (*Psalter Hymnal* [Grand Rapids: Board of Publications of the Christian Reformed Church, 1976], 77).

> ## Key Distinction:
> ### person/nature (Christology)
>
> In the incarnation, the eternal Son assumed fully our human nature (in both body and soul). He is therefore one person, but in two natures. His becoming human in no way changed his deity into humanity or his humanity into deity. The divine and human natures are united in one person without being confused.

distinction of natures being taken away by such union."[10] In fact, all of these christological heresies were decisively rejected at this ecumenical council.

Still, the same christological heresies erupt periodically throughout church history, with only slight mutations. Adoptionism and Arianism are alive and well in quite disparate sects, such as Unitarianism, liberalism, and the Jehovah's Witnesses. In the Reformation era, debates over Christ's presence in the Eucharist provoked charges of Nestorianism (by the Lutherans against the Reformed) and Monophysitism (by the Reformed against the Lutherans). Neither party actually embraced the heresy ascribed to it, but such charges were part and parcel of the fierce polemics of the Reformation era.

Largely dormant after the fourth century, Gnosticism erupted again in the medieval era. Though ruthlessly rooted out in massive extermination campaigns by the medieval church, the docetic tendency nevertheless continued through Anabaptist "spiritualists." Calvin charged Menno Simons with a revival of Gnosticism for believing that Mary was merely a "channel" through whom the Christ was born, the Son taking "celestial flesh" from heaven rather than from Mary.[11] With the ecumenical creeds, the Reformed have emphasized that "Christ was born *ex Maria virgine* [from the virgin Mary], which is explained to mean *ex substantia matris suae* [from the substance of his mother], rather than simply *per* (through) her."[12]

In this context the Belgic Confession states that Jesus Christ was "conceived in the womb of the blessed virgin Mary by the power of the Holy Spirit, without male participation ... and did not only assume a human nature as to the body, but also a true human soul, that He might be a real

---

10. "The Chalcedonian Definition," in *The Creeds of the Churches: A Reader in Christian Doctrine from the Bible to the Present* (ed. John Leith; Louisville: Westminster John Knox, 1983), 34–36.

11. Calvin, *Institutes* 2.13.3.

12. Charles Hodge, *Systematic Theology* (Grand Rapids: Eerdmans, 1946), 2:400.

man." Following the Athanasian argument against the Apollinarians, this Reformed confession adds, "For since the soul was lost as well as the body, it was necessary that He should take both upon Him, to save both. Therefore, we confess (in opposition to the heresy of the Anabaptists, who deny that Christ possessed the human flesh of His mother) that Christ *partook of the flesh and blood of the children* ... descended from the Jews according to the flesh ... so that in truth He is our Immanuel, that is to say, *God with us*."[13] The confession adds that "by this conception the person of the Son is inseparably united and connected with the human nature, so that there are not two Sons of God, nor two persons, but two natures united in one single person; yet each nature retains its own distinct properties." Even after his resurrection, Jesus shares his humanity in common with us, since "our salvation and resurrection also depend on the reality of His body."

> But these two natures are so closely united in one person that they were not separated even by His death. Therefore, that which He, when dying, commended into the hands of His Father, was a real human spirit, departing from His body. But in the meantime the divine nature always remained united with the human, even when He lay in the grave.... Wherefore we confess that He is very God and very man: very God by His power to conquer death; and very man that He might die for us according to the infirmity of His flesh.[14]

The Heidelberg Catechism confesses "that the eternal Son of God, who is and remains true and eternal God, took to himself, through the working of the Holy Spirit, from the flesh and blood of the virgin Mary, a truly human nature so that he might become David's true descendant, in all things like us his brothers except for sin."[15] Similarly, the Westminster Confession declares that "the Son of God, the second person in the Trinity," was "conceived by the power of the Holy Ghost in the womb of the virgin Mary, *of her substance*" (emphasis added).[16] Not because the divine attributes are communicated *to the human nature*, but because the divine and human natures are united in *one person*, it is entirely appropriate to say that Mary is the mother of God, that God suffered temptation, and that God the Creator died for our sins and rose again.

---

13. Belgic Confession, art. 18, in *Psalter Hymnal*, 77. Perhaps the best book on this subject is still J. Gresham Machen's *The Virgin Birth of Christ* (New York: Harper, 1930).

14. Belgic Confession, art. 18, in *Psalter Hymnal*, 78.

15. Heidelberg Catechism, q. 35, in *Psalter Hymnal*, 21.

16. Westminster Confession, ch. 8, in *Trinity Hymnal* (Atlanta: Great Commission Publications, 1990), 853.

With this background, we can summarize the orthodox conception of Christ's incarnation: The eternal Word, God the Son, assumed our human nature by the power of the Holy Spirit from the virgin Mary. In this humiliation, he emptied himself of his glorious privileges that he enjoyed at the Father's right hand, but not of his deity (Php 2:6–8). If it is true that he did not redeem what he did not assume, it is also true that he could not redeem if his divine nature had been diminished in any degree. In this marvelous union, each nature had to remain intact. Monophysitism blends the two natures into one, collapsing his humanity into his deity. In modern theology there was a move toward a **kenotic Christology** (from the Greek word *kenōsis*, "emptying") with the obverse direction: collapsing his deity into his humanity, so that in the incarnation the Son empties himself of his deity in order to share our human nature. Either way, Jesus could not be truly our Savior. If his deity had been collapsed into his humanity, he would be someone other than Immanuel, "*God* with Us." If his humanity had been collapsed into his deity, he would not be "God *with Us*." So the divine nature did not become something that it was not before. Every attribute of God belonged to Jesus of Nazareth, so that his action is God's action. Nor was his human nature deified in the sense of being confused with the divine nature.

This consensus also affirms that the eternal Son assumed our humanity, not an already existing person. Of course, Jesus was and remains a particular human being: a Jewish male born in Roman-occupied Palestine (specifically, Bethlehem) and raised in Nazareth. However, he could be the Savior of the world only by assuming our generic human nature, which belongs to everyone from Adam and Eve to the end of the age. We should resist any analogy with reincarnation, in which supposedly immortal and divine souls—the true identity of the self—come to indwell different bodies at different times. The Son did not assume the body of Jesus; rather, this person came into existence for the first time when the eternal Son became human. *God* saves; therefore, just as our salvation is not a cooperative venture, the incarnation is not a synergistic activity of divine and human natures. The eternal Son assumed our humanity, and apart from this unique work of God there is no person Jesus of Nazareth.

The triumph of orthodoxy could have occurred only at a time when the whole church submitted its judgments to God's Word, allowing the "new thing" God was doing in history to redefine their inherited horizon of possibilities. The ecumenical councils reveal the amazing conversion not only of Jews, but of Greeks and Romans to the gospel of Jesus Christ. It is a mystery to be adored rather than resolved.

Christological Heresies Spectrum	
Denying Christ's Divinity	**Denying Christ's Humanity**
Ebionitism	Docetism/Gnosticism
Subordinationism	Apollinarianism
Adoptionism	Monothelitism
Arianism/Semi-Arianism	
Confusing the Two Natures	**Dividing the Two Natures**
Monophysitism/Eutychianism	Nestorianism

Ecumenical Councils		
Nicaea	325	Formal statement on the Trinity
Constantinople I	381	Rejection of Apollinarianism, Monophysitism (also known as Eutychianism), and Nestorianism
Chalcedon	451	Consolidation of "one person in two natures"
Constantinople III	681	Monothelitism condemned; two intelligences and wills: one human, one divine, united in one person

C. The Threefold Office of Christ

If it is true that God can be known only by his works, then the same may be said of Christ. We have already seen the inextricable connection between Christ's person and work. This intersection is especially evident in the threefold office (*munus triplex*) of Christ, in whom otherwise distinct offices converge. We have already seen that these offices of prophet, priest, and king lie at the heart of the vocation of human beings, who are created in God's image. The tragedy was that Adam and Israel became false prophets, priests, and kings, but the good news is that Christ—the Last Adam and True Israel—has fulfilled this calling not only for himself, but for us.

1. Prophet

Various non-Christian religions are willing to acknowledge Jesus as a great prophet. Following Maimonides, many Jewish scholars have considered Jesus an important figure in bringing Judaism to the Gentile world. According to Islam, Jesus (*'Isa*) was the "Seal of the Israelite Prophets," the last in this noble line. He was the Messiah, born of a virgin, but in no sense divine. God performed miracles through him, he proclaimed the eternal rule of Allah, and he prepared the way for the great prophet Muhammad. Jesus was not crucified, but ascended bodily, and will return to defeat the antichrist before the Last Judgment. At that time he will correct the blasphemous misunderstanding of his followers concerning his divinity and, with the prophet Muhammad, will acknowledge the sole sovereignty of Allah.[17]

Among contemporary Buddhists and Hindus, there is a place for Jesus as a bodhisattva, or "enlightened soul," who did much good for others by his deeds, teaching, and example. For all of their other differences, this view of Jesus prevailed in Enlightenment deism and Romanticism. In the United States, for example, deists like Thomas Jefferson and transcendentalists like Ralph Waldo Emerson rejected the Christian confession of Jesus Christ as God incarnate with polemical fervor, while praising his legacy as the world's greatest prophet. The Baha'i religion considers Jesus a great prophet, as does liberal Protestantism.

However, the New Testament not only proclaims Jesus as more than a prophet, but interprets even his prophetic office as unique. Jesus taught that all of Israel's prophets spoke of him (Lk 24:27, 44–48). "You search the Scriptures because you think that in them you have eternal life," Jesus told the religious leaders; "and it is they that bear witness about me, yet you refuse to come to me that you may have life" (Jn 5:39–40). Jesus not only leads the way; he is the destination. He not only teaches; he is the subject. He not only shows us how to live; he is "the way, the truth, and the life" (Jn 14:6). Jesus not only proclaims God's promises; he is the one in whom they are all fulfilled (2Co 1:20). He not only brings God's Word; he is God's Word incarnate (Jn 1:1, 14). "Long ago, at many times and in many ways, God spoke to our fathers by the prophets, but in these last days he has spoken to us by his Son" (Heb 1:1–2). Moses, the greatest Old Testament prophet, "was faithful in all God's house as a servant, to testify to the things that were to be spoken later, but Christ is faithful over God's house as a son" (Heb 3:5–6). This is no slight to Moses, who himself prophesied a coming final prophet (Dt 18:15; Ac 3:22–23). Peter tells us that the Holy Spirit, speaking through the prophets, concentrated all attention on "the sufferings of Christ and the subsequent glories"—namely, "the good news" (1Pe 1:10–12). The heart of this prophetic revelation is "the gospel of God, which he promised beforehand through his prophets in the holy Scriptures, concerning his Son" (Ro 1:1–3a).

If Jesus' prophetic office is unique, it is nevertheless grounded in the prophetic heritage of Israel. We often use the term *prophet* loosely, as if anyone who brings meaningful instruction and moral guidance is a prophet or

---

17. J. L. Esposito, ed., *The Oxford Dictionary of Islam* (New York: Oxford Univ. Press, 2003), 158.

prophetic. "Prophets" in our culture are specially gifted sages or reformers who have an unusual way of restating eternal truths in a fresh and relevant manner. However, even the Old Testament prophets held a far greater office than this suggests.

First, Israel's prophets were not philosophers, moralists, or monks. They were not merely enlightened sages of eternal truths. To be sure, they brought instruction. However, unlike Buddha or Muhammad, Israel's prophets were first of all witnesses to God's speech and acts in history. Even when they tell us about unchanging and eternal truths—such as God's attributes—it is in the context of a dramatic plot that is unfolding in history. Their words consist primarily of divinely revealed testimony to impending judgment and deliverance. Beyond the dreary cycle of Israel's renewed commitment and broken promises, prophecy announced the "new thing" that God would do in the future, in spite of the covenant partner's faithlessness. Thus, the primary purpose of prophecy is to preach Christ. If the church in any age desires to be "prophetic" in its time and place, it will do the same.

Second, prophecy in Israel was not merely a series of doctrines to be believed and rules to be followed. Of course, there are doctrines and commands. Nevertheless, the word of God spoken by the prophets is "living and active." It not only tells the truth, but does the truth; God's speech not only explains reality but creates it. We have seen that Israel's grammar for its relationship with Yahweh was taken not from the field of religion, but politics. Hence, Israel's prophets are not spiritual gurus and life coaches, but ambassadors and attorneys who prosecute and defend God's people in the great trial of covenantal history. God creates, sustains, judges, justifies, kills, and makes alive by the word of his mouth. After a criminal is convicted, it is the judge's declaration, "I sentence you to life in prison," that changes the whole life of the defendant—and many others as well. The prophets, therefore, not only tell us about God and his purposes; they receive and speak a word by which the Spirit actually brings the announcement to fruition in history. God's declaration of the curses, through the prophets, actually sends Israel into exile. Yet God's word of gracious pardon and promise actually comforts Israel in exile, creating faith in the coming redemption. The Spirit creates despair through his law's condemnation and creates faith through the gospel promise. In his vision, Ezekiel "prophesies" (preaches) to the dry bones, "Live!," and by this performative speech they come to life (Eze 37).

Jesus is surely a prophet in this traditional sense. He pronounces the covenant blessings (e.g., the Beatitudes in Mt 5:2–16) and the covenant curses (Mt 23:1–39). Nevertheless, as the last old covenant prophet (John the Baptist) announced, "I baptize you with water for repentance, but he who is coming after me is mightier than I, whose sandals I am not worthy to carry. He will baptize you with the Holy Spirit and fire" (Mt 3:11). Jesus is the one who brings into history the consummated blessing and judgment of his kingdom that the old covenant merely foreshadowed. Jesus calls himself a prophet (Lk 13:33) and foretells his death and resurrection, as well as the destruction of the temple, the interim era between his advents, and his return in glory to judge the living and the dead (Mt 24; Mk 13; etc.). Nevertheless, whereas the prophets proclaimed the coming Messiah, Jesus Christ is the prophet and the prophecy now fulfilled. He speaks with an authority that is unlike that of the scribes (Mt 7:29), authenticates it with signs, and is thus recognized as a prophet by the people (Mt 21:11, 46; Lk 7:16; 24:19; Jn 3:2; 4:19; 6:14; 7:40; 9:17).

Like the other prophets, Jesus submits to the Father and his word. Moses received God's word from a mount, and Jesus also delivered his Sermon on the Mount. And yet Jesus also speaks of being one with the Father, and instead of saying, "Thus says the LORD," as Moses and the other prophets did, Jesus in this famous sermon astonishes his hearers by speaking in the first person, as the lawgiver himself: "You have heard that it was said to those of old.... But I say to you ..." (Mt 5:21–22, 27–28, 31–32, 33–34, 38–39; 43–44). He is not only the ambassador, but the King; not only the messenger, but the Message. In proclaiming his everlasting kingdom in word and deed, he is actually inaugurating it within history.

2. Priest

The New Testament attributes Jesus' appointment as High Priest to a higher order than the one prescribed under the old covenant: namely, the Melchizedek priesthood, after the priest-king whom Abram recognized as his superior in Genesis 14:18–20 (cf. Ps 110:4; Heb 7:1–7) long before the giving of the law and therefore long before the Aaronic priesthood. In Hebrews 5–7 the argument is made that Jesus was installed as high priest "after the order of Melchizedek" (5:6, 10). The writer contrasts the Abrahamic covenant/Melchizedek priesthood and the Mosaic covenant/Levitical priesthood. The one covenant is an unchangeable oath sworn by God (Ps 110:4; Heb 7:21), while the other depends on the obedience and mediation of sinful human beings (Heb 7:11–13). "This makes Jesus the guarantor of a better covenant" (vv. 18–22). Thus, priesthood and covenant are inextricably connected; a change in one requires a change in the other. Or rather, since covenants cannot be amended, an inferior one must become "obsolete" in the inauguration of the superior one (8:13).

Christ's priesthood is therefore not grounded in history, but in eternity; not at Sinai, but in the heavenly Zion. Reference to the "unchangeable oath," with God himself (rather than Moses or angels) as Mediator, is further evidence of the eternal *covenant of redemption* between the persons of the Godhead. Therefore, the Son did not become the Mediator in his incarnation, but is the trustee of the elect from eternity to eternity.

Nevertheless, the Son did execute this office in history through his incarnation. Before we even arrive at his crucifixion, where the obvious sacrificial imagery is fulfilled, Christ's priestly service begins already in his birth and life. In Calvin's expression, "from the time when he took on the form of a servant, he began to pay the price of liberation in order to redeem us."[18] Not only in his death but already in his life his mission is "to fulfill all righteousness" (Mt 3:15; 5:17), to be "born of woman, born under the law, to redeem those who were under the law, so that we might receive adoption as sons" (Gal 4:4–5). Thus, Christ is not only the Mediator of the covenant of redemption, but the Servant of the *covenant of works*.

So significant was his life that Jesus could speak of the saving work that he had already accomplished prior to the crucifixion: "I glorified you on earth, having accomplished the work that you gave me to do" (Jn 17:4). He does this not only for himself, nor merely as a prerequisite for being the spotless sacrifice for sinners, but as a saving work in its own right: a federal or covenantal act of obedience: "And for their sake I consecrate myself, that they also may be sanctified in truth" (v. 19). In this way, he not only bears our sins on the cross in his passive obedience, but fulfills all righteousness in our place by his active obedience. Both of these aspects of Christ's work will be taken up in the next chapter.

3. King

The offices of prophet, priest, and king were sharply distinguished in Israel. The monarch could never assume liturgical duties in the temple, just as in general, the priest was neither a prophet nor a king. However, in Christ all of these offices are united in one person.

We have already encountered many of the significant passages concerning Christ's identity as the messianic King: Son of David, Son of Man, Son of God, the true and faithful servant of the covenant who drives the serpent from the garden of God and establishes a universal kingdom that will last forever. Psalm 2 celebrates the enthronement of the Son as the anointed Messiah-King on God's holy hill. Psalm 24 is a song of ascent—so-called

---

18. Calvin, *Institutes* 2.16.5.

because it was sung as Israel ascended the hill to the temple for its feasts. Who is worthy to stand on God's holy hill, in his presence? the Psalmist asks. The reply returns, "He who has clean hands and a pure heart, who does not lift up his soul to what is false and does not swear deceitfully" (v. 4). Properly speaking, this does not even describe King David, whom God kept from building the temple because of his blood-stained hands. If not David, then who of those singing this psalm on the ascent could hope to receive a welcoming reception by Yahweh, the Great King?

> Lift up your heads, O gates!
>> And be lifted up, O ancient doors,
>> that the King of glory may come in.
> Who is this King of glory?
>> The LORD, strong and mighty,
>> the LORD, mighty in battle. (Ps 24:7 – 8)

This song must have seemed strange to many of the original worshipers. It would appear that the only one who is worthy to ascend into God's holy presence is God himself: the King of Glory, Yahweh strong and mighty. Echoes of Eden again ring in our ears, with God entering his Sabbath throne of glory in victory after completing the work (trial) of creation, and Adam his image-bearer called to fulfill an analogous commission before entering the Sabbath day with him in triumph, with the whole creation in his train. Yahweh alone is worthy of receiving tribute, for he is the one who has vanquished Israel's enemies in battle, cleansing his own garden.

A similar song appears in Psalm 68, celebrating God's march through the wilderness in conquest, "though you men lie among the sheepfolds," fast asleep (v. 13a). God himself enters victoriously into the sanctuary: "You ascended on high, leading a host of captives in your train and receiving gifts among men, even among the rebellious, that the LORD God may dwell there" (v. 18). As we will see in the next chapter, these songs of ascent refer ultimately to the ascension of Jesus Christ as the "King of glory" who commands the gates of the heavenly Zion to open before his triumphal entry, with the redeemed in his train.

There is therefore no basis for separating Christ's office of Savior (priest) from his office of Lord (king). There is no choice to be made between Christ as Savior and Lord. In any case, we do not *make* him our personal Lord or Savior; it is because he *is* the Lord and Savior that he has become our priest-king. He reigns over sin and death. His royal lordship and his sacrificial service mutually define each other. As we have seen, the title *Son of Man* invokes the divine King of Daniel 7. Nevertheless, Jesus tells us by his words and deeds what true sovereignty means: "Even as the Son of Man came not to be served but to serve, and to give his life as a ransom for many" (Mt 20:28). Rulers are sometimes called upon to demand the blood of their subjects and citizens for the commonwealth, but this universal King willingly surrenders his own life and sheds his own blood to secure the liberty and life not of friends but of those who were his enemies. Never was there such a patriot, nor greater love of a greater King for an unfaithful realm. The next chapter focuses on the achievement through which Jesus fulfills this threefold office.

Key Terms

- Biblical titles: Messiah, Son of Man, Son of God, Servant, only begotten Son
- Christological heresies: Ebionitism, adoptionism, Docetism, Gnosticism, Subordinationism, Arianism/Semi-Arianism, Apollinarianism, monothelitism, monophysitism, Nestorianism
- kenotic Christology

Key Distinctions

- covenant of law/covenant of grace
- person/nature (Christology)

Key Questions

1. Discuss the place of Jesus in Israel's history, referring to his messianic titles.
2. How did the earliest Jewish believers come to confess Jesus as God?
3. "Two natures in one person" is the orthodox formula for Christ's person. Review the various heresies regarding the person of Christ. How does each one deviate from this formula?
4. Is it appropriate to speak of God dying on the cross, or should we attribute this only to Jesus? How would you defend your answer?
5. Does God change because of the incarnation?
6. What is Christ's threefold office? How is his priesthood grounded in the covenants of redemption, creation, and grace?
7. How does Christ's fulfillment of these three offices comfort you?

Chapter Eight

The Work of Christ

All of God's purposes intersect in Jesus Christ (2Co 1:20). Already in eternity he is the Mediator in the *covenant of redemption* that was made between the persons of the Trinity. As the Last Adam, he has fulfilled the *covenant of creation*. The law is not set aside, but is fully satisfied; the law's sentence against his coheirs has been borne fully by him, and because of his resurrection as the beginning of the new creation, its effects will be finally and forever removed "far as the curse is found." He dispenses the spoils of his victory by his Word and Spirit in the *covenant of grace*. All of the many other covenants in Scripture are in service to the eternal covenant of redemption, executed in time through the covenant of creation (fulfilled by Christ) and the covenant of grace (delivered in Christ by the Word and Spirit). The plot that unfolds from Adam to Abraham turns on the mysterious identity of the Last Adam and Abraham's seed in whom all the nations will be blessed.

Therefore, we should be wary of allowing Christ's person and his work to float apart from each other, as if they were quite different topics. Christ's identity is "Mediator" from eternity to eternity, at least in terms of the decree. Mary is told that her son will be named Jesus, "Yahweh Saves!" Jesus Christ is Lord and Savior: the Anointed King (Messiah). So who he is and what he does are inseparable. Indeed, weak views of Christ's person are always grounded in weak views of his work. Bearing this in mind, we focus now on the latter.

I. The Life of Jesus: Active Obedience

There is a tendency sometimes to treat the incarnation merely as the necessary precondition for the saving work of Christ—namely, his death and resurrection. In truth, it is the Son's assumption of our nature that is the beginning of our salvation. His life is as essential to our salvation as his death and resurrection. In his obedience, we finally have a representative human being who has fulfilled the goal of our creation.

While Adam and Israel demanded the perishable food they craved rather than obeying the will of God, one of our own brothers is able to say without hypocrisy, "My food is to do the will of him who sent me and to accomplish his work" (Jn 4:34). "I glorified you on earth, having accomplished the work that you gave me to do. And now, Father, glorify me in your own presence with the glory that I had with you before the world existed" (Jn 17:4–5). Forever, into eternity, God the Son is a human being, reigning not only as God but as the faithful shepherd-king that Adam and Israel's kings refused to be.

Crucial as background for the priestly service of Christ in his life and death are the sacrifices commanded in the Old Testament. There are various sacrifices, each with its own purpose and material element. Yet they may be grouped generally under two broad types: *thank offerings* and *guilt (or sin) offerings*. The first could also be called a tribute offering, since once again the relationship between suzerain (great king) and vassal (servant) is emphasized. Like a tax (or tithe), the tribute offering was, more than anything else, an acknowledgment from every subject and from the vassal-nation corporately that they owed their prosperity and security to the suzerain (great king or emperor). God created human beings to lead the cosmic choir in an unending hymn of thanksgiving. The whole of life was meant to be doxological: an expression of praise, thanksgiving, and worship. In fact, Paul describes the fall in terms of a transition from thanksgiving to ingratitude, which bears the fruit of foolishness and futility (Ro 1:21). Before the fall, the only appropriate response to God was a thank offering, as a token of the whole life of gratitude. This thank offering was the fruit of the ground, a tithe or firstfruits, a way of acknowledging that the earth is the Lord's and that he provides everything we need. Those who gave the thank offering were reminded that they were not the masters of their own fate. Rather than hoarding the wealth of a world of scarcity, they were to delight together in the abundance they had received from God's hand.

After the fall, God could have left humanity mired in its guilt, but instead he promised his gospel (Ge 3:15) and confirmed it by replacing their own cover-up clothes with the skins of animals that he had sacrificed for them (Ge 3:21). *It was no longer sufficient to bring the thank offering now.* The guilt offering was also needed, the worshiper's acknowledgment of guilt and the divine provision for its transfer to the sacrificial animal—as faith in "the Lamb of God, who takes away the sin of the world" (Jn 1:29). Now we can see the significance of the religious war between Cain and Abel. "In the course of time Cain brought to the LORD an offering of the fruit of the ground, and Abel also brought of the firstborn of his flock and of their fat portions. And the LORD had regard for Abel and his offering, but for Cain and his offering he had no regard" (Ge 4:3–5). And the rest, as they say, is history.

Jesus identified Abel as the first martyr for the faith (Mt 23:35). We are also told, "By faith Abel offered to God a more acceptable sacrifice than Cain, through which he was commended as righteous, God commending him by accepting his gifts. And through his faith, though he died, he still speaks" (Heb 11:4). By offering the guilt sacrifice, Abel was acknowledging his transgressions and his trust in a redeemer. His act of making the offering did not justify him, but it witnessed to his justification that he possessed through faith in Christ. And that is why, "through his faith, though he died, he still speaks." Every time he brought the acceptable sacrifice he was proclaiming the gospel, and does so still today every time his story is told. It is not going too far to suggest that Cain, by contrast, was the first "Pelagian."[1] Cain might perhaps pay his membership dues (the thank or tribute offering) in the covenant of creation, but he failed to acknowledge that he stood guilty of violating that covenant and needed to be transferred into the covenant of grace. Cain did not believe that a bloody atonement offering for his guilt was *needed*. This is the oldest and most perennial heresy, the default setting of our fallen heart. It may seem reverent for us to tip our hat in perfunctory gratitude to God, perhaps even tithing to the church and performing various duties, but we innately resist acknowledging our radical guilt and our need for God's equally radical forgiveness. This was precisely the problem that Jesus identified in the religious leaders of his day, whom he linked to the spiritual line of Cain in the passage cited above.

---

1. As a reminder, Pelagianism (named after the fourth-century monk Pelagius) taught (and teaches) that we are not born in original sin and can therefore save ourselves by keeping God's law. Christ's death is therefore not a guilt offering; rather, Jesus serves primarily as a moral example. Although seeds of resurgent Pelagianism were evident in the medieval church, they came to full flower in radical Protestantism, especially Socinianism, the Enlightenment, and Unitarianism.

Genesis 4 therefore grounds the sacrificial system commanded by God at Mount Sinai in the history of creation, fall, and redemption. It is not just Israel, but humankind in general, that needs this guilt offering, as the sacrificial rites of diverse religions attest. Yet not even the guilt offerings commanded in the law could actually take away the guilt and tyranny of sin. They could only serve as a shadow—a placeholder, if you will—for the coming Lamb.

This point is elaborated extensively in Hebrews. Although the annual sacrifice covered over guilt for the time being (the Hebrew word *kipper*, translated *atone*, means "cover over"), "in these sacrifices there is a reminder of sins every year" (Heb 10:3). The conscience is never freed from its bondage to the fear of condemnation and death. "For it is impossible for the blood of bulls and goats to take away sins" (Heb 10:4). The writer places Psalm 40 on Jesus' lips:

Consequently, when Christ came into the world, he said,
"Sacrifices and offerings you have not desired,
     but a body you have prepared for me;
in burnt offerings and sin offerings
     you have taken no pleasure.
Then I said, 'Behold, I have come to do your will, O God,
     As it is written of me in the scroll of the book.'" (Heb 10:5–7)

The writer explains,

When he said above, "You have neither desired nor taken pleasure in sacrifices and offerings and burnt offerings and sin offerings" (these are offered according to the law), then he added, "Behold I have come to do your will." He does away with the first [the old covenant sacrificial system] in order to establish the second [his own obedience]. And by that will we have been sanctified through the offering of the body of Jesus Christ once for all. (Heb 10:8–10)

The point made here is clear, but there are at least two parts to the argument. First, the only reason that God commanded and accepted these animal sacrifices was in lieu of the only sacrifice that can truly remove guilt. Acknowledging their guilt and their need for a substitute, worshipers were looking to Christ through these types and shadows. Hence, they were, like us, justified through faith in Christ, as chapter 11 of Hebrews emphasizes. Second, what we need is not only something (or rather, someone) greater than animal sacrifices, but something greater than even a *guilt* offering. Our salvation requires nothing less than the complete, perpetual, personal *obedience* for which God created humankind.

Even in our own experience as parents, we know how rewarding it is to see our children do the right thing, without nagging or threatening but simply as a mature response of loving gratitude. We may take some pleasure in forgiving them, but forgiveness always highlights a breach of trust. What fills us with delight is when they build our trust by intentional obedience. As Hebrews 10:8–10 explains, in Psalm 40 itself God contrasts the guilt offerings of animals not with the guilt offering of Christ, but with Christ's offering of himself as a *living* sacrifice—a thank offering that is never interrupted by the need for a guilt offering. Psalm 40 does not contrast the guilt offerings with Christ's death but with his life: "Then I said, '*Here I am*—it is written about me in the scroll—I have come *to do your will*, O God'" (Heb 10:7, paraphrase; emphasis added). This is what is meant by the *active obedience* of Christ. Jesus comes not only to bear our sins, but to fulfill all righteousness on our behalf. And then he offers himself as a guilt offering. "For by a single offering he has perfected for all time those who are being sanctified" (Heb 10:14). Jesus not only brings atonement (covering over), but forgiveness of sins. "Where there is forgiveness of these, there is no longer any offering for sin" (v. 18). Thus, the guilt offering is finished. Jesus is the sacrifice to end all sacrifices.

So the thank offering (fulfillment of the covenant of creation) and the guilt offering (bearing our curses for having violated it) converge in Christ's priestly office. Since "there is no longer any offering for sin," all that is left for us is the sacrifice of praise—the thank offering. Even here, the *perfect* living sacrifice of praise has been offered up to God on our behalf. We need not be paralyzed by the fear of falling short; we do and will fall short of Christ's covenantal obedience. However, none of that matters finally. God has in his Son that righteous life and justice-satisfying sacrifice that his holiness requires of us. Forgiveness is not enough, since it merely clears the slate and cancels the debts; God requires a living sacrifice of positive obedience. It is precisely this full and joyful obedience that he has in Jesus Christ, and this righteousness is imputed to us in justification. On this basis, justification is not merely forgiveness ("just-as-if-I'd-never-sinned"), but God's crediting us with Christ's fulfillment of the law.

Far from inhibiting good works, this freedom is the only source of the Spirit's fruit. Not even the sinfulness clinging to our best works can keep our grateful obedience from bringing pleasure to God, who is now our Father rather than our Judge. "I appeal to you therefore, brothers, by the mercies of God, to present your bodies as a *living sacrifice*, holy and acceptable to God, which is your spiritual worship" (Ro 12:1, emphasis added).

Discipleship under Jesus is no longer even remotely involved with offering any of our own sacrifices or works of atonement, but only of grateful living in the joy of the God of our salvation. At last, it is not dead sacrifices for guilt, but the living sacrifice of thanksgiving, that Jesus inaugurates for his coheirs in a world that lies under the bondage of fear and death. Guilt drives us to Christ for grace, and grace drives us out to our neighbors in grateful love and service.

II. The Death of Jesus: Passive Obedience

Much of what has already been said above introduces Christ's death for sinners. Especially when distinguished from "active," "passive" here may give the impression that Jesus was a helpless victim in this aspect of his work. Nothing could be further from the truth, as we will see below. From the Latin *passio*, *passive* means "suffering" (as in "the passion of Christ"). So what we are really talking about when we refer to the **passive obedience** of Christ is his suffering obedience, his willing submission to death for our sakes.

The New Testament — both the Gospels and the Epistles — is incomprehensible apart from the recognition that it is a collection of Jewish texts, the fulfillment of the laws and prophecies that God gave to Israel. George Hunsinger observes, "The blood of Christ is repugnant to the Gentile mind, whether ancient or modern."[2] Answering Jesus' question to Peter, "Who do people say that I am?" Gentiles are not likely to give the same answers that Peter related, much less the one that he himself gave: "You are the Christ, the Son of the living God." Answering this question without going back to the Old Testament is like imagining that we could explain a film's plot by walking into the theater in the middle of the movie.

Already in 1 Corinthians the apostle realized that the gospel is "folly to Greeks" because its message was not "wisdom" in the ordinary philosophical and ethical sense, but "Christ crucified." Our native "Pelagianism," which we have traced all the way back to Cain, lives on in our modern world, where it has only gained strength. Natural theology tells us that wisdom is found in law, techniques, and good examples and instructions to follow in order to live the good life. But according to Paul, the highest "wisdom" is found in Christ's substitutionary death for our sins.

In the Middle Ages, Abelard (1079 – 1142) contested the prevailing view

---

2. George Hunsinger, *Disruptive Grace: Studies in the Theology of Karl Barth* (Grand Rapids: Eerdmans, 2000), 16.

> ## Key Distinction:
> ### active/passive (obedience of Christ)
>
> Christ's lifelong fulfillment of all righteousness (active obedience) is imputed or credited to believers, while their sins are imputed to Christ in his death (passive obedience).

that Christ's death was a substitutionary sacrifice that satisfied God's justice and turned aside his wrath. Ultimately, Abelard's objection was grounded in his doctrine of God. For the apostles, God's nature is one. None of his attributes trumps others. No matter how loving God is, he cannot set aside his righteousness, justice, and holiness. Because of who he is, he must pour out his wrath on transgressors of his covenant. The good news is not that God is so loving that he ignores our sin, but that "God put forward [Christ] as a propitiation by his blood, to be received by faith.... It was to show his righteousness at the present time, *so that he might be just and the justifier* of the one who has faith in Jesus" (Ro 3:25–26, emphasis added). For Abelard, however, all of God's attributes must surrender to his love. Thus, all that was left to say about Christ's work at the cross was that he demonstrated God's love and that this demonstration should move us to repentance, following Christ's example. It is our repentance, then, and not Christ's work, that serves as the basis for our acceptance before God. This is a subjective view of Christ's work: namely, that it changes *our* attitude toward God, not *God's* attitude toward sinners.

Again, we see that this view reflects a Pelagian assumption of moral ability after the fall. Furthermore, it opens the door to an Arian Christology. If we are basically good people who have lost our way, we require no more than a special messenger from God to get us back on the right path. A divine deliverer is hardly necessary; we need only a superior human being to follow. It was just this step that was taken by the Socinians in the Reformation era. Their views, in substance, formed the working theology of many Enlightenment philosophers, such as Kant.[3] Sharing the same basic assumptions, Protestant liberalism can be generally characterized as Socinian (combining the Arian and Pelagian heresies). More recently, renewed criticism of sacrifice-and-substitution has appeared in Protestant (including

---

3. Kant, *Religion and Rational Theology*, in *The Cambridge Edition of the Works of Immanuel Kant* (ed. and trans. Allen W. Wood, George di Giovanni, et al.; Cambridge: Cambridge Univ. Press, 1996), 76–97, 104–45.

evangelical) circles as well, especially through resurgent Arminian and Anabaptist theologies.[4]

Besides philosophical and theological factors, contemporary reactions are fueled by a transformation in cultural conceptions of justice. The very idea of penal (i.e., punishment-bearing) **satisfaction** is receding in legal theory, in favor of a therapeutic-managerial ideal of social education. This perspective holds that criminals ought not to be punished, as satisfaction of the claims of justice, but need to be rehabilitated and reformed. I will not enter into that complicated debate here, nor will I dismiss the importance of rehabilitation. Yet regardless of whether there are other interests to be pursued in criminal law, it is a plain fact that the penal aspect—satisfaction of justice—has been increasingly diminished in our culture. This reflects a wider cultural transformation, summarized by Philip Rieff in *The Triumph of the Therapeutic* (University of Chicago Press, 1987). Sociologist Christian Smith even recently characterized American spirituality as "moralistic, therapeutic deism."[5]

This is not to dismiss thoughtful criticism of traditional atonement doctrine, but it is important to remind ourselves that there are cultural reasons why we find the traditional doctrine difficult to believe. With the rise of modernity, humanity has replaced God at the center. Now, if it is admitted that God (or a higher power) exists, the purpose of such existence must surely be to ensure our "life, liberty, and the pursuit of happiness." It is perfectly reasonable to expect such a human-centered deity to provide moral direction and perhaps even to offer correction—so that we will be happy. However, any concept of a God who is independent of the world and whose righteousness, holiness, and justice are as essential as his love; a God who therefore must pass sentence on the guilty; and a human race that is individually and

---

4. Anabaptists emphasized the example of Christ over his substitution, and some contemporary Anabaptists argue that the traditional view legitimizes violence, grounding it in God. See Anthony W. Bartlett, *Cross Purposes: The Violent Grammar of Christian Atonement* (Harrisburg, Pa.: Trinity Press International, 2001); Robert Hamerton-Kelly, *Sacred Violence: Paul's Hermeneutic of the Cross* (Philadelphia: Fortress, 1992); Denny Weaver, *The Nonviolent Atonement* (Grand Rapids: Eerdmans, 2001). These scholars share much in common also with liberation and feminist critiques, such as Rosemary Radford Ruether, *Introducing Redemption in Christian Feminism* (Sheffield, UK: Sheffield Academic, 1998); Joanne Carlson Brown and Rebecca Parker, "For God So Loved the World?," in *Christianity, Patriarchy and Abuse: A Feminist Critique* (ed. Joanne Carlson Brown and Carole R. Bohn; New York: Pilgrim Press, 1989). Following this critique, some, like Brian McLaren and Stephen Chalke, characterize the sacrificial view as "cosmic child abuse." From its inception, Arminianism has represented a broad range of responses, from an explicit rejection of substitution-sacrifice (in favor of moral influence and governmental theories, as in Hugo Grotius, Charles Finney, John Wiley, and Clark Pinnock) to its warm embrace (as in Arminius, Wesley, and Roger Olson).

5. Christian Smith and Melinda Lundquist Denton, *Soul Searching: The Religious and Spiritual Lives of America's Teenagers* (New York: Oxford Univ. Press, 2005), 118–71.

corporately guilty of death strikes most people in Western societies today as not only wrong but inconceivable.

With these challenges in mind, we begin with a biblical-theological exploration of the atonement and then briefly engage alternative views.

A. The Cross in Scripture

At Mount Sinai, Moses delivered the covenant to the people, with its commands and sanctions: long life in the land for obedience and the threat of being cut off, exiled from the land of the living, for disobedience. "We will do everything the LORD has said," the people replied. To seal the covenant Moses sprinkled blood on the people "in accordance with all these words" (Ex 24:7–8). Israel did not fulfill its commission and was exiled from the temporal and typological garden of God. "For thus says the LORD: Your hurt is incurable, and your wound is grievous. There is none to uphold your cause, no medicine for your wound, no healing for you" (Jer 30:12–13). There is nothing that the covenant people can do to reconcile themselves to God. They are not sick, but, like the Gentiles, "dead in your trespasses and sins" (Eph 2:1).

And yet once again God promises a new covenant that will not be "like the covenant that [he] made with their fathers" at Sinai. It will be dependent on his performance rather than theirs. In this new covenant God will renew their hearts and join them to himself: "for I will forgive their iniquity, and I will remember their sin no more" (Jer 31:31–34). After finishing the Passover meal in the upper room in Jerusalem, Jesus took bread and said, " 'Take, eat; this is my body.' And he took a cup, and when he had given thanks he gave it to them, saying, 'Drink from it, all of you, for this is my blood of the covenant, which is poured out for many for the forgiveness of sins' " (Mt 26:26–28). Christ will offer himself up to death in order to put into effect the "last will and testament" that makes his brothers and sisters coheirs of his estate. In the upper room, Jesus in effect splashes the blood upon himself, bearing the curse that lies upon his people, drinking the cup of wrath so that they may drink the cup of salvation.

1. Lamb of God: sacrifice and satisfaction

Blood atonement lies at the heart both of the wonder and of the offense of the Christian proclamation. Instead of offering a bloody sacrifice for sin, Cain shed the innocent blood of his brother out of jealousy. God threatened to strike Moses dead for delaying his son's circumcision because of his Midianite wife Zipporah's disapproval of the bloody rite. Just in time, though, Zipporah herself "took a flint and cut off her son's foreskin and touched Moses' feet with it and said, 'Surely you are a bridegroom of blood to me!'" However, God "let him alone" (Ex 4:24–26). God passed over the houses of his people when he saw the blood on the doorpost, as he had commanded. Priests in the temple were covered with blood from head to toe during their atonement ministry. "Indeed, under the law almost everything is purified in blood, and without the shedding of blood there is no forgiveness of sins" (Heb 9:22).

This is not an arbitrary command of a bloodthirsty deity. Rather, it belongs to the covenantal context of God's law. God's wrath is an expression of his righteous judgment, and blood is shorthand for the whole life of the person that God requires of transgressors: "For the life of every creature is its blood: its blood is its life" (Lev 17:14).

Substitution is made vividly explicit in a priest's act of laying his hands on the head of the sacrifice, transferring guilt from the offerer (Lev 1:4; 4:20–35; cf. 5:10; 6:7; 16:7, 21–22; 17:11). The burnt offering—singled out for atonement—was to be either from the flock or the herd, but in either case "a male without blemish" (Lev 1:3). Further, the priest would sprinkle the blood of the sin offering on the altar and mercy seat, which covered the treaty tablets in the ark of the covenant. "Thus the priest shall make atonement on your behalf, and you shall be forgiven" (4:30–31 NRSV; cf. 16:21–27).

The Old Testament not only foreshadows Christ's sacrifice by its Levitical system but points, through the words of the prophets, to the Suffering Servant. Most famously, in Isaiah 53 the Servant is the bearer of the iniquities of those whom he represents, and then is exalted in glory. From the very beginning of his ministry, Jesus' mission was marked, as John the Baptist announced, "Look, the Lamb of God, who takes away the sin of the world!" (Jn 1:29).

In the series of actions that Jesus performs on the Temple Mount that will lead to his crucifixion, he assumes the role of the temple itself: forgiving sins directly, to the outrage of the religious leaders. Proclaiming himself the true temple, cursing the fig tree, and casting the religious leaders in the role of antagonists who will deliver him up to death even as they did the prophets since Abel (Mt 21–22), Jesus pronounces his curses upon the scribes and Pharisees (chap. 23), laments over Jerusalem (23:37–39), and predicts the destruction of the temple and the coming of the Son of Man in glory to judge the nations (chaps. 24–25). Jesus' roles of prophet, priest, and king converge in these words and deeds on the Temple Mount after his triumphal entry.

Instead of reviving Israel's national hopes for a reinstitution of the theocracy, centering on the temple, Jesus brings about the end of the old age and the beginning of the new. N. T. Wright observes at this point that even in his ministry, Jesus "regularly acted as if he were able to bypass the Temple system in offering forgiveness to all and sundry right where they were."[6] "'When you make his life an offering for sin' [Isaiah 53:10] by the first century was certainly taken to refer to a sacrifice."[7] But Jesus also saw his death as a battle and the victory of God.[8] All of these themes are brought together in a fully orbed atonement doctrine, as we will see. In Christ's flesh, both his life and his death, we have a thank offering that restores what we owed to God's law—a fragrant life well pleasing to the Lord—and a guilt offering that propitiates God's wrath.

Israel's sacrificial system of guilt offerings, the prophetic anticipation of the Suffering Servant, and the main narrative and doctrinal themes of the New Testament converge in the concept of **penal substitution.** From the Latin word for "penalty" (*poena*), it reflects the church's proper recognition that Christ's sacrifice was the payment of a debt to divine justice in our place. It is impossible to understand the New Testament terms *anti* and *hyper* (in place of) as intending anything other than a substitution: Christ in the place of sinners; the guiltless for the guilty; the righteous for the unrighteous. "For our sake [God] made him to be sin who knew no sin so that in him we might become the righteousness of God" (2Co 5:21). The penal aspect is evident in the phrase "made sin" (Greek, *harmartian epoiēsen*), and its substitutionary aspect in the words "for us" (*hyper hēmōn*). He "suffered for sins once for all, the righteous for the unrighteous" (1Pe 3:18), "suffered for you" (*hyper hymōn*, 2:21), "bore ... sins in his body on the tree" (2:24). He was made a "curse for us" (Gal 3:13) and was "offered once to take away the sins of many" (Heb 9:28).

Just as the sacrificial system was at the heart of Israel's worship, Christ's sacrificial death was at the heart of his self-consciousness. In his anticipation of arrival at Jerusalem, he repeatedly refers to his impending death and resurrection (Mk 8:31–33; 9:30–32; 10:32–35), although in each instance the disciples do not understand and grow impatient with Jesus' talk of crucifixion. After his triumphal entry into Jerusalem, which buoys the disciples' anticipation of imminent glory, Jesus says, "Now my soul is troubled. And what should I say—'Father, save me from this hour'? No, *it is for this reason that I have come to this hour*. Father, glorify your name." Not for his sake

---

6. N. T. Wright, *Jesus and the Victory of God* (Minneapolis: Fortress, 1996), 605.
7. Ibid.
8. Ibid., 606–10.

but for theirs, the voice from heaven declares, "I have glorified it, and I will glorify it again." "Now is the judgment of this world; now will the ruler of this world will be cast out," Jesus explains. "'And I, when I am lifted up from the earth, will draw all people to myself.' He said this to show by what kind of death he was going to die" (Jn 12:27–33, emphasis added).

In instituting the Last Supper, Jesus gives central place to his role as the substitutionary sacrifice who will save his people by his blood (1Co 11:24; Lk 22:19–20). He gives his flesh for the life of the world (Jn 6:51). He "laid down his life for us" (1Jn 3:16), was given up for us (Ro 8:32; Eph 5:2), died for us (Ro 5:8), for our sins (1Co 15:3), as "a ransom for all" (1Ti 2:6), gave himself up for the church (Eph 5:25), came to "give his life as a ransom for many" (Mt 20:28; Mk 10:45). The goal of the substitution is that "in him we might become the righteousness of God" (2Co 5:21) and be brought to God (1Pe 3:18). He carried away our sins into the wilderness.

The New Testament sees these Old Testament sacrifices as prefiguring Christ's work — not only his death and resurrection but his faithful life — as the shadow is related to the substance or type to fulfillment (Col 2:17; Heb 9:23–24; 10:1; 13:11–12; 2Co 5:21; Gal 3:13; 1Jn 1:7). The Christian claim is that Jesus is "the Lamb of God, who takes away the sin of the world" (Jn 1:29); he is "our Passover" (1Co 5:7; cf. 1Pe 1:19). Circumcision was a partial cutting-off, to spare the whole person. Yet it is because Jesus was cut off in his circumcision-death, not only in the foreskin but in his whole person, that we go free (Col 2:11–15).

While the law announces only condemnation to Jew and Gentile alike, "now the righteousness of God has been manifested apart from the law, although the Law and the Prophets bear witness to it — the righteousness of God through faith in Jesus Christ for all who believe" (Ro 3:20–22a). Christ's death brings peace with God (5:1, 6–10). Of first importance in the gospel is "that Christ died for our sins in accordance with the Scriptures" (1Co 15:3). He "loved us and gave himself up for us, a fragrant offering and sacrifice to God" (Eph 5:2), "and he is the propitiation for our sins" (1Jn 2:2; cf. 4:10). Jesus summarized his own mission in terms of the sacrificial motif: "The Son of Man came not to be served but to serve and to give his life as a ransom for many" (Mk 10:45). "I am the good shepherd [of Ezekiel 34]. The good shepherd lays down his life for the sheep" (Jn 10:11). Nothing was more central to Jesus' own understanding of his mission than his priesthood, which would render him both vicar and victim.

Peter adds his testimony to the expiatory nature of Christ's death: "He himself bore our sins in his body on the cross, so that, free from sins, we might live for righteousness; by his wounds you have been healed" (1Pe 2:24). "For Christ also suffered for sins once for all, the righteous for the unrighteous, in order to bring you to God" (3:18). Just as all who looked to the brass serpent in the wilderness were healed from the bites of venomous snakes, all who look to Jesus Christ are saved (Mk 10:45; Jn 3:14–15; 1Pe 2:24).

Throughout the Gospels and Epistles we discover references to redemption through "the blood of Christ" (Mt 26:27–28 and parallels; Ac 20:28; 1Co 11:25; Eph 5:2; 1Pe 1:2, 19). As the only atoning sacrifice that truly avails in the heavenly courtroom, it is not only sufficient but final. *Hapax* or *ephapax* (once and for all) appears repeatedly throughout Hebrews (Heb 9:12, 26, 28; 10:10). Christ's sacrifice is successful because of the superiority of the one who offers and is offered (Heb 1:1–2:18; 3:1–6; 4:14–16).

All three persons of the Trinity are involved in this sacrifice: the Father gives his only Son out of his love (Jn 3:16); the Spirit sustains him in his grief and vindicates him in his resurrection. The Son himself is not an unwilling victim of divine or human violence, as many critics of sacrificial atonement suggest.

We have to admit that some rather crude presentations of the gospel have provided fodder for this misunderstanding. When the Father is regarded as the angry judge who takes out his frustrations on his passive and loving Son, we do indeed have something like cosmic child abuse. However, this is not the biblical story. Rather, the Father acted out of love, both for his Son and for sinners, and the Son joyfully embraced his mediatorial office in the eternal covenant of redemption. God did not first demand satisfaction and then love, but was moved by his love to send his Son to make satisfaction. Calvin's citation from Augustine on this point is an excellent summary: "For it was not after we were reconciled to him through the blood of his Son that he began to love us. Rather, he has loved us before the world was created."[9]

At the cross, therefore, we do not see an angry Father taking out his anger on a helpless Son. Rather, the Father "so loved the world, that he gave his only Son" (Jn 3:16), and the Son, for his part, embraced his vocation as a terrifying means to the end of reconciling sinners to God. From the day of his baptism, when Jesus first heard the benediction of the Father and the Spirit on his new creation ministry, he knew that he was executing the plan of redemption together with the Father and the Spirit. Irenaeus taught that Christ's entire life was a recapitulation (lit., "reheadshiping") of Adam's race. Echoing Irenaeus,

---

9. Calvin, *Institutes* 2.16.4.

Calvin observed, "In short, from the time when he took on the form of a servant, he began to pay the price of liberation in order to redeem us."[10]

The Good Shepherd himself says that *he* lays down his life for the sheep, adding, "No one takes it from me, but I lay it down of my own accord. I have power to lay it down, and I have power to take it up again" (Jn 10:18). While those involved in carrying out the execution, both Jews and Gentiles, can be blamed in one sense, ultimately they did "whatever [God's] hand and [God's] plan had predestined to take place" (Ac 4:28). As "a lamb without defect or blemish," Peter declares, "He was destined before the foundation of the world, but was revealed at the end of the ages for your sake" (1Pe 1:19–20 NRSV).

Jesus, "for the joy that was set before him endured the cross, despising its shame, and is seated at the right hand of the throne of God" (Heb 12:2). He is a willing sacrifice (Jn 10:11, 18; cf. Mt 16:23; Lk 9:51; Jn 4:34; Heb 10:5–10), knowing that his suffering will lead to glory not only for him but for his people. And yet it is an agonizing struggle (Lk 12:50; Mk 10:38). Jesus sees it as a baptism (Lk 12:50). "He learned obedience through what he suffered," even with "loud cries and tears" (Heb 5:7–10). Yet in spite of his grief, he determines, "Shall I not drink the cup that the Father has given me?" (Jn 18:11). His obedience undoes Adam's disobedience (Ro 5:12–21). The cross itself was far from a joy, but he endured it for the joy that lay beyond it. The fact that the Father did not reply to Jesus' agonizing question in Gethsemane demonstrates that there was no other way, and Jesus embraced it. Thus, apart from the vicarious sacrifice of Christ, there is no salvation.

To the sacrificial imagery is added the economic analogy of **ransom** or **redeem**: we were slaves whom God bought back (*agorazō, exagorazō, lytroō*; cf. noun redemption: *apolytrōsis, antilytron*) in order to liberate us and reconcile us to himself. Where such terms appear, they are in the context of redemption from sin: its curse and tyranny. The price is paid in the marketplace (Mt 20:28; Mk 10:45; Ro 3:24; Eph 1:7; Col 1:13–14; Tit 2:14; Heb 9:12; 1Pe 1:18–19). Because this price is paid to God's justice, it frees us from the evil powers that hold us in bondage—especially Satan. However, the price is paid to God's justice rather than to Satan. Christ is the redeemer who buys back his people by paying their debt at the highest personal price (Ac 20:28; 1Co 6:20; 7:23).

Closely related to penal substitution is **propitiation. Expiation** takes away the guilt, while propitiation appeases God's wrath provoked by it. From the

---

10. Ibid., 2.16.5.

Greek verb *hilaskomai* and its cognate noun *hilastērion, propitiation* refers to the necessity for the satisfaction of God's justice. Because God is holy and righteous, he cannot overlook transgression (Ex 34:7; Nu 14:18; Ps 5:4–6; Na 1:2–3). "For the wrath of God is revealed from heaven against all ungodliness and unrighteousness of men, who by their unrighteousness suppress the truth" (Ro 1:18). Propitiation, therefore, focuses on God's relationship to the sinner. God must be just in his justification of sinners (Ro 3:25–26).

God's wrath is not arbitrary or capricious but is the necessary response to the violation of his justice, righteousness, holiness, and goodness. God is not essentially full of wrath, but is only stirred to anger in the presence of sin. God is not "bloodthirsty," like the violent deities of ancient paganism. Rather, he is righteous, and his law requires that "the wages of sin is death" (Ro 6:23). "But now apart from law the righteousness of God has been made known, to which the law and the prophets testify. This righteousness is given through faith in Jesus Christ to all who believe" (3:21–22). Although "all have sinned and fall short of the glory of God," Paul adds, now they "are justified by his grace as a gift, through the redemption that is in Christ Jesus, whom God put forward as a propitiation [*hilastērion*] by his blood, to be received by faith" (Ro 3:21–25).

The result of God's just wrath being satisfied is **reconciliation** (reconcile: *katallassō*; reconciliation: *katallagē*). Just as we are first of all passive subjects of God's wrath before God is propitiated, we are passive subjects of God's reconciliation at the cross. We do not reconcile ourselves to God; God reconciles himself to us and us to him. Paul especially emphasizes this point in Romans 5. Perhaps on rare occasions someone might die for a righteous person. "But God shows his love for us in that while we still were sinners, Christ died for us. Since, therefore, we have now been justified by his blood, much more shall we be saved by him from the wrath of God. For if while we were enemies we were reconciled to God by the death of his Son, much more, now that we are reconciled, shall we be saved by his life." We boast in Christ, "through whom we have now received reconciliation" (Ro 5:7–11). Central to the gospel's announcement, then, is the fact that "in Christ God was reconciling the world to himself, not counting their trespasses against them, and entrusting to us the message of reconciliation.... For our sake he made him to be sin who knew no sin, so that in him we might become the righteousness of God" (2Co 5:19, 21). The Old Testament background here is the transition from a state of war to a state of peace (*shalôm*), a kingdom in which only righteousness dwells. This transition is not only the lifting of the covenant's curses but the positive harmony between erstwhile foes (Ro 5:10–11; Col 1:19–20; Eph 2:11–22, especially v. 14; 2Co 5:18–21).

2. Conquering liberator: victory over the powers

In Scripture, sacrificial, judicial, and economic images of Christ's atoning work combine with those of the battlefield. Christ's cross is a *military conquest*. Christ is King not only in his resurrection and ascension but already at the cross—precisely at the place where Satan and his principalities and powers of death think that they have triumphed. The event that appears in the eyes of the world to display God's weakness and the failure of Jesus to establish his kingdom is actually God's mightiest deed in all of history. Jesus is **Christus Victor**.

Throughout redemptive revelation, from the promise of the serpent-defeating seed of the woman in Genesis 3, the plot turns on the war between Satan with his human followers and Yahweh with his covenant people, as attempts are made all along the way to extinguish the ancestral line leading to the Messiah. All of this comes to a head in Satan's persecution of the church, filled with rage that his time is short and his kingdom is being looted by the one over whom he thought he triumphed at the cross (Rev 12).

This war between the serpent and the seed of the woman looms large across Jesus' whole life and ministry, as he casts out demons, heals the sick, reconciles outcasts to himself, and announces the arrival of his kingdom. The real conquest is now underway. What Adam and Israel failed to do—namely, drive the serpent from God's holy garden and extend his reign to the ends of the earth—the Last Adam and True Israel accomplishes once and for all. The serpent's head is crushed, and the powers of evil are disarmed (Ro 16:20; Col 2:14–15). Death and hell no longer have the last word. Oppressors and those who perpetrate violence, injustice, and suffering throughout the earth have been delivered their own death warrant. In the meantime, it is a time of grace—when enemies are reconciled and even Satan's coconspirators can be forgiven, justified, and renewed as part of God's new creation.[11]

From this brief survey it is evident that Christ's priestly work on the cross is more than a vicarious (substitutionary) sacrifice for sinners. However, it is not less. In fact, apart from this aspect, none of the other marvelous consequences has any basis. Various **atonement theories** have been formulated in church history.[12] It is true, as we have seen, that Christ's active obedience is a **recapitulation** of Adam's aborted trial. Reformed (covenant) theology shares close affinities with the emphasis of Irenaeus on Christ's work as recapitula-

---

11. On this important aspect of Christ's reconciliation in this time between the times, see especially Miroslav Volf, *Exclusion and Embrace: A Theological Exploration of Identity, Otherness, and Reconciliation* (Nashville: Abingdon, 1996).

12. For a survey of these views, see Michael Horton, *The Christian Faith* (Grand Rapids: Zondervan, 2011), 501–9.

tion. However, as Irenaeus himself clearly held, Christ's sacrificial death is as important as his vicarious life. The cross is also a triumph over powers and principalities, especially death. Yet not even death is the ultimate source of our woes. "The sting of death is sin, and the power of sin is the law" (1Co 15:56). Death is the sentence for a guilty verdict, and only when a different verdict is rendered can death lose its power. According to Colossians 2:13–15, Christ's death was a victory over the powers only because in it he bears away the guilt for sin, "canceling the record of debt that stood against us with its legal demands ... nailing it to the cross." As we have seen above, Jesus himself said of his impending death as our sacrifice, "It is for this reason that I have come to this hour." Yet by offering himself in our place for sin, he accomplishes much more: "Now is the judgment of this world; now the ruler of this world will be driven out," Jesus explained. "'And I, when I am lifted up from the earth, will draw all people to myself.' He said this to indicate the kind of death he was to die" (Jn 12:27–33 NRSV). So clearly, there is more to Christ's death than penal substitution, but precisely because penal substitution lies at its heart.

However, when penal substitution is denied, we are left with subjective theories that reduce Christ's work to its effect *on* us (in relation to our own repentance) rather than *for* us (in relation to God's justice). According to the **moral influence** and **governmental theories**, Christ's death incites us to virtue, converts us through a demonstration of God's love, warns us about how seriously God takes sin, and encourages us to join God in his work of bringing peace and reconciliation to the world. Yet apart from an objective satisfaction of God's justice, how is Christ's death a demonstration of God's love? Unless it is a vicarious sacrifice in the place of sinners that *actually* saves them, is it not a rather cruel object lesson? And how can the cross be seen as reestablishing God's moral government if it does not actually satisfy the full demands of his justice? Even if we were morally able to repent simply as a result of a moving image of Golgotha, is this not to turn the gospel into law: namely, to atone for our own sins by responding to an object lesson?

As alternatives to an objective satisfaction of God's holy law, these subjective theories simply fail to deliver—even on their own promises. The one thing that the cross *cannot* be, according to these theories, is the means by which "we have now been justified by his blood [and] ... saved by him from the wrath of God" (Ro 5:9). Subjective theories rest on a weak view of sin. Less an assault against the will of a holy God that provokes his wrath and demands his justice than injuries to ourselves, sin as a condition is also reduced to specific sins that can be overcome with proper instruction and motivation. In Scripture, however, the problem is deeper, and so is the solution.

Atonement Theories	
THEORY	DESCRIPTION
Substitution	Christ died in our place, bearing God's wrath, satisfying his justice, and reconciling us to the Father.
Recapitulation	Associated especially with Irenaeus and Eastern theology, this view underscores Christ's life as well as death as undoing humanity's collective transgression, replacing Adam's headship over the human race with his own. This view also emphasizes immortality as the supreme gift of Christ's saving work.
Ransom	Also known as the "classic" theory (because of its association with Origen and other early Alexandrian theologians), this view held that Christ's death was a ransom paid to Satan for the ownership of humanity. However, Scripture represents Christ's death as a payment of our debt to God's justice, not to Satan.
Christus Victor	A key aspect of atonement theology especially in the East (as well as in Lutheran and Reformed teaching), this theory emphasizes Christ's victory over the powers of death and hell at the cross. Yet this can be true only because his death cancels the law's death sentence for us.
Satisfaction	Associated especially with the eleventh-century theologian Anselm, this view understands Christ's atonement primarily as an appeasement of God's offended dignity rather than divine justice.
Moral Influence	This view interprets the atonement as a demonstration of God's love rather than as a satisfaction either of God's dignity or of his justice. The effect of the atonement is to provide a moving example of God's love that will induce sinners to repent. This view is associated with Abelard (1079–1142), has been held by Socinians and Arminians, and has been the central idea in Protestant liberalism.
Moral Government	According to this view, Christ's atonement exhibits God's just government of the world and thereby establishes repentance as the basis on which human beings approach God. It was formulated in Arminian theology, especially by Hugo Grotius (1583–1645).

B. The Extent of Christ's Atonement

For whom did Christ die? Not only Calvinists, but Arminians also recognize that this is not a speculative question, but necessarily affects our view of the nature of Christ's atonement as well. For example, Arminian theologian John Miley wrote, "The penal substitutionary theory leads of necessity either to universalism on the one hand, or unconditional election on the other." Miley observes that "such an atonement, by its very nature, and by immediate result forever frees [believers] from all guilt as a liability to the penalty of sin."[13] Thus, the nature of the atonement is bound up with the question of its extent. In broad terms, three main answers have been given in church history.

One answer is that Christ's death objectively redeemed every person. The Scriptures unmistakably teach that God loves the world and that Christ died for the world (Jn 1:29; 3:16; 6:33, 51; Ro 11:12, 15; 2Co 5:19; 1Jn 2:2). Therefore, advocates of this first view conclude that it was Christ's purpose to save each and every person who has ever lived or will ever live. Officially condemned in the sixth century, Origen's theory of universal restoration (*apokatastasis*) held that all spirits (though not bodies), including Lucifer, would be reunited in heavenly bliss.[14] Refusing to bind God's freedom, Barth stopped short of a formal doctrine of universal salvation, although his doctrine of election and reconciliation suggests it.[15] Confessional Lutheranism also teaches a universal and objective atonement, although it also holds to a limited and unconditional election. Only the elect will be finally saved, but some receive the saving benefits of Christ's work only for a time and then lose these benefits through mortal sin or unbelief. In this view, then, not all of those for whom Christ died will be saved, in spite of his death's universal intention.

A second option is that Christ died to make salvation of every person possible. The intent of Christ's death, according to the Dutch Remonstrants (Arminians), was to make it possible for God to offer salvation to all by their grace-enabled cooperation: namely, their faith and evangelical obedience. A mediating position between the orthodox Calvinism defined by the Synod of Dort in 1618 – 19 and Arminianism became known as "hypothetical universalism" (also "Amyraldianism," after its architect, Moises Amyraut). Christ bore the sins of every person without exception, but since God knew that no one would embrace Christ apart from the gift of faith, he elected some

---

13. John Miley, *Christian Theology* (New York: Hunt and Eaton, 1889; repr., Peabody, Mass.: Hendrickson, 1989), 2:246.

14. See *The Seven Ecumenical Councils* (*NPNF²*, vol. 14; ed. Henry R. Percival; Grand Rapids: Eerdmans, 1971).

15. Karl Barth, *Church Dogmatics* (trans. G. W. Bromiley; Edinburgh: T&T Clark, 1957 – 1975), vol. 2, pt. 2, 417 – 23; vol. 3, pt. 2, 136; vol. 4, pt. 1, 91, 140, 410. For responsible evaluations, see esp. G. C. Berkouwer, *The Triumph of Grace in the Theology of Karl Barth* (trans. H. R. Boer; London: Paternoster, 1956), 215 – 34; Garry J. Williams, "Karl Barth and the Doctrine of the Atonement," in *Engaging with Barth: Contemporary Evangelical Critiques* (ed. David Gibson and Daniel Strange; Nottingham: Apollos, 2008), 232 – 72.

to receive the benefits of Christ's work. Many evangelical Protestants hold to an Arminian view, as expressed by Lewis Sperry Chafer: "Christ's death does not save either actually or potentially; rather it makes all men savable."[16]

A third view is that Christ died for all of the sins of the elect, thereby redeeming them at the cross. According to this view, expressed by the Canons of Dort (ch. 2, art. 3), Christ's death is "of infinite worth and value, abundantly sufficient to expiate the sins of the whole world," although he objectively and effectively bore the sins of the elect alone. Dort was repeating a common formula found in various medieval systems, including that of Aquinas and of Luther's mentor, Johann von Staupitz: "sufficient for the whole world but efficient for the elect alone."[17]

As the formula indicates, this view does not limit the sufficiency or availability of Christ's saving work. Christ's death is proclaimed to the whole world, as **sufficient** to save each and every person. At the same time, this view holds that the specific intention of Christ as he went to the cross was to save his elect. His death was **efficient** for them alone. Sometimes identified as "limited atonement," this view is better described as *particular redemption*. As the seventeenth-century Puritan John Owen observed, every position that recognizes that some will finally be lost places a limit on the atonement at some point: it is limited either in its extent or in its effect. Owen summarizes the options: Christ died for (1) all of the sins of all people; (2) some of the sins of all people, or (3) all of the sins of some people.[18] If unbelief is a sin, and some people are finally condemned, then there is at least one sin for which Christ did not make adequate satisfaction.

Extent of the Atonement		
THESIS	EXTENT AND NATURE	POSITION
Christ saved every person	Unlimited in extent and effect	Universal salvation
Christ made possible the salvation of every person	Unlimited in extent, but limited in effect	Hypothetical universalism
Christ saved all the elect	Sufficient for all, efficient for the elect	Definite atonement (or particular redemption)

---

16. Lewis Sperry Chafer, "For Whom Did Christ Die?" *Bibliotheca sacra* 137 (October–December 1980): 325.

17. Canons of Dort, ch. 2, art. 3, in Doctrinal Standards of the Christian Reformed Church, in *Psalter Hymnal* (Grand Rapids: Board of Publications of the Christian Reformed Church, 1976), 99.

18. John Owen, "The Death of Death in the Death of Christ," in *Works of John Owen* (London: Johnstone and Hunter, 1850–54; repr., Carlisle, Pa.: Banner of Truth Trust, 1965–68), 10:233.

Key Distinction:
sufficient/efficient (atonement)

Christ's redeeming work is unlimited in its ability to save everyone in the world. Hence, it is proclaimed to every human being as sufficient for his or her salvation. Yet in accord with the eternal covenant of the triune God, Christ actually secured the redemption of the elect.

Among the arguments in favor of particular redemption are the following. First, this view emphasizes the relationship between the Trinity and redemption. In the eternal councils of the Trinity (the covenant of redemption), the Father elected a certain number of the human race and gave them to his Son as their Guardian and Mediator, with the Spirit pledging to bring them to Christ in order receive all of the benefits of his mediation. Besides explicit passages on this eternal pact (Eph 1:4–13; 2Th 2:13:14; Tit 3:4–8), there are several references to Jesus' intention to redeem his elect (Ro 8:32–35), his sheep (Jn 10:11, 15), his church (Ac 20:28; Eph 5:25–27), and his people (Mt 1:21).

Jesus says that he came not to make salvation possible but to actually save "all those the Father gives me." He adds, "And this is the will of him who sent me, that I shall lose nothing of all that he has given me, but raise them up at the last day.... This is why I told you that no one can come to me unless it is granted him by the Father" (Jn 6:37–39, 65). In John 10, Jesus says, "The good shepherd lays down his life for the sheep...., I am the good shepherd. I know my own and my own know me, just as the Father knows me and I know the Father. And I lay down my life for the sheep" (Jn 10:11, 14–15), which includes Gentiles as well as Jews (v. 16). With Golgotha heavy on his heart, Jesus prays to the Father, "Father, the hour has come; glorify your Son that the Son may glorify you, since you have given him authority over all flesh, to give eternal life to all whom you have given him.... Yours they were, and you gave them to me, and they have kept your word.... I am praying for them; I am not praying for the world but for those whom you have given me, for they are yours" (Jn 17:1–2, 6, 9). And once more Jesus includes all "who will believe in me through their word, that they may all be one" (vv. 20–21).

In the Epistles as well, there is the correspondence between the will and work of the Father, the Son, and the Spirit in election, redemption, and calling which creates an unshakable ground of comfort (Ro 8:30–34;

Eph 1:4–13).[19] The Savior entered Paradise as conqueror with the triumphant announcement, "Behold, I and the children God has given me" (Heb 2:13). All of this shows "the heirs of the promise the unchangeable character of his purpose," which was "guaranteed …. with an oath, so that by two unchangeable things, in which it is impossible for God to lie, we who have fled for refuge might have strong encouragement to hold fast to the hope set before us" (Heb 6:17–18).

Second, this view emphasizes the efficacy and objectivity of Christ's saving work. How do I know if I am one for whom Christ died? The only answer given in Scripture is that we look to Christ, in whom we were chosen, and whose death is sufficient for a thousand worlds. However, short of affirming universal salvation, the alternative views hold that in spite of Christ's objective work many for whom he died will be finally lost, bearing their own judgment. But what then of Christ's promise above that he will not lose any of those whom the Father had given him? This possibility of Christ's redeeming work falling short of its intention is not eliminated even in Barth's conception, since he allows for the possibility of final condemnation of some.

Because it is not hypothetical but actual, we can proclaim to everyone with confidence, "God so loved the world, that he gave his only Son, that whoever believes in him should not perish but have eternal life" (Jn 3:16). Again, as we have seen, particular redemption does not limit the *sufficiency* of Christ's death. With the New Testament, advocates of particular redemption can cheerfully proclaim, "Christ died for sinners," "Christ died for the world," and "Christ's death is sufficient for you," acknowledging also with the Scriptures that the assurance, "Christ died for you," is to be given only to believers. If Christ's sin-bearing does not actually bear away God's wrath for every person for whom he died, then, as Bavinck concludes, "The center of gravity has been shifted from Christ and located in the Christian." Instead of Christ's objective work, "Faith is the true reconciliation with God."[20] There is a world of difference between saying that faith is the instrument of receiving Christ and his benefits and saying that it is itself the reason for or basis of our salvation.

Far from being thwarted, the clear invitations of Scripture for all to come to Christ (Mt 11:28; Jn 6:35; 7:37) are even more fully justified by the fact

---

19. See Stephen M. Baugh, "Galatians 3:20 and the Covenant of Redemption," *Westminster Theological Journal* 66, no. 1 (2004): 49–70.

20. Herman Bavinck, *Reformed Dogmatics* (ed. John Bolt; trans. John Vriend; Grand Rapids: Baker Academic, 2004), 3:469.

that the Spirit will use this universal good news to draw his elect to Christ. The Sinai covenant focused Israel's hopes on the Messiah through types and shadows, but the Abrahamic covenant promising salvation for the nations is now announced to the world. It is in this sense that we understand the verses that refer to Christ's death on behalf of "all" and "the world." Since Christ's blood "ransomed people for God from every tribe and language and people and nation" (Rev 5:9), there is no distinction any longer between Jew and Gentile, male and female, slave and free (Gal 3:28). Through the flood, God simultaneously judged and saved the world—even though only eight persons were rescued. How much greater then is the salvation that is ensured by the triune God that there will be a remnant from every nation streaming joyfully into the heavenly sanctuary as his new humanity.

III. The State of Exaltation: The Servant Who Is Lord

As the eternal Word of the Father, Christ has a kingship that does not begin at Golgotha but in creation (Jn 1:1–4, 10; Col 1:15–20; Heb 1:2–3). The Son reflects the Father's glory in eternity as well as in time (Heb 1:3). As we have seen, in every external work of the Godhead, the Father speaks in the Son and by the Spirit. Everything that Jesus performs by his speaking and priestly mediation he accomplishes for the good of his coheirs, and when he rose and ascended in glory as King, he took up his scepter for the same purpose. Christ rules history and nature in the service of redeeming, creating, and ruling his church. Death, the last enemy, lost its legal foothold in creation by the cross (Heb 2:14; 2Ti 1:10), although it awaits its final abolition at Christ's return (1Co 15:23–26). In Christ's ascension, the age to come has already dawned. He is the forerunner who is already glorified as the church's head but will not rest until his body shares in his consummated life.

There can be a church in history only because in this same history the Lord who became the servant was the servant who became Lord. Of course, Jesus Christ was always Lord in his consubstantiality with the Father, but he "was declared to be the Son of God in power according to the Spirit of holiness by his resurrection from the dead" (Ro 1:4). There is a church because there is one who stood in his resurrected flesh and declared, "All authority in heaven and on earth has been given to me. Go therefore and make disciples of all nations" (Mt 28:18).

Not only the cross, but the incarnation, life, resurrection, ascension, and return of Christ belong to the kerygma, that is, the gospel proclaimed by the apostles. The whole gospel is marvelously summarized in the sermons of Acts. Peter proclaims to his hearers that although they crucified "the Author of life," it is he "whom God raised from the dead."

> To this we are witnesses.... And now, brothers, I know that you acted in ignorance, as did also your rulers. But what God foretold by the mouth of all the prophets, that his Christ would suffer, he thus fulfilled. Repent therefore, and turn back, that your sins may be blotted out, that times of refreshing may come from the presence of the Lord, and that he may send the Christ appointed for you, Jesus, whom heaven must receive until the time for restoring all the things about which God spoke by the mouth of his holy prophets long ago.... You are the sons of the prophets and of the covenant that God made with your fathers, saying to Abraham, "And in your offspring shall all the families of the earth be blessed." God, having raised up his servant, sent him to you first, to bless you by turning every one of you from your wickedness." (Ac 3:14–15, 17–21, 25–26)

This pattern—"whom you crucified, [but] whom God raised from the dead" (Ac 4:10), appealing to Old Testament prophecies, and announcing salvation in no other name—marks all of the sermons in Acts (4:10–12, 24–30; 5:30–32, 42; 7:1–53; 10:39–43; 13:16–39; 17:30–32; 25:19; 26:4–8; 26:22–23; 28:20, 23–24). In fact, before the Jewish council Paul noted with some irony, since the Pharisees were distinguished by their belief in the resurrection of the dead, "Brothers, I am a Pharisee, a son of Pharisees. It is with respect to the hope and the resurrection of the dead that I am on trial" (23:6).

We should not allow the threefold office of Christ to be too rigidly tied to the so-called states: humiliation and exaltation. It is easy to identify Christ's kingship exclusively with his resurrection and ascension in glory. However, this misses the paradox that lies at the heart of the kingdom he brings. In this age, it is a kingdom of grace. The King's glory is hidden under the form of suffering and rejection. At no point was Jesus without a kingdom even in his ministry under the cross, and as we have seen, he is even now "ever-living" at God's right hand to intercede for us. The crucifixion itself can be seen as a kind of exaltation, as we find in the fourth gospel: "And I, when I am lifted up from the earth, will draw all people to myself" (Jn 12:32). We might be inclined at first to take this as a reference to Jesus' ascension, but the next verse corrects that impression: "He said this to show by what kind of *death* he was going to die" (v. 33). He is the "brass serpent" raised in the wilderness, so that all who look upon him will be saved (Jn 3:14 with Nu 21:8–9).

> ### Key Distinction:
> ### *humiliation/exaltation*
>
> This distinction refers to Christ's voluntary descent to us, in our nature, under the conditions of a servant. Sharing in our common suffering as well as the uncommon suffering of his enemies and even the judgment of his Father due to us for our sins, he was raised in glorious exaltation on the third day as the King of kings and Lord of lords.

So we see not *simply* a progression from the state of humiliation to that of exaltation, or from prophet to priest and finally king. Even as he was hanging on the cross in dereliction as the enemy of God and humanity, Christ was winning our redemption as our conquering King. "There is no tribunal so magnificent," Calvin wrote, "no throne so stately, no show of triumph so distinguished, no chariot so elevated, as is the gibbet on which Christ has subdued death and the devil."[21] At the same time, there is a progressive unveiling of Christ's ministry from humiliation to exaltation, evident especially in Philippians 2:5–6. First suffering, then glory.

Reformed as well as Lutheran theology has typically followed the eschatological distinction of Christ's kingship between the reign in grace (*regnum gratiae*) and his reign in glory (*regnum gloriae*). God has installed his king on his holy mountain and now demands universal homage (Pss 2:6; 45:6–7, with Heb 1:8–9; 132:11; Isa 9:6–7; Jer 23:5–6; Mic 5:2; Zec 6:13; Lk 1:33; 19:27, 38; 22:29; Jn 18:36–7; Ac 2:30–6). But this kingdom is not simply an extension or reinvigoration of the kingship in Israel, as many of Jesus' admirers had expected—even the disciples after the resurrection (Ac 1:6). During the trial Pilate asked Jesus, "Are you the King of the Jews?" and Jesus replied, "Do you say this of your own accord, or did others say it to you about me?" (Jn 18:33–34).

Pilate answered, "Am I a Jew? Your own nation and the chief priests have delivered you over to me. What have you done?" Jesus answered, "My kingdom is not of this world. If my kingdom were of this world, my servants would have been fighting, that I might not be delivered over to the Jews. But my kingdom is not from the world." Then Pilate said to him, "So you are a king?" Jesus answered, "You say that I am a king. For this purpose I was born, and for this purpose I have come into the world—to bear witness

---

21. John Calvin, *Commentary on Philippians-Colossians* (Grand Rapids: Baker, repr. 1979), 191.

to the truth. Everyone who is of the truth listens to my voice." Pilate said to him, "What is truth?" (Jn 18:35 – 38)

A kingdom of truth and grace rather than a kingdom of power and glory: this surely confused the Romans even more than the Jews.

The kingdom of Christ, then, is, in its present phase — before the second advent — weak and foolish in the eyes of the world. Even though this kingdom is more global in its reach than any empire has ever been and claims a deeper allegiance from its subjects than the powerful rulers of the world have ever attained, it can hardly compare in outward pomp and glory with the kingdoms of the world that it nevertheless outlasts. The kingdom lives not only from the cross but from the resurrection, and yet it is very much in a state of humiliation when empirical criteria are applied. While in the old covenant the kingdom was typologically concentrated in the outward glory of Israel's cultic and civil structures, in the kingdom of Christ during "this present age" its glory is hidden under the cross. It claims hearts, not geopolitical lands. It brings new birth (Jn 3:3 – 7) from the future reign of the Spirit and an anticipation of the consummation that the "Lord and giver of life" will bring in "the resurrection of the body and the life everlasting."

Throughout his ministry, Christ was God's "No" to the powers of sin and death. Healing the sick, casting out demons, and even raising the dead, Jesus provided morsels of that victory that would be consummated on the basis of his resurrection, ascension, the sending of the Spirit at Pentecost, and his triumphant return in glory. Even at the cross, as we have seen, Christ's royal office is publicly displayed as he triumphs over the powers of this present age. Right where those powers can see him only as rejected, helpless, foolish, and weak, he is in fact accomplishing his most decisive victory over his enemies and ours.

Since I have discussed the resurrection claim at length in chapter 1, I will focus in this section on its significance for the royal priesthood that Christ exercises even now on our behalf and the hope of the elimination of sin and suffering forever.

A. The King Raised

The resurrection is not simply proof of Christ's divine identity and the success of his atoning work; it is the dawn of the new creation. Christ's sin-bearing is the *sine qua non* of this cosmic restoration, but his resurrection from the dead brings justification and everlasting life. As goes the King, so goes the kingdom. God did not abandon his messiah to the grave (Ps 16:10). In his Pentecost sermon, Peter cited Psalm 16:8 – 11 as the proof text for his announcement of God's saving work in Christ: "God raised him up, loosing the pangs of death, because it was not possible for him to be held by it" (Ac 2:24–28). Since David's tomb is not empty, he could only have been referring to "the resurrection of the Messiah." "This Jesus God raised up, and of that we all are witnesses. Being therefore exalted at the right hand of God, and having received from the Father the promise of the Holy Spirit, he has poured out this that you yourselves are seeing and hearing. . . . Let all the house of Israel therefore know for certain that God has made him both Lord and Christ, this Jesus whom you crucified" (vv. 29–36).

Christ's kingship, like the other titles we have explored, involves both a human and a divine aspect. Not only as the divine (archetypal) Great King, but as the human (ectypal) servant-king, Jesus accomplished what Adam and David failed to achieve. This can be especially seen in Hebrews 2:5–13, where the "dominion" entrusted to God's image-bearers is finally realized in Jesus Christ.

Only on the basis of the resurrection can we say that the righteous and peaceful dominion of humanity has been restored. It certainly cannot be discerned from the daily headlines or from the state of the church throughout the world. Yet it has been recovered and fulfilled in Christ as our Living Head. By his sanctification, we are sanctified, and by his reign the world is assured its participation in the cosmic glory that he has already inherited in his investiture as "King of kings and Lord of lords" (1Ti 6:15). His investiture at the right hand of God is a reward for his meritorious obedience (Ps 2:8–9; Mt 28:18; Eph 1:20–22; Php 2:9–11).

The already–not yet dialectic is at work in this understanding of Christ's kingly office, in relation both to the cosmos and to the church. The concept of the kingdom of God is broader than that of the church, but in this present age it is especially in the church that the kingdom of Christ comes to visible expression. There, at least in principle, Christ's heavenly reign is openly acknowledged, embraced, and experienced as a living reality. There, through the waters of baptism, the breaking of bread, the hearing of the Word, and the guidance of Christ's people through the ministry of pastors, elders, and deacons, the Spirit makes "dry land" appear for God's dwelling in the world. Just as the regeneration and justification of the wicked anticipates or, better, is in fact the "firstfruits" of the bodily resurrection and glorification that awaits us, the existence of the church is the down payment on "the time for restoring all things about which God spoke by the mouth of his holy prophets long ago" (Ac 3:21). As Paul confirms, the resurrection of Christ is not distinct from the resurrection of believers, but the "first fruits" of the whole harvest (1Co 15:21–26, 45, 49).

We should not be surprised, then, by all of these organic metaphors for the relationship of Christ to his church: vine and branches, tree and its fruit, living stones being built into a Spirit-indwelled temple, and the head and its body. God put this power to work in Christ

> when he raised him from the dead and seated him at his right hand in the heavenly places, far above all rule and authority and power and dominion, and above every name that is named, not only in this age but also in the one to come. And he put all things under his feet and gave him as head over all things to the church, which is his body, the fullness of him who fills all in all. (Eph 1:20–23)

None of these analogies reflects a model of sheer domination of one person over another, but an intimate union. Christ rules *over* by ruling *within* those who are identified as part and parcel of his own body.

In the resurrection of Christ, then, we see the power of the age to come exercised in the present. It is a power that reigns over every other power and authority (a general sovereignty in creation and providence) in the service of his covenant people (cf. Eph 4:15; 5:23; 1Co 11:3). He rules in, not just over, his church through the ministry of the keys (Mt 16:18–19) as well as the fellowship of believers. The Spirit justified Jesus Christ by raising him from the dead, and so too he "was delivered up for our trespasses and raised for our justification" (Ro 4:25). We have been baptized into his death and resurrection (Ro 6:1–10).

Therefore, as Berkhof summarizes, the kingdom of grace is founded upon Christ's redemption, not creation.[22] The creation mandate to rule and subdue was given to all image-bearers in the beginning, but the Great Commission is entrusted to the saints, and it is fulfilled by their testimony to the gospel, baptism, and teaching others everything that he has declared. It is not a geopolitical kingdom as in the theocracy (Mt 8:11–12; 21:43; Lk 17:21; Jn 18:36–37), much less one like the Gentile empires (Mk 10:42–43), although it will one day be revealed in power and glory. In fact, it is interesting that in Mark's Gospel, after each of the three episodes in which Jesus foretells his death and resurrection, the disciples erupt in jealousy and controversy about who will be greatest in the kingdom (implied in 8:34–38, explicit in 9:33–37 and 10:35–45). Just as the empirical reality that we see all around us, epitomized by the decay of our bodies, speaks against the claim that a "new creation" has truly dawned, the weaknesses of the church witness against the participation of the earthly body, the church, in its heav-

---

22. Louis Berkhof, *Systematic Theology* (Grand Rapids: Eerdmans, 1949), 407.

enly head. Yet the resurrection of Christ makes it so, not only because it sets the rest of the redemptive economy in motion but because it is the first installment on the full consummation.

The principle that Paul applies to the physical body — sown in mortality, raised in immortality, sown in dishonor, raised in glory, sown in weakness, raised in power (1Co 15:42 – 43) — is illustrative of the **already – not yet** scheme involved in the manifestation of the kingdom in history. Entered by the new birth (Jn 3:3 – 5), this kingdom nevertheless cannot remain a merely spiritual reality. It must one day become as tangible and complete as the resurrection itself will be for the human person. But for now, it is a mustard seed (Mk 4:30 – 31), leaven being worked into the dough of humanity generally (Mt 13:33). The kingdom is present (Mt 12:28; Lk 17:21; Col 1:13), yet not consummated (Mt 7:21 – 22; 19:23; 22:2 – 14; 25:1 – 13, 34; Lk 22:29 – 30; 1Co 6:9; 15:50; Gal 5:21; Eph 5:5; 1Th 2:12; 2Ti 4:18; Heb 12:28; 2Pe 1:11). The decisive victory has been accomplished, but we have yet to hear that the cities of oppression and violence have been destroyed and that "the kingdom of the world has become the kingdom of our Lord and of his Christ, and he shall reign forever and ever" (Rev 11:15). Jesus' resurrection not only confirms but effects his status as the Israel of God, the eschatological temple in whom each member, Jew or gentile, fits as "chosen" and as a "living [stone]" (1Pe 2:4 – 5).

The claim, "Jesus is Lord," is not simply a confession of his deity. It is that and more. The important eschatological point that this claim makes is

Key Distinction:
"already" / "not yet"

Christ's kingdom is present now, but not yet consummated. It is a "semirealized" kingdom. Even now, the blessings that Christ has won for us are being distributed by him through his Spirit in the ministry of preaching and sacrament. We are already chosen, redeemed, called, justified, and renewed; we are being sanctified, and we will one day be glorified. For now, though, we live in the tension between the kingdom's inauguration and its consummation. A related distinction is drawn in the New Testament between *this age* and *the age to come*. Even now the age to come is breaking in upon this passing age, but not yet in the visible and completed form that will be universally evident at Christ's appearing.

that in Jesus Christ the threats to God's promises being fulfilled have been conquered objectively and that in the same Lord those promises will be realized fully in the age to come. There are no powers, authorities, thrones, or dominions that can thwart his purposes, although they may present fierce opposition until they are finally destroyed. Far greater than a restorer of Israel's national destiny, much less the founder of a new religion, Jesus Christ is the forerunner of the new creation, the firstfruits from the dead, the pioneer of salvation. In this one person, the end-time renewal of all things has begun. The king dies for his kingdom, is raised into the age to come, and sends his Spirit to usher his coheirs into it with him.

To say "Jesus is Lord," one must try to hear it with Jewish as well as Gentile ears. It means that the God of Israel — the one who won the duel with Egypt's gods and led his people through the sea and wilderness into the promised land, is the one who raised Jesus from the dead and, in turn, gave the human person thus raised the name above every name. It is to say that he is the one who will restore Israel's fortunes, not simply by reinvigorating a typological theocracy but by bringing about the universal judgment of sin and vindication for his people that the Abrahamic covenant promised and the Mosaic economy could only foreshadow. To hear "Jesus is Lord" as a slogan for nothing more than "my personal relationship with Jesus" is not to hear it as it is meant to be heard. It is to truncate the message that Jesus both *is* and *proclaims*. Salvation cannot be reduced to an inner, personal experience. Rather, it reaches in ever-widening circles, from the "inner person" (the new birth) to the whole person (the resurrection) until the whole cosmos is the Sabbath land.

Therefore, the announcement of Christ's lordship is as much a part of the gospel as Christ's prophetic and priestly ministry. Christ's reign topples all rivals who hold us in bondage, so that even death has lost its legal authority to keep us in the grave. Jesus "was delivered up for our trespasses and raised for our justification" (Ro 4:25).

We will not learn that Christ is King from the empirical condition of the world — or even of the church in its present form of existence. Death comes to us all. The righteous suffer, while proud oppressors enjoy prosperity. Even with Christ as its one foundation, the church is "by schisms rent asunder, by heresies distressed," as the hymn has it. Hypocrisy, scandal, division, and jealousy often seem as evident among the sheep as among the goats. Yet in all of this, we do have one infallible proof that the new age has dawned: Jesus of Nazareth has been raised, glorified in our flesh, as the firstfruits of the new creation. The future glory of the consummated Sabbath has been inaugurated already. Jesus' resurrection is not actually a different one from ours, but is the beginning of the full harvest.[23] The age to come has already begun, in a semirealized way. The powers of this present evil age capture the world's headlines, but the powers of the age to come have broken in already, with Christ as the firstborn from the dead. As he is now, so shall we be.

B. The King Ascended

Appointed for annual feasts when pilgrims would make their way together up the hill leading to the temple, various psalms of ascent would be sung. Psalm 24 is especially poignant, with its antiphonal (responsive) pattern. It begins with the image of the whole earth (not only Jerusalem) as God's possession, and the question is asked, "Who shall ascend the hill of the LORD? And who shall stand in his holy place?" Only one who has "clean hands and a pure heart" is qualified (vv. 1–6). However, as the liturgy unfolds, it becomes clear that the only one qualified to ascend Yahweh's hill and stand in his holy place is "the King of glory." As he enters in conquest, the order is announced by the choir he leads in his train:

> Lift up your heads, O gates! And be lifted up, O ancient doors, that the King of glory may come in. Who is this King of glory? The LORD, strong and mighty, the LORD, mighty in battle. Lift up your heads, O gates! And lift them up, O ancient doors, that the King of glory may come in. Who is this King of glory? The LORD of hosts, he is the King of glory. (vv. 7–10)

Finally, the Last Adam has triumphed, fulfilling the covenantal trial, and now ascends to his throne at the Father's right hand in Sabbath glory.

Jewish as well as Christian commentators have pointed out that this psalm encapsulates Israel's military march from the desert of Sinai to Jerusalem — God's earthly Zion (see also Ps 68, with the reference to Yahweh's "solemn processions" from wilderness to Zion). Only Jesus Christ perfectly fulfills this commission and is qualified to demand that the ancient doors of the heavenly throne room open to his triumphal entry with his liberated hosts behind him. He claims his victory, announcing, "Behold, I and the children God has given me" (Heb 2:13).

1. The ascension in the New Testament

The most direct ascension account comes from Luke. Meeting two of his disillusioned disciples on the road, the recently risen (though as yet unrecognized) Jesus pushes them regarding their knowledge of the Scriptures:

---

23. Richard B. Gaffin Jr., *Resurrection and Redemption: A Study in Paul's Soteriology* (Phillipsburg, N.J.: P&R, 1987).

"Was it not necessary that the Christ should *suffer these things* and *enter into his glory*?' And beginning with Moses and all the Prophets, he interpreted to them in all the Scriptures the things concerning himself" (Luke 24:13–27). Jesus commanded the disciples to remain in Jerusalem until the promised Spirit was given, so that they might be "clothed with power from on high." "Then he led them out as far as Bethany, and lifting up his hands, he blessed them. While he blessed them, he parted from them and was carried up into heaven. And they worshiped him and returned to Jerusalem with great joy; and they were continually in the temple blessing God" (vv. 49–53).

Acts 1 reprises this episode in its opening verses. The promise that the Holy Spirit would endow the disciples for their witness to the ends of the earth is reiterated, followed by the ascension report:

> And when he had said these things, as they were looking on, he was lifted up, and a cloud took him out of their sight. And while they were gazing into heaven as he went, behold, two men stood by them in white robes, and said, "Men of Galilee, why do you stand looking into heaven? This Jesus, who was taken up from you into heaven, will come in the same way as you saw him go into heaven." (Ac 1:6–11)

Thus the ascension (and still future *parousia*, or second coming) now became part of the gospel itself. Not only was Jesus crucified and raised according to the prophets, Peter preaches, but the Messiah will be sent again, that is, Jesus, "whom heaven must receive *until the time for restoring* all the things about which God spoke by the mouth of his holy prophets long ago" (Ac 3:20–21, emphasis added).

As they were taught by Jesus in the Olivet and Upper Room Discourses (Mt 24–25 and Jn 14–16, respectively) and on the road to Emmaus (one can presume, in the rest of the days leading up to the ascension itself), the apostolic preaching that we find in Acts follows the familiar pattern of descent-ascent-return, justifying the confession in the eucharistic liturgy: "Christ has died, Christ is risen, Christ will come again." His departure is as real and decisive as his incarnation, and he "will come [again] in the same way as you saw him go into heaven" (Ac 1:11)—that is, in the flesh. In the meantime, Jesus of Nazareth is physically absent from the earth. And yet, in this interim, the Spirit causes the Word to spread and bear fruit, through preaching, baptism, and the Supper. It is this eucharistic tension, occasioned by the ascension, that begins to rearrange our questions, not to mention our answers, with respect to the identity, mission, marks, and ministry of the church.

In the Epistles, the ascension marks the present heavenly work of Jesus Christ on behalf of his church (Ro 8:33–34; Eph 4; 1Jn 2:1), as the firstfruits of the harvest (1Co 15), who will return from heaven (1Th 4:13 – 5:11) in judgment and salvation to fulfill the "Day of the Lord" (Ro 2:5; 1Th 5:2; cf. Heb 10:25; Jas 5:3; 2Pe 3:10). The ascension is attested in Stephen's vision as he was martyred, not to mention Paul's on his way to Damascus. United to Christ, believers have been seated with him in the heavenly places (Eph 2:6 – 7), and there is explicit mention of the ascension (interpreting Ps 68:18) as the source of the gifts being poured out on the church (Eph 4:7 – 10). The writer to the Hebrews appeals to the ascension as part of the contrast between old and new covenant worship (Heb 7:23 – 26; 9:25).

In his heavenly exaltation, Jesus Christ exercises all three offices. As prophet, he continues to declare both his law and his gospel, judging and absolving sinners through the frail ministry of human beings in the power of the Spirit. We have been given rest in a greater land through the gospel, led by a greater prophet than Moses (Heb 3:1 – 19) or Joshua (4:1 – 12) and with a greater priest than Aaron or his descendants. "Since then we have a great high priest who has passed through the heavens, Jesus, the Son of God, let us hold fast our confession" (4:14). Chapters 8 – 10 of Hebrews argue that not only does our High Priest minister in the true sanctuary rather than in its earthly copy; he has entered with his own blood, ending the sacrificial system, and cannot have his service interrupted by his death. "He holds his priesthood permanently, because he continues forever. Consequently, he is able to save to the uttermost those who draw near to God through him, since he always lives to make intercession for them" (Heb 7:24 – 25). "But when Christ had offered for all time a single sacrifice for sins, he sat down at the right hand of God, waiting from that time until his enemies should be made a footstool for his feet' " (10:12 – 13).

Therefore, Christ's priesthood does not end at the cross but continues in heaven. Believers are not only saved by Christ's work in the past; God has "raised us up with him and seated us with him in the heavenly places in Christ Jesus, so that in the coming ages he might show the immeasur-able riches of his grace in kindness toward us in Christ Jesus" (Eph 2:6 – 7). Christ's ongoing priestly work is connected to his ascension again in Ephe-sians 4. There the apostle paraphrases Psalm 68:18 (the paraphrase [Eph 4:8]: "When he ascended on high he led a host of captives, and he gave gifts to men") in the light of its fulfillment: "He who descended is the same one who ascended far above all the heavens so that he might fill all things. The gifts he gave were apostles, prophets, evangelists, pastors and teachers, to complete the saints through the work of [their] ministry, for building up the body of Christ, until all of us come to the unity of the faith and of the knowledge of the Son of God, to maturity, to the measure of the full stature of Christ." With the Head now raised, and the Spirit poured out, the members of his body grow together in truth and love (Eph 4:10–16, author's trans.).[24]

Through the ministry of these ambassadors on earth, Jesus himself exercises his heavenly reign. With these keys of the kingdom, that which is loosed and bound on earth is loosed and bound in heaven (Mt 16:19; 18:18–20). Even now, God's kingdom is coming and his will is being done on earth as it is in heaven, because the King has ascended and now reigns in grace. Similarly, Christ intercedes on behalf of his people. John assures, "But if anyone does sin, we have an advocate with the Father, Jesus Christ the righteous" (1Jn 2:1). "Who is to condemn?" Paul asks. Not only has Christ died and been raised; he "is at the right hand of God, [and] indeed is interceding for us," so that even in our suffering we can say that "we are more than conquerors through him who loved us" (Ro 8:34, 37). The Angel of the LORD who stood in the heavenly courtroom to justify Joshua the high priest (Zec 3) is the same who intercedes at the Father's right hand, but now without Satan admitted into the chamber. The prosecutor has been bound, and his house looted, with the victor leading captives in his train.

Jesus prepared his followers for his absence by promising "another *paraklētos*"—defense attorney whom he will send when he ascends to the Father (Jn 14:16). The Son returns to the Father so that they may send the Spirit to complete the earthly work that needs to be done in order to bring about the consummation of all things in God. The Psalms make their way through the Gospels (especially Jn 14) to Pentecost: "Being therefore exalted at the right hand of God, and having received from the Father the promise of the Holy Spirit, he has poured out this that you yourselves are seeing and hearing" (Ac 2:33). That the kingly reign of Christ exists to serve his priestly work is seen in Revelation 12:10, with the song of defeat of the dragon: "And I heard a loud voice in heaven, saying, 'Now the salvation and the power and the kingdom of our God and the authority of his Christ have come, for the accuser of our brothers has been thrown down, who accuses them day and night before our God." It is in this intercession that believers take their assurance of never being "cut off" by God (Ro 8:31–35).

From his incarnation to his reign at the Father's right hand, Jesus is not only the Lord who became the servant, but the servant who is Lord and continues even in this exalted state to serve his Father's will and his people's good. From eternity to eternity, he offers his "Here I am" to the Father on

---

24. For the rationale in the translation I have offered here (similar to the rendering in the King James Version), see Andrew Lincoln, *Ephesians* (Word Biblical Commentary 42; Dallas: Word, 1990), 253.

behalf of those who have gone their own way. For now, Christ reigns in grace; when he returns in judgment and vindication, his kingdom will be consummated in everlasting glory. The one who sits on the throne of all power and authority in heaven and on earth is our older brother.

2. The significance of the ascension

Given the significance of the ascension in the New Testament (especially the Epistles), it is surprising that it plays a comparatively minor role in the faith and practice of the church. Though affirmed, it does not seem to occupy the same status as Christ's incarnation, death, and resurrection. Douglas Farrow has sought to remedy this marginalization of the ascension in theology, seeing it as "the point of intersection in Christology, eschatology, and ecclesiology."[25] One problem in the history of interpretation has been the treatment of the ascension as little more than a dazzling exclamation point for the resurrection rather than as a new event in its own right. Collapsing the ascension into the resurrection "puts in jeopardy the continuity between our present world and the higher places of the new order established by God in Christ," says Farrow.[26]

Christ's ascension is not merely an exclamation point to his resurrection, confirming his deity. Jewish legend taught that Moses had ascended, and Islam proclaims Muhammad's ascension. However, in neither case is the alleged ascension regarded as introducing a new era of human history in its own right; these stories serve merely to confirm the status that the prophet had already before his ascension. By contrast, *the ascension of Christ actually created a new state of affairs in the world*. In other words, it is an eschatological, not just historical, event. It not only happens within history, but transforms history in the process. The kingdom of heaven descends to earth in the person of its King, and returns through the triumphal arch of heaven with our flesh and our history raised to his eschatological glory. Like his humanity, history is not left behind, but is fundamentally altered in its destiny. With Christ's ascension, the dreary history of "this present evil age," in bondage to sin and death, draws to a close, and a new history dawns within the old epoch. It is not yet the consummation, but it is the beginning of the consummation, with its King as the already-glorified Lord of heaven and earth.

---

25. R. Maddox, *The Purpose of Luke-Acts* (Edinburgh: T&T Clark, 1982), 10, cited in Douglas Farrow, *Ascension and Ecclesia* (Edinburgh: T&T Clark, 1999), 16. I draw significantly on Farrow for my own interpretation of the ascension in *People and Place: A Covenant Ecclesiology* (Louisville and London: Westminster John Knox, 2008), ch. 1.

26. Farrow, *Ascension and Ecclesia*, 29.

Academic theology over the last century has been divided between those who favor history and those who favor eschatology—a kingdom that unfolds gradually and one that descends in one moment of radical divine activity. However, in the New Testament they are held together. As with the resurrection, if the ascension were only historical, then regardless of its importance, it could not produce the beginning of the final restoration of all things any more than other events. At the same time, if the ascension were only eschatological (as many, like Rudolph Bultmann, have argued), then the gospel could change only my personal existence—my outlook in the world, but not the world itself. Eschatology without history is basically a gnostic or "docetic" approach that is typical of our Gentile (especially Greek) heritage.

Giving the ascension a "docetic" interpretation not only separates this event from Old Testament expectations, Farrow notes, but it "eventually rebounds on the doctrine of the resurrection itself—if indeed it is not already the sign of a docetic version of that doctrine—and binds it closely to an otherworldly eschatology that has little in common with that of scripture." "Resurrection comes to mean 'going to heaven,' which in some theologies makes it rather hard to distinguish from dying!" The promise of the angels that "this same Jesus" will return in the flesh simultaneously affirms the *continuity* between our resurrection and Christ's and the *dis*continuity between Jesus-history and the common history of this passing age. Apart from this discontinuity, we substitute "our own story (the story of man's self-elevation) as the real kernel of salvation history in the present age."[27] Since Christ is the beginning of the new creation, a docetic (nonphysical) ascension means a docetic consummation for us as well. The ascension can be no less real, no less historical and bodily, than the incarnation, death, and resurrection.

Jesus did not downplay his ascension but comforted his disciples with the promise of the Spirit and his Word. The same point is made by Paul in Romans 10, when he says that we do not have to ascend to the heavens to bring Christ down or into the depths as if to bring him up from the dead—since he comes near to us through his Word. Only when we take seriously Christ's real absence in the flesh are we able to appreciate the significance of eschatology (our being seated with him yet not yet seeing him face to face), pneumatology (the Spirit as the one who now mediates Christ's presence through preaching and sacrament), and ecclesiology (the church as a pilgrim

---

27. Ibid.

community lodged precariously between the two ages). This eschatological orientation also reinforces rather than undermines the historical character of our hope: not until Jesus returns bodily to earth will world history finally be identical with the personal history of Jesus Christ.

When Christ's real absence in the flesh is faced, the Spirit's work of uniting us to Christ and causing us to long for his return qualifies the church's tendency to substitute itself for the glorified Lord who was born of Mary. Otherwise, the confident claim in the eucharistic liturgy, "Christ will come again," becomes easily allegorized, spiritualized, or moralized as something that happens again and again even now (whether through the Mass or through private devotions). However, Christ is truly present here and now through word and sacrament, and yet it is precisely in this way that the Spirit keeps us longing for his return in the flesh at the end of history.

Christ's ascent has opened up a hole in these last days of our present history, through which the Spirit descends, dispensing the spoils of Christ's victory. Because of the ascension, there is now present—even in this passing evil age—a new order at work, an underground resistance to the principalities and powers of sin and death. Though we are still living in this present evil age, the powers of the age to come are breaking in upon us in the Spirit through preaching and sacrament (Heb 6:4–5). Because Jesus Christ is Lord, we are made alive by the Spirit, drawn away from our alliance with death, and made cosufferers as well as coheirs with Jesus Christ. It is the ascension that both grounds the struggle of the church militant and guarantees that one day it will share fully in the triumph of its King.

Key Terms

- penal substitution
- propitiation and expiation
- reconciliation
- atonement theories: satisfaction, *Christus Victor*, ransom, recapitulation, moral influence (exemplary), moral government

Key Distinctions

- active/passive (obedience of Christ)
- humiliation/exaltation
- "already"/"not yet"
- sufficient/efficient (atonement)

228 • Pilgrim Theology

Key Questions

1. Discuss the distinction between thank offerings and guilt offerings. How does this relate to the active and passive obedience of Christ?
2. Identify some of the key interpretations or theories of the atonement that have been offered in church history. Evaluate them in the light of the biblical passages we've reviewed.
3. What's the difference between propitiation and expiation?
4. What is "penal substitution"? And why is this view foundational for all of the other important aspects of Christ's work?
5. What is meant by the phrase "sufficient for the world, efficient for the elect" in relation to the purpose and extent of Christ's work?
6. In what sense was Christ exalted even at the cross?
7. Discuss the significance of the ascension in the New Testament and in the history of theology. Is this an important doctrine—and if so, why?

Chapter Nine

The Spirit and the Kingdom

Ascended to the right hand of the Father, Jesus Christ is absent from us in the flesh. Although Jesus' earthly ministry recapitulated Israel's (and Adam's) commission of **exodus** and **conquest**, the disciples were still wondering even at his ascension, "Lord, will you at this time restore the kingdom to Israel?" (Ac 1:6). This side of the cross and resurrection, they now understood Christ's teaching concerning a greater exodus from death and destruction. In his conversation with the two disciples along the Emmaus road, Jesus said, "O foolish ones, and slow of heart to believe all that the prophets have spoken! Was it not necessary that the Christ should suffer these things and [then] enter into his glory?" (Lk 24:25–26). As Jesus proclaimed himself from all of the Scriptures for the next forty days, the disciples finally recognized that this was the real exodus. It was resurrection life in the renewed creation, not long life in the land of Canaan; liberation from death, sin, and hell, not just from Egypt; good news for the world, not just for Israel, and therefore it was about the justification of the ungodly, both Jew and Gentile, in Jesus Christ.

So far, so good on Christ as the fulfillment of the *exodus*. Yet they were still thinking of the *conquest* in terms of a replay of the Sinai covenant: driving God's enemies from his holy land and re-instituting the earthly theocracy. Their vision was too narrow. The field of Christ's conquest was the whole cosmos, not merely a plot of land in the Middle East, and it included the nations as well as Israel. Yet this conquest would proceed by his word and Spirit, not by chariots and swords:

> Then he opened their minds to understand the Scriptures, and said to them, "Thus it is written, that the Christ should suffer and on the third day rise from the dead, *and that repentance and forgiveness of sins should be proclaimed in his name to all nations, beginning from Jerusalem.* You are *witnesses* of these things. And behold, I am sending the promise of my Father upon you. But *stay in the city until you are clothed with power from on high.*" (Lk 24:45–49, emphasis added)

So, in his answer to their final question — "Lord, will you at this time restore the kingdom to Israel?" — Jesus neither postpones the kingdom to a future age nor leads them into a military insurrection against the Roman Empire. Rather, he answers,

> "It is not for you to know times or seasons that the Father has fixed by his own authority. But you will receive power when the Holy Spirit has come upon you, and you will be my witnesses in Jerusalem and in all Judea and Samaria, and to the end of the earth." And when he had said these things, as they were looking on, he was lifted up, and a cloud took him out of their sight. (Ac 1:6–9)

A great deal happens in Acts 2. From the throne of the ascended Christ the Spirit is sent, creating and indwelling a body that will witness to Christ from Jerusalem to the ends of the earth (vv. 1–13). Its first sign is Peter's sermon, which announces that the Old Testament promises have been fulfilled in Jesus Christ's life, death, resurrection, ascension, and the sending of the Spirit (vv. 14–36). From this announcement a new covenant community is born. "Repent and be baptized every one of you in the name of Jesus Christ for the forgiveness of your sins, and you will receive the gift of the Holy Spirit. For the promise is for you and for your children and for all who are far off, everyone whom the Lord our God calls to himself" (vv. 38–39). While individuals — "about three thousand souls" — were "cut to the heart" by this message, repented, believed, and were baptized, they were organized by the Spirit into a new human community. "And they devoted themselves to the apostles' teaching and the fellowship, to the breaking of bread and the prayers" (v. 42). From this shared union with Christ, these pilgrims from faraway regions were so united with each other that the worshiping community itself was a witness to the world. "And the Lord added to their number day by day those who were being saved" (v. 47).

Though converts entered as individual believers, they were added to the church, baptized into Christ's body. Henceforth they would be "catholic" persons, citizens of the age to come who are strangers and aliens in this present age. No longer mere individuals, they have become parts of Christ's covenantal body. This organization of creation into a new creation was never as fully realized even in Christ's earthly ministry as it was at Pentecost and has been ever since. The Spirit has come to apply the benefits of Christ, making all things new. Furthermore, the promise is for them and for their children. As in its Old Testament administration, the covenant of grace includes the children of believers. Yet it also reaches outside of this community, to bring the gospel to those who are far off.

The link, therefore, between Christ's present reign in his threefold office and the kingdom that he has inaugurated is the person and work of the Holy Spirit.

I. The Spirit of Promise

In treating the doctrine of the Trinity, I observed the danger of separating the work of the Father, the Son, and the Spirit in terms of creation, redemption, and the application of salvation. In every act of the Godhead, each person is engaged. Each has a distinct work to perform in this economy, but every work is done from the Father, in the Son, through the Spirit.

A. The Spirit in Creation and Redemptive History

One of the first things that builders have to do is to separate things before they can put them together. Everything has to be organized according to the architect's plan and the piles of materials that have been purchased. As the builder among the Godhead, the Spirit is associated especially with separating and then putting things back together, making them fit together. Since he is identified in Scripture particularly with his work within people, the building analogy must be combined with the organic metaphor, as it often is in the biblical images of the people of God, with vine and branches, head and body, cornerstone and living stones. In the power of the Spirit, the building "grows up" and functions properly, with each part fulfilling its design.

In both the Hebrew and the Greek, the root of the verb "to sanctify" is "to cut." God's sanctification cuts people, places, and things *away* from their ordinary association *for* his own use. The Spirit's career as the sanctifying divider-and-uniter is evident as early as the Bible's account of creation (Ge 1:1–10).

In the flood narrative in Genesis 8, we encounter the first instance of the Spirit appearing as a dove, announcing the appearance of dry land (Ge 8:8–12), but earlier in this chapter it is said, "And God made a wind [*ruach*] blow over the earth, and the waters subsided" (v. 1b). Given the parallelism with the creation account (of waters being divided for human habitation), there is no good reason not to translate *ruach* "Spirit" rather than "wind" in 8:1b. After the flood in Genesis 9, Yahweh pledges, "I establish my covenant with you, that never again shall all flesh be *cut off* by the waters of the flood..." (v. 11, emphasis added).

The exodus narrative (Ex 19) also invokes this creation imagery with the Spirit descending, hovering over the waters, and separating them in order for dry land to appear, then leading the redeemed host by pillar and cloud to the Sabbath rest.[1] The Spirit leads the Israelites by pillars of cloud and fire through the *tohu wabohu* (darkness and void), cutting or separating the waters for safe passage, but cuts off Pharaoh's armies in the process (Ex 13:17–15:27). The Spirit's leading in the cloud by day and pillar of fire by night is the visible assurance that God is with his people, distinguishing them from the nations (Ex 33:14–16). The Spirit also descends over, upon, and within the tabernacle and then the temple, as well as resting upon the prophets for their unique mission.

Thus, *cutting* is a covenantal term, which comes to expression especially in the rite of circumcision, a partial cutting-off that points to the seed who will be wholly "cut off" for sinners (Isa 53:8). In contrast to pagan cosmologies, the strange new world of the Bible "cuts" between the holy and the common, not between spirit and matter or higher and lower worlds. To be "cut off" is to be excommunicated. In the prophets, the full realization of circumcision is the gift of the Spirit, a circumcision of the heart, which the law could not accomplish (Dt 10:16; 30:6; Jer 4:4; Ro 2:29; 3:30; Gal 6:13–15; Col 2:11; 3:11). At Pentecost Peter's hearers were "cut to the heart" by this circumcision performed by the Spirit through the gospel (Ac 2:37).

In all of these diverse works — from creation to glorification — sanctification therefore involves a negative and positive aspect. Negatively, it is God's definitive act of cutting away his people from the common curse: namely, condemnation and corruption. Yet, positively, it is the definitive ingrafting of dead branches onto the Living Vine, so that they can bring forth the fruit of the Spirit. In both the fiat declaration " 'Let there be light!' And it was so" and the continual word of flourishing, " 'Let the earth bring

---

1. M. G. Kline, *Images of the Spirit* (S. Hamilton, Mass.: self-published, 1986), 14–15.

forth. . . .' And the earth brought forth . . . ," the Spirit is the one who makes God's word effectual.

As we have seen, Jesus' self-consciousness as the Servant of the LORD prophesied by Isaiah was inseparable from the endowment of the Spirit (Lk 4:18 – 21, quoting Isa 61:1 – 2). His conception was attributed to the Spirit as well (Lk 1:34 – 35). The language used here to speak of the Spirit's work in the virginal conception ("The Holy Spirit will *come upon* you, and the power of the Most High will *overshadow* you") echoes creation (esp. Ge 1:1 – 2). In every work of the Trinity, the Spirit is the one who brings about within creation that marvelous fruition of the Father's speech. In Matthew's Gospel, before the engagement and conjugal union of Mary and Joseph, Mary "was found to be with child from the Holy Spirit" (Mt 1:18). After his baptism by John, Jesus, "full of the Holy Spirit . . . was led by the Spirit in the wilderness for forty days, being tempted by the devil" (Lk 4:1 – 2a; cf. Mt 4:1), recapitulating Adam's temptation and Israel's forty years in the wilderness. Jesus performs his miracles by the Spirit — in fact, attributing them to Satan is "blasphemy against the Holy Spirit" (Mk 3:28 – 30; Lk 12:10). Jesus also bestows the Spirit on his disciples (Jn 20:22).

In Exodus 19, the momentous event of the Spirit's descent is represented by the sound of the trumpet blast in a moving cloud, a scene that is repeated throughout Ezekiel and returns at Pentecost with the erection of the end-time sanctuary "not made with hands" (Heb 9:11) that Ezekiel prophesied. To the Spirit particularly is attributed the dignity of transforming created space into covenantal place: a home for communion between Creator and creatures, extending to the ends of the earth in waves of kingdom labor. In the prophets, the Spirit is associated with a glory cloud (Isa 63:11 – 14; Hag 2:5) and divine wind or breath — *ruach*, the same Hebrew word for spirit/ the Spirit (Ps 104:1 – 3). It is, in fact, by this Spirit that all things are created and renewed (v. 30). The presence of the Spirit always signals the arrival of God's kingdom in judgment and salvation.

The Creator Spirit is, even in the very beginning, a divine witness to the goal of creation: namely, the consummation. Thwarted by Adam in the first creation, this goal is finally achieved by the Last Adam in the new creation, but he accomplishes this as our representative by constant dependence on the Spirit. *The age to come is the Father's to give, Christ's to win, and the Spirit's to actually bring into the present, even in the midst of this present evil age.* No wonder, then, that the outpouring of the Spirit is identified with the "last days" and the age to come. The Spirit comes from the consummated future of Sabbath glory, like the dove that brought Noah a leafy twig in its beak as a harbinger of new life beyond the waters of judgment. Already in creation, therefore, we meet the Spirit of promise: the one who propels creation toward its goal, which is nothing less than the consummation at the end of the trial. This interpretation of the relationship between the Spirit of Glory and the Spirit of judgment is especially supported by 2 Corinthians 3 and 4. The Spirit removes the veil that prevents us from seeing the glory of God in the face of Christ.

The Spirit who clothed Christ in our flesh and in consummated glory now clothes us with Christ. In all of these various ways, the appeal is to the old covenant history of royal investiture that begins in Eden, with the Spirit's in-breathing, followed by all of the priestly imagery of glorious temple vestments and the event of Christ breathing on his disciples. "When the investiture figure is used," writes Kline, "what is 'put on' is the new man created in the image of God (Eph. 4:24; Col. 3:10), or Christ the Lord (Rom. 13:14; Gal. 3:27; cf. Eph. 2:15; 4:13), or the resurrection glory of immortality (I Cor. 15:53; II Cor. 5:2ff.).... In the vocabulary of Peter, 'partakers of the divine nature' expresses renewal in the image of God (II Peter 1:4)."[2] Believers are now, in Christ, "the image and glory of God" (1Co 11:7).

Having departed the earthly sanctuary, this Spirit of glory now fills the end-time temple: the church as Christ's body. If the Son is the place in God where covenant community is created, then the Spirit is the one who turns a house into a home. Jesus is Immanuel, God *with* Us, and the Spirit is given by the Father and the Son in these last days to be God *within* Us. This is why the Spirit is especially identified with sanctification: consecrating natural, creaturely reality—people, places, and things. Not only created to worship God, humanity was created to be the temple of God, filled with the Spirit of Glory. The in-breathing of the Spirit that makes humanity a living being in Genesis 2:7 reappears throughout redemptive history, as in the temple-filling episode in Ezekiel 37, as well as Mary's annunciation (Luke 1:35), culminating in the prophetic anticipation of Pentecost, when Jesus breathed on the disciples and issued his performative utterance, "Receive the Holy Spirit" (Jn 20:22).

Echoing the original creation, the Father and the Spirit issue their heavenly benediction on Jesus in his baptism (Mk 1:10–11), repeated by the Father at the Transfiguration (Mk 9:7), testifying from heaven. Yet by themselves the words and signs of the Father, the Son, and the Spirit would not have won the consent of those who are "dead in trespasses and sins" (Eph 2:1)

---

2. Ibid., 29.

apart from the Spirit's ministry of testifying *within us* to the word of Christ *outside of us*. Even after the resurrection and Jesus' instruction, the disciples needed to wait in Jerusalem until the Spirit descended to make them witnesses (Lk 24:48–49). The Spirit, who witnesses to Christ (Jn 16:14), is at work within us to embrace that witness through his Word and then to make us a "cloud of witnesses" in the world. Again, the context is political and judicial. The setting of Pentecost is a courtroom scene in which the Spirit as the heavenly attorney convicts us of sin and convinces us of the gospel, just as Jesus had prophesied in the upper room (Jn 14–16). It opens up a gracious reprieve for judgment and justification, before the final day of reckoning when the court will execute justice without mercy.

B. The Spirit at Pentecost

Acts 1 marks the transition from the ascension to Pentecost. Jesus ordered the disciples to remain in Jerusalem "for the promise of the Father": the baptism with the Holy Spirit "not many days from now" (Ac 1:1–5). About 120 people were gathered in the upper room, near the temple, where pilgrims had gathered for the feast from far-flung regions.

> When the day of Pentecost arrived, they were all together in one place. And suddenly there came from heaven a sound like a mighty rushing wind, and it filled the entire house where they were sitting. And divided tongues as of fire appeared among them and rested on each one of them. And they were all filled with the Holy Spirit and began to speak in other tongues as the Spirit gave them utterance. (Ac 2:1–4)

Astonished that uneducated Galileans were proclaiming the gospel in their own languages, the visitors' reactions ranged from "amazed and perplexed" to outright incredulity: "They are filled with new wine" (vv. 12–13).

Just as the Spirit's presence in Christ's ministry was identified with his proclamation of the gospel (Isa 61:1–2; Lk 4:18–21), the consequence of the Spirit's descent at Pentecost was not unrestrained pandemonium but the public proclamation of the gospel by Peter, with the other apostles standing at his side (Ac 2:14–36). The one who had cowardly denied Christ three times was now risking his life for the message that the one who had been crucified a short distance from there had been raised, was at God's right hand, and would return to judge the earth. Stringing together a series of citations from the prophets and the Psalms, Peter proclaimed Christ and this remarkable descent of the Spirit as the fulfillment of everything the Scriptures had foretold. "Cut to the heart," three thousand people embraced

Peter's message and were baptized (2:37–41). Reflecting a church united to the true and faithful witness in heaven, and empowered by the indwelling Spirit as witnesses, the rest of Acts can be summarized by the theme, "The word of God spread."

Like a rocket piercing the clouds, Christ's ascension opens up a hole in history through which the Spirit descends. This hole is the space for repentance and faith. It is precisely because Christ has ascended bodily that the need for the Holy Spirit is so urgently felt. This hole will close when Christ returns. The productive intermission between Christ's two advents will be over, and the kingdom of grace will become the kingdom of glory. The human race will be divided between the "sheep," who receive everlasting life, and the "goats," who will inherit everlasting condemnation. Were it not for Christ's ascent, we sinners would not have the continuing intercession of our King or the guarantee of our own share in the new creation. And were it not for the Spirit's descent, no one would ever embrace in faith the work that Christ has performed for us. Far from being a replacement for Jesus, the Spirit is the one who unites us to our glorified head, indwells us, and keeps us longing for our Lord's return. Once more the eternal covenant of redemption comes into view. The Father gave a bride to the Son; the Son redeemed her, and now the Spirit unites them in everlasting communion.

C. The Spirit's Ongoing Ministry (John 14–16)

The Father spoke in the Son to create the world, and yet it was the Spirit who brought about within the unformed cosmos thus created that ordered realm of which they spoke. Even in common grace, as Calvin noted, wherever goodness, truth, and beauty flourish in this fallen world, it is because the Spirit grants wisdom, health, and other benefits that we do not deserve.[3] Thus, even in the old creation the Spirit is at work, holding up the columns of the earthly city while bringing the heavenly Jerusalem into this age.

In the new creation, the Spirit inwardly convicts us of God's judgment and convinces us of God's mercies in Christ. Jesus' discourse in the upper room recorded in John 14–16 highlights the way in which the Spirit will mediate (and now mediates) Christ's prophetic, priestly, and kingly reign. Christ now reigns over us in exalted grace and glory, and by his Spirit he also reigns within us, bringing us from death to life, so that we will at last answer the triune Creator, "Here I am."

---

3. Calvin, *Institutes* 2.2.15.

First of all, the Spirit's ongoing ministry is judicial. The Spirit is sent not only to announce the coming judgment, but "convict the world concerning sin and righteousness and judgment," with unbelief in Christ as the focus of that conviction (Jn 16:8). We see the empirical effects of this promise in Peter's Pentecost sermon, and indeed throughout the book of Acts—even as we do today wherever the Great Commission spreads Christ's fame. The Spirit will not speak another word, but will inwardly renew, convicting and persuading us of our guilt and Christ's righteousness.

Second, as the Son is the sole embodiment of all truth, the Spirit will be sent to "guide you into all truth." The Spirit is the guide, while the Son is the destination. Just as the Son did not speak on his own authority, but related everything he himself heard from the Father, the Spirit "will not speak on his own authority, but whatever he hears he will speak, and he will declare to you the things that are to come" (Jn 16:13). The Spirit is the one who "does not in fact present himself but the absent Jesus," as Farrow notes. Through word and sacrament, the Spirit seizes us for his future. "The Spirit's work is an infringement on our time, an eschatological reordering of our being to the fellowship of the Father and the Son, and to the new creation."[4] The Spirit is not a resource that we use, but the God who claims us for his purposes, sweeping us unexpectedly and disruptively into his new world. The Spirit divides and unites, cutting us out of our covenantal solidarity with Adam and grafting us into Christ. The Upper Room Discourse underscores the point that the Spirit comes not to verify our religious experience or assist us in our enthusiastic efforts to establish the ethical kingdom in the world, but to prove us wrong about sin, righteousness, and judgment. Of course, his judgment has its profound effects in our experience and ethical action, but the focus of his work is to convince us of our guilt and of Christ's imputed righteousness and to lead us into all truth as it is in Christ. Although the Spirit preaches Christ rather than himself, Jesus Christ's personal history must be for us a distant and fading memory, except for the Spirit's work of ushering us into the courtroom where even now Christ pleads on behalf of his witnesses on earth and prepares a place for them.

Yet this means conflict, not conquest. Like Jesus in his earthly humiliation, the church militant is a witness (*martys*, from which we get the word "martyr"), that part of the world that, seized by the Spirit in the powers of the age to come, issues an "amen" to Christ that contradicts the powers and principalities of this age. Apart from the Spirit's work, the church would

---

4. Douglas Farrow, *Ascension and Ecclesia* (Edinburgh: T&T Clark, 1999), 257.

always prefer to reign with Christ now (or in his absence, here below) rather than be witnesses.

When it is no longer content to be visible as the eucharistic community, gathered in the upper room to be scattered in witness and martyrdom, the church begins to resemble more the disciples on their way to Jerusalem before the solemn events that unfolded there, expecting Jesus to restore the earthly theocracy to its visible splendor. Even while they stood in the presence of the true temple who would be torn down and raised after three days, "[Jesus'] disciples came to point out to him the buildings of the temple" (Mt 24:1). What an impressive structure, with its sprawling colonnades and piercing pinnacles! "But [Jesus] answered them, 'You see all these, do you not? Truly, I say to you, there will not be left here one stone upon another that will not be thrown down" (v. 2). We cling by nature to the high and exalted places, even when God is among us in the flesh. Sure, Jesus says and does some interesting things, but look at our impressive buildings, history, and cultural contributions; or observe the headlines we have made with our movements and charismatic leaders! We point out to Jesus all of our works, all of our magnificent cathedrals of stone and piety, our noble traditions, holy ecstasy, and press releases, and Jesus replies, "What are these to me? I am the temple, the high priest, the king, and the prophet rolled into one. I am the Way, the Truth, and the Life."

In this interim, the Spirit inwardly convicts the guilty and conveys forgiveness by making them hearers of the Word. This is the presence of the kingdom in this age. Even the Spirit is a hearer of the Word. As the divine missionary in the earth today, the Spirit will speak "whatever he hears" (Jn 16:13). The Spirit not only has stood in the council of Yahweh as a witness, like the prophets and apostles, but is one with the Father and the Son. The one by whom the Word was conceived in the flesh is the source and the interpreter of the word concerning him. And he will tell the truth not only about the past (what God *has* done in Christ), but about the future (what God *will do* in Christ): "and he will declare to you the things that are to come" (Jn 16:13). Although the Spirit works within us, it is with the intention of drawing us outside of ourselves to focus on this economy of grace. The Spirit is an extrovert, always going forth on missions with his Word, creating an extroverted community who can at last look up to God in faith and out to the world in love, witness, and service. We see the first impact of this promise at Pentecost, with Peter's proclamation of Christ as the fulfillment of all prophecy as well as with the response of the hearers.

Third, Jesus says concerning the Spirit, "He will glorify me" (v. 14). This surely denotes the point of the Spirit's testimony, just as verses 14b and 15 underscore this mutuality (perichoresis) between the Son and the Spirit in the covenant of redemption: the Spirit and the Son share a common treasure, a treasure that they together with the Father intend to share also in common with us. The Father chose a bride for his Son, who gave his life for her; now the Spirit is the matchmaker, uniting us to Christ. This comes to fullest expression perhaps in Jesus' prayer in chapter 17. Jesus glorified the Father and now the Father and the Spirit glorify the Son. The Son is the content, but the Spirit brings all of God's words to pass and makes them fruitful, convincing us inwardly to embrace Christ. When he ascends, Jesus will prepare a place for us in his kingdom (Jn 14:2–3). Because the King still has a history, so do his coheirs, and because he has a place, we will have one also—where he is. And he will come again to take us there.

In the meantime, his departure opens a fissure in history where the Spirit—for the first time in redemptive history—will not only lead, guide, and light above or upon the temple-people, but will permanently indwell them. "I will not leave you as orphans," says Jesus, but "I will ask the Father, and he will give you another Helper, to be with you forever"—"the Spirit of truth" (Jn 14:16–18). Jesus Christ indwells believers and the church, but by his Spirit, not immediately in the flesh (2Co 1:22; cf. Ro 8:16, 26; 1Co 3:16; Gal 4:6; Eph 5:18). For this immediate presence nothing short of Christ's bodily return is required. Because of the ascension, the church on earth is not triumphant and must wait for the bodily return of its head in the future for the renewal of all things. However, because Christ already reigns now from heaven and has sent his Spirit, the church is never defeated; on the contrary, "the gates of hell shall not prevail against it" (Mt 16:18).

The disciples may have seen Jesus Christ in the flesh, but we know him in the power of the Spirit through the proclamation that they were authorized by Christ and endowed by his Spirit to deliver to us. Although they walked and ate with him, the disciples did not recognize him as their Redeemer until the Spirit opened their eyes (Mt 16:17; Lk 24:31). Their relationship with Jesus was conditioned (both for Jesus and for them) by the realities of "this age" that came crashing down upon the Savior at Golgotha, but their saving relation to Christ came from the realities of the age to come, on the other side of the death that could not hold him. We know him now not simply as a historical figure or a model to be emulated, but as the firstfruits of the harvest to which we belong. It is the Spirit who causes us to recognize the Jesus of history as the Christ of faith (2Co 5:16–17). The Spirit takes what belongs to Christ and gives it to us, so that our Lord's absence in the flesh from earth does not stand in the way of our being located even now "with [Christ] in the heavenly places" (Eph 2:6). The Father speaks the liturgy of grace, while the Son is himself its embodiment, and the Spirit then works in "the sons of disobedience" (Eph 2:2) to create a choir of antiphonal response that answers its appropriate "amen" behind its glorified forerunner (2Co 1:19–22). "He who has prepared us for this very thing"—immortality—"is God, who has given us the Spirit as a guarantee" (2Co 5:5).

The Spirit's presence announces that the epochs are turning: this present age is giving way to the age to come. The outpouring of the Spirit will guarantee a believing community in "these last days," one that not only remembers Christ's completed work, but is actually inserted into the covenantal history (and eschatology) of its glorified head. In fact, as Paul teaches, the Spirit is sent not only *among* believers but *into* them, to indwell them. It is precisely because we "have the firstfruits of the Spirit" that "we ourselves ... groan inwardly as we wait eagerly for adoption as sons, the redemption of our bodies" (Ro 8:23; cf. Gal 4:6). As the **arrabōn** (down payment) of our final redemption, the Spirit gives us the "already" of our participation in Christ as the new creation, and it is the Spirit within us who gives us the aching hope for the "not yet" that awaits us in our union with Christ (Ro 8:18–28; cf. 2Co 1:22; 5:5; Eph 1:14). The *more we receive* from the Spirit of the realities of the age to come, the *more restless we become*. Yet it is a restlessness born not of fear but of having already received a foretaste of the future.

From John 14–16 we also see that the Spirit applies the benefits of Christ's threefold office in these last days. As *prophet*, the Spirit bears the covenant word of judgment and justification, conviction of sin and faith-creating promise. This is what it means for the Spirit to be poured out on all flesh (Joel 2). As Barth put it, "The Lord of speech is also the Lord of our hearing."[5]

The Spirit also mediates Christ's *priestly* ministry, as "another paraclete" (attorney), not by replacing Christ but by inwardly convicting us of sin, giving us faith in Christ, and assuring us of forgiveness. The content of the Spirit's teaching ministry is Christ (Jn 15:26b). As the builder of God's house, the Spirit follows the architect's plan and works with the materials that have been purchased. The Spirit does not have his own strategy, content, and methods, but convinces us inwardly of what the Father has said outwardly, through the means that Christ ordained: preaching and sacrament.

---

5. Karl Barth, *Church Dogmatics* (trans. G. W. Bromiley; Edinburgh: T&T Clark, 1957–1975), vol. 1, pt. 1, 182.

Mediating Christ's *royal* ministry, the Spirit subdues unbelief and the tyranny of sin in the lives of believers, creating a communion of saints as a body ruled by its living head through the prophets and apostles, evangelists, pastors, and teachers that Christ has poured out as the spoils of his victory (Eph 4:11–16). Through this ministry of the Spirit, Moses' request in Numbers 11:29 ("Would that all the LORD's people were prophets, and that the LORD would put his Spirit on them!") will be fulfilled beyond his wildest dreams. Not only the seventy elders, but the whole camp of Israel is made a Spirit-filled community of witnesses. The spiritual gifts bestowed on the whole body are orchestrated by the Spirit through the ordained office-bearers, who differ only in the *graces* (vocation), but not in the *grace* (ontic status) of the Spirit. Thus, the mission of the twelve in Luke 9:1–6 widens to the seventy in chapter 10. Yet this was but a prelude to the commissioning ceremony of Pentecost. Through the Spirit's ministry, we too are remade in Christ's likeness as prophets, priests, and kings: true and faithful witnesses in the cosmic courtroom, a choir answering antiphonally in praise to our Redeemer. Today, millions have joined the 120 assembled in the upper room, with tongues ablaze, to proclaim the gospel to the ends of the earth.

II. The Spirit and the Bride

In Revelation 21 one of the angels says to John, " 'Come, I will show you the Bride, the wife of the Lamb.' And he carried me away in the Spirit to a great, high mountain, and showed me the holy city Jerusalem coming down out of heaven from God" (Rev 21:9–10). In the closing verses, "The Spirit and the Bride say, 'Come.' And let the one who hears say, 'Come.' And let the one who is thirsty come; let the one who desires take the water of life without price" (Rev 22:17). Just as the Spirit works within the material creation to bring to fruitfulness the word of the Father in the Son, so also he works through the ministry of the church in salvation. The Father has chosen a bride for his Son, and the Spirit brings her to the Son for the wedding day. In Revelation 21, the Bride is also a city. Unlike the pretentious Tower of Babel, it does not arise like a pyramid from earth, but is even now "coming down out of heaven from God" (21:2). Rather than building this kingdom, "we are receiving a kingdom that cannot be shaken" (Heb 12:28). "Fear not, little flock, for it is your Father's good pleasure to give you the kingdom" (Lk 12:32). The King creates his kingdom and raises his subjects to the status of coheirs, "a kingdom of priests" (Ex 19:6 with 1Pe 2:9 and Rev 5:10).

The kingdom is a gift of the King, not an achievement of his subjects.

It comes into being and grows because its King reigns from his heavenly throne and has sent his Spirit into the world to bring conviction of sin and to grant faith to sinners to embrace Christ with all his benefits. The same Spirit who hovered over the waters to create dry land, led Israel through the watery grave of the Red Sea on dry land, filled the temple, and overshadowed Mary's womb so that the one to whom she gave birth was no less than the incarnate God who now sweeps across the valley of dry bones to raise those dead in sin. Wonder of all wonders, this same Spirit indwells not only the church corporately but each believer as Christ's living temple. The indwelling Spirit assures us of our justification by the gospel (Ro 8:1). His living and life-giving presence within us is the source of our sanctification and the down payment on our final resurrection (Ro 8:11, 23).

As a "mixed body," the visible church as we now know it is neither hidden under the types and shadows of the old covenant theocracy nor fully revealed as the elect spouse of Christ in glory. A bride is not yet the wife, just as justified and renewed believers are not yet glorified. The kingdom of God is present in a semirealized way even now in and through the church, yet it is a more encompassing reality than the church and will be fully realized only when the groom returns for his wedding day.

Theologians have sought to identify this difference between the present and future states of the kingdom and the church in various ways. Familiar ever since the medieval era is the distinction between *the church militant* and *the church triumphant*. Echoing Christ's states of humiliation and exaltation, this distinction is useful up to a point; however, it refers to the generations of the church who are now alive (the church below) and those who have died in the Lord (the church above). More eschatological is the distinction between the **kingdom of grace** and the **kingdom of glory**. With either distinction, it is not a question of two churches, but of the two different phases of Christ's reign. The status and character of Christ's kingdom are always determined by

---

Key Distinction:
kingdom of grace / kingdom of glory

United to Christ, the church too lives under a period of humiliation, bearing its cross in testimony to Jesus, in order to reign with Christ when he returns. For now, Christ's kingdom expands by his Word and Spirit, proclaiming the forgiveness of sins to the ends of the earth. At Christ's return, this kingdom will be consummated and the kingdoms of this age will be finally judged and absorbed into his everlasting reign.

the status and character of its King. Like its Lord during his earthly ministry, this kingdom at present has a glory that lies hidden under the cross, even though its power is at work as the Spirit makes the rays of the age to come penetrate into the darkness of this present evil age.

Like its gospel, the kingdom's form, means, government, and effect seem weak in the eyes of the world. It is often persecuted or simply ignored by the powers and principalities of this present age, and yet it grows precisely in and through the apparent weakness of its message and ministry. The release of Satan's prisoners does not attract the world's attention, but it is indeed headline news. And one day the announcement will ring out, "'The kingdom of the world has become the kingdom of our Lord and of his Christ, and he will reign forever and ever'" (Rev 11:15). On that day, the hole in history—the intermission—will be closed. The kingdom of grace that has grown throughout the world by word and Spirit, distinct from the kingdoms of this age, will welcome the King of Glory. The old covenant theocracy was merely typological of the union of cult and culture, worship and geopolitics, church and state, that will occur when Jesus Christ returns in judgment and vindication, setting all things right in the earth forever.

Key Terms

- exodus and conquest
- *arrabōn*

Key Distinction

- kingdom of grace/kingdom of glory

Key Questions

1. Discuss the Spirit's role in history, from creation to consummation. How does the Spirit's ministry differ from and also serve Christ's ministry?
2. What are some of the key insights we glean from Jesus' Upper Room Discourse (John 14–16) concerning the Spirit's work in these last days?
3. How does the Spirit mediate Christ's royal office today?
4. What is the relationship between the covenant and the kingdom? How does this differ from its form in the old covenant?

Chapter Ten

Chosen and Called

W e turn now to the spoils of Christ's triumph that are poured out by his Spirit upon people "from every tribe and language and people and nation," being made into "a kingdom and priests to our God" (Rev 5:9). What a wondrous thing it is that even though Jesus Christ has been exalted to the throne of God, absent from us in the flesh, we may nevertheless only now be united to him in a manner far more intimate than the fellowship enjoyed by the disciples with Jesus during his earthly ministry. Having united himself to us in our flesh, sharing in our suffering and death, he now unites us to himself in his victorious life by his Spirit.

The covenant of redemption entered into by the persons of the Godhead in eternity is the anchor of Paul's *ordo salutis* (order of salvation) in Romans 8:30–31, which William Perkins aptly called the golden chain. "Those whom he predestined he also called, and those whom he called he also justified, and those whom he justified he also glorified." Behind all of the covenants in history lies the "eternal purpose in election" to which Paul repeatedly refers (Ro 8:28; 9:11; Eph 1:4–5, 11; 3:11; 2Ti 1:9). **Election** is God's choice of particular people as recipients of his merciful grace in his Son out of the mass of condemned humanity. Though united to Christ in history, through faith, within the covenant of grace, the elect were chosen in Christ from all eternity in the covenant of redemption.

Key Distinction:
history of salvation/order of salvation

When were you saved? I'll never forget the day the answer hit me between the eyes: "Two thousand years ago." My pastor looked puzzled. I didn't know it then, but I was talking about the **history of salvation** (*historia salutis*), and he was thinking about the **order of salvation** (*ordo salutis*). In reality, though, "salvation" in Scripture encompasses both. Jesus Christ *accomplished* our redemption at the cross and in his resurrection, but the Spirit *applies* it when he calls us effectually through the gospel and unites us to Christ. So *history of salvation* refers to the unfolding stages from promise to fulfillment, while the order of salvation focuses on the various stages in the believer's experience of salvation's blessings.

The order of salvation is of crucial significance and may be drawn from many clear passages, including Romans 8:29–30: "Those whom he predestined he also called, and those whom he called he also justified, and those whom he justified he also glorified." We were chosen in eternity and redeemed at the cross. We have been justified the moment we trusted in Christ alone for our salvation. We are being sanctified. And we will be glorified.

I. The State of the Controversy

According to Pelagius and his disciples, every human being is born in the same state as Adam before the fall, free to choose good and gain eternal life or sin and eternal death.[1] Semi-Pelagianism holds that grace is necessary for the continuance of salvation, but that free will initiates the process. Aided especially by Augustine, the church condemned Pelagianism, and even Semi-Pelagianism, in no uncertain terms. From a common Augustinian heritage, many Roman Catholic as well as Protestant theologians have affirmed that God's grace precedes all human decision and effort. In fact, the sixth-century Second Council of Orange condemned the view that God gives his grace in response to human decision and effort.[2] This Semi-

---

1. See B. R. Rees, *Pelagius: Life and Letters* (London: Boydell Press, 2004); *Pelagius's Commentary on St. Paul's Epistle to the Romans* (trans. Theodore De Bruyn; Oxford Early Christian Studies; Oxford: Oxford Univ. Press, 1998).

2. See *Creeds of the Churches* (ed. John H. Leith; 3rd ed.; Louisville: Westminster John Knox, 1982), 37–44.

Pelagian position was revived in the late Middle Ages, and is illustrated in the common formula, "God will not deny his grace to those who do what lies within them" (repeated substantially in Benjamin Franklin's famous proverb, "God helps those who help themselves"). Nevertheless, a strain of Augustinian teaching persisted throughout this era and formed much of the positive influence on Martin Luther, John Calvin, and other Reformers.[3]

Within Protestantism, however, consistent Augustinianism was challenged by various groups, most notably the **Arminians.** Arising from within the Dutch Reformed Church, the followers of James Arminius issued their Five Points of the Remonstrants in 1610: (1) God's election of sinners is conditional (based on foreseen faith); (2) Christ died to make salvation possible for every person; (3) all human beings are born in sin and therefore incapable of being saved apart from grace; (4) this grace is offered to all and may be resisted; (5) it is possible for regenerate believers to lose their salvation. Arminianism soon divided into two trajectories: one was more liberal (Pelagian-Socinian), and the other more evangelical (following Arminius and, later, Wesley).

According to evangelical Arminians, original sin has so corrupted the heart that no one can be saved apart from God's *prevenient* grace (that is, grace that "goes before"). Nevertheless, God has given sufficient prevenient grace to every person for regeneration, so it is now up to each person to choose Christ and, consequently, to be born again or to reject Christ and be condemned. The important difference from the Reformed position defined at Dort is that this grace is (a) potentially rather than actually saving and (b) granted to every person rather than to the elect alone.

At the Synod of Dort (1618–19), with the representation of various Reformed bodies throughout the Continent as well as the Church of England and the Church of Scotland, Arminianism was carefully analyzed and refuted. The Canons, to which we will return, locate unbelief in the total inability of sinners to effect their own liberation from the bondage of the will and locate faith in the unconditional election, redemption, and effectual

---

3. Staunch Augustinianism persisted throughout the Middle Ages, especially through the work of Gregory of Rimini (1300–1358) and Archbishop Thomas Bradwardine (1290–1344). Luther's mentor and the head of the Augustinian Order in Germany, Johann von Staupitz, defended this tradition as well. Bradwardine's "Against the New Pelagians" and Staupitz's "On the Eternal Predestination of God" are included in Heiko A. Oberman, ed., *Forerunners of the Reformation: The Shape of Late Medieval Thought* (London: James Clarke, 2003). Interestingly, Staupitz (like most Augustinians) affirmed what would later be associated with the "five points of Calvinism," including particular redemption. Although he later seems to have questioned reprobation (God's decision to condemn the nonelect), and Lutheranism came to reject particular redemption, Luther included these emphases in his Romans commentary and in *The Bondage of the Will.*

calling of the triune God alone. God gives not only *sufficient grace* (that is, enough grace to enable sinners to respond positively to God if they choose to do so), but *efficient grace* (that is, regeneration as well as faith and repentance as gifts).

Eastern Orthodoxy and Roman Catholicism identify effectual calling (or regeneration) with baptism — though with different formulations. Largely removed from the Western controversy between Augustine and Pelagius, the East nevertheless teaches a view that is similar to Arminianism, with "preparatory grace and means sufficient for the attainment of happiness" given to all.[4] "In the exposition of the faith by the Eastern Patriarchs, it is said, 'As [God] foresaw that some would use well their free will, but others ill, he accordingly predestined the former to glory, while the latter he condemned.'"[5]

For Rome, baptism infuses a new habit or disposition into the soul: negatively, washing away original sin and (in the case of adults) actual sins up to that point, and positively, strengthening the soul to cooperate with grace. This baptismal regeneration is called the "first justification" and is said to be followed by an increase in inherent holiness through cooperation with grace, with the ultimate hope of attaining to final justification through grace and merit.[6] At any stage along the way, this justification (as an infused habit) may be lost, but there is in most cases the possibility of renewing one's beginning in justification through the sacrament of penance.[7]

Confessional Lutheranism also ties regeneration closely to baptism, but clearly distinguishes justification (a declaration of righteousness) from sanctification (an actual transformation in the moral life of the baptized). Imputation, not infusion, is the Lutheran (as well as Reformed) understanding of justification. In the Lutheran view, new life (*regeneratio prima*) is begun in baptism but is constantly renewed throughout the Christian life (*regeneratio secunda* or *renovatio*). Although the principle of new life is given in baptism, this new birth flowers through the preaching of the gospel. Since Lutherans do not distinguish (as the Reformed do) between external calling and inward or effectual calling, they regard this ministry of the Spirit as effectual except in the case of those who willfully resist it. Confessional Lutheranism teaches total depravity and unconditional election while also holding to God's universal grace (*gratis universalis*). Accordingly, all of the elect will believe and

---

4. The Longer Catechism of the Orthodox, Catholic, Eastern Church, q. 123, in *The Greek and Latin Creeds* (vol. 2 of *The Creeds of Christendom*, comp., ed., and with commentary by Philip Schaff; New York: Harper and Brothers, 1905, 1919), 273.

5. Ibid., q. 125, in *Creeds of Christendom*.

6. *Catechism of the Catholic Church* (Liguori, Mo.: Liguori Publications, 1994), 321–25.

7. Ibid., 363–69.

persevere, but others who have been regenerated and justified may lose their salvation.[8] Free will "does nothing" in preparing for, cooperating with, or completing God's gracious work of calling sinners to himself; in fact, the Lutheran confessions regard this as the essence of works righteousness.[9] Nevertheless, they also teach that this calling can be resisted.

II. Why Do Some Believe and Others Not?

With Lutheranism, the confessions of the Reformed and Presbyterian churches teach that human beings are conceived in sin, spiritually dead in relation to God, unable to prepare themselves for grace because their will is in bondage to sin. These traditions are agreed also in their confessional affirmation of unconditional election. Both agree that the outward calling of Christ by his Spirit, through his Word, can be resisted. However, the Reformed are distinguished by their belief that all of those for whom Christ died will be effectually (inwardly) called by the Spirit and none of those who are justified and regenerated will fail to persevere to the end. The following summary extrapolates this view.

A. Unbelief: The Bondage of the Will

Calvinism does not locate unbelief in God's sovereignty but in human depravity. Before addressing the question as to why some people believe (turning to election), we need to recognize the universal bondage that would keep all from embracing Christ if left to themselves.

Our will can choose only that in which our nature delights. If our nature is in bondage to unbelief, then our will is not free with respect to God. By nature, we "by [our] unrighteousness suppress the truth" (Ro 1:18). It is not that we are ignorant, but that we willfully reject, distort, and deny even that which we know about God from creation (vv. 20–32). Paul asks his fellow

---

8. Edmund Schlink, *Theology of the Lutheran Confessions* (trans. Paul F. Koehneke and Herbert J. A. Bouman; Philadelphia: Muhlenberg, 1961): "Embraced by God's election and act at the beginning and at the end, the believer is completely secure.... According to A. C. [Augsburg Confession] V, the Holy Spirit works faith 'when and where he pleases' ('ubi et quando visum est Deo')," which is "to be understood in a predestinarian sense even though it speaks only of God's volition [election] and not of his nonvolition [reprobation]" (289). The Formula of Concord (art. 11) rejects conditional election (i.e., based on foreseen faith) but also rejects reprobation (election to judgment). Luther taught reprobation as well as election in *The Bondage of the Will* (as did the earlier Melanchthon) but related it to the hidden God (*deus absconditus*) rather than to the God who is revealed in Christ (*deus revelatus*). Lutheran theology typically reconciles the apparent contradiction of unconditional election and universal grace by appealing to this distinction.

9. Ibid., 90.

Jews, "Are we Jews any better off? No, not at all; for we have already charged that all, both Jews and Greeks, are under sin, as it is written: 'None is righteous, no, not one; no one understands; no one seeks for God'" (3:9–11). The fallen mind is darkened to the gospel apart from the Spirit's gift of faith (1Co 2:14). Believers "were dead in the trespasses and sins in which [they] once walked.... But God, being rich in mercy, because of the great love with which he loved us, *even when we were dead* in our trespasses, *made us alive* together with Christ" (Eph 2:1–2, 4–5, emphasis added). Even faith belongs to the gift that is freely given to us by God's grace (vv. 5–9). We are saved *for* works, not *by* works (v. 10). Therefore, salvation "depends not on human will or exertion, but on God, who has mercy" (Ro 9:16).

In our fallen condition, we try to justify ourselves. We assume that while we may commit sins from time to time, we are basically good "deep down." At least our hearts are right. However, Scripture challenges this perspective. Jeremiah lamented, "The heart is deceitful above all things, and desperately sick; who can understand it?" (Jer 17:9). The Sinai covenant required Israel to circumcise its own heart (Dt 10:16), but the command could not effect any change. Even in this canon of the Sinai covenant itself God anticipates Israel's disobedience and the new covenant in which he will circumcise their heart and the heart of their children (Dt 30:1–10). This is more clearly prophesied in Jeremiah 31, where God's circumcision of the hearts of his people will be based on his forgiveness and grace alone. God's commands — even the command to repent and believe — cannot change hearts so that they can obey them. Through the law the Spirit inwardly convicts, but only the gospel — the announcement of Christ's saving person and work — can absolve us and give us a new heart. Jesus, too, emphasized that wickedness is not first of all perverse actions, but that these acts themselves have their fountainhead in a perverse heart (Mt 12:34). We cannot change our own heart by an act of will or by changing our behavior.

On the basis of such clear passages, evangelical Arminians, Lutherans, and Calvinists agree that human beings, born in sin, are incapable of any movement toward God apart from grace. However, Lutheran and Reformed confessions teach that God not only gives sufficient grace for us to cooperate toward our own rebirth but actually grants the new birth and faith prior to any human decision or activity. In other words, our rebirth is **monergistic** (one working, namely God) rather than **synergistic** (cooperation). With respect to the doctrine of salvation (soteriology), it is this single point that most decisively distinguishes the churches of the Reformation from all other traditions.

Key Distinction:
monergism/synergism

Monergism ("one working") holds that God saves sinners without their assistance, while synergism ("working together") teaches that salvation depends on our cooperation. In all of its varieties, synergism teaches that God's grace makes everything possible, but our response makes everything actual. However, monergism teaches that God's grace accomplishes everything, even granting us repentance and faith.

B. Belief: Electing, Redeeming, and Regenerating Love

The churches of the Reformation, Lutheran and Reformed (including Anglicanism, according to its Thirty-Nine Articles), also agree that election is unconditional: that is, not dependent on anything that God foresaw in us (either willing or doing), but on his merciful purpose in his Son. The London/Philadelphia Confession of the Baptists agrees.

All of us would refuse Christ were it not for the marvelous fact that "those whom he predestined he also called" (Ro 8:30). Jesus explained, "No one can come to me unless the Father who sent me draws him. And I will raise him up on the last day.... This is why I told you that no one can come to me unless it is granted him by the Father" (Jn 6:44, 65). This is why Jesus told Nicodemus that "unless one is born again," one cannot even "see the kingdom of God" (Jn 3:3). As the conversation unfolds, it becomes clear that Jesus is not telling Nicodemus how he can bring about his new birth but how the Spirit accomplishes it. Jesus explains, "The wind blows where it wishes, and you hear its sound, but you do not know where it comes from or where it goes. So it is with everyone who is born of the Spirit" (v. 8). The new birth is a mysterious work of the Spirit in his sovereign freedom, not an event that we ourselves can bring about any more than our natural birth.[10] Two chapters

---

10. Reflecting Arminian presuppositions, much of contemporary evangelicalism understands the new birth as something that is in our power (at least partially) to effect. Especially in its American expression, this form of synergism (cooperative regeneration) is combined with a pragmatic and almost technical apparatus of formulas for being born again. For example, this can be seen even in the title of a best-selling book by Billy Graham from the 1970s, *How to Be Born Again* (Nashville: Nelson, 1977, 1989); cf. Billy Graham, *The Holy Spirit: Activating God's Power in Your Life* (Nashville: Nelson, 1978, 1988, 2000). Shaped by the Keswick "Higher Life" movement, this broad stream of contemporary evangelical piety tends to treat the Spirit's person and work as a resource that we can access, activate, and manage through various steps and techniques. For a balanced critique of this view see especially B. B. Warfield, *Studies in Perfectionism* (Phillipsburg, N.J.: P&R, 1958); J. I. Packer, *Keep in Step with the Spirit* (Old Tappan, N.J.: Revell, 1987), 146–63.

earlier, we read, "But to all who did receive him, who believed in his name, he gave the right to become children of God, who were born, not of blood nor of the will of the flesh nor of the will of man but of God" (Jn 1:12–13).

God's predestination encompasses election and reprobation (rejection), but these are not two sides of the same coin. Often, when the term *Calvinism* is mentioned, people think of an arbitrary God who drags some people into heaven kicking and screaming, while telling others who want to be saved that they're simply not on the list. Sometimes this caricature is actually given life by hyper-Calvinists. However, it has never had any place in the Reformed system. In strong terms, the Canons of the Synod of Dort (1618–19) declared, "Reformed Churches ... detest with their whole soul" the view "that in the same manner in which the election is the fountain and cause of faith and good works, reprobation is the cause of unbelief and impiety."[11] Although God glorifies himself even in his righteous judgment of the reprobate (Ps 76:10; Ro 9:21–24), he takes no pleasure in the death of the wicked (Eze 18:32) but delights in the salvation of the elect (Eph 1:5–6). No one is saved by divine coercion, and no one is rejected apart from his or her own will.

God is not active in hardening hearts in the same way that he is active in softening hearts. Scripture does speak of God hardening hearts (Ex 7:3; Jos 11:20; Isa 63:17; Jn 12:40; Ro 9:18; 11:7; 2Co 3:14). Yet it also speaks of sinners *hardening their own hearts* (Ex 8:15; Ps 95:8; Mt 19:8; Heb 3:8, 13). However, no passage speaks of sinners *softening their own hearts* and regenerating themselves. Human beings are alone responsible for their hardness of heart, but God alone softens and in fact re-creates the hearts of his elect (1Ki 8:58; Ps 51:10; Isa 57:15; Jer 31:31–34; Eze 11:19; 36:26; 2Co 3:3; 4:6; Heb 10:16). In short, God has only to leave us to our own devices in the case of reprobation, but it requires the greatest works of the triune God to save the elect, including the death of the Father's only begotten Son.

If we are to be saved, God must graciously grant us faith; if we are not to be saved, God need only leave us to our own decision. Given what has already been said concerning the bondage of the will, the real question is why any believe at all. Scripture is hardly silent on this point, but celebrates this amazing grace. In fact, Jesus said, "You did not choose me, but I chose you and appointed you that you should go and bear fruit and that your fruit should abide" (Jn 15:16). In the New Testament, the new birth and the pres-

---

11. Canons of Dort, ch. 5, conclusion, in Doctrinal Standards of the Christian Reformed Church, in *Psalter Hymnal* (Grand Rapids: Board of Publications of the Christian Reformed Church, 1976), 115.

ence of the Spirit in our hearts are harbingers of the age to come. In some remarkable sense, the future consummation has already penetrated this evil age, so that even now it is beginning to make all things new from the inside out. This is God's work.

Chosen in Christ before the creation of the world, redeemed by Christ in history, receiving an inheritance in Christ, and being sealed in Christ by the gospel, we have a salvation that from start to finish is the work of the Father, in the Son, by the Spirit (Eph 1:3–14). In fact, in Romans 8 it is this realization of God's gracious election, calling, justification, and glorification (vv. 29–30) that leads Paul to the summit of doxology, first in verses 31–39, and then again finally in 11:33–36. In the application of this salvation by the Spirit no less than in its accomplishment by Christ can we sing, "Salvation is of the LORD" (Jnh 2:9). All of this means that the gospel is not an experience that we have, much less one that we can bring about. It is an announcement that creates faith in the Redeemer who makes It. It comes to us from the outside, and the Spirit opens our hearts to receive it. It *creates* new experiences and inner transformation that yields good works, but the gospel itself—and the Spirit's effectual calling through that gospel—remain distinct from anything done by us or within us. The gospel is God's life-giving word, creating a new world out of nothing (Ro 4:16–17; 1Pe 1:23, 25).

Predestination is clearly taught in Scripture, but debates over its interpretation and meaning have occupied the greatest minds in church history. The Old Testament refers to the "counsel" (*'etsah*) of God, as in Job 38:2 and Isaiah 14:26 as well as 46:10–11. Other expressions include the verb "to purpose" (*zamam*), as in Jeremiah 4:28; 51:12; and Proverbs 30:32 (ESV "devising"); "pleasure" (*haphets*), as in Isaiah 53:10 (KJV; ESV "will"); and "sovereign will" (*ratson*), as in Isaiah 49:8 (ESV "favor"). That nothing comes to pass (including the sinful actions of human beings) apart from God's sovereign governance is attested in many passages, including Genesis 50:20; Daniel 4:34–37; Acts 2:23; and Ephesians 1:11. In fact, an implication of God's omniscience is that the future is determined. God knows the future exhaustively because he has decreed the future exhaustively.

The close connection of foreknowledge and foreordination is further established by the force of the Hebrew word *yada'* and the Greek *ginōskein/proginōskein*, which occur frequently in contexts in which more than a bare awareness is in view, as in Genesis 18:19 (ESV "have chosen"), Amos 3:2 (ESV "have known"), and Hosea 13:5 (ESV "knew"). Adam's "knowing" Eve (Ge 4:1 KJV) or Mary's conception of Christ before she "knew" a man

(Lk 1:34 KJV) clearly intends something more than mere awareness of the other's existence. It is an intimate knowledge of the person in question. In Romans 8:29 we are told, "Those *whom* he foreknew he also predestined" (emphasis added), rather than *that which* he foreknew. In other words, Paul's point is not that God foreknew human choices, but that he knew his elect before they came to exist. Similarly, in 1 Peter 1:20, Jesus Christ is said to have been "foreknown before the foundation of the world." God not only foreknows; he chooses—elects—some for salvation out of a condemned race. The Hebrew word *bachar* implies choice, along with the Greek equivalents *eklegesthai* and *eklogē*, as the latter two appear in connection with divine election explicitly in Romans 9:11; 11:5 and Ephesians 1:4. The Greek verb *proorizō* and its cognates mean to "fore-horizon" (i.e., predetermine), and this word group appears in close connection also with predestination in passages such as Acts 4:28, Romans 8:29, 1 Corinthians 2:7 and Ephesians 1:5, 11.

In addition to being stated explicitly, predestination is demonstrated in the biblical narratives, including sinful actions (Ge 50:20). Nebuchadnezzar eventually learned the lesson of God's sovereignty over all things, including his own kingdom (Da 4:34–37). The times and places of every person's life are included in God's decree (Ac 17:26). Even the falling of a bird and the number of hairs on each person's head are encompassed by God's sovereign wisdom (Mt 10:29–30). Although humans are held responsible for their wicked acts in Christ's crucifixion, he was "delivered up according to the definite plan and foreknowledge of God" (Ac 2:22–23). Using the same term, *boulē*, and adding the phrase *proōrisen genesthai*, the believers later praised God saying, "For truly in this city there were gathered together against your holy servant Jesus, whom you anointed, both Herod and Pontius Pilate, along with the Gentiles and the peoples of Israel, to do whatever your hand and your plan (*boulē*) had predestined to take place (*proōrisen genesthai*)" (Ac 4:27–28). Once more, this passage does not tell us *how* God can decree the sins of sinners while holding them responsible; it simply states that this is the case.[12]

Therefore, not only the good deeds of human beings but sinful actions

---

12. Charles Hodge, *Systematic Theology* (Grand Rapids: Eerdmans, 1946), 1:547: "It is vain to argue that a holy and benevolent God cannot permit sin and misery, if sin and misery do in fact exist. It is vain to say that his impartiality forbids that there should be any diversity in the endowments, advantages, or happiness of his rational creatures.... So it is utterly irrational to contend that God cannot foreordain sin, if He foreordained (as no Christian doubts) the crucifixion of Christ. The occurrence of sin in the plan adopted by God is a palpable fact; the consistency, therefore, of foreordination with the holiness of God cannot rationally be denied."

[handwritten marginal notes: "we choose to commit sins ↓ our responsibility"]

as well are simultaneously said to be included in God's plan, yet freely willed by humans. Hebrews speaks of "the unchangeable character of his purpose" (boulē) (Heb 6:17). Ephesians 1:11 refers to the "counsel of [God's] will" (boulē tou thelēmatos) according to which "God works everything." The motivating cause of our election in Christ is God's "good pleasure" (eudokia; Eph 1:5, 9), a term that is also employed in Matthew 11:26 and Luke 2:14.

According to Paul's argument in Romans 9, God's prerogative to elect whom he will and to leave the rest in their just condemnation has been exercised all along even within Israel. In this chapter, Paul clearly teaches that election is not based on anything in or foreseen in those who are chosen (vv. 9–13). Yet God is not unfair, since everyone is in a state of condemnation and God is not bound by any necessity to save anyone (vv. 14–15). "So then it depends not on human will or exertion, but on God, who has mercy" (v. 16). Out of the same mass of fallen humanity God chooses some and rejects others (vv. 17–24). Nor can the scope of this argument be limited to Israel, since Paul concludes that those whom God "has prepared beforehand for glory" include "even us whom he has called, not from the Jews only but also from the Gentiles" (v. 24).

Finally, God's sovereignty is not only demonstrated in narratives and described in doctrines; it is celebrated in praise. For example, in each of the arguments for God's predestining purposes in Christ, Paul moves from narratively grounded doctrinal arguments to scenic vistas where he pauses to adore. Immediately after teaching, "And those whom he predestined he also called, and those whom he called he also justified, and those whom he justified he also glorified" (Ro 8:30), he exclaims, "What then shall we say to these things? If God is for us, who can be against us? ... Who shall bring any charge against God's elect? It is God who justifies" (Ro 8:31, 33). Then in chapter 11, after treating the same topic in the context of Israel's unfolding narrative, again he is left in wonder at the riches of God's unfathomable knowledge and grace (Ro 11:33–36). Only when we are led, beyond debates (and away from speculation), to *praise* have we truly understood that part of the mystery of God's decree that he has revealed.

Those whom God chose before the creation of the world he also calls in due time by his Spirit (Eph 1:4–15). The connection between election and calling is well attested, both in Paul's letters (Ro 9:6–24; Eph 1:4–13; 2Th 2:13–15; 2Ti 1:9) and elsewhere (Jn 6:29, 37, 44, 63–64; 15:16, 19; Ac 13:48; 1Pe 1:2; 2Pe 1:10), and it proceeds as the execution of an eternal covenant of redemption within the context of a historical covenant of grace.

In effectual calling, the Spirit unites us here and now to the Christ who redeemed us in the past.

We see Jeremiah's prophecy fulfilled throughout the book of Acts: as Christ is proclaimed, people respond in repentance and faith. As the businesswoman Lydia heard Paul's message, "the Lord opened her heart to pay attention to what was said by Paul," and she and her household were baptized (Ac 16:14–15). The accused become the justified and then witnesses in the courtroom. When the Gentiles in Antioch heard the gospel, "they began rejoicing and glorifying the word of the Lord; and as many as were appointed to eternal life believed" (Ac 13:48). Far from inhibiting evangelism, God's electing and regenerating grace ensured that "the word of the Lord was spreading throughout the whole region" (v. 49). Left to ourselves, none of us would receive this Word. God's sovereign grace guarantees the success of evangelism and missions.

C. Effectual Calling and the Question of Coercion

Now we come to the heart of the debate over **effectual calling**. Reformed theology understands the divine call in terms of an **outward call**, by which God summons the whole world to Christ through the preaching of the gospel, and an **inward** or **effectual call**, as the Spirit illumines the hearts of his elect and gives them faith through the gospel. Yet it is crucial to recognize that, according to this view, the internal (effectual) calling of the elect occurs through the same gospel that is announced externally to everyone.[13] The Father preaches, the Son is preached, and the Spirit is the "inner preacher" who illumines the understanding and inclines the will to receive him.

Although the means of grace (preaching and sacrament) will be explored later, it is important to add here that the Spirit delivers the gift of faith through the preaching of the gospel and confirms and strengthens it through the sacraments.[14] Yet some are attracted to the light, others repelled by it.

---

13. The Reformed scholastic Johann Heinrich Heidegger, for example, writes, "The word is the same which man preaches and which the Spirit writes on the heart. There is strictly one calling, but its cause and medium is twofold: instrumental, man preaching the word outwardly; principal, the Holy Spirit writing it inwardly in the heart" (quoted in Heinrich Heppe, *Reformed Dogmatics* [rev. and ed. E. Bizer; trans. G. T. Thomson; London: G. Allen and Unwin, 1950; repr., London: Wakeman Trust, 2002], 518). Heidegger adds, "The first effect of calling is regeneration" (ibid.).

14. See, for instance, the Heidelberg Catechism, q. 65: "You confess that by faith alone you share in Christ and all his blessings: where does that faith come from? A. The Holy Spirit produces it in our hearts by the preaching of the holy gospel, and confirms it through our use of the holy sacraments" (Doctrinal Standards of the Christian Reformed Church, in *Psalter Hymnal* [Grand Rapids: Board of Publications of the Christian Reformed Church, 1976], 32).

Key Distinction:
outward/inward (effectual) call

Scripture proclaims the gospel to everyone. In this *outward call*, Christ delivers himself to all as the only Savior. Yet only when the Spirit *inwardly* and effectually draws sinners to Christ do they actually receive the gift announced to them in the gospel.

Those who do come to trust in Christ are represented as "dead in ... sins" (Eph 2:1–5), unable to respond until God graciously grants them the gift of faith to freely embrace what they would otherwise reject (Isa 65:1; Jn 1:13; 3:7; 6:44; Ac 13:48; 16:14; 18:10; Ro 9:15–16; 1Co 2:14; Eph 2:1–5; 2Ti 1:9–10; 2:10, 19).

So the gospel is proclaimed to everyone without exception. It is proclaimed as good news not merely for the elect, but for each and every human being. Everyone who believes will be saved, and Christ's redeeming work is sufficient for the whole world. At the same time, the Spirit supervenes upon this external call by drawing sinners inwardly to Christ. Traditionally, Reformed theology has referred to this as *effectual calling* rather than *irresistible grace*. However, the latter term became more widespread as the "I" in popular presentations, with the advent of the famous "TULIP." Prior to the twentieth century, there is no evidence of the famous acronym being used in Reformed circles.[15] "Irresistible" suggests coercion, the sort of causal impact that is exercised when force is applied to someone or something. As we will see, this idea of coercion is excluded from the classic Reformed formulations. Like the "L" (limited atonement), "irresistible grace" is a liability, wreaking havoc on the noble flower.

We encounter again that useful distinction between *natural* and *moral* ability from our discussion of original sin. In Adam, we freely choose our alliance with sin and death. The fall has destroyed not our natural ability to reason, observe, experience, and judge, but our moral ability to reason, observe, experience, and judge our way to God as our Lord and Redeemer. It is not God's sovereignty but our moral blindness to God's word that keeps us from raising our eyes to heaven to say, "God, be merciful to me, a sinner!" (Lk 18:13). The problem is not the *power* to will and to do,

---

15. See Kenneth J. Stewart, *Ten Myths about Calvinism: Recovering the Breadth of the Reformed Tradition* (Downers Grove, Ill.: IVP Academic, 2011), 75–96.

but the *moral* determination of that willing and doing by slavery to sinful autonomy. The will is moved by the mind and affections; it cannot act in isolation.

It is clear from Reformed confessions that the source of unbelief is neither sovereign coercion on God's part nor any natural defect in the creature. Like Calvin, a number of Reformed confessions affirm that Adam fell by his own free will, not by any necessary compulsion. The Westminster Confession states, "God hath endued the will of man with that natural liberty that it is neither forced, nor by any absolute necessity of nature determined to good or evil." Before the fall, the will was entirely free to choose good or evil, but after the fall, humanity "has wholly lost all ability of will to do any spiritual good accompanying salvation," rendering every person "dead in sin ... not able, by his own strength, to convert himself, or to prepare himself thereunto."

> When God converts a sinner and translates him into the state of grace, he frees him from his natural bondage under sin and, by his grace alone, enables him freely to will and to do that which is spiritually good; yet so as that, by reason of his remaining corruption, he does not perfectly or only will that which is good, but does also that which is evil. The will of man is made perfectly and immutably free to good alone in the state of glory only.[16]

Such statements reflect a basic Augustinian consensus, filtered through the Reformation. The Westminster divines add that God is pleased "in his appointed and accepted time, effectually to call, by his Word and Spirit," all of the elect "out of that state of sin and death in which they are by nature, to grace and salvation by Jesus Christ." He accomplishes this by "enlightening their minds ... taking away their heart of stone ... renewing their wills ... and effectually drawing them to Jesus Christ; *yet so as they come most freely, being made willing by his grace*" (emphasis added).[17]

Employing the traditional Aristotelian categories, Reformed theologians affirmed that the Holy Spirit is the *efficient cause* of regeneration. Especially in the wake of the Arminian controversy, some Calvinists have distinguished regeneration from effectual calling. They do so in order to emphasize that the former occurs as a direct and immediate work of the Spirit, while the latter is mediated by the gospel. In this way, regeneration not only occurs prior to human response (which all Reformed as well as Lutheran churches confess), but even precedes the hearing of the gospel. However, our confes-

---

16. Westminster Confession of Faith, in *The Trinity Hymnal*, ch. 9, p. 854.
17. Ibid., ch. 12.

sions treat these as synonymous terms, and this conclusion seems to me to have the exegetical weight behind it.[18] I offer here only a brief summary in defense of this position.

First, regeneration is not treated in Scripture as the action of a sovereign subject on an object; nor is it represented as an infusion of a new principle, but rather as the result of the Spirit's work in making effectual *within* us that saving Word spoken *to* us by the Father in the Son. To repeat again Calvin's formula, echoing the ancient fathers, "To the Father is attributed the beginning of activity, and the fountain and wellspring of all things; to the Son, wisdom, counsel, and the ordered disposition of all things; but to the Spirit is assigned the power and efficacy of that activity."[19] The Father objectively reveals the Son, and the Spirit inwardly illumines the understanding to behold "the glory of God in the face of Christ" (2Co 4:6; cf. Jn 1:5; 3:5; 17:3; 1Co 2:14), liberating the will not only to assent to the truth but to trust in Christ (Eze 36:26; Jer 32:39–40; Heb 8:10; Eph 2:1–9). Because the word of God is not mere information or exhortation but the "living and active" energies of the triune God, it is far more than a wooing, luring, persuasive influence that might fail to achieve the mission on which it was sent. In both regeneration and effectual calling, it is the work of the Father, in the Son, by the Spirit. Separating regeneration from effectual calling breaks up the Trinitarian logic, as if the Spirit's work in regeneration could occur apart from the Father's speech in the Son. As the inspiration of Scripture depends equally on the Father who speaks, the Son as the content, and the Spirit as the one who brings about the powerful effect within creatures, regeneration is the Spirit's work through the gospel. By itself, the gospel would fall on deaf ears, but it is never by itself; it is accompanied by the Spirit. Therefore, every purpose for which the Father sends his word will be fulfilled (Isa 55:11). The Father is the playwright

---

18. A standard way of putting this earlier view is stated by Herman Witsius: "Regeneration is that supernatural act of God whereby a new and divine life is infused into the elect person, spiritually dead, and that *from incorruptible seed of the word of God, made fruitful by the infinite power of the Spirit*" (emphasis added) (Herman Witsius, *The Economy of the Covenants between God and Man* [trans. William Crookshank; 2 vols.; London: Edwards Dilly, 1763; repr., lithographed from 1822 ed., Phillipsburg, N.J.: Den Dulk Christian Foundation / P&R, 1990], 357). In this, Witsius is simply following the Canons of Dort (chs. 3 and 4), which is consistent with the assumption of the Westminster Confession (10.2) that regeneration and effectual calling are one and the same event. Similarly, q. 65 of the Heidelberg Catechism teaches that the Spirit creates faith "in our hearts by the preaching of the holy gospel, and confirms it through our use of the holy sacraments" (Doctrinal Standards, in *Psalter Hymnal*, 32). Here, as in the Canons of Dort, even the language of "new and divine life infused" is employed, but this is said to occur *through* the ministry of the gospel.

19. Calvin, *Institutes* 1.13.18.

and director, the Son is the central character, and the Spirit is the casting director in this divine drama.

Second, God's word is not therefore only the speech of the Father concerning the Son, which we then make effective by our own decision; rather, it is the instrumental action through which the Spirit brings about within us the corresponding response. It is a *performative* word. In effectual calling, the Spirit draws us into the world that the Word not only *describes* but *brings into existence*. Through this word, the Spirit not only works to propose, lure, invite, and attract, but actually kills and makes alive, sweeping sinners from their identity "in Adam" to the riches of their inheritance in Christ. This view of the divine word as "living and powerful" renders pointless any worry that by identifying regeneration with effectual calling through the gospel, this sovereign work can be thwarted. When the Spirit effectually calls us through the gospel, it is a fiat word that regenerates, as when God said, "'Let there be light.' And it was so." As we will see below, conversion (repentance and faith) is the human response ("'Let the earth bring forth fruit.' ... And the earth brought forth fruit") that this fiat word produces. When God declared, "Let there be ..." he did not persuade or lure things into being. He spoke and it was so. Whether in creation, providence, or redemption, God accomplishes his works through his speech. In fact, this is how actual instances of conversion are described in the New Testament, as in the case of Lydia: "The Lord opened her heart to pay attention to what was said by Paul" (Ac 16:14).

Third, there is no passage in Scripture that implies that the new birth occurs apart from the Word. Rather, Scripture locates it explicitly in the hearing of the word, specifically the gospel (Mt 4:23; Mk 13:10; Ac 14:7; 15:7; Ro 1:16; 10:8, 17; 1Co 1:18; 9:16, 23; 2Co 4:3; 8:18; 10:16; Gal 1:9; Eph 1:13; 3:6; Col 1:5, 23; 1Th 2:4; 1Pe 1:23, 25; 4:6; Rev 14:6). The gospel is not simply the good news concerning Christ, but Christ's own declaration to sinners of that reality of which the gospel speaks. Christ himself declares his absolution to the ungodly through the lips of his messengers (Ro 10:8–17). In attributing all efficacy to the Spirit's power, Scripture nevertheless represents this as occurring through the word of God that is "at work" in its recipients (1Th 2:13; cf. Ro 8:14–16; 1Co 2:4–5; 4:12–13; 2Co 4:13; Gal 3:2; Eph 1:17; Tit 3:4–5) — specifically, that message of the gospel, which is "the power of God for salvation" (Ro 1:16; 10:17; 1Th 1:5). We "have been born again ... through the living and abiding word of God" — specifically, "the good news that was preached to [us]" (1Pe 1:23, 25), "the word of the gospel" (Ac 15:7), "the word of Christ" (Ro 10:17), "the word of the cross"

(1Co 1:18). "Of his own will he brought us forth by the word of truth, that we should be a kind of firstfruits of his creatures" (Jas 1:18). In John 6 Jesus says, "No one can come to me unless the Father who sent me draws him" (v. 44). This comes only from the Spirit, and yet Jesus adds, through his speech: "The words that I have spoken to you are spirit and life" (v. 63).

This does not mean, of course, that the preached gospel works automatically; it is the Spirit who creates faith through it, when and where he will. Nevertheless, when the Spirit does regenerate people, he does so through that medium. Apart from effectual calling, one hears merely the external Word, but in effectual calling the external word is embraced inwardly through the Spirit. Calvin comments, "We must also observe that form of expression, *to believe through the word*, which means that faith springs from hearing, because the outward preaching of men is the instrument by which God draws us to faith. It follows that God is, strictly speaking, the Author of faith, and men are *the ministers by whom we believe*, as Paul teaches (1Co 3:5)" (emphasis added).[20] Commenting on Romans 10:17 ("Faith comes from hearing, and hearing through the word of Christ"), Calvin writes,

> And this is a remarkable passage with regard to the efficacy of preaching; for he testifies that by it faith is produced. He had indeed before declared that of itself it is of no avail; but that when it pleases the Lord to work, it becomes the instrument of his power. And indeed the voice of man can by no means penetrate into the soul; and mortal man would be too much exalted were he said to have the power to regenerate us; the light also of faith is something sublimer than what can be conveyed by man: but all these things are no hindrances, that God should not work effectually through the voice of man, so as to create faith in us through his ministry.[21]

Against both the medieval doctrine of justification according to infused habits and the Anabaptist emphasis on a direct and immediate work of the Spirit within us, the Reformers insisted upon the mediation of the word — specifically, the gospel. In the account I have offered thus far, believers are seen to be "worded" all the way down: in election, through the covenant of redemption; in creation, and now in the covenant of grace. The Spirit has voluntarily bound himself in his activity to the word spoken by the Father in the Son.

---

20. John Calvin, *Commentary on the Gospel of John* (trans. William Pringle; Grand Rapids: Baker, repr. 1996), comment on Jn 17:20.

21. John Calvin on Ro 10:17, in *Commentary on the Epistle of Paul the Apostle to the Romans* (ed. and trans. John Owen; vol. 19 of Calvin's Commentaries; Edinburgh: Calvin Translation Society, 1843–55; repr., Grand Rapids: Baker, 1993), 401.

III. Conversion: "Let the Earth Bring Forth..."

If there is no reason to distinguish **regeneration** and effectual calling, there is nevertheless every reason to distinguish this event from **conversion**. In regeneration we are passive; the new birth is a gift, not the result of our decision or effort. We hear the gospel, and the Spirit creates faith in our hearts to embrace it. However, in conversion we are active. There are commands to repent and believe. In conversion (unlike regeneration), we are told, "Work out your own salvation with fear and trembling, for it is God who works in you, both to will and to work for his good pleasure" (Php 2:12–13). This does not mean that in conversion our salvation shifts from God's sovereign grace in Christ to our activity and cooperation, but that the salvation that has been given is worked out by that same Spirit, through the same gospel, in a genuine relationship in which we become covenant partners who are now alive to God in Christ. Apart from our repentance and faith, there is no justification or union with Christ.

"Repent, and believe the good news": this command forms the two aspects of conversion: repentance from sin and faith toward God. In repentance, we say no to the idols, powers, rulers, and lies of this present evil age, and in faith, we say yes to Christ, "for all the promises of God find their Yes in him. That is why it is through him that we utter our Amen to God for his glory" (2Co 1:20). Yet even this human response is a gift of the Spirit through the gospel.

A. Repentance

Christ does not come to improve our lives—the "old self," to use Paul's vocabulary—but to crucify it and bury it with him so that we may be raised with him in newness of life (Ro 6:1–4). To return to the analogy of a drama, the Spirit does not help us write our script; in this scene, the character we have written for ourselves dies and we find ourselves cast in an entirely different play.

Key Distinction:
regeneration/conversion

In *regeneration* (or effectual calling), we are passive recipients of God's grace: "Even when we were dead in our trespasses, [God] made us alive together with Christ—by grace you have been saved—and raised us up with him and seated us with him in the heavenly places" (Eph 2:5–6). In *conversion*, however, those now quickened by God's Spirit through the gospel respond in repentance and faith, though these too are the gift of God.

The Greek word translated "**repentance**" (*metanoia*) denotes "change of mind." It is not only modifying a few convictions here and there, but realizing that your whole interpretation of reality—God, yourself, your relation to God and the world—is misguided. It is not finding your way back to the "straight-and-narrow," after wandering off the beaten path a bit, but acknowledging before God that you are not—and never have been—even in the right vicinity. What you once counted pious is idolatry and self-righteousness. You saw yourself at the center of the universe, but now you realize that you exist for God's pleasure and glory, and that changes how you look at everything. The right to determine for yourself what you believe and how you will live is surrendered.

Repentance is treated in Scripture as first of all the knowledge of sin produced by the law (Ro 3:20). As we have seen above from Jesus' Upper Room Discourse, the Spirit is an attorney sent "to convict the world concerning sin and righteousness and judgment" (Jn 16:8), to convict us inwardly of our guilt and his gift of justification. This change of mind is not just intellectual, but shakes the whole person to the very foundations. Repentance is what we might call today a "paradigm shift."

We see the features of repentance finely exhibited in David's prayer of confession:

> Have mercy on me, O God, according to your steadfast love; according to your abundant mercy blot out my transgressions. Wash me thoroughly from my iniquity, and cleanse me from my sin! For I know my transgressions, and my sin is ever before me. Against you, you only, have I sinned and done what is evil in your sight, so that you may be justified in your words and blameless in your judgment. Behold, I was brought forth in iniquity, and in sin did my mother conceive me. Behold, you delight in truth in the inward being, and you teach me wisdom in the secret heart. Purge me with hyssop, and I shall be clean; wash me, and I shall be whiter than snow. Let me hear joy and gladness; let the bones that you have broken rejoice. Hide your face from my sins, and blot out all my iniquities. (Ps 51:1–9)

David is not simply ashamed of his behavior but guilty. Furthermore, although he has sinned cruelly against Bathsheba and plotted the death of her husband, David recognizes that his sin is first and foremost against God. Repentance is not only remorse for having wronged our neighbors or ourselves, but is a recognition that God is the most offended party. David does not try to atone for his sins or pacify God's just anger by his remorse. He confesses that before God's throne he is condemned, and he does not try to justify himself. Finally, David acknowledges not only his sinful *actions* but his sinful *condition* from the hour of conception. Repentance pertains not simply to certain sins; pagans can be remorseful for their immoderate behavior. Rather, it is the revulsion of the whole soul toward its alliance with sin and death.

Although such godly sorrow leads David to despair of his own righteousness, it does not lead him to the final despair that often leads the ungodly to either self-destruction or a searing of their conscience. As Paul observes, "For godly grief produces a repentance that leads to salvation without regret, whereas worldly grief produces death" (2Co 7:10). After all, "God's kindness is meant to lead you to repentance" (Ro 2:4). While the law by itself produces a *legal repentance* (fear of judgment), the gospel engenders an *evangelical repentance* that bears the fruit of real change. David turns outside of himself to his merciful God. Here we see the closest possible link between repentance and faith. By itself repentance is merely the experience of damnation—until one looks by faith to Jesus Christ. The life of believers is perpetual repentance that is provoked by the law and yet sweetened by the gospel. Only because the Father freely loves and accepts us in his Son are we free to accept the awful truth about ourselves and cling to Christ in faith.

Often repentance is more broadly defined to include actual change in character and behavior, but Scripture describes this as "the fruit of repentance" (Mt 3:8) or "deeds in keeping with ... repentance" (Ac 26:20; cf. Mt 7:16; Lk 3:8; 8:15; Jn 12:24; Ro 7:4; Gal 5:22; Col 1:10). Of course, repentance is always partial, weak, and incomplete in this life. Nor is it a one-time act. As the first of Luther's Ninety-Five Theses states, "Our Lord and Master Jesus Christ, in saying 'Repent ye,' etc., intended that the whole life of believers should be penitence."

In Roman Catholic theology and practice, this call to repentance is replaced with a system of penance. As the Renaissance scholar Erasmus discovered, the Latin Vulgate had erroneously translated the Greek imperative "Repent!" (*metanoēsate*) as "Do penance! (*poenitentium agite*). Rome defines such penance as involving four elements: contrition, confession, satisfaction, and absolution.[22] Since few are able to rise to the level of true contrition (genuine sorrow for sin), attrition (fear of punishment) is deemed suitable for this first stage. For forgiveness, each sin must be recalled and orally con-

---

22. *Catechism of the Catholic Church*, 364–67. "Christ instituted the sacrament of Penance for all sinful members of the Church: above all for those who, since Baptism, have fallen into grave sin, and have thus lost their baptismal grace and wounded ecclesial communion. It is to them that the sacrament of Penance offers a new possibility to convert and to recover the grace of justification. The Fathers of the Church present this sacrament as 'the second plank [of salvation] after the shipwreck which is the loss of grace'" (363).

fessed to a priest, who then determines a suitable action or series of actions to perform in order to make satisfaction for the sin. Only then can the penitent receive the absolution.[23]

In Arminian theology, repentance—understood not only as a change of heart or mind but as a new obedience—is regarded as a condition rather than result of the new birth and justification. Even in broader evangelical circles, some Christians struggle to the point of despair over whether the quality and degree of their repentance is adequate for them to be forgiven, as if repentance were the ground of forgiveness and the former could be measured by the intensity of emotion, resolve, and victory over specific sins.

However, according to Scripture it is not our tears but Christ's blood that satisfies God's judgment and establishes peace with God (Ro 5:1, 8–11). In the words of "Rock of Ages," "Though my tears forever flow; / Though my zeal no respite know, / Naught for sin could these atone—/ Thou must save, and Thou alone." God heals the bones that he crushes and raises up those whom he has cast down. "But he gives more grace. Therefore it says, 'God opposes the proud, but gives grace to the humble'" (Jas 4:6). The law exposes our guilt, by convicting us of sin, but only the gospel can lead us to boldly claim God's promise with David: "Let me hear joy and gladness; let the bones that you have broken rejoice. Hide your face from my sins, and blot out all my iniquities" (Ps 51:8–9).

When repentance is marginalized in conversion, it is usually because of an inadequate sense of God's holiness and the just demands of his righteous law. The consequence is that conversion is represented merely as moral improvement: the *addition* of certain distinctives of Christian piety. Biblical repentance, however, involves a fundamental *renunciation* of the world, the flesh, and the devil: including the spirituality, experiences, and moral efforts in which one has trusted. The whole self must be turned away both from self-trust and from the autonomy that demands final say as to what one will believe, whom one will trust, and how one will live. Although the fruit of repentance is never perfect or complete in this life, the change of mind is decisive. Even when we sin, we now acknowledge it as sin—an offense against God—and accept God's holy judgment as true and good.

B. Faith

Arrested, arraigned, and indicted, in repentance we turn away *from* ourselves—our untruths, sins, and fraudulent claim to righteousness—and in faith we look *to* Christ for salvation and for every spiritual gift. To put it

---

23. Ibid.

differently, in repentance we confess (with David) that God is justified in his verdict against us, and in faith we receive God's justification. Dead to sin and alive to Christ once and for all in regeneration (Ro 6:1 – 11), we are called to die daily to our old self and live daily by "the free gift of God," which "is eternal life in Christ Jesus our Lord" (vv. 12 – 23).

Faith is not only knowledge of and assent to gospel truths, but trust in Christ as one's own Redeemer. In the Hebrew Scriptures to believe (*he'emin*, in the hiphil form of *'aman*) means to acknowledge as an established fact. However, this is not merely intellectual assent. It is, literally, to say "amen" to what God has performed as pertaining to oneself. Other words (*chasah*, "to take refuge"; *batach*, "to trust or lean upon") also convey the idea of faith as involving trust as well as knowledge and assent.

The Greeks believed in the existence of their gods, but the New Testament carries over from the Old Testament this understanding of faith as trust in and reliance upon the saving action of a personal God. Faith (*pistis*) is understood as trust or belief in what is said on the testimony of another (Php 1:27; 2Co 4:13; 2Th 2:13; and especially in John). More often still, faith is specifically exhibited as trust in Jesus and his declarative word (Jn 4:50; 5:47; Ro 3:22, 25; 5:1 – 2; 9:30 – 32; Gal 2:16; Eph 2:8; 3:12), a trustful reliance in Jesus Christ (*en*: Mk 1:15; Jn 3:15; Eph 1:13; *epi* plus dative: Isa 28:16, quoted in Ro 9:33; Ro 10:11; 1Ti 1:16; 1Pe 2:6; cf. Ac 16:34; Ro 4:3; 2Ti 1:5, 12). The use of *epi* with the accusative or *eis* ("into") emphasizes the transfer of trust from ourselves to God in Christ (Jn 2:11; 3:16, 18, 36; 14:1; Ro 10:14; Gal 2:16; Php 1:29; etc.). Such faith is described as looking to Christ (Jn 3:14 – 15, with Nu 21:9); hungering, thirsting, and drinking (Mt 5:6; Jn 4:14; 6:50 – 58); and coming and receiving (Jn 1:12; 5:40; 6:44, 65; 7:37 – 38). These instances (besides many others) underscore the role of faith *in the act of justification* as a passive receiving and resting in Christ, although the faith of the justified is also active in good works (Jas 2:26).

In other cases we find references to "*the* faith"—that is, the doctrinal content (Ac 6:7; 1Ti 1:19; 3:9; 5:8; 6:12; Jude 3). Therefore the distinction often made in theology between *the* faith that is believed (*fides quae creditur*) and faith as the personal act of believing (*fides qua creditur*) seems well founded. This means that the personal act of faith has an object (Christ as he is clothed in the gospel), a content (the doctrine concerning Christ and his gospel), and a subject (the believing sinner).

Faith is the same in both testaments, both in its act and its object. Abraham is especially paradigmatic as the one who was justified by faith and is the father of all who have faith in Christ (Ro 2:28–29; ch. 4; Gal 3; Heb 11; Jas 2). Throughout the New Testament this continuity is assumed (Jn 5:46; 12:38–39; Hab 2:4; Ro 1:17; 10:16; Gal 3:11; Heb 10:38). As Berkhof reminds us, "The giving of the law did not effect a fundamental change in the religion of Israel, but merely introduced a change in its external form. The law was not substituted for the promise; neither was faith supplanted by works."[24]

Paul's legalists had misunderstood the true nature of the law: to lead us to Christ, not to lead us to self-salvation. The demand for faith does not turn faith into a work. On the contrary, it is a command to cease our labors and enter God's rest (Heb 4:10). We are commanded to repent not only of our immoral life that we once approved but of self-trust, which is the greatest sin of all—the chief form of idolatry.

Faith is not only something we believe or even the act of personal faith. It is something that arrives in history, part of the "new thing" that has dawned with Christ's resurrection and Pentecost. A comparison may be made with regeneration. Usually, when we speak of regeneration we have in mind our own personal rebirth. However, "the time for restoring [regenerating] all the things" (Acts 3:21) is a wider event. The "new creation" is not just an individual believer, but a new condition of humanity in Christ that sweeps us into its dawning light. Just as "the grace of God has appeared" (Tit 2:11), so Paul also speaks of faith as arriving: "Now before faith came, we were held captive under the law, imprisoned until the coming faith would be revealed." Because "Christ came," "faith has come" (Gal 3:23–25). Again, this cannot mean that the Old Testament saints were not justified through faith—especially since this same chapter underscores continuity on this point. Rather, the contrast for Paul lies in the fact that the old covenant (Sinai) was an external form of government for the nation that established cultic and legal practices that clearly pointed to Jesus Christ (hence, the contrast between the "two covenants" in 4:21–31). Yet this Sinai covenant did not—and could not—replace the Abrahamic covenant of grace (Gal 3:15–18).

While upholding the continuity of faith in Christ from Abraham (indeed, from Adam and Eve after the fall) to the present, the New Testament also announces that something new has dawned. The law itself could not create faith, hope, or love but because of sin could only place the world in prison awaiting the redeemer (Gal 3:22–23) or under a guardian

---

24. Louis Berkhof, *Systematic Theology* (Grand Rapids: Eerdmans, 1949), 498.

—awaiting its maturity in order to receive the inheritance (v. 24). The faith that the Old Testament saints had was just as true as ours, but the object was far off in the distance, whereas for us it has already arrived. In Hebrews, the great fathers and mothers of Israel are commended for having faith in the promise even though they did not yet see its fulfillment (Heb 11:1 – 12:2). Moses and his liberated followers, according to Paul, "drank from the spiritual Rock that followed them, and the Rock was Christ" (1Co 10:4). In fact, the wilderness generation is said to have "put Christ to the test" when they rebelled (v. 9).

Faith involves the intellect, the will, and the affections. It is knowledge (*notitia*), assent (*assensus*), and trust (*fiducia*). Given definition by doctrine, faith is nevertheless directed to a person: the triune God as he has revealed himself in Christ as our Redeemer. It would be mere assent to say even that Christ died for sinners generally, without recognizing that he died *for me*. According to the Lutheran confessions, "The faith here spoken of 'is not that possessed by the devil and the ungodly, who also believe the history of Christ's suffering and resurrection from the dead, but we mean such true faith as believes that we receive grace and forgiveness of sin through Christ.'" It is not merely acknowledging the truth of Christ's person and work but receiving and clinging to Christ himself.[25] The same view is expressed on the Reformed side in the Heidelberg Catechism (q. 21): "True faith is not only a knowledge and conviction that everything God reveals in his Word is true; it is also a deep-rooted assurance, created in me by the Holy Spirit through the gospel, that, out of sheer grace earned for us by Christ, *not only others, but I too*, have had my sins forgiven, have been made forever right with God, and have been granted salvation" (emphasis added).[26]

Nor is faith's justifying power located in any inherent quality or virtue of faith itself. Faith is only the instrument rather than the basis for justification: it simply lays hold of Christ and his merits. Hence, the common Reformation formulation of justification: *per fidem propter Christum* (through faith because of or on the basis of Christ). Strictly speaking, one is not justified *by* faith but by Christ's righteousness which is received *through* faith. Therefore, faith is always extrospective: looking outside of itself. Faith does not arise within the self but comes to us from the outside, through the preaching of the gospel (Ro 10:17).

We must always distinguish what faith *is* from what faith *does*. Faith does

---

25. Schlink, *Theology of the Lutheran Confessions*, 96.
26. Heidelberg Catechism, q. 21, in Doctrinal Standards, in *Psalter Hymnal*, 14.

> ## Key Distinction:
> ### *passive/active righteousness*
>
> Faith receives Christ for everything: not only for salvation from judgment, but for the fruit of good works. However, in justification faith is passive: receiving, resting, clinging to Christ alone for an imputed righteousness even while we are still ungodly. This same faith, in sanctification, is active in good works. Having received everything in Christ, faith goes to work in love and service to our neighbors. There is no justification by works. However, there is no genuine faith (and therefore justification) that fails to bear the fruit of good works. Faith is passive with respect to God (receiving rather than giving), but active toward our neighbors (giving without demanding anything in return).

many things; it is always active, bearing fruit. However, *in the act of justification, faith only receives, embraces, and clings to Christ; it does not do anything but receives everything.* Faith is not a probable opinion or conjecture, nor mere assent to an external authority—even the Bible or the church. Nor is faith an immediate certainty, like the knowledge of logical, geometrical, or mathematical axioms. Nor is it merely something we infer from sense experience. It is not a general attitude, characteristic, or virtue—such as an optimistic outlook or positive thinking. Faith is not a genus of which faith in Christ is a species, as is often assumed especially in our day when we speak of various religions as "faith communities" or the importance of "faith." Faith is not even a general trust in God and his promises. Evangelical faith—that is, faith as defined by the gospel—is the specific conviction of the heart, mind, and will that God is gracious to us in Jesus Christ on the basis of God's Word. Faith is clinging to Christ.

Key Terms

- election
- Arminianism
- conversion
- repentance
- faith

Key Distinctions

- history of salvation/order of salvation
- monergism/synergism
- outward/inward (effectual) call
- regeneration/conversion
- passive/active righteousness

Key Questions

1. Why do some people believe in Christ and others not? Explain.
2. What is the order in our salvation? Are we born again because we believe, or do we believe because we are born again? Why is this an important distinction?
3. How would you explain the difference between monergism and synergism?
4. Is "irresistible" a good way of talking about effectual calling? Why or why not?
5. What is repentance? What is faith? How are they related?

Chapter Eleven

Union with Christ

In effectual calling the Spirit grants us faith in Christ as he is clothed in his gospel. Through this faith we are united to Christ with all of his benefits, as beneficiaries not only of his gifts but of the Giver himself. Chosen in Christ and redeemed In Christ, we are united to Christ by the Spirit through faith. We identify this wonderful reality as **union with Christ**.

I. The Meaning of Union

Union with Christ incorporates various aspects of our salvation. As in the union of man and woman, the marriage of the church to Christ involves a *forensic* or *legal* aspect. *Forensic* pertains to the courts: as in forensic evidence used in a trial. In this case, the forensic aspect is an inheritance: the legal transfer of debts and riches. "For you know the grace of our Lord Jesus Christ, that though he was rich, yet for your sake he became poor, so that you by his poverty might become rich" (2Co 8:9). In Ephesians 5:25–27, Paul invokes the marriage analogy for the loving self-sacrifice of the redeeming husband for his sinful bride.

This marital analogy was explored richly by the French abbot Bernard of Clairvaux (1090–1153), and Luther and Calvin echoed his emphasis on the "**marvelous exchange**" in which Christ assumes our debts and we inherit his wealth. Christ instituted the Lord's Supper as the sacrament of his last will and testament, offering the cup as "my blood of the covenant, which is poured out for many for the forgiveness of sins" (Mt 26:28). Paul speaks of this covenant in precisely the same terms, as a will that has been ratified and cannot be amended or annulled (Gal 3:15). The writer to the Hebrews adds that Jesus is "the mediator of a new covenant, so that those who are called may receive the promised inheritance." However, the Mediator must himself die. "For a will takes effect only at death, since it is not in force as long as the one who made it is alive" (Heb 9:17). Underage, the church in the old covenant looked forward to its maturity, and now this will is executed, with Christ's death. No longer held in a trust fund, the inheritance is being poured out on the church as Christ's bride (Gal 3:15 – 4:7). In our former marriage, united to Adam, we accrued nothing but debts, but in Christ our debts are imputed to him and his righteousness is imputed to us. Thus, to the covenantal headship of Adam and Christ in Romans 5 Paul adds the marriage analogy in chapter 7.

We have seen that Christ's work at the cross was more than a legal substitution, but that none of the other aspects of his redemptive work is secured only on that basis. The same is true of our union with Christ. On this legal ground, it is also a *mystical* union. In marriage, two persons become "one flesh" without losing their distinct identities. "This mystery is profound, and I am saying that it refers to Christ and the church" (Eph 5:32). Therefore, "husbands should love their wives as their own bodies.... For no one ever hated his own flesh, but nourishes and cherishes it, just as Christ does the church, because we are members of his body" (vv. 28 – 30). It is a mystery in part because the husband and wife are not fused into one person and yet they are no longer who they are without the other. The goal is neither fusion with nor mere imitation of the Savior, but fellowship and communion (*koinōnia*).

Yet this union is also *organic*. On the basis of the legal security of the union, husbands and wives grow more and more into each other; so too do those who are united to Christ. Being in Christ is a fact that can never be improved, diminished, or withdrawn; nevertheless, we grow experientially in this union as we come to know, communicate with, and respond to each other. This aspect of our union is typically highlighted in Scripture by metaphors of vine and branches, tree and fruit, head and members, firstfruits and full harvest, cornerstone and stones in a building, and so forth. In union with Adam, we inherit not only guilt and condemnation, but corruption. In Christ, we inherit not only justification, but sanctification and finally glorification. Decisively cut off from the cursed vine and grafted onto the Living Vine, we begin to produce the fruit of righteousness. As we have seen in considering the atonement, Christ speaks in John 6, 10, and 17 of the Father's gift of a people to the Son, "that they may all be one, just as you, Father, are in me, and I in you, that they also may be in us, so that the world may believe that you have sent me" (Jn 17:21–22).

Salvation is a new exodus, in which we are identified with a Mediator far greater than Moses and a deliverance from a servitude far more serious than bondage in Egypt (1Co 10:1–4). God prophesied through Ezekiel, "I will sprinkle clean water on you, and you shall be clean from all your uncleanness, and from all your idols I will cleanse you. And I will give you a new heart, and a new spirit I will put within you; and I will remove the heart of stone from your flesh and give you a heart of flesh.... I will make the fruit of the tree and the increase of the field abundant" (Eze 36:22–33). This is the meaning of our being baptized into Christ: into his death and resurrection (Ro 6:1–23; cf. 1:3–4; 4:25; 1Co 15:35–36; 1Pe 3:21–22; 2Pe 3:5–7). More and more, the Spirit takes what belongs properly to Christ and makes it our own (Jn 16:14), working within us so that we bear the fruit of the Spirit (Jn 15:1–11; cf. Gal 5:22–26).

Through the centuries many have emphasized the Christian life as the imitation of Christ. There are certainly calls to imitate Christ's humility and service in the New Testament. However, even these imperatives are based on the indicative fact of union. In other words, Jesus Christ is not simply a great man, even a divine man, who calls us to become like him. The gospel proclaims something far more wonderful than the law of moral striving. It announces that all who are in Christ are actually coheirs with him of his estate, members of his body. Grafted by the Spirit onto this Vine, we bear fruit that is not just *like* his own, as if he were merely a model to imitate, but is in fact the fruit that ripens from the sap of his own eschatological life, because he is our covenant head (Jn 15:1–10).

All of these aspects were affirmed in the Reformation understanding of union with Christ. Far from rejecting the believer's actual righteousness (sanctification), Luther wrote that Christ's imputed righteousness "is the basis, the cause, the source of all our own actual righteousness."[1] "We conclude, therefore, that a Christian lives not in himself, but in Christ and his neighbor. Otherwise he is not a Christian. He lives in Christ through faith, in his neighbor through love. By faith he is caught up beyond himself into God. By love he descends beneath himself into his neighbor. Yet

---

1. Martin Luther, "Two Kinds of Righteousness," in *Luther's Works* (ed. Harold J. Grimm; Philadelphia: Fortress, 1957; repr., 1971), 31:298.

he always remains in God and in his love."[2] Faith not only justifies; it "unites the soul with Christ as a bride is united with her bridegroom," says Luther.[3]

In fact, Luther so stressed this mystical aspect alongside the forensic that his colleague Andreas Osiander (1498 – 1552) lodged justification in the idea of Christ dwelling within the believer essentially (that is, in his very essence) rather than in the imputation of Christ's alien righteousness. Luther rejected this position, and the Lutheran Flacius as well as John Calvin wrote extended rebuttals of Osiander's confusion of Creator and creature. Osiander's view, revived in the past by radical Pietists, and today by some mainline Lutherans, reveals the influence of Plato more than of Paul.

Union with Christ is a recurring theme in Calvin's writings. Here, the forensic aspects of our salvation (such as justification) are held together with the mystical or subjective aspects (such as sanctification) — yet without confusing them. Christ's work outside of us is the basis of our salvation. Yet "we must understand that as long as Christ remains outside of us, and we are separated from him, all that he has suffered and done for the salvation of the human race remains useless and of no value for us. Therefore, to share with us what he received from the Father, he had to become ours and to dwell within us." He does not do this by pouring his divinity into us, but by "the secret energy of the Spirit," through whom "we come to enjoy Christ and all his benefits.... To sum up, the Holy Spirit is the bond by which Christ effectually unites us to himself."[4] So the believer is never confused with Christ or vice versa. We do not find Christ by ascending into heaven or by descending into our hearts, but by the work of the Spirit through his Word. This point is explicitly developed by Paul in Romans 10:1 – 17.

Drawing directly, like Luther, on Bernard (at least twenty-one times in the *Institutes*), Calvin writes,

> For in Christ [the Father] offers all happiness in place of our misery, all wealth in place of our neediness; in him he opens to us the heavenly treasures that our whole faith may contemplate his beloved Son, our whole expectation depend upon him, and our whole hope cleave to and rest in him. This, indeed, is that secret and hidden philosophy which cannot be wrested from syllogisms. But they whose eyes God has opened surely learn it by heart, that in his light they may see light [Ps 36:9].[5]

---

2. Martin Luther, *The Freedom of a Christian*, in *Luther's Works*, 31:371.
3. Ibid., 31:351.
4. Calvin, *Institutes* 3.1.1.
5. Ibid., 3.20.1.

So where more mystical versions drawn from Christian Platonism speak of the soul's union with God, as if both were divine substances, Calvin clearly distinguishes God from the believer and offers a more Trinitarian account: the Father unites us to his Son by his Spirit.[6] We are "one with the Son of God; not because he conveys his substance to us, but because, by the power of his Spirit, he imparts to us his life and all the blessings which he has received from the Father."[7] "Since we are clothed with the righteousness of the Son" in justification, "we are reconciled to God and renewed by the power of the Spirit to holiness."[8] In fact, "with a wonderful communion, day by day, [Christ] grows more and more into one body with us, until he becomes completely one with us."[9]

So for the Reformers, the mystical and subjective aspects of union are inseparable from the objective and legal. Nevertheless, we do not find Christ by descending into our hearts, but by being drawn out of ourselves to Christ as he is clothed in his gospel. "If you contemplate yourself," Calvin counsels, "that is sure damnation."

> But since Christ has been so imparted to you with all his benefits that all his things are made yours, that you are made a member of him, indeed one with him, his righteousness overwhelms your sins; his salvation wipes out your condemnation; with his worthiness he intercedes that your unworthiness may not come before God's sight. Surely this is so: We ought not to separate Christ from ourselves or ourselves from him. Rather we ought to hold fast bravely with both hands to that fellowship by which he has bound himself to us. So the apostle teaches us: 'Now your body is dead because of sin; but the Spirit of Christ which dwells in you is life because of righteousness' [Ro 8:10].[10]

Through the same act of faith, one receives the *whole* Christ, Lord and Savior, with *all* of his gifts, including justification and renewal.

II. Misunderstandings of Union

Two obvious misunderstandings of union with Christ are represented by the tendencies to reduce it either to the forensic (legal) or mystical-organic

---

6. Ibid., 4.15.16.
7. Ibid.
8. John Calvin, *Commentary on Romans* (ed. David W. Torrance and Thomas F. Torrance; Grand Rapids: Eerdmans, 1964), 138.
9. Calvin, *Institutes* 3.2.24.
10. Ibid.

aspect. The former is evident when the horizon of salvation is reduced to the objective work of Christ and the gifts of justification and adoption. To be sure, the objective fact of one's marriage provides the security of the relationship, but there is more to marriage than the ceremony and legal documents. The latter is evident when the subjective aspect of our relationship with Christ is so emphasized that our legal entitlement to Christ with all of his benefits is made the goal rather than the basis.

The other danger is to subordinate the legal to the mystical aspect. The legal or forensic aspect of this union remains the basis for the mystical and organic effects. As in marriage, the legal transfer of identity and possessions secures the relationship of growing trust and mutual communion. Every subjective blessing that we experience *within* us is the result of Christ's objective work *for* us, outside of us, in history. We are not declared righteous legally nor caused to abide in Christ forensically because we bear the fruit of the Spirit, but vice versa. We do not base our assurance of God's favor on our experience of or growth in godliness; rather, we experience and grow in godliness because we are assured of God's favor. As Geerhardus Vos expressed it,

> In our opinion Paul consciously and consistently subordinated the mystical aspect of the relation to Christ to the forensic one. Paul's mind was to such an extent forensically oriented that he regarded the entire complex of subjective spiritual changes that take place in the believer and of subjective spiritual blessings enjoyed by the believer as the direct outcome of the forensic work of Christ applied in justification. The mystical is based on the forensic, not the forensic on the mystical.[11]

Throughout the history of the church, there has been a marked tendency to emphasize the mystical over the forensic. Often aided by a Platonic-Neoplatonic philosophical paradigm, a mysticism emerges that confuses the Creator with the creature and Christ with the believer. Recall from Ephesians 5 the point that the two are made "one flesh" not by fusion (so they are one person), but by communion (so they are two persons together). Plato and his heirs have held that the human mind or soul is divine, fallen from its original and eternal unity with the divine One. Cast into bodily prisons of time and space, the soul strives through contemplation to ascend to the beatific vision:

---

11. Geerhardus Vos, "The Alleged Legalism in Paul's Doctrine of Justification," in *Redemptive History and Biblical Interpretation* (ed. Richard B. Gaffin Jr.; Phillipsburg, N.J.: P&R, 1980), 384. The same point is made by Louis Berkhof, *Systematic Theology* (Grand Rapids: Eerdmans, 1949), 452, against those who would make the imputation of Christ's righteousness depend on mystical union rather than vice versa. See also John V. Fesko, *Justification: Understanding the Classic Reformed Doctrine* (Phillipsburg, N.J.: P&R, 2008), ch. 10.

beholding the Good itself in all its glory. Influenced by this philosophical map, Christian monasticism encouraged braver souls to strive toward this union, by upward ascent through contemplation or by descending into the soul to find Christ within.

Many of the radical mystics of the medieval era and spiritualists of the Reformation era (especially the Anabaptists) emphasized moral and spiritual ascent toward union with God. Later, Pietism focused more on the Christ who dwells within the human heart than the objective work of the historical Jesus. Along this line, the forensic aspect of our union was subordinated to the mystical and in some cases even forgotten (or rejected) entirely. Furthermore, in this mysticism Christ is so fused with the believer that the "fully surrendered" believer's identity is simply replaced with Christ's.

However, in the Scriptures, union with Christ is no more a matter of ascending or descending into oneself than is a marriage. Rather, it is the covenantal relationship of two distinct persons, in loving fellowship.

Particularly in Paul's interpretation, union with Christ corresponds to the new creation: the new world of grace, faith, promise, justification, and life, in contrast to the old world of sin, unbelief, law, condemnation, and death. In spite of appearances, everything outside of Christ is dead and everything in Christ is alive. The Old Testament saints share with us in the reality for which they hoped. In fact, this *koinōnia* between the old and new covenant believers is so strong that the writer to the Hebrews can say of the former, "And all these, though commended through their faith, did not receive what was promised, since God had provided something better for us, that apart from us they should not be made perfect" (Heb 11:29–40). United to Christ through faith, which the Spirit "produces ... in our hearts by the preaching of the holy gospel, and confirms ... through our use of the holy sacraments,"[12] we are made coheirs with Christ. In union with Christ, we are also united in the same fellowship with each other in the communion of saints. What then are the effects of this union? That is the focus of the next two chapters.

Key Terms
- union with Christ
- *koinōnia*
- the "marvelous exchange"

---

12. Heidelberg Catechism, q. 65, in Doctrinal Standards of the Christian Reformed Church, in *Psalter Hymnal* (Grand Rapids: Board of Publications of the Christian Reformed Church, 1976), 32.

Key Questions

1. Union with Christ is "mystical." What does that mean? What are other defining aspects of union with Christ?
2. What is the difference between union with Christ and imitation of Christ?
3. Distinguish Reformation views of union from alternative perspectives.
4. Who is Osiander, and why is his view relevant for modern discussions of the doctrine?

Chapter Twelve

Justified and Adopted

Chosen in Christ from all eternity, we are called effectually through the gospel and united to Christ through faith. In clinging to Christ, the believer receives with him all of his estate. This chapter considers two of these blessings: **justification** and **adoption**. The next chapter will focus on sanctification and glorification.

I. Justification

"*God justifies the wicked.*" As counterintuitive as it is simple, that claim which lies at the heart of the good news has brought immeasurable blessing—and trouble—to the church and the world. It is not the Pharisee, confident in his own righteousness, who went home justified, said Jesus, but the tax collector who could not even raise his eyes to heaven but cried out, "God, be merciful to me, a sinner!" (Lk 18:9–14). It was precisely such outcasts as he who would be seated at the wedding feast clothed in the wedding garment, said Jesus, while those who entered in their own attire would be cast out (Mt 22:1–14).

It was this simple claim that caused the apostle Paul to look back on all of his zealous obedience as "a Pharisee of Pharisees" and call it "dung," "in order that I may gain Christ and be found in him, not having a righteousness of my own that comes from the law, but that which comes through faith in Christ, the righteousness from God that depends on faith" (Php 3:8–9). As the revelation of the righteousness *of* God, the law condemns all and leaves no one standing. Yet the gospel is the revelation of the righteousness *from* God, the good news that sinners "are justified by his grace as a gift, through the redemption that is in Christ Jesus, whom God put forward as a propitiation by his blood, to be received by faith" (Ro 3:24–25). "Therefore, since we have been justified by faith, we have peace with God through our Lord Jesus Christ" (Ro 5:1). Paul considered this doctrine to be so central that he regarded its explicit denial as "anathema"—that is, an act of heresy that the Galatian church was on the verge of committing (Gal 1:8–9). For Paul, a denial of *justification* was tantamount to a denial of grace and even to a denial of Christ, "for if justification comes through the law, then Christ died for nothing" (Gal 2:21 NRSV).

God justifies *the wicked*—not those who have done their best yet have fallen short, those who might at least be judged acceptable because of their sincerity, but those who, at the very moment of being pronounced righteous, are in themselves unrighteous. "And to the one who does not work but believes in him who justifies the ungodly, his faith is counted as righteousness, just as David also speaks of the blessing of the one to whom God counts righteousness apart from works" (Ro 4:5–6).

Numerous passages testify to the imputation or crediting of our sins to Christ (on the basis of his substitutionary atonement) and of his righteousness to us (on the basis of his active obedience). Following Paul's banking, clothing, and courtroom analogies from our everyday experience, the Reformers called this the "marvelous exchange." Jesus Christ, sinless in himself, becomes, representatively, the greatest sinner who ever lived, while "in him we become the righteousness of God" (2Co 5:21).

A. The State of the Controversy

This claim that God justifies the wicked brought enormous controversy to the apostolic church and has continued to do so throughout the history of the church.[1] And in spite of the heroic efforts of representatives on

---

1. The teaching of the ancient church is ambiguous with respect to justification. On one hand, there are marvelous testimonies to God's justification of sinners, as Thomas Oden observes in *The Justification Reader* (Grand Rapids: Eerdmans, 2002). On the other hand, there are many threads of synergism that later Eastern Orthodoxy developed in Byzantine theology in a manner that parallels Western (medieval) developments.

both sides during the sixteenth century, the Council of Trent (1545 – 63) in no uncertain terms condemned the Reformation's understanding of justification.

1. The Reformation debate

With respect to justification, the Reformation debate turned on different answers to the following major questions: (1) Is justification only a legal (forensic) verdict, or is it a process of moral renewal (sanctification) that leads to a legal verdict? (2) Is justification a declaration that is pronounced solely by virtue of Christ's imputed righteousness, while the believer is actually unrighteous in himself/herself, or is it a declaration that is pronounced upon those who have cooperated with grace by doing what lies within them? (3) Is Christ's merit the only basis for justification, or do our merits (and those of Mary and the saints) also contribute to this right standing before God? (4) In the act of justification, is faith merely resting in and receiving Christ alone (knowledge, assent, and trust), or is faith merely assent to church teaching and therefore something that must be transformed into love in order to be justifying? (5) Can one know with assurance that he or she is justified now, or is this the sin of presumption, since even those who die in a state of grace require the fires of purgatory to pay the temporal penalty for their sins? To each of these questions, the Reformers gave the first answer and Rome the second.

In Scripture, especially in Paul, Luther discovered that the righteousness that God is, which condemns us, is the same righteousness that God *gives*, freely, as a gift, through faith in Jesus Christ (Ro 3:19 – 31). As we have seen, the "marvelous exchange" of Christ's riches and righteousness for our poverty and sin received attention and wonderful articulation in ancient and medieval piety. It would be dishonoring to the Spirit, as well as historically inaccurate, to suggest that there was no evangelical light in the medieval church. However, the understanding of justification as an exclusively forensic (legal) declaration, based on the imputation of Christ's righteousness through faith alone, was recovered in the Reformation.

The inextricable connection between doctrine and experience is acutely evident in Luther's spiritual wrestling that led to his fresh interpretation of Scripture. Nevertheless, his insight into justification evolved principally through exegesis. A decade earlier than Luther's own "breakthrough," the eminent French humanist and biblical scholar Jacques Lefèvre d'Étaples (1455 – 1536) had arrived at the same conclusions while making the first French translation of the Bible from the Latin Vulgate. Erasmus

(1466–1556) also had made important textual contributions that paved the way for Luther's work, and Luther's own mentor and the head of Germany's Augustinian Order, Johann von Staupitz, also set the Reformer on his course. However, Luther's own exegesis in the original languages led him to further insights with radical implications, particularly after Staupitz appointed him professor of Bible at the new Wittenberg University. If Luther's own breakthrough cannot be explained away by psychoanalysis (i.e., his personal struggle with anxiety), then it is surely a caricature to allege that many of the brightest biblical scholars of the age were merely following in the wake of one person's morbid introspection. The Reformation was, first of all, a revolution in biblical scholarship.

To cut the story short, the magisterial Reformation coalesced around the view summarized in the fourth article of the apology of the Augsburg Confession: God justifies the wicked on the basis of Christ (*propter Christum*), apart from our inherent righteousness. This is the *solo Christo* (by Christ alone). And he credits this righteousness through faith alone (*sola fide*), apart from works. Believers are just before God not to the extent that they are inherently righteous; rather, they are "simultaneously just and sinner" (*simul iustus et peccator*).

All of the Reformers were at one on this point, over against both Roman Catholic and Anabaptist interpretations. Calvin regarded justification as "the primary article of the Christian religion," "the main hinge on which religion turns," "the principal article of the whole doctrine of salvation and the foundation of all religion."[2] In fact, Philipp Melanchthon and John Calvin influenced each other in working out the refinements of this common evangelical position.[3] This righteousness "consists in the remission of sins, and in this: that the righteousness of Jesus Christ is imputed to us."[4]

According to this evangelical interpretation, justification is not a process of transformation from a condition of sinfulness to a state of justice. Believers are *simultaneously* justified and sinful.[5] Sin's dominion has been toppled, but sin still indwells believers.[6] Consequently, whatever works believers perform will always fall short of that righteousness that God's law

---

2. Calvin, *Institutes* 3.2.1, 3.11.1; John Calvin, "Sermon on Luke 1:5–10," in *Corpus Reformatorum* (101 vols.; ed. K. G. Bretschnider et al., Berlin: Schwetschike, 1834–1900), 46.23.

3. See, for example, Richard Muller, *The Unaccommodated Calvin* (New York: Oxford Univ. Press, 2000), 126–27. Calvin, however, sharply criticized Melanchthon's later synergistic turn, which the orthodox (Gnesio) Lutherans also rejected.

4. Calvin, *Institutes* 3.11.2.

5. Ibid., 3.3.10.

6. Ibid., 3.3.11.

requires; nevertheless, believers themselves are accepted as fully righteous already through faith in Christ. Justification as a finished verdict is not the *terminus ad quem* (goal) of sanctification, as Thomas Aquinas taught, but the *terminus a quo* (basis) of the Christian life.

This orientation stood in sharp contrast not only with Rome, but with the radical sects. "Certain Anabaptists of our day conjure up some sort of frenzied excess instead of spiritual regeneration," Calvin relates, thinking that they can attain perfection in this life.[7] Rome teaches that Christ's sacrifice remits the guilt but not the punishment of sins.[8] In either case, justification is understood as a process of inner transformation, rather than as God's free acquittal of sinners for the sake of Christ and his imputation of Christ's righteousness to their account. Of course, a diversity of moral character is evident to us as human beings, but Calvin reminds us (repeating Luther's contrast) that righteousness before humanity (*coram hominibus*) is not the same as righteousness before God (*coram deo*).[9] "Therefore," Calvin responds, "we explain justification simply as the acceptance with which God receives us into his favor as righteous. And we say that it consists in the remission of sins and the imputation of Christ's righteousness."[10]

The logic of Calvin's argument in the *Institutes* may be summarized as follows:

> To save us from judgment, the Son became flesh and merited our salvation (2.15 – 17).
>
> Thus, the righteousness by which we are saved is alien to us (3.11.2, etc.).
>
> Yet Christ must not only be given *for* us; he must be given *to* us (3.1.1).
>
> We are recipients not only of Christ's gifts but of Christ himself with his gifts (3.1.1.; 3.1.4; 3.2.24; 4.17.11).[11]
>
> Faith unites us to Christ (3.1.1), but it is the Holy Spirit who gives faith, and it is Christ who always remains the sole ground of salvation rather than faith itself. In other words, faith is nothing in itself; it receives *Christ* and with him all treasures (3.11.7; 3.18.8). After all, "if faith in itself justified one by its own virtue, then, seeing that it is always weak and imperfect, it would be only partly effectual and give us only a part of salvation" (3.11.7).

---

7. Ibid., 3.3.14.
8. Ibid., 3.4.30.
9. Ibid., 3.12.2.
10. Ibid., 3.11.2.
11. Cf. *Corpus Reformatorum*, 9:88; *Opera Selecta*, 1:41, 88.

One of the clearest summaries of the evangelical doctrine of justification is found in chapter 13 of the Westminster Confession:

> Those whom God effectually calls, he also freely justifies: not by infusing righteousness into them, but by pardoning their sins and by accounting and accepting their persons as righteous; not for anything wrought in them or done by them, but for Christ's sake alone; not by imputing faith itself, the act of believing, or any other evangelical obedience to them as their righteousness; but by imputing the obedience and satisfaction of Christ unto them, they receiving and resting on him and his righteousness by faith; which faith they have not of themselves, it is the gift of God. Faith, thus receiving and resting on Christ and his righteousness, is the sole instrument of justification; yet is it not alone in the person justified, but is ever accompanied with all other saving graces, and is no dead faith, but works by love.

The justified may fall into grave sin and "fall under God's Fatherly displeasure," but they "can never fall from the state of justification."[12]

The Heidelberg Catechism also emphasizes that this divine verdict has Christ's righteousness, not ours, as its basis, so that through faith alone we who "have grievously sinned against all the commandments of God and have not kept any one of them" are nevertheless regarded as though we had never sinned and had perfectly kept the commands. Not even the gift of faith itself can be considered the ground of justification, but simply the empty hand that receives it. This teaching cannot be used to justify moral carelessness, however, for "it is impossible for those grafted into Christ by true faith not to produce fruits of gratitude."[13] Similar summaries can be found, of course, in the Lutheran Book of Concord, the Anglican Thirty-Nine Articles, and the London/Philadelphia (Baptist) Confession.

It was this understanding that Rome officially anathematized at the Council of Trent in its longest decree, which included the following:

> Canon 9. If anyone says that the sinner is justified by faith alone ... let him be anathema.
>
> Canon 11. If anyone says that men are justified either by the sole imputation of the righteousness of Christ or by the sole remission of sins ... let him be anathema.

---

12. Westminster Confession of Faith, in *The Book of Confessions* (Louisville: General Assembly of the Presbyterian Church in the USA, 1991), ch. 13.

13. Heidelberg Catechism, qs. 60–64, in Doctrinal Standards of the Christian Reformed Church, in *Psalter Hymnal* (Grand Rapids: Board of Publications of the Christian Reformed Church, 1976), 30–31.

Canon 12. If anyone says that justifying faith is nothing else than confidence in divine mercy, which remits sins for Christ's sake, or that it is this confidence alone that justifies us, let him be anathema.

Canon 24. If anyone says that the justice [righteousness] received is not preserved and also not increased before God through good works, but that those works are merely the fruits and signs of justification obtained, but not the cause of the increase, let him be anathema.

Canon 30. If anyone says that after the reception of the grace of justification the guilt is so remitted and the debt of eternal punishment so blotted out to every repentant sinner that no debt of temporal punishment remains to be discharged either in this world or in purgatory before the gates of heaven can be opened, let him be anathema.

Canon 32. If anyone says that the good works of the one justified are in such manner the gifts of God that they are not also the good merits of him justified; or that the one justified by the good works that he performs by the grace of God and the merit of Jesus Christ, whose living member he is, does not truly merit an Increase of grace, eternal life, and in case he dies in grace the attainment of eternal life itself and also an increase of glory, let him be anathema.[14]

Much has happened since the Council of Trent, especially in the fruitful ecumenical discussions since the Second Vatican Council. Nevertheless, Trent remains binding dogma, and even if it could be amended, the official statements of the magisterium to the present day continue to deny the evangelical view.[15] Still today, Rome teaches that "'justification is not only the remission of sins, but also the sanctification and renewal of the interior man.'"[16] Justification is therefore regarded as a process of becoming actually

---

14. *Canons and Decrees of the Council of Trent: Original Text with English Translation* (trans. H. J. Schroeder, OP; St. Louis: Herder, 1960), 43, 45–46.

15. *Joint Declaration on the Doctrine of Justification: The Lutheran World Federation and the Roman Catholic Church* (Grand Rapids: Eerdmans, 2000). Among other problems, the declaration teaches, "The justification of sinners is forgiveness *and being made righteous*" (4.3.27, emphasis added), and particular acts of sin require the sacrament of penance (4.3.30). Thus, the Roman Catholic position is not altered on this fundamental point; it is the evangelical view that is surrendered. Only on that basis can both partners conclude that the condemnations of the sixteenth century no longer apply to each other's respective communions. It should be noted that the Lutheran World Federation, like the World Alliance of Reformed Churches, represents the more liberal wing of Lutheranism. Their confessional rivals (including the Lutheran Church Missouri Synod) rejected the Joint Declaration, because they do still hold the views condemned by the Council of Trent and all subsequent reaffirmations by the magisterium. Furthermore, the Vatican warned against concluding that the Joint Declaration represented a consensus on justification (reported in the official Vatican newspaper, *L'Osservatore Romano*, weekly edition in English, 8 July 1998, p. 2). Citing the Council of Trent, the official statement reminded Roman Catholics that they must hold as dogma that "eternal life is, at one and the same time, grace and the reward given by God for good works and merits."

16. *Catechism of the Catholic Church* (Liguori, Mo.: Liguori Publications, 1994), 492, quoting the Council of Trent (1574): DS 1528.

> ## Key Distinction:
> ### imputed/infused (righteousness)
>
> "Imputed" means credited: Christ's fulfillment of the law is credited to us. By contrast, "infusion" refers to an inner strengthening of the soul to cooperate with God's grace in attaining righteousness.

and intrinsically righteous. The first justification occurs at baptism, which eradicates both the guilt and corruption of original sin.[17] Due entirely to God's grace, this initial justification **infuses** the habit (or principle) of grace into the recipient. By cooperating with this inherent grace, one merits an increase of grace and, one hopes, final justification.[18] So while initial justification in baptism is by grace alone, final justification depends also on the works of the believer, which God graciously accepts as meritorious.[19] Since the believer's progress in holiness is never adequate to cancel the guilt of actual sins, he or she must be refined in purgatory before being welcomed into heaven. In all of the ecumenical consultations, the Vatican has never had to modify, much less deny, any of Trent's positions.

The Roman Catholic Church has never denied the necessity of grace — indeed, its priority. The Council of Trent expressly repeated the condemnations of Pelagianism, in fact. However, the addition of works to faith as the instrument of justification is as strongly affirmed today as it was in the sixteenth century. From the evangelical perspective, the strongest affirmation of the importance of God's grace does not mitigate the corruption of the gospel by including our own merits. "But if it is by grace, it is no longer on the basis of works; otherwise grace would no longer be grace" (Ro 11:6).

Differences over justification are motivated by different understandings of grace. In Roman Catholic theology grace is understood as a medicinal substance infused into a person at baptism, elevating nature to supernatural appetites. In Reformation theology grace is understood as God's favor to those who are dead in sins and ungodly, on account of Christ's merit alone. Through faith, God gives believers nothing less than Christ and all of his benefits. Among these gifts is rebirth and sanctification, but this renewal is the consequence of justification rather than part of its definition.

---

17. Ibid., 482.
18. Ibid., 483.
19. Ibid., 486–87.

2. Divergences among Protestants

Though in some respects more radical in distancing itself from the medieval church than were the Reformers, *Anabaptists* were closer to Rome on justification. Contemporary Anabaptist theologian Thomas Finger observes, "Robert Friedmann found 'A forensic view of grace, in which the sinner is ... undeservedly justified ... simply unacceptable' to Anabaptists. A more nuanced scholar like Arnold Snyder can assert that historic Anabaptists 'never talked about being "justified by faith." ' "[20]

Rejecting any conception of a forensic (substitutionary) atonement, *Socinians* (forerunners of modern Unitarianism) rejected a forensic justification in favor of a basically Pelagian soteriology and this became the presupposition of Enlightenment rationalism. Kant rejected a forensic doctrine of justification as counter-productive to moral striving.

Although the classical *Arminianism* of the original Remonstrants (led by Arminius) affirmed justification through faith alone, the atonement came to be understood along the lines of Grotius's governmental theory. Rather than a satisfaction of God's justice in the place of sinners, Christ's atonement was seen as the basis for the propriety of God's offering salvation on the basis of the sinner's repentance and new obedience. Some Arminians, like Philip von Limborch, moved in a Pelagian (Socinian) direction. Evangelical Arminians, such as John Wesley, taught God's free justification of sinners, but sometimes confused it with sanctification and in general subordinated it to the inner renewal and perfection of personal holiness.[21]

---

20. Thomas A. Finger, *A Contemporary Anabaptist Theology: Biblical, Historical, Constructive* (Downers Grove, Ill.: InterVarsity Press, 2004), 109. Finger believes that Anabaptist soteriological emphases (especially on divinization) can bring greater unity especially between marginalized Protestant groups (Pentecostals and Quakers) and Orthodox and Roman Catholic theologies of salvation (110). Finger observes that recent Anabaptist reflection is no more marked in its interest in this topic than its antecedents, with discipleship ("following Jesus") and the inner transformation of the believer as central (132–33).

21. William B. Pope (*A Compendium of Christian Theology* [New York: Hunt and Eston, 1880], 2:414) states that the verb "to justify" in the New Testament denotes both "a declaratory and imputed righteousness, and at the same time the power of a righteousness internal and inherent" (2:404). At the same time, Pope properly insists that we are justified through faith (*dia pisteōs* or *ek pisteōs*), not on account of faith (*dia pistin*). Nevertheless, "Faith, with works, justifies instrumentally the person believing: inasmuch as its works give evidence of its genuineness as a permanent living principle. It retains the soul in a state of justification, and is the power of a Divine life by which the righteousness of the law is fulfilled" (2:415). Pope states that "Arminianism was in its doctrine of the Atonement a mediation between Socinianism and the Anselmic teaching as revived at the Reformation," although "Arminianism gradually declined from its first integrity" and "does not now represent any fixed standard of confession" (2:442). He points out that original Arminianism (including the belief of Arminius himself), which Pope affirms, denied the active obedience of Christ as well as the imputation of Christ's righteousness (2:443). However, Limborch went further than this, toward "the Romanist error" and Socinianism (ibid.). Pope denies, however, that the English Arminians (Methodists) denied the Refor-

From the New Haven divinity Nathaniel Taylor, some Arminians (especially in the United States) moved in a more Pelagian direction. Justification by the imputation of Christ's righteousness not only is "absurd," said evangelist Charles Finney, but undermines all motivation for personal holiness. The new birth is not a divine gift, but the result of a rational choice to turn from sin to obedience. Christians can perfectly obey God in this life if they choose, and only in this way are they justified. In fact, "full present obedience is a condition of justification." No one can be justified "while sin, any degree of sin, remains in him."[22] Finney declared concerning the Reformation formula "simultaneously justified and sinful," "This error has slain more souls, I fear, than all the universalism that ever cursed the world." For, "Whenever a Christian sins, he comes under condemnation and must repent and do his first works, or be lost."[23] "As has already been said, there can be no justification in a legal or forensic sense, but upon the ground of universal, perfect, and uninterrupted obedience to law."[24]

> The doctrine of an imputed righteousness, or that Christ's obedience to the law was accounted as our obedience, is founded on a most false and nonsensical assumption, for Christ's righteousness could do no more than justify himself. It can never be imputed to us.... It was naturally impossible, then, for him to obey in our behalf. Representing the atonement as the ground of the sinner's justification has been a sad occasion of stumbling to many.[25]

Finney's peculiar rationalism and moralism, virtually identical to the arguments against justification offered by Enlightenment philosophers like Kant, embraces the Pelagian positions that were condemned even by the Counter-Reformation Council of Trent.

---

mation doctrine of justification, although they taught the doctrine of entire sanctification (perfection) and stressed forgiveness rather than the imputation of Christ's righteousness (2:444–48). Watson explicitly denies that justification includes the imputation of Christ's righteousness (Richard Watson, *Theological Institutes* [New York: Phillips and Hunt, 1887], 2:215). After warning that the Reformation view tends to treat justification merely as a change in legal status, John Lawson writes in his *Introduction to Christian Doctrine* (Grand Rapids: Francis Asbury, 1967, 1986), "To be justified, therefore, is the first and all-important stage in a renewed manner of life, actually changed for the better in mind and heart, in will and action" (226). In fact, "regeneration" is "an alternative word for 'the initial step' " (227). This is the Roman Catholic view. On the other hand, Methodist theologian Thomas Oden has labored to defend the Reformation doctrine of justification, especially in *The Justification Reader* and his *Systematic Theology*, vol. 3, *Life in the Spirit* (New York: HarperOne, 1994). See also Roger Olson, *Arminian Theology* (Downers Grove, Ill.: InterVarsity Press, 2006), 200–220.

22. Charles G. Finney, *Systematic Theology* (repr., Minneapolis: Bethany, 1976), 46.

23. Ibid., 57.

24. Ibid., 320–22.

25. Ibid., 321–22. Referring to "the framers of the Westminster Confession of faith" and their view of an imputed righteousness, Finney wondered, "If this is not antinomianism, I know not what is" (ibid.).

3. Justification in modern and contemporary theology

In *Protestant liberalism* (especially Schleiermacher and Ritschl), justification loses its objective and forensic character as a verdict before God in favor of a consciousness of the realization that God never really was at enmity with the believer in the first place. We have already observed this in relation to the atonement. In this conception, justification is not an objective change in status from wrath to grace (as Paul states explicitly, for example, in Ro 5:8–11); rather, the believer merely overcomes estrangement—the subjective *feeling* that one is alienated from God.

While affirming, against liberalism, the necessity and fact of God's wrath being turned away by Christ's death, *Karl Barth* refused to see the various elements of the *ordo salutis* as occurring successively in time. Rather, they are simultaneous, belonging to a single event in God's eternal history of election: objectively true of every person yet ever new in every moment of faith and obedience.[26] God's justification of the ungodly is a major theme in Barth. He sought to recover the insights of the Reformation over against a Protestantism that was at least as guilty as Roman Catholicism for rejecting those insights, that is, for trading an objective, complete, perfect, and finished justification by God alone in Christ alone received through faith alone and a subjective, progressive, incomplete, and unfinished justification by the believer's cooperation with grace.[27] Nevertheless, if the usual temptation is to collapse justification into sanctification, for Barth the tendency is to collapse justification into election (conceived in universal terms) and the law into the gospel. As a consequence, the necessity of faith for receiving this justification is denied. Faith simply acknowledges the status that pertains objectively to every person.

More recently, there has been growing criticism of the evangelical doctrine of justification within Protestant circles. First, trends in New Testament scholarship (especially identified with the "New Perspective on Paul")

---

26. See Michael Horton, "A Stony Jar: The Legacy of Karl Barth for Evangelical Theology," in *Engaging with Barth: Contemporary Evangelical Critiques* (ed. David Gibson and Daniel Strange; New York and London: T&T Clark, 2008), 346–81.

27. This concern was already evident in Karl Barth, *The Epistle to the Romans* (trans. Edwyn C. Hoskyns from the 6th ed.; London: Oxford Univ. Press, 1933), 366: "The Church must therefore know that nothing is gained by replacing an objective by a subjective religion, by transforming the service of God into 'pious practices' and righteousness into *a law of righteousness*, because even so it does not find what it is seeking. The Church can, of course, pursue religion and busy itself in the human work of the law. It can cultivate religious experience aesthetically, ethically, and logically. But it cannot do more than this: for religious experience is not the same thing as faith or righteousness; it is not the presence and reality of God, nor is it the divine 'Answer.' Religious experience is our human and, consequently, our very questionable, relation to God."

sharply criticize the Reformation interpretation both of Judaism and Paul. Although there is some diversity among proponents of this perspective, they agree that justification does not mean for Paul the imputation of Christ's righteousness to the believing sinner.[28] Second, trends in historical and ecumenical theology criticize the confessional Lutheran and Reformed interpretations of Luther and Calvin and try to draw the Reformers closer to Eastern Orthodox and/or Roman Catholic positions that the critics contend were lost to later orthodoxy.[29] An impressive movement in theology known as Radical Orthodoxy (led by John Milbank) has attracted many Protestants, including evangelicals, to its renewal of Christian Neoplatonism over against the "extrinsicism" and "forensicism" of Reformation theology.[30] Third, resurgent Anabaptist and Arminian theologies as well as various types of liberation theology combine to challenge the emphasis on justification and in many cases the doctrine itself, as inhibiting personal and social transformation.[31]

For the remainder of this chapter I will summarize the exegetical basis for the classic evangelical doctrine of justification, interacting along the way with contemporary criticisms.

B. Justification in Scripture

"And those whom he called he also justified" (Ro 8:30). Understanding what Paul meant by justification depends on whether we can come to terms with his anthropology (universal human depravity)[32] and therefore his compelling interest in, as Peter Stuhlmacher puts it, "whether Jews and Gentiles will or will not survive before God's throne of judgment."[33] The gospel is not

---

28. I interact at length with these views in the first half of *Covenant and Salvation: Union with Christ* (Louisville: Westminster John Knox, 2007).

29. One prominent example is the "evangelical catholic" circle associated with Robert Jenson and Carl Braaten and the New Finnish interpretation of Luther led by Tuomo Mannermaa and others (Tuomo Mannermaa, *Christ Present in Faith: Luther's Doctrine of Justification* [ed. Kirsi Stjerna; Minneapolis: Fortress, 2005]). I interact with these views in *Covenant and Salvation*, 127–260.

30. John Milbank et al., *Radical Orthodoxy: A New Theology* (London and New York: Routledge, 1999).

31. Stanley Grenz challenged the older evangelical preoccupation with "Christ alone" as the material principle and "Scripture alone" as the formal principle of the Christian faith (Stanley Grenz, *Revisioning Evangelical Theology* [Downers Grove, Ill.: InterVarsity Press, 1993], 62). Similarly, Brian McLaren, in *A Generous Orthodoxy* (Grand Rapids: Zondervan, 2004), faults Reformation theology for its commitment to the solae: Christ alone, Scripture alone, grace alone, through faith alone, and to God alone be glory (221). For both writers, as for the generation of evangelicals that preceded them, the heart of Christianity is our imitation of Christ's example, which — at least for McLaren — does not even require one to become a Christian, but only to be better Buddhist, Muslim, or Jewish followers of Jesus (ibid.).

32. See Timo Laato, *Paul and Judaism: An Anthropological Approach* (Atlanta: Scholars Press, 1995).

33. Peter Stuhlmacher, *Revisiting Paul's Doctrine of Justification: A Challenge to the New Perspective*

simply that Jesus was crucified and raised, or that these events demonstrate his lordship, but that he "was delivered up *for our trespasses* and raised *for our justification*" (Ro 4:25, emphasis added).

1. Declarative (judicial) meaning

Among biblical scholars it is generally recognized, even by Roman Catholics and Protestants unsympathetic to the Reformation doctrine, that the verb *to justify* means "to declare righteous." It is a forensic (legal) term taken from the courtroom. This is the case in the Old Testament (*tsadaq*).[34] And it is just as true in the New Testament: *dikaioō*, "to declare just," is unmistakably judicial in character. This verb was erroneously rendered *iustificare* (to make righteous) in the Latin Vulgate, and this mistake contributed significantly to the idea of justification as a process, synonymous with sanctification.[35]

Though hardly motivated by doctrinal concerns, Erasmus had pointed out these translation errors even before Luther. A number of Roman Catholic New Testament scholars have pointed out in recent years that *dikaioō* has to do with a legal vindication.[36] The lexical definition of *to justify* is "to be cleared in court,"[37] which, as Sanders has said above, is found even in the Old Testament (*tsadaq* and cognates) and can be amply attested. That significant consensus can be reached on this point even among those who stand in some critical relation to the Reformation interpretation demonstrates that we are quite far from witnessing the destruction of a forensic definition of justification on *exegetical* grounds.

While the verb is judicial or forensic (that is, referring to a declaration rather than a process), this fact by itself does not indicate the basis on which or the means by which one is justified before God. It simply stipulates that the demands of the law have been fully met (Ac 13:39; Ro 5:1, 9; 8:30–33; 1Co 6:11; Gal 2:16; 3:11). In Scripture, the opposite of justification is not corruption but condemnation, which is quite evidently a judicial concept as well (Jn 3:17–18; Ro 4:6–7; 8:1, 33–34; 2Co 5:19).

(Downers Grove, Ill.: InterVarsity Press, 2001), 43.

34. E. P. Sanders, *Paul and Palestinian Judaism* (Philadelphia: Fortress, 1977), 198–99.

35. Alister E. McGrath, *Iustitia Dei: A History of the Christian Doctrine of Justification* (Cambridge: Cambridge Univ. Press, 1986), 11–14.

36. See, for instance, Joseph Fitzmyer, "The Letter to the Romans," and "The Letter to the Galatians," in *The Jerome Biblical Commentary* (ed. Raymond S. Brown, Joseph A. Fitzmyer, Roland E. Murphy [Englewood Cliffs, N.J.: Prentice-Hall, 1968], esp. 241–44 and 303–15, respectively).

37. See Walter Bauer, rev. and ed. by Frederic W. Danker, *A Greek-English Lexicon of the New Testament and Other Early Christian Literature* (3rd ed.; Chicago: Univ. of Chicago, Press, 2000), 246–50.

2. The righteousness of God

In medieval theology, the righteousness of God was identified exclusively with God's moral character. Mention of the phrase provoked the image of scale pans, in which our merits are weighed against demerits. There are many passages that support this interpretation. In the lawcourt setting, God's righteousness is his own standard by which he makes true judgments. In this sense, his judgment is inflexible. Under the terms of the Mosaic covenant, God describes himself as one who "will by no means clear the guilty," but in fact will punish successive generations for the ancestor's sin (Ex 34:7 – 8). Similarly, in the first two chapters of Romans, Paul presses the argument that the righteousness of God in this sense — as his moral character (the righteousness that he is) — condemns us all. By this standard, "None is righteous, no, not one" (Ro 3:10). This is as far as the law can go, revealing God's righteousness, which is like a mirror showing us our guilt. "For by works of the law no human being will be justified in his sight, since through the law comes knowledge of sin" (Ro 3:20). God cannot clear the guilty according to his law (Ex 34:7).

However, Paul's very next sentence provides the transition from the righteousness that God *is*, which condemns us all, to the righteousness that God *gives* to all who believe in Christ:

> But now the righteousness of God has been manifested apart from the law, although the Law and the Prophets bear witness to it — the righteousness of God through faith in Jesus Christ for all who believe. For there is no distinction: for all have sinned and fall short of the glory of God, and are justified by his grace as a gift, through the redemption that is in Christ Jesus, whom God put forward as a propitiation by his blood, to be received by faith. (Ro 3:21 – 25a)

In this way, God's law is not set aside or relaxed, nor is his righteousness diminished. He does not — indeed, cannot — simply clear the guilty according to his righteous judgment. Nevertheless, he has charged his Son with our guilt and credited us with Christ's righteousness, so that we are not simply cleared but justified, not only forgiven but declared righteous. With Jesus "put forward" as our vicarious law-keeper and sin-bearer, God is "just and the justifier of the one who has faith in Jesus" (v. 26). "Do we then overthrow the law by this faith? By no means! On the contrary, we uphold the law" (v. 31). Though unrighteous in ourselves, we are credited with Christ's righteousness through faith alone. The law cannot condemn us because we have in Jesus Christ everything that it requires of us before God's judgment.

Therefore, *the righteousness of God* bears two senses: according to the law, as the revelation of God's moral character, which condemns us as sinners, and according to the gospel, as the revelation of God's free gift of his Son for all who believe. The righteousness *of* God is our death sentence, but the gift of righteousness *from* God is our justification.

Medieval theology was so preoccupied with Platonic and Aristotelian philosophical categories that it could not recognize the quite different paradigm with which Paul, and indeed the whole New Testament, was working. For medieval theologians, righteousness was the goal toward which we were to strive, and grace was likened to a medicinal substance that is infused into our soul, so that we may do what lies within us. Begun in baptism, justification increased with our cooperation, anticipating a future justification according to works. Of course, if it were a strict judgment according to works (condign merit), no one could be saved—even after centuries of purgatorial fires. However, God accepts our earnest attempts to cooperate with grace *as if* they were meritorious (congruent merit). Ironically, this is actually a weak view of God's righteousness and judgment as revealed in the law. In this way of thinking, Paul could not have properly concluded that "we uphold the law." Rather, the law is relaxed. However, Paul does not say that the law was given so that everyone might try harder to attain final justification, assisted by God's grace, but rather "so that every mouth may be stopped, and the whole world may be held accountable to God" (3:19). The law reveals that God is just (and therefore must condemn all transgressors), but the gospel reveals that God is just and justifier (v. 26).

The Reformers and their heirs affirmed the inflexibility of God's righteous character and judgment, recognizing that according to the gospel Jesus Christ has accomplished everything for us that the law requires of us. They labored the point that it is Christ's successful fulfillment of the trial of the covenantal representative that is imputed or credited to all who believe. This is what keeps justification from being abstract or a legal fiction, since the justified do in fact possess in Christ the status of those who have perfectly fulfilled all righteousness. This is the covenantal language that is everywhere presupposed but so clearly comes to expression in Romans 5, where Adam's covenantal headship imputes guilt and condemnation as well as imparting inherent corruption, while Christ's covenantal headship imputes righteousness and imparts his inherent new life. The forensic language of the courtroom and the organic language of head and body, tree and fruit, vine and branches converge without being confused. In Christ we have both justification and new life, an alien righteousness imputed and Christ's own resurrection life imparted. However, it is complete justification alone, rather than partial sanctification, that assures us of objective peace with God (Ro 5:1).

To build on Paul's banking analogy, for one to not only have one's debts canceled but have a full account by a transfer of funds from someone else renders that wealth no more a fiction than if it were the fruit of one's own labors. As Paul looks over his ledger in Philippians 3, he places all of his own righteousness in the liabilities column and all of Christ's righteousness in his assets column. His only confidence is the **alien righteousness** of Christ imputed to him.

3. Imputed righteousness

The sin of Adam was imputed to the human race as a covenantal entity in solidarity because it was imputed to each member (Ro 5:12). This notion of imputing the sin of one person to each Israelite—and thus to the nation generally—is found elsewhere, as in Achan's theft (Jos 7:10–26). Just as our guilt is imputed to us in Adam, our covenantal head, righteousness is imputed to us in Christ. Original sin and justification by imputed righteousness stand or fall together.

The Reformation view of justification rests on the declarative character of the verb and the twofold meaning of the righteousness of God as that justice that God is, which condemns us, and the justice that God gives, which saves us. Yet it requires a further point: namely, **imputation** as the way in which God gives this righteousness or justice to the ungodly through faith.

The verb translated "to impute" (*logizomai*) is used explicitly in Romans, especially in chapter 4, where Paul refers to Abraham, quoting Genesis 15:6: "Abraham believed God, and it was counted to him as righteousness" (Ro 4:3). Notice how imputation fits in Paul's argument: "Now to the one who works, his wages are not counted [imputed] as a gift but as his due. And to the one who does not work but believes in him who justifies the ungodly, his faith is counted as righteousness" (vv. 4–5). Clearly something is being transferred or given from one person (employer) to another (employee): namely, wages. But in this case it is different: God does not justify those who work for it but only imputes righteousness to those who trust in the justifier of the ungodly. David is another example of one "against whom the Lord will not count his sin" (v. 8). Abraham could not even count his circumcision as the instrument of his justification before God (vv. 9–12). "But the words 'it was counted to him' were not written for his sake alone, but for ours also. It will be counted to us who believe in him who raised from the dead Jesus our Lord, who was delivered up for our trespasses and raised for our justification" (vv. 23–25).

In Galatians 3, with the contrast between "the works of the law" and "hearing with faith," Paul repeats the quotation from Genesis 15:6. "Counting as" or "being counted as," *logizomai eis*, is also found in Romans 2:26; 9:8; 2 Corinthians 12:6, as well as in Acts 19:27 and James 2:23. Although the term does not appear in Romans 5, the idea is evident throughout Paul's comparison and contrast between Adam and Christ. Under Adam's headship, the whole race is guilty and corrupt; under Christ's headship, many are justified and made alive. These passages unmistakably teach that the righteousness by which the believer stands worthy before God's judgment is *alien*: that is, belonging properly to someone else. It is Christ's righteousness imputed, not the believer's inherent righteousness—even if produced by the gracious work of the Spirit. In the quotation from the Westminster Confession above, the clause is added that not only works "done by us" but even works "wrought in us"—by the Holy Spirit—are excluded from justification. Far from denying the Spirit's work within us, the confession is simply saying that this is not justification.

The notion of one person's righteousness being imputed to another is already present in Second Temple Judaism (the "merit of the fathers").[38] Furthermore, if one grants that our sins can be credited to Christ as our vicarious substitute, then surely there is no contradiction in saying that his righteousness can be credited to us. If Christ's work provides forgiveness for our *debts*, we still lack that *righteousness* that God requires of his image-bearers.

Paul appeals to the examples of Abraham and David (especially in Romans 4 and Galatians 2–4). In fact, the familiar prophecy of Isaiah 53 describes this imputation or exchange. The suffering Servant bears our sins, suffers in our place, and by his righteous act "shall ... make many to be accounted righteous, and he shall bear their iniquities" (v. 11). Our sins are *charged* to him, and his righteousness is *credited* to us. In Zechariah 3, there is the prophecy of Joshua the high priest in the heavenly courtroom, with Satan as the prosecuting attorney and the angel of the Lord as his defender. Although Joshua is condemned in himself, his filthy clothes are removed, and instead he is arrayed in a spotless robe. All of these passages flood the New Testament's testimony to Jesus Christ as "the LORD is our righteousness" (Jer 23:5–6, with 1Co 1:30–31; 2Co 5:21). "There is therefore now no

---

38. Hermann Lichtenberger, "The Understanding of the Torah in the Judaism of Paul's Day," in *Paul and the Mosaic Law: The Third Durham-Tübingen Research Symposium on Earliest Christianity and Judaism* (ed. James D. G. Dunn; Grand Rapids: Eerdmans, 2001), 16. He refers to a prayer in the rabbinical sources that God will keep petitioners from sin so that they "may find joy at the end of the age ... this being counted to you for righteousness if you do what is true and good before God for the salvation of yourself and of Israel."

condemnation for those who are in Christ Jesus" (Ro 8:1). Nothing remains to be done; all has been accomplished for us by Christ, and in him we are already holy and blameless before the Father.

Apart from the imputation of Christ's righteousness, there is no justification. In fact, it is precisely this imputation that keeps justification from being the "legal fiction" that critics often call it. God pronounces us just, not because we are just in ourselves, but also not as a useful fiction. Rather, he declares us righteous because Christ's righteousness is imputed to us through faith. The husband assumes his bride's debts and shares with her his whole estate. Besides the lawcourt and banking analogies, the Scriptures draw on a rich variety of metaphors: our fig leaves are removed and we are clothed in Christ's righteousness; the Benefactor has died, thus putting his will into effect so that we receive all of his estate. On we could go with the scriptural analogies for this marvelous exchange.

Critics of the evangelical doctrine of justification have frequently judged that it has no place for sanctification; the effective and transformative aspects of salvation are reduced to a legal verdict. However, it simply does not follow that to affirm a strictly forensic justification is to deny sanctification. In fact, we affirm both, while critics of the view deny the former.

II. Adoption

Adoption is a good transition from justification to sanctification, since it consists of both forensic and transformative aspects. Adapting the ancient Near Eastern treaties to God's covenantal purposes, Scripture indicates that to be adopted by the Great King, the vassal "puts on" the identity of the suzerain, including his regal glory. It is this lost glory that is recovered — and, because it is no less than the glory of the God-Man, it is greater than the original glory of "the first man ... from the earth, a man of dust" (1Co 15:47). "Just as we have borne the image of the man of dust, we shall also bear the image of the man of heaven" (v. 49).[39] "To be the image of God is to be the son of God."[40] To "put on Christ" is to derive all of one's righteousness from him, both for justification and for sanctification. That is not only because he is the eternal Son, but because he is the justified covenant head

---

39. Appealing to the research of Phyllis Bird, I pointed out in *Lord and Servant: A Covenant Christology* (Louisville, Ky.: Westminster John Knox, 2005), ch. 4, that Ge 1–2 exploits Egyptian mythology for polemical purposes. While the Pharaoh was thought to be the son of the gods, in Genesis this royal sonship extends beyond the king, and not only to all sons but to all human beings: "male and female" created in God's *image*, the language of sonship.

40. M. G. Kline, *Images of the Spirit* (Eugene, Ore.: Wipf & Stock, 1999), 35.

of his people, "and was declared to be Son of God in power according to the Spirit of holiness by his resurrection from the dead" (Ro 1:4). In Christ, our rags are exchanged for robes of regal splendor, and we are seated at the same table with Abraham, Isaac, and Jacob.

The clothing analogy is not original to Pauline theology. It occurs first with God's clothing of Adam and Eve after the fall, the vision of Joshua the high priest having his filthy clothes exchanged for a robe of righteousness in Zechariah 3, and a host of other passages. In Isaiah 61:10–11, we read, "I will greatly rejoice in the LORD; my soul shall exult in my God, for he has clothed me with the garments of salvation; he has covered me with the robe of righteousness, as a bridegroom decks himself like a priest with a beautiful headdress, and as a bride adorns herself with her jewels" (cf. Rev 21:2, which paraphrases this verse). The guests at the wedding feast in Jesus' parable are adorned in festive garments (Mt 22:1–14), and the prodigal son is decked out by the father in the best clothes upon his return (Lk 15:11–32). So when Paul says that Christ is "our righteousness and sanctification and redemption" (1Co 1:30), and refers repeatedly to our being "clothed with Christ" and "having put on Jesus Christ," and calls us on that basis to "put on Christ" in our daily conduct, this same connection between justification and sanctification is being drawn. Or, to shift to the drama analogy once again, our character in the "Adam story" has been killed off, and we have been written into a different script as a completely different character, "in Christ."

In common with the practices of its neighbors, Israel's law made the first-born son heir of the estate, which was also the inheritance law of the Greco-Roman world. Yet in the new covenant (fulfilling the promise to Adam and Eve as well as the covenant with Abraham and Sarah), with Christ as the head, "There is neither Jew nor Greek, there is neither slave or free, there is no male and female; for you are all one in Christ Jesus. And if you are Christ's, then you are Abraham's offspring, heirs according to promise" (Gal 3:28–29). Everyone who is in Christ is a "firstborn son," coheir of the entire estate.

A lodestar for justification, Galatians 3 and 4 are also crucial for our understanding of adoption. After all, the same logic that announces freedom from the bondage of the law for righteousness also pertains to the right of inheritance, which is a question of "sonship." Paul unfolds his argument redemptive-historically: with the law (here intending the whole old covenant administration) as the "guardian until Christ came, in order that we might be justified by faith" (3:24).

I mean that the heir, as long as he is a child, is no different from a slave, though he is the owner of everything, but he is under guardians and managers until the date set by his father. In the same way we also, when we were children, were enslaved to the elementary principles of the world. But when the fullness of time had come, God sent forth his Son, born of woman, born under the law, to redeem those who were under the law, so that we might receive adoption as sons. And because you are sons, God has sent the Spirit of his Son into our hearts, crying, "Abba! Father!" So you are no longer a slave, but a son, and if a son, then an heir through God. (Gal 4:1–7)

These "sons" who are legally entitled to the inheritance include females as well as males, Gentiles as well as Jews, slaves as well as free citizens, without distinction (Gal 3:28–29). This is the legal significance of Paul's identification of not only males but females also as "sons." It breaks all of the time-honored institutions of inheritance.

To be sure, as we have seen, Israel was identified in the Old Testament as God's son as well as a slave or servant. Yet this is exactly why we need to distinguish the Abrahamic covenant from the Mosaic covenant. In terms of the former, those who share Abraham's faith belong to the covenant of grace and are therefore sons. In terms of the latter, though, the theocratic nation is described in the law as a servant, even a tenant, in God's land (Lev 25:23). "For the Israelites are My slaves. They are My slaves that I brought out of the land of Egypt; I am Yahweh your God" (Lev 25:55 HCSB).[41]

However, the true spiritual heirs of Abraham, in both testaments, constitute the true Israel of God, and they are "sons." Furthermore, these brothers and sisters are not only heirs of whatever is left over from the spoils of the firstborn son's inheritance. In fact, the very passage we are using for the structure of the *ordo salutis* (Ro 8:30) begins with the statement, "For those whom he foreknew he also predestined to be conformed to the image of his Son, in order that he might be the firstborn among many brothers" (v. 29). Jews and Gentiles alike are "fellow heirs, members of the same body, and partakers of the promise in Christ Jesus through the gospel" (Eph 3:6). Properly speaking, it is Christ who is the "heir of all things" (Heb 1:2; cf. Lk 20:14), but precisely because he possesses all things not only as a private but as a public person, his inheritance is a public trust. Believers hold all things in common with Christ and therefore with each other.

In the economy of the Sinai covenant, Moses is a servant in God's house,

---

41. I have used the Holman Christian Standard Bible translation here, since it consistently translates *'ebed* "slave," whereas other translations render it "servant" when it refers to Israel — even when the same word is rendered "slave" in connection with non-Hebrews (e.g., Lev 26:13).

while Jesus Christ is the firstborn son (Heb 3:1–6). So even Moses' adoption is dependent not on the condition of his personal fulfillment of the law-covenant made at Sinai but on Christ's personal fulfillment of that covenant by which he has won the inheritance for his brothers and sisters in the covenant of grace: "For he who sanctifies and those who are sanctified all have one source. That is why he is not ashamed to call them brothers, saying … 'Behold, I and the children God has given me'" (Heb 2:11–13). As with justification, this adoption is not a legal fiction, since the law is fulfilled: the firstborn Son has won the entire estate by his victorious service to the crown, but, as established in the mutuality of the covenant of redemption (i.e., election), every adopted child has an equal share.

Having merited his estate by his loyal service to the Great King, Christ passes on this inheritance in perpetuity to all of those coheirs included in his last will and testament. Jesus' high-priestly prayer in John 17 is pregnant with this covenantal language, even to the point of linking his own fulfillment of his earthly mission to the intra-Trinitarian covenant of redemption, referring to "those whom you gave me," who are now to be included in the *koinōnia* (fellowship) of the Trinity itself.

The children need not worry about their future or jockey for their Father's favor (as Jacob and Esau). After all, "He who did not spare his own Son but gave him up for us all, how will he not also with him graciously give us all things?" (Ro 8:32). As Calvin comments on Ephesians 1:23,

> This is the highest honour of the Church, that, until He is united to us, the Son of God reckons himself in some measure imperfect. What consolation is it for us to learn, that, not until we are along with him, does he possess all his parts, or wish to be regarded as complete! Hence, in the First Epistle to the Corinthians, when the apostle discusses largely the metaphor of a human body, he includes under the single name of Christ the whole Church.[42]

If union with Christ in the covenant of grace is the matrix for Paul's *ordo*, justification is nevertheless the legal basis for our adoption, sanctification, and glorification. "Adoption of its own nature requires and presupposes the reconciliation found in justification," William Ames reminds us. "The first fruit of adoption is that Christian liberty by which all believers are freed from the bondage of the law, sin, and the world."[43]

---

42. John Calvin, *Commentaries on the Epistles of Paul to the Galatians and Ephesians* (trans. William Pringle; Grand Rapids: Eerdmans, 1957), 218.

43. William Ames, *The Marrow of Theology* (trans. J. D. Eusden; orig. 1629; Boston: Pilgrim, 1968), 165.

Adoption, like justification, is simultaneously legal and relational, as is the obverse: alienation and condemnation. Adoption is not a goal held out to children who successfully imitate their parents; nor is it the result of an infusion of familial characteristics or genes. Rather, it is a change in legal status that issues in a relationship that is gradually reflected in the child's identity, characteristics, and actions. From the courtroom, with the legal status and inheritance unalterably established, the child moves into the security of a growing and thriving future. While the relationship must never be reduced to the legal aspect, it is inconceivable—especially in this case—without it. Legally adopted children no longer have to wonder if they really belong to the family and are heirs of the estate along with their siblings.

God's Word declares us to be righteous heirs of the kingdom, and this same word immediately begins to conform us existentially, morally, and socially to this new-creation reality, the firstborn Son being its archetype. Though justification and sanctification remain distinct, the gospel is the source of both. The legal act of making a child an heir together with the firstborn son gives that child a new name, a new identity, a new family, and a new future that can never be stolen or surrendered. The world's King has become our Father in Christ. He has adopted us not only from the hospital or a foster home, but from the prison in which his own justice held us as rebels. And his own Spirit, who raised Jesus from the dead, is given to us as a down payment, causing us even now to raise our eyes to heaven, crying, "Abba! Father!" (Gal 4:6). As with all sound teaching, the goal of the doctrine is to bring us to doxology, giving all praise to God with nothing left for ourselves. "What then shall we say to these things? If God is for us, who can be against us?.... Who shall bring any charge against God's elect? It is God who justifies. Who is to condemn?.... Who shall separate us from the love of Christ?" (Ro 8:31–35).

Key Terms
- justification
- imputation, forensic (legal)
- alien righteousness
- adoption

Key Distinctions
- imputed/infused (righteousness)

Key Questions

1. "[God] justifies the ungodly" (Ro 4:5–6). What does Paul mean by this statement?
2. What is meant by the phrase "the righteousness of God"?
3. Define *imputation*. How would you respond to the charge that this makes justification a "legal fiction": in other words, that God unjustly judges someone to be righteous who isn't?
4. Discuss Roman Catholic (and some Arminian) objections to the Reformation view of justification.
5. How does adoption highlight both the legal and relational aspects of our union with Christ?

Chapter Thirteen

Sanctification and Perseverance

We have seen that one reason for the ongoing criticism of the evangelical doctrine of justification is that it undermines sanctification.[1] However, this assumption presupposes a false choice that the Reformers did not make between the imputation of Christ's righteousness and the renewal of believers according to Christ's image. While Rome simply assimilated justification to sanctification, the Reformation position affirmed both as distinct yet inseparable gifts. Whereas Rome maintains that God's justifying verdict is a future reward for our faithful cooperation, evangelical faith teaches that this verdict is the present gift that motivates our faithful response. We do not work for a secure future, but from a secure present.

Our union with Christ comprehends all of our saving blessings. Through the gospel preached, the Spirit creates faith in our hearts and confirms it by the sacraments. Faith embraces Christ in the indivisible unity of his person and work, inheriting everything that belongs to Christ himself as the Mediator of the covenant. We do not find some gifts, like justification, in Christ

---

1. According to an uncharacteristically ill-informed assertion of the great Roman Catholic historian of philosophy, Étienne Gilson, "For the first time, with the Reformation, there appeared this conception of a grace that saves a man without changing him, of a justice that redeems corrupted nature without restoring it, of a Christ who pardons the sinner for self-inflicted wounds but does not heal them" (Étienne Gilson, *The Spirit of Medieval Philosophy* [London: Sheed and Ward, 1936], 421).

and then other gifts, like sanctification, in ourselves or even in the Spirit apart from Christ. In the same act of faith, one is justified and renewed. These are distinct gifts that must never be confused, but they are given together—with every other blessing—through faith in Christ.

In the Greek language there are two distinct moods (among others): the *indicative* mood, which is declarative—simply describing a certain state of affairs—and the *imperative* mood, setting forth commands. For example, in Romans Paul first explains who believers were in Adam and their new status and life in Christ and then reasons from this indicative to the imperatives as a logical conclusion: "Do not present your members to sin as instruments for unrighteousness, but present yourselves to God as those who have been brought from death to life" (Ro 6:13). He concludes with what at first appears to be a command but is really an indicative: "For sin will have no dominion over you, since you are not under law but under grace" (v. 14). Paul does not exhort us to keep sin from having dominion over us; he says that it *doesn't* have this dominion because we "are not under law but under grace."

As counterintuitive this may seem to our natural way of thinking, Paul says that the gospel is the answer not only to our guilt and condemnation but to our corruption and slavery to sin. As strange as it sounds to say that God pronounces the wicked just, it is even stranger to imagine that what we need most for sanctification is *more* proclamation of God's free grace in Christ. Perhaps guilt can be assuaged by the preaching of grace, but now that we are justified, don't we need directions for practical living? Indeed, we do. It is always the case that we need God's law to *direct* us. However, it is dangerous to assume that the law can *empower* us in sanctification any more than in justification.

In his hymn "Rock of Ages," Augustus Toplady spoke of the gospel as "the double cure," saving us from both sin's guilt and its power. The gospel announces that we are free not only from condemnation but from the cruel tyranny of sin. In the act of justification, works and grace are totally opposed. However, precisely on the basis of justification, good works are the fruit of faith. The faith that receives Christ *apart from works for justification* also receives Christ *for works in sanctification.* We are saved by grace alone, through faith alone, for a life of good works (Eph 2:8–10). The order is first justification, then good works; not first good works, then justification. The Spirit creates faith through his word; faith clings to Christ alone, and this faith produces the fruit of the Spirit. The gospel indicative is not only that we are justified, but that we are buried and raised with Christ in resurrection life

> ## Key Distinction:
> ### *faith/works*
>
> In determining the basis for our relationship with God, **faith** and **works** are completely opposed. However, the justified are free finally for the first time to pursue good works out of love for God and neighbor. Fear is no longer in the driver's seat, so love can flourish. The proper order is the word (specifically the gospel), then faith (created by the Spirit through the gospel), then love (which expresses itself in good works). In seeking justification, faith and works are opposed; in sanctification, however, works are the fruit of faith.

(Ro 6:1–11). The imperative naturally follows: "Let not sin therefore reign in your mortal body" (v. 12).

There are not two Christs (one who is Savior and the other who is Lord), nor two acts of faith (one to "make Jesus our personal Savior" and another to "make him Lord of our life"). We do not make Jesus anything, as if faith were a work, but receive everything, as a free gift. The Savior is Lord and the Lord is the Savior. The tyranny of sin over your life has been toppled; therefore do not live as though this has not happened: this is the order of Paul's logic. In fact, presenting our bodies as a living sacrifice, according to Paul, is "our spiritual [*logikēn*] worship" in the light of "the mercies of God" that have been explored to that point (Ro 12:1). It is the good news that produces faith, which not only justifies but yields a harvest of good works.

In Romans 4:17, God's work in justification is compared to his work in creating the world out of nothing. Justification is the fiat declaration, "Let there be righteousness!" even where, at present, there is nothing but guilt and unrighteousness in the sinner, because Christ's righteousness is imputed through Spirit-given and gospel-created faith. As in creation, only after God's declarative word of justification ("'Let there be....' And there was ...") can there be an appropriate creaturely response ("Let the earth bring forth ...").

I. Justification and Sanctification: The "Double Benefit" of Union with Christ

As G. C. Berkouwer reminds us, we are not moving from theory to practice when we turn from justification to sanctification. Even in our sanctification, we keep our eye on Christ and his all-sufficient righteousness imputed as the only basis for our growth in holiness. *Separating* justification from sanctification is as serious as *confusing* them, because it means that the latter is "cut loose or abstracted from justification."[2] When that happens, says Berkouwer, justification is easily seen as the gracious act of God, while sanctification becomes the result of human striving.[3] Paul teaches that believers are "sanctified in Christ Jesus" (1Co 1:2, 30; 6:11; 1Th 5:23; cf. Acts 20:32; 26:18). As Herman Bavinck puts it, "Many indeed acknowledge that we are justified by the righteousness of Christ, but seem to think that—at least they act as if—they must be sanctified by a holiness they themselves have acquired."[4] Something close to this error seems to have been held by Paul's opponents in Galatia (Gal 3:1–9).

I have pointed out that union with Christ is different from imitation of Christ. There are calls in Scripture to imitate Christ, but this is only possible because of that deeper reality of our being actually united to Christ through faith alone. The evangelical call of the New Testament is not to be *like* Christ, but to be *in* Christ. In other words, while sanctification finds its direction in the law, it finds its ground in the gospel. George Lindbeck reminds us that the proper category for discipleship and *imitatio Christi* is not the atonement or justification, but the third use of the law (i.e., to direct believers in the way of obedience).[5] Otherwise, the Christian life is reduced to a moralistic attempt to live *up to* Christ's example rather than our living *out of* the realities of Christ's saving work. Writes Lindbeck: "From a traditional perspective, the error here is in the reversal of the order: Jesus is not first Example and then Savior, but the other way around."[6] As Paul notes in 1 Corinthians 9:21, as a saved believer he is "under the law of Christ."

This view puts to flight two perennial temptations: legalism and antinomianism. The law cannot heal; it can only pronounce a just sentence in view of the facts. Basing sanctification on our imitation of Christ or following his commands can only yield self-righteousness, hypocrisy, and ultimately condemnation for having failed. Only when Christ steps forward as our law-keeping and curse-bearing Mediator are we no longer "under the law"—that is, subject to its demand, "Do this and you shall live." At the same time, this

---

2. G. C. Berkouwer, *Studies in Dogmatics: Faith and Sanctification* (Grand Rapids: Eerdmans, 1952), 20.
3. Ibid., 21.
4. Herman Bavinck, quoted in ibid., 22.
5. George Lindbeck, "Justification and Atonement: An Ecumenical Trajectory," in *By Faith Alone: Essays on Justification in Honor of Gerhard O. Forde* (ed. Joseph A. Burgess and Marc Kolden; Grand Rapids: Eerdmans, 2004), 208.
6. Ibid., 209.

> ## Key Distinction:
> ### justification/sanctification
>
> With the distinction between faith and works in mind, we can also distinguish (without separating) **justification** and **sanctification**. Both gifts are given in union with Christ. Through the same act of faith we embrace Christ for the imputation of righteousness (justification) and gradual conformity to his likeness (sanctification). Justification is a legal verdict pronounced on us; sanctification is the Spirit's work within us, bringing forth good works.

gospel creates faith that bears the fruit of righteousness. Because of our justification, the law no longer can condemn us before God's throne. Yet far from leading to moral anarchy, this justification is precisely the basis on which the deepest intent of the law—love of God and neighbor—is written on our hearts by the finger of God. We are liberated now to seek God's moral will for our lives without fear. We are free to struggle earnestly against sin and temptation, to love and serve our neighbors, and to obey the calls to active discipleship because we know that in spite of the corruption still clinging to our best motives and works, we are no longer under the law's condemnation. Furthermore, we have been given the Spirit of God, who renews us day by day, conforming us to the image of Christ.

The law remains the *standard* for righteousness, but no more in sanctification than in justification does our obedience to the law become the *basis* for our righteousness before God. Otherwise, we would place ourselves under a covenant of works again, proposing to fulfill the conditions of justification, instead of the covenant of grace, with Christ as the fulfiller of all righteousness for us. We must always bear in mind throughout our Christian pilgrimage that the Christ who commands is already also the one who has taken care of the guilt not only for past failures but for present and future ones—and even for our failure to do anything as fully and faithfully as we ought.

How can we despise that holy will of the Father that Jesus not only fulfilled for us out of duty but of which he said, "My food is to do the will of him who sent me and to accomplish his work" (Jn 4:34)? How can we set aside God's commands when Jesus rebuffed Satan's temptation with his submission to "every word that comes from the mouth of God" (Mt 4:4)? How can we cherish those sins from which Christ has liberated us by his death and resurrection? Believers hate their sin, and they love God's law, longing to keep it not out of fear of punishment or hope of merit, but because they belong to Christ, who loved us and God's law to the point of death on a cross. With such an inheritance, it would be not only ungrateful but foolish for us to disparage our adopting Father, redeeming older brother, the Spirit of grace, and the family of coheirs.

So we must beware of seeking a *balance* between legalism and antinomianism. After explaining the justification of the ungodly, Paul anticipates the logical question: "Are we to continue in sin that grace may abound?" (Ro 6:1). The legalist replies to Paul's question, "Not on your life! Don't you know that if you still fall into sins—especially the same ones repeatedly—you either lose your salvation or never had it to begin with?" If our view of justification does not provoke this charge of antinomianism, it has missed Paul's point. Yet Paul clearly refutes any antinomian conclusion. He does not teach that one who is justified (i.e., has accepted Jesus as Savior) might nevertheless still be under the tyranny of sin (i.e., not having accepted Jesus as Lord). There simply is no such thing as a "carnal Christian," one who does not bear fruit and may not even still trust in Christ.

Instead, Paul's answer stands in sharp contrast to both legalism and antinomianism. He does not advocate balance between these extremes. Rather, he turns to the gospel as an alternative to both: "By no means! How can we who died to sin still live in it? Do you not know that *all* of us who have been baptized into Christ Jesus were baptized into his death? We were buried therefore with him by baptism into death, in order that, just as Christ was raised from the dead by the glory of the Father, we too might walk in newness of life" (Ro 6:2–4, emphasis added). No one can be united to Christ's death, for the forgiveness of sin, without also being united to his resurrection life (vv. 5–6). We *have died* (a completed act in the past) and now *are alive*. So instead of issuing an imperative with a threat, Paul proclaims an indicative with a promise. The answer to the antinomian and legalist alike is the gospel. The antinomian has too narrow a view of the gospel, as if it were mere fire insurance—canceling our debt without actually marrying us to Christ—while the legalist turns the gospel into law. However, Paul returns to the gospel and simply announces that through our union with Christ by faith we have not only justification but sanctification. No one who is justified is in fact under the reign of sin and death. Drawing on the wide vista of this triumphant indicative, the imperative follows: "Let not sin therefore reign in your mortal body, to make you obey its passions" (v. 12).

Instead of a double source (synergism), redemption is concerned with a double grace: justification and inner renewal. It is all the work of God, in Christ. In Lesslie Newbigin's words,

> The idea of a righteousness of one's own is the quintessence of sin. Against this, therefore, against every trace of a holiness or righteousness which does not depend simply upon God's mercy to the sinner, we have to set our faces as relentlessly as Paul did. But equally with Paul we have to recognise that if any man be in Christ there is a new creation, not a fiction but a real supernatural new birth, the life of the risen Christ in the soul.[7]

Just as Paul's treatment of justification led logically to the question, "Are we to continue in sin that grace may abound?" (Ro 6:1), the Reformation unleashed radical elements that went well beyond the views of the Reformers. Gerhard Forde reminds us, "Luther had hardly begun to proclaim the freedom of the Christian before he had to fight against abuse of the term. He did not do this in such a way as to speak about the good works that must be added to faith. Instead, he did so by calling people back to that faith that occurs 'where the Holy Spirit gives people faith in Christ and thus sanctifies them.' "[8]

Luther's response at this juncture was precisely Paul's: to infer from justification that we are free to remain in sin is to ignore the vast scope of what justification actually secures. Though we are justified through faith alone, this faith "is never alone, but is always accompanied by love and hope."[9] Sanctification does not just happen to us automatically, apart from our conscious engagement. This conscious engagement is always an act of receiving, but precisely because it receives Christ, his gospel, and his Spirit, it is always an act also of living, working, doing. Faith is created by receiving and expresses itself by giving. Far from leaving us passive, God's regenerating grace activates us, so that our renewed will "is not idle in the daily practice of repentance but cooperates in all the works of the Holy Spirit that He accomplishes through us."[10]

Exactly the same points are made in the Reformed confessions. The Westminster Confession states, "They who are effectually called and regenerated, having a new heart and a new spirit created in them, are further sanctified, really and personally, through the virtue of Christ's death and resurrection, by his Word and Spirit dwelling in them."[11] All of this is "in

---

7. Lesslie Newbigin, *The Household of Faith* (London: SCM, 1953), 128–29.

8. Gerhard Forde, *On Being a Theologian of the Cross: Reflections on Luther's Heidelberg Disputation, 1518* (Grand Rapids: Eerdmans, 1997), 56–57.

9. See *Formula of Concord* (Epitome 3, 11; cf. Solid Declaration 3, 23, 26, 36, 41).

10. Ibid., Solid Declaration 2, 88.

11. Westminster Confession of Faith, in the *Book of Confessions* (Louisville: General Assembly of the Presbyterian Church in the USA, 1991), ch. 15.

Christ," not in ourselves.[12] We have to get the order right: through the gospel the Spirit produces faith, faith produces love, and love goes out to others in good works. Apart from our union with Christ and especially the imputation of righteousness in that union, sanctification is simply another religious self-improvement program determined by the powers of this age (the flesh) rather than of the age to come (the Spirit).

Good works now may be freely performed for God and neighbors without any fear of punishment or agony over the mixed motives of each act. Because of justification in Christ, even our good works can be "saved," not in order to improve either God's lot or our own, but our neighbor's. As Calvin explains,

> Those bound by the yoke of the law are like servants assigned certain tasks for each day by their masters. These servants think they have accomplished nothing and dare not appear before their masters unless they have fulfilled the exact measure of their tasks. But sons, who are more generously and candidly treated by their fathers, do not hesitate to offer them incomplete and half-done and even defective works, trusting that their obedience and readiness of mind will be accepted by their fathers, even though they have not quite achieved what their fathers intended. Such children ought we to be, firmly trusting that our services will be approved by our most merciful Father, however small, rude, and imperfect these may be.... And we need this assurance in no slight degree, for without it we attempt everything in vain.[13]

My father was a bomber mechanic in the Second World War; he once built a boat from scratch. However, in my case the apple not only fell far from the tree, but rolled down the street and was crushed by heavy traffic. Nevertheless, watching him work on our car as a child, I often heard him say, "Now push that down," directing my hand to the appropriate lever for the last operation. We would go inside the house and he would tell my mother, "Mike fixed the car." I was not an employee or a hired mechanic taking credit for contracted labor, but a son being treated indulgently by a loving parent. This is how God relates to us now. Far from making us lazy, this frees us from the paralyzing fear that whatever we do is not good enough. Good enough for what: for justification or for grateful obedience? And good enough for whom: for a judge or for a father? Our good works can never make us accepted children of God, but they are pleasing to God when they are done in faith and serve the good of our neighbors. Conversely, our selfishness grieves the Spirit (Eph 4:30). Our attitudes and actions matter in

---

12. For a fine elaboration of this point, see again John Webster, *Holiness* (Grand Rapids: Eerdmans, 2003), 81.

13. Calvin, *Institutes* 3.19.5.

this new family, even though they are not the meritorious basis or condition of our being God's children.

II. What Is Holiness? absence of sin p. 83

Sanctification is grounded in election, the incarnation, and redemption, but most immediately in effectual calling, justification, and adoption. Called into union with Christ by the Spirit through the gospel, the elect are adopted into God's family as joint heirs with Christ, renewed according to the image of their elder brother. This sanctification begins with a decisive break with the old life, sharing by the Spirit in Christ's death and resurrection. This new birth is the sovereign work of the Spirit, without our cooperation, but it gives rise to our response in repentance and faith. Although our whole life is repentance and faith, dying daily to sin and self, there is a decisive claim that God makes on us prior to all gradual conformity to Christ's image.

God alone *is* holy; creatures are *made* holy by God. But what is holiness? In both the Hebrew and the Greek, the root of the verb translated "to sanctify" is "to cut." God's act of sanctifying cuts people, places, and things *away* from their ordinary association *for* his own use. Conversely, to be unholy is to be "cut off" from the covenant and its blessings. Although we will come to the sense in which sanctification is more commonly understood as moral renewal, it is important to recognize at the outset that it is *God's* action of electing, separating or cutting, claiming a people for himself. It is not the gold that makes the sanctuary sacred, nor the gift on the altar that sanctifies the altar, but the sanctuary that sanctifies the gold and the altar that sanctifies the gift, Jesus reminded the religious leaders (Mt 23:16–21). Jesus even refers to himself as "sanctified [set apart] by the Father and sent into the world" (Jn 10:36). Paul reminds us that we have been chosen out of the same lump of clay, to be vessels of mercy rather than vessels of wrath (Ro 9:22–23). He tells Timothy that approved ministers in God's house are vessels set apart from ordinary use for special use (2Ti 2:21). Holiness is not determined by what things are in themselves, but by what God makes of them in his economy of grace.

At the same time, holiness is frequently associated in Scripture with an inherent moral quality. It is first of all an attribute of God. When Isaiah, commissioned to declare God's judgment on Israel and the nations, encounters a vision of God in his majesty, he is overwhelmed with his own sinfulness (Isa 6:1–5). Only after God absolves him is Isaiah relieved of his fear and enabled to cheerfully accept his vocation (vv. 6–8). God's holiness highlights his otherness or difference from human beings, both in terms of his transcendent majesty (compared to our creatureliness) and his ethical purity (compared to our sinfulness). In the Lord's Prayer, Jesus calls us first to regard the Father's name as sacred (*hagiastheto to onoma sou*). Similarly, Peter instructs believers not to fear the world, "but in your hearts sanctify [*hagiasate*] Christ as Lord" (1Pe 3:15 NRSV).

It is therefore a marvelous wonder that God can speak of anyone or anything as holy other than himself. Nevertheless, in his condescending kindness, God claims certain people, places, and things as the site for his blessing and communion: again, not because they share univocally in his essence, as the Sun, but because they are recipients of his gracious energies, which are like the rays that warm the earth. The whole earth is the Lord's (Ps 24:1–2), yet he has claimed Zion, like Eden of old, as his holy hill and Israel as his holy land (vv. 3–6).

To Israel God says that as long as the people obey his law, they will be "my treasured possession among all peoples, for all the earth is mine; and you shall be to me a kingdom of priests and a holy nation" (Ex 19:5–6). It is this same description that Peter applies to the church because of Christ's faithfulness, even to those who "were not a people" and "had not received mercy" (1Pe 2:9–10). In his baptism, their baptism is sanctified. In his active obedience, they are holy. "And for their sake I consecrate myself," says Jesus, "that they also may be sanctified in truth" (Jn 17:19). In his death, burial, and resurrection they die and are raised to new life. They have been saved out of the world. Therefore, even before Jesus tells the disciples about their own fruit-bearing life as part of the Vine, he declares, "Already you are clean because of the word that I have spoken to you" (Jn 15:3).

In his message to the Ephesian elders, Paul said, "And now I commend you to God and to the word of his grace, which is able to build you up and to give you the inheritance among all those who are sanctified" (Ac 20:32). He addresses his letters to the churches as those "who are ... called to be saints [*hagiois*]" (Ro 1:7), "to those sanctified [*hegiasmenois*] in Christ Jesus" (1Co 1:2; cf. 2Co 1:1; Eph 1:1; Php 1:1; Col 1:2). Similarly, Peter addresses his first letter to Christians of the Jewish diaspora as those "who are elect exiles ... according to the foreknowledge of God the Father, in the sanctification [*hagiasmo*] of the Spirit, for obedience to Jesus Christ and for sprinkling with his blood" (1Pe 1:1–2), and his second letter "to those who have obtained a faith of equal standing with ours by the righteousness of our God and Savior Jesus Christ" (2Pe 1:1).

Everything outside of Christ is "common," ultimately to be "set apart" for destruction. All that is found in Christ is holy, because it is in Christ. He is our sanctification — "the LORD is our Righteousness" (1Co 1:30 with Jer 23:6), our Holy Place. The sprinkling of Christ's blood is vastly superior to that of the blood of goats and bulls in sanctifying, since it purifies "our conscience from dead works to serve the living God" (Heb 9:13–14)! "And by [God's] will we have been sanctified through the offering of the body of Jesus Christ once for all" (Heb 10:10). It is this "blood of the covenant by which he [each covenant member] was sanctified" (v. 29). Jesus suffered outside the camp "in order to sanctify the people through his own blood" (Heb 13:12). God "saved us and called us to a holy calling, not because of our works but because of his own purpose and grace, which he gave us in Christ Jesus before the ages began, and which now has been manifested through the appearing of our Savior Christ Jesus, who abolished death and brought life and immortality to light through the gospel" (2Ti 1:9–10).

Before we can speak of our being put to holy use and growing in grace, we must see that sanctification is first of all God's act of setting us apart from the world for himself. Even though the Corinthian church has become filled with immorality, strife, division, and immaturity, Paul begins both letters to this body by addressing them as "saints" (holy ones) and re-introduces the wonder of the gospel. Precisely because their status was defined by the gospel's indicatives, the apostle could recall them to repentance as the only legitimate response. This looks back retrospectively to our election in Christ, which is frequently mentioned as the ultimate source of our sanctification (Jn 15:16; Eph 1:4; Col 3:12; 1Th 1:2–7; 2Th 2:13–16; 2Ti 1:9–10; 1Pe 1:2). Yet when we are called effectually by the Spirit through the gospel, not only the condemnation but also the dominion of sin is definitively toppled. This does not mean that we no longer sin, but that sin has lost its command — objectively, once and for all. We no longer belong to this passing evil age, although we still live in it. We are now, already, citizens of the new creation. Our sanctification lies not in our claim on God but on God's gracious and sovereign claim to us and upon us.

Whereas most people think that the goal of religion is to get people to become something that they are not, the Scriptures call believers to become more and more what they already are in Christ. Because they were definitively sanctified or set apart as holy to the Lord, the Corinthians must reestablish proper relationships, order, and behavior in the church. Their practice must be brought in line with their identity. Here again the indicative is the basis for the imperative. We are holy (definitive sanctification); therefore we are to be holy (progressive sanctification).

The same point can be discerned in John 15:3, where Jesus says, "Already you are clean because of the word that I have spoken to you," and only then calls them to bear fruit that is consistent with this objective declaration.

III. Growth in Sanctification

So far, everything I have said about our holiness is objective: it is God's act of claiming us as his people, his possession, the field of his gracious labors. However, when God elects, redeems, and calls us out of the world, to himself, he works within us by his Spirit, through the word, to bring forth fruit. Again, the comparison with creation is apt: The "Let there be" gives rise to "Let the earth bring forth fruit." Just as the temple vessels were not intrinsically holy before they were set aside for holy purposes, there is no preparation on our part that can make us holy.[14] However, set apart definitively by election, redemption, and effectual calling, we are being set apart progressively from this passing age as the Spirit conforms us to Christ's image. The gospel not only announces God's work *for* us in Christ; it is also "the power at work *within* us" (Eph 3:20), so that despite our own weakness Christ's energies are at work within us by his Spirit (2Co 12:9–10). Believers are called to pursue purity, to dwell on excellent things, and to "practice these things [i.e., what you have learned and received and heard and seen in me], and the God of peace will be with you" (Php 4:8–9). Such holiness distinguishes itself by producing the fruit of wisdom, purity, peace, gentleness, without partiality or hypocrisy (Jas 3:13–18). We are called to discipline ourselves and to submit to the government and discipline of Christ's church. We do not spontaneously burst forth from death to life with maturity, godly wisdom, and new habits. These are the fruit of the Spirit that require patience, love, struggle, and intentional effort.

Already holy in Christ, we are to offer ourselves as "a living sacrifice, holy and acceptable" (Ro 12:1), as stones in a holy temple and those who offer a spiritual sacrifice of holy living (1Co 3:17; 1Pe 2:4–5). Therefore, Paul says, we are not only freed *from* the rigor and condemnation of the law, much less the legalistic regulations of ascetic sects (Col 2:16–23), but freed *for* our heavenly calling, which the moral law defines: "If then you have been raised with Christ, seek the things that are above, where Christ is, seated at the right hand of God.... Put to death therefore whatever is earthly in you: sexual immorality, impurity, passion, evil desire, and covetousness, which is

---

14. For an excellent treatment of this topic, see Webster, *Holiness*, esp. ch. 4.

idolatry" (Col 3:1, 5). God's moral law, then, continues to show us the right path, but only the gospel can give us arms and legs.

This growth in holiness has its source in God alone, but it is something we are called to pursue, making full use of the means that he has appointed for it. The indicative (definitive sanctification) leads to the imperatives (progressive sanctification): "Put on then, as God's chosen ones, holy and beloved, compassionate hearts, kindness, humility, meekness, and patience, bearing with one another and, if one has a complaint against another, forgiving each other; as the Lord has forgiven you, so you also must forgive. And above all these put on love, which binds everything together in perfect harmony" (Col 3:12–14). We must not marginalize the many New Testament imperatives to do certain things, to respond in certain ways, to strive earnestly, and so forth. They do not (or should not) haunt or threaten us. We need not (must not) recoil from them, precisely because they are not a condition for life but the way of life that can at last begin in this passing age because the new creation has dawned. There is a lot of work to do, not for our salvation but because of it. And all good works flow from love, which is the fruit of faith, produced by the Spirit through the gospel.

A wild branch is definitively changed in its identity when it is grafted onto a cultivated vine, but it begins to change progressively in its character by virtue of belonging to the vine. Similarly, we are holy in Christ, but are called to holiness in our character and affections, to bear the fruit of the Spirit. While they are distinct, the organic and the legal are two sides of the same covenantal coin. This harmony can be found in the confessional treatments, as in the Second Helvetic Confession, chapter 15: "Wherefore, in this matter we are not speaking of a fictitious, empty, lazy and dead faith, but of a living, quickening faith. *It is and is called a living faith because it apprehends Christ who is life and makes alive, and shows that it is alive by living works*" (emphasis added). It is not the quality of faith itself, but of the person it apprehends (Christ), that makes it the sufficient means of receiving both our justification and sanctification. Not because of what faith is, but because of who Christ is, faith in Christ cannot fail to bring forth good works. In fact, precisely because believers do not trust at all in their own piety, the works that spring from faith are truly pious.[15]

---

15. Second Helvetic Confession, ch. 15, in *The Book of Confessions*: "This all the pious do, but they trust in Christ alone and not in their own works. For again the apostle said: 'It is no longer I who live, but Christ who lives in me; and the life I now live in the flesh I live by faith in the Son of God, who loved me and gave himself for me. I do not reject the grace of God; for if justification were through the law, then Christ died to no purpose' (Gal 2:20)."

In a moving and friendly letter to Cardinal Sadoleto, Calvin made much the same point, when he argued that only by being freed of having to love our neighbor in the service of our own salvation are we able to really love them for their own sake.[16] Sanctification is a life not of acquiring but of receiving from the excess of divine joy that then continues to overflow in excess to our neighbor and from our neighbor to us. Ascetic, moralistic, and introspective programs of sanctification keep us in that very condition of being "curved in on ourselves" that defines sin. This individualistic concern with pacifying God or improving our own character only inflames God's wrath and does nothing for our neighbors. It is precisely in seeing that God does not need our works and they will do nothing for us before God that we are liberated to do them simply because they are what our neighbors need from us.

Our identity is no longer something that we fabricate in our bondage that we mistake for freedom. C. S. Lewis observes, "Out of our selves, into Christ, we must go."[17] "Your real, new self (which is Christ's and also yours, and yours just because it is His) will not come as long as you are looking for it," he adds. "It will come when you are looking for Him." To be in Christ is to be "very much more themselves than they were before."[18] "He invented — as an author invents characters in a novel — all the different people that you and I were intended to be. In that sense our real selves are all waiting for us in Him. It is no good trying to 'be myself' without Him."[19] "To enter heaven," he writes elsewhere, "is to become more human than you ever succeeded in being on earth."[20]

IV. Eschatology: The "Already" and "Not Yet" of Sanctification

Romans 6 completes Paul's proclamation of the triumphant indicative: what is already true of us because of what Christ has accomplished for us. His emphasis on the fact of our deliverance from sin's reign in chapter 6 was provoked by the question, "Are we to continue in sin that grace may abound?" His argument in chapter 7 is provoked by an implied question,

---

16. John Calvin, *A Reformation Debate: Sadoleto's Letter to the Genevans and Calvin's Reply* (ed. John C. Olin; Grand Rapids: Baker, 1966), 56.

17. C. S. Lewis, *Mere Christianity* (San Francisco: HarperSanFrancisco, 2001), 224.

18. Ibid., 161.

19. Ibid., 225.

20. C. S. Lewis, *The Problem of Pain* (San Francisco: HarperSanFrancisco, 2001), 127–28.

"If we are no longer under sin's reign, then why do we still sin?" This is an important question, because many sensitive believers hear about the victory that Paul describes in chapter 6 and, looking at their own experience, can conclude only that they are not truly united to Christ. Ever the good pastor and teacher, Paul addresses this directly. Once again, he does not look for balance, a middle path between activistic perfectionism and lazy pacifism. For one thing, Paul is too profoundly taken with eschatology to settle for such a static way of looking at the matter. By *eschatology* here, I mean the new creation that has dawned with Christ's resurrection.

Christ's resurrection from the dead is the beginning of the general resurrection of the dead and the restoration of all things. Having been judged for our sins, he is vindicated (justified) and is already glorified. We are in Christ already, but always at a different place. Everything awaiting us still in the future is already his now. Because we are inseparably joined to him, even these future realities are already secured for us. They are not in question, but certain, because they are already true of our head. The Spirit is sent into our hearts as the security deposit on our final glorification (Ro 8:11, 14–17, 23). At the same time, "we ourselves, who have the firstfruits of the Spirit, groan inwardly as we wait eagerly for adoption as sons, the redemption of our bodies" (v. 23). We are not yet raised in glory, but "we wait for it with patience" (v. 25).

So, like the kingdom itself, its heirs find themselves in this eschatological tension between the "already" and the "not yet." Like the kingdom, our renewal is already here but not yet consummated. Errors on this aspect of sanctification are therefore similar to errors concerning the kingdom. Some err in denying the reality of the new creation here and now, postponing it to the future state. There is a kind of passivity that allows us to ignore the wonderful indicatives that announce, "Therefore, if anyone is in Christ, he is a new creation. The old has passed away; behold, the new has come" (2Co 5:17). Others err in denying or downplaying the ongoing struggle with sin that Paul describes in Romans 7. This is especially evident in the Wesleyan doctrine of Christian perfection: a triumphalistic eschatology that divides Christ's body into the "victorious" and the "ordinary" believers. Over against both errors, Paul argues that the person described in Romans 6— definitively freed from the reign of sin—is the same conflicted person he describes in chapter 7, and the one who nevertheless looks with assurance to Christ for future glorification in chapter 8.

An emphasis on measurable progress can shift our focus from Christ back to ourselves. In fact, genuine holiness actually makes us more progressively aware of and disturbed by our ongoing struggles with indwelling sin. We grow more aware of our need for Christ, not our own growth in virtue. Rather than measurable progress in virtue, we should think of sanctification as "grow[ing] in the grace and knowledge of our Lord and Savior Jesus Christ" (2Pe 3:17–18). The biblical balance that we find in Scripture reminds us that sanctification is more a matter of going deeper into the gospel than of getting better through the law. The law guides, but it does not give. Of course, there is progress, but that is usually something that *others* observe. (It is interesting that in Matthew 25 the sheep seemed unaware of the acts of mercy they had done in Christ's name, while the goats protest their judgment by appealing to their good works.)

Some believers, like John Wesley, may be able to identify their initial conversion with precision (a quarter to nine in the evening on the twenty-fourth of May, 1738), but this experience cannot be made into a rule. Those who struggled with drug addiction or sexual immorality before conversion will ordinarily struggle with it afterward. Nevertheless, sanctification is the radical in-breaking of the powers of the age to come into this present evil age. The Spirit's transcendent grace can never be domesticated to the ordinary powers of nature, however well programmed and effectively managed.

Sanctification is not treated in Scripture mainly as a matter of getting better and better (a more individualistic approach centered on the self), but as a life of looking up to Christ and out to our neighbors in love and service. If we focus on our experience rather than on Christ, on what we see in ourselves rather than on what we hear in God's promise, then instead of drawing us out of ourselves in faith this focus will drive us deeper into ourselves in alternating moods of self-trust and despair. Again, this is counterintuitive, especially when we have been raised to think that sanctification is about programs for reengineering our soul. If, as Augustine suggested, the essence of sin is to be "turned in on ourselves," then many popular approaches to sanctification only perpetuate this disease. We often nurture our native narcissism even under the name of personal growth and sanctification. There is a place for introspection, but if we are honest, that leads us not only to some encouraging signs of grace but ultimately to question the intensity of our zeal, the purity of our motives, and the reality of our experience. Faith does not look within for its object; it looks up to Christ in faith and out to our neighbors in love.

We have seen how God created human beings as covenantal, social, embodied creatures. Sanctification is the restoration of that image. The Spirit is at work, not drawing us further away from other people, wrapped in a cocoon of spiritual navel-gazing, but leading us out to Christ and his body, out to our family, our neighborhood, and wider society. That is why the vast majority of passages — even on the "fruit of the Spirit" — have to do with our relationship to others, rather than a concentration on taking our spiritual temperature (Gal 5:16 – 26). We are not to be "carried about by every wind of doctrine.... Rather, speaking the truth in love, we are to grow up in every way into him who is the head, into Christ, from whom the whole body, joined and held together by every joint with which it is equipped, when each part is working properly, makes the body grow so that it builds itself up in love" (Eph 4:14 – 16). As Paul makes clear in this passage, growing up in Christ is not something we can do by ourselves. Private spiritual disciplines are part of it, but they are far less grueling than living with other people in community every day and every week. Only through encountering others do I become aware of my weaknesses and offenses and my need to receive forgiveness daily not only from God but from my neighbors. Instead of being obsessed with our own measurable growth, we should be focused on Christ our head and on how we can build up his body. In the process of looking after others, others are looking after us as well, and Christ is looking after us all. The Ten Commandments and the many New Testament commands that unpack the moral law are all concerned with the way we relate to others: to God and to fellow human beings, as well as to the wider creation. They stand in striking contrast with more individualistic approaches.

Like initial conversion, sanctification is a process of growth and maturation that requires a diligent use of the public means of grace as well as the ecclesial, familial, and private disciplines of private prayer, meditative reading of Scripture, witness, fellowship, service to those in need, and the discerning care of faithful elders. The "already" makes it wonderful, while the "not yet" makes it difficult, as Paul relates: "Not that I have already obtained this or am already perfect, but I press on to make it my own, because Christ Jesus has made me his own. Brothers, I do not consider that I have made it my own. But one thing I do: forgetting what lies behind and straining forward to what lies ahead, I press on toward the goal for the prize of the upward call of God in Christ Jesus" (Php 3:12 – 14).

V. Mortification and Vivification

Sanctification has two parts: **mortification** (dying) and **vivification** (rising), "both of which happen to us by participation in Christ," as Calvin notes.[21] These occur simultaneously and continuously throughout the Christian life, rather than in stages. Christ's death alone is atoning, and cannot be repeated. He died *for* our sins, but we die *to* our sins. Christ took up his cross once and for all as a sacrifice for sin, but he calls his disciples to "take up [their] cross daily," facing persecution from within and without (Lk 9:23). Subjectively experiencing this definitive reality signified and sealed to us in our baptism requires a daily dying and rising.

This is what the Reformers meant by sanctification as a living out of our baptism. We were circumcised by the Spirit; "having been buried with him in baptism ... you were also raised with him through faith in the powerful working of God, who raised him from the dead" (Col 2:11–12; cf. Ro 6:4–5, 11). Every day we return to our baptism for the strength we need to die to ourselves and live to God in righteousness, because in doing so we are returning again to Christ. Sanctification includes our own activity as enabled by God's grace (Jn 15:2, 8, 16; Ro 8:12–13; 12:9, 16–17; 1Co 6:9–10; 2 Cor 7:1; Gal 5:16–23; 6:7–8, 15; Col 3:5–14; 1Pe 1:22). It is not Christ but we who die daily, take up our cross, and follow in the way of righteousness. As those who were spiritually dead and incapable of pleasing God, we could in no way cooperate with grace for our regeneration and justification. We were not active but acted upon by the Spirit through the gospel. However, as those who are now alive in Christ, we are exhorted, "Work out your own salvation with fear and trembling; for it is God who is at work in you, enabling you both to will and to work for his good pleasure" (Php 2:12–13). Although we cannot work *for* our own salvation, we can and must work *out* that salvation in all areas of our daily practice, realizing more and more the amazing truth of our identity in Jesus Christ. When God calls, "Adam, where are you?" the Spirit leads us to answer, "In Christ," to the glory and pleasure of the Father.

We believe that we are new creatures because God has told us so, and he is in the business of *ex nihilo* creation. We therefore joyfully say "amen" to this truth because he is also in the business of *continual* creation, bringing about by his Spirit the effects of the Word that he has spoken in his Son. Just as the fiat declaration, "Let there be ..." was complemented by the imperative, "Let the earth bring forth ...," God's justifying verdict creates a state of affairs in which it is now possible for fallen creatures to bear the fruit of righteousness. As a result of *having been turned* toward the Living Word by

---

21. Calvin, *Institutes* 3.3.2, 9. The "mortification/vivification" distinction was first formulated by Philipp Melanchthon in his *Commentary on Romans*, in *Corpus Reformatorum* (ed. K. G. Bretschneider et al., Berlin: Schwetschike, 1834–1900), 15:636.

his word and Spirit, the believer, in conversion, also decisively *turns him- or herself* toward God once and for all in faith and repentance in response to God's calling. This conversion yields lifelong mortification and vivification, "again and again." Yet it is crucial to remind ourselves that in this daily human act of turning, we are always turning not only from sin but toward Christ rather than toward our own experience or piety. Regeneration is a gracious work that happens to us, without our aid; this mortification and vivification is something that we pursue actively as those who are filled with the Spirit.

VI. Perseverance of the Saints

If there is "now no condemnation for those who are in Christ Jesus" (Ro 8:1), on the sole basis of Christ's righteousness imputed, then a reversal of the court's verdict is impossible. That verdict has already set into motion the irreversible process of inward renewal, as the believer has been inserted by the Spirit into the powers of the age to come (2Co 5:17–18). Even our sanctification is the result of "the power [of God] at work within us" (Eph 3:20), and not only our justification but our walking in good works is predestined by God (Eph 2:10). Not only some but all of those *and only those* whom God chose before time began in Christ are effectually called, justified, and glorified (Ro 8:30).

Jesus taught, "All that the Father gives me will come to me, and whoever comes to me I will never cast out. For I have come down from heaven, not to do my own will but the will of him who sent me. And this is the will of him who sent me, that I should lose nothing of all that he has given me, but raise it up on the last day" (Jn 6:37–39). There is no indication in Scripture that God effectually calls (i.e., regenerates) those whom he has not chosen or that he draws into vital union with his Son those whom he allows finally to perish. The believer's **perseverance** is guaranteed by God's perseverance, so that Paul can say, "And I am sure of this, that he who began a good work among you will bring it to completion at the day of Jesus Christ" (Php 1:6). And to Timothy he writes, "But I am not ashamed, for I know whom I have believed, and I am convinced that he is able to guard until that Day what has been entrusted to me" (2Ti 1:12).

God *does* what he *declares*. When he pronounces someone righteous in Christ, he immediately begins also to conform that person to Christ. Left to ourselves, we not only could but would fall from grace, but God "is able to keep you from stumbling" (Jude 24). Crucial to grasping the organic character of this covenantal relationship are the botanical and biological images of Scripture. Christ is the Vine and we are his branches (Jn 15:1–11; cf. Mt 13:24–30; 17:20; 20:1–6). The New Testament member of the covenant of grace is in the same position as a covenant member in the Old Testament: though outwardly received by Christ as belonging to his people, yet each member must also inwardly receive Christ as his Savior. Just as John the Baptist and Jesus warned of the breaking off of unproductive branches, and as Pentecost initiated the fulfillment of the annual Jewish feast of harvest or ingathering, Paul, too, can speak of Gentiles as wild branches grafted onto the living vine of Israel, which may also be broken off if they do not yield the fruit of faith (Ro 11:16–24). Thus, the New Testament indicates that there are dead *and* living branches on the vine: those who are related merely outwardly and visibly and those who are united to Christ inwardly and invisibly in the communion of the elect.

So apostasy is not only hypothetical; it actually happens. "Therefore I endure everything for the sake of the elect, that they also may obtain the salvation that is in Christ Jesus with eternal glory. The saying is trustworthy, for: If we have died with him, we will also live with him; if we endure, we will also reign with him; if we deny him, he also will deny us; if we are faithless, he remains faithful—for he cannot deny himself" (2Ti 2:10–13). Unfaithfulness continues to plague our lives, but apostasy (rejecting Christ) leaves us without any remedy for its guilt or power. Jesus warned that "every branch in me that does not bear fruit [the Father] takes away" (Jn 15:2), yet he tells his disciples, "Already you are clean because of the word that I have spoken to you.... You did not choose me, but I chose you and appointed you that you should go and bear fruit, and *that your fruit should abide*" (15:3, 16, emphasis added).

Although Peter denied him three times, our Lord did not put out the smoldering wick or break off the bruised reed and brought him back to faith by his Spirit after the resurrection. Yet those who deny Christ to the very end, even though they may perhaps have been outward members of the visible church, are lost because they were never living members through faith. "They went out from us," says John concerning those who deny Christ, "but they were not of us; for if they had been of us, they would have continued with us. But they went out, that it might become plain that they all are not of us. But you have been anointed by the Holy One, and you all have knowledge" (1Jn 2:19–20).

In this light we are better able to understand the dire warnings against **apostasy** or falling away in Hebrews 6. The writer describes those who belong only outwardly to the covenant community as "those who have once been enlightened, who have tasted the heavenly gift, and have shared in the Holy Spirit, and have tasted the goodness of the word of God and the powers of the age to come, and then have fallen away … " (vv. 4–6a). Those who apostatize have been beneficiaries of the Spirit's ministry through the means of grace—*even as merely formal or external members of the covenant community.* Having been baptized ("enlightened"), they have also "*tasted* the heavenly gift" in the Supper and "*tasted* the goodness of the word of God and the powers of the age to come," but they have not actually received or *fed upon* Christ for eternal life, which Jesus linked to faith (Jn 6:27–58, 62–65).

According to Hebrews 6, then, those who apostatize by returning to the shadows of the law after Christ has come are basically "crucifying once again the Son of God to their own harm and holding him up to contempt" (v. 6). Belonging to the visible church places one in the very heart of the Spirit's activity of uniting sinners to Christ through the means of grace. It is therefore a tremendous benefit; yet it is also a greater threat for those who do not actually trust in Christ. "Land that has drunk the rain that often falls on it, and that produces a crop useful to those for whose sake it is cultivated, receives a blessing from God. But if it bears thorns and thistles, it is worthless and near to being cursed, and its end is to be burned" (vv. 7–8). The blessings of the covenant ordinarily lead to salvation, but when instead one hardens his or her heart to these blessings and does not receive the Christ who gives them, they become curses. Happily, this severe warning is followed by the encouragement of verse 9: "Though we speak in this way, yet in your case, beloved, we feel sure of better things, *things that belong to salvation.*" In the case of these who are actually saved, this salvation is exhibited by the fruit that it yields (vv. 10–12). The writer then goes on to assure them of the unchangeable character of God's promise in Jesus Christ, so that "we who have fled for refuge might have strong encouragement to hold fast to the hope set before us" (v. 18). So these warning passages themselves target those who are visible members of the covenant community, in some sense benefiting from the Spirit's ministry, who have nevertheless failed to embrace the gift of salvation and, in this case, have returned to Judaism.

The doctrine of the perseverance of the saints I have defended here is not exactly the same as the view commonly known as **eternal security**. It is not the case that those who are born again by making a decision for Christ are secure because of that one-time act of faith. Rather, it is that the God who begins a good work will complete it (Php 1:6). This gives all glory to God alone, for electing, redeeming, calling, and keeping his people to the end. In spite of the weakness of our faith and repentance, we are "more than conquerors through him who loved us," so that nothing "will be able to separate us from the love of God in Christ Jesus our Lord" (Ro 8:37, 39).

Key Terms

- mortification and vivification
- perseverance
- apostasy
- eternal security

Key Distinctions

- faith/works
- justification/sanctification

Key Questions

1. If sanctification is to be distinguished from justification, is there nevertheless a necessary connection? How would you describe the relationship between the two?
2. What is the role (if any) of God's law in the Christian life?
3. What are mortification and vivification, and are these done mainly by imitating Christ?
4. What is meant by perseverance of the saints? How does this compare and contrast with the concept of eternal security?
5. Does this doctrine encourage zeal to grow in Christ, or discourage it from growing?
6. How do we explain apostasy, especially in the light of Hebrews 6?

Chapter Fourteen

The Doctrine of Glorification

As Jesus is now, we will be also together with him: head and members joined in unending joy. This future hope is what theology identifies as **glorification**. In glorification, the apparent contradiction between God's verdict and our actual lives is finally and forever resolved. The "already" and the "not yet" converge, completing immediately and perfectly that which the Spirit began when he called us into fellowship with Christ by the gospel (Php 1:9–10). Even here, at the very end of the golden chain of salvation, we see the inextricable connection between the forensic verdict of God's Word that inaugurates the new creation and our progressive re-creation according to Christ's image. Indeed, no doctrine better exhibits the busy intersection of all the key highways of God's saving work. Here our union with Christ in election, the incarnation, active and passive obedience, justification, adoption, and sanctification reach their glorious destination. When this day dawns, there will no longer be a "not yet" to our salvation; no longer a *simil iustus et peccator* (just and sinner simultaneously). Rather, God's declaration that we are righteous in Christ will actually correspond fully to the actual reality of our lives. The branches, once dead, will not only flourish but be exactly the same in their character, appearance, quality, and fruitfulness as the Vine. The body will be as beautiful as its head, and the kingdom as glorious as its King.

I. Differing Views of Glorification

In comparing differing views of the doctrine of glorification, we can identify two broad streams of thought. The first stream leads from Origen, teaching that our glorification leads to an *essential* union with God. Origen's teaching is similar to both Plato and the Indian (Buddhist and Hindu) idea of karma or samsāra.[1] Origen believed that souls existed in eternity and through a primordial fall were incarcerated in material bodies, varying in status according to the degree of their preincarnate fault. He held that the distinction between "vessels of glory" and "vessels of wrath" in Romans 9 rests "not on the basis of unmerited election, but on the basis of those souls' behavior before they were conceived in the womb."[2] Just as being emanates from the One, returning again to its source, Origen (like Plato and much of Eastern thought) thought of the goal (eschatology) in terms of an eternal circle rather than a historical line from promise to fulfillment. For Origen, "the end is always like the beginning."[3] Since the goal is the soul's liberation from its bodily incarnation, Origen regarded the resurrection of the body as "crude" literalism. Biblical passages that taught otherwise had to be interpreted allegorically.[4]

Although Origen speculated on the possibility of reincarnation (*Peri Archon* 2.8.5), he clearly taught that upon death the soul enters a process of purgation: the beginnings of the dogma of purgatory. The soul could reach Paradise only by purifying fires, depending on its merits. Even if they are not drawn explicitly from Origen, all of the classic images in Christian spirituality that speak of climbing the ladder of ascent toward *fusion* of the divine soul with God's essence belong to this trajectory. All souls will be purified—even Satan and the fallen angels—and will become one with the divine. The inner divinity of the soul and its ascent through contemplation away from the realm of the body, history, and matter were central to his Platonic worldview. Glorification (or deification) arrives when the soul takes flight from the body; it will "return like an eagle to the house of its master."[5]

This all stands in sharp contrast to the biblical story, in which Adam is the covenantal head of the race, created mortal from the beginning (with no eternally preexistent soul), with the Tree of Life—resurrection and immor-

---

1. John Anthony McGuckin, *The Westminster Handbook to Origen* (Louisville: Westminster John Knox, 2004), 58.

2. Joseph W. Trigg, *Origen: The Early Church Fathers* (London and New York: Routledge, 1998), 29.

3. Origen, as quoted in ibid., 30.

4. Ibid., 32.

5. Origen, *An Exhortation to Martyrdom, Prayer and Selected Works* (trans. Rowan Greer; Mahwah, N.J.: Paulist, 1979), 67.

tality—as the goal. In the biblical drama, Adam and Eve never experienced the consummation, either in eternity or in time. Therefore, it's not a question of going back to an origin, but of going forward to a place where we've never been. The goal is not the loss of individual identity, as the soul is finally absorbed into the unity of the One (what the Greek philosophers called *henōsis*), but the fullness of our identity in Christ as God's image and likeness (*theōsis*). Our resurrection is not allegorical—an ascent of spirit—nor even a return to the original state; it is something that "no eye has seen, nor ear heard, nor the heart of man [has] imagined" (1Co 2:9, from Isa 64:4). And it is bodily, with the whole creation restored in its wake (Ro 8:22–25).

These two visions or doctrines are grounded in two different dramas: the one pagan and the other biblical. Irenaeus, a second-century father and ardent opponent of Gnosticism, represents the second, biblical trajectory. Rejecting the cyclical view of an end that is always like its beginning, Irenaeus concentrated his attention on the historical economy of creation, redemption, and the consummation, with Christ as the Last Adam who recapitulates ("reheadships") the fallen race. As we have seen (p. 59), Irenaeus understood this history of redemption in connection with specific covenants, especially a covenant "under Adam" and a gospel covenant in Christ. God became like us, even flesh of our flesh, so that we might become what he is—never merging with God's essence, but like God in true righteousness and holiness. God doesn't save us from the body and the material world, as Origen and the gnostics taught, but became flesh in order to win back the creation that had fallen into sin and death. It is in history, in the flesh, not away from it in contemplative ascent, where God works out his purposes.

Origen's stream of thinking is based on union (deification) as *methexis*: a fusion of the creature with the Creator. Irenaeus's stream is based on union (deification) as *koinōnia*: a covenantal communion with God in body and soul that transforms both into the likeness of God in Christ as much as is possible for creatures. Origen's barely Christianized Platonism was condemned as heresy at the Second Council of Constantinople (553), yet his basic system of thought continued to influence Christian theology and piety, especially through Evagrius the Solitary (345–99) and other leaders in the rising monastic movements. Even though later developments in doctrine often fell somewhere between Origen and Irenaeus, we can speak only loosely of Origenist and Irenaean "trajectories," since they often intersected and combined in the early teaching of both the Christian East and West.

A. Eastern Orthodoxy: Theōsis (Deification)

Coined by Gregory of Nazianzus in the fourth century, the term **theōsis** referred less to a distinct dogma than to a way of speaking of the believer's transfiguration through union with God in Christ.[6] Especially to the extent that it followed Irenaeus and Athanasius, the concept of *theōsis* (deification) is close to what Western theology has called the "marvelous exchange." Irenaeus put it this way: "In his immense love he became what we are, that he might make us what he is."[7] Centuries later, this concept was refined into a central doctrine of the Christian East, the jewel in the chain of salvation.[8] "For Orthodoxy our salvation and redemption mean our deification," writes Bishop Kallistos Ware.[9] Taking its coordinates from 2 Peter 1:4, where God's promises to believers include their becoming "participants in the divine nature," this prominent patristic theme attained systematic formulation especially by the Byzantine theologian Gregory Palamas (1296–1359).

For Orthodoxy, deification has never meant that the soul becomes one with God in essence. The ancient theologians of the Eastern church were at great pains to emphasize the Creator-creature distinction. They taught that God so transcends creation in his incomprehensible majesty that we can know him only according to his works (or energies), not according to his essence. Generally speaking, Western theology operates with two categories: whatever is not *created* is *divine*. The Eastern church added a third category: divine *energies*. We say commonly that we are warmed by the sun, but what we mean is the sun's rays; to be absorbed into the sun itself would be death. Similarly, there is no merging of the creature with the Creator. To experience fully our union with God is to participate in his energies, not to share his essence.[10] Without this middle category of energies, "deification" or

---

6. Stephen Finlan and Vladimir Kharlamov point out, "Deification played an important, but not definitive, role in early Patristic theology. Despite Patristic fascination with deification, the fathers do not develop a 'doctrine' of theosis. Nor do the doctrinal controversies and decisions of the Church Councils deal with the subject" (Stephen Finlan and Vladimir Kharlamov, eds., *Theōsis: Deification in Christian Theology* [Princeton Theological Monograph Series; Eugene, Ore.: Pickwick Publications, 2006], 4).

7. Irenaeus, *Against Heresies* 5, pref. (*ANF*, 1:526).

8. Jaroslav Pelikan, *The Spirit of Eastern Christendom (600–1700)* (vol. 2 of *The Christian Tradition: A History of the Development of Doctrine* [Chicago: Univ. of Chicago Press, 1977]), 125.

9. Timothy (Kallistos) Ware, *The Orthodox Church: New Edition* (New York: Penguin, 1997), 231.

10. Ibid., 231. See also Timothy (Kallistos) Ware, *The Orthodox Way* (Crestwood, N.Y.: St. Vladimir's Seminary Press, 1995), 22–23: "While God's inner essence is forever beyond our comprehension, His energies, grace, life and power fill the whole universe, and are directly accessible to us.... The essence signifies the whole God as he is in himself; the energies signify the whole God as he is in action.... The essence-energies distinction is a way of stating simultaneously that the whole God is inaccessible, and that the whole God in his outgoing love has rendered himself accessible to man. By virtue of this distinction... we are able to affirm the possibility of a direct or mystical union between

union with God can mean only that our spiritual essence merges with God's essence, a belief more akin to pantheism. Theologians in the East point to this recurring tendency in Western mystical traditions as the logical outcome of overlooking this distinction.[11]

Reflecting this emerging distinction, Athanasius affirmed, "[God] is outside all things according to his essence, but he is in all things through his acts of power."[12] Similarly, the church father Basil writes, "We know the essence through the energy. No one has ever seen the essence of God, but we believe in the essence because we experience the energy."[13] Here we find deification without pantheism, union without fusion.[14] Furthermore, these deifying energies come to us not from "the One," but from the Father, in the Son, by the Spirit. To be deified is also to be *transfigured*, so that the rays of God's energies (again, not the divine essence) permeate (rather than obliterate) the creature. The Old Testament theophanies, as well as the Transfiguration of Christ and the experience of Paul on the Damascus road, represent such events.[15] In the Transfiguration, Christ himself underwent no change, but the apostles were able to see during that time the glory (energies) that was always present yet hidden from their view. In this light, they saw light. "The apostles were taken out of history and given a glimpse of eternal realities."[16]

At the same time, Plato continued to cast a long shadow over the East as well as the West, especially in the ascetic spirituality of monasticism. Even though it was qualified by the essence-energies distinction, the myth of the exiled soul and its return through contemplative ascent continued to shape the piety of both traditions. Furthermore, in Eastern Orthodoxy *theōsis* is inextricably connected with *synergism* (divine-human cooperation). "The Eastern tradition has always asserted simultaneity in the synergy of divine grace and human freedom," according to Lossky.[17] In other words, there is no point in the *ordo salutis* (order of salvation) at which human beings will and work apart from grace or God wills and works apart from human

---

man and God—what the Greek Fathers term the *theōsis* of man, his 'deification'—but at the same time we exclude any pantheistic identification between the two: for man participates in the energies of God, not in his essence."

11. Vladimir Lossky, *The Mystical Theology of the Eastern Church* (Crestwood, N.Y.: St. Vladimir's Seminary Press, 1976), 221.

12. St. Athanasius, *On the Incarnation* 17, in *Athanasius: Contra Gentes and De Incarnatione* (trans. R. W. Thomson; Oxford: Clarendon, 1971), 174, quoted in Ware, *Orthodox Way*, 22.

13. Basil, *Doctrina Patrum de Incarnatione Verbi* (ed. Franz Kiekamp; 2nd ed.; Münster: Aschendorff, 1981), 88–89.

14. Ibid., 23.

15. Ibid., 223.

16. Ibid.

17. Lossky, *Mystical Theology*, 199.

cooperation. Also, whereas judicial categories (e.g., original sin and vicarious substitution) dominate Western thinking about Christ's work, the Christian East focuses on redemption as the bestowal of immortality.

The Western church shared with the Orthodox many sources and emphases on deification, especially as mediated by the late fifth- or early sixth-century writer Dionysius. Plato's "beatific vision" was transformed in varying degrees by ancient and medieval writers. However, in the West the lack of a clear distinction between God's essence and energies, in combination with Dionysius' pantheistic tendencies, gave rise to a sturdy tradition of "Christian" pantheism or panentheism from Dionysius to John Scotus Erigena, Meister Eckhart, and Nicholas of Cusa, revived again in radical Protestant sects and German idealism.

B. The Doctrine of Glorification in Reformed Theology

From a Reformed perspective, the problem is not that human beings have simply lost their way from the path of the soul's upward ascent but that they are guilty of breaking the covenant of creation, lie under the penalty of the law, and are therefore in bondage to sin and death. Consequently, salvation is viewed as a forensic or judicial matter that brings about a new condition of actual existence. The gift of immortality in our glorification is key, but it can come about only because, in union with Christ, the legal sentence of death has been removed. Furthermore, Reformed theology is critical of the synergism that dominates Eastern and Western ideas of deification. Yet despite these criticisms, there are surprising parallels between the Reformed understanding of glorification and the notion of theōsis — parallels that were recognized by older orthodox writers and should be rediscovered for the enrichment of our Christian hope.

Reformed theologians have often criticized the idea of grace elevating nature (like helium in a balloon), and the modified Platonism that underlies it. Instead of making us something *more than* human, grace saves and liberates humans to become *more human*: finally to glorify and to enjoy God forever. Following Irenaeus rather than Origen, Reformed theology maintains that God became flesh not to make us divine but to make us fully human — not only God's image-bearers but sharers in his Sabbath glory.[18] The total person is the subject

---

18. Reformed theology would concur with Sergei Bulgakov's point that God's relationship with Adam was "no donum superadditum" — a gift added to nature — and that theōsis is a fulfillment rather than transcendence of our humanity (cited and discussed in Andrew Louth, "The Place of Theōsis in Orthodox Theology," in *Partakers of the Divine Nature: The History and Development of*

of glorification; there is no elevation of a privileged aspect of humanity (i.e., the soul) above its own created nature. Not surprisingly, then, Ireneaus occupies a leading role as a patristic source, although other ancient Greek theologians also occupy a privileged place in Calvin's reading, especially John Chrysostom and even Cyril of Alexandria.[19] Exploring these connections should be of great importance, for greater mutual enrichment of both traditions.[20]

As we have seen in our discussion of sanctification, justification and inner renewal are completely distinct. "Yet you could not grasp this [imputed righteousness] without at the same time grasping sanctification also," Calvin insists. "For he 'is given unto us for righteousness, wisdom, sanctification, and redemption' [1 Cor. 1:30]."[21] The forensic emphasis of Calvin and the Reformed tradition generally is the basis for rather than the alternative to the actual transformation of creaturely reality in anticipation of its glorification. While Orthodoxy and Roman Catholicism deny forensic justification in favor of deification and sanctification, respectively, Reformed theology affirms all of these aspects of our union with Christ. Calvin can even say, "Let us mark that the end of the gospel is to render us eventually conformable to God, and, if we may so speak, to deify us."[22]

The way in which Calvin and other Reformed theologians explain this gift shares interesting parallels with the Orthodox East.

First, deification is qualified by the essence-energies distinction. In fact, immediately after saying that the gospel's goal is "to deify us," Calvin adds,

---

Deification in the Christian Traditions [ed. Michael J. Christensen and Jeffery A. Wittung; Grand Rapids: Baker, 2007], 39).

19. See Irena Backus, "Calvin and the Greek Fathers," in *Continuity and Change: The Harvest of Later Medieval and Reformation History* (ed. Robert J. Bast and Andrew C. Gow; Leiden: Brill, 2000), 253–76; cf. Johannes Van Oort, "John Calvin and the Church Fathers," in *The Reception of the Church Fathers in the West: From the Carolingians to the Maurists* (ed. Irena Backus; Leiden: Brill, 1997).

20. Further, as J. Todd Billings cautions, a certain account of deification (the Byzantine version of *theōsis* articulated by Palamas) is often read back into the earlier tradition as the definitive Eastern position. Whatever convergences might obtain between this position and Reformed theology, Billings wisely suggests that they should be related to the concept of *divinization* more broadly rather than to the doctrine of *theōsis* with its distinct Palamite refinements. See J. Todd Billings, "United to God through Christ: Assessing Calvin on the Question of Deification," *Harvard Theological Journal* 98, no. 3 (2005): 315–34. While pointing out potential parallels, Billings carefully distinguishes Calvin's references to "deification" (which are sparse to begin with) from the distinctively Palamite notion of *theōsis*. This relationship has been fruitfully explored in the Orthodox-Reformed discussions, especially (on the Reformed side) by Thomas F. Torrance. However, Billings is, in my view, a more reliable guide for interpreting Calvin's relationship to the topic of divinization. See especially his book, *Calvin, Participation, and the Gift: The Activity of Believers in Union with Christ* (New York and Oxford: Oxford Univ. Press, 2008).

21. Calvin, *Institutes*, 3.16.1.

22. John Calvin on 2Pe 1:4, in *Commentaries on the Catholic Epistles* (trans. and ed. John Owen; repr., Grand Rapids: Baker, 1996), 371.

But the word nature is *not here essence but quality*. The Manicheans formerly dreamt that we are a part of God, and that after having run the race of life we shall at length revert to our original. There are also at this day fanatics who imagine that we thus pass over into the nature of God, so that his swallows up our nature. Thus they explain what Paul says, that God will be all in all (1 Cor 15.28) and in the same sense they take this passage. But such a delirium as this never entered the minds of the holy Apostles; they only intended to say that when divested of all the vices of the flesh, we shall be *partakers of divine and blessed immortality and glory*, so as to be as it were *one with God as far as our capacities will allow*. This doctrine was not altogether unknown to Plato, who everywhere defines the chief good of man to be an entire conformity to God; but as he was involved in the mists of errors, he afterwards glided off to his own inventions. But we, disregarding empty speculations, ought to be satisfied with this one thing—that the *image of God in holiness and righteousness is restored* to us for this end, that we may at length be partakers of eternal life and glory *as far as it will be necessary for our complete felicity*. (emphasis added)[23]

This is a gloss on 2 Peter 1:4, the only biblical passage that speaks directly of our sharing in the divine nature. Nevertheless, while cautioning us against "empty speculations," Calvin here seems to affirm a sharing in the energy ("quality") rather than in the essence of God and even includes under this many of the attributes that the East has identified (divine immortality and glory through the restoration of the image of God in holiness and righteousness). We saw in chapter 2 how Calvin and Reformed theologians emphasized knowing God according to his works (energies) rather than in himself (essence).

Calvin's interpretation bears affinities to the great Syrian theologian John of Damascus (676–749), who gave systematic expression to Orthodox teaching, when the latter expresses the goal of salvation: that goal, he said, is "becoming deified, in the way of participating in the divine *glory* and not in that of a change into the divine *being*" (emphasis added).[24] Calvin, too, affirms this distinction, even quoting Eastern fathers in making the point, as do the classic Reformed orthodox treatments of glorification.[25] As Francis Turretin (1623–87) argued, the created glory that causes the saints to shine in beauty forever results from the uncreated energies of God's glory.[26] His

23. Ibid., 371–72.
24. John of Damascus, "An Exact Exposition of the Orthodox Faith," in *NPNF²*, 9:31.
25. For only a few references, see Calvin, *Institutes* 1.2.2, 1.10.2; John Calvin on Ro 1:19 in his *Commentary on Paul's Epistle to the Romans* (trans. and ed. John Owen; repr., Grand Rapids: Eerdmans, 1948), 69.
26. Francis Turretin, *Institutes of Elenctic Theology* (Philadelphia: P&R, repr. 1992), 609.

view can be contrasted with that of Aquinas when the latter writes, "When ... a created intellect sees God in his essence, the divine essence becomes the intelligible form of that intellect."[27]

Second, in continuity more with the East, Reformed theology identifies *theōsis*-glorification with our sharing in Christ's bodily resurrection on the last day rather than with the ascent of mind. In other words, the focus is on our being united to Christ's historical and eschatological career rather than on returning to a supposedly primordial union with God prior to embodiment. Reformed theology is even willing to speak of glorification in terms of the **beatific vision**, but here again it is closer to an Eastern (Irenaean) emphasis on the resurrection of the body than it is to the preoccupation of much of Western reflection on beholding and ascending into the divine essence. In fact, Reformed theology can be said to affirm the beatific vision only in a form radically revised from its pedigree in Christian Platonism.

In Reformed theology, redemption does not make humans something more than human, nor does it simply restore them to the original status of being innocent image-bearers; rather, it transforms them into the state of glorified images of God, a state that was never attained by the first Adam. The eschatological emphasis of Irenaeus, with the consummation as something beyond a mere return to an original state, is also a crucial working assumption of covenant theology. Christ's covenantal recapitulation ("reheadshiping") begins already with his incarnation. Echoing Irenaeus, Calvin wrote, "Christ aggregated to his body that which was alienated from the hope of life: the world which was lost and history itself."[28] Creation is saved, not escaped, in the consummation.

In this sense, *theōsis* (or the beatific vision) does have a discernible place in Reformed theology, but only on a non-Platonist map. It's called **glorification**. It is not a movement of the soul away from the body and history, but of a new creation and a new history that makes us more truly human; that saves nature, beyond the reach of corruption. Though we still wait patiently for our own glorification, we participate even now in the new kind of human being that Jesus Christ has already become. In this way, glorification is both a humanization and a deification. To be fully and consummately human is to be like God as much as is possible for a creature.

---

27. Thomas Aquinas, *Summa theologica* i.12.5 (trans. Fathers of the English Dominican Province; repr., Westminster, Md.: Christian Classics, 1948).

28. John Calvin, *Corpus Reformatorum* (101 vols.; ed. K. G. Bretschneider et al., Berlin: Schwetschike, 1834–1900), 55:219.

Our union with Christ does not make us divine beings, but brings us into that same relationship of children that Christ enjoys. His Father becomes our Father. His justification and glorification become our own. Francis Turretin writes that this glory will be bestowed "both as to the soul and as to the body," to be "enjoyed by the whole person in communion with God forever, which on this account Paul calls 'a far more exceeding and eternal weight of glory' (2 Cor 4:17) under which the mind is so overwhelmed that it is better expressed by silence and wonder than by eloquence."[29] It is described as light, a nuptial feast, treasures of richest gems, an estate, a garden full of fruit-bearing trees and a land flowing with milk and honey, a royal priesthood and a kingdom, an eternal Sabbath free of oppression.[30]

Therefore, this deification or glorification is not a deliverance from our body; rather, we are " 'delivered from the bondage of corruption and from vanity' (Rom. 8:21)."[31] Christ's transfiguration was a foretaste of this "weight of glory," and his resurrection its beginning.[32] Although God alone possesses immortality (1Ti 6:16), "the saints are immortal *by grace* from the beatific vision of God" (emphasis added).[33] There is no contrast drawn between an immortal soul and a mortal body: the whole person is mortal by nature but is raised in immortality by grace. "Now as dishonor denotes the meanness of human nature liable to various defects, so this glory will consist of a splendor and beauty of the body by which [believers] will shine and glitter like the stars and the sun, hardly capable of being looked at by mortal eyes." Foreshadowed by Moses' face (Ex 34:29) and even more so in Christ's transfiguration (Mt 17:2), "that splendor will flow both from the blessed vision of God, whom we shall see face to face, and from the glorious view of Christ exalted in his kingdom; and it will be nothing else than the irradiation of God's glory, from which the bodies will be made to shine."[34] They will be agile bodies: "vigorous, firm and strong, able to perform their duties rightly."[35] As to spirituality, "this spiritual does not refer to the very substance of the soul, as if it [the spiritual body] was to be changed into a spirit, for thus it could no longer be called a body, but a spirit." Their bodies will be "spiritual"—not meaning nonmaterial, but rather "purged from all

29. Turretin, *Institutes*, 3:612.
30. Ibid., 3:614–15.
31. Ibid., 3:618.
32. Ibid.
33. Ibid.
34. Ibid., 3:619.
35. Ibid., 3:620.

impurity and defilement."[36] Once more the Irenaean emphasis prevails: since Jesus' humanity was not swallowed by his deity, the consummation will not render us something more than human but perfectly human—which is to say, like God while never sharing the divine essence.

Language will even continue to characterize the society of the age to come. "If the body no less than the soul was created and redeemed by God and is to be glorified by the same, what is more just than that this body glorified by him should glorify him both in works and in word?" Turretin also cites "the vocal language" of the doxologies in the Apocalypse and the conversation in the transfiguration.[37] With a common tongue, glorified and glorifying "in body and soul, we may in unison sing an eternal Hallelujah to him."[38]

This emphasis on the participation of the body in the new age is characteristic of many Reformed writers. The seventeenth-century divine Thomas Watson quotes the answer to question 38 of the Westminster Shorter Catechism: "At the resurrection, believers being raised up in glory, shall be openly acknowledged and acquitted in the day of judgment, and made perfectly blessed in the full enjoyment of God to all eternity." He then interprets: "Some hold that we shall be clothed with a new body; but then it were improper to call it a resurrection, it would be rather a creation. 'Though worms destroy this body, yet in my flesh shall I see God.' Job xix 26. Not in another flesh, but my flesh. 'This corruptible must put on incorruption.' I Cor xv. 53."[39] This bodily resurrection is required by the fact that believers are mystically united to Christ's flesh, which has been raised. Further, "if the body did not rise again, a believer would not be completely happy; for, though the soul can subsist without the body, yet it has appetitus unionis; 'a desire of reunion' with the body; and it is not fully happy till it be clothed with the body. Therefore, undoubtedly, the body shall rise again. If the soul should go to heaven, and not the body, then a believer would be only half saved."[40] Anticipating the resurrection, then, Watson exults, "What a welcome will the soul give to the body! Oh, blessed body! When I prayed, thou didst attend my prayers with hands lifted up, and knees bowed down; thou wert willing to suffer with me, and now thou shalt reign with me; thou wert sown in dishonour, but now art raised in glory. Oh, my dear body! I will

---

36. Ibid.
37. Ibid., 3:635.
38. Ibid., 3:637.
39. Thomas Watson, *A Body of Divinity Contained in Sermons upon the Westminster Assembly's Catechism* (Edinburgh: Banner of Truth Trust, repr., 1965), 305–6.
40. Ibid., 306.

enter into thee again, and be eternally married to thee."[41] In fact, he goes so far as to conclude, "The *dust* of a believer is part of Christ's mystic body" (emphasis added).[42]

In sum, wherever the Reformed typically addressed glorification and the beatific vision, it was ordinarily in connection with the resurrection of the body, as it is throughout the New Testament epistles. Paul encourages the Philippians with these words: "But our citizenship is in heaven, and from it we await a Savior, the Lord Jesus Christ, who will transform our lowly body to be like his glorious body, by the power that enables him even to subject all things to himself. Therefore, my brothers, whom I love and long for, my joy and crown, stand firm thus in the Lord, my beloved" (Php 3:20–4:1).

Although the soul departs the body at death, there can be no glorification of the soul apart from its reunion with the body at the end of the age.[43] Not the mere intellectual vision of God (which can supposedly in some measure be attained at least by some saints now), but the bodily presence of the whole church with its glorified head in the everlasting presence of the triune God on the last day, is the emphasis that one finds in Reformed theology under consideration of this topic.

Third, as in the East, restoration of the imago dei is also crucial in Reformed treatments of the Spirit's work of making us participate in Christ and all of his benefits. The Son is God's image, Calvin writes, not only according to his deity but according to his humanity—the true image of the Adamic representative.[44] In fact, the whole purpose of the gospel is to restore this image. Also like the Christian East, Reformed theology emphasizes that Christ began winning our redemption from the moment of his conception. Not only his death and resurrection, but his incarnation and active obedience, are the basis for our salvation.

This correlation of deification or glorification with restoration (indeed, *consummation*) of the image of God reflects an important convergence between Reformed theology and patristic teaching. However—and this is a critical point that reflects a more Eastern than Western emphasis—human participation in this image is mediated by the Son in the Spirit; it is *not* an immediate participation in God's deity. Particularly in his debates with Servetus and Osiander, Calvin emphasized that the Spirit is the source of this

---

41. Ibid., 308.

42. Ibid., 309.

43. See the quotations in Heinrich Heppe, *Reformed Dogmatics* (rev. and ed. E. Bizer; trans. G. T. Thomson; London: G. Allen and Unwin, 1950; repr., London: Wakeman Trust, 2002), 695–712.

44. John Calvin, *Commentary on the Gospel of John* (trans. William Pringle; Grand Rapids: Baker, repr. 1996), comment on 17:21.

restoration rather than any infusion of divinity flowing into human beings.[45] Against views of deification suggesting that creatures somehow merge with God's essence or teaching that grace is a created substance infused into the soul,[46] the Reformers insisted that in salvation the gift is Christ—the God-Man himself. We cannot receive Christ's gifts, Calvin argued (along with Luther), without receiving Christ himself.

This interpretation of participation in God is eschatological. In other words, the believer shares in the new creation, whose head Christ has become by his own resurrection-glorification. As Christ's humanity was deified (glorified), we too will share in the same kind of eschatological life that he already enjoys. As goes the King, so goes the kingdom; what has happened to the head will happen to the whole body. The soul is not moving upward, out of the body and away from history, but creation is moving forward toward the fulfillment of history. This consummation does not arise naturally from history itself, including human activity, but by the descending grace of God within history, from the Father, centering in Christ, and in the power of the Spirit. Because of an emphasis on the historical economy of grace, Calvin and the wider tradition emphasized the future resurrection of the dead as the place where the consummation occurs.

II. Deification and the Beatific Vision as Resurrection and Sabbath

In sharp contrast with Western mysticism and monasticism, Reformed theology affirms that the dignity of this glory or beatific vision belongs to *every* believer, while denying that *any* believer attains it in this age—it is a fruit of the final consummation. Jesus Christ is not just a prototype, example, or even the first Christian. He did more than open up a path that

---

45. John Calvin, *Harmony of the Evangelists*, on Luke 17:20, quoted in Philip Walker Butin, *Revelation, Redemption, and Response* (New York: Oxford Univ. Press, 1995), 69. Butin writes, "He inferred from II Corinthians 3:18 that a human being 'is made to conform to God, not by an inflowing of substance, but by the grace and power of the Spirit'... Eschatological categories ultimately shape the way in which Calvin understands the progressive and gradual nature of this trinitarian restoration ... 'we now begin to be reformed to the image of God by His Spirit so that the complete renewal of ourselves and the whole world may follow in its own time.'"

46. This is the ontology that supports the dogma of transubstantiation, according to which bread and wine no longer retain their creaturely essence but become the divine body and blood, worthy of adoration. However, with the middle category of energies, God's gracious working ("the powers [*dynameis*] of the age to come," Heb 6:5) may be seen as divine action without being collapsed into the divine essence; the rays, but not the sun. We do not worship the Bible, baptism, or the Lord's Supper, but we also do not regard them simply as created things. United to God's activity, they are means of grace. Similarly, believers are never sharers in the divine essence, but they are made beneficiaries of God's gracious energies, glorified to the degree that creatures can ever be like God.

we can follow into the consummation. Rather, he is the only victor over sin and death, the only human being who secured the beginning of the new creation. We share in it because we are united to him, not because we cooperate in a process of grace-empowered deification. We will be everything he is in his humanity because he has done everything for us in our humanity. He is not only the eternal God-made-man but the first man-made-divine (in the sense of being glorified).

The resurrection-justification of Jesus and his glorification (Ro 1:3–4)—his triumphal entry into the heavenly sanctuary—both ground and anticipate our justification in the present, which will be verified in our own glorification: our resurrection to life everlasting. Thus, the "heavenly man" (Jesus) is the eschatological person who was raised from the dead and ascended to heaven to reign at the Father's right hand. The comparison of the "man of dust" (*anthrōpos ek gēs choikos*) and the "man ... from heaven" (*anthrōpos ex ouranou*) in 1 Corinthians 15:47 is instructive here. Far from drawing a contrast between Adam as a mere human being and Christ as divine, Paul is saying that while our first covenant head was mortal (and never attained immortality), the Last Adam is raised in immortal glory. We may have our natural existence from Adam (along with his guilt and corruption), but we have our heavenly-consummated existence from Christ. "Thus it is written, 'The first man Adam became a living being' "—the source of our mortal existence under probation (and subsequent death); "the last Adam became a life-giving spirit" (1Co 15:45).

Jesus' resurrection was therefore not only the divine stamp of approval on the judicial work of the cross, but was itself a judicial act. Paul summarizes the Christian message as "the gospel ... concerning [God's] Son, who was descended from David according to the flesh and was declared to be the Son of God in power according to the Spirit of holiness by his resurrection from the dead..." (Ro 1:1–4). Paul is not referring here to Christ's two natures but to "two successive stages in His life." His life "according to the flesh" originated from David, while his life "according to the Spirit" had its source in his resurrection from the dead.[47] While Jesus is the Son from all of eternity, his resurrection actually gives rise to "a new status of sonship" that is distinct from his essential deity.[48] To put it differently, we are saved by Jesus not only because he is also God (as true as that is), but because he

47. Geerhardus Vos, "Paul's Eschatological Concept of the Spirit," in *Redemptive History and Biblical Interpretation: The Shorter Writings of Geerhardus Vos* (ed. Richard B. Gaffin Jr.; Phillipsburg, N.J.: P&R, 1980), 104.
48. Ibid.

is the appointed and anointed human servant of the covenant who has completed his work. We are justified in his justification and will be glorified in his glorification.

Paul's point in all of this is that our conformity to Christ, which begins in sanctification, is consummated when we are actually made like him, *not in his eternal deity but in his resurrection and glorification*. The Spirit is not simply waiting in the wings as the Son fulfills his mission, so that he can then work exclusively within individual believers. Rather, the Spirit by whom Jesus was conceived, who upheld Jesus in his mission, and who raised him from the dead outside of our hearts is the same one who indwells us, ensuring that he will raise us as also (2Co 4:13–18; 5:1–5).[49]

Seeing the work of the Spirit through this wide-angle lens, we recognize that it is the Spirit who gives birth to the new age, an age that is called into being by the Father in the Son. It is the Spirit by whom humanity was created as an image of the archetypal image-Son, who declares to the entire cosmos that those whom he now clothes with bodily glory are heavenly (glorified) rather than merely earthly (created and fallen) beings. *In other words, the day of judgment is the day of resurrection: they are one and the same event.*[50] The judgment that would have been pronounced upon humanity in Adam after successful completion of the trial is now pronounced upon Christ and all of those in union with him. Jesus authorizes the expectation of rewards not at some event subsequent to the resurrection, but "at the resurrection of the righteous" (Lk 14:14; cf. 20:35). Those in their graves "will hear his voice and come out, those who have done good to the resurrection of life, and those who have done evil to the resurrection of judgment" (Jn 5:28–29).[51]

As Reformed exegesis has done, N. T. Wright and others have pointed up the judicial aspect of the resurrection as the last judgment. However, Wright sees this as final justification rather than glorification.[52] He correctly identifies the resurrection with the judicial atmosphere of the last judgment, yet fails to recognize that justification is the "already" verdict. There is no

---

49. Geerhardus Vos, "Our Lord's Doctrine of the Resurrection," in *Redemptive History and Biblical Interpretation*, 322.

50. See John Fesko, *The Doctrine of Justification: A Contemporary Restatement of the Classic Reformed Doctrine* (Phillipsburg, N.J.: P&R, 2008), 299–331.

51. Only if this refers to justification is it susceptible of being interpreted as resurrection on the basis of works. However, such passages (as well as the Olivet Discourse) merely identify the just(ified) as those who have been renewed and thus have begun even in this age to produce the fruit of the Spirit.

52. N. T. Wright, *Climax of the Covenant: Christ and the Law in Pauline Theology* (Minneapolis, Fortress, 1992), 203.

future aspect to justification itself. In justification, the believer has *already* heard the verdict of the last judgment. Glorification is the final realization, not of our justification itself, but of its effects.

This future event both *discloses* the true identity of the covenant people as an act of the cosmic revelation of the justified children of God (ecclesiology) and *actually transforms* the whole justified person into a condition of immortality and perfect holiness (soteriology). The great verdict awaiting the world at the end of the age is therefore with respect not to justification, but to glorification. All who have been justified are inwardly renewed and are being conformed to Christ's image, but their cosmic vindication *as* the justified people of God will be revealed in the resurrection of the dead. It will be not only a verdict that we hear (justification), but the glorious correspondence of that verdict with the reality that we all behold together. "And just as it is appointed for man to die once, and after that comes judgment, so Christ, having been offered once to bear the sins of many, will appear a second time, not to deal with sin but to save those who are eagerly waiting for him" (Heb 9:27–28). Through faith in Christ, the *verdict* of the last judgment itself has already been rendered in our favor, but, as our meager growth in holiness and the unabated decay of our bodies attest, the full *consequences* of this verdict await a decisive future completion. We receive our justification through believing what we have heard; we will receive our glorification by seeing face-to-face the one whose voice we have heard. Thus, the beatific vision is the sight of God's glory in the face of Christ, without veil, without corruption, without the mediation of preaching and sacrament. For now, we are creatures of the word, hearers of the promise, with the hope of glory, expressing our faith imperfectly in love. On the last day, however, there will be no need for faith or hope. Faith will yield to sight. Hope will be fulfilled. All that will be left is love, forever (1Co 13:8–13).

"The resurrection of the dead in general, therefore, is primarily a judicial act of God," Bavinck notes.[53] United to Christ, the "inner person" is being invisibly renewed through faith day by day according to the glorious image of the exalted Son even while the "outer self" is visibly wasting away (2Co 4:16–5:5). On the last day, however, the whole person—and the whole church—will be radiant with the light that fills the whole earth with the glory of God, and this new humanity will be joined by the whole creation as it is led by the Servant-Lord of the covenant into the day whose sun never sets.

---

53. Herman Bavinck, *The Last Things* (ed. John Bolt; trans. John Vriend; Grand Rapids: Baker, 1996), 133.

The following litany of the benefits of our union with Christ indicated by Calvin offers a fitting summary of the golden chain that we have considered:

> We see that our whole salvation and all its parts are comprehended in Christ. We should therefore take care not to derive the least portion of it anywhere else. If we seek salvation, we are taught by the very name of Jesus that it is "of him." If we seek any other gifts of the Spirit, they will be found in his anointing. If we seek strength, it lies in his dominion; if purity, in his conception; if gentleness, it appears in his birth. For by his birth he was made like us in all respects that he might learn to feel our pain. If we seek redemption, it lies in his passion; if acquittal, in his condemnation; if remission of the curse, in his cross; if satisfaction, in his sacrifice; if purification, in his blood; if reconciliation, in his descent into hell; if mortification of the flesh, in his tomb; if newness of life, in his resurrection ... if inheritance of the heavenly kingdom, in his entrance into heaven; if protection, if security, if abundant supply of all blessings, in his kingdom; if untroubled expectation of judgment, in the power given him to judge. In short, since rich store of every kind of good abounds in him, let us drink our fill from this fountain, and from no other.[54]

Key Terms

- glorification
- *theōsis*
- beatific vision

Key Questions

1. What is the relationship between justification, sanctification, and glorification?
2. Compare and contrast the Eastern Orthodox, Roman Catholic, and Reformed views on this doctrine.
3. What is the relationship between glorification and the resurrection of the dead at the end of the age?

---

54. Calvin, *Institutes* 2.16.19.

Chapter Fifteen

Word and Sacraments

After several weeks of working together in adjoining cubicles, Jeff and Sharon picked up hints that they were both Christians. One day, Jeff asked his coworker, "Are you saved?" Sharon replied, "I think I am," not because she wasn't sure that she belonged to Christ but because she was unfamiliar with this way of putting it. Jeff asked Sharon how she came to know Christ—to give her personal testimony, and she said that she was baptized, grew up hearing sermons and participating in the public service, was catechized, and was eventually confirmed. After making a public profession of faith before the elders and then the whole congregation, she received her first Communion and was still a communicant member at her church. "Yes," Jeff pressed, "but do you have a personal relationship with Jesus?" "What do you mean by that?" Sharon wondered. "I mean, you've talked a lot about 'churchy' stuff, but when were you born again?" Sharon was stumped. "I don't know," she shrugged. "I guess I've always been a Christian." With genuine concern, Jeff began to talk to Sharon as someone who didn't really know Christ in a saving way.

For many Christians, especially evangelicals, the public *means of grace* (preaching, baptism, and the Lord's Supper) are "churchy," different from—if not antithetical to—one's private, personal, and unmediated relationship

Key Distinction:
means of grace/means of gratitude

Means of grace are creaturely media through which the Spirit delivers Christ and all of his benefits. We are effectually called into union with Christ by the preaching of the gospel. Through this ministry of the word the Spirit gives us faith in Christ. He further ratifies his gracious promise by baptism and the Lord's Supper, the signs and seals of the covenant of grace.

Means of gratitude are our appropriate response to the gift that is given to us through the means of grace. Chief among these is prayer, as well as witness, mutual instruction and admonition (including through singing, Col 3:16), church discipline, meditation on God's word, and service to others (our families, fellow saints, and neighbors).

with Christ. For many of us, it's counterintuitive to speak of the Spirit's work *through creaturely means*. The assumption quite often is that the Spirit's canvas is noncreaturely—a divine spirit or soul within each individual—and that he paints with secret strokes of invisible oils. Perhaps when we think of the Father, creation of the material world comes to mind. When we think of the Son, Jesus of Nazareth, the *incarnate* God is in view. However, when we think of the Holy Spirit, we see him working directly, immediately, spontaneously, and inwardly in our hearts—in the realm of the invisible. For Jeff, mention of the Holy Spirit does not ordinarily provoke thoughts about preaching, baptism, and the Lord's Supper, except perhaps as a way of contrasting genuine rebirth and external rituals.

Many of us were raised with the assumption that people who talk about sacraments trust in rituals rather than in Christ. Belonging to Christ and belonging to the visible church were seen as two different things. Often in this environment, preaching is simply teaching: instruction and exhortation. It can be done as effectively in small group settings or in personal devotions as in formal church services, and a teacher need only be ordained from within, by the Holy Spirit, not outwardly by the visible church. In Jeff's thinking, ordinary sacraments of baptism and the Lord's Supper are not God's means of grace, but our means of obedience. The purpose of preaching is to teach us what to believe and to do, in baptism we testify to our commitment to follow Christ, and in the Lord's Supper we strengthen our love for and commitment to Jesus by remembering his death for us. The emphasis throughout falls on *getting us to do something*: to learn and follow (in preaching), to commit (in baptism) and to recommit (in the Lord's Supper). For Jeff, these activities may be resources he can use in his personal relationship with Jesus, but he doesn't think of them as the means that the Spirit uses to bring about and confirm this relationship.

At the other extreme, however, many Christians have tended toward an almost superstitious attachment to rituals, leading to a barren formalism. It may in fact be the case that Sharon was trusting in her churchly socialization, rather than in Christ. Perhaps, for her, being a Christian was like being a Republican or a Democrat. Who knows whether Christ was actually proclaimed to her each week or whether her public profession of faith was genuine? She may think of baptism or first Communion as a rite of passage to adulthood, like countless rituals that mark coming-of-age in different societies and religions. According to surveys, most young people raised in the church (across the whole spectrum) cannot tell you what their church teaches concerning the Lord's Supper. So perhaps her church experience is nothing but an empty ritual that Sharon goes through, mumbling the prayers along with everyone else, while she's thinking about meeting up with her friends after the service. Yes, people can indeed trust in rituals rather than in Christ. In fact, this happens in evangelical contexts, too, where the "Are you saved?" question is answered by referring not to their baptism, which Christ did ordain, but to the altar call or the sinner's prayer, which he did not.

In contrast to both cold, ecclesiastical formalism and warm, enthusiastic individualism, Scripture provides us with a completely different paradigm for thinking about the relationship between the Spirit, the church, and the means of grace. We shouldn't let ourselves be pressed into a false choice between trusting in external forms that have power *in themselves* to save and believing that the Spirit ordinarily works *apart from* these forms. As we have seen, created matter has been the medium of the Spirit's artistry in creation, providence, the history of Israel, and the incarnation, life, death, and resurrection of Jesus Christ. The same is true in his application of Christ's work to us here and now.

In the last few chapters we have explored the benefits that we have in union with Christ. Now, as we make the transition to the doctrine of the church (ecclesiology), our primary question is *how* the Spirit unites us to Christ and confirms and strengthens this communion. The short answer is found in Question 65 of the Heidelberg Catechism: "Where ... does that true faith come from? The Holy Spirit produces it in our hearts by the preaching of the holy gospel, and confirms it through our use of the holy sacraments."[1] Faith is not something we can manufacture within ourselves; it is a gift of the Spirit, which he gives us through tangible, unspectacular, earthly means: another sinner's speech in the name of Christ, water, bread and wine. What could be more common? And yet, consecrated by God, they become his means of salvation.

In short, the Spirit worked with matter in creating and sustaining the old world and does so also in the new creation; the gospel testifies to the incarnate God and his saving work in the flesh; the Spirit gives us the faith to embrace Christ through visible means in a historical institution, and the result of the Spirit's work is a visible body, not just the private experience of individuals.

I. The Sacramental Word: Preaching as a Means of Grace

Churches in the Reformation traditions understand "sacrament" as "means of grace." Even before we get to baptism and the Lord's Supper, we encounter preaching as God's **sacramental word**, which always remains God's primary means of grace. It could also be called God's performative word, because it is speech that does what it says; it not only teaches and exhorts, but is the means through which something new is actually brought about. Jesus Christ is the Word of God in his essence, while Scripture is the canonical word (norming our preaching and practice), and preaching is the sacramental word. In Scripture we find the normative canon of saving speech, and in preaching, the ongoing means by which this saving speech generates a new creation, so that even in this present evil age we "[taste] the goodness of the word of God and the powers of the age to come" (Heb 6:5). This is *how* the kingdom comes. God himself preached the world into existence; through the prophets and apostles he preached a new covenant community into being, and by the continual ministry of the word today he continues to preach his kingdom into existence, expanding its borders and adding immigrants daily. Even through the speech of his ambassadors, the triune God is the speaker. When the message is normed and drawn from the canonical word (Scripture), preaching is sacramental — that is, a means of grace, the living and powerful word of God.

From this line of thinking it has been said that the church is the **creation**

---

1. Heidelberg Catechism, in Doctrinal Standards of the Christian Reformed Church, in *Psalter Hymnal* (Grand Rapids: Board of Publications of the Christian Reformed Church, 1976), 32.

of the word (*creatura verbi*). The new birth, as part of the new creation, is effected *in* the church (i.e., through its ministry of the Word), but not *by* the church. Neither the individual nor the community gives birth to itself, but is born from above (Jn 3:3–5). The preaching of this gospel is not merely instruction concerning Christ and an exhortation to believe, but the means by which the Spirit creates faith in our hearts to embrace Christ and all of his benefits. The origin and source of the church's existence is neither the autonomous self nor the autonomous church: "So then it depends not on human will or exertion, but on God, who has mercy" (Ro 9:16). It is not the effects (faith and its fruits) that define the church's existence, but the word that is proclaimed.

Just as creation began with a command, "Let there be.... And there was ...," so too does the new creation originate in the womb of the word. The church is "a chosen race" and a "holy nation," "that you may proclaim the excellencies of him who called you out of darkness into his marvelous light" (1Pe 2:9). Although "the gospel is veiled, it is veiled only to those who are perishing.... For God, who said, 'Let light shine out of darkness,' has shone in our hearts to give the light of the knowledge of the glory of God in the face of Jesus Christ" (2Co 4:3, 6). It is not surprising that Paul also thinks of new creation as analogous to *ex nihilo* creation (Ro 4:17–18). By speaking righteousness (imputed in justification and merited in sanctification) into a condition of unrighteousness, God brings into existence not only a collection of justified and renewed individuals but a living community: his church.

We use language to do certain things. Sometimes we want to inform, but there are many other things that we do by speaking. For example, saying the words "I do" in a marriage ceremony is not only a proposition—that is, a statement about reality. It is an act of making a promise. When the minister or justice of the peace says, "I now pronounce you husband and wife," it is not merely a description of truth; it brings about a union of a man and a woman.

Our speech is analogous to God's. Sometimes God teaches, explains, and proposes things to be believed and practiced. However, in many other instances God actually brings about a new reality by speaking. "I will be your God and you will be my people"; "I forgive all your transgressions and remember your sins no more"; "I give you a new heart"; "This is my body, broken for you ... the blood of the new covenant, shed for many for a remission of sins." In these actions, God is actually creating a new covenant, a new relationship through his pledge, and the communication of his pledge is the very means that the Spirit uses to draw us inwardly to Christ. "For all the promises of God find their Yes in him. That is why it is through him that we utter our Amen to God for his glory" (2Co 1:20). When God speaks his word of judgment, we stand condemned; when he speaks comfort to his people—the good news of his unconditional promise—hope is renewed.

God's words are performative: powerful, event-generating discourse. They are not only enlightening or informative; they are *fulfilled* (Eze 12:28; cf. Isa 55:10–11). The scene of the prophet preaching to the valley of dry bones in Ezekiel 37 vividly portrays this living and active word that creates the reality of which it speaks. And in the same way, the preaching of the gospel draws us out of our self-enclosed prison of sin and death, effectually calling, justifying, and renewing us from the inside out. By the word of the gospel the Spirit builds a temple-house for the Father in the Son.[2]

Is this to say that the sermons you'll hear next Sunday are equal to the Bible? Certainly, there is a qualitative difference between Scripture and preaching. Scripture is directly *inspired* by the Holy Spirit, preserved from error, and serves as the written constitution for the covenant community. Preaching, on the other hand, is *illumined* by the Spirit, is not preserved from error, and is the Word of God only as it draws its substance from the biblical canon. However, when preaching stands under this authority—not only formally, but in substance—it is God's Word in exactly the same sense as Scripture. Though it is inspired and inerrant, Scripture itself is mediated by God's preachers: the prophets and apostles. Jesus Christ is the Word of God in *essence*, while Scripture and preaching are God's Word in his *energies*. Whether through the infallible written Scriptures or fallible preaching, the same Spirit delivers the same gift—Christ and all his benefits. It is the same Word that is given through Scripture, preaching, and the sacraments. Both in the canonical, written Word and in preaching, there are two speakers: the Creator and a creature. In both cases, the Spirit unites the divine and the creaturely in what theologians call a "sacramental union": where the creaturely action becomes the medium of his divine activity.

Whether through the written Scriptures or the preached Word, it is Christ himself who addresses us by his Spirit and delivers himself to us with all of his benefits, even opening our ears, eyes, and hands to receive the gift. We see this in the event of Pentecost itself, where the first public evidence is Peter's proclamation of the gospel (Ac 2:14–36). Repeatedly in Acts, the growth of the church is attributed to the fact that "the word of God spread" and "prevailed" (Ac 6:7; 13:49; 19:20), and "proclaiming the good news"

---

2. As I have noted elsewhere, M. G. Kline's treatment of this theme is richly suggestive, in *The Structure of Biblical Authority* (Grand Rapids: Eerdmans, 1989), ch. 3.

is the central activity described in this history of the early church. In fact, the spreading of the word is treated as synonymous with the spreading of the kingdom of God. By the word we are legally adopted, and by the Spirit we receive the inner witness that we are the children of God (Ro 8:12–17). Through the word *of* Christ the Spirit creates faith *in* Christ. Where this is present, there is the church.

Preaching involves teaching, but it is much more. It is often assumed that our job is to teach the gospel as information and then the Holy Spirit does something else within the hearer, apart from this human task. According to this view, it is when the *hearer* does something with the information or exhortation that he or she is born again. Yet this misses the wonderful truth that the ordinary manner in which the Spirit works savingly in our hearts is *through* the preaching of the gospel, not by doing something apart from it. The secret working of the Spirit is not separated from the publicly audible proclamation of Christ. In preaching, Christ proclaims himself and the Spirit brings about the new birth when and where he chooses.

Specifically, the *gospel* is that part of God's word that gives life (1Pe 1:23–25, Ro 10:6–17, etc.). The gospel is "the power of God for salvation" (Ro 1:16). While everything that God says is true, useful, and full of impact, not everything that God says is *saving*. Sometimes God's speech brings judgment, disaster, fear, warning, and dread, Calvin reminds us.[3] "For although faith believes every word of God, it rests solely on the word of grace or mercy, the promise of God's fatherly goodwill," which is realized only in and through Christ.[4] The only safe route, therefore, is to receive the Father through the Incarnate Son. Christ is the saving content of Scripture, the substance of its canonical unity. "This is the true knowledge of Christ: if we take him as he is offered by the Father, namely, clothed with his gospel."[5]

The Word is a ladder, to be sure, but, like the incarnation, one that God always descends to us (Ro 10:6–17). In Romans 10, Paul tells us that we do not have to ascend to heaven to bring Christ down or descend into the depths to bring him up from the dead, as if we could make him present or relevant by our zeal. Rather, Christ himself is present, addressing us in preaching. "'The word is near you, in your mouth and in your heart' (that is, the word of faith that we proclaim)" (v. 8). Paul's logic is clear: "And how shall they believe him whom they have never heard? And how are they to

---

3. Calvin, *Institutes* 3.2.7; 3.2.29.
4. Ibid., 3.2.28–30.
5. Ibid., 1.13.7.

hear without someone preaching? And how are they to preach unless they are sent?" (vv. 14–15).[6] Ambassadors do not send themselves; they are sent by the King to herald the message. When they speak from Christ's canon, in Christ's name, it is Christ's voice that is heard. In the appropriate context, the appropriate person may communicate another person's intentions. An ambassador is authorized to speak for the head of state.

Luther famously declared that one is made a "Christian" by "the hearing of the Word of God, that is, faith." "Therefore, the ears alone are the organs of a Christian man, for he is justified and declared to be a Christian, not because of the works of any member but because of faith."[7] The choice of preaching as a medium is not incidental. Putting us on the *receiving* end of things, not only does justification come through faith alone, but faith itself comes through hearing.[8] "For Calvin as for Luther," as John H. Leith observes, " 'The ears alone are the organ of the Christian.' "[9] Calvin summarized, "When the Gospel is preached in the name of God, it is as if God himself spoke in person."[10]

According to the Second Helvetic Confession,

> The preaching of the Word of God is the Word of God. Wherefore when this Word of God is now preached in the church by preachers lawfully called, we believe that the very Word of God is proclaimed, and received by the faithful; and that neither any other Word of God is to be invented nor is to be expected from heaven: and that now the Word itself which is preached is to be regarded, not the minister that preaches; for even if he be evil and a sinner, nevertheless the Word of God remains still true and good.[11]

Regardless of the subjective piety or intention of the minister, the word of God is effective.

---

6. Verse 14 is my own translation. The point Paul is making is not simply that Christ is as near as the discourse concerning him that somehow informs us of him or brings him to mind, but that he is present in and through the preaching.

7. Martin Luther, *Lectures on Titus, Philemon, and Hebrews* (vol. 29 of *Luther's Works* [ed. Jaroslav Pelikan; St. Louis: Concordia, 1968]), 224.

8. This comparison between hearing and seeing is not meant to suggest that there is some magical quality to hearing or that God is bound by this medium. Rather, it is to say that God has bound himself to the spoken word as the *ordinary* method of self-communication. Like Augustine, many Christians would refer to their reading of Scripture as a moment of conversion. Furthermore, physical disabilities such as deafness are no obstacle to God's grace. Stephen H. Webb offers a well-informed treatment of this issue in *The Divine Voice: Christian Proclamation and the Theology of Sound* (Grand Rapids: Brazos, 2004), 51–55.

9. John H. Leith, "Doctrine of the Proclamation of the Word," in *John Calvin and the Church: A Prism of Reform* (ed. Timothy George; Louisville: Westminster John Knox, 1990), 212.

10. Ibid., 211.

11. Second Helvetic Confession, ch. 1, in *Book of Confessions: Study Edition* (Louisville: Westminster John Knox, 1999), 53–54.

This should caution us against identifying effectiveness either with the antiquity and prestige of a particular office or with the charisma and communicative gifts of a particular person. The medium is consistent with the message of the cross. Far from putting the spotlight on the preacher, this argument shifts the emphasis on preaching as *Christ's* activity, by his Spirit. It is his word, wisdom, and power—not the preacher's—that brings life. The fact that some of the most significant witnesses in the history of redemption are characterized as inferior speakers—Moses (Ex 4:10), Isaiah (Isa 6:5–8), and Paul (1Co 2:5) among others—is surely of some consequence. All of this is "so that your faith might not rest in the wisdom of men but in the power of God" (1Co 2:5). The power of the Word lies in the ministry of the Spirit, not in the ministers themselves. We do not need great preachers, but faithful preaching of the word.

Far from marginalizing lay witness, Bible reading, and mutual instruction, this emphasis on the proclaimed word by one who is authorized and sent ensures that the whole body will have what it needs to function properly. Far from eliminating our activity, God's means of grace give rise to our response through means of gratitude. This is Paul's argument in Ephesians 4:7–16. Timothy's chief job description, according to the apostle, is to "preach the word" (2Ti 4:2) so that the church will be built up in the truth and live out their high calling in Christ. From the public ministry of the word, Christ delivers himself with all of his benefits, cascading as from a fountain to every nook and cranny of our lives. We speak this word to each other in our homes with our families, in our neighborhoods with friends, and in the public places where our lives intersect with the wider world. Our lives, shaped by this word, become a fragrance of life, attracting people to hear the gospel. So the public preaching of the word *makes* all of us witnesses and disciples. God's word is spread in more ways, but its public preaching is the fountain from which it flows to us and out, through us, to the world.

II. The Sacraments

So great is God's love and care for his people that he not only calls them into fellowship with his Son by his Word; he assures them of his goodwill, binding himself to them and binding them to himself and to each other through **sacraments** that he has personally instituted. Together with the word, these sacraments are means of grace and the essential marks of the true church.

Lutheran and Reformed theologians have traditionally affirmed that in order for a practice to be considered a sacrament it must be *instituted by Christ* and *evangelical* (i.e., a means of grace) in substance. When it comes to "high church" traditions, we are alert to the invention of rituals without scriptural authorization. However, evangelical Protestantism is rife with methods, techniques, and rituals in public worship that have no biblical foundation. In many churches, the "altar call" is an essential weekly ritual, while the Lord's Supper has a relatively marginal place in the ordinary life of the church.

Scripture attributes great significance to baptism and the Lord's Supper. Christ commanded baptism in the Great Commission (Mt 28:19). At Pentecost, Peter exhorted, "Repent and be baptized every one of you in the name of Jesus Christ for the forgiveness of your sins, and you will receive the gift of the Holy Spirit" (Ac 2: 38). "And now why do you wait? Rise and be baptized and wash away your sins, calling on his name" (Ac 22:16). Through baptism, we are buried and raised with Christ (Ro 6:1 – 11; Col 2:12; Gal 3:27). Baptism is identified with the "washing away of sins" (1Co 6:11; cf. Tit 3:5). Christ "gave himself up for [the church], that he might sanctify her, having cleansed her by the washing of water with the word" (Eph 5:25). In fact, "one baptism" is right up there with "one Lord, one faith" as the defining mark of the church (Eph 4:5; cf. 1Co 12:13). The deliverance of Noah and his family through water is typological of the greater deliverance: "Baptism, which corresponds to this, now saves you, not as a removal of dirt from the body but as an appeal to God for a good conscience, through the resurrection of Jesus Christ" (1Pe 3:20 – 21). This baptism always involves water and the word, administered in the name of the Father, and of the Son, and of the Holy Spirit (Mt 3:13; Lk 3:21; Jn 1:31; 3:5; 4:1; Ac 8:36 – 37; 10:47).

Instituting the Lord's Supper, Jesus took the cup, saying, "This is my blood of the covenant, which is poured out for many for the forgiveness of sins" (Mt 26:26 – 29; cf. Mk 14:22 – 25; Lk 22:18 – 20; 1Co 11:23 – 26). In fact, Paul says, "The cup of blessing that we bless, is it not a participation in the blood of Christ? The bread that we break, is it not a participation in the body of Christ?" (1Co 10:16). Participation in pagan sacrifices unites people to demons, but in the sacrament they are identified with Christ (vv. 18 – 22). And just as circumcision and the Passover meal can be identified simply as "the covenant," baptism and the Lord's Supper are connected to the reality they signify and seal. "Whoever, therefore, eats the bread or drinks the cup of the Lord in an unworthy manner will be guilty concerning the body and blood of the Lord" (1Co 11:27).

> ## Key Distinction:
> ### sign/reality
>
> We distinguish without separating *sign* and *reality*, applied to the church and the sacraments. Some confuse them, as if the water, bread, and wine were transformed into the body and blood of Christ. Others separate them, as if the signs only point to but do not convey Christ and his benefits.

These passages have to be taken at face value. To interpret them in the light of other passages is essential, but to explain them away is a way of subordinating Scripture to our own theological assumptions. Scripture tells us that we receive baptism for the forgiveness of sins and the gift of the Spirit; that in the Lord's Supper we receive Christ's body and blood for everlasting life. At the same time, Scripture teaches with equal clarity that salvation comes only through faith in Christ. How do we reconcile these facts? This question comes down to the relationship between the **reality** (Christ and all his benefits) and the **sign** that is performed.

A. Historical Views

According to its fragmentary liturgies and writings, the postapostolic church regarded the sacraments as real means of grace. That is, through baptism and the Lord's Supper, Christ truly gives himself along with all of his benefits. So the sign is bound closely together with the reality. Distinguishing without separating the sacramental sign from the reality signified, Augustine taught that the efficient cause of all grace is God rather than the sacraments themselves. Therefore, he did not believe that recipients truly received the reality signified in baptism and the Supper apart from faith.[12]

1. Roman Catholic interpretations

With the increasing dominance of Neoplatonism and the concept of grace as a disposition (*habitus*) infused into the soul to elevate it from natural to supernatural ends, the sacraments were seen as conduits for this process. Because grace was understood as a substance (i.e., a healing medicine) infused into the soul, the sacraments themselves came to be regarded as causing initial regeneration (in baptism) and increasing it (in the sacrifice of the Mass).

---

12. See Calvin's citations and interpretation of Augustine on this point in *Institutes* 4.17.34.

The medieval formulation of this idea is expressed in the phrase *ex opere operato*: in the doing of it, it is done. By the time of the Reformation (especially in late medieval nominalism), *ex opere operato* came to mean that sacraments work automatically and meritoriously, causing grace to flow into the soul—provided that the recipient does not place any obstacle in its path.[13] Throughout the medieval period there were debates over the sacraments (especially the Supper), but the trajectory was set toward an inflated ecclesial ego. Increasingly, the church substituted itself for Christ's physical body as the ladder of grace. Claiming authority to institute new sacraments that are not explicitly appointed in Scripture, the medieval church added confirmation, penance, ordination, marriage, and extreme unction and gave a quasisacramental status to relics, pilgrimages, and shrines, as well as to pictures, icons, and statues. To each additional sacrament there could be further acts bearing sacramental efficacy. For example, the sale of indulgences (still offered today), which could purchase time off in purgatory for oneself as well as for friends and relatives, was an extension of the sacrament of penance.

Beginning especially with the Fourth Lateran Council (1214), official Roman Catholic teaching on the sacraments received its most elaborate formulation by Thomas Aquinas and attained its clearest dogmatic status at the sixteenth-century Council of Trent. According to Aquinas, unlike just any sign of a sacred thing, a sacrament "makes people holy."[14] Thus, "only those are called sacraments which signify the perfection of holiness in man."[15] The sacraments accomplish this by causing grace to be infused into the recipient, and this is where the different understandings of grace underlying the sacraments emerge.[16] If grace is the medicine of the soul, as Roman Catholic theology teaches, then the sacraments are the intravenous tube.

2. Anabaptist interpretations

A diverse movement arising more out of late medieval spirituality than the Reformation, Anabaptism gave rise to communities united by a mysti-

---

13. *Catechism of the Catholic Church* (Liguori, Mo.: Liguori Publications, 1994), 211.

14. Thomas Aquinas, *Summa theologica*, q. 60, art. 2, pt. 3 (trans. Fathers of the English Dominican Province; repr., Westminster, Md.: Christian Classics, 1948), vol. 4, p. 2340.

15. Ibid.

16. Ibid., q. 69, art. 9, pt. 3, vol. 4, p. 2409: "While infants, all being equal in capacity, receive the same effect in baptism, adults, who approach Baptism in their own faith, are not equally disposed to Baptism; for some approach thereto with greater, some with less, devotion. And therefore some receive a greater, some a smaller share of the grace of newness," just as those who come closer to the fire receive more of its heat. Grace is obviously a power (*potentia*) and a substance (*substantia*) with which one must cooperate in order to receive its fullest effect: "Consequently in order that a man be justified by Baptism, his will must needs embrace both Baptism and the baptismal effect.... Wherefore it is manifest that insincerity hinders the effect of Baptism."

cal tendency to sharply contrast the inner work of the Spirit with the outer work of the church in its official ministry.[17] With its strong emphasis on personal decision and moral perfection, baptism and the Supper became chiefly means of discipline. They became less means of grace than instruments of law.

Of course, this meant that only those who publicly professed faith in Christ could be baptized. (The label "Anabaptist" came from the practice of rebaptizing those who had been baptized as infants.) The Supper, too, is often treated merely as a memorial with social (horizontal) implications rather than as a means of grace.[18] While the social dimension is important for a biblical conception as well, as I will argue, Berkhof's judgment seems substantially correct:

> The Anabaptists, and other mystical sects of the age of the Reformation and later times, virtually deny that God avails Himself of means in the distributing of His grace. They stress the fact that God is absolutely free in communicating His grace, and therefore can hardly be conceived of as bound to such external means. Such means after all belong to the natural world, and have nothing in common with the spiritual world. God, or Christ, or the Holy Spirit, or the inner light, works directly in the heart, and both the Word and the sacraments can only serve to indicate or to symbolize this internal grace. The whole conception is determined by a dualistic view of nature and grace.[19]

Eventually, some groups so emphasized the inner work of the Spirit apart from external means that the sacraments were regarded as unimportant. Some, like the Society of Friends (Quakers) and the Salvation Army have dispensed with the sacraments altogether. However, for most Anabaptists—as well as Baptists—baptism of adults is treated with seriousness as an essential mark of discipleship.

3. Reformation interpretations

The Reformation introduced a view of the sacraments that differed substantially from both medieval Rome and Anabaptism. The church is

---

17. Thomas N. Finger offers helpful nuances in interpreting various strands of Anabaptist teaching on this subject in *A Contemporary Anabaptist Theology* (Downers Grove, Ill.: InterVarsity Press, 2004), ch. 6.

18. For a contemporary statement, see John Howard Yoder, *Body Politics* (Nashville: Discipleship Resources, 1992), 16; Thomas Finger recognizes, "[Balthasar] Hubmaier stressed the Supper's communal dimension and its expression through concrete, outward ethical activity"; quoting Hubmaier, he adds, "For the Supper has to do 'completely and exclusively with fraternal love'" (*Contemporary Anabaptist Theology*, 187). Like Zwingli, many of the Anabaptists presupposed that "an ontological barrier separated spirit and matter" (ibid., 190).

19. Louis Berkhof, *Systematic Theology* (Grand Rapids: Eerdmans, 1949), 607.

not itself a means of grace, Martin Luther insisted, but the servant of the word that created the church in the first place and sustains and expands it. Therefore, the sacraments have efficacy only in connection with the word. Together with the word, the sacraments promise God's favor on account of Christ. They are a "visible Word" (Apology 13, 5), "a seal and confirmation of the Word and promise" (Apology 24, 70). Yet because God gives his promise—indeed, Christ himself—through these signs, they are not separated from the reality that they signify (Apology 24, 70; Larger Catechism 5, 30).[20]

Because the word embraces the baptismal water, it becomes "a gracious water of life and a washing of regeneration in the Holy Spirit." Baptism removes the guilt of original sin and brings "God's grace, the entire Christ, and the Holy Spirit with his gifts"[21] Because Christ is objectively present and is given bodily in baptism and Communion, every recipient of these sacraments receives Christ, although unbelievers receive them to their judgment. Faith therefore contributes nothing to the nature and efficacy of the sacraments; they are what they are and do what they do, regardless. However, there can be no saving profit if one refuses the gift that Christ gives through these means.

Crucial to Luther's view is the belief that Christ is *bodily* present, not only at the altar but in the words of proclamation and the waters of baptism. This is predicated on the belief that in the unity of Christ's person as God incarnate the characteristics (or attributes) of divinity are communicated to his humanity (in this case, omnipresence). Consequently, Christ can be present physically wherever he wills. Not only according to his divinity but according to his humanity, he is present at every altar with the bread and wine (which remain unchanged).[22]

The Zurich Reformer Ulrich Zwingli (1484–1531) differed from Luther's view of sacraments on several points. Assuming a sharp dualism between spiritual and material things as well as between the divine and human natures of Christ, Zwingli came to regard the sacraments more as a human than a divine pledge. Consequently, he viewed the sacraments as teaching and motivating ordinances more than means of grace. Meeting at Marburg in 1529, Luther and Zwingli, along with several other repre-

---

20. See Apology of the Augsburg Confession, in *The Book of Concord: The Confessions of the Evangelical Lutheran Church* (ed. and trans. Theodore G. Tappert; Philadelphia: Fortress, 1959), 13.5; 24.70; also Larger Catechism, 5.30.

21. For the quotes in this paragraph see Smalcald Articles 4.10; Apology of the Augsburg Confession 2.35; Larger Catechism 4.41, in ibid.

22. Formula of Concord, Solid Declaration 7.36–38, in ibid., 575–76.

sentative Reformed leaders, were able to agree on fourteen out of fifteen points that had been in dispute. The final point of disagreement, however, concerned Christ's real presence in the Supper. The majority of Reformed leaders rejected both Zwingli's view and Luther's notion of Christ's omnipresent body. Thus, despite several points of agreement, there remained a split between the Lutheran and the Reformed over the issue of the real presence of Christ in the Supper, a breach that was never healed.

It was in this context that John Calvin gained prominence, giving refinement to the view that would eventually become standard in the Reformed and Presbyterian confessions. It is through the Word that the Spirit creates faith, Calvin insisted, "But the sacraments bring the clearest promises."[23]

Convinced that Luther's notion of an omnipresent human body emptied Christ's glorified flesh of its reality, Calvin affirmed with Zwingli the significance of Christ's bodily ascension. Nevertheless, Calvin agreed with Luther on the principal definition of a sacrament; namely, that God does in fact bring about spiritual effects through physical means and that sacraments are primarily God's action rather than that of the recipients. In the **sacramental union** of sign and thing signified, Calvin emphasized, God truly offers and gives his saving grace *through* earthly means. Just as the preaching of the Word is valid in and of itself, apart from human response, baptism and the Supper remain objective sacraments even apart from one's faith. Faith does not *make* a sacrament, but it does *receive* the reality of the sacrament; otherwise one receives only the sign without the thing signified. A sacrament, then, consists of both a visible sign and spiritual grace.[24] According to Reformed interpretation, the sacramental union is not a fusion of substances, but a relational act of God in the covenantal economy; that is, an exchange of gifts from one person (God) to others (believers).

4. Contemporary evangelical interpretations

Throughout much of its history (especially in pietism and revivalism) the broad movement known as 'evangelicalism' has been reacting against sacramentalism. Consequently, the evangelical movement is more sympathetic to its Anabaptist than to its Reformation roots. Personal practices and spiritual disciplines are often regarded as more central than the sacraments

---

23. Philip Walker Butin, *Revelation, Redemption and Response: Calvin's Trinitarian Understanding of the Divine-Human Relationship* (New York: Oxford Univ. Press, 1995), 103.

24. Ibid., 618; cf. the Belgic Confession, art. 33, in Doctrinal Standards of the Christian Reformed Church, in *Psalter Hymnal* (Grand Rapids: Board of Publications of the Christian Reformed Church, 1976), 85–86; Heidelberg Catechism, q. 66, in Doctrinal Standards, 32; and Westminster Confession, in *Trinity Hymnal* (Atlanta: Great Commission Publications, 1990), ch. 27.

of the church in the ordinary nurture and sustenance of faith. According to Stanley Grenz, "the ordinances symbolize the gospel,"[25] and he titles his chapter treating baptism and the Supper, "Community Acts of Commitment." Grenz explains that from the perspective of the Radical Reformers and their Baptist heirs, baptism and the Supper "are basically human, and not divine acts." "At the heart of this theology was a focus on obedience. Believers participate in the ordinances out of a desire to be obedient to the one who ordained these acts for the church. The ordinances, therefore, are signs of obedience."[26]

Viewing the sacraments as our own acts of obedience rather than as God's means of grace has enormous implications for ecclesiology more generally, as we will see, but also for soteriology (the doctrine of salvation). Millard Erickson recognizes that the Reformed view, which "is tied closely to the concept of the covenant," emphasizes "the objective aspect of the sacrament."[27] In opposition to this view Erickson argues, "The act of baptism conveys no direct spiritual benefit or blessing." "It is, then, a testimony that one has already been regenerated," and is performed only after candidates "have exhibited credible evidence of regeneration" and have therefore "met the conditions for salvation (i.e., repentance and active faith)."[28] "It is a public indication of one's commitment to Christ."[29] Concerning the Supper, Erickson notes that in the Reformed view, "There is, then, a genuine objective benefit of the sacrament. It is not generated by the participant; rather, it is brought to the sacrament by Christ himself." Erickson disagrees with this understanding, stating that the Supper is "basically commemorative."[30]

B. The Efficacy of the Sacraments: A Biblical-Theological Interpretation

The preceding survey identifies two extreme positions. At one end is the tendency to collapse any distinction between sign and reality. The sign simply is (or becomes) the reality itself, as in the Roman Catholic doctrine of transubstantiation, in which the creaturely substance of bread and wine is annihilated. Grace elevates nature beyond itself, transforming it into some-

---

25. Stanley Grenz, *Theology for the Community of God* (Nashville: Broadman & Holman, 1997), 644.

26. Ibid., 670.

27. Millard Erickson, *Christian Theology* (Grand Rapids: Baker, 1985), 3:1093–94.

28. Ibid., 3:1096.

29. Ibid., 3:1101.

30. Ibid., 3:1120, 1122.

thing supernatural. The natural sign no longer exists after the priestly consecration, but is replaced with the supernatural reality. At the other end is the tendency to separate sign and reality. In this approach, sacraments can only be human acts of testifying, remembering, and commitment; they are not means of grace. As we will see, these different views of the sacraments have an enormous impact on differing views not only of the application of redemption but also of the nature of the church. Though differing sharply from the Roman Catholic as well as the Lutheran position, the Reformed view is nevertheless in agreement with the catholic heritage, over against Anabaptist traditions, in regarding the sacraments as objective means of grace. As Francis Turretin put the matter, "The question is not whether or not the sacraments are efficacious in some sense. This is granted by both sides. The question is *how* they exert their efficacy."[31]

Scripture identifies sacraments as **signs and seals** of the covenant. They outwardly ratify the new relationship between Lord and servant. International treaties or covenants in ancient Near Eastern politics bear remarkable similarities to the biblical rites. This should not be surprising, when we consider that in Scripture God's relationship with human beings always takes the form of a covenant. Of course, there are radical differences. Only in Israel is the nation's God also its head of state. Furthermore, given the uniqueness of this King, and the heavenly ministry of his Holy Spirit through his "living and active" word, the covenantal rituals that he commands are means of grace in a sense that could never be said of secular rites. Nevertheless, since God appropriates this political structure of "covenant" as a way of communicating with his people, we should examine first of all what "signs and seals of the covenant" would have meant to the original audience rather than develop an elaborate philosophical explanation.

In the secular treaties, a great ruler would save a lesser kingdom from an invading army and then annex the liberated party to his empire. The covenant would be imposed, not negotiated. And then the lesser king (or vassal) would ratify the treaty on behalf of his people in a public ceremony. Often this ceremony took the form of walking through the pieces of severed animals, sealing the words he had sworn, in complete fealty to the new suzerain. The rite was so identified with the words that making a covenant was called *cutting* a covenant.

In the Abrahamic covenant, God is the oath maker, and his promise is confirmed and ratified first by the vision of the theophany passing through

---

31. Francis Turretin, *Institutes of Elenctic Theology* (Philadelphia: P&R, repr. 1992), 3:343.

the severed halves, and then by circumcision (Ge 15 – 17). God, not Abraham, is the oath maker in this covenant; Abraham is the recipient of the pledge. We read that Abram "believed the LORD, and he counted it to him as righteousness" (Ge 15:6), Abram asks, "O Lord GOD, how am I to know that I shall possess it?" (v. 8), and God accedes to the request by ratifying the spoken promise in the vision of Yahweh passing through the halves (vv. 9 – 21). As a sign and seal of God's promise, then, a sacrament not only serves to assure the believer of God's favor in Christ but to "remind" *God* of his commitment, even when our sins provoke his anger. Here, the words of the covenant are not those of a conditional treaty, in which the vassal swears the oath to fulfill the stipulations or die the death; rather, the Great King is the one making all of the promises, and the words of his covenant are sealed not by making the servant pass through the halves but by assuming the role commonly assigned to the servant. "May I be cut in half like these animals if I fail to fulfill my promises": this is what God is swearing not only in the words but in the public ceremony that ratifies them. Obligations are imposed on Abraham, but they are not conditions of justification. Abram "believed the LORD, and he counted it to him as righteousness" (Ge 15:6).

This covenant differs from other major covenants in Scripture, in which the human partner is the oath maker who swears to fulfill the commands and ratifies the oath by identifying with the slaughtered animals. The Adamic covenant was signified and sealed by the Tree of Life, through which God would grant everlasting life and confirmation in righteousness upon the human being's completion of his task. The right to eat from the Tree was the goal, not the basis; everlasting confirmation in righteousness and blessing was the end point, not the starting point. The Sinai covenant was also sworn by the people and was ratified by Moses' sprinkling of blood on the people, "in accordance with the words that they spoke, saying, 'All this we will do'" (Ex 24:3, 6 – 8). The ritual is consistent with the words that it confirms. "See the blood of the covenant that the LORD has made with you in accordance with all these words" (v. 8). Together, the words and the ratification ceremony constitute a covenant.

The Sinai covenant has the people for the oath makers, Moses for its mediator, and temporal promises (death/exile or long life in the land) based on the fulfillment of temporal conditions. It still shares in the Abrahamic covenant, by providing temporal shadows that direct Israelites to the everlasting gospel in Jesus Christ. Nevertheless, in form and substance, it is a law-covenant.

Unlike the law-covenant, the covenant of grace is a bequest or inheritance that God pledges as an outright gift. It is the covenant of promise that God makes immediately after the fall to Adam and Eve and in both the Abrahamic and Davidic covenants. In all of these cases, God is the oath maker who assumes full responsibility for seeing the covenant through to completion. No matter how faithless David and his heirs will be, God promises, and although he will punish them, there will be a Davidic heir on David's throne forever. This is as firm as God's "covenant with the day ... and night" (2Sa 7:16; 1Ki 2:4; Ps 89:3 – 4; Jer 33:20). The covenant of grace continued through a remnant, even as Israel thoroughly violated the law-covenant that it swore as a nation at Mount Sinai.

When God later sends the prophets to prosecute his case against the nation, it is clearly Israel — not God — who must bear the sanctions of the law-covenant: "And the men who transgressed my covenant and did not keep the terms of the covenant that they made before me, I will make them like the calf that they cut in two and passed between its parts" (Jer 34:1 – 22). By contrast, through the covenant of grace, renewed in the New Covenant (see Jer 31), God promises a new creation and a new exodus. God renews *his* oath: "And they shall be my people, and I will be their God" (Jer 32:38).

So it is important to see not only the covenantal context of sacraments in the Bible, but also how these signs and seals function in different covenants. In both cases (covenants of law and of promise), someone swears the oath and ratifies it through a bloody rite; it all depends on who is the speaker (promise maker) and whose head the sanctions will fall on, as confirmed by the ceremony. The action of "cutting a covenant" is itself neither a magical annihilation of natural substances by supernatural substances nor a merely symbolic gesture. Rather, God consecrates nonmysterious, ordinary and natural substances as means by which he performs his mysterious, marvelous, and miraculous work. Precisely in using elements that remain ordinary creaturely, sanctified by the word and Spirit, God's pledge is concrete and tangible for us.

In a covenantal context, words and signs together create a covenant: a legally binding and personal union, as in marriage or adoption. As signs and seals of the covenant (and every covenant involves two parties), sacraments oblige the human partner to faith and obedience. However, baptism and the Supper are first and foremost *means of grace* because they are the sacraments of the *covenant of grace*.

In instituting circumcision, Yahweh pledges, "And I will establish my covenant between me and you and your offspring after you throughout their generations for an everlasting covenant, to be God to you and to your offspring after you" (Ge 17:7). Circumcision not only symbolizes this promise but assures each recipient of his entitlement to it: "So shall my covenant be in your flesh an everlasting covenant" (v. 13). It was the "seal" of their justification (v. 11). Similarly, an adult convert is justified the moment he or she trusts in Christ, but this justification is sealed or ratified by baptism. The choice, then, is not between salvation by grace through faith and salvation by sacraments; *the latter signify and seal the former.* Precisely for that reason, they must not be withheld from entitled recipients. In fact, withholding the visible sign and seal excommunicates one from the visible covenant community: "Any uncircumcised male who is not circumcised in the flesh of his foreskin shall be cut off from his people; he has broken my covenant" (Ge 17:14). Furthermore, just as the old covenant sacraments promised grace and threatened judgment for those who did not receive the reality signified, the New Testament provides the same dire warnings (1Co 10:1–22; 11:27–32; Heb 4:1–13; 6:1–12).

In the covenantal economy, the function of signs is not primarily to express an inner experience or wish. The sign does not stand for something else. It is not a question of something that is present representing something that is absent or of somehow making the beloved present in one's mind (like looking at a picture). It is not an object lesson or illustration. "Remembering" the covenant is not simply recalling it to mind. Rather, to remember the covenant on the basis of the sign is to acknowledge once again one's pledge, and for God to remember his covenant is for him to act in the present on the basis of a past promise, in spite of the good reasons in the present that God might have for doing otherwise. Unlike the pagan feasts, which celebrated natural cycles, Israel's feasts solemnized a perpetual, present participation in the redemptive events of the past and an expectation of their fulfillment in the future. The Israelites who left Egypt "were baptized into Moses in the cloud and in the sea," and drank of the rock in the wilderness, "and the Rock was Christ" (1Co 10:1–4). Furthermore, each generation celebrating the Passover was to recognize its participation in this "baptism."

What, then, does it mean then for signs to "participate" in the reality they signify? Instead of beginning with the usual philosophical solutions, we will avail ourselves of the ancient Near Eastern answer. "This is the head of Mati'ilu and his sons," begins a Hittite treaty in which the suzerain goes on to say that the severed head of the goat is no longer "a goat's head but the head of Mati'ilu and his sons."[32] This treaty includes an explanation

---

32. This example is cited in Dennis J. McCarthy, *Treaty and Covenant: A Study in the Ancient Oriental Documents and in the Old Testament* (Rome: Biblical Institute Press, 1963), 195.

that distinguishes this use of the goat's head from uses of it in religious festivals and public barbeques. In this treaty, an ordinary goat's head was set apart for special purposes. The *use* of the goat's head—not its *essence*—was changed by this political act of consecration. Witnesses to such a ceremony knew what was intended. They did not imagine that the goat's head was magically transformed into the head of Mati'ilu and his sons, nor that it was merely symbolic. Rather, they recognized that in swearing the oath along with performing the ritual they were sealing their own doom if they failed to keep its terms.

The biblical sacraments closely parallel the sign-signified relation that was presupposed in these secular treaties or covenants. So close was the representative identification of the forswearer with the ritual animal, and the sign with the thing signified, that circumcision was called simply "the covenant," just as Jesus designated the cup he raised in the upper room as "my blood of the covenant" (Mt 26:25–28). In these actions, we encounter neither mere illustrations nor some kind of magical transformation, but *performative communication* that actually places Jesus under the sword of judgment. He offers his followers the "cup of salvation" because he will drink the "cup of wrath" to its dregs, a cup that he will dread in Gethsemane but will accept for us. It is no wonder, then, that Paul called the cross "the circumcision of Christ" (Col 2:11).[33] After all, it was he of whom Isaiah prophesied "that he was *cut off* out of the land of the living, *stricken* for the transgression of my people.... He bore the sin of many, and makes intercession for the transgressors" (Isa 53:8–12).

United to Christ in his circumcision-death, the baptized also come under God's sword of judgment. As Peter affirms, baptism, foreshadowed by the salvation of Noah and his family in the flood ordeal, "now saves" not by cleansing the body but "as an appeal to God for a good conscience, through the resurrection of Jesus Christ, who has gone into heaven and is at the right hand of God" (1Pe 3:21–22). Now when the people pass through the waters, they will not be drowned, because God is with them as he was in the exodus (Isa 43:1–3).

Just as circumcision could be called "the covenant" because of the close

---

33. M. G. Kline reminds us that like Isaac, Jesus as an infant underwent circumcision, "that partial and symbolic cutting off"—the "moment, prophetically chosen, to name him 'Jesus.' But it was the circumcision of Christ in crucifixion that answered to the burnt-offering of Genesis 22 as a perfecting of circumcision, a 'putting off' not merely of a token part but of 'the [whole] body of the flesh' (Col. 2:11, ARV), not simply a symbolic oath-cursing but a cutting off of 'the body of his flesh through death' (Col. 1:22) in accursed darkness and dereliction" (*By Oath Consigned* [Grand Rapids: Eerdmans, 1968], 45).

union of the sign and the thing signified, the Passover ritual was itself called "the LORD's passing over," with successive generations called upon to regard themselves as representatively (i.e., covenantally) present with the founding generation, dressed for the road in anticipation of their redemption (Ex 13:14–16). So too, in the Supper's words of institution, Jesus simply calls the cup and the bread "the new covenant in my blood" (Lk 22:20). "This is my body.... This is my blood of the covenant, which is poured out for many for the forgiveness of sins" (Mt 26:26–28).

The same cup that was filled with judgment for the Messiah (Mt 26:39) is now drunk by those who, united to his death and resurrection, receive from it only forgiveness and life. The sacraments correspond to the Word as the ratification of covenantal sanctions: "The cup of blessing that we bless, is it not a participation [koinōnia] in the blood of Christ? The bread that we break, is it not a participation in the body of Christ? Because there is one bread, we who are many are one body, for we all partake of the one bread" (1Co 11:16–17). Thus the union is covenantal and centers on legal and relational mediation between erstwhile enemies.

Again, the focus is not upon divine *presence* per se but divine *action*. Aquinas spends eight articles in his *Summa theologica* providing a series of philosophical arguments for "the way in which Christ is in this sacrament."[34] This is consistent with his treatment of grace as a metaphysical substance whose infusion is caused by baptism and subsequent sacraments. However, in a covenantal understanding, sacraments involve an exchange of gifts from one person to another, not an exchange of substances. What is important is not what happens *to the signs* but what happens *between persons through them*; not *how* Christ is present in the sacraments, but *that through them he is present in saving action toward us*. Grace is God's favor, and the sacraments ratify God's favor toward us. Their purpose is to reconcile enemies, not to elevate nature beyond itself. When God commanded Moses to erect a pole with a brass serpent in the wilderness to heal anyone who looked at it, there was no change in the wood and the metal. Nor was it merely an object lesson or

---

34. Thomas Aquinas, *Summa theologica*, q. 76, pt. 3, vol. 4, p. 2550. Thomas does not deny the reality of the ascension, and he carefully distinguishes his understanding of presence from natural and local concepts (involving movement from one place to another, for example). Yet for all that, "the whole substance of the bread is changed into the whole substance of Christ's body, and the whole substance of the wine into the whole substance of Christ's blood. Hence this is not a formal, but a substantial conversion; nor is it a kind of natural movement: but, with a name of its own, it can be called *transubstantiation*" (q. 75, art. 5, pt. 3, vol. 4, p. 2444). I am inclined to believe that such an account (and rival accounts that remain in this circle) could evolve only within Neoplatonic-Aristotelian frame of reference. Even when Thomas engages in proof texts from Scripture, Aristotle is everywhere in the treatment of the sacraments the dominant voice.

illustration. Rather, ordinary elements were set apart for extraordinary purposes. They became holy because God was using them for certain purposes, not because they were transformed essentially. The brass serpent was a means of grace, like Moses' staff or the rock in the desert.

Through the Word and the sacraments, the Spirit dislocates us from this present age of sin and death "in Adam" and relocates us "in Christ," as citizens of the age to come. No longer under the dominion of the flesh (i.e., the possibilities inherent in this present age), we are under the reign of the Spirit (i.e., the powers of the age to come). The recipient must *receive* the gift; otherwise, the sacrament becomes a sign and seal of the judgment that he or she will have to bear personally, apart from the substitutionary judgment borne by the Covenant Mediator. As the writer to the Hebrews emphasizes, to share in the dignity and privilege of covenant membership while rejecting the promised inheritance is the greatest offense not only to God's justice but to his mercy. There is an analogy with marriage. A man and woman do not become husband and wife merely by showing up for the ceremony, but it is in that ceremony that they exchange their vows and are acknowledged publicly as married.

Once strangers and enemies of the Great King, we are now brought near by the blood of Christ. We know this because God has sworn his covenant mercies in the gospel and ratified them in our baptism and in the Supper. The Father gave his Son for us, objectively, in history; now he gives his Son to us, objectively, through preaching and sacrament. Christ is truly *given* to all who hear the gospel and receive baptism and the Lord's Supper, yet he must be *received* for everlasting life. The gospel preached is God's means of grace, whether anyone believes it or not; nevertheless, simply hearing it is not saving unless the promise proclaimed is received and embraced by faith. Christ delivers himself to us, gift-wrapped in the creaturely means of preaching and sacrament. In this way, the transcendent and majestic God makes himself "havable." However, we must never forget that salvation is found in the Gift, not in the package in which it is delivered.

Key Terms

- sacramental word
- creation of the Word
- sacraments
- *ex opere operato*
- sacramental union
- signs and seals

Key Distinctions

- means of grace/means of gratitude
- sign/reality

Key Questions

1. Do you identify more with Jeff or with Sharon in the opening illustration of this chapter? How might you respond to both?
2. Why is preaching especially emphasized as a means of grace? Discuss this in the light of Romans 10:1 – 15. What difference does it make, practically speaking, to think of preaching not only as instruction or exhortation but as sacramental — i.e., a means of grace?
3. Compare and contrast different interpretations of sacraments: especially the Roman Catholic view of *ex opere operato* and Lutheran, Anabaptist, and Reformed interpretations.
4. What is a "covenantal" interpretation of sacraments?
5. Are sacraments chiefly our actions or God's?
6. Why is it important to talk about the sacraments in the church today?

Chapter Sixteen

Baptism and the Supper

The covenant of grace continues unbroken from the promise in Genesis 3:15 to Abraham and David all the way to us now, as coheirs with Christ in the new covenant. However, this one covenant of grace has been administered differently under the old and new covenants, with different sacraments. Scripture itself tells us that circumcision is now replaced by baptism (Col 2:11 – 12), and the Lord's Supper was instituted after the conclusion of the Passover meal (Mt 26:26 – 29).

I. Baptism
A. The Nature and Administration of Baptism

Paul appeals to the analogy of the "baptism" of the children of Israel into Moses through the Red Sea for this union (1Co 10:2), and Peter refers to the Noahic deluge ordeal as a baptism foreshadowing the baptism that now saves us (1Pe 3:21). Jesus emphasized over against the theologians of glory at his own side that none but he could bear the "baptism" of the cross (Lk 12:50; cf. Mk 10:38), yet we now are included in the benefits of his circumcision-death and resurrection-life. As the promises are greater in the new covenant, so also are the curses for refusing to receive the substance that it promises

(Mt 8:12; Jn 15:1 – 8; Ro 11:17 – 21; Heb 4:2; 6:4 – 8; 12:25). Earthly exile from the geopolitical theocracy is merely typological of being cut off from the heavenly rest.

The sign and thing signified are treated in the New Testament, as in the Old, as intimately connected. Christ has "cleansed [the church] by *the washing of water with the word*" (*katharisas tō loutrō tou hydatos en rhēmati*, Eph 5:26) and "saved us, not because of works done by us in righteousness, but according to his own mercy, by the washing of regeneration and renewal of the Holy Spirit" (Tit 3:5).[1] Believers have been "buried with Christ in baptism" and raised with him in newness of life. Baptism, in fact, is now the true circumcision (Col 2:11 – 12). The contrast between baptism and works righteousness points up that the sacraments cannot be treated as human works, much less as attempts to attain righteousness before God.

Baptism itself does not effect this in an *ex opere operato* fashion. That is to say, the sacrament performed by a priest does not automatically regenerate recipients. Rather, baptism is a visual confirmation of God's act of communicating his covenant promise. It achieves its effect when and where the Spirit chooses. "The efficacy of baptism is not tied to that moment wherein it is administered," according to the Westminster Confession (28.7), "yet, notwithstanding, by the right use of this ordinance, the grace promised is not only offered, but really exhibited and conferred, by the Holy Ghost, to such (whether of age or infants) as that grace belongeth unto, according to the counsel of God's own will in His appointed time." In fact, Reformed theology and piety emphasize the perpetual significance and efficacy of baptism for the whole life of believers.[2]

Therefore, a covenantal view of the sacraments serves rather than undermines the crucial point that this is a covenant of *grace*. The Reformers and their heirs emphasized that baptism was, first of all, an action of the whole Trinity. Calvin writes,

> For he [Christ] dedicated and sanctified baptism in his own body in order
> that he might have it in common with us as the firmest possible bond of the
> union and fellowship which he has deigned to form with us.... All the gifts

---

1. So, for example, Karl Barth, *Church Dogmatics* (trans. G. W. Bromiley; Edinburgh: T&T Clark, 1957 – 1975), vol. 4, pt. 4, 113 – 14. Despite considerable technical skill and knowledge of a wide variety of classical and contemporary interpretations of each passage (acknowledging in the preface the debt to his son, Markus Barth, in this regard), Barth's exegesis presupposes from the outset that these passages cannot be interpreted in a sacramental manner.

2. Calvin, *Institutes* 4.15.3; Belgic Confession, art. 34, in Doctrinal Standards of the Christian Reformed Church, in *Psalter Hymnal* (Grand Rapids: Board of Publications of the Christian Reformed Church, 1976), 86 – 87.

of God displayed in baptism are found in Christ alone. Yet this cannot take place unless he who baptizes in Christ invokes also the names of the Father and the Spirit.... For this reason we obtain and, so to speak, clearly discern in the Father the cause [*causa*], in the Son the matter [*material*], and in the Spirit the effect [*effectio*] of our purgation and our regeneration.[3]

Just as Calvin had earlier insisted that through the Scriptures believers hear God as if he were standing before them, he asserts that they also in baptism "see with their very eyes the covenant of the Lord engraved upon the bodies of their children."[4] Like the preaching of the gospel, the sacraments are God's pledge of goodwill toward us. God's work comes first, and this generates our repentance and faith. God first serves us; the church comes into existence (not just in the beginning but throughout the life of the individual Christian and the corporate body) as a *recipient* of grace. We are not building a kingdom, either as individuals or as a church, but can only "be grateful for receiving a kingdom that cannot be shaken" (Heb 12:28).

The New Testament does not lay down any absolute rule concerning the mode of baptism: immersion, pouring, or sprinkling. Baptism was already in use as a purification rite when John began his ministry. As the vessels in the sanctuary were used in rituals of sprinkling and pouring, such washings were administered by sprinkling or pouring (Nu 8:7; 19:13, 18–20; Ps 51:7; Eze 36:25; Jn 3:25–26; Mk 7:3–4 with Lk 11:38; Ac 2:38; 22:16; Ro 6:4–5; 1Co 6:11; Tit 3:5; Heb 9:10; 10:22; 1Pe 3:21; Rev 5:1). Immersion does seem more suggestive of being buried and raised with Christ and of being drawn out of God's waters of judgment alive. At the same time, those who "passed through the sea and ... were baptized into Moses in the cloud and in the sea" in the exodus from Egypt (1Co 10:1–2) actually escaped immersion in the waters. In view of the varied examples and precedents for ritual purification, the church's historical acceptance of immersion, sprinkling, and pouring as valid modes of baptism seems entirely justified. Partisans on all sides should beware of rejecting the validity of one's baptism on the basis of the amount of water administered.

However, Scripture does seem to restrict the proper administration of baptism to ordained ministers. In fact, even though the apostles (as extraordinary ministers) were authorized to baptize, Paul makes a point of saying that his calling was to preach the gospel where it was unknown. With a few exceptions (administered by the apostles), the administration of the

---

3. Calvin, *Institutes* 4.15.6.
4. Ibid., 4.16.9.

sacraments was the proper province of settled, ordinary ministers (1Co 1:16–17).

Furthermore, baptism is a public-covenantal rite, to be administered ordinarily in the regular service in which the word is preached and the assembly of God's people is present. It is not merely a private, personal affair, nor an informal celebration among family members and friends. Christ himself baptizes, through his ambassadors who are called and set apart by ordination for this task.[5] Apart from the word, the signs have no efficacy. Reformed churches also reject the practice of allowing parents, midwives or nurses in extreme cases to administer baptism, which arose in connection with the doctrine of baptismal regeneration. It is not the lack of baptism that excludes one from the covenant but its refusal. The thief on the cross was saved without baptism (Lk 23:43), Abraham received circumcision as a "seal of the righteousness that he had by faith while he was still uncircumcised" (Ro 4:11), and adult converts are justified through faith before they are baptized. Christian parents should not doubt that their children who die in infancy before they can receive baptism in the public assembly are elect in the Lord (2Sa 12:23; 1Co 7:14). Consequently, there is no need to suspend the ordinary and proper administration of baptism in any case.

Furthermore, based on the Great Commission, Reformed churches recognize the validity of all baptisms administered with water in the name of the Father, the Son, and the Holy Spirit. Against sectarian movements (especially the Donatists), Augustine rightly argued that the validity of the ministry of word and sacraments in no way depends on the piety or sincerity of the administrator. As long as it is administered with water, in the triune formula of Matthew 28:19, baptism is a valid sacrament of Christ and his church, regardless of the personal faith or piety of its ministers. As a public and covenantal rite rather than a private religious experience, a valid baptism is never to be repeated. There is "one Lord, one faith, one baptism" (Eph 4:5).[6]

---

5. Louis Berkhof, *Systematic Theology* (Grand Rapids: Eerdmans, 1949), 631: "The Reformed Churches always acted on the principle that the administration of the Word and of the sacraments belong together, and that therefore the teaching elder or the minister is the only lawful administrator of baptism."

6. From the Anabaptist perspective, the name given to them (Anabaptists = "rebaptizers") is a misnomer, since they have always believed that they were baptizing Christians for the first time. With regard to the validity of Roman Catholic baptism, Robert L. Dabney and James Thornwell, both Southern Presbyterian theologians in the nineteenth century, argued that since the Church of Rome did not bear the marks of the true church its baptisms were to be regarded as invalid. However, as Hodge points out, this view is an exception to the general consensus of Reformed and Presbyterian practice.

B. The Proper Subjects of Baptism

Until the sixteenth century, the churches of the East and the West were united in affirming that the children of believers are included with their parents in baptism. All Christians agree that adult converts must be baptized. In fact, adult baptisms are evident throughout the book of Acts, just as we would expect to see in any situation in which the gospel was brought by missionaries. At the same time, there are examples in Acts of household baptisms (Ac 16:15, 31, 33; cf. 1Co 1:16). However, this question cannot be decided merely by trading proof texts. It involves a broader hermeneutic, or way of interpreting the Bible. Though others could be added, two questions highlight these broader differences.

1. What is the covenant of grace, and who belongs to it?

Refusing to administer the sign and seal of the covenant to young children presupposes that they are not part of the covenant community. In fact, this has usually been the devout position of many Anabaptist and Baptist believers: their children are considered unbelievers—non-Christians—until they experience a definable (ideally, datable) conversion. So how does Scripture treat the children of professing Christians? Are they considered unbelievers—in effect, excommunicated from the covenant? Paul reminds Gentiles that they were once "separated from Christ, alienated from the commonwealth of Israel and strangers to the covenants of promise, having no hope and without God in the world" (Eph 2:11–12). Now, they are "no longer strangers and aliens" (v. 19), but what does this change in status mean for their children?

We begin answering this by acknowledging that new covenant believers are children of Abraham, belonging to the same covenant that was pledged to him (Mt 19:14; Mk 10:13–16; Ac 2:39; 4:12; 10:43; 15:10–11; Ro 3:27–4:25; 1Co 7:14; Gal 3:16; 1Ti 2:5–6; 1Pe 1:9–12). Abraham was justified *before* he was circumcised, and this is the pattern also for baptism of adult converts; but the patriarch also obeyed the command to circumcise his sons. Are believers today heirs of the Abrahamic covenant? With wonderful clarity and repeated emphasis, Jesus and his apostles answer, "Yes!—This is part of the gospel's good news!" Gentile sinners now sit at the same table with Abraham, Isaac, and Jacob for the wedding feast. The two peoples have been made one in Christ. "And if you are Christ's, then you are Abraham's offspring, heirs according to promise" (Gal 3:29), "the Israel of God" (Gal 6:16).

Yet the principle of covenant succession—that is, the inclusion of believers' children—remains constant. It is still true, as Peter announced, that "the promise is for you and for your children." Peter makes this statement in the context of baptism (Ac 2:39). As the Belgic Confession argues, children in the new covenant, as in the old, should be baptized, since "Christ shed his blood no less for the washing of the children of believers than for adult persons.... Moreover, what circumcision was to the Jews, baptism is to our children. And for this reason St. Paul calls baptism the *circumcision of Christ* [Col 2:11]" (emphasis original).[7] If anything, there is a trend toward inclusion rather than exclusion as we move from old to new covenants: not only males but females also will be circumcised in heart and filled with the Spirit (Joel 2:28–29), and Peter announced that this was fulfilled at Pentecost (Ac 2:17).

From a covenantal perspective, it is impossible to separate the claim that the children of believers are holy (1Co 7:14) from the seal of the covenant that designates them as such. According to the traditional Anabaptist/Baptist view, the children are not regarded as holy until they personally repent and believe. However, although the New Testament preserves the clean/unclean distinction, it pertains now not to Jew and Gentile, circumcised and uncircumcised, but to believing and unbelieving families, with baptism as the covenant's ratification. In fact, Paul especially labors the point that all, Jew and Gentile, circumcised and uncircumcised, are Abraham's children and heirs of the Abrahamic covenant through faith alone, just as Abraham (Ro 4:3 with Ge 15:6; cf. Gal 3–4). The church, in its unity of Jew and Gentile in Christ, is understood as the fulfillment of Israel's existence (Mt 21:43; Ro 9:25–26; 2Co 6:16; Tit 2:14; 1Pe 2:9; Gal 6:16; Rev 5:9). Everything turns on whether we assume continuity or discontinuity as most fundamental to interpreting the relationship between the Old and New Testaments. Given the way that the New Testament itself interprets the Old, we should privilege continuity.

If this is the case, then, the burden of proof shifts from paedobaptists (i.e., infant baptizers) to Baptists. Given the Jewish background of the first Christians, it would not be the command to *administer* the sign and seal of the covenant to their children that would have been surprising but the command to *cease administering* it to them. However, we are not left to an argument from silence. This promise for believers and their children is exhibited in the conversion and baptism of Lydia. After she believed the gospel, "she was baptized, and her household as well" (Ac 16:15). Later in the same chapter, we read of the conversion of the Philippian jailer. He too is told, " 'Believe in the Lord Jesus, and you will be saved, you and your household.'... And he

---

7. Belgic Confession, art. 34, in *Psalter Hymnal*, 87.

was baptized at once, he and all his family" (vv. 31, 33). Paul recalls having baptized the household of Stephanas (1Co 1:16). If children are included in the covenant of grace under its Old Testament administration, surely they are not excluded in the new covenant administration, which the writer to the Hebrews calls "better" than the old (Heb 7:22).

2. What is baptism, and who should receive it?

Arguments over infant baptism usually involve a fundamental difference concerning the nature of baptism itself. Is baptism God's means of ratifying his promise to be our God and our children's God forever? Or is it our means of testifying to our own pledge? Nothing confirms the gracious sovereignty of God in our salvation more than the baptism of a child who cannot yet respond in even the most rudimentary way. Only if the efficacy of baptism depends on God's act of grace, rather than our act of obedience, is it possible to include children. Certainly baptism creates an obligation to repent and believe, but does it presuppose such conversion as having already happened in the case of covenant children? This was not assumed by Abraham, whose circumcision was "a seal of the righteousness that he had by faith while he was still uncircumcised" (Ro 4:11). Nevertheless, he was commanded also to circumcise his sons, for whom the sacrament had precisely the same purpose — namely, as a seal of the righteousness that was truly theirs by faith alone.

A final point in relation to the exegetical argument should be made. The Anabaptist/Baptist traditions have traditionally defended the notion of an age of accountability, when individuals are old enough to decide for themselves whether they will become Christians.[8] In addition, many of these bodies practice infant dedication. Nevertheless, there is no reference to an age of accountability or to the practice of infant dedication in the New Testament, while there are references to household baptism.

With respect to the historical argument, Baptists point out the paucity of evidence for infant baptism in the earliest postapostolic communities. This has been a matter of debate among church historians for some time, but there is considerable evidence in favor of infant baptism in the early church.[9] Regardless, the same response can be made here as is offered in

---

8. See, for example, Millard Erickson, *Christian Theology* (Grand Rapids: Baker, 1985), 639. However, Wayne Grudem sees no exegetical basis for the view and offers a sound rebuttal on the basis of the participation of all people from conception in original sin (*Systematic Theology* [Grand Rapids: Zondervan, 1994], 499–500).

9. For support of infant baptism as the practice of the early church, see especially Joachim Jeremias, *Infant Baptism in the First Four Centuries* (trans. David Cairns; Philadelphia: Westminster, 1962).

relation to the lack of New Testament commands to baptize infants. We have no evidence of any commands to *forbid* infant baptism, and by the second century the literature is replete with references to the practice. Just as the exclusion of believers' children would have provoked controversy among early Jewish Christians, surely such a radical change from apostolic to postapostolic practice on such an important matter would have sparked considerable debate. On the contrary, Tertullian in the second century, due largely to his involvement in the Montanist movement, questioned the propriety of infant baptism (*Baptism* 18), and his contemporary, Origen, said that "the Church had from the apostles a tradition (or, order) to give baptism even to infants" (*Commentary on Romans* 5).[10] Taking infant baptism for granted, the Council of Carthage (253) debated whether it should be performed on the eighth day (like circumcision).[11]

II. The Lord's Supper

Although the priority lies with God's gracious action, baptism also involves the responsive pledge of the whole church, the family, and eventually the children who will profess faith later in life. If baptism is the bath for the beginning of this journey, the Supper is the table that God spreads in the wilderness along the way. I have already indicated that covenant meals were part and parcel of the treaty-making events in the ancient Near East, and in Israel particularly. As with baptism, then, I will begin with the covenantal context.

A. The Cup of Salvation: The Supper in Its Covenantal Context

Covenant meals both celebrated and ratified a treaty, as when the mysterious king of Salem, "priest of the Most High God," "brought out bread and wine" and then pronounced Yahweh's blessing on Abraham (Ge 14:17–20). Similarly, the Passover meal is the participation of the generations to come in their night of safely passing under God's sword because of the blood on the doorpost (Ex 12). The prophets frequently speak of God's judgment as a "cup of wrath." And in Jesus' announcement, "This is my body" and "This is my blood of the covenant," when he speaks of his own crucifixion as the drinking of the cup (presumably the cup of wrath) to its dregs in the place

---

10. Quoted in Berkhof, *Systematic Theology*, 635.
11. Ibid.

of those he represents (Mk 10:38; Lk 22:42), we find this same covenantal background. That very night, Jesus sealed his fate as the one upon whose head the covenant curses would fall.

For those who embrace the reality signified and sealed in the sacraments, the ordeal is liberation, but those who embrace only the signs and not the reality must personally bear their own guilt. Thus anyone who in the Supper does not discern the Lord's body and blood (the reality) "eats and drinks judgment on himself" (1Co 11:29). Those who receive Communion unworthily do in fact receive Christ, but as judge rather than as justifier. Just as God sought to kill Moses until Zipporah circumcised his son and threw the skin at his feet, the Corinthian profanation of the Supper provoked God's temporal judgments, including sickness and even death (1Co 11:30). The sacraments are not playthings, but are signs and seals of the covenant.

Covenantal meals are not simply state dinners that follow a treaty-making ceremony; they are part of it. We recall Moses, Aaron, and the elders at the top of Sinai eating with Yahweh the Great King (Ex 24:9–11). The motif of "eating and drinking in the presence of the LORD" that is especially prominent in the patriarchal narratives is explicitly carried over in Luke's Gospel.[12] Unlike the covenant-*breaking* meal enjoyed in God's absence by Adam and Eve, through which their eyes were "opened" to recognize their guilt, the two disciples along the Emmaus road heard the resurrected Christ proclaim himself from all the Scriptures, and "their eyes were opened" to recognize him in the breaking of the bread.[13]

In the Passover meal, "remembering" was not merely an intellectual recollection of past events but a contemporary act of deliverance. Invoking the name of the Great King for rescue, the participants in the meal took up the Passover cup: "I will lift up the cup of salvation and call on the name of the LORD" (Ps 116:13). Like the rainbow in the Noahic covenant, the Supper involves *God's* remembering the oath that he made. The close bond between sign and signified in Passover is carried over into the New Testament celebration of the Lord's Supper.

If we allow ourselves to be distracted at the outset by metaphysical questions alien to these sorts of actions in their original covenantal context, we will miss crucial points. In Luke's account (22:14–23; cf. Mt 26:26–30; Mk 14:22–25), Jesus emphasizes twice that he will not share this meal with his

---

12. For the significance of meal fellowship, see especially David P. Moessner, *Lord of the Banquet: The Literary and Theological Significance of the Lukan Travel Narrative* (Minneapolis: Fortress, 1989).

13. Douglas Farrow, *Ascension and Ecclesia: On the Significance of the Doctrine of the Ascension for Ecclesiology and Christian Cosmology* (Edinburgh: T&T Clark, 1999), 7n23, drawing on the insights of Earl Ellis.

disciples "until the kingdom of God comes" in all of its fullness (vv. 16 and 18). Even in the physical presence of Jesus at this unique table, there is the expectation of absence, "till he come again." This will keep the celebration tethered not only to the past (the fulfillment of Passover) and the present (Christ's sacrifice), but to the future, as Paul will include in his words of institution (1Co 11:26). However, because the Spirit runs interference, as it were, between these tenses, they are not impenetrable compartments. "The relation between the Eucharist and eating and drinking in the coming kingdom of God is *not merely that between symbol and reality, but that between commencement and fulfillment,*" Herman Ridderbos argues. "In a word, it is the meal in which 'the powers of the world to come' have been released in Christ's coming, and in which the 'heavenly gift' and the Holy Spirit have been given and tasted' [Heb 6:4ff.]" (emphasis added).[14]

In our contemporary celebration of the Supper, we are participating in a foretaste of that greater meal, to be sure, but its primary reference is to a present participation in the past sacrifice.[15] (Hence, the significance of Paul's instruction in 1 Corinthians 11:26: "For as often as you eat this bread and drink the cup, you proclaim the Lord's death until he comes.") For now, the disciples must regularly eat the bread and drink the wine that Jesus allows to pass by his lips precisely because he will drink the cup of wrath instead. "Only, they must do so realizing that what they in this way will henceforth eat and drink is *the body and the blood of the Lord*" (emphasis added).[16] So in this age, Christ is the food and drink; in the age to come, he will eat and drink together with us. For now, it is a sacrificial meal, although it will be fully realized as the eschatological feast with Christ when he returns.[17] The Supper is not the Passover meal, but is inaugurated after they have celebrated the old covenant feast. Yet it is not the Marriage Supper of the Lamb.[18] The Supper not only reminds us of the tension between the "already" and the "not yet," but actually places us in that precarious intersection between the two ages.

We are invited to a table, not an altar. Like the paschal meal, the Supper is not a *sacrifice*, but it is a *sacrificial meal*: receiving Christ's crucified body and shed blood on our behalf.[19] Wherever "Christ's body and blood are eaten

---

14. Herman Ridderbos, *The Coming of the Kingdom* (ed. Raymond O. Zorn; trans. H. de Jongste; Philadelphia: P&R, 1962), 412–13.
15. Ibid., 416.
16. Ibid.
17. Ibid., 417.
18. Ibid., 431.
19. Ibid., 428.

and drunk at the Communion table, the cross becomes an actual and living reality in the midst of the congregation" and a witness to the world.[20] Thus, it is not the action of the individual or the church, but God's action through these creaturely means, an action that traverses the temporal gap between the "then and there" of Golgotha, the "here and now" of our existence, and the future feast. For now, Christ is not a fellow guest with whom we eat and drink, but rather the one who gives himself as the meal.

Instead of the blood dashed on the people at Sinai, confirming their oath to do everything prescribed in the law, Jesus inaugurates the new covenant by saying, "This is my body, which is *given for you.*... This cup that is *poured out for you* is the new covenant in my blood" (Lk 22:19–20, emphasis added). Fulfilling the oath to Abraham that was confirmed by the vision of the smoking torch (Ge 15), this action in the upper room is an unmistakably legal, covenantal event. Jesus, God and human, bears our sanctions. As the writer to the Hebrews explains, even appealing to the role of sprinkling blood in old covenant worship, Christ's death is both a sacrifice for sin and an inauguration of a new covenant in the sense of a last will and testament, which is rather different from a conditional arrangement. In the new covenant, believers are simply beneficiaries of an estate. The death of the testator puts the will into effect (Heb 9:17–22). The writer then goes on to declare the superiority, finality, and unrepeatable character of Christ's sacrifice.

When we come to his treatment of the Supper, Paul represents the sign and signified as distinct yet united (1Co 10:16). In a covenantal conception, the Supper can never be reduced to an individualistic encounter with Jesus. In fact, Paul's discussion of the Supper in 1 Corinthians is occasioned by the divisiveness of the community. Christ's existence as the head of his body makes us coheirs of his last will and testament. Therefore, the horizontal vector is immediately linked to the vertical: "Because there is one bread, we who are many are one body, for we all partake of the one bread" (1Co 10:17). By contrast, those who share in idol feasts are "participants in the altar" of false gods (v. 18).

To put it somewhat crudely, the church *is* what it *eats*. The point at issue is covenantal identification: with which Lord and under which constitution and therefore to which communion does one belong? In this sense, the Reformed tradition can concur with the position that the *eucharistic* body (the consecrated bread), appended to the word, gives unity to the

---

20. Ibid., 432.

ecclesial body (the church) because it truly communicates the energies of the *natural* body of Christ, the church's life-giving and glorified head. In this interpretation, then, there is still an important place for remembering and testifying to Christ's work in history. There is also an important horizontal dimension, uniting us to each other in a bond of fellowship in which we grow more and more into a family. Yet all of this is possible because the meal is nothing less than Christ himself. Because he has risen and sent his Spirit with his word, the event not only celebrates the past acts of redemption but allows us here and now to receive Christ and proclaim his death as well as his resurrection and return. And because each of us shares or participates in Christ himself through this meal, we are bound together with each other as one body (1Co 10:17).

B. Historical Views of the Lord's Supper

All of the ancient church writers held to the view that Christ was truly offered and given in the Supper and received through faith. That is, they held to the **real presence** of Christ in Communion. Beyond this, one may find support for any number of later theories as to the *model* of Christ's presence and its relation to the elements. Recognizing that the Supper is a mystery to be celebrated rather than a philosophical conundrum to be resolved, the Christian East embraces a realism (i.e., that we receive nothing less than the whole Christ in the Supper) without a technical argument about how this happens. Among these writers we discern a special emphasis on the Spirit and eschatology that is often less evident in Western views—except, I will argue, in the Reformed position.

Since I treat the different historical positions elsewhere,[21] I will offer only a brief summary before explaining the Reformed view. First, it is helpful to begin with agreement. Roman Catholic, Lutheran, Reformed, and Anabaptist traditions agree that Christ instituted the Supper, that it proclaims Christ's death until he returns, and that it has ongoing significance in the life of the church today. Further, the first three traditions agree, over against the fourth, that it is a mystery whose substance is nothing less than Jesus Christ himself. That is, in the Supper nothing less is given to us than the crucified body and shed blood of Christ.

Over against the first and fourth views, Lutheran and Reformed views agree that the Supper is a gift that is given by God to us—that is, a means

---

21. See Michael Horton, *The Christian Faith* (Grand Rapids: Zondervan, 2011), 803–4, 809, 814–18.

of grace; it is not a gift of the church to God (either an atoning sacrifice of the church or the believer's gift of obedience)—and that the gift is Christ himself, with all of his work. Every sacrament includes a sign and the reality, joined in a "sacramental union" by the word and the Spirit. The confessions of both Lutheran and Reformed traditions teach that Christ is present in the Supper—not merely figuratively, but really and truly—while rejecting the Roman Catholic view that at the priest's consecration of the elements the bread and wine are converted in their essence into the body and blood of Christ (i.e., the dogma of **transubstantiation**).[22]

The breach between Lutheran and Reformed traditions is, first of all, christology. That is, while both embrace the Chalcedonian definition of Christ's person (two distinct natures, yet united inseparably in one person), they have different nuances that give rise to rather different views as to the mode of Christ's presence in the sacrament. The Lutheran confession teaches that the two natures are so united as to allow a **communication of the divine attributes** to the human nature. Accordingly, Christ may be said to be omnipresent not only in his divinity but in his humanity. Consequently, even though the bread and wine are not transformed, Christ is bodily present wherever he wills, and he promises to be present bodily in the word and the sacraments.[23]

The earliest reaction within the evangelical movement against Luther's view came from Ulrich Zwingli. Not only did the Zurich Reformer reject Luther's concept of an omnipresent (or at least multipresent) human body; he harbored a Platonist antithesis between the visible (material) and invisible (immaterial). Consequently, he could see sacraments only as badges of Christian profession, testimonies to the reality that we have by faith. He could not see sacraments as means through which God actually delivers that reality to us. The primary significance of the Supper, then, became a communal act of remembering Christ's work in the past as a pledge of the future. But what happens in the present? Basically, it is our action in the present rather than God's. The sacraments provide an occasion for the Spirit to work in our hearts, but are not the means through which the Spirit works. The substance of the Supper is not Christ but the memory of Christ, and the results

---

22. For a contemporary statement of the Roman Catholic view, see *Catechism of the Catholic Church* (Liguori, Mo.: Liguori Publications, 1994), 335, 342–47.

23. For some important statements of the Lutheran view, see Martin Luther, *Luther's Works* (ed. Jaroslav Pelikan and Helmut Lehmann; 55 vols.; American Edition; St. Louis and Philadelphia: Concordia and Fortress, 1955–86), 37:187; Apology of the Augsburg Confession, 8; Formula of Concord, Solid Declaration 7 and Epitome 7; cf. Edmund Schlink, *Theology of the Lutheran Confessions* (trans. Paul F. Koehneke and Herbert J. A. Bouman; Philadelphia: Muhlenberg, 1961), 161–62.

are primarily horizontal: the deepening of union and communion (as well as obedience) among believers.[24]

As soon as Zwingli advocated this view, his Reformed colleagues criticized it. They shared Zwingli's worry that Luther's view tended to collapse the distinction between the two natures and, as a result, turned Christ's natural body, now ascended, into a "monstrous phantasm." A body that can be everywhere is in fact nowhere. Why would Jesus tell them to celebrate the Supper "until he comes [again]" (1Co 11:26) if in fact he returns bodily at every celebration? Yet Reformed leaders began to distance themselves from Zwingli's view. In the Second Helvetic Confession, even Heinrich Bullinger offered a rather sharp, if veiled, criticism of his predecessor's view. Martin Bucer, Peter Martyr Vermigli, John Calvin, and others were even more robust in their criticisms and developed a formulation that became standard in the Reformed and Presbyterian confessions and catechisms.

Although Bucer and other Reformed leaders had already reached a provisional agreement with Luther and Philipp Melanchthon (as in the Wittenberg Concord), it was especially Vermigli and Calvin who filled in the arguments for a Reformed consensus. Affirming with Luther the maxim *distinctio sed non separatio*, Calvin refused to separate the sign (bread and wine) from the signified (body and blood of Christ). Yet with Zwingli he held that the **doctrine of ubiquity** (Christ's omnipresence even in the flesh) was strange and veered toward a confusion of natures (a Monophysite/Eutychian Christology). How can we long for Christ's return in the flesh at the end of the age if he is already present bodily, on earth, at every Eucharist? And what is our resurrection hope if the body of our glorified head is so radically different from those of his members? The easy solution to this problem was Zwingli's: Christ is omnipresent in his divinity, but absent from us in his humanity.

Yet if Luther's view sounded too Monophysite (confusing the two natures), Reformed leaders like Calvin agreed with Luther that Zwingli verged on Nestorianism (separating Christ's two natures). Instead, the Reformed churches offered a unique formulation that differs as much (on key points, even more) from Zwingli as it does from Lutheranism. Reformed theology affirmed that Christ is ascended bodily and will return at the end of the age. As the angel told the disciples at Christ's ascension, "Men of Galilee, why do you stand looking into heaven? This Jesus, who was taken

---

24. Geoffrey W. Bromiley, *Zwingli and Bullinger* (Library of Christian Classics 24; Philadelphia: Westminster, 1953), 179–84; Zwingli, *Commentary on True and False Religion* (ed. Samuel Macauley Jackson and Clarence Nevin Heller; trans. Samuel Macauley Jackson; Durham, N.C.: Labyrinth Press, 1981), 214.

up from you into heaven, will come in the same way as you saw him go into heaven" (Ac 1:11). However, in the New Testament—as well as the early theologians of the East—Reformed writers discovered a key missing ingredient: the Holy Spirit.[25] In his Upper Room Discourse (Jn 14–16), Jesus prepared his disciples for his departure by promising the Spirit—"another Paraclete" (Attorney)—who would take what was Christ's and give it to us. The Spirit will unite us to Christ. In fact, because of the Spirit's ministry of the Word, Paul tells us that we are even now "seated … with [Christ] in heavenly places" (Eph 2:6). Therefore, Christ can be truly and really present in the Word and the sacraments, even though he is not yet on earth bodily, because the Spirit unites us to him by his mysterious operation. The Spirit effects this union and deepens our communion with Christ through preaching and sacrament. So the "sacramental union" of sign and reality is brought about not simply by the action of the sacrament or the priest, but by the Spirit, who "produces [faith] in our hearts by the preaching of the holy gospel, and confirms it through our use of the holy sacraments."[26]

So whereas Rome, Luther, and Zwingli concentrated on how Christ was or was not present *in the bread and the wine*, Calvin directed his attention to how Christ is present *in action* in the sacrament even though he is absent from earth in the flesh until his return. As strongly as Calvin rejected the Lutheran doctrine of ubiquity, he and his Reformed colleagues (other than those in Zurich) were convinced that they did not disagree with Wittenberg over the question of *what* was received in the Supper.[27] They affirmed the real presence of Christ in the *Supper*, but *through* the giving and receiving of the bread and the wine rather than *in* them. Christ gives himself with the bread and the wine, without being enclosed in these elements.

As in preaching and baptism, in the Supper the Spirit unites the sign to the reality. Here below are the bread and the wine, while Christ is bodily seated at the Father's right hand. Yet because of the Spirit's work, we too are seated with him. Although we do not see Christ bodily until his second coming, we nevertheless receive the whole Christ bodily in the Supper, through

---

25. Calvin, *Institutes* 4.14.9 and 4.14.12.

26. Heidelberg Catechism, q. 65, in Doctrinal Standards of the Christian Reformed Church, in *Psalter Hymnal*, 32.

27. B. A. Gerrish, *Grace and Gratitude: The Eucharistic Theology of John Calvin* (Minneapolis: Augsburg Fortress, 1993), 8. "Later, after Marburg," as Gerrish points out, "it was repeatedly argued that the point at issue between the Lutherans and the Reformed was no longer whether, but only how, the body and blood of Christ were present in the Sacrament. Calvin himself so argued." Since even Heinrich Bullinger (Zwingli's successor) came to embrace the sacramental union of sign and signified, the focus was on *what* is received (Christ and all of his benefits) in the Supper, rather than on the *manner* of eating—in other words, presence as such.

faith. Rather than transform the sign into the signified (Rome), confuse the sign and the signified (Luther), or separate the sign and the signified (Zwingli), Calvin affirmed that signs were "guarantees of a present reality: the believer's feeding on the body and blood of Christ."[28] In explicit contrast with Zwingli, Calvin held that the reality—Christ and his benefits—could be truly communicated to believers through earthly means. Otherwise, he says (appealing to Chrysostom), faith becomes a "mere imagining" of Christ's presence.[29]

Although Calvin's formative influence cannot be denied, it is important to recognize that he was articulating a view that was also taught by his Reformed peers (like Bucer, Vermigli, Musculus, Knox, and the later Cranmer) and their confessional successors. Therefore, with respect to *what* is received in the sacrament, the Reformed unanimously answered, in the words of the Belgic Confession, that it is nothing less than "the proper and natural body and the proper blood of Christ."[30] Reflecting Calvin's contention that there is no communication of Christ's benefits apart from his person, the Confession adds that "Christ communicates *himself with all his benefits* to us, and gives us there to enjoy *both Himself and the merits of His sufferings and death*: nourishing, strengthening, and comforting our poor comfortless souls by the eating of His flesh, quickening and refreshing them by the drinking of his blood" (emphasis added).[31]

---

28. Ibid., 165.

29. Calvin, *Institutes* 4.17.5–6.

30. Belgic Confession, art. 35, in Doctrinal Standards of the Christian Reformed Church, in *Psalter Hymnal*, 87–88. For the Reformed, the Supper gives the believing sinner the knowledge "that he personally was the object of that incomparable love" in Christ's sacrifice, "the personal assurance that all the promises of the covenant and all the riches of the gospel offer are his by a divine donation, so that he has a personal claim on them"; the Supper also "assures him that the blessings of salvation are his in actual possession." As a consequence, participation in the Supper is a profession of allegiance to Christ as King (Berkhof, *Systematic Theology*, 651). For Zwingli, although it is not entirely clear what he believed about the Supper consistently throughout his life, "for him the emphasis falls on what the believer, rather than on what God, pledges in the sacrament.... He denied the bodily presence of Christ in the Lord's Supper, but did not deny that Christ is present there in a spiritual manner to the faith of the believer. Christ is present only in His divine nature and in the apprehension of the believing communicant" (ibid., 653). The Reformed view followed Calvin, who rejected Zwingli's view on several counts, including the following: "(a) that it allows the idea of what the believer does in the sacrament to eclipse the gift of God in it; and (b) that it sees in the eating of the body of Christ nothing more nor higher than faith in His name and reliance on His death." For Calvin, the Supper has to do not only with Christ's work in the past, but with his work in the present. Though not present locally in the bread and wine, Christ's nevertheless gives "His entire person, both body and blood," through the meal (ibid., 653). The efficient agent of this sacramental union is the author of the mystical union itself: namely, the Holy Spirit. "This view of Calvin is that found in our confessional standards" (ibid., 654, citing Belgic Confession, art. 35, in *Psalter Hymnal*, 87–88; Heidelberg Catechism, qs. 75–76, in *Psalter Hymnal*, 36–37; and "Celebration of the Lord's Supper," in Liturgy of the Christian Reformed Church, in *Psalter Hymnal*, 143–59).

31. Belgic Confession, art. 35, in *Psalter Hymnal*, 87–88.

Typical of Reformed confessions, the Westminster Larger Catechism points out that the *mode*, not the *substance*, is spiritual.[32] Furthermore, it is crucial to bear in mind that "spiritual" here refers to a person—the Holy Spirit—and not to a merely intellectual or imaginary mode of feeding.[33] While Christ is not present on earth in the flesh until his return in glory, he is active in grace from his heavenly throne through the agency of his Spirit. Therefore, he can make himself the substance of the sacrament without bodily descending to the bread and the wine. Because of the agency of the Spirit, who unites us to the whole Christ in the first place, there can be a real communication of Christ's person and work to the church. It is not simply Christ's divinity but the Spirit who makes Christ's reign universally present, so that even Christ's true and natural body and blood can be communicated to believers. Thus, "the Spirit makes things which are widely separated by space to be united with each other, and accordingly causes life from the flesh of Christ to reach us from heaven."[34]

So the question is not how to relate spirit and matter, or divinity and humanity, but how Christ, being glorified in heaven, can be related to us in our present condition. Since this feeding is the work of the Spirit, its precise mode remains mysterious—something to be marveled at and enjoyed rather than explained. The Belgic Confession declares that while the mode "cannot be comprehended by us, as the operations of the Holy Spirit are hidden and incomprehensible ... we err not when we say that what is eaten and drunk by us is the proper and natural body and the proper blood of Christ."[35] The Spirit, in this view, is not a substitute for Christ, but is the agent who unites us to Christ and therefore communicates Christ and his benefits to believers.

How often should we celebrate the Supper? In answering this question, Reformed Christians have invoked the distinction between elements (that which Christ has ordained in worship) and circumstances (matters left to godly wisdom). Since the church has no authority to bind consciences

---

32. See, for example, the Westminster Larger Catechism, q. 170, in *Book of Confessions* (Louisville: General Assembly of the Presbyterian Church in the USA, 1991), 7.280. The catechism underscores this point by confessing that believers truly "feed upon the body and blood of Christ" (the substance of the sacrament), "not after a corporeal but in a spiritual manner; yet truly and really, while by faith they receive and apply to themselves Christ crucified and all the benefits of his death."

33. A. A. Hodge, *Evangelical Theology: Lectures on Doctrine* (Edinburgh: Banner of Truth Trust, 1976), 355.

34. John Calvin, "The Best Method of Obtaining Concord," in *Selected Works of John Calvin: Tracts and Letters* (ed. Henry Beveridge and Jules Bonnet; trans. Henry Beveridge; repr., Grand Rapids: Baker, 1983), 2:578.

35. Belgic Confession, art. 35, in *Psalter Hymnal*, 87–88.

beyond God's word, and there is no express command concerning frequency of Communion, this should be left to the discretion of each congregation.

At the same time, it should be said that one's view of the efficacy of Communion largely determines one's views concerning frequency. If the Supper not only is an occasion for us to exercise and strengthen our faith, but is itself a means appointed by Christ for the strengthening of our faith, then its celebration should be frequent. Paul referred to the Supper as being celebrated "when you come together as the church" (1Co 11:18; the phrase is repeated in verses 17, 20, 33, and 34—all in connection with Communion). Acts 2:42 gives us the elements of the service: "the apostles' teaching and the fellowship ... the breaking of bread and the prayers."

It has been noted often that the confessional theology of Reformed and Presbyterian churches often differs from their practice, with long seasons of preparation for Communion. Against the traditional medieval practice of infrequent communion Calvin offered a sustained plea that the Supper should be celebrated whenever the Word is preached, "or at least once a week."[36] "The Eucharist is the communion of the body and blood of the Lord," so infrequent communion is in effect, says Calvin, a withholding of Christ and his benefits from the covenant assembly.[37] In fact, only a year after the city of Geneva officially embraced the Reformation, Calvin's articles for worship (1537) stated, "It is certain that a Church cannot be said to be well ordered and regulated unless in it the Holy Supper of our Lord is always being celebrated and frequented."[38]

From the beginning Reformed and Presbyterian church orders and liturgical dictates called for "frequent" observance. "Calvin articulated a new conceptualization of 'liturgy' itself," according to Lee Palmer Wandel. "For him, certainly, the Supper was a drama, but the source of that drama was God. No human movement could add to that meaning in any way, no crafted object could draw greater attention to those earthly elements." She adds, "Perhaps most important of all, however, was Calvin's insistence on frequency. Most evangelicals condemned the medieval requirement of annual communion as nonscriptural.... But no other evangelical so explicitly situated the Eucharist within a dialogic process not simply of deepening faith,

36. Calvin, *Institutes* 4.17.44–46.

37. Mary Beaty and Benjamin W. Farley, eds., *Calvin's Ecclesiastical Advice* (Louisville: Westminster John Knox, 1991), 165.

38. John Calvin, "Articles concerning the Organization of the Church and of Worship at Geneva Proposed by the Ministers at the Council, January 16, 1537," in *Calvin: Theological Treatises* (ed. and trans. J. K. L. Reid; Library of Christian Classics 22; Philadelphia: Westminster, 1954), 48.

but of the increasing capacity to read the signs of the Supper itself, and by extension, of God, in the world."[39]

In both Roman Catholic and Zwinglian conceptions, the Eucharist was chiefly a human work, either of offering Christ again for sacrifice, or of remembering and pledging. However, says Wandel, "The Supper, for Calvin, was not 'external'—a ceremony ... nor even 'worship' in the sense that other evangelicals, such as Zwingli and Luther, used: a mode of honoring God." Rather, it is a means of binding us together more and more with Christ in an ongoing relationship in which "Christ 'is made completely one with us and we with him.'"[40] At the same time, God's grace establishes a union and communion with Christ that is simultaneously a union and communion with his body. To the extent that the Supper is at the heart of the church's life, it will generate a familial and communal bond of love.

We did not choose these people who eat and drink Christ's body and blood with us; the Father chose them in the Son, and the Spirit has united us to Christ and therefore to them. This is the ultimate family table that relativizes every other community, including our own blood relatives. Precisely because God gives the same gift—Christ with all of his benefits—to us all, equally, there are no first-class or second-class guests at the feast. That is Paul's point in 1 Corinthians 10 and 11. The church had imported social hierarchies into its worship and they must suspend the Supper's celebration until they examine themselves. This self-examination turns especially on their recognition of what the Supper is: the kind of body it gives to us (namely, Christ's) and the kind of ecclesial body that results. To eat and drink the bread and wine is to share in the body and blood of Christ (1Co 10:16–17), and to be made by the Spirit into his covenantal body. This inseparable connection between the vertical aspect (feeding on Christ) and its horizontal aspect (communion with his people) is underscored throughout Paul's argument. Like the word, the sacraments draw us out of our private rooms into the public dining room. Here we are coheirs at the family table, not consumers of exotic or meaningful religious experiences. Christ gives his body and we thereby become "one body by such participation."[41]

No part of the body can be injured without pain to the whole body, and the Supper not only illustrates this point, but is a means through which Christ actually effects our unity. "Accordingly, Augustine with good reason

---

39. Lee Palmer Wandel, *The Eucharist in the Reformation: Incarnation and Liturgy* (Cambridge: Cambridge Univ. Press, 2006), 171.

40. Ibid.

41. Calvin, *Institutes* 4.17.38.

frequently calls this Sacrament 'the bond of love.'"[42] In this sacrament, Christ makes himself the common property of all believers, Calvin insists, no believer possessing any greater or lesser participation in Christ or any of his benefits than the others.[43] There can be no participation in Christ that is not simultaneously a participation in each other.

Key Terms

- real presence
- transubstantiation
- communication of divine attributes/doctrine of ubiquity

Key Questions

1. What is the Old Testament background to baptism? How does the New Testament speak of baptism?
2. Who should be baptized, and is it appropriate to be baptized more than once?
3. What is the Old Testament background to the Lord's Supper? How is it connected to the "new covenant," especially in Jesus' institution and Paul's treatment in 1 Corinthians 10:16?
4. Discuss the different views of the Supper. Which one do you think is most biblical, and why?
5. How does the Supper bring together the vertical relation to God and the horizontal relation to each other, as well as to the wider world to which the event witnesses?
6. How important is the Lord's Supper to your own Christian life?

---

42. Ibid.
43. Ibid.

Chapter Seventeen

The Church

"Ecclesiology": study of church.

W ith Constantine's conversion and Edict of Milan (313), the era of imperial persecution of the church came to an end. Almost overnight, it seemed, pastors had gone from being human candles in Nero's garden to sitting at his successor's side at public functions. As Christ's kingdom became privileged and quickly fused with the empire, Christendom emerged. No longer the suffering flock to whom the book of Revelation was written, the church now seemed to hear the seventh angel announce, "The kingdom of the world has become the kingdom of our Lord and of his Christ, and he shall reign forever and ever" (Rev 11:15). The plea at the end of Revelation, "Come, Lord Jesus!" could still be heard in the liturgy of the great cathedrals, but it did not have quite the same urgency. After all, in the words of church historian Eusebius, "Our divinely favored emperor [Constantine], receiving, as it were, a transcript of the divine sovereignty, directs, in imitation of God himself, the administration of this world's affairs." With divine mandate, therefore, the emperor "subdues and chastens the open adversaries of the truth in accordance with the usages of war."[1]

Similarly, the modern era was shaped early in its infancy by the religious wars that divided Christendom. It was easy to go along with the official policy of the state church (engendering nominal membership), since dissenters were often persecuted. Once again, one had to *decide* to become a disciple of

---

1. Eusebius, *Praise of Constantine* 1.6–2.5 (*NPNF²*, 1:583).

Jesus, even in some cases with the possibility of martyrdom. With the rising emphasis on the freedom of the individual, the power of personal choice in a marketplace of goods and services, and the waning alliance of the powers in Christendom, the temptation to become assimilated to the culture was just as real as it had been under Christendom. However, in this case, it was a culture of individual choice and consumerism. Many churches became more like voluntary associations: a supermarket of personal spiritual identities.

It is perhaps easier for us today to see the ways in which the political culture of Christendom warped Christian discipleship and ecclesiology in the past, but more difficult to see the ways in which our beliefs about the church and its ministry are warped by democratic, egalitarian, and free-enterprise models of community. In our culture, formal communal ties crumble under the forces of consumer preferences and demographic affinities. Far from offering a counternarrative, with its distinctive doctrines, doxology, and discipleship, churches in our culture today are often captive in ways that we don't even recognize. We think we are a transforming influence when in fact we are in our own way, like Eusebius, christening the powers of this present evil age as if they were harbingers of the age to come. A church that fails to diagnose its own cultural infections will be absorbed into the bloodstream of this age that is passing away.

The last two chapters identified and explored the source of the church's existence: the Word, as the Spirit draws sinners to Christ—and they grow in Christ—through preaching and sacrament. Only after asking where the church comes from can we determine what the church is and why its mission is so crucial.

I. The Marks of the Church

Different views of the Word and the sacraments generate different views of the church. For example, it is of decisive importance whether one thinks that faith is assent to everything the magisterium teaches (as in Roman Catholic teaching), a personal choice that the individual makes to become born again (as in evangelical Arminianism), or the gift that the Spirit gives from the Father, in the Son, because the triune God chose us, redeemed us, and now calls us effectually to Christ. Understandably, the first view will tend to generate hierarchical models stressing the unity of the church in terms of a strict numerical "oneness"; the second fosters a more egalitarian and individualistic approach.

There are several points that distinguish the third view.

First, it emphasizes once again our union with Christ and therefore with fellow saints in all times and places in a covenant of grace. God's work, not the church's or the individual believer's willing and working, is the source of the church's existence. Preparing his disciples for his departure, Jesus taught,

> I am the true vine, and my Father is the vinedresser.... You did not choose me, but I chose you and appointed you that you should go and bear fruit and that your fruit should abide, so that whatever you ask the Father in my name, he may give it to you. These things I command you, so that you will love one another.... If you were of the world, the world would love you as its own; but because you are not of the world, but I chose you out of the world, therefore the world hates you.... But when the Helper comes, whom I will send to you from the Father, the Spirit of truth, who proceeds from the Father, he will bear witness about me. And you also will bear witness, because you have been with me from the beginning. (Jn 15:1, 16–17, 19, 26–27)

The church is neither a central agency with branch offices nor a group of individuals who decide to follow Jesus and therefore decide to start a church. Rather, it is a supernatural and eschatological reality that descends from heaven in the power of the Spirit through the means of grace (see Rev 21:9–27). On one hand, we cannot be born naturally into the kingdom; nor, on the other hand, is our new birth the result of human decision and effort. It is the gift of God from heaven. Just as each believer's salvation finds its origin in God's sovereign grace, so too the church collectively is the result of God's gracious plan, not ours. It is not simply a voluntary association that exists as the result of people choosing the same preferences.

Second, the view of the church that I defend in this chapter arises from the conviction that the Spirit unites us to Christ and makes us grow more and more into Christ (and therefore in communion with each other) through creaturely means. If the reality (the word of Christ) simply were *identical* with the sign (the word of the church), then the church's actions would simply cause God's grace to flow down the hierarchical ladder. If the reality is *separated* from the sign, then the Spirit's work will be reduced to immediate and private operations within individuals without any mediated and public ministry. At most, that public ministry of preaching, sacrament, and discipline can be only instructive, therapeutic, and advisory, but not authoritative in any sense. In such a view, public ministry is merely the ministry of human beings, not the ministry of Christ. The result is a church that exists because of the inner experience of individuals whose gathering together is primarily a means of fellowship, sharing each other's experiences of personal transformation.

Because it originates in the ministry of Word and sacrament, the church shares in but is not yet the fully realized kingdom of God. Its words and actions are always provisional and fallible—ministerial, but not magisterial. The church is the servant, not the Master. And yet it is through the ministry of this visible church that Christ's kingdom is present, growing in depth and breadth in all times and places. The church's *ministry*, not the authority of its servants or the piety of those who are served, determines whether there is a church. Though not fully realized, the kingdom is present—because the King is present in action by his Word and Spirit—wherever this ministry that he has ordained is executed. There are not two churches (visible and invisible), the real church consisting only of those who are truly born again and the false church of mere professors who go merely through the motions. The ministry of the church is not simply a witness to Christ and his work by his Spirit but is the service of Christ by his Spirit to and through his church.

All of these differences may be discerned in the definition of the "marks" of the church. In the Roman Catholic view, the true church is present wherever a local body is related organizationally and hierarchically to the papal office. The true church simply is the Roman Catholic Church: because it has the right ministers (the papal hierarchy in direct succession from the apostles), it has the right ministry—and always will have it. The church and its ministers guarantee the ministry, rather than vice versa. It is impossible for any local expression of this body to lose its ecclesial status as long as it remains in communion with its visible head, the pope, who is the vicar of Christ on earth. In fact, Christ is made present bodily on the altar by the priest's actions. This tends to emphasize the church as a historical organization. The Roman Catholic Church is the realized kingdom of God in earth in history.

In the radical Protestant (Anabaptist) view, affirmed by many evangelicals today, the chief mark of the church is the new birth; the true church is found wherever people are truly born again and exhibiting signs of genuine conversion and transformation. This tends to emphasize the church not as a historical organization but as a purely vertical (eschatological) event between God and the individual. It also gives priority to the activity of believers over the electing, redeeming, and renewing work of the triune God; the fruit over the root. Notice the reversal of this church-ministry relation, for example, in Menno Simons's claim, "Where the church of Christ is, there His Word is preached purely and rightly."[2] Elsewhere, he adds that "wherever sincere, brotherly love is found without hypocrisy, with its fruits, there we find the

---

2. Menno Simons, "Reply to Gellius Faber," in *The Complete Writings of Menno Simons* (ed. J. C. Wenger; trans. Leonard Verduin; Scottdale, Pa.: Herald Press, 1984), 623.

church of Christ."[3] By contrast, Calvin says, "If they have the ministry of the Word and honour the administration of the sacraments, they are undoubtedly entitled to be ranked with the Church, because it is certain that these things are not without a beneficial result."[4] These "marks" don't justify dead formalism; rather, the conviction is that where they are present, the Spirit is at work, because these are the means of grace that Christ appointed for the blessing and salvation of his pilgrim people.

A sound ecclesiology does not force a choice between the history and eschatology, organization and organism, letter and Spirit. Because it depends at every moment on the free work of the Father, in the Son, by the Spirit, the church can never take its existence for granted. It is always "hanging by a thread," as it were, and that thread is the Word and Spirit. Any particular church can lose its status as a true church when its ministry loses the true proclamation of God's word, so the only guarantee that a professing body is part of the true church is in heaven, where Christ is seated, not on earth where religious leaders and centers of power or charisma are located. The church is not evolving out of history, from acorn to oak tree, but is coming down from heaven as the gift of a bride for the Son. And yet, because God works through creaturely and historical means, there is a church throughout the world that endures from age to age.

The Reformation consensus has held that the true church is present "wherever the gospel is purely preached and the sacraments are properly administered according to Christ's institution."[5] There is one church, which is neither wholly invisible nor visible, but partially visible in word and Spirit. The terms *visible* and *invisible* refer to eschatological rather than philosophical categories. Inasmuch as it is "already" here, the kingdom is visible, but it remains invisible to the extent that it is "not yet" consummated.

Until Christ returns, the church will always be a mixed body of professing members with their children, consisting of wheat and weeds that must grow up together until the harvest (Mt 13:24–30). Regeneration is not the prerequisite for covenant membership; rather, it is through covenant membership that most people have actually come to a living faith. Christ hands over to ministers the authority to preach, teach, and administer the sacraments. He gives them, together with the elders, authority also to certify credible professions of faith and to look after the flock in his name. However,

---

3. Ibid., 740.

4. Calvin, *Institutes* 4.1.9.

5. The Belgic and Westminster confessions added discipline as a third mark. I discuss that mark below.

Christ never hands over to them the authority to determine whether the Spirit has truly regenerated someone. Not only is the church corporately a mixed body of regenerate and unregenerate; its regenerate members are also caught in this tension between the "already" and "not yet," simultaneously just and sinner.

Wherever Christ is present by his Spirit through the gospel, there is a church where faith is born and produces the fruit of righteousness. The objective Word always comes first, and we believe it even when we do not see or experience subjectively the full reality that it is calling into being. These marks are identified explicitly by Jesus in the Great Commission: preaching the gospel, baptizing, and teaching people to observe everything he commanded the apostles. The marks are also identified repeatedly in Acts as the means through which the Spirit created, expanded, and nurtured Christ's kingdom. At the same time, these marks are never exhibited perfectly in any church. Rather, they are exhibited in varying degrees.

In broad outline, then, these are some of the points that distinguish the different approaches to the questions before us in this chapter. The Reformed view seeks to avoid the extremes that are represented by (though by no means limited to) Roman Catholic ecclesiology on one hand and radical Protestant (Anabaptist, pietist, and revivalistic) views on the other.[6]

Roman Catholic	Radical Protestant
The one	The many
Corporate faith (assent to church teaching)	Personal faith (individual decision)
Sign and reality fused	Sign and reality separated
Hierarchical-aristocratic	Democratic-egalitarian
Centralized	Decentralized
Formal/ordered	Functional/spontaneous
Visible organization	Invisible fellowship

Whatever marks we identify as defining the church's very existence will reveal the message and the methods that define the church's mission. If the Roman Catholic tendency is simply to collapse the message (i.e., the gospel) into the methods (the sacraments) and secure their efficacy in the ministers (ultimately, the papal office), the radical Protestant impulse is to separate

---

6. I realize that I have so far (especially in the following chart) identified only extreme tendencies, leaving out a wide variety of views in between. I hope to rectify that in what follows.

them, as if the message is clearly defined in Scripture but the methods are indifferent, changing according to pragmatic circumstances.

As Paul makes clear in Romans 10, the means of grace that God has chosen are essential to and inseparable from the message that they deliver to us. "The righteousness that is by works" and "the righteousness that is by faith" yield completely different paths. The one ascends to the heights of heaven or descends into the depths, while the other path is from God to us: we are told simply to sit down and listen to Christ as he meets us in his word. He will create faith in our hearts to embrace this word by his Spirit. The marks of the church are the unchanging methods that guard the safe delivery of the unchanging message.

If this interpretation is correct so far, then there can be no contrast between the marks (the formal ministry) and the mission of the church (the informal activity of believers). The mission of the church is to exhibit the marks, and the purpose of the marks is to fulfill the Great Commission. Indeed, when the church is fulfilling this mandate through its formal ministry of Word, sacrament, and discipline, the whole body is built up and lavished with every good gift to distribute to their neighbors in daily witness and service.

II. The Attributes of the Church

The marks of the church disclose the source: that which distinguishes the church from all earthly societies. Different messages generate different methods, and together these generate different entities. The next question naturally follows: what then is the entity that the Spirit creates through Word and sacrament? What are its characteristics? Following common precedent, I will address this question by following the attributes mentioned in the Creed: "one holy, catholic, and apostolic church."

In treating each of these characteristics, it is worth bearing in mind the coordinates to which I have already referred.

First, there is the eschatological coordinate, with its "already/not yet" tension. Here we are dealing with the relationship between the church as an institution in history and the church as an eschatological event. The tendency is either to secure the identity of the church identity in an ancient and unbroken history (Roman Catholic view) or to emphasize its invisible, heavenly aspect to the point of obscuring God's covenant faithfulness from generation to generation (radical Protestant view).

Yes, the church is coming down out of heaven, from God, not simply enduring and evolving throughout history. Each citizen of this kingdom enters through the new birth, one by one. Nevertheless, it is also a covenant of grace extending from generation to generation. The same gospel, the same faith, the same Spirit, and the same ministry deliver the same gift—Christ and his benefits—to the same race of corrupt and condemned humanity. The message and the methods are already determined by the King; ambassadors do not change the policy of state according to their own authority. Because of the continuity of this message and the ministry for delivering it, the church endures from age to age—even though particular branches may wither or apostatize. No longer drawing their life from the Vine, they die and are cut off. However, God preserves a remnant throughout all times and generations in an unbroken succession of faithful ministry. Just as Communion participates in the wedding feast in the age to come while not yet being that consummated event, the church shares in the eschatological life of its Lord without yet experiencing his glorified existence. We live in that "already"/"not yet" tension.

The second coordinate is *union with Christ in the power of the Spirit*. Here again, the Roman Catholic tendency is to emphasize the outward, visible, and historical form of the church, while the radical Protestant tendency is to underscore the inward, invisible, and spiritual form of the church. How can we affirm the church's ever-essential dependence on the Spirit for its existence at every moment while also affirming that Christ's ministry by his Spirit is exercised through the ordinary service of his ambassadors?

In a Reformed perspective, although the Spirit is never the prisoner of the church, he binds himself freely to its outward ministry. Therefore, apart from this inner work of the Spirit, the church and its ministry are ineffectual, but the Spirit ordinarily works through the church and its ministry. The church is always dependent on the Spirit and can never take its identity for granted, but where this external ministry of the gospel exists, the Spirit is active among us. We look for the Spirit not in the extraordinary events that we might stage and manage, but in the ordinary events in which Christ has pledged his saving action.

Third, there is the *covenantal coordinate*. This one comes into play at many points in our ecclesiology. One important example is the tension between the church as "one" and "many." Once more, Roman Catholic ecclesiologies emphasize the former, and radical Protestants the latter. One of the most vivid ways in which the New Testament describes the covenantal union is by the concept of the *body of Christ*, with the related analogy of marriage. The body is united, not confused, with its head. Husband

(Christ) and wife (church) become "one flesh" mystically and covenantally (Eph 5:31–32). They become *one with* each other (*koinōnia*), *not one person* (*methexis*). Much less does the church replace Christ's natural body, which is glorified at the Father's right hand.

On the other hand, the church is not a collection of sovereign individuals. The source of the church's existence is not our willing or running, but God's election, redemption, and calling (Ro 9:16). This covenantal principle expresses itself not only in the local church, but in ever-expanding circles of communion. Just as the many members have fellowship in one local body, the many churches have fellowship with each other in one visible body throughout all times and places.

Now let's apply these coordinates to the attributes of the church.

A. Unity and Catholicity

Catholic means "universal," but although there are many global religions and corporations, they are not catholic in the sense that Christians intend. The catholicity of the church is distinguished by having been chosen by the Father, in the Son, and formed by the Spirit through the gospel. We are one in Christ: "one Lord, one faith, one baptism" (Eph 4:5). There is no catholic church in the world apart from the local churches that are covenantally (or federally) related to each other. It is not merely the case that the many churches are assimilated to the one visible church (as in a traditional Roman Catholic understanding), any more than the many churches are independent or autonomous (as in independent/congregationalist ecclesiologies). Rather, each local church is itself the church in the fullest sense, though only in communion with the other churches. Although there are important differences on church government, this point is strongly affirmed by Eastern Orthodox as well as Reformed churches.

The most common Greek noun for the church is *ekklēsia*, a compound meaning "those called out." The passive form underscores the fact that this community is not a voluntary association of those with similar interests, choices, and activities; rather, it comes into being as a result of God's purpose and energy. The church does not vote itself into being as the collective willing of the many. Nor are its unity and catholicity determined by an organizational connection to a particular office or minister; it is summoned into existence by the living and active speech of the triune God, who calls his people out of the world through the ministry that he has ordained. It is his act of speaking, not our act of faith (corporately or individually), that comes first. Hierarchy and democracy focus on human decisions and actions, while a covenantal view of catholicity focuses on God's decisions and actions through his ordained means.

In fact, the unity of the church is grounded in the covenant of redemption: the eternal election of a people in the Son and called into fellowship with Christ by the Spirit. Here we are talking about the invisible church—that is, the communion of God's elect. According to the Heidelberg Catechism, to affirm "one holy catholic church" means first of all, "I believe that the Son of God, through his Spirit and Word, out of the entire human race, from the beginning of the world to its end, gathers, protects, and preserves for himself a community chosen for eternal life and united in true faith. And of this community I am and always will be a living member."[7] In this sense, the one church consists of all who were chosen "in [Christ] before the foundation of the world" (Eph 1:4). Echoing Augustine, Calvin writes, "Now this society is catholic, that is, universal, because there could not be two or three churches. But all God's elect are so united and conjoined in Christ that, as they are dependent upon one Head, they also grow together into one body." It is this church that cannot be destroyed. It must always have its visible expression in every era. Nevertheless, this visibility is always ambiguous, because the visible churches bear the marks of faithfulness in varying degrees, the church is a mixed assembly, and even the elect are simultaneously justified and sinful.[8] Nevertheless, "God's firm foundation stands, bearing this seal: 'The Lord knows those who are his'" (2Ti 2:19).

Thus, when we talk of the **invisible** and **visible** church, we are not referring to two different churches (much less do they correspond to true and false, as sectarians often assume), but to the body of Christ as known to God in eternity and as known to us now as a mixed assembly. The Westminster Confession first defines the catholic church as "*invisible*," which "consists of the whole number of the elect, that have been, are, or shall be gathered into one, under Christ the Head thereof; and is the spouse, the body, the fullness of him that filleth all in all" (emphasis added). Yet in the next article, "The *visible* church, which is *also catholic* or universal under the gospel (not confined to one nation, as before, under the law), consists of all those throughout the world that profess the true religion; and of their children: and is the kingdom of the Lord Jesus Christ, the house and family of God, out of which there is no ordinary possibility of salvation" (emphasis added).[9]

---

7. Heidelberg Catechism, q. 54, in Doctrinal Standards of the Christian Reformed Church, in *Psalter Hymnal* (Grand Rapids: Board of Publications of the Christian Reformed Church, 1976), 27.

8. Calvin, *Institutes* 4.1.2–3.

9. Westminster Confession, ch. 25, in *Trinity Hymnal* (rev. ed.; Philadelphia: Great Commission Publications, 1990), 863.

Key Distinction:
invisible/visible church

It is helpful to distinguish between the *invisible* and *visible church*. Many confuse them, as if the visible church were identical to the full number of elect and regenerate — as if everyone who is baptized is united to Christ even apart from exercising faith in Christ. Others separate them, as if the visible church were merely a "man-made" organization unrelated to the spiritual church of the "truly saved." These are not two churches, but the church as God knows it now (as the communion of his glorified elect) and the church that is visible to us now in history (as a mixed body with even the elect as simultaneously just and sinner).

For all of its ambiguities, the visible church is Christ's flock, and no one can presume to belong to Christ without belonging to a true church.

Often, the church's unity seems questionable, to say the least. There are divisions between churches, even within churches, and some members fall away from the covenant. So how can we affirm the church's catholicity when there are so many independent denominations and local churches? Some Protestants are attracted to the easy resolution of this eschatological tension by embracing Rome or Orthodoxy, or perhaps a fundamentalist sect, as the one, true, visible, catholic church. This sort of move certainly relieves the burden of having to exercise spiritual discernment, but there are too many passages enjoining believers to that responsibility for us to surrender our mind, heart, and conscience to anyone or anything other than the Lord Jesus Christ.

With Scripture we must accept the fact that we are, for now, living at the intersection of this present evil age and the invading powers of the age to come. Where the means of grace are present, the Spirit is making the invisible church partially visible. And yet, "the creation waits with eager longing for the revealing of the sons of God" (Ro 8:19). We do not know the church yet as God knows it eternally, but we will share in this glorious revelation in the consummation. Furthermore, the church's Head is now already glorified, guaranteeing the participation of his whole body in his consummated existence. This one catholic church of those chosen, holy and blameless before the Father, is the reality in which the visible church now shares, but in an already and not-yet tension. Not only is this church a mixed body; even the elect are justified and sinful — pilgrims on the way, not the glorified saints who have arrived.

Once more we see how decisive it is that we determine first where the church comes from—that which constitutes its identity and is the source of its being.

The ministry of preaching and sacrament creates community, to be sure. Yet it is a covenantal communion (*koinōnia*) of persons united to Christ, not a fusion of persons. In the Reformed understanding, the church must always receive its existence anew. Because its existence depends on the Spirit through the ministry of Word and sacrament, that existence is always precarious. That is, the identity of any professing body as part of *the church* is always a gift to be received again and again, not a given to be taken for granted. Candlesticks can be removed, and branches can be broken off. The history of Christendom and liberal Protestantism testifies to the danger of being absorbed back into the bloodstream of this present evil age.

At the same time, there is covenantal succession, from generation to generation. Precisely because there is a written canon given once and for all, and proclamation of it, "the faith once and for all delivered to the saints" (Jude 3) continues to give birth to churches and keep them in that one catholic faith. The same Spirit who scattered the proud nations, confusing their languages to thwart the building of the Tower of Babel, united people from different tribes and tongues at Pentecost. Luke reports:

> Now there were dwelling in Jerusalem Jews, devout men from every nation under heaven. And at this sound [of people speaking the gospel in different languages] the multitude came together, and they were bewildered, because each one was hearing them speak in his own language. And they were amazed and astonished, saying, 'Are not all these who are speaking Galileans? And how is it that we hear, each of us in his own native language? Parthians and Medes and Elamites and residents of Mesopotamia, Judea and Cappadocia, Pontus and Asia, Phrygia and Pamphylia, Egypt and the parts of Lybia belonging to Cyrene, and visitors from Rome, both Jews and proselytes, Cretans and Arabians—we hear them telling in our own tongues the mighty works of God. (Ac 2:5–11)

One gospel, and many languages. It is not culture, socioeconomic position, education, market niches or language that unites. Nor is it one minister who unites. It is the one gospel that unites. In so doing, it preserves cultural, social, and linguistic diversity intact—just as the bread and wine remain what they are even when they are set aside for holy use in the sacrament.

In a bewildering variety of languages and tunes, we sing God's word together. The covenant draws people together in unity without subverting the rich diversity. Catholicity means not only that we are one, nor even that we are one in spite of our diversity; it means that we are one precisely with our diversity. Diverse gospels and methods for delivering it create niche markets rather than the catholic church. Although there will always be historical circumstances (such as slavery or immigration) that justify churches of one ethnic or linguistic background, this should never be regarded as the ideal over the long term. If individual consumer choice creates the church, then its local expressions will be divided along cultural, political, socioeconomic, or generational lines. Even within the same congregation today there may be essentially different churches (especially when they meet in different services). However, each local church is meant to be a microcosm of the "one catholic church." The only demographic location that unites us is "in Christ": "one Lord, one faith, one baptism." Each church should therefore strive to exhibit this catholicity in its common life together.

There are always churches within history that bear the marks of gospel ministry. In Reformed ecclesiology, it is not just the message — the doctrine — that endures, but the practices that convey it. This is why we confess the faith together in local and wider ecclesial connections, through the ecumenical creeds, confessions, and catechisms. It is why, when we gather for public worship, we sing a common faith across the generations, especially the Psalms; pray together with the whole church; and support the church's mission in the world and each other's spiritual and material welfare. After all, we are the children of Abraham, heirs of the covenant of grace.

We also experience concretely the unity and catholicity of the church when our local church participates covenantally in wider assemblies for mutual deliberation, correction, mission, and diaconal care. As I point out below, our ecclesiology is neither hierarchical (aristocratic) nor democratic (egalitarian), but representative (covenantal). Thus, we can affirm the church as a historical institution, with visible ministry and government enduring through generations, with the awareness that this is always a gift, not a given. God's gift comes from heaven to us, but the Spirit delivers it through creaturely-historical means. Again, this view fits with our understanding of the sign and reality in the sacraments. Although the Spirit's saving work cannot be held captive to the church's ministry (*ex opere operato*), that mysterious work is ordinarily done through the church's ministry. Just as there is a sacramental union of sign and reality, without fusion or separation, there is a historical succession of God's covenant people that is nevertheless dependent entirely on God's sovereign grace. If Christ's kingdom is not identical with its visible and historical institution, it also cannot be separated from it.

When Christ promised to build his church, he was not referring merely to a collection of believers but to a concrete organization.

A covenantal interpretation of the unity and catholicity of the church presses upon us the controversial question of church offices and government. By treating this question here, I am not suggesting (as some unfortunately have) that the specific form of government is somehow essential to the church's identity. However, I do believe that Scripture teaches a particular form of government that is consistent with its covenantal view of the church.

Eastern Orthodoxy holds that each local church is catholic through the representation of the bishop in the Eucharist, and true bishops must be consecrated in historical succession from the apostles. Each local church under episcopal[10] oversight is *autocephalous*—that is, with its own head, though in collegial communion with other churches. Bishops may be challenged or deposed, even by the laity, if they contradict the faith, but there can be no true church without a duly consecrated bishop. In the Roman Catholic understanding, it is not enough to have bishops who can (allegedly) trace their ordination to the apostles; the bishop of Rome is the "Supreme Pontiff of the Universal Church." This assertion of papal sovereignty, reflected in the oxymoron "Roman Catholic," has been regarded historically in the Christian East as an act of schism. The Catholic Church is *by definition* irreducible to one of its particular jurisdictions.

Protestant groups hold a variety of different perspectives on the question of church government. Lutheranism places church government in the category of "things indifferent" (*adiaphora*), and this is reflected in the diversity of its denominational expressions (ranging from episcopal to congregational in polity). Independent churches arose largely within the established church of early seventeenth-century England. A number of Anabaptist groups retained the office of bishop, but their bishops function more like pastors in the traditional Protestant sense, and episcopal government is by no means considered essential. Later, the "churchly pietists" basically adopted the Lutheran position on the question, while the "radical pietists" differed little from the position of the Society of Friends (Quakers), who rejected any distinct offices in the church.

Although some significant Reformed churches were episcopal (such as the Hungarian Reformed church and the Church of England) or congregational (such as the independents in England and New England), most are presbyterian. With some notable exceptions, especially during the Eng-

---

10. From *episkopos*, the NT word for "overseer" (e.g., Ac 20:28; 1Ti 3:2), from which we get the word *bishop*.

lish controversies of the late sixteenth and early seventeenth centuries, most Reformed churches have adopted the view that the form of government neither determines the very being (*esse*) of the church nor is indifferent (*adiaphora*). Rather, they hold that it is essential for the well-being (*bene esse*) of the church. It cannot be essential for the church's existence, since it is not explicitly identified as a mark of the church (though some Presbyterians have argued that presbyterian polity is included under "discipline"). Yet it cannot be indifferent if Scripture clearly teaches it. This is the position of the major Reformed confessions (French, Belgic, Scots, and Westminster).

I do believe that the basic structure of presbyterian government can be demonstrated from the New Testament. The covenantal connections that obtain between the members of the one body extend organically and organizationally between the churches. The New Testament refers to the church as wider than a local congregation (Ac 9:31; 1Co 12:28; Eph 4:4–16). Presbyterian government (from Gk. *presbyterion*, presbytery; i.e., council of elders) is connectional government, with spiritual authority spread out among elders and ministers — not only locally (the session), but in wider assemblies: presbyteries, general assemblies, and sometimes international synods.[11] We see this pattern in Acts 15, where a local church (probably a presbytery or group of congregations in Antioch) appealed its dispute to the broader assembly of the church. It is striking that several times the report refers to "the apostles and the elders" as the decision-making body. Commissioners (including Paul and Barnabas) were sent from Antioch to this synod at Jerusalem. In fact, it was James rather than Peter who said, for his part, "Therefore my judgment is that we should not trouble those of the Gentiles who turn to God" (v. 19). Still, the final verdict awaited the assent of the full assembly. "Then it seemed good to the apostles and the elders, with the whole church, to choose men from among them and send them to Antioch with Paul and Barnabas," to relate the written decision to that local church (vv. 22–29).

Already in the following chapter we see the wonderful effect of this decision, when Timothy joins Paul and Silas. "As they went on their way through the cities, they delivered to them for observance the decisions [*dogmata*] that had been reached by the apostles and elders who were in Jerusalem. So the churches were strengthened in the faith, and they increased in numbers daily" (Ac 16:4–5). A split was averted by the mutual correction and deliberation of this synod. Through these representatives, "the whole church" spoke with one voice and the Gentile mission exploded.

---

11. In the Continental Reformed churches, these same assemblies are designated consistories (local), classes (regional [CLASS-eez]; singular, "classis"), and synods (national).

One of the glories of the presbyterian system is that authority is spread out among many: to paraphrase Paul, "one session, many elders." The pastor is an elder who preaches and teaches (1Ti 5:17). Ministers are not distinguished from the other leaders by ruling authority but by their calling to the ministry of Word and sacrament. Furthermore, the other leaders (elders/overseers) are laypeople who are ordained to ruling office: hence, "ruling elders." This guards against clericalism, since the pastor is only one elder, with limited authority. No more than any other elder can the pastor exercise discipline or determine the church's confession and worship. Rather, pastors serve together with the ruling elders, and only *together* does this body exercise spiritual government. This same sharing of authority is evident in wider assemblies. It is therefore ironic when some evangelicals claim that the presbyterian system is hierarchical and clerical, leaving little place for nonpastors to exercise spiritual and diaconal leadership. On the contrary, in many independent churches today a local church or network is organized around the founder or lead pastor, with other teachers, preachers, and pastoral administrators in ranking order. In effect, this is an episcopal (sometimes even "papal") government, but without the checks and balances that even these more explicitly hierarchical models include.

In a presbyterian system, each local session is accountable to other sessions in the presbytery; if there is strife and if fraternal admonition is unsuccessful, the presbytery can exercise oversight and censure or even dismiss a minister. The presbytery and general assembly (or synod) are not *higher* offices than a local session, in a hierarchical sense, but merely a *broader* group of ministers and elders. Authority does not flow down the ladder, but back and forth between the churches in mutual edification and admonition. The model is not a pyramid but a network: that is, a covenantal community that is spread throughout the world. Like the embassies of nations, local and regional expressions of the visible church reflect their distinctive cultures and yet are never independent of the wider kingdom that endures in all times and places.

Elder-led government is clearly attested by the apostles, along with qualifications for holding this office (1Ti 3:1–13). Pastors and elders are "worthy of double honor," though for that reason, "Do not be hasty in the laying on of hands [in ordination]" (1Ti 5:17, 22). So important was this to Paul that he could remind Titus, "This is why I left you in Crete, so that you might put what remained into order, and appoint elders in every town as I directed you," again listing the qualifications (Tit 1:5–9). Significantly, when Timothy was discouraged because some criticized his youth, Paul replied, "Do not neglect the gift you have, which was given you by prophecy when the council of elders [*presbyterion*] laid their hands on you" (1Ti 4:11, 13–14). Even Peter addresses the elders as "a fellow elder" (1Pe 5:1). Pastors are "shepherds" who preach and teach (Eph 4:7–16; cf. 1Ti 4:11; 5:17).

Together, the ministers and elders are "overseers" or "bishops" (*episkopoi*), distinct from deacons (Ac 20:28; Php 1:1). Paul uses *presbyteros* and *episkopos* interchangeably (Tit 1:5–7). This point is affirmed in Clement of Rome's *Letter to the Corinthians* (AD 95).[12] Likewise, the *Didache* (AD 98) acknowledges "bishops [overseers] and deacons" as the only two orders.[13] Even as late as the fourth century, a theologian of such stature as Jerome could assume the presbyterian government of the early church and trace the gradual migration toward episcopacy (bishops as holding an office distinct from that of pastors). After adducing various passages in which the apostles "clearly teach that presbyters are the same as bishops," Jerome observed that presbyters selected one of their number as moderator of their meetings. Yet presbyters were "all alike of equal rank" in the apostolic era. In a letter, he repeated the point that "with the ancients these names [bishops and presbyters] were synonymous," and only grew into separate orders by later custom rather than from "an arrangement by the Lord."[14] In fact, the Second Helvetic Confession invokes Jerome's statement: "Before attachment to persons in religion was begun at the instigation of the devil, the churches were governed by the common consent of the elders."[15]

Writing in AD 376, Ambrose noted:

> After churches were planted in all places, and officers ordained, matters were settled otherwise than they were in the beginning. And hence it was that the Apostles' writings do not, in all things, agree with the present constitution of the Church; because they were written under the first rise of the Church; for [Paul] calls Timothy, who was created a Presbyter by him, a Bishop, for so, at first, the Presbyters were called.[16]

Even Pope Benedict and Orthodox theologian John Zizioulas observe that presbyterian government was the earliest form of polity.[17] This should

---

12. Clement of Rome, *1 Corinthians*, in *The Apostolic Fathers: Greek Texts and English Translation* (ed. Michael W. Holmes; 2nd ed.; Grand Rapids: Baker, 1989), 22–100.

13. *Didache*, in *Apostolic Fathers*, 246–69.

14. Jerome, "Letter 146 to Evangelus" and "Letter 64 to Oceanus," in "Earliest Textual Documentation," in *Paradigms in Polity* (ed. David W. Hall and Joseph H. Hall; Grand Rapids: Eerdmans, 1994), 57–58.

15. Second Helvetic Confession, in *Book of Confessions* (Louisville: General Assembly of the Presbyterian Church in the USA, 1991), ch. 18, 5.160–62.

16. Quoted in Samuel Miller, "Presbyterianism: The Apostolic Constitution," in *Paradigms in Polity*, 81.

17. Joseph Cardinal Ratzinger, *Called to Communion: Understanding the Church Today* (trans. Adrian Walker; San Francisco: Ignatius, 1996), 122–23; John Zizioulas, *Being as Communion: Studies in Personhood and the Church* (Crestwood, N.Y.: St. Vladimir's Seminary Press, 1993), 195.

at least qualify the claim of apostolic succession, much less the insistence that it is constitutive of ecclesial existence.

The same passages also challenge the arguments of independents (congregationalists). Could such local assemblies today receive the decisions of an ecumenical synod as binding dogma "to be observed" in every church, as we find in Acts 15 and 16? How can the term "church" belong only to a local congregation when the New Testament designates groups of churches as "the church"? It is difficult to know how an independent ecclesiology can affirm the reality of "one catholic" church except as the invisible church. For the visible church that we know and inhabit now, though, which is exclusively each congregation, visible unity and catholicity do not seem relevant categories.

B. Holy

Paul refers to the Corinthian church as holy, even though many of its members are scandalous in doctrine and life and there seems to be little discipline by the officers. Many ministers today address their congregations as holy and beloved, the chosen of God, redeemed, and "saints" in Christ even though there are probably some members who are not and even the regenerate members are "holy and blameless" objectively in Christ alone and will not be subjectively complete in Christ until their glorification. This view of "ecclesial holiness" stands in some contrast with both Roman Catholic and Anabaptist/pietist alternatives. Both tend to lodge the church's holiness in some quality inherent in the institution or in the collective piety of its individual members. However, Scripture locates this attribute, like the others, in the triune God and his covenantal grace.

I have argued that the Roman Catholic paradigm tends toward confusing things that ought to be distinguished: head and members, the one and the many, sign and reality, the "already" and the "not yet." This is evident also with respect to the church's holiness. According to official teaching, the Roman Catholic Church is "spotless": without error or sin. The one (church) is sinless, regardless of what the many (individual believers) do. According to the Catechism of the Catholic Church, "If they live her life, her members are sanctified; if they move away from her life, they fall into sins and disorders that prevent the radiation of her sanctity."[18] Although the Church itself already "exists without spot or wrinkle, the faithful still strive to conquer sin and increase in holiness. And so they turn their eyes to Mary:

---

18. *Catechism of the Catholic Church* (2nd ed.; Liguori, Mo.: Liguori Publications, 1994), sec. 827, citing Pope Paul VI.

in her, the Church is already the 'all-holy.'"[19] So the one church possesses this inner perfection in its essence, with holiness radiating or emanating in degrees from the highest to the lowest rungs. Over against the Augustinian emphasis on the church's holiness rooted in God's electing grace, Hans Urs von Balthasar writes that we therefore see "in the Church all gradations of holiness from the highest, most unsullied sanctity of Mary to the very brink of damnation, in fact even beyond it, in the case of the gravely sinful who are not yet, in some way, members of the Church."[20]

I have also argued that the radical Protestant paradigm separates these coordinates. In contrast to the Roman Catholic paradigm of *fusion*, radical Protestant movements have tended to lodge the church's holiness in the identifiable experience of the many (regenerate believers) as opposed to the collective identity of the one church. In the Roman Catholic perspective, the church makes the saints, while in the radical Protestant view, the saints make the church. This draws a sharp contrast between the Spirit's sanctifying work within believers and the visible means of grace. Like some of the more extreme monastic movements in the medieval era, Anabaptism defined the church not as a mixed body but as a pure congregation of the truly regenerate; radical pietism followed, first by developing conventicles and holy clubs of the truly converted within the established churches, which eventually became distinct denominations.

Both views, however, tend to lodge the church's holiness *within the inner condition of the church itself.* This is where we find the most striking contrast with a covenantal ecclesiology.

In a covenantal ecclesiology the church is holy because the covenant of grace is the sphere within which the Holy Trinity gathers, protects, and keeps a people set apart from the world. God has claimed certain ordinary times, places, and things as the theater of his gracious economy. What makes the Lord's Day holy is that the triune God has set it apart as a special time of his saving and sanctifying activity. What makes human speech, water, and bread and wine holy is that the triune God has set these apart as special media to which he has attached his promise. What makes the church holy is its election, redemption, and calling. The church—as both the one and the many—exhibits the fruit of this holiness in myriad ways, but *these are effects rather than sources of its holiness.* The body is not holy apart from the many members who compose it, but it is not holy because of the many members

---

19. Ibid., sec. 829.
20. Ibid., sec. 152.

who compose it. Neither the one church nor the many members, but the unique Head, constitutes the holiness of his body.

The Reformers and their heirs identify the church's holiness with its Head, Jesus Christ, in whom alone the visible church receives its "righteousness and sanctification and redemption" (1Co 1:30). The church's holiness is always a gift, not an attainment either of an institution or of a movement of individual believers. It is first and foremost God's claim on us, not our claim on God, that constitutes this holiness. This means that churches must struggle "to maintain the unity of the Spirit in the bond of peace" (Eph 4:3), even though this unity is already a gift that we have received by virtue of belonging to "one body and one Spirit" (v. 4). There is no pure church on earth, but only churches that bear the ecclesial marks in varying degrees, as the Westminster Confession puts well: "This catholic church hath been sometimes more, sometimes less visible. And particular churches, which are members thereof, are more or less pure, according as the doctrine of the gospel is taught and embraced, ordinances administered, and public worship performed more or less purely in them."[21]

On one hand, we do not believe that the visible church is perfectly holy and blameless subjectively now, but only objectively in Christ. Like its catholicity and unity, the church's holiness is constituted outside of itself, in the crucified, risen, and ascended Christ. The very people whom Paul "could not address ... as spiritual people, but as people of the flesh, as infants in Christ," are nevertheless infants *in Christ* (1Co 3:1). The letter is even addressed "to the *church* of God that is in Corinth, to those *sanctified* in Christ Jesus, *called to be saints* together with all those who in every place *call upon the name of our Lord Jesus Christ*, both their Lord and ours: Grace to you and peace from God our Father and the Lord Jesus Christ" (1Co 1:2–3, emphasis added). A church that is not sinful and does not sin is not a church at all, but a religious society that stands in defiance of grace and forgiveness.

"The purest churches under heaven," according to the Westminster Confession, "are subject both to mixture and error; and some have so degenerated, so as to become no churches of Christ, but synagogues of Satan. Nevertheless, there shall be always a church on earth, to worship God according to his will."[22] Even if only one parent is a believer, the children are holy (1Co 7:14). This is due not to any inner transformation or infused grace, but simply to God's promise. In covenantal thinking, the tree is holy even if some of its

---

21. Westminster Confession, 25.4–5, in *Trinity Hymnal*, 863.
22. Ibid.,

branches will finally fail to yield fruit and be broken off to make room for others (Ro 11:16–24). The tree is holy neither because it is collectively identical to Christ nor because it is the sum total of the regenerate, but because of the visible connection of the covenant people to their living root (v. 16, 18–20). At any given moment, in any local expression, the church will be a "mixed assembly" and yet the field of God's action where faith is created and sustained. The whole field is holy in this ecclesial sense, even though there are weeds sown among the wheat. This covenantal holiness means also that now in the new covenant the "clean" (holy) / "unclean" (common) distinction is no longer interchangeable with Jew/Gentile (Ac 10:1–11:18). In Christ, even the "unclean" are holy; strangers to the covenants and promises can become children of Abraham (Lk 3:8; Jn 1:12; Gal 3:13–18; 4:21–5:1; 1Pe 2:10), and their children can be holy to the Lord (1Co 7:14).

On the other hand, this objective holiness that the true church already possesses in Christ is partially revealed in this present age by the fruit of the Spirit. As the gospel claims and renames strangers to the covenant, the kingdom of God spreads in holiness. Yet in this time between the times, there is still the conflict between the holy and the common, the heirs of promise and a world that prefers the darkness to light. The divine claim that makes us holy also makes us aliens and strangers in this age. The church's holiness is attributed not only to the invisible church (i.e., those who are elect and regenerated), but to the visible church even as a mixed company. Cain, Esau, and Judas may sell their covenantal birthright. John could lament concerning those who denied Jesus as God in the flesh, "They went out from us, but they were not of us; for if they had been of us, they would have continued with us" (1Jn 2:19). Just as the visible catholicity of the church is threatened when we allow other lords to locate us under their dominion, the church's visible holiness is threatened when its words and ways become assimilated to cultural traditions and fashions. Nevertheless, neither the apostasy of some of its members nor the sins, errors, and weaknesses of the rest can vitiate the objective fact that in Christ the church is holy and is the sacred field that the Spirit tends.

Weary of its ambiguous location between the two ages (this present age and the age to come), a church that preaches another gospel or corrupts the sacraments is no longer holy, but is assimilated into the world—the age that is passing away—despite its outward forms (Gal 1:6–9; 1Co 3:10–17). We cannot deny that there will be those finally who hear these chilling words of Jesus Christ: "I never knew you; depart from me," although they protest that they performed wonders in his name (Mt 7:22–23). The lampstand of any particular church or group of churches can be removed when that body ceases to bear illuminating witness to Christ in the world (Rev 2:5). This tragic end may come upon a church not only for abandoning the doctrine of the gospel itself, but for failing to bear witness to it. Yet we have Christ's promise that he will build his church. Despite the church's compromised, ambiguous, schismatic, and sinful character, the covenant of redemption ensures that our unfaithfulness will not have the last word.

Grounded in the proper preaching of the gospel and administration of the sacraments, *discipline* holds its proper place as a mark of the true church. Christ's flock must be led not only in the pulpit, at the font, and at the table, but through faithful elders to whom he has given oversight of the sheep in doctrine and life. This is part of the ministry of the keys, taught by Jesus in Matthew 18, where the keys of the kingdom are given to the church's pastors.[23]

There is a remarkable similarity between Roman Catholic and Anabaptist conceptions of discipline. Both exhibit legalistic features. In the former case, sins can be forgiven only through the sacrament of penance. This includes private confession (with sorrow) of each sin committed and making satisfaction. The priest prescribes certain acts to make up for the offense, such as saying so many prayers, making a pilgrimage, even payment of money in the case of indulgences. Completing these steps, the penitent is absolved. However, the Reformers discerned a legalistic rigor among the Anabaptists as well. "Certain Anabaptists of our day conjure up some sort of frenzied excess instead of spiritual regeneration," Calvin warns. "The children of God, they assert, restored to the state of innocence, now need not take care to bridle the lust of the flesh, but should rather follow the Spirit as their guide, under whose impulsion they can never go astray."[24] They "imagine such a perfection as can never be found in a community of men."[25] The radical pietists often followed a more antinomian course. For these groups, church discipline was part and parcel of the externalism and formalism that subverted the individual's direct and spontaneous relationship with the Spirit.[26]

While avoiding these theories of penance and perfection, the Reformed

---

23. Although some Reformed theologians (Calvin, Bullinger, Zanchius, Junius, Gomarus, Van Mastricht, à Marck) identified only the preaching of the gospel and the administration of the sacraments as the marks of the church, others added discipline (Hyperius, Vermigli, Ursinus, de Brès), and the last came to expression in the Belgic as well as the Westminster confession.

24. Calvin, *Institutes* 3.3.14.

25. Ibid., 4.20.2.

26. Martin H. Schrag, "The Impact of Pietism upon the Mennonites in Early American Christianity," in *Continental Pietism and Early American Christianity* (ed. F. Ernest Stoeffler; Grand Rapids: Eerdmans, 1976), 115.

tradition has a high view of the biblical justification and spiritual good of church discipline. The church is a historical institution—a covenant community—to which Christ has entrusted the power of the keys, the authority to act in his name (Mt 16:19; 18:15–20; Jn 20:22–23). At the same time, Christ remains the sole head of the church. Ordinarily, he acts through his officers, but he is always free, by his word and Spirit, to have the last word. Yet we have access only to his human administration of this kingdom and must therefore respect the authority that Christ has given to ministers and elders in our spiritual affairs.

In Reformed teaching, the goal of church discipline is always restorative rather than punitive. The Westminster Confession explains,

> Church censures are necessary for the reclaiming and gaining of offending brethren, for deterring of others from like offenses, for purging out that leaven which might infect the whole lump, for vindicating the honor of Christ, and the holy profession of the gospel, and for preventing the wrath of God, which might justly fall upon the church, if they should suffer his covenant and the seals thereof to be profaned by notorious and obstinate offenders.[27]

Following Matthew 18, this goal is emphasized in our confessions and church orders. Excommunication is never the goal of discipline, but the last step after due process, which ordinarily requires the approval of the wider body (presbytery/classis). In fact, subjects of such discipline may appeal their case to these wider bodies. Sometimes not only individuals but local congregations are disciplined by the wider body for breaches in doctrine or practice, sometimes as much for too much severity as for too much laxity in local discipline. Again, the goal is not a perfect church, but one in which Christ reigns by his word, exercising his threefold office as prophet, priest, and king, for the good of his kingdom.

Actually, all members (including officers) are under church discipline in one way or another. That is, we are all under the spiritual and diaconal care of the church through its officers. Our Savior loves us too much to redeem his sheep only to leave them to wander or fall prey to wolves. "Remember your leaders, those who spoke to you the word of God. Consider the outcome of their way of life.... Obey your leaders and submit to them, for they are keeping watch over your souls, as those who will have to give an account. Let them do this with joy and not with groaning, for that would be of no advantage to you" (Heb 13:7, 17). As this passage underscores, discipline is a privilege

---

27. Westminster Confession, 30.3, in *Trinity Hymnal*, 866.

of church membership, not a liability. Any visible church that refuses to be regulated by God's Word loses its place in the holy church. This happens not when preaching sometimes veers from the true sense of Scripture or when there is an occasional irregularity in the administration of the sacraments, nor when there are occasions of too much laxity or too much severity in church discipline. Rather, a local church ceases to belong to the holy church when it no longer proclaims the gospel, completely vitiates the meaning and administration of the sacraments, or no longer recognizes the authority of God's Word over the doctrine, life, worship, mission, and government of the church.

Even the church's unregenerate members are in some sense beneficiaries of the Spirit's activity in the covenant community, which, according to Hebrews (esp. chs. 4, 6, 10), makes them all the more responsible for embracing the promises signified and sealed to them in baptism. The church is never the effectual agent, but the recipient and field of God's sanctifying work in the world: the theater in which the Spirit is casting and staging dress rehearsals of the age to come.

C. Apostolicity: The Mission of the Church

Chosen, redeemed, justified, and sanctified in Christ, we are made into "a holy nation": one, holy, catholic, and apostolic church. Each of these attributes of the church is vitally connected with the church's mission. More than that, they *are* the church's mission. The church's mission is to incorporate strangers into the family of God, calling sinners out of this passing evil age into the age to come. This church is brought into being, is sustained, and expands across all times and places only as a recipient of the gospel, in the power of the Spirit, through the means of grace.

Today, churches often seem to be polarized between the marks of the church and the mission of the church, and there are frequent debates between those who favor "traditional" and those who favor "missional" ministry. But there is not first of all a church, which then has a mission; the church is itself the result of the mission entrusted to it. It has been said that the church exists by mission as a fire exists by burning. Only as it proclaims the gospel to all nations, baptizes, and teaches everything that Christ commanded can we say that the church exists, much less that it fulfills its mission.

Of course, there is a certain attractiveness to this choice between traditional and missional approaches. Traditionalists may rest contentedly that they are fulfilling their responsibility simply by guarding sound doctrine and the public ministry each Lord's Day, undistracted by outreach. Missional churches may pride themselves in their outward-looking focus, undistracted by "churchianity." However, Christ's mandate imposes a greater responsibility on all of us. The mission of the church is to bear the marks of the church, not only "for [us] and for [our] children," but "for all who are far off, everyone whom the Lord our God calls to himself" (Ac 2:39). If we are not preaching the gospel, administering baptism and Communion, exercising spiritual oversight and temporal care for the saints, then we are not missional. Conversely, if we are not making disciples by these means, for both the upbuilding of the saints and the incorporation of strangers to the covenant, then we are not actually bearing the marks. *The mission is to bear the marks and to therefore plant churches that are part of the "one holy catholic and apostolic church."* In this statement the two aspects of this one calling are brought together.

To say that the church is apostolic, then, is to say not simply that it belongs to a long tradition deriving from the apostles, but that it is to be engaged in the mission that Christ entrusted to the apostles. In other words, to be apostolic is to be both confessional *and* confessing: to take the gospel to the world. Once again the same extremes are to be avoided. At one end is the tendency to identify apostolicity simply with a historical institution that claims an unbroken succession of *ministers*, from the apostles to the present. In this view, the church need not ask whether it is in touch with the faith of the apostles; it is apostolic—and will always be apostolic—simply because of an alleged historical continuity with the apostles themselves. On the other hand, there is the danger of separating apostolic mission from the marks, offices, and ministry of the church.

1. Apostolicity and apostleship

A professing church community cannot be identified as apostolic apart from its doctrine. It is the relation of our churches to the apostles' teaching, not to their persons or genealogy of ordination, that determines apostolicity. Accordingly, the gospel is the criterion for apostolicity, which means that because there is "one faith"—meaning the *fides quae creditur* (the faith that is believed)—there is historical continuity with the apostles. "The faith that was once for all delivered to the saints" (Jude 3) is the unbroken thread running from the prophets and apostles to us today.

In very different ways, Orthodoxy and Roman Catholicism as well as many Pentecostal groups identify the apostolicity of the church with the *office* of apostle. Accordingly, the Spirit's presence and activity are identified visibly with those holding this position, whether they received this office through historical succession or immediately from the Spirit. By contrast, churches of the Reformation identify the presence of the Spirit and the mark of apostolicity, once

again, with the word properly preached and the sacraments rightly administered. As I will argue below, Reformed traditions hold that the apostolic office ceased with the end of the apostolic era and therefore distinguish between the extraordinary ministry of the apostles and the ordinary ministry of pastors.

In the second century, Irenaeus emphasized that the authorized form of Christian faith and practice was defined by the apostolic writings and the ministers (bishops) who could trace their ordination to the apostles. Given the confusion of competing claims resulting from his ongoing conflict with gnostic sects, his apologetic is understandable. However, this argument from historical succession later evolved into a formal doctrine of **apostolic succession**. Today, the Orthodox East still holds that it is the "one holy, catholic, and apostolic Church," corporately preserved from error by an unbroken succession of its bishops from the apostles.

Though ancient Christian leaders of the East accorded great respect to the Roman bishop, they never accepted his supremacy. Cyprian, among others, warned that any assertion of episcopal primacy would constitute schism. Such a privilege was even rejected by Pope Gregory the Great in the sixth century. He expressed offense at being addressed by a bishop as "universal pope": "a word of proud address that I have forbidden.... None of my predecessors ever wished to use this profane word ['universal'].... But I say it confidently, because whoever calls himself 'universal bishop' or wishes to be so called, is in his self-exaltation Antichrist's precursor, for in his swaggering he sets himself before the rest."[28]

It is impossible on historical grounds to support a definition of apostolicity based on the doctrine of apostolic succession. However, my concern at this point is more theological. Aside from the question of papal authority or even apostolic succession through a valid episcopate, the deeper issue is *whether the church is saved by law or gospel*. Christ's commands for the government and discipline of his church are to be obeyed. However, any understanding of the church that defines a particular polity into the essence of the church *assimilates* the gospel to law. The danger is that we end up substituting the church — perhaps even a single denomination — for the gospel itself, a move that, as Yves Congar laments, is actually made in Roman Catholic theology.[29] According to the Cardinal Hosius, a theologian of Trent, "the living gospel is the Church itself."[30]

---

28. Gregory I, *Letters* (in *NPNF²*, vol. 12), i.75–76; ii.170, 171, 179, 166, 169, 222, 225.
29. Yves Congar, *I Believe in the Holy Spirit* (New York: Crossroad, 1999), 154.
30. Ibid., 153.

Mercifully, the church is not the living gospel, but is instead the recipient of the good news that despite its unfaithfulness God will keep his promise. What remains inviolable is the "election of grace," a gift of God rather than a given of historical existence. There will always be a visible church with a valid ministry and public forms; however, because this visibility is constituted by the word and sacraments, any professing community can lose its connection to this apostolicity. Whether by privileging the visibility of a historical institution or the invisible power of the Spirit at work in the lives of its members, the church can lose its focus on God, yet the church is apostolic only to the extent that it is the site of the Trinity's disrupting and reorganizing grace through the Word.

2. Offices and gifts

According to the **regulative principle** embraced by Reformed Christians, the church cannot prescribe as necessary for true faith and practice anything that is not commanded in Scripture. In public worship, for example, there are *elements* (such as preaching, confession of sin, prayer, baptism, the Supper, singing, and alms giving) and *circumstances* (such as the appointed time and order of services, liturgical forms, architecture, musical style, and so forth). Making everything in the church's worship and church order an element, even apart from any biblical warrant, is legalistic; making everything a circumstance, in spite of biblical command, is antinomian. Since they were matters not specifically commanded in Scripture, decisions regarding circumstances were left to sanctified wisdom, and churches were free to change them at their discretion, in the light of their time and place.

The Spirit, who sometimes disorders the settled life of the church when it does not conform to his word, also reorders it, so that the church is always being built up. This upbuilding takes place across generations through a public, ordered, and disciplined ministry. Wherever the word is preached and the sacraments are administered, a desert blossoms into a lush garden with the streams of living water. In the chaotic use of spiritual gifts in the church, one may edify oneself, but will not build up the church, Paul warns (1Co 14:4, 15–17). "Let all things be done for building up," he exhorts. "For God is not a God of confusion but of peace" (vv. 26, 33).

For Lutheran and Reformed traditions, apostolicity is identified with the apostolic preaching of Christ by which the church's speech and action are determined. A church is not apostolic because its office bearers trace their ordination to the apostles nor because it enjoys an ongoing charismatic ministry of revelation and prophecy—nor, I should add, because of its presbyterian government. Rather, it is apostolic because it passes on what it has heard from this qualitatively unique circle of ambassadors appointed by Christ in his earthly ministry. As an *eschatological* and *Spirit-filled* community, the church is always put in question as to its apostolicity and must receive it ever anew from the word and Spirit. As a *covenantal* community, it is historically continuous from generation to generation. A biblical view of apostolicity refuses to set the formal against the informal, the external and visible against the internal and invisible.

An apostle was Christ's own representative, even if perhaps "an ambassador in chains" (Eph 6:20). Even Timothy, who is a minister in the ordinary office rather than an apostle, is said to be "our brother and *God's coworker* [*synergon tou theou*] in proclaiming the gospel of Christ" (1Th 3:2, author's trans.). Even when the apostles were living, the saints were gathered weekly for the ministry of Word and sacrament. "They devoted themselves to the apostles' teaching and the fellowship, to the breaking of bread and the prayers" (Ac 2:42). Through this ministry, "day by day the Lord added to their number those who were being saved" (v. 47). The centrality of the word is incontestable from the apostolic mission in Acts. Wherever growth occurs, it is attributed to the Word (Ac 6:7; 12:24; 19:20). It is the Word (more accurately, the Spirit through the word) that prevails against unbelief.

At a bare minimum, then, a true visible church is recognized by this continuity with the apostolic proclamation. "Where the gospel is preached," there is a church; where a professing body fails to proclaim this message, or distorts and contradicts it, it cannot be considered a valid visible church. If it is possible for a church that is in fellowship with the living apostles to become a false church (Gal 1:6–9; 3:1–10; 4:11, 20; Rev 2–3), then it is surely possible for churches in fellowship with their ministerial successors to have their lampstand removed.

The Reformers identified Roman Catholicism and Anabaptism as evidencing "enthusiasm" by insisting that the apostolic office remains open, and that from holders of that office there may still come fresh revelations. The New Testament, however, draws a clear line between the *extraordinary ministry* of the apostles and the *ordinary ministry* of pastors and elders (1Ti 6:20; 2Ti 1:13–14). The apostles were eyewitnesses of Christ, and Paul himself asserts his apostleship on the basis of having received it directly and immediately from Christ rather than from the church (Gal 1:11–23). However, the apostles clearly distinguished their extraordinary office from the ordinary one of ministers. What the apostles received directly from Christ, they pass on—without ecclesiastical sanction. However, assisted by elders, ministers must diligently teach and must refute anything that "is contrary to sound

> ## Key Distinction:
> ### extraordinary/ordinary (ministry)
>
> Sometimes the triune God works directly and apart from means, as in the creation of the world. This is his extraordinary work. More regularly, though, God works through ordinary means. Even in miraculous activity, God usually works through creaturely means. Applied to the Spirit's ministry in the history of revelation, this distinction holds that the extraordinary ministry of the prophets and apostles is qualitatively distinct from the ordinary ministry of the pastors, elders, and deacons who followed the foundation-laying era of the old and new covenants.

doctrine, in accordance with the gospel of the glory of the blessed God *with which I have been entrusted*," says Paul (1Ti 1:10–11, emphasis added). The distinction is qualitative, not quantitative. The apostles heard Christ directly, and their proclamation and writings were "breathed out" by the Spirit (2Ti 3:16), whereas we now, illumined by the Spirit, hear Christ through the word of the prophets and apostles, through the mouth of pastors and teachers.

While there were certainly unwritten traditions in the apostolic era that were nevertheless binding on those who received them, all of those traditions that are normative for the whole church in all times and places have been committed to the canon. Furthermore, the offices for which Paul provides instruction to Timothy, in transition from the extraordinary apostolic ministry to the ordinary ministry that Timothy signals, are those of pastor/overseer (*poimēn, episkopos*), elder (*presbyteros*), and deacon (*diakonos*). While God "gave apostles and prophets" (Eph 4:11), and the gifts of healing, languages, and prophecy were exhibited in the extraordinary ministry of the apostolic era, there are no instructions in these epistles for the ordination of the apostles' successors to their office.

Through the extraordinary ministry of the prophets and apostles the Spirit delivered Christ's canon by inspiration, constituting the new covenant community; through the ordinary ministry of pastors, the Spirit guides the church by illumination as it is being shaped and normed by that constitution. Just as the event to which the apostles bore witness is unique, unrepeatable, and completed, their office is extraordinary and unique in the church's history.[31] Paul describes himself as part of the foundation-laying episode in

---

31. See especially Richard Gaffin Jr., *Perspectives on Pentecost* (Phillipsburg, N.J.: P&R, 1989).

the church's history, adding, "For no one can lay a foundation other than that which is laid, which is Jesus Christ" (1Co 3:11). I take this to be a reference not only to the content but to the historical-eschatological uniqueness of the apostolic ministry. Paul is not issuing an imperative not to lay another foundation but is simply stating an indicative: another foundation *cannot* be laid.

Now at last, the typological offices of prophet, priest, and king that had been reserved for special office-bearers in the old covenant were realized in Christ as the Head and in his whole body as his members. In the new creation, the office of prophet, priest, and king that was part and parcel of being created in God's image was restored. "But you are a chosen race, a royal priesthood, a holy nation," Peter tells believers in Christ (1Pe 2:9). All believers hold this threefold office in Christ. They receive the same gift of grace, but are also given different graces for specific tasks. *different purposes*

In Ephesians 4:7–16, the apostle says that the offices of prophets and apostles as well as pastors, teachers, and evangelists are gifts of Christ's heavenly ascension. Through this ministry, Christ builds up his body in sound doctrine. All believers are prophets, priests, and kings in their **general office**. Together they walk in godliness and spur each other on in the apostolic doctrine, faith, and good works. They are "filled with the Spirit, addressing one another in psalms and hymns and spiritual songs … submitting to one another out of reverence for Christ" (Eph 5:15–21).

Romans 12 and 1 Corinthians 12 expand the list. In addition to the gifts pertaining to the ministry of the Word (prophecy, teaching, and exhortation), there are the gifts of service and hospitality, healing, helping, administrating, tongues and their interpretation, giving, and mercy. Some of these gifts are exercised in the special offices of elders and deacons, but all of them are exercised in a general way by the whole body. Therefore, Christ exercises

Key Distinction:
general/special office

The church is both a divinely ordained organization and a Spirit-empowered organism, with special offices (pastors, elders, and deacons) as well as the general office (prophet, priest, and king) shared by all believers equally. All believers are priests, with Christ as their only Mediator; nevertheless, only some believers are called to special offices in Christ's body for the service of all.

his public ministry of Prophet, Priest, and King through the special office of pastors, deacons, and elders, respectively, but these gifts are also distributed in varying degrees beyond the officers to the wider body.

The controversial question arises as to whether any of these gifts has ceased in the church. Particularly in the wake of the Pentecostal and charismatic movements, this question has divided Christians into two camps: cessationists (believing that the gifts of healing, prophecy, and tongues have ceased) and noncessationists. Noncessationists find no exegetical reason to distinguish some of these gifts and offices from others in terms of their perpetuity. However, cessationists hold that the New Testament itself makes a distinction between the foundation-laying era of the apostles and the era of building the church on their completed foundation (1Co 3:10–11). Although the New Testament establishes the offices of pastors/teachers, elders, and deacons, it does not establish perpetual prophetic or apostolic offices with their attendant sign-gifts.

Miraculous signs always cluster in the Bible around significant turning points in redemptive history. Like the temporary prophesying of the elders in Moses' day, the extraordinary gifts of signs and wonders are given to validate the sacred ministry of human ambassadors. Once that ministry is validated, it no longer requires further confirmation.[32] It would seem, then, that the gift of prophets and apostles (along with the gifts of miracles, prophecy, and tongues) was given but fulfilled its foundation-laying function. Just as Paul's understudy Timothy is an ordinary minister, we find no evidence that his ministry was attended by extraordinary signs and wonders.

Today, the Spirit validates this ordinary ministry of the gospel. Today, God continues to speak his word of judgment and grace, but through illumined rather than inspired preaching. Today, the sacraments are the signs and wonders that Christ instituted to confirm his word to us.

Apostolic succession, like all other attributes of the church, is therefore determined by the *content* of the church's ministry rather than by the historical succession of *persons* ordained to office. At the same time, those who minister in Christ's name must be called to that office by Christ through the agency of the church: they cannot send themselves on the basis of an inward call alone, but must be sent, which again emphasizes the mission as concerned chiefly with heralding good news (Ro 10:14–15). Analogous to the Father's sending of the Son and the sending of the Spirit by the Father and

---

32. For an excellent treatment of this topic, see Gaffin, *Perspectives on Pentecost*, esp. 94–95, in relation to Wayne Grudem's contention that "prophets" and "apostles" in 1Co 12:28 and Eph 4:11 refer to the same group.

the Son, and their joint-commission of the apostles, the calling and sending of pastors and elders to their local post comes from the wider church, and the local church sends its representatives to its wider assemblies. Because these leaders do not send themselves (any more than the Son or the Spirit sent himself), and their commission from God is tested and validated by the church that bears the marks, their hearers can be assured that the leaders are not speaking on their own authority when they bring good news. The ordinary ministers do not receive their gift and commission directly from God alone, as the apostles did, but through "the laying on of the hands of the eldership [*presbyteriou*]" (1Ti 4:14, author's translation).

The church's order, government, liturgy, and discipline do not create the church; the Spirit does this, working through the Word. Nevertheless, God's Word creates a real, concrete, visible society over which Christ reigns as Savior and Lord. Under Christ, each believer has been gifted for a particular function in the one body. "If the whole body were an eye, where would be the sense of hearing?" (1Co 12:12–26). Every part, therefore, does not do the same thing. As the pastoral epistles elaborate, the transferable aspects of the extraordinary apostolic vocation have been entrusted to the ordinary offices of pastors and elders. The authority that Christ delegates to ministers, elders, and deacons is real, but it is unlike the domination exercised by Gentile rulers. Although all believers are prophets, priests, and kings in Christ, this identity depends on the fact that Christ has called some believers to particular offices as servants of the word, deacons, and elders.

The triumphant indicative ("All authority in heaven and on earth has been given to me") is the basis for the imperative ("Go therefore and make disciples of all nations, baptizing … [and] teaching," Mt 28:18–20). This explains the link between Christ's bestowal of the Spirit on the disciples and his commission to them to mediate his royal authority. The ministry of reconciliation draws together the marks (word, sacrament, and discipline) and further links the marks and mission of the church. We must therefore resist the false choice between looking after the sheep already gathered through preaching, sacrament, and discipline (the marks) and reaching out to the lost sheep, who have yet to hear and believe (the mission). Peter draws no contrast between ministering the gospel to covenant members (believers and their children) and mission to the world (Ac 2:39). Instead, there is an ever-widening circumference, as the ecclesial body expands through the apostolic teaching, the Supper, the fellowship, and the prayers (vv. 40–47). Confessional Protestants typically focus on the apostles' teaching, independent evangelicals and Pentecostals on fellowship and evangelism, and more liturgical bodies on "the breaking of the bread and the prayers," while more liberal groups concentrate on caring for material needs. However, a genuinely apostolic and missional church must strive to integrate all of these concerns.

The church therefore not only makes disciples; it is the place where disciples are made, not just once but throughout their Christian life. The orderly worship of the saints gathered in weekly assembly for preaching, teaching, and witness *is* missional (1Co 14:23–25). The word that is preached, taught, sung, and prayed, along with baptism and the Eucharist, not only prepares us for mission; it is itself *the* missionary event, as visitors are able to hear and see the gospel that it communicates and the communion that it generates. To the extent that the marks define the mission and the mission justifies the marks, the church fulfills its apostolic identity.

Key Terms

- apostolic
- apostolic succession
- regulative principle

Key Distinctions

- invisible/visible church
- ordinary/extraordinary (ministry)
- general/special office

Key Questions

1. What is the source of unity and catholicity according to the Scriptures?
2. What is the difference between the visible and invisible church? How are the two related?
3. How do the churches relate to the one church in the New Testament teaching?
4. Are there apostles (or their apostolic successors) today?
5. What are the *marks* and *attributes* of the church? How do we relate the eschatological (i.e., the church as God's work from above) and the historical (i.e., the church as an institution in history)?
6. What is the church's mission?

Chapter Eighteen

The End Times

Human beings were created as covenantal creatures and given a commission. We were aimed at the glory that lay up ahead after the trial: namely, confirmation in everlasting blessedness in God's Sabbath rest. But we, in the person of our covenantal head, failed to execute our office and were corrupted. Now, in our current situation we have a problem. Apart from hearing God's law, we still think we are capable of fulfilling the trial ourselves, doing what Adam failed to do. We may admit that we have lost our way a bit, but we tend to believe that with the proper instructions and the right motivation, we will be able to ascend the hill of the Lord and stand in his holy place. Our follies may take individualistic or collective forms of mysticism, moralism, and cultural advancement, but they are all towers of Babel. On our various paths of foolish ascent our Lord passes us by in his descent to save sinners. As we build our towers reaching to the heavens, the New Jerusalem descends to the earth as a gift.

By nature, we are creatures who hope, longing for someone to tell us not only who we are but where we're going. Is there something more than life "under the sun"? Is our destiny greater than just a random accident on an accidental planet, where we create a few thrills for ourselves until our lives dissolve into the abyss of nothingness? Tell me something that I haven't heard before, something that gives me a reason to look forward to the future, so that my life even now will be more than a succession of events, more than Post-It notes to myself.

We need a paradigm shift. Our orientation needs to be recalibrated to Christ's victory rather than to our projects and programs. All of this leads us to a question, as we wind our way from creation through the fall and redemption and its application by the Spirit through the means of grace to our lives as pilgrims in Christ's church.

What comes next?

I. Death and the Intermediate State

There is no part of us that is divine or that possesses divine attributes, such as eternity and immortality. From our soul to our fingernails, we are creatures through and through. Christ may return before you die, but in case he does not, everyone—believer and unbeliever alike—will face the reality of death at some point. Death is not theoretical. It is a well-established fact. God is "the blessed and only Sovereign ... who alone has immortality" (1Ti 6:15–16; cf. 1Ti 1:17), and yet this creaturely worldliness God pronounced "very good" (Ge 1:10, 18, 21, 25, 31). Forming man from the dust, God "breathed into his nostrils the breath of life, and the man became a living creature" (Ge 2:7). God created Adam as mortal: as subject to the possibility of death, though not yet its actuality. Just as Adam was capable of obedience and disobedience, he was capable of living and dying. Had he fulfilled the covenant of creation, Adam would have secured for himself and Eve and all of us the right to eat from the Tree of Life. This immortal life is not merely a continuation of unfallen existence (*bios*), but the entrance of humanity for the first time into a new way of being alive (*zōē*). As it is after the fall, we are dying from the moment that we are born. Immortality is not something that we possess by creation, but is a gift of redemption in Christ, "who abolished death and brought life and immortality to light through the gospel" (2Ti 1:10). And it is not only the soul but the body that "must put on immortality" in the resurrection (1Co 15:53). Indeed, the soul will not be saved *from* the body and this world of matter; rather, as whole persons we will be redeemed fully with "the redemption of our bodies" (Ro 8:23), and even the whole created world will share in this liberation (vv. 20–23).

This means that the death of human beings is not part of a natural cycle; it is the curse for disobedience (Ge 2:17; 3:19, 22; 5:5; Ro 5:12; 8:10; 1Co 15:21). As such, it is not a friend. Rather, it is "the last enemy" (1Co 15:26). Looking to our glorified Head, we are already assured of our future destiny; therefore, we do not fear death as an everlasting curse (Ps 23:4; Heb 2:15;

Ro 8:38–39; 1Co 15:55–57; Php 1:21–23; 2Co 5:8). For unbelievers, this death is merely the harbinger of "the second death": everlasting judgment (Rev 20:14).

It is striking to see news images of Middle Eastern people wailing over their deceased loved ones, compared to the relative calm that marks funerals in more stoic cultures. Jesus belonged to the former world. With each step closer to the tomb of his friend Lazarus, Jesus lost his composure. Even though he knew that he would raise Lazarus (temporarily) and be raised himself as the everlasting Life of his coheirs, Jesus was gripped with angry awe as he stared his gruesome enemy in the face (Jn 11:33–36). The same "great lamentation" ensued among the faithful gathered at Stephen's martyrdom (Ac 8:2). Christ has removed the sting of death for believers, because he has borne its curse: "the sting of death is sin, and the power of sin is the law" (1Co 15:54–57; cf. Jn 14:2–3; Php 1:21; 2Co 5:8). However, believers still feel death's bite.

We refer to what happens at death as the **intermediate state**, not the ultimate or **final state**. The soul does not "pass on" into an eternity from which it allegedly came. Rather, it is preserved in blessedness until it is finally reunited with our resurrected flesh on the last day. A Christian perspective on death is poised between two extremes. At one end is the Greek myth of the exiled soul, perhaps best articulated in Plato's *Phaedo* (esp. 64a–67b). Immortal and eternal, the soul of each person belongs to the universal soul from which it has fallen but is now imprisoned in a material body. In this view, the *goal* of life is death, understood as liberation from the bodily carapace to ascend finally to its original home. Among others, Philo of Alexandria imported this vision into early Judaism, as Origen of Alexandria brought it into Christianity. Remarkably similar views may be found in Eastern religions (especially in doctrines of karma, samsara, and reincarnation) and in the popular mysticism of the West, from Gnosticism to the New Age movement. From Mary Baker Eddy, founder of Christian Science, the language of

Key Distinction:
intermediate/final state

At death, the souls of believers are immediately present with the Lord (2Co 5:8). This is a wonderful consolation. Nevertheless, this condition is only temporary (hence, "intermediate"), as we anticipate "the resurrection of the body and the life everlasting" in a new heavens and earth.

"passing on" has come into the Christian vocabulary. People don't die, they just fade away. Like all evils (including the body), death, according to Eddy's theosophy, is an illusion that we must resist through intellectual enlightenment: "mind over matter." In this trajectory of mysticism, death is a friend, our portal to eternity.

If the Platonizing trajectory makes the intermediate state ultimate, the opposite extreme denies the intermediate state altogether. This view, known as **physicalism** or materialism, denies that there is a soul that can exist separately from the body. This view is held by atheistic materialism, though some modern Jews and Christians have recently argued that the distinct existence of a soul, and thus its immortality, is a Greek rather than biblical concept.[1] Only with the resurrection does the person come to self-consciousness again. This, in my view, is an overreaction.[2] Although biblical eschatology gains greater clarity and detail as the story of redemption unfolds, Jon D. Levenson (among others) has documented the early Jewish belief in the soul's survival at death.[3] In addition, a denial of the intermediate state is impossible to reconcile with clear passages in Scripture, which are hardly influenced by Greco-Roman visions of souls wandering throughout the realm of shadows or crossing back and forth over the River Styx ferried by Charon. Rather, they are made part of the company assembled at the true Zion, with "innumerable angels in festal gathering" and "the assembly of the firstborn who are enrolled in heaven, and to God, the judge of all, and to the spirits of the righteous made perfect, and to Jesus, the mediator of a new covenant" (Heb 12:22–24). Scripture teaches that immediately upon death the soul of a believer joins the saints at "Abraham's side," in the conscious presence of the Lord with inexpressible joy (Pss 16:10; 49:7–15; Ecc 12:7; Lk 16:22; 23:43; Php 1:23; 2Co 5:8; Rev 6:9–11; 14:13). Jesus told the believing criminal, "Today you will be with me in Paradise" (Lk 23:43), even though Jesus himself would not be raised until the third day, and when Jesus died, he cried out, "Father, into your hands I commit my spirit!" (v. 46). The body apart from the spirit is dead (Jas 2:26); yet for believers, to be absent from the body is to be present with the Lord (2Co 5:8).

---

1. This view is taken by G. B. Caird, *The Language and Imagery of the Bible* (Philadelphia: Westminster, 1980), 244; Wolfhart Pannenberg, *What Is Man?* (trans. Duane A. Priebe; Philadelphia: Fortress, 1972), 46–47; Nancey Murphy, *Bodies and Souls, or Spirited Bodies?* (Cambridge: Cambridge Univ. Press, 2006).

2. For an excellent defense of the orthodox view, see John W. Cooper, *Body, Soul, and Life Everlasting: Biblical Anthropology and the Monism-Dualism Debate* (Grand Rapids: Eerdmans, 1989).

3. Jon D. Levenson, *Resurrection and the Restoration of Israel: The Ultimate Victory of the God of Life* (New Haven, Conn.: Yale Univ. Press, 2006); cf. Kevin J. Madigan and Jon D. Levenson, *Resurrection: The Power of God for Christians and Jews* (New Haven, Conn.: Yale Univ. Press, 2008).

At the same time, the intermediate state is just that: intermediate. It is an unspeakable pleasure to be in the presence of God, but ultimate salvation is not "going to heaven when you die." Even in heaven, "the souls of those who had been slain for the word of God and for the witness they had borne" cry out from before God's throne, "O Sovereign Lord, holy and true, how long before you will judge and avenge our blood on those who dwell on the earth?" (Rev 6:9–10). Until the resurrection and last judgment, then, our final deliverance is not yet complete (Ro 8:23). We possess immortality in promise, with Christ's resurrection as the firstfruits and the Spirit within us as the security deposit; only at our bodily resurrection will we possess it in reality.

II. The Millennium and Its Debates

In his Olivet Discourse (Mt 24–25), Jesus laid out a clear sequence of events between his two advents. This was in answer to his disciples' query, "Tell us, when will these things be, and what will be the sign of your coming and of the end of the age?" (Mt 24:3). This question itself was provoked by Jesus' remark that the temple will be destroyed (vv. 1–2). First, Jesus said, there will false messiahs, "but the end is not yet" (v. 6); wars, earthquakes, and famine, but "all these are but the beginning of the birth pains" (v. 8). Enemies of his followers will "deliver [them] up," as they did Jesus, with many falling away. "But the one who endures to the end will be saved" (vv. 9, 13). None of this counts against Christ's promise that he has inaugurated his kingdom and that the gates of hell will not prevail against it, for even through such persecution he will build his kingdom by his gospel. "And this gospel of the kingdom will be proclaimed throughout the whole world as a testimony to all nations, and then the end will come" (v. 14).

Here Jesus gives us a wide-angle view of the time between his two comings: the first, when he came in grace, and the second, when he comes in glory. First, "the abomination of desolation": the temple will be destroyed, and some of his hearers will live to see this (v. 15, 34). Disciples will be scattered from Jerusalem in the wake of this momentous event, and should be warned against false claims that Christ has returned (vv. 16–27). "Immediately after the tribulation of those days," Jesus tells us, "all the tribes of the earth ... will see the Son of Man coming on the clouds of heaven with power and great glory. And he will send out his angels with a loud trumpet call, and they will gather his elect from the four winds, from one end of heaven to the other" (vv. 29–31). We do not know how long "the tribulation of those days" (v. 29) is going to last. No one knows when Jesus will return—even

Jesus himself—but only the Father; it will come when no one is expecting it (vv. 36–44). Then the Son of Man will sit on his throne, judging the world, welcoming his sheep into everlasting glory and sending the goats "into the eternal fire prepared for the devil and his angels" (25:31–46).

It is easy to summarize Jesus' sequence of events: (1) destruction of the temple in Jerusalem ("the abomination of desolation" [Mt 24:15], which occurred in AD 70); (2) "the tribulation of those days" (v. 29), involving a long period of persecution, apostasy, general calamities, and yet the progress of the gospel throughout the world; (3) the coming of the Son of Man from heaven; (4) the gathering of the elect; and (5) the last judgment.

The immediate recipients of the book of Revelation would certainly have recognized themselves in our Lord's description of the great tribulation, as would believers today who are enduring fierce persecution for the name of Christ. In a series of snapshots, Revelation moves back and forth between heavenly and earthly scenes of persecution and ultimate victory. In vivid apocalyptic imagery, Revelation reprises the history that Jesus summarized in his Olivet Discourse. In both of these accounts, the next event we are awaiting is the return of Christ to judge the living and the dead and to consummate his everlasting kingdom.

On the basis of such summaries, most Christians through the ages have held that the present age is marked simultaneously by suffering and the triumph of the gospel. Christians confess that Jesus Christ "will come again in glory to judge the living and the dead, whose kingdom shall have no end." This hope includes "the resurrection of the body and the life everlasting." Given our propensity for disagreement over end-times scenarios, this represents a remarkable Christian consensus. We cling to the angel's promise at Christ's ascension: "This Jesus, who was taken up from you into heaven, will come in the same way as you saw him go into heaven" (Ac 1:11). He came first in humility and grace, but will return in glory and power.

Where paths diverge among Christians today is on the question of a literal **millennium**—that is, a thousand-year reign of Christ. The only biblical passage that speaks directly of such an era is Revelation 20. In a vision John beholds an angel descending from heaven to bind "that dragon, that ancient serpent, who is the devil and Satan ... so that he might not deceive the nations any longer, until the thousand years were ended" (vv. 2–3). "After that he must be released for a little while" (v. 3).

> Then I saw thrones, and seated on them were those to whom the authority to judge was committed. Also I saw the souls of those who had been beheaded for the testimony of Jesus and for the word of God.... They

came to life and reigned with Christ for a thousand years. The rest of the dead did not come to life until the thousand years were ended. This is the first resurrection. Blessed and holy is the one who shares in the first resurrection! Over such the second death has no power, but they will be priests of God and of Christ, and they will reign with him for a thousand years. (vv. 4–6)

After the thousand years, Satan is released for a final time (the "little while" mentioned in verse 3), before the last battle, which concludes with the final banishment of Satan and the false prophet to the flames where "they will be tormented day and night forever and ever" (vv. 7–10). These events are followed by the last judgment, with Death and Hades thrown into the lake of fire along with all whose names are "not found written in the book of life" (vv. 11–15), and the arrival of the new heavens and earth (chs. 21–22).

Interpreting the "thousand years" in Revelation 20 symbolically (along with other numbers in this highly symbolic book), the church has traditionally held that the kingdom of Christ is present on earth now, but will be consummated only when Christ returns. This perspective is usually called amillennialism (no-millennium).[4] However, this is a bit of a misnomer. Far from denying the reality expressed symbolically by "a thousand years," with Satan chained so that the gospel may have free sway, amillennialists embrace the present rather than the future as this golden age of harvesting the nations.

Obviously missing from Jesus' summary as well as from Revelation 20 are events that many other Christians today are expecting before the return of Christ, especially the following: (1) the rapture of believers before a seven-year tribulation period, (2) the beginning of the tribulation, with the rise of something like the United Nations or European Union, (3) the emergence of the Antichrist, a false messiah who will lead this empire, (4) a war that Antichrist will wage against Israel (perhaps with the aid of Russia or, more recently,

---

4. Among the best recent defenses of amillennialism are Kim Riddlebarger, *A Case for Amillennialism* (Grand Rapids: Baker, 2003); G. K. Beale, *The Book of Revelation: A Commentary on the Greek Text* (New International Greek Testament Commentary; Grand Rapids: Eerdmans, 1998), especially his excursus on the kingdom. Recent defenses of postmillennialism include Keith Mathison, *An Eschatology of Hope* (Phillipsburg, N.J.: P&R, 1999), and John Jefferson Davis, *The Victory of Christ's Kingdom: An Introduction to Postmillennialism* (Moscow, Ida.: Canon, 1996). George Eldon Ladd's works remain standard as an interpretation of historic premillennialism, but an outstanding recent defense of this view is found in Craig Blomberg and Sung Wook Chung, eds., *The Case for Historic Premillennialism: An Alternative to "Left Behind" Eschatology* (Grand Rapids: Baker Academic, 2009). A classic statement of classic dispensational premillennialism is Charles Ryrie's *Dispensationalism* (rev. and exp. ed.; Chicago: Moody Press, 2007), and the view known as progressive dispensationalism (considered below) is defended in Craig A. Blaising and Darrell L. Bock, *Progressive Dispensationalism* (Grand Rapids: Baker Academic, 2000).

Islamic nations), and (5) the return of Christ with his saints (including those raptured) to establish his millennial kingdom, a literal one-thousand-year reign, with the renewal of the Sinai theocracy, including sacrifices in a rebuilt temple. After this, there will be (6) another fall or rebellion in the millennial kingdom itself, after which Christ will (7) return with all of the saints, including those who had been raptured, to (8) judge the nations and then (9) judge the saints for rewards in heaven. Then finally arrives (10) the eternal state. This view is associated with **dispensational premillennialism**, formulated by John Nelson Darby (1800 – 1882). This view of the end times was popularized by the C. I. Scofield Reference Bible, prophecy conferences, Bible colleges, and a vast network of Christian pastors and radio and television ministries. Revived especially by the popular *Left Behind* novels of Tim LaHaye and Jerry Jenkins, dispensationalism is taught by John MacArthur, Charles Ryrie, and many others; it is popular also among evangelicals and Pentecostals in the Global South. Dispensationalists believe that Israel and the church are two completely different groups and that God has a distinct program for each.

Besides amillennialism and dispensational premillennialism, there are other major end-time views among evangelical Christians: especially, **historic premillennialism**. This view differs from dispensationalism in various ways. It does not necessarily distinguish so sharply between Israel and the church and either rejects or questions many of the details in the dispensationalist scheme. Nevertheless, historic premillennialists agree that Christ will return before a literal thousand-year millennium. As its name suggests, **postmillennialism** holds that Christ will return after a literal thousand-year reign. Where premillennialism tends to think of history in terms of decline and catastrophe (especially in the dispensationalist version), postmillennialism expects the gradual improvement of the church and, as a result of its influence, the world at large.

In contrast with all these views, amillennialism cannot be characterized as optimistic or pessimistic. Rather, it is a paradoxical view of these last days: optimistic about the success of the gospel throughout the world, while expecting this triumph to proceed through an era marked by common ills (natural disasters, wars, injustice) and the persecution of the church from without and the continuing struggle with sin, false teaching, and schism from within. Only when Christ returns to establish his everlasting reign will this tension between the "already" and the "not yet," this present age and the age to come, be finally resolved. In the meantime, God's common grace keeps this present evil age from total entropy—especially for the purpose of keeping open that hole in history that Jesus' ascension created for the planting and growth of a vast field that he will harvest on the last day.

According to an amillennial interpretation, we should not assume that biblical prophecy is weighted toward the past or the future. Rather, it is part of the "already"/"not yet" dialectic of redemptive history. Since Christ's ascension and the descent of the Spirit at Pentecost, we have been living in "the/these last days" (Ac 2:17; 2Ti 3:1; Heb 1:2; Jas 5:3; 2Pe 3:3; Jude 18; 1Pe 1:20; 1Jn 2:18), before the "last day" (Jn 6:39, 40, 44, 54; 11:24; 12:28). Paul says that "the end of the ages has come" (1Co 10:11). Nevertheless, there is more ahead. Christ appeared "at the end of the ages" (Heb 9:26), yet spoke of "the coming age." That "age to come" is even now breaking in upon us through preaching and sacrament (Heb 6:5). It is a period in which the kingdom has been inaugurated by Christ's earthly ministry, empowered by the Spirit, advanced through witness to the gospel, consistently opposed by the world even to the point of great tribulation for the saints. Christ is reigning in grace from heaven by his Word and Spirit. Yet he will return in power and glory on the earth. With his second coming will arrive the resurrection of all the dead and the last judgment as one single and sweeping event. In this perspective, believers are not awaiting a series of intervening events and regimes, but Christ's return in judgment and resurrection-power. Although he favors the premillennial view, Wayne Grudem observes, "This [amillennial] scheme is quite simple because all of the end time events happen at once, immediately after Christ's return."[5]

Paul understood Christ's reign as "already" and "not yet": "For he must reign until he has put all his enemies under his feet. The last enemy to be destroyed is death" (1Co 15:25 – 26). Even those who receive the signs and seals of the covenant without embracing the reality itself are nevertheless "enlightened ... have tasted the heavenly gift, and have shared in the Holy Spirit, and have tasted the goodness of the word of God and the powers of the age to come" (Heb 6:4 – 5). If this is true of those who eventually fall away, how much greater is the reality that believers embrace (v. 9)? The presence of the Spirit in our hearts as a pledge (*arrabōn*) of the consummation ensures that what he has begun in us he will complete. The Spirit brings the blessings of the age to come into the present, which fills us not only with unspeakable joy but also with unutterable longing for the "more" still up ahead. The strong man is bound (Mt 12:28 – 29; Lk 10:18), so that the

---

5. Wayne Grudem, *Systematic Theology* (Grand Rapids: Zondervan, 1994), 1110.

veil of unbelief may be torn from the eyes of Satan's prisoners. Christ has triumphed over Satan at the cross, and in his resurrection and ascension he has led captivity captive. According to the epistles, Christ is now reigning (Ac 2:24–25; 3:20–21; 1Co 15:25; Heb 1:3, 8, 13; 8:1; 10:12–13). For this reason, Jesus can assure his persecuted saints, "Fear not, I am the first and the last, and the living one. I died, and behold I am alive forevermore, and I have the keys of Death and Hades" (Rev 1:17–18).

In this interim period, the kingdom advances alongside the suffering and even martyrdom of its witnesses. Yet Christ "will appear a second time, not to deal with sin but to save those who are eagerly waiting for him" (Heb 9:28; cf. 10:37). As we have seen, the regeneration of all things works in concentric circles, beginning with the inner person and then, at the consummation, including the resurrection of the body and the complete renewal of creation. Wherever the New Testament treats the complex of Christ's return, the resurrection, and the last judgment, no intervening raptures, resurrections, or judgments are mentioned. Grudem believes that in John 5:28–29 Jesus refers to two resurrections, with "those who have done good [coming out] *to the resurrection of life*, and those who have done evil to *the resurrection of judgment.*"[6] However, Jesus' reference here is not to two separate *events* but to two separate *destinies*.

If Revelation 20 were straightforward historical narrative—or even prophecy—we would follow the dictum of dispensationalism to interpret it "literally wherever possible." However, the apocalyptic genre of the entire book is to be taken seriously on its own terms. To take symbols literally is not to take them in their natural sense. Dispensationalists certainly recognize that there is much in Revelation that is symbolic. In fact, symbolic interpretations sometimes border on the fanciful.[7] So both positions allow for symbolic interpretation of what are obviously symbols.

The question, then, is whether we should interpret Revelation in the light of biblical apocalyptic (especially in Ezekiel and Daniel) or as secret codes to be cracked by daily news headlines. The prophets used numbers not as a

---

6. Ibid., 1119.

7. For example, Hal Lindsey identifies the "two wings of the great eagle" in Revelation 12 with a massive airlift of Jews fleeing the Antichrist's pursuit. "Since the eagle is the national symbol of the United States, it's possible that the airlift will be made available by aircraft from the U. S. Sixth Fleet in the Mediterranean" (*There's a New World Coming: A Prophetic Odyssey* [Santa Ana, Calif.: Vision House, 1973], 179). Similarly, the locusts in Rev 9 are probably Cobra helicopters. The means of torment described may even be "a kind of nerve gas sprayed from its tail" (ibid., 138–39). For decades, dispensationalists have identified the Antichrist and other end-times figures with contemporary individuals, movements, and nations. Even though these predictions prove erroneous, the same author often finds a willing audience for a new set of predictions.

secret language but as another way of conveying truth. For example, "Ten thousand times ten thousand" is an idiom referring to a great multitude (Da 7:10). Also in Daniel, the saints will suffer tribulation at the hand of a blaspheming king for "a time, times, and half a time" (7:25): three and a half times—that is, half of the total time of seven judgments (4:16; 9:27). Seven is the number of God, enthroned in his Sabbath rest, and six is the number of the sinful empire that sets itself against Yahweh and his Anointed. Every seventh day is a Sabbath, and in the old covenant there were also annual and jubilee-year Sabbaths: the "sevens" multiply, layer upon layer, to lead Israel to hope in a greater Sabbath rest. The detailed measurements of the heavenly city in Revelation 21 (vv. 10–17) are based especially on Ezekiel's prophecies. If we were to take these as literal measurements of an edifice, it would contradict the point that the rich symbolism supports: namely, that in the age to come there is no local temple at all, since the whole cosmos is the sanctuary, "for its temple is the Lord God the Almighty and the Lamb" (v. 22). These prophetic symbols direct us to Christ, not to the nation of Israel or political intrigues in the daily news. Especially in the light of the straightforward statements of Jesus and the rest of the New Testament, it makes better sense to interpret the thousand years of Revelation 20 as symbolizing the present reign of Christ. In this perspective, the part of John's vision that we find in Revelation 20 happens in heaven, not on earth, and in the present day, not simply in a future event. The whole book is meant to be read not chronologically but as snapshots of the current age of the church from a heavenly point of view and to provide comfort and assurance to the suffering church by testifying to the final triumph of the Lamb.[8]

With good reason, premillennialists wonder how we could interpret Revelation 20 as occurring now, when it seems obvious to them that Satan is not bound and that he is in fact deceiving the nations. Yet if Satan were not currently bound—if he were free to rule and reign over the earth—there could be no church, much less one that endures through the centuries despite heresy and schism. Christ clearly promised that he would build his church and that not even the gates of Hades would be able to withstand its assaults (Mt 16:18). In addition, premillennialism must somehow explain how Christ's glorious reign in power for a thousand years following his return can conclude with yet another "falling away."

---

8. On this interpretation, see Richard Bauckham, *The Theology of the Book of Revelation* (Cambridge: Cambridge Univ. Press, 1993), 7. In Revelation John was "taken up into heaven in order to see the world from the heavenly perspective. In fact, John mentions that it was 'on the Lord's day,' which highlights the Christian Sabbath as the sign participating in the reality." See also Dennis Johnson, *Triumph of the Lamb: A Commentary on Revelation* (Phillipsburg, N.J.: P&R, 2001).

It is true, as Grudem observes, that Revelation 20 speaks not only of Satan being bound but of his being thrown into the bottomless pit.[9] Yet here again it is quite consistent with prophecy, especially apocalyptic, to understand this as a telescoping of this action, encompassing both the period of his being bound (now) and the consummation of his judgment (destruction in the future). He still "prowls around like a roaring lion, seeking someone to devour" (1Pe 5:8), but this is consistent with an amillennial interpretation of Revelation 12, where Satan is cast out of the heavenly sanctuary, unable to affect the outcome of redemption, and yet persecutes the church on earth. This interpretation underscores the point that it is the ministry in the heavenly courtroom that is decisive and that whatever Satan is allowed to do on earth is finally nothing more than the desperate and futile struggle of a defeated foe.

Grudem refers also to 2 Corinthians 4:4, where it is said that "the god of this world has blinded the minds of the unbelievers, to keep them from seeing the light of the gospel of the glory of Christ."[10] Yet it is precisely Satan's being bound that finally thwarts this effort. To the ends of the earth, the blind see. Grudem also refers to 1 John 5:19, where it is said that "the whole world is in the power of the evil one."[11] However, when read together with the many passages indicating that the kingdom has been inaugurated, is progressing through the gospel, and that all authority now belongs to Christ in heaven and on earth, such passages reveal that the imprisonment of the world is precisely *the condition that Christ's kingdom of grace is overturning*. At present, he is looting Satan's kingdom, liberating captive hosts in his train. The world lies in darkness, but a growing remnant in every nation has seen a great Light.

For amillennialists, the already/not yet tension will not be resolved until Christ returns. Just as Christ's life was both humiliation and exaltation, the church suffers even as it fulfills its mission to bring the gospel to the ends of the earth. Neither a kingdom for which we are still waiting nor a kingdom that we must bring about, Christ's reign in grace is a kingdom that we are even now receiving from heaven.

Moreover, in response to Grudem's argument that the Old Testament prophecies (such as the wolf dwelling with the lamb) anticipate "a momentous renewal of nature that takes us far beyond the present age,"[12] we may again

---

9. Grudem, *Systematic Theology*, 1118.
10. Ibid.
11. Ibid.
12. Ibid., 1128.

appeal to principles of prophetic interpretation. Apocalyptic language draws on natural images to express the force of major turning points in redemptive history. Even in secular literature of the ancient Near East, wolves and lambs, serpents and doves, routinely describe the violent and peaceful condition of nations. Furthermore, the telescoping pattern of prophecy anticipates penultimate (semirealized) and ultimate (fully realized) fulfillments.

We have to recall the context and purpose of the Apocalypse. John's strange and wonderful visions were given by Christ first of all for the comfort of early Christians who were suffering extreme persecution under the Roman Empire. The book begins, "The revelation of Jesus Christ, which God gave [John] to show to his servants *the things that must soon take place*.... Blessed is the one who reads aloud the words of this prophecy, and blessed are those who hear, and who keep what is written in it, *for the time is near*" (Rev 1:1, 3, emphasis added). A greeting is then offered to the seven churches in Asia Minor.[13] These are actual churches in John's day. They are to be comforted by the fact that Christ is now already "the firstborn of the dead, and the ruler of kings on earth," who "has freed us from our sins by his blood and made us a kingdom, priests to his God and Father.... Behold, he is coming with the clouds, and every eye will see him, even those who pierced him, and all tribes of the earth will wail on account of him. Even so. Amen" (1:5–7). Jesus is preparing his flock for imminent slaughter, assuring them that he is now already king over all powers and authorities and that he will, in due time, return to set everything right (1:17–18). Great persecution did come upon the church and has continued uninterrupted in various parts of the world ever since. The events interpreted in Revelation lie neither entirely in the past nor entirely in the future, but encompass "these last days" that begin with Pentecost and end with the full arrival of the age to come at Christ's appearing.

According to an amillennial interpretation, then, we are presently living in the "thousand years" of Revelation 20, longing not for a literal millennium with yet another fall into sin but for the everlasting kingdom of righteousness and peace that will dawn with Christ's return in judgment and restoration. Borrowing imagery from the natural world, we can say that God promises a state of affairs in which erstwhile enemies (wolves, lambs, and lions) will be at peace.

---

13. In many popular versions of dispensational teaching, these seven churches are taken to represent different periods of church history. So, ironically, the nonapocalyptic introduction to Revelation is in some sense "spiritualized," while the apocalyptic visions that follow are largely interpreted according to a more literalistic hermeneutic.

Often in the popular imagination at least, the future hope is less physical and earthly. The old spiritual "I'll Fly Away" expresses this sentiment. The transition is from earth to heaven, from matter to spirit, from this world to another world. However, in Scripture this pagan map is exposed as false. For now, the "inner self" shares already in Christ's resurrection, while the "outer self" wastes away (2Co 4:16). The kingdom is flourishing through the Spirit's work within human hearts, uniting them to Christ through the gospel, even while the visible condition of this world seems relatively unchanged by this reality. However, it is not an eternal dualism (spirit vs. matter) but an eschatological duality ("this age" and "the age to come") that is determinative here. Though the inner self is raised now, the outer self will be raised as well—and the whole creation will share in this restoration of all things (Ro 8:18–25). God's kingdom will not be less "worldly," but more: the whole earth will be filled with his glory, and there will be no longer any distinction between heaven and earth. God's plan is to save this world, but not this present evil age, which, ever since Christ's resurrection, is passing away.

For now, the kingdom is bringing peace on earth by reconciling individuals into one holy and catholic church. This, in fact, is "the mystery of Christ, which was not made known to the sons of men in other generations as it has now been revealed to his holy apostles and prophets by the Spirit." "This mystery is that the Gentiles are fellow heirs, members of the same body, and partakers of the promise in Christ Jesus through the gospel" (Eph 3:4–6). Although once "separated from Christ, alienated from the commonwealth of Israel and strangers to the covenants of promise, having no hope and without God in the world," believing Gentiles "have been brought near by the blood of Christ. For he himself is our peace, who has made us both one and has broken down in his flesh the dividing wall of hostility" (Eph 2:12–14). Unless Christ is reigning now, Gentiles still have no hope in the world—and neither can Jews, since they too lie under the law's condemnation. But the kingdom is not yet revealed in glory, as it will be when Christ returns. Then his kingdom will indeed be entirely visible, complete, unopposed, and fully realized in the public sphere. The peace that reconciles us to God and to each other will be realized in a global peace that will never again be disturbed by violence. Paul's description of these last days in 2 Timothy 3:1–9 and Jesus' query, "Nevertheless, when the Son of Man comes, will he find faith on the earth?" (Lk 18:8) leave little place for confidence in a golden age prior to Christ's return. And yet these passages occur alongside Christ's promise to build and preserve his church to the end of the age.

Views on the Millennium	
Amillennialism	Interpreted symbolically, the "thousand years" in Rev 20 refers to the present age in between Christ's two advents.
Dispensational premillennialism	Expectation of a literal thousand-year kingdom in the future that will also culminate in human failure. Israel and the church represent two distinct peoples with different programs in salvation history.
Historic premillennialism	A literal millennium in the future, but with less discontinuity between Israel and the church than in the dispensationalist view.
Postmillennialism	A literal millennium that dawns gradually now, at the end of which Jesus returns.

III. Israel, the Rapture, and the Antichrist

Defending the amillennial view, I have referred to the New Testament statements indicating that "these last days" encompass the whole era between Christ's advents; "the tribulation of those days" began with Jesus' hearers and continues until his return in glory (Mt 24:3–29). We are still living in that era of the great tribulation. It is an era of global peace, reconciliation, salvation, and grace as the kingdom is spread by the Spirit through the Word. And yet it is simultaneously an era of suffering for the church.

What then do we make of the biblical references to a coming rapture of the church and of "Antichrist"? Should we expect a revival of Israel as a theocracy, with a rebuilt temple and sacrificial system?

A. The Antichrist

One of the most explicit references to the **Antichrist** or "man of lawlessness" is found in 2 Thessalonians 2:1–12. From this passage we notice that the revealing of "the man of lawlessness" occurs as a precursor to Christ's return and gathering of his saints—with no intervening periods of tribulation or a millennium mentioned. At the same time, Paul explicitly warns against the teaching of some "that the day of the Lord has come." It is a future event, with the Antichrist taking "his seat in the temple of God, proclaiming himself to be God." If we are to take this straightforward prophecy literally, it could not have been fulfilled after the destruction of the temple, nor is there any reference here (or elsewhere) to his taking his seat in a rebuilt temple.

Paul (writing most likely in the early 50s) may have been prophesying any number of future Caesars: the reign of Nero or perhaps Titus, who sacked Jerusalem in AD 70, offered a pig on the altar, and burned the temple to the ground (with not one stone left upon another, as Jesus prophesied [Mt 24:2]). The Arch of Titus was built in Rome to commemorate the deified emperor's sacking of Jerusalem. Although he (like Satan himself) is being restrained, "the mystery of lawlessness is already at work." At the same time, the apostle seems to indicate that this satanic figure will be destroyed by Christ's return. Given the telescoping pattern of biblical prophecy, it does not seem unreasonable to conclude that this antichrist figure, truly mimicking Christ, appears in two advents: first as the self-deifying Roman emperor and then as a climactic figure at the end of the age, or perhaps more generally as the world powers. In the meantime, such antichrists come and go on the world stage as echoes and foreshadowings.

Various groups throughout the medieval period identified the Antichrist with a pope or with the papal office more generally. In fact, this view goes all the way back to the early fathers. Not only Cyprian in the East but Gregory the Great, a sixth-century bishop of Rome, warned that any bishop who accepted the title "universal bishop" "is in his self-exaltation Antichrist's precursor."[14] With such precedent, the Protestant Reformers concluded that the papal office had become this seat of that Antichrist. This interpretation is difficult to sustain, however, for various reasons. Most evidently, as Kim Riddlebarger observes, such a view would mean that John's Apocalypse was addressed not to the first-century witnesses and martyrs "but to Christians living centuries later."[15] Although it was the dominant Protestant interpretation (among advocates of all three millennial positions), it finds little support among serious commentators today.[16] John warns, "Children, it is the last hour, and as you have heard that antichrist is coming, so now many antichrists have come. Therefore we know that it is the last hour." John identifies these "antichrists" as those in the midst of his readers' commu-

---

14. Gregory the Great, Letters (in NPNF[2] vol. 12), 1.75–76; 2.170, 171, 179, 166, 169, 222, 225.
15. Riddlebarger, Case for Amillennialism, 22; see also Kim Riddlebarger, Man of Sin (Grand Rapids: Baker, 2006).
16. With Riddlebarger, Case for Amillennialism, 22, I would recommend the commentaries on Revelation by Beale (Book of Revelation) and Johnson (Triumph of the Lamb), which regard the Apocalypse as a series of snapshots that characterize the entire era between Christ's two advents. Although the Roman Empire is in the immediate foreground, Babylon (like its precursor, Babel) represents all of the Promethean regimes that oppose Yahweh and his Messiah, persecuting the saints.

nity who have denied that Jesus is God in the flesh (1Jn 2:18 – 27). So once again, it seems that "antichrist" refers to figures in the past, the present, and the future — perhaps with a culminating representative of Christless religion prior to Christ's return.

B. The Rapture and Christ's Return

I have argued that the most obvious reading of the relevant New Testament passages leads us to expect Christ's return in glory as the next great event in the history of redemption. However, many Christians today believe that believers will be secretly caught up to heaven prior to a seven-year tribulation period and then return with Christ in judgment. The concept of a secret rapture was first formulated by John Nelson Darby in the nineteenth century, on the basis of 1 Thessalonians 4:13 – 18. Several problems arise with the dispensationalist reading of this passage, however.

First, Paul expresses his purpose to comfort those who mourn the death of loved ones in the Lord. Second, he does this by assuring them that their fellow saints are already with the Lord and will return with him at "the coming of the Lord" — and only one "coming" is mentioned here. Third, he says that we who are alive at this coming will *not* precede those who have died, and his reference is not to a secret rapture prior to the resurrection but to the latter itself: "And the dead in Christ will rise first," followed by the changing of those who are still alive, so that all of the elect may join Christ's retinue as he comes on the clouds of the final judgment. Fourth, far from being a secret event that is discovered only after millions of earth's inhabitants are unaccounted for, this event is described by Paul in the most public terms. Compare this passage with the event described in Matthew 24:30 – 31, which Jesus not only identifies with his second coming "with power and great glory," but describes as an event that will provoke the mourning of "all the tribes of the earth." Jesus even refers here to "a loud trumpet call" at which the angels "will gather his elect from the four winds, from one end of heaven to the other." Finally, Paul says that this event — the second coming, the resurrection, and the last judgment — will culminate in the final state: "and so we will always be with the Lord" (1Th 4:17). There does not appear to be any room in this series for the insertion of a secret rapture.

C. The Church and Israel

Finally, we must ask with the apostle Paul, "Has God rejected his people?" — referring, of course, to ethnic Jews (Ro 11:1). Many premillennialists, especially dispensationalists, distinguish sharply between the end-time events that culminate God's program with Israel and others that culminate his program with the church. Is it not "spiritualizing" to interpret promises and prophecies made to Israel as fulfilled in Christ's expanded Israel composed of "people ... from every tribe and language and people and nation" who form his "holy nation" (Rev 5:9)?

We may consider Amos 9:11 – 12, for example, a key passage on the restoration of Israel: " 'In that day I will raise up the booth of David that is fallen and repair its breaches, and raise up its ruins and rebuild it as in the days of old, that they may possess the remnant of Edom and all the nations who are called by my name,' declares the LORD who does this." In that day, Israel's fortunes will be restored, and "they shall plant vineyards and drink their wine, and they shall make gardens and eat their fruit" (v. 14). "They shall never again be uprooted" (v. 15). This is a vision of an everlasting paradise. Premillennialists (especially dispensational premillennialists) treat this as referring exclusively to the restoration of the nation of Israel, in its geopolitical land, with the restoration of the temple sacrifices, and the earthly kingship of Messiah. The amillennial interpretation—namely, that the passage refers to this present age of the church's mission under Christ's reign—is regarded as a "spiritualizing" exegesis that does not take such prophecies at face value. However, there are several difficulties with the dispensational approach to a passage such as Amos 9.

First, Amos 9 speaks of a condition of everlasting, uninterrupted, unconditional blessing, whereas according to dispensational exegesis this can be true only of the millennial period. Second, and most decisively, the apostles typically interpreted these prophecies as being fulfilled now in Jesus Christ and his gathering of a remnant from Israel and the nations by his Spirit. In fact, Amos 9 is quoted by James in his defense of Gentile inclusion in the church:

> Simeon [Peter] has related how God first visited the Gentiles, to take from them a people for his name. And with this the words of the prophets agree, just as it is written, "After this I will return, and I will rebuild the tent of David that has fallen; I will rebuild its ruins, and I will restore it, that the remnant of mankind may seek the Lord, and all the Gentiles who are called by my name, says the Lord, who makes these things known from of old." (Acts 15:14 – 18)

For James, the application of this passage is not future but present: do not make the entrance requirements of the church depend on Jewish distinctives (v. 19).

James's interpretation is typical of the Christocentric reading of the whole of Scripture that Jesus Christ himself taught his disciples (Lk 24:25–27, 31–32; 44–49). Jesus Christ is the true temple, the high priest and the sacrifice to end all sacrifices. The whole burden of the Epistle to the Hebrews is to emphasize that the old covenant is "obsolete" (Heb 8:13), that there is no going back in redemptive history to the shadows now that the reality has arrived. This grand announcement that all of the types and shadows of promise have now been fulfilled in Christ is put in jeopardy by any expectation of a renewed old covenant, with the nation of Israel, its laws, and its sacrificial worship being restored.[17]

Now the core designations of the people of Israel — "a chosen race, a royal priesthood, a holy nation, a people for his own possession" (Ex 19:6; Dt 7:6; 10:15; Isa 43:20; 61:6; 66:21; Mal 3:17) — are applied to all who have faith in Christ (1Pe 2:9). In fact, the inclusion of Gentiles in this identification is explicit in 1Pe 2:10: "Once you were not a people, but now you are God's people; once you had not received mercy, but now you have received mercy." There are not two centers of Scripture, Israel and Jesus Christ, but one. Jesus is the seed of Abraham in whom all the nations are blessed. The Sinai covenant was temporary; it is this Abrahamic covenant that is everlasting.

Paul's contrast between the heavenly and earthly Jerusalem in the allegory of Sarah and Hagar (Gal 4:21–31) redraws the boundaries of Israel around Jesus Christ. Earthly descent no longer means anything, since the Mosaic covenant is no longer in force and it could never annul or revise the earlier Abrahamic covenant, which promised blessing to the nations through the seed of Abraham and Sarah. As a result, the Jew-Gentile distinction no longer has any religious or ecclesial significance (Gal 3:15–4:7). It is the promise, not the law, that determines inheritance — and this is true now for everyone. "This means that it is not the children of the flesh who are the children of God, but the children of the promise are counted as offspring" (Ro 9:8). The church is not a parenthesis in the history of redemption between national Israel's rejection and embrace of the kingdom.[18] Rather, the national theocracy was a parenthesis in what Paul calls the mystery of the church (Eph 1:9; 3:4; 5:32; Col 1:26). The church is Israel — the truly circumcised remnant within the nation that clung to God's promises

---

17. For a statement of the dispensationalist view I am challenging here, see Lewis Sperry Chafer and John Walvoord, *Major Bible Themes* (Grand Rapids: Zondervan, 1974), 357–58.

18. For the opposite view, see Charles C. Ryrie, *The Basis of the Premillennial Faith* (New York: Loizeaux Bros., 1953), 136.

even through the exile, now with natural branches broken off and foreign branches grafted in. The expansion of Israel to include a remnant from the nations was a key message of the Old Testament prophets. The apostles announce that this is now being fulfilled. If God has two peoples (or wives), then there are two gospels: good news for a restored nation of Israel and good news for the world of salvation in Christ. However, Paul treats the mystery of the church (Jew and Gentile united in Christ) as part of the one gospel.

Just as some premillennialists have acknowledged the New Testament's identification of Israel and the church, some amillennialists have argued that God still has a purpose for ethnic Jews, anticipating a wide-scale ingathering of Jews to Jesus Christ at the end of the age—after, in Paul's words, "the fullness of the Gentiles has come in." "And in this way," the apostle adds, "all Israel will be saved" (Ro 11:25–26).[19] In my view, this conclusion follows plausibly from the flow of Paul's argument in Romans 9–11.

Salvation has come to the world through the Jews; Jesus was sent to the Jews; the gospel was first brought to the Jews and was delivered to the world by Jews, and the kingdom grew from Jerusalem to the ends of the earth. In the end, it will be brought full circle, from the ends of the earth back to Jerusalem again.

Key Terms

- physicalism
- millennium
- antichrist

Key Distinctions

- intermediate/final state
- amillennial, postmillennial, premillennial views (including historic and dispensational premillennialism

---

19. Although the minority view among amillennialists, it has Geerhardus Vos, Herman Ridderbos, and John Murray among its defenders. I have especially been persuaded by the arguments in David E. Holwerda, *Jesus and Israel: One Covenant or Two?* (Grand Rapids: Eerdmans, 1994). A good defense of the amillennial majority report is offered by Robert Reymond, *A New Systematic Theology of the Christian Faith* (Nashville: Nelson, 1998), 1027–30.

Key Questions

1. Is the goal of salvation going to heaven when we die? Why or why not?
2. How do you understand the "thousand years" (millennium) in Revelation 20? How would you respond to other interpretations?
3. What are some of the key passages that amillennialists draw on to support their view?
4. Do you believe God has two different covenantal programs today: one with the nation of Israel and the other with the church? How does the New Testament speak of the relationship of Israel and the church?
5. Does biblical prophecy lead us to expect a mass conversion of ethnic Jews in the future?
6. What does Scripture teach concerning the Antichrist and a secret rapture?
7. What should we be expecting next in terms of God's eschatological timetable?

Chapter Nineteen

The Resurrection of the Body and the Life Everlasting

M any people today are not sure that heaven sounds like an enjoyable place to spend eternity: bouncing on clouds, playing harps, and singing in the choir. Since "no eye has seen, nor ear heard, nor the heart of man imagined, what God has prepared for those who love him" (1Co 2:9; cf. Isa 64:4), we cannot help but associate visions of heaven with popular images from our childhood. Yet far different from popular images of heaven in our Western culture is the biblical vision of Isaiah 25:

> On this mountain the LORD of hosts will make for all peoples a feast of rich food, a feast of well-aged wine, of rich food full of marrow, of aged wine well refined. And he will swallow up on this mountain the covering that is cast over all peoples, the veil that is spread over all nations. He will swallow up death forever; and the Lord GOD will wipe away tears from all faces, and the reproach of his people he will take away from all the earth, for the LORD has spoken. It will be said on that day, "Behold, this is our God; we have

waited for him, that he might save us. This is the LORD; we have waited for him; let us be glad and rejoice in his salvation." (vv. 6–9)

It is significant that the Christian creed ends with "the resurrection of the body and the life everlasting"—not with the hope of a disembodied heavenly existence after death. As wonderful as it is to rejoice in the hope of being with the Lord upon our death, how much greater still is our expectation of being raised bodily in a world that is full of the glory, peace, justice, and love of the triune God. This is the consummation of our hope.

I. The Resurrection of the Body

Jesus walked through a curtain that no mortal has walked through before. He died and was raised to life in glory. As the prototype of the new creation, Jesus ate and drank with his disciples after his resurrection. "Touch me, and see," he invited. "For a spirit does not have flesh and bones as you see that I have" (Lk 24:39). Not only is the bodily resurrection of Christ affirmed in the Gospels, where Jesus eats with his disciples and even invites Thomas to inspect his wounds; it is clearly taught in the letters of Paul, particularly 1 Corinthians 15.

In 1 Corinthians 15 we find a lodestar for the Christian hope of the resurrection. Paul's whole point in this section of his letter is to challenge a sect that is teaching that the resurrection has already happened as a "spiritual" event. Paul treats the resurrection of believers as belonging to the same event (though in two stages) as that of their forerunner, Jesus Christ.[1] He also considers the way in which the renewal of all things takes place. The resurrection of the body, first witnessed in the resurrection of Christ and then in the resurrection of believers, indicates the shape of the life everlasting. Even now, writes Paul, the resurrection of the dead in the age to come is being realized partially in the present by the renewal of the inner person (regeneration). Those "dead in trespasses and sins" are already raised spiritually and are seated with Christ (cf. Eph 2:1–6; Ro 6). In 1 Corinthians 15:26, 54–55, Paul makes it clear that there is an *order* to this renewal: first, spiritual resurrection, and then bodily resurrection, completing the total renewal of believers. As is also taught in 2 Corinthians 4:16–18, the "outer person" is wasting away while the "inner person" is being renewed day by day in the image of Christ (cf. Ro 8:9–30; 2Ti 1:10; Col 3:1–17). In 1 Corinthians 15:50 Paul says, "Flesh and blood

---

1. This is the thrust of Richard Gaffin's richly insightful argument in *Resurrection and Redemption: A Study in Paul's Soteriology* (Phillipsburg, N.J.: P&R, 1987).

cannot inherit the kingdom of God, nor does the perishable inherit the imperishable." Yet notice the comparison: "As was the man of dust, so also are those who are of the dust.... Just as we have borne the image of the man of dust, we shall also bear the image of the man of heaven" (vv. 48–49).

In its present condition, our nature cannot withstand the glory of the heavenly city; it must be glorified, as Christ's was, in order to participate in the age to come. There is something to be noted about Paul's analogy in 1 Corinthians 15:42–44 of the seed that is planted in the earth and rises as a plant. Whatever the apparent discontinuities between an apple seed and an apple tree, it is the same substance. Flesh and blood in its present, fallen condition cannot endure the joys of Zion. Nevertheless, our bodies will be *changed* (1Co 15:51), not *replaced*. "For ... the *dead* will be raised imperishable, and we shall be changed. For *this* perishable body must put on the imperishable, and *this* mortal body must put on immortality" (v. 53, emphasis added). We cannot imagine the glory of our future existence, but we can look to Christ as our forerunner: "He who raised Christ Jesus from the dead will also give life to your mortal bodies" (Ro 8:11), and Christ "will transform our lowly body to be like his glorious body" (Php 3:21). So the contrast is not between this body and another body but between *this body* in its lowly condition and the same body *changed* into the glorious condition of Christ's own body.

The Scriptures teach that whatever happened to Jesus in his resurrection from death will also happen to us. Whatever details that involves, at the very least it means this world's transformation—rather than its abandonment. "But according to his promise we are waiting for new heavens and a new earth in which righteousness dwells" (2Pe 3:13). Significantly, the one "seated on the throne said, 'Behold, I am making all things new'" (Rev 21:5), not creating all things *ex nihilo*. It is not that we will no longer live on the earth, much less that we will no longer be embodied. Rather, "God himself will be with them as their God. He will wipe away every tear from their eyes, and death shall be no more, neither shall there be mourning, nor crying, nor pain anymore, for the former things have passed away" (Rev 21:3–4).

We are creatures of time and space. The resurrection and the new creation will not transcend our humanity; rather, we will be set free from the bondage of our humanity to the conditions of sin and death. Wayne Grudem is exactly right when he argues, "Although a popular hymn speaks of the time 'when the trumpet of the Lord shall sound and time shall be no more,' Scripture does not give support to that idea."[2] Rather, all of our times will

---

2. Wayne Grudem, *Systematic Theology* (Grand Rapids: Zondervan, 1994), 1162.

be gathered together in the fullness of God's Sabbath rest: everlasting joy. If there has been love on earth, it will be deepened and purified in glory; if pleasure, it will be fuller, richer, and enduring; if friendship, these bonds will be only stronger. We will not cease learning and growing, but will never reach that peak beyond maturity when we begin to slide down the other side of the hill. Every evening we've ever spent laughing with friends and loved ones around a sumptuous feast or warm fire will have been a mere foretaste of heavenly company. It is not another world, but this world that, like us, will be more truly itself than we've ever known it. The life everlasting is not even "Paradise Restored," as if we returned to the innocence of Eden. Rather, it will be "Beyond Paradise": the eschatological Sabbath that Adam never knew and that he forfeited by his disobedience.

II. Hell and Eternal Punishment

From the ancient Greeks to Dante all the way to Billy Sunday, there have been imaginative construals of hell, many of which sit loosely on the biblical text. Heaven and hell appear together, affirmed side by side, in the New Testament (Mk 9:42–48; 2Th 1:7–9; 1Pe 3:22; 2Pe 2:4–10; 3:13; Jude 5–13; Rev 19:20–21; 21:2–3). John the Baptist pointed to this judgment (Mt 3:11–12), but the most detailed references to the reality of hell come from Jesus himself. Jesus warns against the whole body being cast into hell (Mt 5:30); in fact, no prophet or apostle spoke so vividly and repeatedly of the last judgment (Mt 8:10–12; 13:40–42, 49–50; 22:13; 24:51; 25:30; Lk 16:19–31). Echoing Isaiah 2 (as well as chapter 11), Jesus says that the nations will appear before the Son of Man in judgment, and all will be separated, as sheep and goats, "into eternal life" and "into eternal punishment" (Mt 25:31, 41, 46). In John's vision in Revelation, Jesus announces, "Fear not, I am the first and the last, and the living one. I died, and behold I am alive forevermore, and I have the keys of Death and Hades" (Rev 1:17–18). The term that Jesus often used, *Gehenna*, has its origins in the perpetually burning fire of the Ben Hinnom valley, where Israel imitated the pagan practices of its neighbors in child sacrifice (Jer 19:5; 32:35). Jesus tells us that the wicked will find themselves facing the same fate.

We encounter the same solemn expectation in the Epistles. Paul writes, "But because of your hard and impenitent heart you are storing up wrath for yourself on the day of wrath when God's righteous judgment will be revealed." For the wicked and unbelieving, "there will be wrath and fury

... tribulation and distress" (Ro 2:5, 8 – 9). First Thessalonians 5 warns that "the day of the Lord will come like a thief in the night," just when everyone is proclaiming peace and security (vv. 1 – 3). This event of salvation-and-judgment will be as final as it is sudden, "when the Lord Jesus is revealed from heaven with his mighty angels in flaming fire, inflicting vengeance on those who do not know God and on those who do not obey the gospel of our Lord Jesus." These "will suffer the punishment of eternal destruction," he says, "away from the presence of the Lord and from the glory of his might, when he comes on that day to be glorified in his saints, and to be marveled at among all who have believed, because our testimony to you was believed" (2Th 1:7 – 10). Elsewhere we read that Sodom and Gomorrah "serve as an example by undergoing a punishment of eternal fire" and that false teachers are "wandering stars, for whom the gloom of utter darkness has been reserved forever" (Jude 7, 13). Second Peter 3:7 speaks of "the day of judgment and destruction of the ungodly."

At the end of history, Satan is "thrown into the lake of fire and sulfur where the beast and the false prophet [are], and they will be tormented day and night forever and ever" (Rev 20:10; see also 19:11 – 20:9). The dead are then judged. "This is the second death, the lake of fire" (20:14 – 15). The finality of this judgment ushers in the new heavens and earth, where there is no longer any judgment, war, pain, suffering, or oppression. And it is there, finally, where the Tree of Life yields its fruit and leaves "for the healing of the nations" (22:2; see also chs. 21 – 22).

A. Is Hell Forever?

The images of the last day — of heaven and hell — are communicated in an apocalyptic form. Such images are not meant to be read like a morning newspaper, yet neither are they meant to be ignored. They indicate realities that are beyond our conceptual grasp, yet are certain to come to fruition. Ours is not the first age to have found the doctrine of everlasting punishment difficult to accept. Let's consider two of the most prominent alternatives to the doctrine of everlasting punishment.

1. Apokatastasis and inclusivism

Origen's doctrine of universal restoration (**apokatastasis**), though condemned at the Fifth Council of Constantinople in 553, has had its admirers throughout the ages, including John Scotus Erigena, and was revived in Anabaptist circles (especially by Hans Denck and Hans Hut). With some modifications, it continues to attract interest among a wide variety of theologians.[3] According to Origen's Platonizing of Christian eschatology, all spiritual essences (including human souls) will be at last freed from the body and reunited with their origin, but only after passing through successive cycles of educative purgation, perhaps through reincarnation in other worlds. Origen conjectured that even Satan and his hosts will be at last reunited with God.[4]

Unwilling to endorse an absolute principle of universal salvation, many Roman Catholic and Protestant theologians in the modern era have embraced **inclusivism**: the belief that although Jesus Christ is the only Savior, people may be saved without explicit faith in Christ. Karl Barth taught a form of universalism that is grounded in God's sovereign grace. According to Barth, the whole human race is elect in Christ, objectively redeemed and justified by grace alone. One may reject this election, but one's response is not finally decisive. "God does not permit [the human being] to execute this No of his, this contradiction and opposition."[5] As with other interpreters since Origen, for Barth Ephesians 1:10 was a key text for this view: namely, God's plan "to unite all things in [Christ], things in heaven and things on earth." Yet Barth's universalism has no parallels in the history of biblical interpretation. While Ephesians 1:10 indeed speaks of God's plan, the context is God's election of many in Christ to be adopted, redeemed, forgiven, and called into union with Christ through faith. "In him you also, when you heard the word of truth, the gospel of your salvation, and believed in him, were sealed with the promised Holy Spirit, who is the guarantee of our inheritance until we acquire possession of it, to the praise of his glory" (vv. 13–14). Eventually, out of concern for God's sovereign freedom, Barth left open the possibility that some may be lost.[6]

Jürgen Moltmann follows a similar interpretation, although he seems less reticent than Barth to affirm universal salvation.[7] Like Barth, he bases his inclusivism on God's grace rather than on human goodness or free will, but unlike Barth he makes God's "suffering love" necessary to God's being

---

3. Many Roman Catholic theologians, especially after the Second Vatican Council, have found Origen's speculations attractive: among them, Hans Urs von Balthasar. Universalism more generally has been favored by the liberal Protestant theologians from Schleiermacher and Ritschl to Paul Tillich and John Hick. It is also the position of Wolfhart Pannenberg and seems to be gaining strength in evangelical circles.

4. Origen, *On First Principles* 1.6.2; 3.6.6 (*ANF*; Grand Rapids: Eerdmans, repr. 1976), 4:260–61, 347.

5. Karl Barth, *Church Dogmatics* (trans. G. W. Bromiley; Edinburgh: T&T Clark, 1957–1975), vol. 2, pt. 2, 13.

6. Ibid., vol. 2, pt. 2, 417.

7. Jürgen Moltmann, "The Logic of Hell," in *God Will Be All in All: The Eschatology of Jürgen Moltmann* (ed. Richard Bauckham; Edinburgh: T&T Clark, 1999), 43–48.

and therefore compromises the very idea of grace as a free decision and act. It is difficult to resist the impression that both theologians reflect a nearly fatalistic interpretation of God's sovereign grace. In fact, Moltmann criticizes the notion of annihilation for making human free will ultimate rather than God's grace. This form of inclusivism is therefore more "Augustinian," but with God's electing grace encompassing every person. The real question, however, is not whether God's "Yes" overcomes our "No," but whether God is free to show this mercy to whomever he will and whether the nonelect are responsible for their rejection of the gospel.

Evangelical Arminians like Clark Pinnock share the presupposition that all of God's attributes are subservient to his love and that his purpose is to save every person. This differs sharply from the inclusivism of theologians like Barth and Moltmann in that it represents salvation as dependent on the free will of individuals. Evangelical Arminian inclusivists also believe that the content of saving revelation can be mediated apart from the gospel, even through other religions, as "means of grace."[8] Whereas Barth and Moltmann ground inclusivism in a notion of God's universal electing grace, Pinnock's inclusivism (like that of the Second Vatican Council) is grounded in a notion of God's universal accessibility of grace for those who respond to it—even apart from explicit faith in Christ. It appeals to the examples of Melchizedek, Job, and Paul's quotation of pagan poets in Acts 17 to defend the idea that God reveals himself in a saving way outside of biblical revelation and that people are responsible only for responding obediently to what they know.

However, are these in fact biblical examples of "noble pagans" who believed the truth even though they did not trust explicitly in Christ? Although revelation progresses from Old Testament shadows to New Testament reality, the object of faith is the same. Meanwhile, the religions of the nations are consistently regarded as idolatrous throughout this history. Ever since Justin Martyr, some Christians have claimed that the pagan philosophers prepared the way for Christ among the Gentiles as Moses and the

---

8. These theses are defended in the following works: Clark H. Pinnock, "An Inclusivist View," in *Four Views on Salvation in a Pluralistic World* (ed. Dennis L. Okholm and Timothy R. Phillips; Grand Rapids: Zondervan, 1995), 93–123, cf. also 251–54; Pinnock, *A Wideness in God's Mercy: The Finality of Jesus Christ in a World of Religions* (Grand Rapids: Zondervan,1992); Pinnock, "Acts 4:12—No Other Name under Heaven," in *Through No Fault of Their Own* (ed. William Crockett and James Sigountos; Grand Rapids: Baker, 1991), 107–115. Arminian defenses of inclusivism are similar to the arguments of Karl Rahner and the Second Vatican Council. Pinnock (*Wideness in God's Mercy*, 34) appeals to "Declaration on the Relationship of the Church to Non-Christian Religions," par. 2, in *The Documents of Vatican II* (ed. Walter M. Abbott and Joseph Gallagher; trans. Joseph Gallagher; New York: Herder & Herder, 1966), 662. A more Augustinian (and guarded) interpretation of inclusivism is argued by John Stackhouse, *What Does It Mean to Be Saved? Broadening Evangelical Horizons of Salvation* (Grand Rapids: Baker Academic, 2002).

prophets prepared the Jews. But this is to confuse general revelation with special revelation and the law with the gospel.

The examples cited above do not demonstrate a saving knowledge of God apart from his revelation to Israel. From what little we know about Melchizedek, he could not have been a "noble pagan."[9] He was "king of Salem" (proto-Jerusalem), "priest of God Most High," "God Most High" (*'El 'Elyon*) being identified as none other than "the LORD [Yahweh], God Most High" (Ge 14:18 – 22). He brought Abram bread and wine, blessed him, and received a tributary tithe—all of these actions reflecting a covenantal context in which Abram recognized Melchizedek as his high priest. Nor can Job qualify as an anonymous believer. His allusion to Psalm 8:4 in Job 7:17 – 18 and to Isaiah 41:20 in Job 12:9 render implausible the long-held view that he was a pre-Israelite figure.

Finally, we should note that Paul quotes pagan poets to his audience of Athenian philosophers in Acts 17 for the express purpose of demonstrating that they are not even living consistently with general revelation. In any case, Paul declares, "The times of ignorance God overlooked, but now he commands all people everywhere to repent, because he has fixed a day on which he will judge the world in righteousness by a man whom he has appointed; and of this he has given assurance to all by raising him from the dead" (Ac 17:30 – 31). However lenient God may have been in "the times of ignorance," the appearance of Christ in these last days leaves everyone without excuse. It is the universal-public character of Christ's decisive work and coming judgment that gives to the missionary enterprise the kind of urgency that is found throughout the book of Acts.

At the same time, I do not believe that we can conclude that no one can be saved apart from explicit faith in Christ. First, it is precisely because God is sovereign and free in his grace that he can have mercy on whomever he chooses. From first to last, "salvation is of the LORD" (Jnh 2:9). Second, since the children of believers are comprehended with their parents in the covenant of grace, in the words of the Canons of Dort, "godly parents ought not to doubt the election and salvation of their children whom it pleases God to call out of this life in their infancy (Gen. 17:7; Acts 2:39; 1 Cor. 7:14)."[10] Third, we are not told what God does in extraordinary cases: e.g., those

---

9. James L. Kugel, *Traditions of the Bible: A Guide to the Bible as It Was at the Start of the Common Era* (Cambridge, Mass.: Harvard Univ. Press, 1988), 276 – 78.

10. Canons of Dort, ch. 1, art. 17, in Doctrinal Standards of the Christian Reformed Church, in *Psalter Hymnal* (Grand Rapids: Board of Publications of the Christian Reformed Church, 1976), 95. There is also the example of the death of David's week-old son. "I shall go to him," David said, "but he will not return to me" (2Sa 12:23).

who are physically or mentally incapable of understanding God's Word. As in all theological questions, we must restrain our curiosity and refuse to speculate beyond God's own instruction. Apart from God's self-disclosure in Scripture, we do not know what God has ordained from all of eternity. Whatever God *might choose to do* in any given case, he has *promised* to save all of those—and only those—who call on the name of his Son.

2. Annihilation

Other Christians have concluded that the exegetical evidence for the reality of hell is impossible to reconcile with universal salvation. The question addressed by **annihilationism** is not the scope of God's mercy, but the nature of hell. Those who hold to this position interpret various passages as teaching that unbelievers are raised on the last day for destruction (the second death) rather than for everlasting, conscious torment. Because they are destroyed forever, Scripture can still speak in apocalyptic terms of "their smoke going up forever" and their being eternally destroyed. However, this need not entail conscious punishment.[11]

Historically, this view has not gained adherents except among the Adventists, Jehovah's Witnesses, Christadelphians, and other groups. More recently, however, it has attracted some support in British evangelicalism, including (possibly) C. S. Lewis, as well as F. F. Bruce, John Wenham, Phillip E. Hughes, and, more tentatively, John Stott.[12] It has also been defended, in more emotional language, by Clark Pinnock and Edward Fudge.[13]

Annihilationists often claim that the notion of eternal, conscious torment is based on the Greek doctrine of the immortality of the soul. In its place, they argue for conditional immortality. At the final resurrection and

---

11. One of the most extensive treatments of eternal punishment from this perspective is Edward W. Fudge, *The Fire That Consumes: A Biblical and Historical Study of the Doctrine of Final Punishment* (Fallbrook, Calif.: Verdict, 1982). Various studies interact thoughtfully with Fudge's thesis, including Robert A. Peterson, *Hell on Trial: The Case for Eternal Punishment* (Phillipsburg, N.J.: P&R, 1995). Cf. Edward W. Fudge and Robert A. Peterson, *Two Views on Hell: A Biblical and Theological Dialogue* (Downers Grove, Ill.: InterVarsity Press, 2000); Christopher W. Morgan and Robert A. Peterson, eds., *Hell under Fire: Modern Scholarship Reinvents Eternal Punishment* (Grand Rapids: Zondervan, 2004).

12. It is difficult to discern exactly what Lewis held on this matter. In *The Problem of Pain* (San Francisco: HarperSanFrancisco, 1940 and 2001) he writes, "The characteristic of lost souls is 'their rejection of everything that is not simply themselves.' Our imaginary egoist has tried to turn everything he meets into a province or appendage of the self. The taste for the other, that is, the very capacity for enjoying good, is quenched in him except in so far as his body still draws him into some rudimentary contact with an outer world. Death removes this last contact. He has his wish—to lie wholly in the self and to make the best of what he finds there. And what he finds there is Hell" (124–25). For Stott's view, see David L. Edwards and John Stott, *Essentials: A Liberal-Evangelical Dialogue* (Downers Grove, Ill.: InterVarsity Press, 1988), 314–20.

13. Clark Pinnock, "The Conditional View," in *Four Views on Hell* (ed. William Crockett; Grand Rapids: Zondervan, 1997), 135–66; Fudge, *Fire That Consumes*.

judgment, the immortal God will grant immortality to believers and condemn unbelievers to destruction. Satan and the false prophet are said to suffer eternal consciousness in hell, but no one else (Rev 14:9–11; 20:10). Jesus' description of the fire as "eternal" and "unquenchable" (Mt 3:12; 18:8; 25:41; Lk 3:17) can be interpreted as annihilation. Positively, advocates of this view appeal to passages that speak of unbelievers perishing (Jn 3:16) and being destroyed (Mt 10:28), and believe that the reference in Revelation 20 to the "second death" (vv. 6, 8, 14) can refer only to this annihilation. In Matthew 10:28, Jesus warns hearers to "fear him who can destroy both soul and body in hell."

However, Jesus' teaching concerning the final separation of the saved and the lost seems to treat punishment and life as equally eternal: "And these will go away into eternal punishment, but the righteous into eternal life" (Mt 25:46). If it is generally assumed that "eternal life" means unending, conscious joy, then it would seem that annihilationists bear the burden of proof in treating "eternal punishment" as otherwise in duration.

Still, regardless of how one finally interprets these passages, our emotional revulsion at the admittedly difficult idea of conscious punishment forever cannot be the basis for our decision to accept or reject the idea of hell. Nor, indeed, can it be decided out of concern to protect the missionary imperative, as if the motive for our evangelism were to be based on the fear of conscious eternal punishment. The only decisive question is whether Scripture teaches it. Furthermore, we must be careful to distinguish scriptural teaching from the popular images of hell that we have inherited from popular mythology, whether pagan or Christian. The critical point to be made from Scripture with regard to eternal punishment is not its degree or duration, but its horrifying reality as God's personal judgment that is final and forever.

III. The Everlasting Sabbath of the New Heavens and Earth

In the old covenant, *some* places were holy. In the present phase of Christ's kingdom there are *no* holy places. However, when Christ returns, cleansing the land in a final judgment, *everything* will be holy. Zechariah prophesies of the day when the true temple will be cleansed of all traders and everything that defiles. The most common household pots and pans—even the bells on the horses—will bear the inscription, "Holy to the Lord!" (Zec 14:20–21). The wasteland will again become a lush garden, from which the violent and the oppressor are banished (Isa 35). One last time the world will be shaken and the nations will come to the "desire of all nations," the end-time temple filled with the glory of the Spirit (Hag 2:6–7 KJV). "'The latter glory of this house shall be greater than the former, says the LORD of hosts. And in this place I will give peace,' says the LORD of hosts" (v. 9).

After the destruction of the first temple, Ezekiel received a vision of the new one (Eze 40–42), and in chapter 43 he relates the return of the glory-cloud to the temple. A man "whose appearance shone like bronze" stood with a measuring rod, six cubits long (40:3–5). He took detailed measurements and gave specific instructions for the temple's construction and furnishings. Recalling to our minds that cherubim were posted at the eastern gate of Eden, barring reentry to the sanctuary after the fall, as was the case when the glory of God evacuated Israel's first temple, the account reports that Ezekiel was now taken in his vision to the gate that faced east: "and it was shut." "The LORD said to me, 'This gate shall remain shut; it shall not be opened, and no one shall enter by it, for the LORD, the God of Israel, has entered by it. Therefore it shall remain shut. Only the prince may sit in it to eat bread before the LORD. He shall enter by way of the vestibule of the gate, and shall go out by the same way" (44:1–3). Nothing profane or unclean will be allowed to enter its sacred precincts (vv. 4–9).

In Revelation 21 and 22 we have a similar description of the new temple as the ultimate dwelling place of God among his covenant people, bringing a final end to suffering, sin, pain, and injustice. "And he who was seated on the throne said, 'Behold, I am making all things new'" (21:5). The inhabitants will drink freely of the water of life, just as they are finally allowed to eat from the Tree of Life. "The one who conquers will inherit these things, and I will be his God and he will be my son. But as for the cowardly, the faithless, the detestable, as for murderers, the sexually immoral, sorcerers, idolaters, and all liars, their portion will be in the lake that burns with fire and sulfur, which is the second death" (vv. 7–8). John is then shown "the Bride, the wife of the Lamb," who is none other than "the holy city Jerusalem coming down out of heaven from God" (vv. 9–10). Rare jewels, high walls, twelve gates and twelve foundations are mentioned. And once more the angel appears with a measuring rod (vv. 9, 15–16). It becomes increasingly clear that the temple is not something *within* the city, but *the city itself.* "I saw no temple in the city, for its temple is the Lord God the Almighty and the Lamb" (v. 22). Unlike the temples of Eden and Jerusalem, it is a temple into which "nothing unclean will ... enter," and therefore this Sanctuary's gates "will never be shut" so that all "who are written in the Lamb's book of life" may enter

(vv. 25–27). There is no sea there, which surely means that just as the wild beasts no longer threaten on land, the chaos monster of the dark and turbulent depths no longer has a home from which to assault the citizens of Zion.

In his remarkable treatment of this theme, G. K. Beale articulates "a biblical theology of the dwelling place of God."[14] Symbolizing the cosmos, Israel's temple consisted of three areas: an outer court (representing "the habitable world where humanity dwelt"), the holy place (representing "the visible heavens and its light sources"), and the holy of holies (representing "the invisible dimension of the cosmos, where God and his heavenly hosts dwelt."[15]

It is not too fanciful to suggest that the movement from the inner court entered only by the high priest once a year, to the precincts of the holy place that immediately surrounded it, and finally to the outer court of the Gentiles is typological of Jesus' answer to the disciples' query at his ascension, "Lord, will you at this time restore the kingdom to Israel?": "He said to them, 'It is not for you to know times or seasons that the Father has fixed by his own authority. But you will receive power when the Holy Spirit has come upon you; and you will be my witnesses in *Jerusalem* in all *Judea and Samaria*, and to the *end of the earth*" (Ac 1:6–8). In its typological-theocratic form, Israel was a centripetal community, separated from the common nations; in its fulfillment, it becomes a centrifugal community, sent out from the Holy of Holies, through the Holy Place, out to the court of the Gentiles. This is the force of Jesus' Great Commission: "All authority in heaven and on earth has been given to me. Go therefore and make disciples of all nations, baptizing them in the name of the Father and of the Son and of the Holy Spirit" (Mt 28:18–19). "Go into all the world and proclaim the gospel to all creation" (Mk 16:15).

In Christ, according to the New Testament, the end-time temple made without hands has appeared in history. The temple curtain is torn from top to bottom, with its corresponding omens in the heavens, as the High Priest enters not a copy but the true Holy of Holies with his own blood. No longer needed, the pictures are replaced by the reality. Not by another attempt to renew the Sinai covenant, but by becoming living stones in the end-time temple built by Yahweh himself, the people become the place: God's home. To his deputies, this Last Adam—now invested in the robes and seat of glory—now gives the keys of the kingdom (Mt 16:18–19; 18:15–18; Jn 20:23; and Rev 3:7, harking back to Isa 22:22), and they are clothed in his righteousness.

---

14. G. K. Beale, *The Temple and the Church's Mission: A Biblical Theology of the Dwelling Place of God* (Downers Grove, Ill.: InterVarsity Press, 2004).

15. Ibid., 32–33.

In John's Apocalypse, the whole cosmos is the city, and the city is the temple. "Not only does the horizontal demarcation between the old temple and city disappear in the New Jerusalem," notes Meredith Kline, "but the vertical distinction between heavenly and earthly temples as well."[16] Not only the prophets and apostles, but the whole people of God are now "caught up in the Spirit" to stand in the heavenly council, covered in priestly vestments, sent from the throne room as witnesses.[17] In the New Testament, the glory of Christ's face (2Co 4:6) reveals judgment from heaven. It is a *parousia*-glory, as Jesus returns on the last day (Mt 16:27; Mk 8:38; Lk 9:26)."[18] In Hebrews 12, this parousia-glory is identified with his voice (cf. Rev 1:10–15).[19] In the heavenly worship scene of the Apocalypse, amid flashes of lightning and peals of thunder, flaming fires burn in front of the throne as the twenty-four elders are seated around God, and behind the throne the bow of judgment is no longer drawn but hangs in peace (Rev 4:2–5).

In Revelation as well, then, the flaming torches are redolent of the church's witness, as at Pentecost. Christ's resurrection is regarded as the rebuilding of Israel's temple, a temple not built "by [human] hands" (Ac 7:48), "because believers have been 'circumcised with a circumcision made without hands, in the removal of the body of the flesh by the circumcision of Christ [i.e., his death]' (Col 2:11)."[20] The new creation is therefore entirely the work of God, and the end-time sanctuary is the temple that God has built for himself. "Judaism highlighted this by saying that God would 'build the temple [of Ex 15:17] ... with his two hands' (*Mekilta de-Rabbi Ishmael, Tractate Shirata* 10.40–42)."[21] It is not built by us but by God, whose indwelling presence is not conditioned on the nation's faithfulness but on his own covenant faithfulness, erected not from inanimate blocks that may be pulled down but from living stones taken from every tribe under heaven with Christ as the cornerstone (1Pe 2:4–8).

Far from the vision of disembodied spirits floating on ethereal clouds with harps, Isaiah 65 speaks of a "new heavens and a new earth" with buildings and vineyards, trees, labor, and fellowship with all of creation. What is gone are not emotions, but "the sound of weeping and the cry of distress" (v. 19). Its inhabitants "shall build houses and inhabit them; they shall plant vineyards and eat their fruit," enjoying the fruit of their labor rather

---

16. M. G. Kline, *Images of the Spirit* (S. Hamilton, Mass.: self-published, 1986), 35.
17. Ibid., 94.
18. Ibid., 121–22.
19. Ibid., 122.
20. Beale, *Temple and the Church's Mission*, 233–34.
21. Ibid., 235n66.

than building and planting only to have their homes occupied by invaders (vv. 21–22a). Not work itself but the curse of tiresome, frustrating, and meaningless labor, will be no more (v. 22b). Children will be a blessing rather than a cause for distress over their future (v. 23). No one will need to cry to the Lord, for "while they are yet speaking I will hear" (v. 24) and it is not the absence of wildlife but of danger that will characterize this Sabbath land (v. 25). The book of Isaiah closes with this prophecy:

> "For as the new heavens and the new earth that I make shall remain before me, says the LORD, so shall your offspring and your name remain. From new moon to new moon, and from Sabbath to Sabbath, all flesh shall come to worship before me, declares the LORD. And they shall go out and look on the dead bodies of the men who have rebelled against me. For their worm shall not die, their fire shall not be quenched, and they shall be an abhorrence to all flesh." (Isa 66:22–24)

The resurrection of the body underscores the anticipation of the final state as redemption of nature rather than its oblivion.

In the New Testament as well, the final heavenly abode is a created place (Lk 24:51; Jn 14:2–4; Ac 1:11; 7:55–56; 1Pe 3:22). To be sure, the renewal is so radical that it can be described only in apocalyptic terms, as passing away (2Pe 3:12–13; Rev 21:2–3). Nevertheless, we should think not in terms of the end of God's creation itself but of the end of creation *in its current condition*. Our heavenly hope is not only of saved souls but of saved creation (Ro 8:19–21). Just as Jesus ate and drank after his resurrection, there will be eating and drinking in the new creation, although this time at the consummated marriage supper of the Lamb (Rev 19:9), with Jesus drinking wine with us (Lk 22:18). The theme of eating and drinking in the presence of the Lord that we find throughout the Old Testament narratives and again so prominently in Luke's gospel will be fully realized in that day.

Revelation 22 employs the imagery of a river flowing through the city, with the tree of life "yielding its fruit each month" (Rev 22:2). Again, it is apocalyptic imagery, but the purchase of such imagery is lost if there is no physical creation. Just as the imagery of fire, outer darkness, and the grave seems contradictory if taken literally and yet, taken together, indicates the horrible condition of hell, the imagery of wedding feasts, rivers, trees, and a city with streets of gold is richly suggestive of a condition that we cannot conceive of apart from such analogies. This does not mean that these are "mere metaphors," since the value of metaphors is to actually convey truth. Whatever the condition of "the life everlasting," it is more, certainly not less, than the embodied joy that such imagery suggests. We are creatures of time and space, and we will transcend not our humanity but the bondage of our humanity to the conditions of sin and death.

Interpreting the apocalyptic imagery of 2 Peter 3:12–13 literally, classic dispensationalism anticipates a complete annihilation of the cosmos.[22] The title of Hal Lindsey's classic bears this point: *The Late Great Planet Earth.* Lewis Sperry Chafer and John Walvoord write, "The day of the Lord, which begins at the Rapture and includes in its introduction the judgments preceding and immediately following the Second Coming, concludes with the end of the millennium and with the final destruction of the present heaven and earth."[23] After the great white throne judgment, "the old creation is destroyed, ... Because of the destruction of the present earth and heaven, the judgment of the great white throne apparently takes place in space."[24] The heavenly Jerusalem coming down from heaven, beautifully described in Revelation 21, is apparently uncreated: "It is most significant that the city is not said to be created, and it apparently was in existence during the preceding period of the millennial kingdom, possibly as a satellite city above the earth; as such, it may be the millennial home of the resurrected and translated saints."[25]

If, however, such apocalyptic language in 2 Peter 3:10–13 is to be interpreted like apocalyptic language elsewhere, there is no reason to interpret these verses as communicating anything more than a complete transition from one condition of existence to another. "This present age" versus "the age to come," not this present world versus another world, reflects the consistent emphasis of New Testament eschatology. This whole creation will be wholly saved, and yet wholly new.

Our actions cannot bring about this cosmic regeneration. Our noblest efforts are incapable of turning Christ's kingdom of grace and suffering into a kingdom of glory and triumph over evil, sin, injustice, and violence. That is why we long for our unsubstitutable Savior to appear from heaven once again, this time to cleanse his garden once and for all of that which defiles us and his creation. At the same time, how can we fail to care for each other and creation in view of this ultimate re-creation that he intends for his world?

---

22. Lewis Sperry Chafer and John Walvoord, *Major Bible Themes* (Grand Rapids: Zondervan, 1974), 353: "In this discussion it will be assumed that prophecy should be interpreted in the same literal sense as any other theme of divine revelation." However, interpreting prophetic and apocalyptic literature—or, for that matter, parables and poetry—as if they were historical narrative results in violence to the actual intention of the text.

23. Ibid., 334–35.

24. Ibid., 367.

25. Ibid., 370.

If our goal is to be liberated from creation rather than the liberation of creation, we will understandably display little concern for the world that God has made. If, however, we are looking forward to "the restoration of all things" (Ac 3:21) and the participation of the whole creation in our redemption (Ro 8:18–21), then our actions here and now pertain to the same world that will one day be finally and fully renewed. Following our Savior's path can mean neither arrogant triumphalism nor passive resignation, but an active—even suffering—love that knows how the story turns out in the end.

> For I consider that the sufferings of this present time are not worth comparing with the glory that is to be revealed to us. For the creation waits with eager longing for the revealing of the sons of God. For the creation was subjected to futility, not willingly, but because of him who subjected it, in hope that the creation itself will be set free from its bondage to corruption and obtain the freedom of the glory of the children of God. For we know that the whole creation has been groaning together in the pains of childbirth until now. And not only the creation, but we ourselves, who have the first-fruits of the Spirit, groan inwardly as we wait eagerly for adoption as sons, the redemption of our bodies. For in this hope we were saved. Now hope that is seen is not hope. For who hopes for what he sees? But if we hope for what we do not see, we wait for it with patience. (Ro 8:18–25)

Key Terms

- *apokatastasis*
- inclusivism
- annihilationism

Key Questions

1. Is there a basic continuity between creation and the new creation, or is this world to be destroyed? How do Christ's resurrection in the past and ours in the future help us to answer that question?
2. How does the New Testament talk about the last judgment?
3. What is *apokatastasis*? Is their biblical support for this view?
4. Does Scripture teach that hell is forever? Evaluate the different views.
5. What do we know about heaven? Is our eternal blessedness non-worldly? How important is our view of this matter for our lives today?

Making Necessary Distinctions: The Call to Discernment

> Do your best to present yourself to God as one approved, a worker who has no need to be ashamed, rightly handling the word of truth. (2Ti 2:15)

Some distinctions are pedantic, part of that "craving for controversy and for quarrels about words" that Paul warned against (1Ti 6:4). On one hand, distinctions should not be endlessly multiplied. On the other hand, there is a kind of "biblicism" that discourages making any distinctions that are not found explicitly in Scripture. Of course, that would spell disaster for the doctrines of the Trinity, Christology, and a host of other core Christian convictions. Good distinctions are an act of discernment. It is the wisdom to recognize things that are required by Scripture even when they are not directly expressed in Scripture. While we must avoid "quarrels about words" (1Ti 6:4), we must also "follow the pattern of sound words" (2Ti 1:13).

One good example is the maxim from the Council of Chalcedon: "distinction without separation." Coined specifically in relation to the person of Christ, this formula holds across all of the distinctions below. In each case, danger lurks whenever we either confuse or separate that which God has distinguished but joined inseparably together.

Our problem today is more often the erosion—or even ignorance—of crucial distinctions and categories. As someone has remarked, "We like to reinvent the wheel, and it's never round." Sometimes, unaware of the discussions and debates that forged Christian consensus in the past, we treat contemporary controversies as if we were the first to encounter them. Starting from scratch, we often end up with our own lopsided confusion of things that ought to be distinguished and separation of things that ought to be held together.

Here is a summary of several key distinctions that are helpful in guiding our own reflection on some of these important questions. Each of these distinctions is explained in the appropriate context throughout *Pilgrim Theology*.

Glossary

Active obedience of Christ: Jesus Christ's fulfillment of the law on behalf of his people.

Adoptionism: Christological heresy that Jesus of Nazareth was conceived as merely a natural human being, but was later adopted as the Son of God at his baptism.

Analogical: the epistemological position that creaturely knowledge is a copy (an analogue) of divine knowledge. This type of knowledge is both similar and dissimilar (cf. **equivocal**, **univocal**).

Apokatastasis: the concept of universal restoration (universal salvation) for all of creation, humanity, and fallen angels alike. Ancient Gnostics and the early church theologian Origen (c. 185–254) taught this view, but it was condemned at the Fifth Council of Constantinople in 553.

Apostles' Creed: Although this creed dates in its final form from the eighth century, most of its elements are present already in second-century creedal affirmations. Along with the Nicene (also known as the Nicene-Constantinopolitan) Creed (325/381), it is the most widely used ecumenical creed in Christian churches.

Archetypal knowledge: the knowledge that only God possesses. It is the original, whereas all else is the copy (cf. **ectypal knowledge**).

Arianism (also, **Subordinationism**): Only the Father is God in the fullest sense; the Son and the Spirit are ontologically inferior. According to Arianism, the Son is the first created being.

Arminianism: Initiated in the seventeenth century, this movement follows the teachings of Jacobus Arminius (1560–1609), who emphasized that God's election is conditioned upon foreseen faith, his grace can be resisted, and Christ's atonement was made on behalf of all humanity. The first confessional statement of Arminian theology is in the *Remonstrance* (1610), to which the Synod of Dort responded with its "Canons," later known as the Five Points of Calvinism.

Baptists: those who believe that only professing believers should be baptized (credobaptism), in contrast to those who believe professing believers and their children should be baptized (paedobaptism).

Barthians: theologians continuing (to varying degrees) the work of Swiss-German theologian Karl Barth, who was one of the most significant twentieth-century theologians.

Beatific vision: The teaching that the angels and souls in heaven will see and experience God face-to-face and enjoy the resulting perfect and supreme blessedness.

Calvinists: named after Protestant Reformer John Calvin (1509–64). Though reductionistic, Calvinism is often associated with the five heads of doctrine articulated at the Synod of Dort: total depravity, unconditional election, limited atonement, irresistible grace, and perseverance of the saints.

Canon: a collection of varied texts that are authoritative for the followers of a religion. When we call the Bible a canon, we means its books are united by their divine source (the Father's speaking), their content (the Son's work of redemption), and their power to generate the world of which they speak (the Spirit's work of inspiration, illumination, and regeneration).

Cappadocian fathers: Basil the Great (330–79), bishop of Caesarea; Gregory of Nyssa (c. 330–95), bishop of Nyssa and Basil's brother; Gregory Nazianzus (329–89), patriarch of Constantinople. They were influential theologians in the development of Christian theology in the East and West, in such areas as the doctrine of the Trinity, theological terminology, and Christology.

Common grace: God's bestowal of a variety of gifts and blessings on Christians and non-Christians alike, such as health, intelligence, friendship, vocation, family, government, art, science, etc. Common grace upholds fallen humanity, but it is not saving.

Communicable attributes: those attributes that may be predicated of God and humans (though only analogically), such as love, mercy, and justice.

Concursus (or, concurrence): the simultaneity of divine and human agency in specific actions and events.

Council of Trent: One of the most important Roman Catholic ecumenical councils in all of the history of the Roman Catholic Church. Meeting between 1545 and 1563, this council discussed Reformation teachings and defined Roman Catholic doctrine on theological topics, such as Scripture and tradition, original sin, justification, and the sacraments. Many of these central Christian doctrines had not received official Roman Catholic statements until this council. It sought not only to state clearly the Roman Catholic position on various topics but also to renew the church in its polity and practice.

Covenant: an oath-based union under given stipulations and sanctions.

Covenant of creation (also, covenant of works; covenant of nature): covenant between the triune Lord and humanity in Adam, with Adam as its covenantal representative (**federal** head). With disobedience, Adam (and humanity whom he represented) would die (Ge 2:15 – 17; Ro 5:12 – 18).

Covenant of grace: postfall covenant between the triune God and Christ with the church, with Christ as its head and mediator. It began with God's promise of salvation to Adam and Eve and continued through the family of faith leading from Seth to Noah and on to Abraham and Sarah all the way to the new covenant as inaugurated by Christ's death. In this covenant, God promises to be our God and to make believers and their children his own redeemed family, with Christ — the Last Adam — as the **federal** representative, head, and mediator. It is the historical unfolding of the eternal plan of God in the covenant of redemption.

Covenant of redemption (also, *pactum salutis*; covenant of peace): covenant entered into by the persons of the Trinity in the councils of eternity, with the Son mediating its benefits to the elect. This covenant is the basis for all of God's purposes in nature and history, and it is the foundation and efficacy of the covenant of grace.

Deism: belief that God created the world but does not intervene miraculously within it.

Demythologization: term coined by Rudolf Bultmann (1884 – 1976), referring to his project of removing what he regarded as the first-century mythic elements of the New Testament, which alienated modern thinkers from Christian faith.

Descartes's *ego cogito*: René Descartes, the father of modern philosophy, proved his existence through doubting everything. He realized that he doubted, so there must be a doubting thing. His famous phrase, "I think, therefore I am" (*cogito ergo sum*), represents the foundation on which he builds the rest of his knowledge.

Dispensationalism: a system of theology that sees God's relationship to humans under distinct economies (dispensations) through history. Dispensationalists hold to a distinction between Israel and the church and a premillennial return of Christ, and many argue for a pretribulation rapture. John Nelson Darby (1800 – 1882) and C. I. Scofield (1843 – 1921) were significant writers in the formation and development of dispensationalism.

Docetism: early church heresy that denied Jesus Christ as fully human.

Dogmatics: a deeper analysis of Christian doctrines than systematic theology, including more exegesis and engagement with alternative views.

Dominicans: Roman Catholic order named after St. Dominic, which began in the thirteenth century. The most famous Dominican is Thomas Aquinas (c. 1225 – 74). Its emphasis was predominantly education and preaching.

Donatism: Similar to the Novatianists, the Donatists sought a church of saints, not sinners. They declared invalid all baptisms that had been performed by bishops and pastors who had apostatized. Augustine (354 – 430) opposed them by arguing that the validity of the ministry of Word and sacraments in no way depends on the piety or sincerity of the administrator.

Economic Trinity: the revealed activity of the triune God in creation and redemption, distinguished from the immanent Trinity. This parallels the distinction between knowledge of God-in-himself (to which we do not have access) and of God-for-us (given by God's revelation).

Ectypal knowledge: creaturely knowledge that is revealed by God and accommodated to our finite capacities. Creaturely knowledge is always imperfect, incomplete, and dependent on God's perfect and complete knowledge.

Effectual call (also, inward call, irresistible grace): occurs when through the hearing of the gospel the Spirit illumines an individual's heart and gives them faith.

Epistemology: branch of philosophy that deals with questions about knowledge, answering the question, "How do we know?"

Equivocal (also, equivocity): In theology, this term means "bearing no relationship" and is used to state the epistemological position that God's knowledge and creaturely knowledge have nothing in common (cf. **analogical**, **univocal**).

Erastianism: political theory that the church's outward administration, worship, and discipline function under the state.

Essence-energies distinction: the Cappadocian fathers' and Eastern Orthodox distinction between the essence of God (which we cannot know) and his energies (which we can know). Eastern Orthodoxy has appealed to Exodus 33 for this distinction between God's inaccessible glory (his essence) and his gracious acts (his energies). Reformation theologians utilized this distinction in a variety of ways: to distinguish between theologies of glory and of the cross, between archetypal and ectypal theology, and between knowing God's being and knowing his acts.

Existentialism: philosophical view that emphasizes authentic individual existence. Significant existentialists have been Søren Kierkegaard (1813 – 55), Friedrich Nietzsche (1844 – 1900), Martin Heidegger (1889 – 1976), and Jean-Paul Sartre (1905 – 80).

Ex opere operato: medieval sacramental formulation meaning, "In the doing of it, it is done."

Federal theology (also, covenant theology): framework for interpreting the Bible that has the biblical idea of "covenant" as its organizing principle. It utilizes the covenantal and representative (federal) headship of Adam and Jesus Christ (the Second and Last Adam) to understand the flow, continuity, and discontinuity in redemptive history.

Fides qua creditur: the personal act of believing.

Fides quae creditur: the faith (the content) that is believed.

Filioque (Latin: "and from the Son"): addition to the Nicene Creed at the Third Council of Toledo (589), affirming the eternal procession of the Holy Spirit from both the Father and the Son. This additional clause created tensions between Western and Eastern Christendom and is considered to be one of the fundamental points of disagreement that led to their split in 1054.

Five Points of Calvinism: based on the five canons given by the Synod of Dort (1618 – 19), which sought to answer Remonstrant (early Arminian) positions by affirming the following: total depravity, unconditional election, limited atonement, irresistible grace, and perseverance of the saints. The acronym used to remember these points is TULIP.

Formula of Concord: Lutheran confessional statement that sought to unite Lutheran churches. Jakob Andreä (1528 – 90) and Martin Chemnitz (1522 – 86) were the main writers of the Formula in 1577.

Gnosticism: the beliefs of a diverse group of writers in the first and later centuries. Its primary underpinning was dualism. Two examples of this dualism are the gnostic contrast between the warring God of the Old Testament and the loving God of the New Testament and the gnostic contrast between matter being evil and spirit being good. The gnostics sought redemption from this evil, material creation through secret knowledge (*gnōsis*) possessed only by the spiritually elite. This heresy was decisively challenged by Irenaeus (AD 115 – 202), bishop of Lyons, in his *Against Heresies*, from which comes much of the information we have about Gnosticism.

Heidelberg Catechism: Reformation document with a question-and-answer format used to teach Christian doctrine and practice. It was written by Caspar Olevianus and Zacharius Ursinus (1534 – 83) and approved by the Synod of Heidelberg in 1563.

Hermeneutics: the study and practice of interpretation.

Historia salutis: literally, the history of salvation. It refers to the historical events of Christ's life, death, resurrection, and ascension and the coming of the Spirit.

Hyper-Calvinism: theological position that so emphasizes the sovereignty of God that it minimizes (or denies) the place of creaturely means and secondary causation (thereby rejecting the need for evangelism).

Hypostatic union: theological term used in the early church to describe the union of the divine and human natures in the one person (hypostasis) of Jesus Christ.

Idealism: philosophical theory that the center and origin of all knowledge is based on mind and ideas. With sources in Plato and Platonism, modern German idealism has exercised enormous influence through Immanuel Kant, G. W. F. Hegel, F. W. J. Schelling, and others.

Immanence: being entirely within creation.

Immanent Trinity: the hidden intratrinitarian communion (distinguished from the economic Trinity).

Incommunicable attributes: those attributes that belong to God alone, such as simplicity, omnipresence, and omniscience.

Infinite-qualitative distinction (also, Creator-creature distinction): the theological teaching that God and creation are qualitatively different.

Kenosis: from a Greek verb in Philippians 2:7 (*kenoō*), meaning "to empty." Nineteenth-century theologians understood this verse and others to argue that the Son of God emptied himself of some (or all) of his divine attributes when he became a human.

Lessing's ugly ditch: the epistemological dilemma that G. E. Lessing (1729–81) expressed, that contingent historical truths could not be used to verify necessary truths of reason. One could not cross from one side of the ditch (contingent history) to the other (necessary truths).

Manichaeanism: in the early centuries of the church, a materialistic dualist group that separated the God of creation (of the Old Testament) from the God of redemption (of the New Testament).

Metanarrative: a story (narrative) that pretends it is not a narrative. It claims that it is "beyond" (*meta*) grand-overarching narratives that sought to explain all of reality and human existence.

Method of correlation: theological paradigm of Paul Tillich (1886–1965), which seeks to correlate Christian theology to the philosophical and existential questions of the contemporary world. Philosophers determine the questions and theologians provide the answers.

Modalism (also, Sabellianism): There is only one person in God, who represents himself in the roles of three persons.

Montanism: early church sect founded by Montanus, who emphasized the work of the Spirit through continuing prophecy and speaking in tongues.

Moral ability: the power to approve, delight in, and fulfill God's moral will.

Mortification: Latin term used by Reformed theologians to refer to the dying of the old self in sanctification.

Narrative theology (also, the Yale School; postliberal theology): begun by professors Hans Frei (1922–88) and George Lindbeck (1923–) of Yale Divinity School, with a focus on the centrality of narrative for the church's confession and as the governing paradigm for theology. Postliberal theology has also brought renewed attention to the connection between a community's practices and its beliefs.

Natural ability: the set of faculties and abilities necessary to fulfill God's commands. Some believe that humans have natural ability but that since these faculties have been marred by sin, human beings lack the moral ability to fulfill these commands.

Natural law: the law of God written on the conscience of every person (Ro 2:14–15).

Neoplatonism: the revival and recasting of Platonism in the third century, mainly through writers such as Plotinus and Porphyry, which influenced theologians such as Origen, Augustine, Boethius, and Bonaventure.

Nicene Creed: the result of the first ecumenical (universal) church council in AD 325, in the midst of orthodox and Arian debates over the divinity of Jesus Christ. In 381 the Council of Constantinople produced a revision of this creed, which is the text commonly used today, although the East retains its original language of the Spirit proceeding from the Father and the West added "from the Father and the Son" (see *Filioque*).

Noetic: of or related to the mind.

Ontology: branch of philosophy that seeks to answer questions dealing with reality and existence.

Open theism: twentieth-century theological movement seeking to affirm the free will of humanity and the openness of the future, which, since it has yet to happen, cannot be known by anyone (including God). Open theists reject the classical attributes of God, such as omniscience, omnipotence, omnipresence, immutability, and impassibility. Main proponents include Clark Pinnock, John E. Sanders, and Gregory Boyd.

Ordo salutis: literally, the order of salvation. It refers to the logical order as to how the Spirit applies the benefits of Christ to individuals.

Original sin: the guilt and corruption brought on the human race as a result of Adam's sin.

Outward call (also, external call): occurs anytime when God summons the world to Christ through the preaching of the gospel.

Panentheism: literally, "all-within-God." This view holds that God (or the divine principle) transcends the world, although God and the world exist in mutual dependence.

Pantheism: literally, "all is divine." It is the theological belief that all of reality is God.

Passive obedience of Christ: Jesus Christ's suffering the penalty of sin and death on behalf of his people.

Pelagianism: school of thought named after Pelagius (354–418?) and promulgated by Julian of Eclanum (c. 386–c. 455). They taught that the human will was capable of spiritual good without the aid of God's grace, and that sinless perfection was possible in this life. Augustine and Jerome were chief critics of Pelagianism, and it was condemned by church councils in 418 and 431.

Penal substitution: doctrine according to which Jesus Christ's sacrifice was the payment of a debt to divine justice as a substitute for his people.

Perfectionism: theological position that teaches that believers can live above sin. The Pelagian view assumed believers can (and must) attain absolute perfection in this life to be acceptable to God. The Arminian version of John Wesley (1703–91) argues for the possibility of believers living without known sin through grace-perfected love.

Perichoresis: a term first used by the Cappadocian fathers, referring to the mutual indwelling and fellowship of the persons of the Trinity.

Postmodernism: a term with a variety of meanings, depending on whether one is speaking of architecture, literature, music, philosophy, theology, or something else. In many ways it is both reaction to and rejection of modern thought, yet can also be seen as its culmination.

Prelapsarian: literally, "before the fall."

Premodernity: in philosophy, a term usually referring to the period in Western intellectual history before the work of René Descartes (1596–1650).

Propitiation: Jesus Christ's death propitiated (satisfied) God's justice and wrath against sin.

Rationalism: epistemological theory that attempts to base theological beliefs on universal principles of innate reason, with absolute certainty as the only legitimate form of knowing.

Regeneration: the Spirit's sovereign work of raising those who are spiritually dead to life in Christ through the announcement of the gospel.

Regulative principle of worship: the Reformed and Presbyterian teaching that only what Christ commands regulates faith, practice, and church worship.

Romanticism: cultural and intellectual movement in the late eighteenth and early nineteenth centuries, seeking aesthetic experience and emotion as a reaction to Enlightenment thought and the mechanization of nature brought about through the rise of science.

Sacrament: a visible sign and seal of a spiritual grace.

Second Helvetic Confession: Reformation statement of faith written by Heinrich Bullinger (1504–75) in 1562, which became popular in many Reformed congregations in geographical areas such as Switzerland, Scotland, and France.

Second Vatican Council: significant twentieth-century (1962–65) Roman Catholic Church council that discussed issues such as the relation between Scripture and tradition, ecclesiology, ecumenism, and the liturgy. It was the twenty-first ecumenical council of the Roman Catholic Church.

Semi-Pelagianism: term coined in the sixteenth century for the teaching that human beings are affected by sin but can still choose the good. In the common formulation of the late medieval period, it asserts that "God will not deny his grace to those who do what lies within them." Salvation is attained by human cooperation with grace.

Simil iustus et peccator: Reformation slogan meaning "both saint and sinner," which points out that the believer in Christ is righteous before God and yet also still sins.

Stoicism: a school of philosophy founded around the third century BC in Athens. It valued independence and the striving for unity with the principles of divine harmony.

Sufficient grace: grace that is enough to enable sinners to respond positively to God if they choose to do so.

Supralapsarianism: The theological position that God's decree to save is logically *prior to* his decree to create and permit the fall.

Suzerainty treaty: a treaty imposed unilaterally by the great king (the suzerain) on the lesser ruler (the vassal), which required strict obedience to specific commands or else the vassal would die.

Synergism (meaning "working together"): the view that salvation is attained through a cooperative process between God and human beings.

Systematic theology: an organized and detailed summary of important topics in theology (cf. **dogmatics**).

Theology of the cross: Phrase used by Protestant Reformer Martin Luther (1483–1546) to emphasize that human knowledge and experience must be based on the foolishness of the cross, not human abilities or human ascent to God (theology of glory).

Theology of glory: Phrase used by Protestant Reformer Martin Luther (1483–1546) to criticize medieval theologians who sought direct access to God without the need of mediation.

Theōsis: deification.

Theotokos: term used of Mary ("the mother of God") at the Council of Ephesus in 431 to affirm the divinity of Jesus Christ.

Thomists: followers of the teaching of Thomas Aquinas (c. 1225–74).

The Three Forms of Unity: The three most widely accepted confessional standards of the Reformed church: the Belgic Confession (1561), the Heidelberg Catechism (1563), and the Canons of Dort (1618–19).

Total depravity: the corruption of every aspect of human nature—body, soul, mind, heart, and will—in the fall; a condition to which, according to Reformed theology, all human beings are subject.

Transcendence: being entirely above and outside of creation.

Transubstantiation: change undergone by the physical elements of the Eucharist, according to Roman Catholic teaching. The bread and wine, in this view, materially change into the body and blood of Christ, although the accidents of the bread and wine (their appearance, taste, and smell, for instance) remain unchanged.

Tritheism: a denial of the essential unity of the Trinity in favor of three Gods.

Ubiquity: ability to be omnipresent. "Ubiquitarianism" teaches that the human nature of the resurrected Christ is omnipresent and therefore is able to be in the elements of the Lord's Supper simultaneously around the world.

Unconditional election: God's election based entirely on his own good pleasure, dependent on no condition in the one he elects.

Union with Christ: phrase referring to the way in which believers share in Christ in eternity (by election), in past history (by redemption), in the present (by effectual calling, justification, and sanctification), and in the future (by glorification). This union is mystical, legal, and organic.

Univocal (also, univocity): exactly the same. In ontology, to say that reality or existence is univocal is to say that it is of only one kind; in epistemology, to say that knowledge is univocal is to say that God's knowledge and creatures' knowledge are identical (cf. analogical, equivocal).

Univocity of being: the character of being univocal with respect to existence. Those who believe in the univocity of being believe that everything that truly exists is one.

Vivification: Latin-based term used by Reformed theologians to refer to the making-alive of the new human being in sanctification.

Voluntarism: school of thought that emphasizes the will (whether human or divine) as that which determines what is good, true, and beautiful. Voluntarism is contrasted with intellectualism, according to which what is good determines the will. This debate is associated especially with the Franciscans (John Duns Scotus [c. 1266–1308]) and Dominicans (Thomas Aquinas [1225–74]), who emphasized the primacy of the will and the intellect, respectively. Nineteenth-century voluntarism finds its source in Immanuel Kant (1724–1804), who elevated the practical reason (the will) over pure reason.

Westminster Standards: confessional statements and catechisms developed and written by the Westminster Assembly in England during the years 1643–48. These standards include the Westminster Confession of Faith, the Westminster Larger Catechism, and the Westminster Shorter Catechism. These documents are the doctrinal standards (subordinate to the Scriptures) in Presbyterian churches throughout the world.

From Drama to Discipleship: Applying the Coordinates to Key Doctrines

	Drama	Doctrine	Doxology	Discipleship
God's Incommunicable Attributes	In his victory over the idols, Yahweh shows himself to be Israel's Lord and the world's only sovereign.	Immutable, eternal life-in-himself, independent of the world, simple, impassible.	Praised for his incomparable greatness, confided in as the only object of faith and worship.	"No other gods." When we worship what God has made instead of God himself, we become slaves of lords that cannot liberate.
God's Communicable Attributes	God acts in judgment and mercy, goodness and grace, wrath and love, displaying his comprehensive knowledge, wisdom, and power.	God is loving, merciful, just, good, righteous, omniscient, and omnipotent.	Swept into his covenant of grace, we find ourselves crying out to God in trials, casting ourselves on him, and reveling in his generosity.	Our lives are founded in God's love, yet subject to God's righteous will. God's attributes never clash; we can always trust in his promises as we glorify and enjoy God.
The Trinity	Throughout God's mighty acts in history we meet three distinct actors who are nevertheless identified as God.	God is "one in essence, three in persons." In every external act of the Godhead, the Trinity is undivided and yet each person's agency is distinct.	Baptized into the triune name, we pray to the Father, in the Son, by the Spirit. Creation, redemption, and the consummation come to us from the Father as origin, in the Son as mediator, through the Spirit as perfector.	Created in God's image, our lives should reflect his unity and diversity. Especially in the church, we are one body with many members. So our lives are intended for community—not because we are all the same, but precisely in the difference that contributes to the upbuilding of Christ's body.
Creation	"In the beginning, God created the heavens and the earth," with human beings as his covenant partner. The eternal and unchanging God created the world with time and change. The Father created everything "visible and invisible" in the Son and by the Spirit.	*Ex nihilo* creation: The world is neither eternal nor necessary, but came into being as a free act of the triune God. We are not our own (autonomous), but depend for our existence and knowledge on God.	"The earth is the Lord's and everything in it." Since God created us for his glory, we realize the purpose of our existence in trusting delight in our dependence on him. Our prayers invoke God for security and strength and praise him as Creator and Redeemer.	No longer treating the world as a given but as a gift, we listen to God's Word—both his commands and his promises—to learn how to live generous and responsible lives that contrast sharply with the autonomy, meaninglessness, and idolatry of a nihilistic culture.
Anthropology	The goal of Adam's representative trial was to lead creation into God's Sabbath rest. Violating the covenant of creation, Adam plunged the human race into sin and death.	Creation in God's glorious image measures the tragedy of the fall. Original sin means that we are all conceived in sin: guilty and corrupt image-bearers of God.	Our worship is characterized simultaneously by praise for our nature and lament for our lives in a fallen world and confession of our own sin against a holy God.	We live in the awareness of our solidarity with all human beings in Adam and our union with Christ as the Last Adam. Autonomy is exchanged for dependence on God not only for our creation but for our redemption and renewal.

	Drama	Doctrine	Doxology	Discipleship
The Person of Christ	In the fullness of time, God sent his Son, conceived by the Spirit, yet of the substance of the virgin Mary from the line of David.	In the incarnation, the eternal Son (Word) assumed our humanity. In this hypostatic union, Jesus Christ is fully divine and fully human (yet without sin).	At last we can celebrate the arrival of the one who is both the Covenant Lord who commands and promises and the Covenant Servant who obeys and fulfills. We worship Christ as God incarnate.	Christ is unique in his person and work. While we are called to follow his example, more importantly we are beneficiaries of his incarnation and saving work. Our lives are therefore first and foremost a matter of being united to Christ rather than merely imitating his example.
The Work of Christ: Substitution	As our covenantal head, Christ fulfilled all righteousness in our place and bore God's wrath in our place on the cross.	The active obedience of Christ (in his life) and passive obedience (on the cross) form the ground of our salvation.	We praise God for all his works, but even these works of God assume a lively color when Christ's redeeming work is the centerpiece of our worship.	When forgiveness and reconciliation with God are the basis rather than the goal of our lives, we are free to live as secure heirs rather than as slaves. Further, we are free to forgive others rather than record their offenses.
The Work of Christ: Victory	As the beginning of the resurrection from the dead, Christ was raised bodily by the Father in the power of the Spirit on the third day. Glorified, he was exalted in his ascension to the right hand of the Father.	Jesus "was crucified for our sins and was raised for our justification." In his resurrection, he has triumphed over Satan, death, hell, and the powers and principalities that held us in bondage. His ascension assures us that he is now, we will one day be—raised in glory.	Our worship centers not only on the forgiveness of sins, but also on the new creation that Christ inaugurated by his victory.	Christ's work frees us not only from sin's guilt but also its power. We live not toward victory, much less as something that we bring about, but from the victory that Christ has already accomplished for us. Sin *cannot* reign over us, because Christ is King!
The Spirit's Application of Redemption: Union with Christ	At Pentecost, the Spirit descended to apply the benefits of Christ's work to sinners, unite the elect to Christ as his body, and expand his church to the ends of the earth.	Those whom the Father chose in Christ are called effectually to Christ. United to him through faith, we inherit justification, adoption, sanctification, and glorification.	The Spirit is worshipped and glorified together with the Father and the Son. As the perfecting (completing) agent of all God's works, he is praised for taking what is Christ's by right and making it ours by gift.	We live in the power of the Spirit, who raised Jesus from the dead. The Spirit is the down payment on our final redemption, indwelling us so that we are now citizens of the new creation. It is the Spirit who makes us cry out, "Abba! Father!" through the mediation of the Son.

	Drama	Doctrine	Doxology	Discipleship
Justification	The Spirit gives us faith to embrace Christ. The first gift is the justification of the ungodly.	Not only forgiven, the elect are justified—declared righteous even while they are in themselves unrighteous. Christ's righteousness is imputed to them.	"What shall we say in response to this? If God is for us, who can be against us?... Who shall bring any charge against God's elect?"	We live from, not toward, the verdict of justification. For all who trust in Christ, the sentence or the Last Judgment has been rendered: "There is therefore now no condemnation for those who are in Christ Jesus." Joy, not fear, is the basis of the Christian life.
Sanctification	The same act of faith that receives Christ for justification receives Christ for renewal of the inner self (sanctification) and one day the outer self (glorification).	While justification is a legal verdict made once and for all, sanctification is a gradual process by which the Spirit conforms us to the image of Christ through the gospel.	Holy in Christ already, believers are more and more conformed to Christ. What can be more glorious than being made like Christ?	While sanctification is God's gracious work, faith bears the fruit of good works. We are exhorted to put to death the deeds of the flesh and to bear the fruit of the Spirit. United to Christ, we grow in communion with his body. Since our good works cannot serve God or ourselves, they go out to our neighbors who need them.
Glorification	"Those whom he justified he glorified." While our sanctification remains incomplete in this life, we will be instantaneously changed into Christ's incorruptible glory at the resurrection of the dead.	Glorification is the public display of God's saving work, when the elect are no longer subject to the fallen condition and the whole creation shares in the victory that Christ has won. Sin, ugliness, and death will yield entirely to righteousness, beauty, and life.	Faith in the "already" of our election, calling, and justification is often tested by the "not yet" that we discern in our sanctification. Hope in our future glorification renews our strength to praise God even in our trials.	We live now in the hope of this future promise. Not only our souls, but our bodies; and not only we, but the whole creation, will be changed forever. This future hope, guaranteed by Christ's glorification already, changes the way we live in the world now.
Baptism	Replacing circumcision as the sign and seal of the covenant of grace, baptism was instituted by Christ to deliver himself with all of his benefits to believers and their children.	Baptism involves the sign (washing with water) and the reality (union with Christ). These cannot be separated or confused. A means of grace, baptism is used by the Spirit to ratify God's promises to us.	We receive baptism as God's pledge, assuring us that he is favorable toward us in his Son. The Spirit creates faith in our hearts through the preaching of the gospel and confirms it by his sacraments.	Once again grounding our assurance in God's promise, baptism also calls us to faith and repentance throughout our lives. "Living out our baptism" is the character of Christian discipleship.

		Drama	Doctrine	Doxology	Discipleship
The Lord's Supper		In the Upper Room after the Passover meal, Jesus instituted the Lord's Supper as the ratification of his sacrificial death.	We participate in Christ's sacrifice by feeding on him through faith. This reality is conferred by the Spirit when we receive the bread and wine in faith.	Since the Supper is not only a memorial of Christ's death, but a feeding on Christ himself—his true body and blood—by faith, we are regularly assured that he died not only for others, but also "for you."	Nourished at Christ's table, we are made one family with co-sharers and are motivated to go out into the alleys of our neighborhood to invite guests to the feast that participates in the wedding supper of the Lamb.
The Invisible Church		Before the creation of the world, the Father gave a bride to his Son, being now gathered by the Spirit in union with Christ.	So called because for now its membership is known to God alone, the invisible church is the full number of the elect in all times and places.	We praise and glorify the triune God for including us in the worldwide family that the Father has chosen for his Son.	Although the church seems difficult to discern at times in this world, God's promise guarantees that there will always be a true church. We live by faith, not by sight.
The Visible Church		Although the invisible church will be fully visible on the last day, Christ promised that he will build his church and the gates of hell will not prevail against it.	A true visible church exists wherever the Word is properly preached and the sacraments are properly administered, and discipline is exercised.	Called out of the world by God's Word and Spirit, we find our communion with Christ in his visible body. Here we receive his gifts and respond in joyful fellowship and worship with his people.	Union with Christ is inseparable from communion with his church. Those who claim to be Christ's disciples are members of his visible church, sharing their gifts, suffering, and experiencing hope with each other.
Last Things		Christ will come again, bodily, to claim his bride and to judge the world.	The bodily return of Christ to judge the living and the dead is an essential Christian doctrine.	A centerpiece of Christian worship is the joyful celebration, "Christ had died, Christ is risen, Christ will come again." It is this hope that animates our hearts to pray, "Even so Lord Jesus, come quickly."	Living in the light of the future judgment and restoration of all things, we acknowledge a dual calling today: to call sinners to repentance and faith, and to love and serve our neighbors in our callings in the world.
Everlasting Life		After the judgment, Christ will hand over all authority to the Father and the whole creation will be under his sovereign sway.	At death, the body is separated from the soul, with believers entering immediately the presence of the Lord (the intermediate state). At the last day, the soul will be reunited with the body. The "sheep" will be raised to an eternal inheritance of life (heaven) while the "goats" will suffer everlasting death (hell).	While believers rejoice that at death they will be received into God's presence, their ultimate hope is the resurrection of the body and the life everlasting in a renewed creation beyond the reach of sin and death.	It makes all the difference in the world (literally) if Christians see "going to heaven when we die" as the ultimate goal of salvation. Rather, this is the intermediate state. Our ultimate hope is that this whole creation, redeemed by Christ, will share in the unending and ever-new beauty of true justice, righteousness, and life in a cosmos with Yahweh as the fountain of joy.

Scripture Index

Subject Index

Note: glossary entries are in boldface type.

Author Index

For Calvinism

Michael Horton

The system of theology known as Calvinism has been immensely influential for nearly five hundred years, but it is often encountered negatively as a fatalistic belief system that confines human freedom and renders human action and choice irrelevant.

Taking us beyond the caricatures, Michael Horton invites us to explore the teachings of Calvinism, also commonly known as Reformed theology, by showing us how it is biblical and God-centered, leading us to live our lives for the glory of God.

Horton explores the historical roots of Calvinism, walking readers through the distinctive known as the "Five Points," and encouraging us to consider its rich resources for faith and practice in the 21st Century.

A companion book to this one is Roger Olson's *Against Calvinism*, by which readers will be able to compare contrasting perspectives and form their own opinions on the merits and weaknesses of Calvinism.

A Place for Weakness

Preparing Yourself for Suffering

Michael S. Horton

In a world of hype, we may buy into the idea that, through Jesus, we'll be healthier and wealthier as well as wiser. So what happens when we become ill, or depressed, or bankrupt? Did we do something wrong? Has God abandoned us?

As a child, Michael Horton would run up the down escalator, trying to beat it to the top. As Christians, he notes, we sometimes seek God the same way, believing we can climb to him under our own steam. We can't, which is why we are blessed that Jesus descends to us, especially during times of trial.

In *A Place for Weakness*, formerly titled *Too Good to Be True*, Horton exposes the pop culture that sells Jesus like a product for health and happiness and reminds us that our lives often lead us on difficult routes that we must follow by faith. This book offers a series of powerful readings that demonstrate how, through every type of earthly difficulty, our Father keeps his promises from Scripture and works all things together for our good.

The Christian Faith

A Systematic Theology for Pilgrims on the Way

Michael Horton

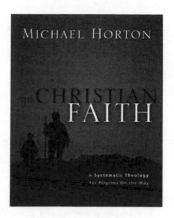

Michael Horton's highly anticipated *The Christian Faith* represents his magnum opus and will be viewed as one of the—if not the— most important systematic theologies since Louis Berkhof wrote his in 1932.

A prolific, award-winning author and theologian, Professor Horton views this volume as "doctrine that can be preached, experienced, and lived, as well as understood, clarified, and articulated." It is written for a growing cast of pilgrims making their way together and will be especially welcomed by professors, pastors, students, and armchair theologians.

Features of this volume include: (1) a brief synopsis of biblical passages that inform a particular doctrine; (2) surveys of past and current theologies with contemporary emphasis on exegetical, philosophical, practical, and theological questions; (3) substantial interaction with various Christian movements within the Protestant, Catholic, and Orthodox traditions, as well as the hermeneutical issues raised by postmodernity; and (4) charts, sidebars, questions for discussion, and an extensive bibliography, divided into different entry levels and topics.

Available in stores and online!

What Is Theology?

A Zondervan Digital Short

Michael S. Horton

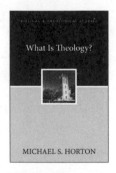

Every seminary in the world offers classes on Christian theology, but what is theology at its core? Is it a practical or theoretical discipline? Is it centrally a matter of faith or of reason? What are its proper means and ends? Derived from Michael Horton's recently released *The Christian Faith*, already one of the most significant systematic theologies of the past fifty years, this digital short explores the discipline of theology through the lens of philosophy, Scripture, ministry, and the church, laying a foundation for pursuing theology as hearing, wisdom, understanding, and more.

"Theology serves the function of articulating the identity of this God so that he may be properly invoked," Horton writes. This short work constructs a conceptual framework for pastors, theologians, and students wanting to think more deeply about the foundational discipline of Christian thought and practice.

Union with Christ

A Zondervan Digital Short

Michael S. Horton

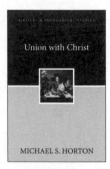

Derived from Michael Horton's recently released *The Christian Faith*, this digital short presents a full theological investigation into the biblical concept of union with Christ. Horton covers the nature of this union, exegetical development of the concept, and both historical visions and contrasting paradigms of it. He also draws connections between a Christian's ongoing union with his or her Savior and grace, ontology, essence and energies, and covenant—an altogether masterful sketch of a beautiful and mysterious spiritual reality.

The Kingdom and the Church

A Zondervan Digital Short

Michael S. Horton

Michael Horton writes, "Some Christians so stress the 'kingdom living' of individual believers in the world that the church and its partial manifestation of the kingdom of God through the means of grace become subordinate. Others confuse the church with that kingdom in its fully realized form." In his development and delineation of a theology of both the kingdom and the church, Horton seeks to show that they are interrelated but not identical. Along the way he explores the difference between the cultural mandate and the Great Commission, biblical images of the church, the ecclesiologies of various Christian traditions, and the integral connection between eschatology, ecclesiology, and kingdom.

Derived from Michael Horton's recently released *The Christian Faith*, already one of the most significant systematic theologies of the past fifty years, this digital short tackles one of today's theological hot topics with insight and charity.

White Horse Inn

White Horse Inn (www.whitehorseinn.org) is a multimedia catalyst for reformation. Our mission is to help Christians "know what they believe and why they believe it" through conversational theology. The conversations take place in talk show, magazine, event, book, blog, and social media formats. Our vision is to see a modern reformation in our churches through a rediscovery of God, the gospel, and the classic Christian confessions proclaimed during the sixteenth-century Reformation.

More than just a talk show and a magazine, White Horse Inn is a conversation for reformation. C. S. Lewis famously remarked that "mere Christianity" is like a hallway. In this hallway, real conversations between Christians of different convictions can begin and develop over time as we emerge from these various rooms to speak of Christ and his gospel to one another. For twenty years, White Horse Inn has hosted this conversation both on the radio (*White Horse Inn*) and in print (*Modern Reformation*) in the spirit of that great hallway of "mere Christianity," bringing the rich resources of the Reformation to bear on American evangelicalism.

At the center of our work are six core beliefs:

1. The five "solas" of the Reformation are more than slogans to be recovered; they are the messages that will renew the church's mission in our age.
2. Gospel-centered preaching that rightly distinguishes between law and gospel rescues the church from "Christless Christianity" while enabling Christians to grow in grace.
3. Word and Sacrament ministry realigns the church's mission and identity from program-driven pragmatism to the means of grace that Christ has ordained for the creation, sustenance, and expansion of his kingdom.
4. A properly missional mindset will identify the church as distinct from but engaged with the world, encouraging individual Christians to pursue their God-honoring vocations.
5. In order to know what they believe and why they believe it, Christians need to be well catechized and grounded in the central doctrines of the faith.
6. Withstanding the onslaught of heresy and persecution requires a confessing church grounded in the witness of the ages and animated by deeds of loving service and witness.

Our vision is to see nothing less than a "modern reformation" take hold in the hearts and lives of Christians in America and around the world. It is our prayer that God would once again pour out his Spirit, granting the church a modern reformation. For Christ's sake. Amen.

White Horse Inn is home to the *White Horse Inn* radio broadcast and Modern *Reformation* magazine.

White Horse Inn · 1725 Bear Valley Parkway · Escondido, CA 92027 · 1-800-890-7556

WHITE HORSE INN.ORG

FOR *a* MODERN REFORMATION